These safety symbols are used in laboratory and field investigations in this book to indicate possible hazards. Learn the meaning of each symbol and refer to this page often. *Remember to wash your hands thoroughly after completing lab procedures.*

PROTECTIVE EQUIPMENT

Do not begin any lab without the proper protection equipment.

GOGGLES	Proper eye protection must be worn when performing or observing science activities which involve items or conditions as listed below.
APRON	Wear an approved apron when using substances that could stain, wet, or destroy cloth.
SOAP	Wash hands with soap and water before removing goggles and after all lab activities.
GLOVES	Wear gloves when working with biological materials, chemicals, animals, or materials that can stain or irritate hands.

LABORATORY HAZARDS

Symbols	Potential Hazards	Precaution	Response
DISPOSAL	contamination of classroom or environment due to improper disposal of materials such as chemicals and live specimens	• DO NOT dispose of hazardous materials in the sink or trash can. • Dispose of wastes as directed by your teacher.	• If hazardous materials are disposed of improperly, notify your teacher immediately.
EXTREME TEMPERATURE	skin burns due to extremely hot or cold materials such as hot glass, liquids, or metals; liquid nitrogen; dry ice	• Use proper protective equipment, such as hot mitts and/or tongs, when handling objects with extreme temperatures.	• If injury occurs, notify your teacher immediately.
SHARP OBJECTS	punctures or cuts from sharp objects such as razor blades, pins, scalpels, and broken glass	• Handle glassware carefully to avoid breakage. • Walk with sharp objects pointed downward, away from you and others.	• If broken glass or injury occurs, notify your teacher immediately.
ELECTRICAL	electric shock or skin burn due to improper grounding, short circuits, liquid spills, or exposed wires	• Check condition of wires and apparatus for fraying or uninsulated wires, and broken or cracked equipment. • Use only GFCI-protected outlets	• DO NOT attempt to fix electrical problems. Notify your teacher immediately.
CHEMICAL	skin irritation or burns, breathing difficulty, and/or poisoning due to touching, swallowing, or inhalation of chemicals such as acids, bases, bleach, metal compounds, iodine, poinsettias, pollen, ammonia, acetone, nail polish remover, heated chemicals, mothballs, and any other chemicals labeled or known to be dangerous	• Wear proper protective equipment such as goggles, apron, and gloves when using chemicals. • Ensure proper room ventilation or use a fume hood when using materials that produce fumes. • NEVER smell fumes directly. • NEVER taste or eat any material in the laboratory.	• If contact occurs, immediately flush affected area with water and notify your teacher. • If a spill occurs, leave the area immediately and notify your teacher.
FLAMMABLE	unexpected fire due to liquids or gases that ignite easily such as rubbing alcohol	• Avoid open flames, sparks, or heat when flammable liquids are present.	• If a fire occurs, leave the area immediately and notify your teacher.
OPEN FLAME	burns or fire due to open flame from matches, Bunsen burners, or burning materials	• Tie back loose hair and clothing. • Keep flame away from all materials. • Follow teacher instructions when lighting and extinguishing flames. • Use proper protection, such as hot mitts or tongs, when handling hot objects.	• If a fire occurs, leave the area immediately and notify your teacher.
ANIMAL SAFETY	injury to or from laboratory animals	• Wear proper protective equipment such as gloves, apron, and goggles when working with animals. • Wash hands after handling animals.	• If injury occurs, notify your teacher immediately.
BIOLOGICAL	infection or adverse reaction due to contact with organisms such as bacteria, fungi, and biological materials such as blood, animal or plant materials	• Wear proper protective equipment such as gloves, goggles, and apron when working with biological materials. • Avoid skin contact with an organism or any part of the organism. • Wash hands after handling organisms.	• If contact occurs, wash the affected area and notify your teacher immediately.
FUME	breathing difficulties from inhalation of fumes from substances such as ammonia, acetone, nail polish remover, heated chemicals, and mothballs	• Wear goggles, apron, and gloves. • Ensure proper room ventilation or use a fume hood when using substances that produce fumes. • NEVER smell fumes directly.	• If a spill occurs, leave area and notify your teacher immediately.
IRRITANT	irritation of skin, mucous membranes, or respiratory tract due to materials such as acids, bases, bleach, pollen, mothballs, steel wool, and potassium permanganate	• Wear goggles, apron, and gloves. • Wear a dust mask to protect against fine particles.	• If skin contact occurs, immediately flush the affected area with water and notify your teacher.
RADIOACTIVE	excessive exposure from alpha, beta, and gamma particles	• Remove gloves and wash hands with soap and water before removing remainder of protective equipment.	• If cracks or holes are found in the container, notify your teacher immediately.

Your online portal to everything you need

ConnectED

connectED.mcgraw-hill.com

Look for these icons to access exciting digital resources

- Video
- Audio
- Review
- Inquiry
- WebQuest
- Assessment
- Concepts in Motion

McGraw Hill Education

INDIANA

GRADE 7

iScience

Glencoe

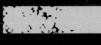

Leopard, *Panthera pardus*

Once common across southern Asia and most of Africa, most leopards exist today in sub-Saharan Africa in rain forests and deserts. They are the smallest of the big cats—tigers, lions, jaguars, and leopards. Leopards are known for their ability to climb trees while carrying prey.

The McGraw-Hill Companies

Mc Graw Hill **Education**

Send all inquiries to:
McGraw-Hill Education
8787 Orion Place
Columbus, OH 43240-4027

ISBN: 978-0-07-888035-3
MHID: 0-07-888035-1

Printed in the United States of America.

3 4 5 6 7 8 9 10 QDB 15 14 13 12 11

Contents in Brief

Indiana's Academic Standards for Science, Grade 7 Correlated to *Indiana* ⓘ *Science Grade 7*

Process Standards	Pages
The Nature of Science **Students gain scientific knowledge by observing the natural and constructed world, performing and evaluating investigations and communicating their findings. These principles should guide student work and be integrated into the curriculum along with the content standards on a daily basis.**	
7.NS.1 Make predictions and develop testable questions based on research and prior knowledge.	NOS 6–NOS 7, NOS 22–NOS 29, 36–37, 108–109, 418–419
7.NS.2 Plan and carry out investigations as a class, in small groups or independently often over a period of several class lessons.	NOS 13, 72–73, 148–149
7.NS.3 Collect quantitative data with appropriate tools or technologies and use appropriate units to label numerical data.	NOS 14–NOS 15, NOS 17–NOS 19, 28, 34, 59, 63, 83, 85, 92, 97, 108–109, 179, 188–189, 203, 209, 220, 321, 362, 391, 411, 418–419
7.NS.4 Incorporate variables that can be changed, measured or controlled.	NOS 22, NOS 24, 13, 28, 59, 63, 85, 97, 99, 105, 123, 144, 166, 213, 215, 224–225, 340, 418–419
7.NS.5 Use the principles of accuracy and precision when making measurement.	NOS 16, 13, 28, 59, 63, 97, 108–109, 144, 173, 179, 203, 209, 220, 290, 321, 340, 411, 418–419, 441
7.NS.6 Test predictions with multiple trials.	108–109
7.NS.7 Keep accurate records in a notebook during investigations.	NOS 18, NOS 22–NOS 29, 9, 13, 18, 20, 28, 34, 36–37, 47, 50, 57, 59, 63, 65, 66, 72–73, 83, 85, 91, 92, 97, 99, 105, 108–109, 119, 123, 128, 130, 136, 142, 144, 148–149, 166, 171, 179, 207, 209, 215, 220, 281, 289, 290, 294, 296, 298, 301, 303, 308–309, 321, 332, 359, 362, 365, 372–373, 387, 391, 395, 403, 405, 407, 413, 418–419, 450–451
7.NS.8 Analyze data, using appropriate mathematical manipulation as required, and use it to identify patterns and make inferences based on these patterns.	NOS 7, NOS 14, NOS 17, 59, 97, 108–109
7.NS.9 Evaluate possible causes for differing results (valid data).	36–37, 72–73, 108–109, 418–419
7.NS.10 Compare the results of an experiment with the prediction.	108–109
7.NS.11 Communicate findings using graphs, charts, maps and models through oral and written reports.	NOS 7, 28, 59, 72–73, 128, 136, 148–149, 188–189, 224–225, 266–267, 308–309, 382–383, 418–419, 450–451
The Design Process: **As citizens of the constructed world, students will participate in the design process. Students will learn to use materials and tools safely and employ the basic principles of the engineering design process in order to find a solution to a problem.**	
7.DP.1 Identify a need or problem that needs to be solved.	NOS 12–NOS 13, 72–73, 148–149, 308–309, 344, 383, 398
7.DP.2 Brainstorm potential solutions.	142, 148–149, 266, 308, 344, 383

Indiana's Academic Standards for Science, Grade 7 Correlated to *Indiana* ⓘ *Science Grade 7*

Process Standards	Pages
7.DP.3 Document the design throughout the entire design process so that it can be replicated in a portfolio/notebook with drawings including labels.	NOS 12–NOS 13, 72–73, 148–149, 344, 383, 398
7.DP.4 Select a solution to the need or problem.	NOS 12–NOS 13, 72–73, 148–149, 344, 383, 398
7.DP.5 Select the most appropriate materials to develop a solution that will meet the need.	NOS 12–NOS 13, 72–73, 128, 130, 266, 308, 344, 398
7.DP.6 Create a solution through a prototype.	NOS 12–NOS 13, 72–73, 144, 266, 336, 344, 383, 398
7.DP.7 Test and evaluate how well the solution meets the goal.	NOS 12–NOS 13, 72–73, 128, 130, 148–149, 266, 344, 398
7.DP.8 Evaluate and test the design using measurement.	266
7.DP.9 Present evidence using mathematical representation (graphs, data tables).	266, 344, 383
7.DP.10 Communicate the solution including evidence using mathematical representations (graphs, data tables), drawings or prototype.	NOS 12–NOS 13, 72–73, 148–149, 344, 383, 398
7.DP.11 Redesign to improve the solution based on how well the solution meets the need.	NOS 12–NOS 13, 128, 130, 148–149, 344, 383, 398
Standard 1: Physical Science	**Pages**
Core Standard **Explain that energy cannot be created or destroyed but only changed from one form into another or transferred from place to place.**	
Core Standard **Describe and investigate how forces between objects can act at a distance or by means of direct contact between objects.**	
7.1.1 Explain that when energy is transferred from one system to another, the total quantity of energy does not change.	18–21
7.1.2 Describe and give examples of how energy can be transferred from place to place and transformed from one form to another through radiation, convection and conduction.	13, 16, 31
7.1.3 Recognize and explain how different ways of obtaining, transforming, and distributing energy have different environmental consequences.	21–24, 164, 334
7.1.4 Recognize and provide evidence how light, sound and other waves have energy and how they interact with different materials.	13, 119–126, 128, 130–138, 142–146, 148–149

Indiana's Academic Standards for Science, Grade 7 Correlated to *Indiana* ⓘ *Science Grade 7*

Process Standards	Pages
7.1.5 Describe and investigate how forces between objects can act at a distance, such as magnetic, electrical or gravitational forces, or by means of direct contact between objects.	58–60
7.1.6 Explain that forces have magnitude and direction and those forces can be added to determine the net force acting on an object.	57, 61, 67–69
7.1.7 Demonstrate and describe how an object's speed or direction of motion changes when a force acts upon it. Demonstrate and describe that an object's speed and direction of motion remain unchanged if the net force acting upon it is zero.	57–61, 65–70, 72–73
Standard 2: Earth and Space Systems	**Pages**
Core Standard **Describe how earth processes have shaped the topography of the earth and have made it possible to measure geological time.**	
7.2.1 Describe how the earth is a layered structure composed of lithospheric plates, a mantle and a dense core.	163, 167, 171–176, 188–189
7.2.2 Recognize that the earth possesses a magnetic field that is detectable at the surface with a compass.	176–177
7.2.3 Characterize the immensity of geologic time and recognize that it is measured in eras and epochs.	235–236, 243–247, 251–255, 259–264
7.2.4 Explain how convection currents in the mantle cause lithospheric plates to move causing fast changes like earthquakes and volcanic eruptions, and slow changes like creation of mountains and formation of new ocean floor.	215–221
7.2.5 Describe the origin and physical properties of igneous, metamorphic and sedimentary rocks and how they are related through the rock cycle.	281–285, 289–292, 296–299, 303–306, 308–309
7.2.6 Describe physical and chemical characteristics of soil layers and how they are influenced by the process of soil formation, including the action of bacteria, fungi, insects, and other organisms.	320, 325, 339, 356, 364–370, 372
7.2.7 Use geological features such as karst topography and glaciation to explain how large-scale physical processes have shaped the land.	319–325, 329–334, 338–342
7.2.8 Compare and contrast fossils with living organisms in a given location to explain how earth processes have changed environments over time.	201, 205, 236, 254, 255, 257

Indiana's Academic Standards for Science, Grade 7 Correlated to *Indiana* ⓘ*Science Grade 7*

Standard 3: Life Science	Pages
Core Standard **Understand the cellular structure of living organisms, both single-celled and multicellular.**	
7.3.1 Explain that all living organisms are composed of one or more cells and that the many functions needed to sustain life are carried out within such cells.	387–391, 395–401, 405–409, 413–416
7.3.2 Understand that water is a major component within all cells and is required to carry out many cellular functions.	389, 406
7.3.3 Explain that although the way cells function is similar in all living organisms, multicellular organisms also have specialized cells whose specialized functions are directly related to their structure.	443–448
7.3.4 Compare and contrast similarities and differences between specialized subcellular components within plant and animal cells, including organelles and cell walls that perform essential functions and give a cell its shape and structure.	390–391, 395–397, 400–401
7.3.5 Explain that cells in multicellular organisms repeatedly divide to make more cells for growth and repair.	429–437
7.3.6 Explain that after fertilization, a small cluster of cells divides to form the basic tissues of an embryo which further develops into all the specialized tissues and organs within a multicellular organism.	443–448
7.3.8 Describe how various organs and tissues serve the needs of cells for nutrient and oxygen delivery and waste removal.	445–448

Standard 4: Science, Engineering and Technology	Pages
Core Standard **Design and construct a device that converts energy from one form to another to perform work.**	
7.4.1 Understand that energy is the capacity to do work.	19, 83–86, 91, 95
7.4.2 Explain that energy can be used to do work using many processes, for example generation of electricity by harnessing wind energy.	22–23, 92–93, 100–106
7.4.3 Explain that power is the rate that energy is converted from one form to another.	13
7.4.4 Explain that power systems are used to provide propulsion for engineered products and systems.	4–5

Indiana Authorship and Review Team

Author
William D. Rogers, DA
Professor of Biology
Ball State University
Muncie, IN

Consultant
Cheryl Wistrom, PhD
Associate Professor of Chemistry
Saint Joseph's College
Rensselaer, IN

Reviewers
Jane E.M. Buckingham
Teacher
Crispus Attucks Medical Magnet High School
Indianapolis, IN

Ginger Shirley
Our Lady of Providence Junior–Senior High School
Clarksville, IN

Tony Spoors
Switzerland County Middle School
Vevay, IN

Nancy A. Stearns
Switzerland County Middle School
Vevay, IN

Driftwood River, Bartholomew County

Authors and Contributors

Authors

American Museum of Natural History
New York, NY

Michelle Anderson, MS
Lecturer
The Ohio State University
Columbus, OH

Juli Berwald, PhD
Science Writer
Austin, TX

John F. Bolzan, PhD
Science Writer
Columbus, OH

Rachel Clark, MS
Science Writer
Moscow, ID

Patricia Craig, MS
Science Writer
Bozeman, MT

Randall Frost, PhD
Science Writer
Pleasanton, CA

Lisa S. Gardiner, PhD
Science Writer
Denver, CO

Jennifer Gonya, PhD
The Ohio State University
Columbus, OH

Mary Ann Grobbel, MD
Science Writer
Grand Rapids, MI

Whitney Crispen Hagins, MA, MAT
Biology Teacher
Lexington High School
Lexington, MA

Carole Holmberg, BS
Planetarium Director
Calusa Nature Center and Planetarium, Inc.
Fort Myers, FL

Tina C. Hopper
Science Writer
Rockwall, TX

Jonathan D. W. Kahl, PhD
Professor of Atmospheric Science
University of Wisconsin-Milwaukee
Milwaukee, WI

Nanette Kalis
Science Writer
Athens, OH

S. Page Keeley, MEd
Maine Mathematics and Science Alliance
Augusta, ME

Cindy Klevickis, PhD
Professor of Integrated Science and Technology
James Madison University
Harrisonburg, VA

Kimberly Fekany Lee, PhD
Science Writer
La Grange, IL

Michael Manga, PhD
Professor
University of California, Berkeley
Berkeley, CA

Devi Ried Mathieu
Science Writer
Sebastopol, CA

Elizabeth A. Nagy-Shadman, PhD
Geology Professor
Pasadena City College
Pasadena, CA

William D. Rogers, DA
Professor of Biology
Ball State University
Muncie, IN

Donna L. Ross, PhD
Associate Professor
San Diego State University
San Diego, CA

Marion B. Sewer, PhD
Assistant Professor
School of Biology
Georgia Institute of Technology
Atlanta, GA

Julia Meyer Sheets, PhD
Lecturer
School of Earth Sciences
The Ohio State University
Columbus, OH

Michael J. Singer, PhD
Professor of Soil Science
Department of Land, Air and Water Resources
University of California
Davis, CA

Karen S. Sottosanti, MA
Science Writer
Pickerington, Ohio

Paul K. Strode, PhD
I.B. Biology Teacher
Fairview High School
Boulder, CO

Jan M. Vermilye, PhD
Research Geologist
Seismo-Tectonic Reservoir Monitoring (STRM)
Boulder, CO

Judith A. Yero, MA
Director
Teacher's Mind Resources
Hamilton, MT

Dinah Zike, MEd
Author, Consultant, Inventor of Foldables
Dinah Zike Academy; Dinah-Might Adventures, LP
San Antonio, TX

Margaret Zorn, MS
Science Writer
Yorktown, VA

Consulting Authors

Alton L. Biggs
Biggs Educational Consulting
Commerce, TX

Ralph M. Feather, Jr., PhD
Assistant Professor
Department of Educational Studies and Secondary Education
Bloomsburg University
Bloomsburg, PA

Douglas Fisher, PhD
Professor of Teacher Education
San Diego State University
San Diego, CA

Edward P. Ortleb
Science/Safety Consultant
St. Louis, MO

Series Consultants

Science

Solomon Bililign, PhD
Professor
Department of Physics
North Carolina Agricultural and Technical State University
Greensboro, NC

John Choinski
Professor
Department of Biology
University of Central Arkansas
Conway, AR

Anastasia Chopelas, PhD
Research Professor
Department of Earth and Space Sciences
UCLA
Los Angeles, CA

David T. Crowther, PhD
Professor of Science Education
University of Nevada, Reno
Reno, NV

A. John Gatz
Professor of Zoology
Ohio Wesleyan University
Delaware, OH

Sarah Gille, PhD
Professor
University of California San Diego
La Jolla, CA

David G. Haase, PhD
Professor of Physics
North Carolina State University
Raleigh, NC

Janet S. Herman, PhD
Professor
Department of Environmental Sciences
University of Virginia
Charlottesville, VA

David T. Ho, PhD
Associate Professor
Department of Oceanography
University of Hawaii
Honolulu, HI

Ruth Howes, PhD
Professor of Physics
Marquette University
Milwaukee, WI

Jose Miguel Hurtado, Jr., PhD
Associate Professor
Department of Geological Sciences
University of Texas at El Paso
El Paso, TX

Monika Kress, PhD
Assistant Professor
San Jose State University
San Jose, CA

Mark E. Lee, PhD
Associate Chair & Assistant Professor
Department of Biology
Spelman College
Atlanta, GA

Linda Lundgren
Science writer
Lakewood, CO

Keith O. Mann, PhD
Ohio Wesleyan University
Delaware, OH

Charles W. McLaughlin, PhD
Adjunct Professor of Chemistry
Montana State University
Bozeman, MT

Katharina Pahnke, PhD
Research Professor
Department of Geology and Geophysics
University of Hawaii
Honolulu, HI

Jesús Pando, PhD
Associate Professor
DePaul University
Chicago, IL

Hay-Oak Park, PhD
Associate Professor
Department of Molecular Genetics
Ohio State University
Columbus, OH

David A. Rubin, PhD
Associate Professor of Physiology
School of Biological Sciences
Illinois State University
Normal, IL

Toni D. Sauncy
Assistant Professor of Physics
Department of Physics
Angelo State University
San Angelo, TX

Series Consultants, continued

Malathi Srivatsan, PhD
Associate Professor of Neurobiology
College of Sciences and Mathematics
Arkansas State University
Jonesboro, AR

Cheryl Wistrom, PhD
Associate Professor of Chemistry
Saint Joseph's College
Rensselaer, IN

Reading

ReLeah Cossett Lent
Author/Educational Consultant
Blue Ridge, GA

Math

Vik Hovsepian
Professor of Mathematics
Rio Hondo College
Whittier, CA

Series Reviewers

Thad Boggs
Mandarin High School
Jacksonville, FL

Catherine Butcher
Webster Junior High School
Minden, LA

Erin Darichuk
West Frederick Middle School
Frederick, MD

Joanne Hedrick Davis
Murphy High School
Murphy, NC

Anthony J. DiSipio, Jr.
Octorara Middle School
Atglen, PA

Adrienne Elder
Tulsa Public Schools
Tulsa, OK

Carolyn Elliott
Iredell-Statesville Schools
Statesville, NC

Christine M. Jacobs
Ranger Middle School
Murphy, NC

Jason O. L. Johnson
Thurmont Middle School
Thurmont, MD

Felecia Joiner
Stony Point Ninth Grade Center
Round Rock, TX

Joseph L. Kowalski, MS
Lamar Academy
McAllen, TX

Brian McClain
Amos P. Godby High School
Tallahassee, FL

Von W. Mosser
Thurmont Middle School
Thurmont, MD

Ashlea Peterson
Heritage Intermediate Grade Center
Coweta, OK

Nicole Lenihan Rhoades
Walkersville Middle School
Walkersvillle, MD

Maria A. Rozenberg
Indian Ridge Middle School
Davie, FL

Barb Seymour
Westridge Middle School
Overland Park, KS

Ginger Shirley
Our Lady of Providence Junior-Senior High School
Clarksville, IN

Curtis Smith
Elmwood Middle School
Rogers, AR

Sheila Smith
Jackson Public School
Jackson, MS

Sabra Soileau
Moss Bluff Middle School
Lake Charles, LA

Tony Spoores
Switzerland County Middle School
Vevay, IN

Nancy A. Stearns
Switzerland County Middle School
Vevay, IN

Kari Vogel
Princeton Middle School
Princeton, MN

Alison Welch
Wm. D. Slider Middle School
El Paso, TX

Linda Workman
Parkway Northeast Middle School
Creve Coeur, MO

Online Guide

Get ConnectED

connectED.mcgraw-hill.com

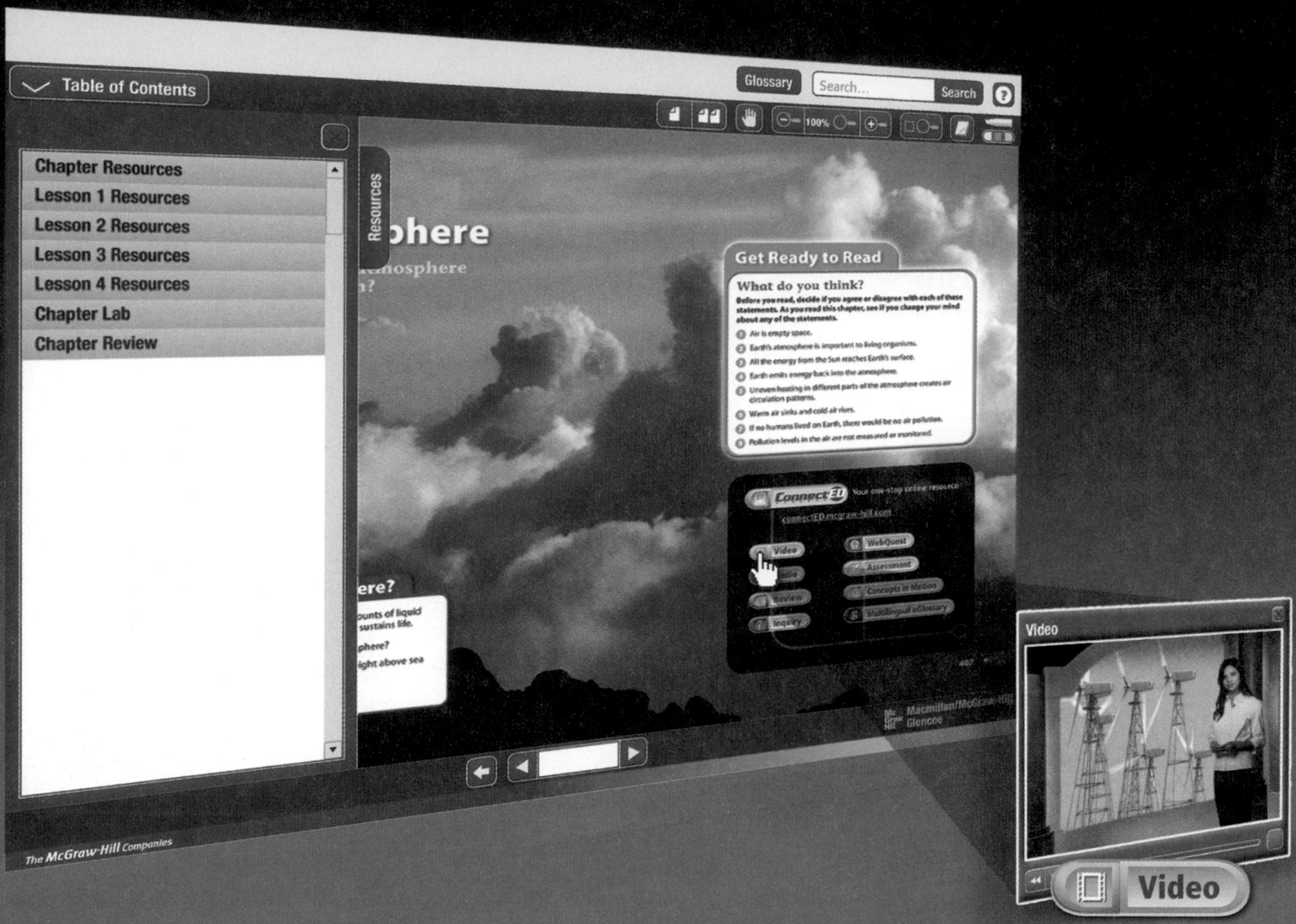

ConnectED

Your Digital Science Portal

Video See the science in real life through these exciting videos.

Audio Click the link and you can listen to the text while you follow along.

Review Try these interactive tools to help you review the lesson concepts.

Inquiry Explore concepts through hands-on and virtual labs.

WebQuest These web-based challenges relate the concepts you're learning about to the latest news and research.

The icons in your online student edition link you to interactive learning opportunities. Browse your online student book to find more.

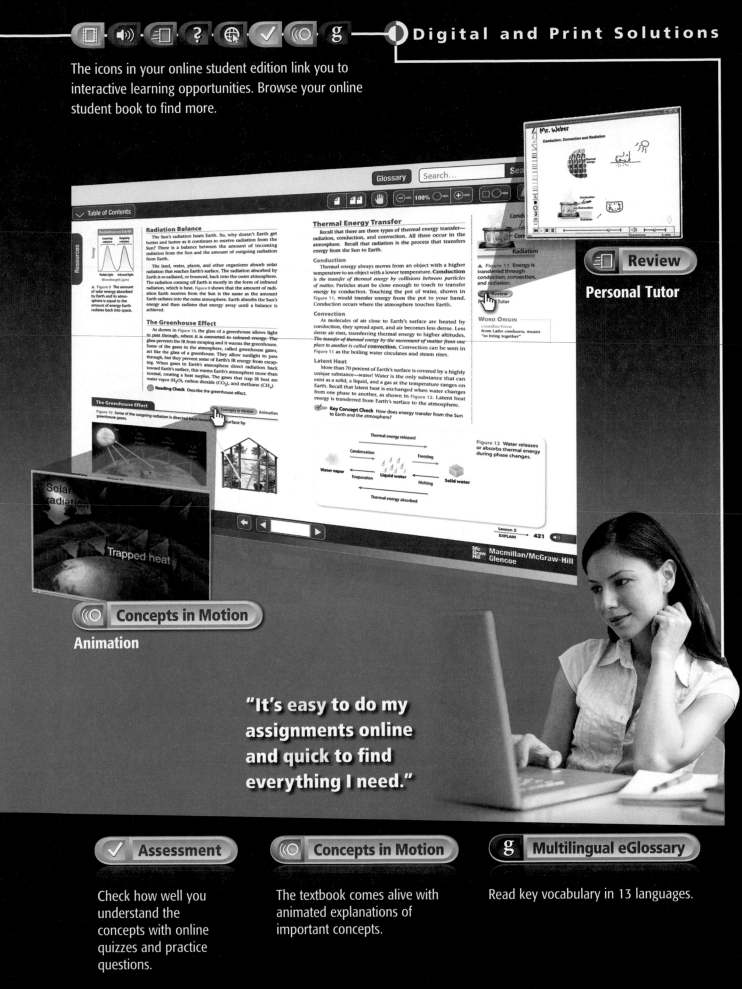

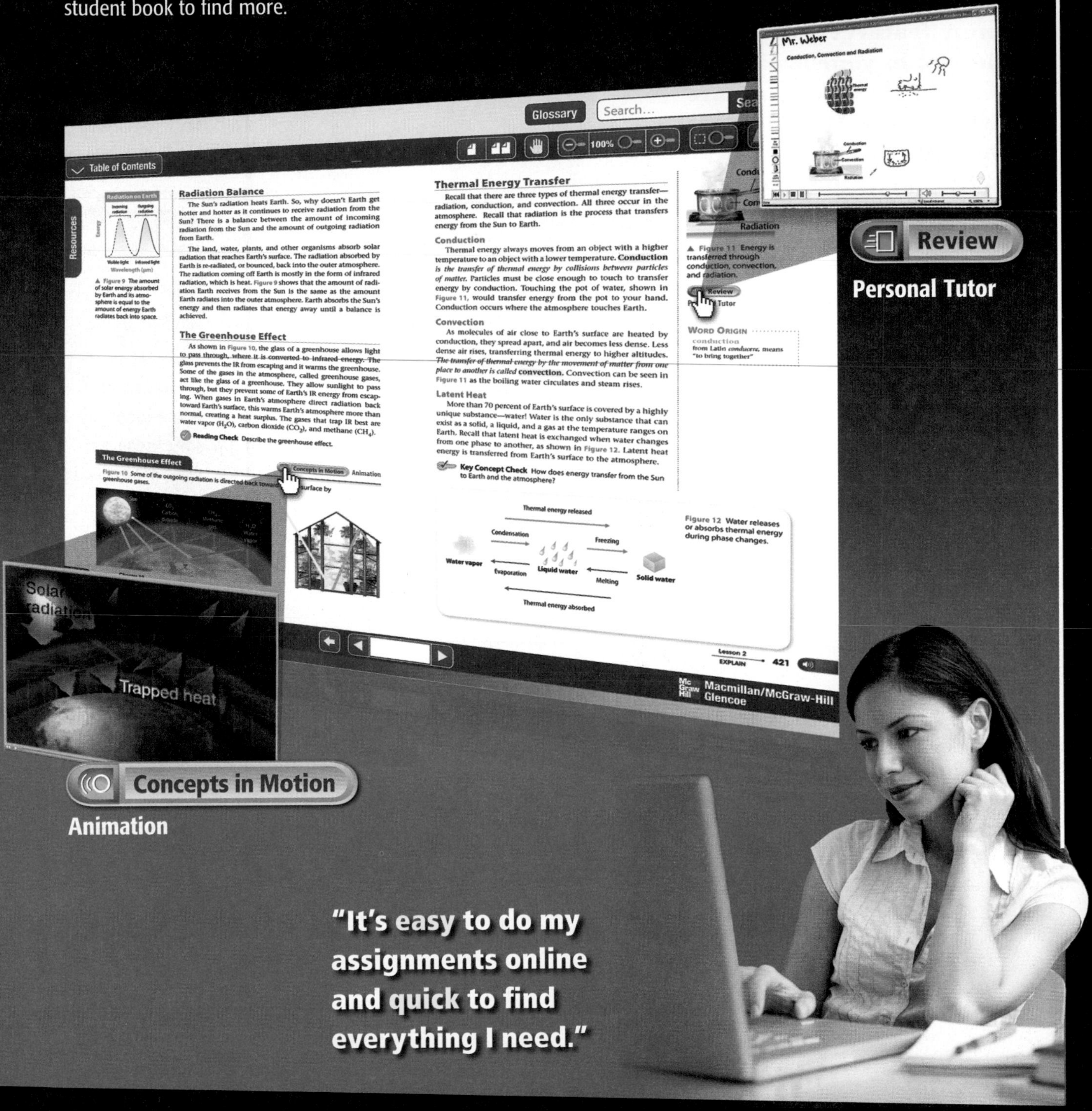

Review

Personal Tutor

Concepts in Motion

Animation

"It's easy to do my assignments online and quick to find everything I need."

Assessment

Check how well you understand the concepts with online quizzes and practice questions.

Concepts in Motion

The textbook comes alive with animated explanations of important concepts.

Multilingual eGlossary

Read key vocabulary in 13 languages.

Treasure Hunt

Your science book has many features that will aid you in your learning. Some of these features are listed below. You can use the activity at the right to help you find these and other special features in the book.

- THE BIG IDEA can be found at the start of each chapter.
- The Reading Guide at the start of each lesson lists **Key Concepts,** vocabulary terms, and online supplements to the content.
- ConnectED icons direct you to online resources such as animations, personal tutors, math practices, and quizzes.
- Inquiry Labs and Skill Practices are in each chapter.
- Your FOLDABLES help organize your notes.

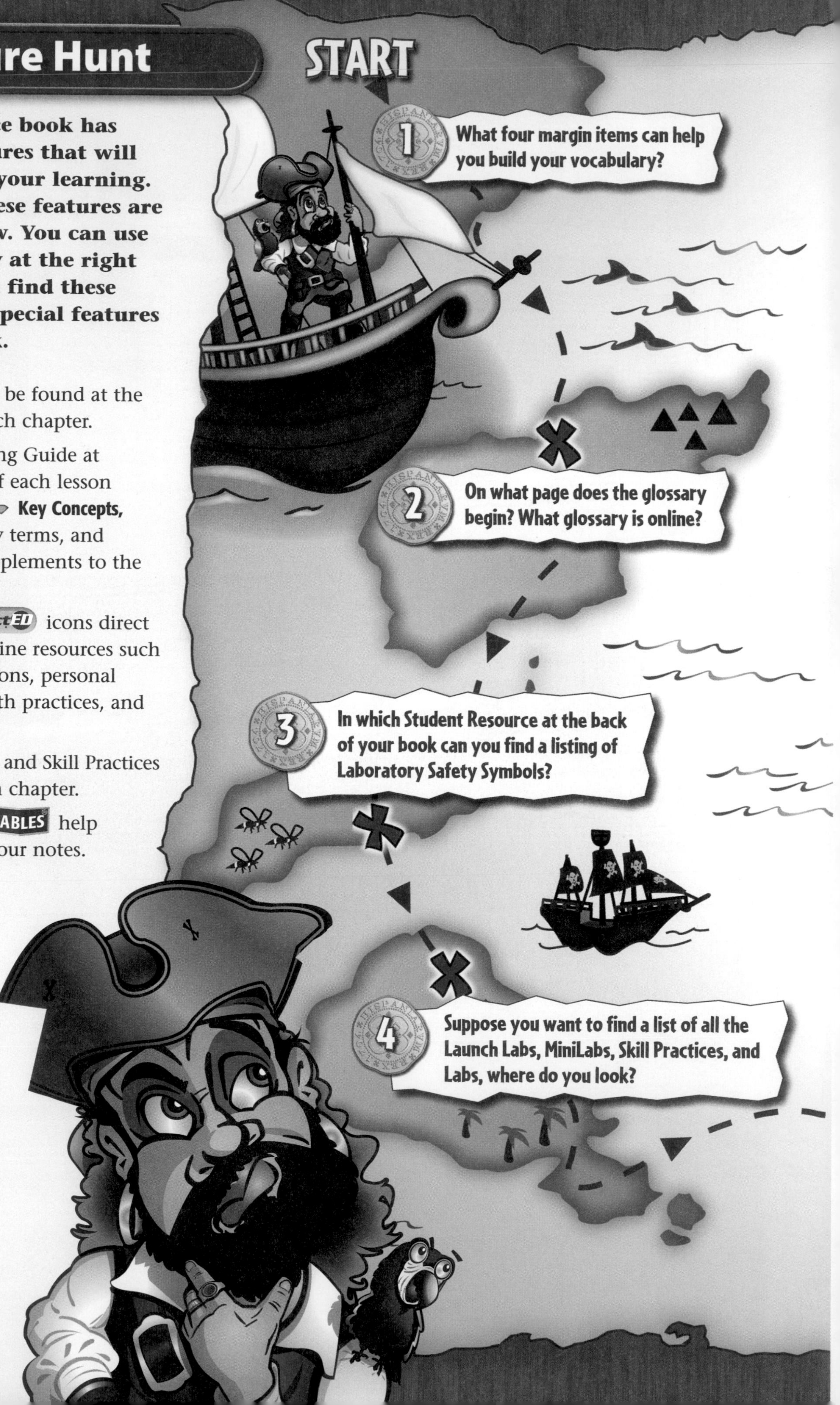

START
1
What four margin items can help you build your vocabulary?
2
On what page does the glossary begin? What glossary is online?
3
In which Student Resource at the back of your book can you find a listing of Laboratory Safety Symbols?
4
Suppose you want to find a list of all the Launch Labs, MiniLabs, Skill Practices, and Labs, where do you look?

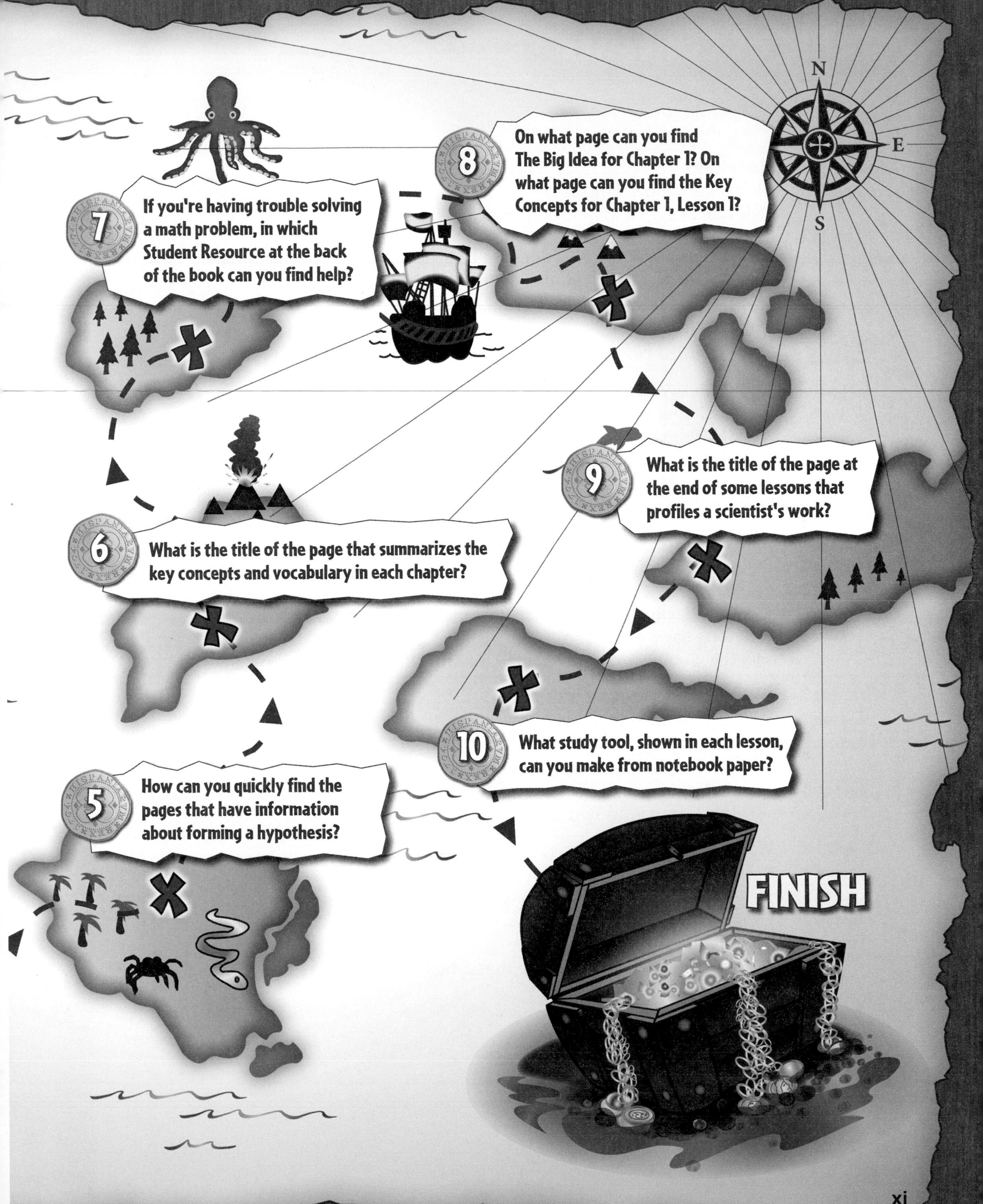
N
E
S
5
How can you quickly find the pages that have information about forming a hypothesis?
6
What is the title of the page that summarizes the key concepts and vocabulary in each chapter?
7
If you're having trouble solving a math problem, in which Student Resource at the back of the book can you find help?
8
On what page can you find The Big Idea for Chapter 1? On what page can you find the Key Concepts for Chapter 1, Lesson 1?
9
What is the title of the page at the end of some lessons that profiles a scientist's work?
10
What study tool, shown in each lesson, can you make from notebook paper?
FINISH

Table of Contents

Table of Contents

Student Resources

Inquiry Launch Labs

Inquiry MiniLabs

Inquiry Skill Practice

Inquiry Labs

Features

GREEN SCIENCE

HOW IT WORKS

SCIENCE & SOCIETY

CAREERS in SCIENCE

HOW NATURE WORKS

Science & Engineering

Scientific Explanations

THE BIG IDEA How can science provide answers to your questions about the world around you?

Inquiry Vacuuming Corals?

No, these two divers are collecting data about corals in waters near Sulawesi, Indonesia. They are marine biologists, scientists who study living things in oceans and other saltwater environments.

- What information about corals are these scientists collecting?
- What questions do they hope to answer?
- How can science provide answers to their questions and your questions?

Methods of SCIENCE

This chapter begins your study of the nature of science, but there is even more information about the nature of science in this book. Each unit begins by exploring an important topic that is fundamental to scientific study. As you read these topics, you will learn even more about the nature of science.

ConnectED Your one-stop online resource

connectED.mcgraw-hill.com

- Video
- Audio
- Review
- Inquiry
- WebQuest
- Assessment
- Concepts in Motion
- Multilingual eGlossary

Lesson 1 Understanding Science

Reading Guide

Key Concepts
ESSENTIAL QUESTIONS

- What is scientific inquiry?
- What are the results of scientific investigations?
- How can a scientist prevent bias in a scientific investigation?

Vocabulary

science p. NOS 4
observation p. NOS 6
inference p. NOS 6
hypothesis p. NOS 6
prediction p. NOS 7
technology p. NOS 8
scientific theory p. NOS 9
scientific law p. NOS 9
critical thinking p. NOS 10

Academic Standards for Science

Covers: 7.NS.1, 7.NS.8, 7.NS.11, 7.DP.1, 7.DP.3, 7.DP.4, 7.DP.5, 7.DP.6, 7.DP.7, 7.DP.10, 7.DP.11

What is science?

The last time that you watched squirrels play in a park or in your yard, did you realize that you were practicing science? Every time you observe the natural world, you are practicing science. **Science** *is the investigation and exploration of natural events and of the new information that results from those investigations.*

When you observe the natural world, you might form questions about what you see. While you are exploring those questions, you probably use reasoning, creativity, and skepticism to help you find answers to your questions. People use these behaviors in their daily lives to solve problems, such as keeping a squirrel from eating bird seed, as shown in **Figure 1.** Similarly, scientists use these behaviors in their work.

Scientists use a reliable set of skills and methods in different ways to find answers to questions. After reading this chapter, you will have a better understanding of how science works, the limitations of science, and scientific ways of thinking. In addition, you will recognize that when you practice science at home or in the classroom, you probably use scientific methods to answer questions just as scientists do.

Figure 1 Someone used reasoning and creativity to design each of these squirrel-proof bird feeders. However, some solutions don't work. Scientists use similar methods to try to solve problems.

Branches of Science

No one person can study all the natural world. Therefore, people tend to focus their efforts on one of the three fields or branches of science—life science, Earth science, or physical science, as described below. Then people or scientists can seek answers to specific problems within one field of science.

WORD ORIGIN

biology
from Greek *bios,* means "life"; and *logia,* means "study of"

Life Science

Biology, or life science, is the study of all living things. This forest ecologist, a life scientist who studies interactions in forest ecosystems, is studying lichens growing on Douglas firs. Biologists ask questions such as

- How do plants produce their own food?
- Why do some animals give birth to live young and others lay eggs?
- How are reptiles and birds related?

Earth Science

The study of Earth, including its landforms, rocks, soil, and forces that shape Earth's surface, is Earth science. These Earth scientists are collecting soil samples in Africa. Earth scientists ask questions such as

- How do rocks form?
- What causes earthquakes?
- What substances are in soil?

Physical Science

The study of chemistry and physics is physical science. Physical scientists study the interactions of matter and energy. This chemist is preparing antibiotic solutions. Physical scientists ask questions such as

- How do substances react and form new substances?
- Why does a liquid change to a solid?
- How are force and motion related?

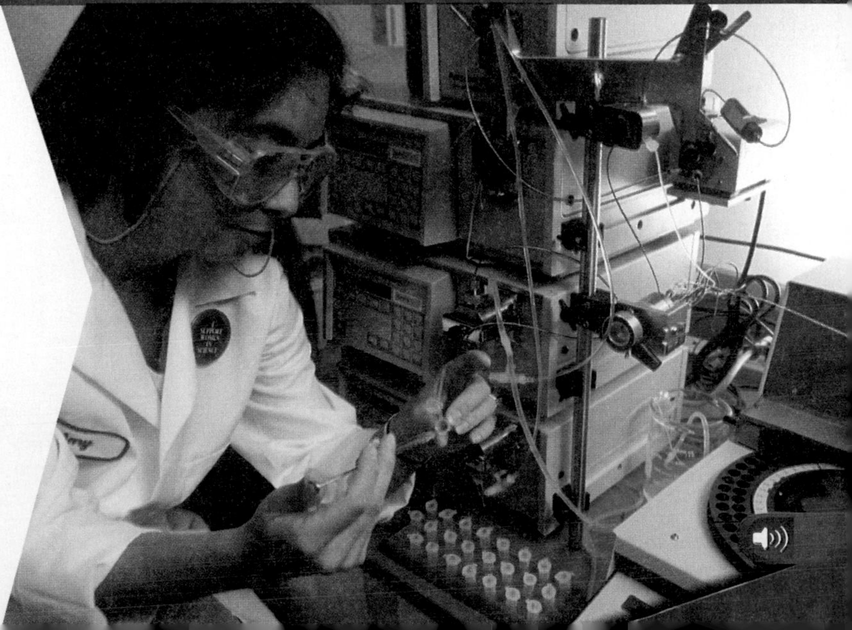

Scientific Inquiry

As scientists study the natural world, they ask questions about what they observe. To find the answers to these questions, they usually use certain skills, or methods. The chart in **Figure 2** shows a sequence of the skills that a scientist might use in an investigation. However, it is important to know that, sometimes, not all of these skills are performed in an investigation, or performed in this order. Scientists practice scientific inquiry—a process that uses a variety of skills and tools to answer questions or to test ideas about the natural world.

Ask Questions

Like a scientist, you use scientific inquiry in your life, too. Suppose you decide to plant a vegetable garden. As you plant the vegetable seeds, you water some seeds more than others. Then, you weed part of the garden and mix fertilizer into some of the soil. After a few weeks, you observe that some vegetable plants are growing better than others. An **observation** *is using one or more of your senses to gather information and take note of what occurs.*

Observations often are the beginning of the process of inquiry and can lead to questions such as "Why are some plants growing better than others?" As you are making observations and asking questions, you recall from science class that plants need plenty of water and sunlight to grow. Therefore you infer that perhaps some vegetables are receiving more water or sunlight than others and, therefore, are growing better. An **inference** *is a logical explanation of an observation that is drawn from prior knowledge or experience.*

Hypothesize

After making observations and inferences, you are ready to develop a hypothesis and investigate why some vegetables are growing better than others. *A possible explanation about an observation that can be tested by scientific investigations is a* **hypothesis.** Your hypothesis might be: Some plants are growing taller and more quickly than others because they are receiving more water and sunlight. Or, your hypothesis might be: The plants that are growing quickly have received fertilizer because fertilizer helps plants grow.

Figure 2 This flow chart shows steps you or a scientist might use during a scientific investigation.

Visual Check What happens if a hypothesis is not supported?

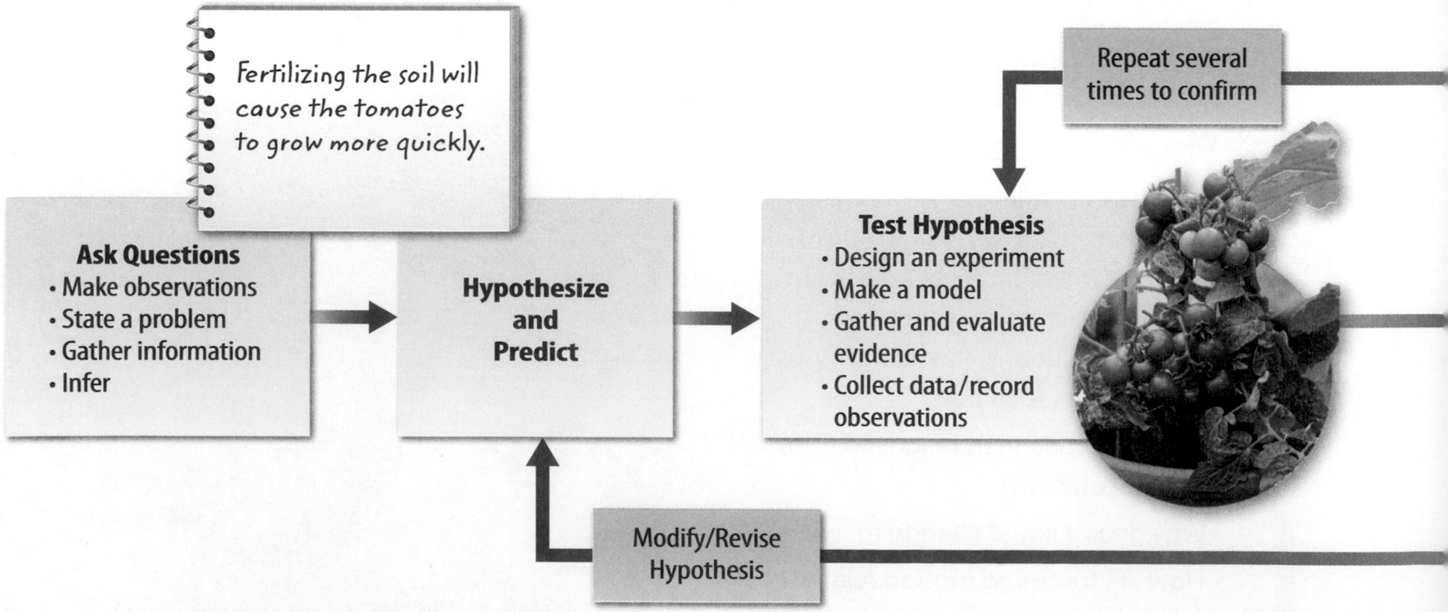

Predict

After you state a hypothesis, you might make a prediction to help you test your hypothesis. *A* **prediction** *is a statement of what will happen next in a sequence of events.* For instance, based on your hypotheses, you might predict that if some plants receive more water, sunlight, or fertilizer, then they will grow taller and more quickly.

Test your Hypothesis

When you test a hypothesis, you often are testing your predictions. For example, you might design an experiment to test your hypothesis on the fertilizer. You set up an experiment in which you plant seeds and add fertilizer to only some of them. Your prediction is that the plants that get the fertilizer will grow more quickly. If your prediction is confirmed, it supports your hypothesis. If your prediction is not confirmed, your hypothesis might need revision.

Analyze Results

As you are testing your hypothesis, you are probably collecting data about the plants' rates of growth and how much fertilizer each plant receives. Initially, it might be difficult to recognize patterns and relationships in data. Your next step might be to organize and analyze your data.

You can create graphs, classify information, or make models and calculations. Once data are organized, you more easily can study the data and draw conclusions. Other methods of testing a hypothesis and analyzing results are shown in **Figure 2.**

Draw Conclusions

Now you must decide whether your data do or do not support your hypothesis and draw conclusions. A conclusion is a summary of the information gained from testing a hypothesis. You might make more inferences when drawing conclusions. If your hypothesis is supported, you can repeat your experiment several times to confirm your results. If your hypothesis is not supported, you can modify it and repeat the scientific inquiry process.

Communicate Results

An important step in scientific inquiry is communicating results to others. Professional scientists write scientific articles, speak at conferences, or exchange information on the Internet. This part of scientific inquiry is important because scientists use new information in their research or perform other scientists' investigations to verify results.

Key Concept Check What is scientific inquiry?

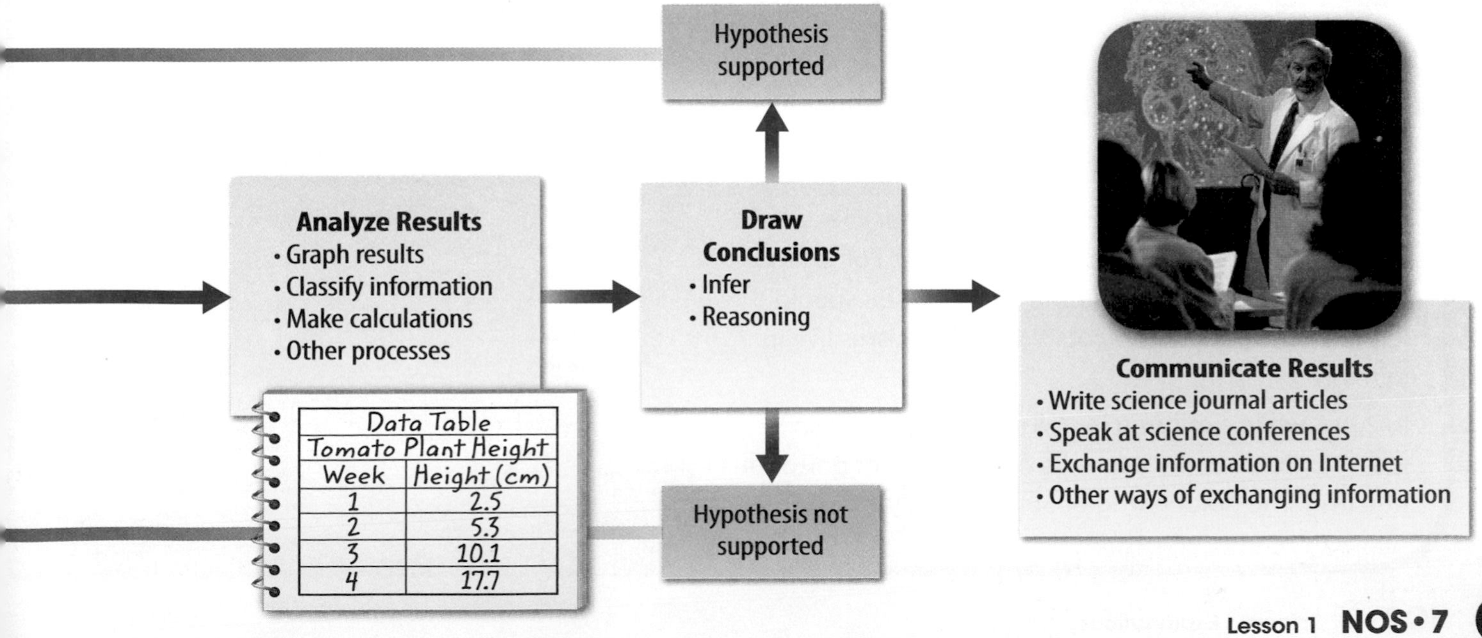

Results of Scientific Inquiry

In science, you perform scientific inquiry to find answers to questions. There are many outcomes of scientific inquiry, such as technology, materials, and explanations, as shown below.

Key Concept Check What are the results of scientific investigations?

Technology

The practical use of scientific knowledge, especially for industrial or commercial use is technology. Televisions, MP3 players, and computers are examples of technology. The C-Leg, shown to the right, is one of the latest designs of computer-aided limbs. The prosthetic leg has sensors that anticipate the user's next move, which prevents him or her from stumbling or tripping. In addition, this new technology has several modes that can enable the user to walk, stand for long periods of time, and even ride a bike.

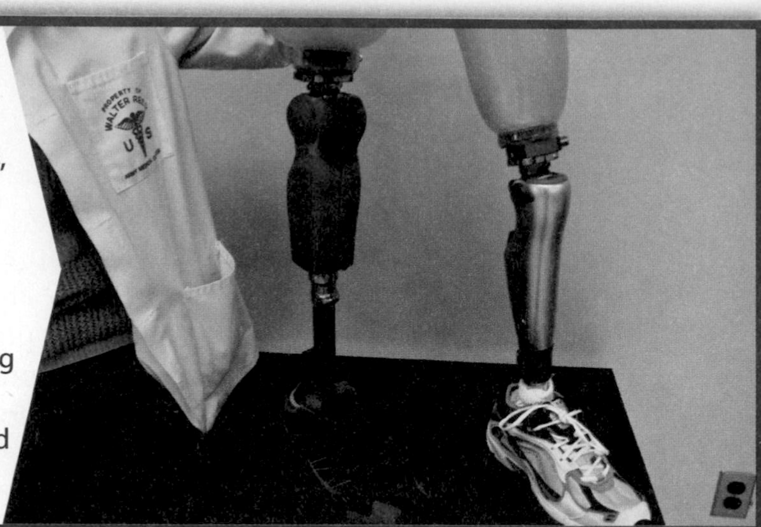

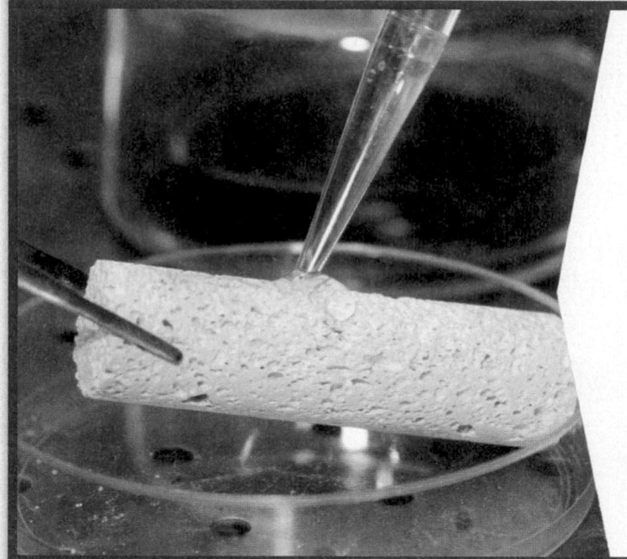

New Materials

Another possible outcome of an investigation are new materials. For example, scientists have developed a bone bioceramic. A bioceramic is a natural calcium-phosphate mineral complex that is part of bones and teeth. This synthetic bone mimics natural bone's structure. Its porous structure allows a type of cell to grow and develop into new bone tissue. The bioceramic can be shaped into implants that are treated with certain cells from the patient's bone marrow. It then can be implanted into the patient's body to replace missing bone.

Possible Explanations

Many times, scientific investigations answer the questions: *who, what, when, where,* or *how*. For example, who left fingerprints at a crime scene? When should fertilizer be applied to plants? What organisms live in rain forests?

In 2007, while exploring in Colombia's tropical rain forests, scientists discovered a new species of poisonous tree frog. The golden frog of Supatá is only 2 cm long.

Scientific Theory and Scientific Laws

Scientists often repeat scientific investigations to verify that the results for a hypothesis or a group of hypotheses are correct. This can lead to a scientific theory.

Scientific Theory The everyday meaning of the word *theory* is an untested idea or an opinion. However, a **scientific theory** *is an explanation of observations or events based on knowledge gained from many observations and investigations.* For example, about 300 years ago, scientists began looking at samples of trees, water, and blood through the first microscopes. They noticed that all of these organisms were made of tinier units, or cells, as shown in **Figure 3.** As more scientists observed cells in other organisms, their observations became known as the cell theory. This theory explains that all living things are made of cells. A scientific theory is assumed to be the best explanation of observations unless it is disproved. The cell theory will continue to explain the makeup of all organisms until an organism is discovered that is not made of cells.

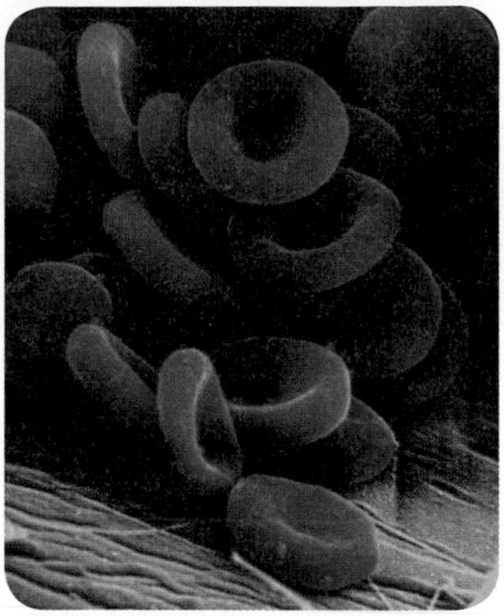

Figure 3 When you view blood using a microscope, you will see that it contains red blood cells.

Scientific Laws Scientific laws are different from societal laws, which are an agreement on a set of behavior. A **scientific law** *describes a pattern or an event in nature that is always true.* A scientific theory might explain how and why an event occurs. But a scientific law states only that an event in nature will occur under specific conditions. For example, the law of conservation of mass states that the mass of materials will be the same before and after a chemical reaction. This scientific law does not explain why this occurs—only that it will occur. **Table 1** compares a scientific theory and a scientific law.

FOLDABLES®

Make a vertical two-column chart book. Label it as shown. Use it to organize your notes on scientific investigations.

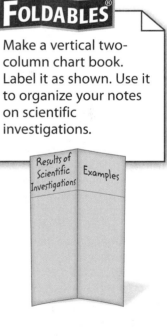

Table 1 Comparing Scientific Theory and Scientific Law

Scientific Theory	Scientific Law
A scientific theory is based on repeated observations and scientific investigations.	Scientific laws are observations of similar events that have been observed repeatedly.
If new information does not support a scientific theory, the theory will be modified or rejected.	If many new observations do not follow the law, the law is rejected.
A scientific theory attempts to explain why something happens.	A scientific law states that something will happen.
A scientific theory usually is more complex than a scientific law and might contain many well-supported hypotheses.	A scientific law usually contains one well-supported hypothesis that states that something will happen.

Skepticism in Media

When you see scientific issues in the media, such as newspapers, radio, television, and magazines, it is important to be skeptical. When you are skeptical, you question information that you read or hear, or events you observe. Is the information truthful? Is it accurate? It also is important that you question statements made by people outside their area of expertise, and claims that are based on vague statements.

Evaluating Scientific Evidence

An important skill in scientific inquiry is critical thinking. **Critical thinking** *is comparing what you already know with the information you are given in order to decide whether you agree with it.* Identifying and preventing bias also is important when conducting scientific inquiry. To prevent bias in an investigation, sampling, repetition, and blind studies can be helpful, as shown below.

Key Concept Check How can a scientist prevent bias in a scientific investigation?

1 Sampling

A method of data collection that involves studying small amounts of something in order to learn about the larger whole is sampling. A sample should be a random representation of the whole.

2 Bias

It is important to remain unbiased during scientific investigations. Bias is intentional or unintentional prejudice toward a specific outcome. Sources of bias in an investigation can include equipment choices, hypothesis formation, and prior knowledge.

Suppose you were a part of a taste test for a new cereal. If you knew the price of each cereal, you might think that the most expensive one tastes the best. This is a bias.

3 Blind Study

A procedure that can reduce bias is a blind study. The investigator, subject, or both do not know which item they are testing. Personal biases cannot affect an investigation if participants do not know what they are testing.

4 Repetition

If you get different results when you repeat an investigation, then the original investigation probably was flawed. Repetition of experiments helps reduce bias.

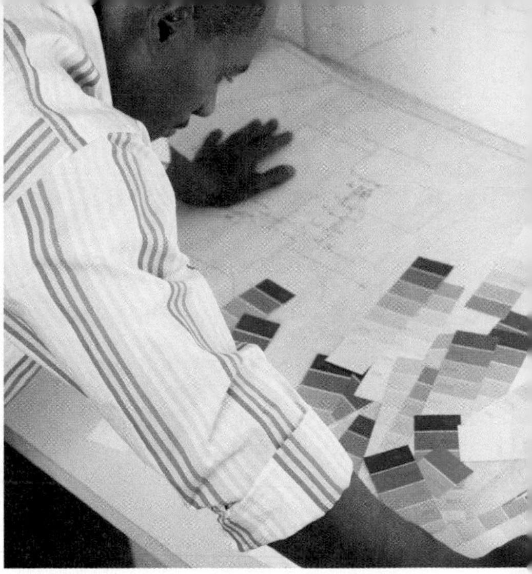

Figure 4 Science cannot answer questions based on opinions or feelings, such as which paint color is the prettiest.

Science cannot answer all questions.

You might think that any question can be answered through a scientific investigation. But there are some questions that science cannot answer, such as the one posed in **Figure 4.** Questions about personal opinions, values, beliefs, and feelings cannot be answered scientifically. However, some people use scientific evidence to try to strengthen their claims about these topics.

Safety in Science

Scientists follow safety procedures when they conduct investigations. You too should follow safety procedures when you do any experiments. You should wear appropriate safety equipment and listen to your teacher's instructions. Also, you should learn to recognize potential hazards and to know the meaning of safety symbols. Read more about science laboratory safety in the Science Skill Handbook at the back of this book.

Ethics are especially important when using living things during investigations. Animals should be treated properly. Scientists also should tell research participants about the potential risks and benefits of the research. Anyone can refuse to participate in scientific research.

ACADEMIC VOCABULARY
ethics
(noun) rules of conduct or moral principles

Lesson 1 Review

Assessment Online Quiz
Inquiry Virtual Lab

Use Vocabulary

1. **Explain** the relationship between observations and hypotheses.
2. **Use the terms** *technology, scientific law,* and *scientific theory* in complete sentences.
3. **Contrast** inference and prediction.
4. **Compare and contrast** critical thinking and inference.

Understand Key Concepts

5. Which should NOT be part of scientific inquiry?
   A. bias
   B. analysis
   C. hypothesis
   D. testing
6. **Describe** four real-life examples of the results of scientific investigations.
7. **Discuss** four ways a scientist can prevent bias in scientific investigations.

Interpret Graphics

8. **Draw** a graphic organizer like the one below. In each oval, list an example of how to test a hypothesis using scientific inquiry.

Critical Thinking

9. **Suggest** Why do you think people believe some theories even if they are not supported by credible evidence?
10. **Evaluate** In a magazine, you read that two scientific investigations attempted to answer the same question. However, the two teams of scientists came to opposite conclusions. How do you decide which investigation was valid?

Science & Engineering

The Design Process

Create a Solution to a Problem

Scientists investigate and explore natural events and then interpret data and share information learned from those investigations. How do engineers differ from scientists? Engineers design, construct, and maintain things that do not occur naturally. Roads, submarines, toys and games, microscopes, medical equipment, and amusement park rides all are the results of engineering. Science involves the practice of scientific inquiry, but engineering involves The Design Process—a set of methods used to find and create a solution to a problem or need.

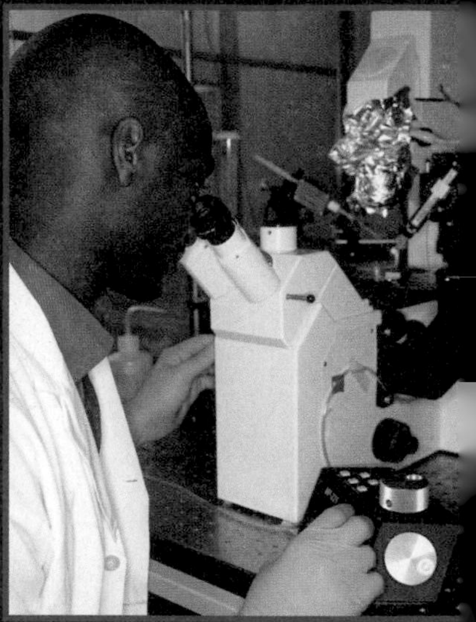

Engineers have developed tools, such as submersibles and microscopes, that enable scientists to better explore the biological, physical, and chemical world, no matter where studies take place—under water, in a lab, or in a rain forest.

Alvin, a deep-sea submersible, has been in operation since 1964. It makes about 200 deep-sea dives each year and has helped scientists discover human artifacts, deep-sea organisms, and seafloor processes. Microscopes enable scientists to examine closely things that are not visible to the naked eye.

The Design Process

1. Identify a Problem or Need
- Determine a problem or need
- Document all questions, research, and procedures throughout the process

2. Research and Develop Solutions
- Brainstorm possible solutions
- Research any existing solutions that address the problem or need
- Suggest limitations of the solutions

3. Construct a Prototype
- Develop possible solutions
- Estimate materials, costs, resources, and time to develop the solutions
- Select the best possible solution
- Construct a prototype

4. Test and Evaluate Solutions
- Use models to test the solutions
- Use graphs, charts, and tables to evaluate results
- Analyze the process and evaluate strengths and weaknesses of the solution

5. Communicate Results and Redesign
- Communicate your design process and results to others
- Redesign and modify solution
- Construct final solution

Design a Magnifying Tool

While on a rain forest field study with a group of fellow scientists, you discover a plant you do not recognize. Because the rain forest contains some plant species that are poisonous, you know not to touch the plant as you examine it. You could become famous with this new discovery. Unfortunately, you lost your scientific backpack earlier when you crossed the Deepenphast River. How can you examine the plant specimen more closely?

Identify the Problem

You are anxious to examine and identify the plant species. You do not have your microscope or other tools to examine the plant's structures. When you were young, you read how microscopes and lenses were first developed. You remember that water and glass were used to view small details of objects. How can you engineer a tool to enlarge your view of the plant using only the limited supplies in your day pack—a bottle of water, a plastic bag of paper clips, a test tube and stopper, a glass slide, a dropper, forceps, and disposable gloves?

Research Existing Solutions

Begin answering your questions by researching existing magnifying devices. How could you design and construct such a tool? Make note of possible limitations to your solutions, such as cost, size, materials, location, time, or other restraints.

Brainstorm Possible Solutions

Record in your Science Journal ideas for engineering a device to magnify tiny objects. Note how curved surfaces change the size and shape of an object, how distance from an object changes the view, and how both the amount of light and the angle of light affect the image. Record any limitations to your construction.

Construct a Prototype

Discuss how the limited supplies could be used to design and construct a magnifying tool. Draw several plans to answer your problem. Use your materials to construct several models of a magnifier.

Test and Evaluate Solutions

Test your models many times to compare the ability to increase the size and clarity of the image. Use graphs, charts, and tables to evaluate the process and identify strengths and weaknesses in your solutions.

Communicate Your Results and Redesign Your Magnifying Tools

Share your design process and solutions with peers using visual displays and models. Discuss and critique your working solutions. Do further research and testing, if necessary. Redesign and modify your solutions to meet design objectives. Finally, construct models of your magnifying tools.

Lesson 2 Measurement and Scientific Tools

Reading Guide

Key Concepts

ESSENTIAL QUESTIONS

- What is the difference between accuracy and precision?
- Why should you use significant digits?
- What are some tools used by life scientists?

Vocabulary

description p. NOS 14
explanation p. NOS 14
International System of Units (SI) p. NOS 14
accuracy p. NOS 16
precision p. NOS 16
significant digits p. NOS 17

g Multilingual eGlossary

Academic Standards for Science

Covers: 7.NS.3, 7.NS.5, 7.NS.7, 7.NS.8

Description and Explanation

How would you describe the squirrel's activity in **Figure 5?** A **description** *is a spoken or written summary of observations.* Your description might include information such as: the squirrel buried five acorns near a large tree. A qualitative description uses your senses (sight, sound, smell, touch, taste) to describe an observation. *A large tree* is a qualitative description. However, a quantitative observation uses numbers to describe the observation. *Five acorns* is a quantitative description. You can use measuring tools, such as a ruler, a balance, or a thermometer, to make quantitative descriptions.

How would you explain the squirrel's activity? An **explanation** *is an interpretation of observations.* You might explain that the squirrel is storing acorns for food at a later time. When you describe something, you report what you observe. But when you explain something, you try to interpret your observations. This can lead to a hypothesis.

Figure 5 A description and an explanation of a squirrel's activity contain different information.

The International System of Units

Suppose you observed a squirrel searching for buried food and recorded that it traveled about 200 ft from its nest. Someone who measures distances in meters might not understand how far the squirrel traveled. The scientific community solved this problem in 1960. It adopted *an internationally accepted system for measurement called the* **International System of Units (SI).**

SI Base Units and Prefixes

Like scientists and many others around the world, you probably use the SI system in your classroom. All SI units are derived from seven base units, as listed in **Table 2.** For example, the base unit for length, or the unit most commonly used to measure length, is the meter. However, you have probably made measurements in kilometers or millimeters before. Where do these units come from?

A prefix can be added to a base unit's name to indicate either a fraction or a multiple of that base unit. The prefixes are based on powers of ten, such as 0.01 and 100, as shown in **Table 3.** For example, one centimeter (1 cm) is one-hundredth of a meter and a kilometer (1 km) is 1,000 meters.

Concepts in Motion **Interactive Table**

Table 2 SI Base Units

Quantity Measured	Unit (symbol)
Length	meter (m)
Mass	kilogram (kg)
Time	second (s)
Electric current	ampere (A)
Temperature	Kelvin (K)
Substance amount	mole (mol)
Light intensity	candela (cd)

Table 3 Prefixes

Prefix	Meaning
Mega– (M)	1,000,000 (10^6)
Kilo– (k)	1,000 (10^3)
Hecto– (h)	100 (10^2)
Deka– (da)	10 (10^1)
Deci– (d)	0.1 (10^{-1})
Centi– (c)	0.01 (10^{-2})
Milli– (m)	0.001 (10^{-3})
Micro– (μ)	0.000 001 (10^{-6})

Conversion

It is easy to convert from one SI unit to another. You either multiply or divide by a power of ten. You also can use proportion calculations to make conversions. For example, a biologist measures an Emperor goose in the field. Her triple-beam balance shows the goose has a mass of 2.8 kg. She could perform the calculation below to find its mass in grams, X.

$$\frac{X}{2.8\text{ kg}} = \frac{1{,}000\text{ g}}{1\text{ kg}}$$

$$(1\text{ kg})X = (1{,}000\text{ g})(2.8\text{ kg})$$

$$X = \frac{(1{,}000\text{ g})(2.8\text{ }\cancel{\text{kg}})}{1\text{ }\cancel{\text{kg}}}$$

$$X = 2{,}800\text{ g}$$

Notice that the answer has the correct units.

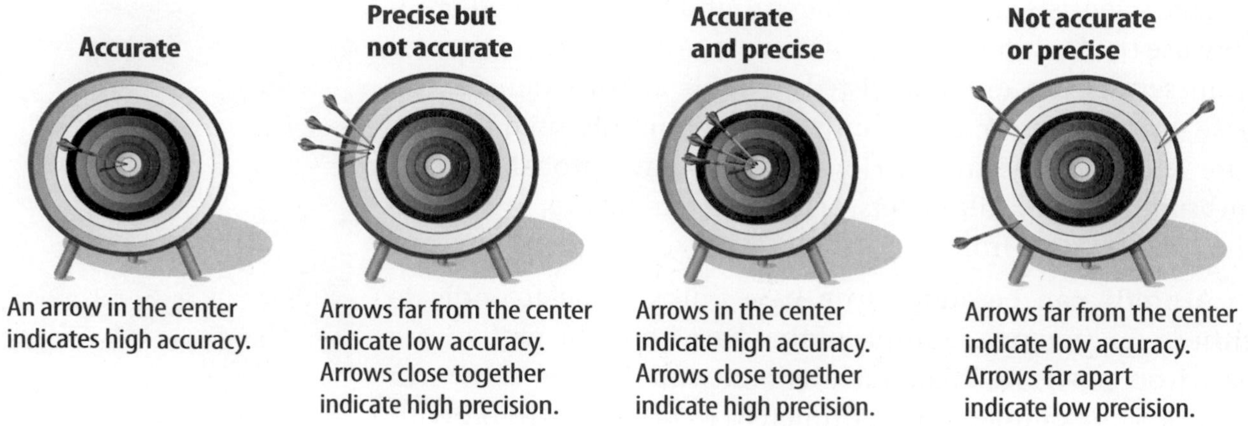

Accurate
Precise but not accurate
Accurate and precise
Not accurate or precise
An arrow in the center indicates high accuracy.
Arrows far from the center indicate low accuracy. Arrows close together indicate high precision.
Arrows in the center indicate high accuracy. Arrows close together indicate high precision.
Arrows far from the center indicate low accuracy. Arrows far apart indicate low precision.

Figure 6 The archery target illustrates accuracy and precision. An accurate shot is in the bull's-eye.

Precision and Accuracy

Suppose your friend Simon tells you that he will call you in one minute, but he calls you a minute and a half later. Sarah tells you that she will call you in one minute, and she calls exactly 60 seconds later. What is the difference? Sarah is accurate and Simon is not. **Accuracy** *is a description of how close a measurement is to an accepted or true value.* However, if Simon always calls about 30 seconds later than he says he will, then Simon is precise. **Precision** *is a description of how similar or close measurements are to each other,* as shown in **Figure 6.**

FOLDABLES®

Make a horizontal two-tab book with a top-tab. Label it as shown. Use it to compare precision and accuracy.

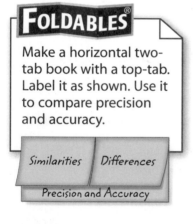

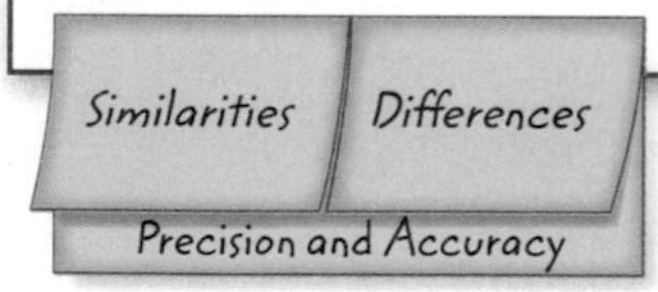

Table 4 illustrates the difference between precise and accurate measurements. Students were asked to find the melting point of sucrose, or table sugar. Each student took three temperature readings and calculated the mean, or average, of his or her data. As the recorded data in the table shows, student A had more accurate data. The melting point mean, 184.7°C, is closer to the scientifically accepted melting point, 185°C. Although not accurate, Student C's measurements are the most precise because they are similar in value.

Key Concept Check How do accuracy and precision differ?

Table 4 The data taken by student A are more accurate because each value is close to the accepted value. The data taken by student C are more precise because the data are similar.

Table 4 Student Melting Point Data

	Student A	Student B	Student C
Trial 1	183.5°C	190.0°C	181.2°C
Trial 2	185.9°C	183.3°C	182.0°C
Trial 3	184.6°C	187.1°C	181.7°C
Mean	184.7°C	186.8°C	181.6°C
Sucrose Melting Point (accepted value) 185°C			

Measurement and Accuracy

The tools used to take measurements can limit the accuracy of the measurements. Suppose you are measuring the temperature at which sugar melts, and the thermometer's measurements are divided into whole numbers. If your sugar sample melts between 183°C and 184°C, you can estimate the temperature between these two numbers. But, if the thermometer's measurements are divided into tenths, and your sample melts between 183.2°C and 183.3°C, your estimate between these numbers would be more accurate.

Significant Digits

In the second example above, you know that the temperature is between 183.2°C and 183.3°C. You could estimate that the temperature is 183.25°C. When you take any measurement, some digits you know for certain and some digits you estimate. **Significant digits** *are the number of digits in a measurement that are known with a certain degree of reliability.* The significant digits in a measurement include all digits you know for certain plus one estimated digit. Therefore, your measurement of 183.25°C would contain five significant digits, as explained in **Table 5.** Using significant digits lets others know how certain your measurements are. **Figure 7** shows an example of rounding to 3 significant digits?

Key Concept Check Why should you use significant digits?

Figure 7 Since the ruler is divided into tenths, you know the rod is between 5.2 cm and 5.3 cm. You can estimate that the rod is 5.25 cm.

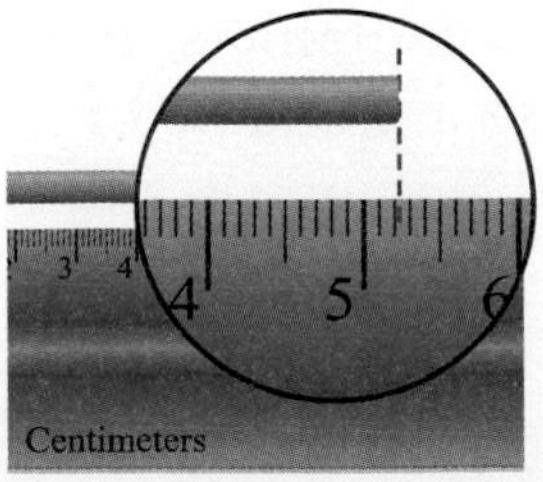

Math Skills

Significant Digits

The number 5,281 has 4 significant digits. Rule 1 in **Table 5** below states that all nonzero numbers are significant.

Practice

Use the rules in **Table 5** to determine the number of significant digits in each of the following numbers: 2.02; 0.0057; 1,500; and 0.500.

Review

- **Math Practice**
- **Personal Tutor**

SCIENCE USE V. COMMON USE

digital

Science Use of, pertaining to, or using numbers (numerical digits)

Common Use of or pertaining to a finger

Table 5 Significant Digits

Rules

1. All nonzero numbers are significant.
2. Zeros between nonzero digits are significant.
3. Final zeros used after the decimal point are significant.
4. Zeros used solely for spacing the decimal point are not significant. The zeros indicate only the position of the decimal point.

* The blue numbers in the examples are the significant digits.

Example	Significant Digits	Applied Rules
1.234	4	1
1.2	2	1
0.023	2	1, 4
0.200	3	1, 3
1,002	4	1, 2
3.07	3	1, 2
0.001	1	1, 4
0.012	2	1, 4
50,600	3	1, 2, 4

Scientific Tools

Scientific inquiry often requires the use of tools. Scientists, including life scientists, might use the tools listed on this page and the next page. You might use one or more of them during a scientific inquiry, too. For more information about the proper use of these tools, see the Science Skill Handbook at the back of this book.

Science Journal ▶

In a science journal, you can record descriptions, explanations, plans, and steps used in a scientific inquiry. A science journal can be a spiral-bound notebook or a loose-leaf binder. It is important to keep your science journal organized so that you can find information when you need it. Make sure you keep thorough and accurate records.

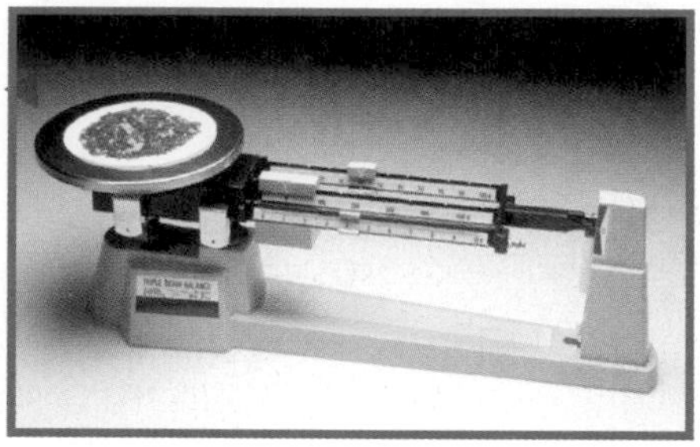

◀ Balances

You can use a triple-beam balance or an electric balance to measure mass. Mass usually is measured in kilograms (kg) or grams (g). When using a balance, do not let objects drop heavily onto the balance. Gently remove an object after you record its mass.

Thermometer ▶

A thermometer measures the temperature of substances. Although the Kelvin (K) is the SI unit for temperature, in the science classroom, you measure temperature in degrees Celsius (°C). Use care when you place a thermometer into a hot substance so that you do not burn yourself. Handle glass thermometers gently so that they do not break. If a thermometer does break, tell your teacher immediately. Do not touch the broken glass or the thermometer's liquid. Never use a thermometer to stir anything.

◀ Glassware

Laboratory glassware is used to hold, pour, heat, and measure liquids. Most labs have many types of glassware. For example, flasks, beakers, petri dishes, test tubes, and specimen jars are used as containers. To measure the volume of a liquid, you use a graduated cylinder. The unit of measure for liquid volume is the liter (L) or milliliter (mL).

◀ Compound Microscope

Microscopes enable you to observe small objects that you cannot observe with just your eyes. Usually, two types of microscopes are in science classrooms—dissecting microscopes and compound light microscopes, such as the one shown to the left. The girl is looking into two eyepieces to observe a magnified image of a small object or organism. However, some microscopes have only one eyepiece.

Microscopes can be damaged easily. It is important to follow your teacher's instructions when carrying and using a microscope. For more information about how to use a microscope, see the Science Skill Handbook at the back of this book.

Concepts in Motion **Animation**

Computers—Hardware and Software ▶

Computers process information. In science, you can use computers to compile, retrieve, and analyze data for reports. You also can use them to create reports and other documents, to send information to others, and to research information.

The physical components of computers, such as monitors and keyboards, are called hardware. The programs that you run on computers are called software. These programs include word processing, spreadsheets, and presentation programs. When scientists write reports, they use word processing programs. They use spreadsheet programs for organizing and analyzing data. Presentation programs can be used to explain information to others.

Tools Used by Life Scientists

Magnifying Lens

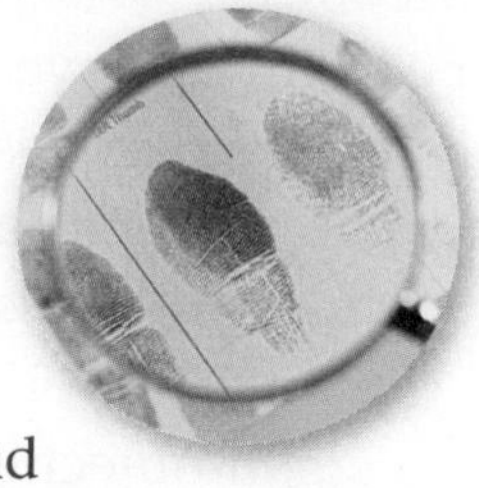

A magnifying lens is a hand-held lens that magnifies, or enlarges, an image of an object. It is not as powerful as a microscope and is useful when great magnification is not needed. Magnifying lenses also can be used outside the lab where microscopes might not be available.

Slide

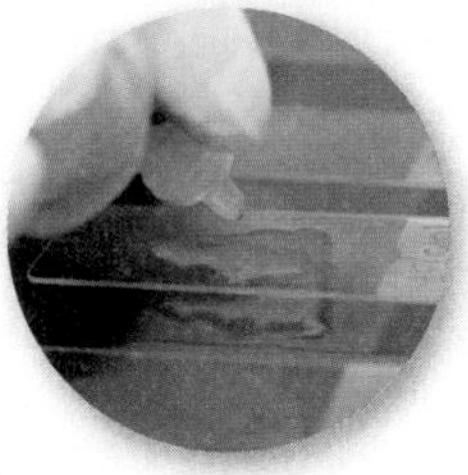

To observe items using a compound light microscope, you must place it on a thin, rectangular piece of glass called a slide. You must handle slides gently to avoid breaking them.

Dissecting Tools

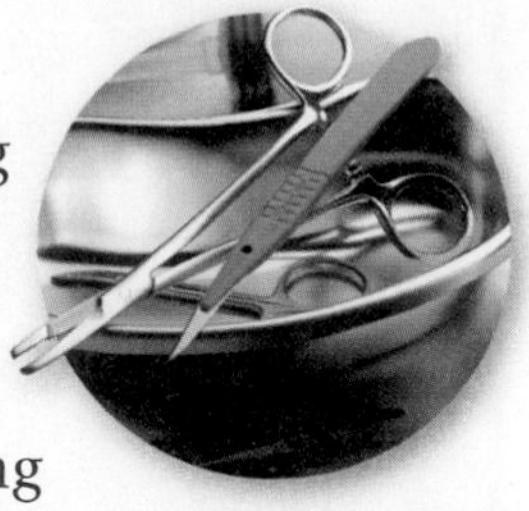

Scientists use dissecting tools, such scalpels and scissors, to examine tissues, organs, or prepared organisms. Dissecting tools are sharp, so always use extreme caution when handling them.

Pipette

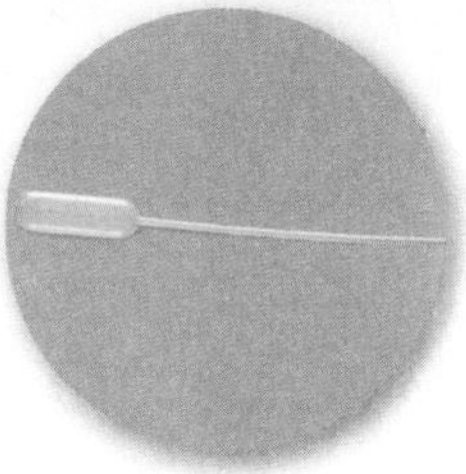

A pipette is similar to an eyedropper. It is a small glass or plastic tube used to draw up and transfer liquids.

Key Concept Check What are some tools used by life scientists?

Lesson 2 Review

Assessment Online Quiz

Use Vocabulary

1. **Define** *description* and *explanation* in your own words.
2. **Use the term** *International System of Units (SI)* in a sentence.

Understand Key Concepts

3. Which tool would a scientist use to view a tiny organism?
   A. computer
   B. compound microscope
   C. test tube
   D. triple-beam balance
4. **Describe** the difference between accuracy and precision.
5. **Explain** why scientists use significant digits.

Interpret Graphics

6. **Draw** a graphic organizer like the one below. Write the name of an SI base unit in each circle. Add additional circles to the graphic organizer as needed.

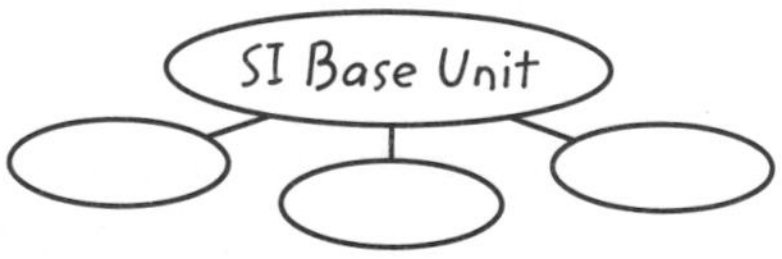

Critical Thinking

7. **Recommend** ways that computers can assist life scientists in their work.

Math Skills

Review Math Practice

8. **Suppose** you measure the mass of a book and it is 420.0890 g. How many significant digits are in this measurement?

How can you build your own scientific instrument?

All organisms take in and release gases. Your cells take in oxygen and release carbon dioxide just like the cells of other animals, plants, fungi, protists, and some bacteria. However, many plant cells, some protists, and some bacteria also can take in carbon dioxide and release oxygen. In this lab, you will follow a procedure and build your own scientific instrument that measures the change in the volume of a gas.

Materials

500-mL Erlenmeyer flask

rubber tubing, 15 cm

2-hole stopper

500-mL beaker

Also needed: short piece of plastic tubing, water, 100-mL graduated cylinder, plastic wrap (10 cm × 30 cm), bendable straws, food coloring (optional)

Safety

Learn It

Scientists often **follow procedures** developed by other scientists to collect data. A procedure is a step-by-step explanation of how to accomplish a task. The steps in a procedure tell you what materials to use, how to them, and in what order to perform specific tasks. Some procedures are simple, while others are more complicated and require a lot of practice and skill.

Try It

1. Read and complete a lab safety form.
2. Into each, an Erlenmeyer flask and a beaker, pour 350 mL of water. Pour 100 mL of water into a graduated cylinder.
3. Seal the graduated cylinder with plastic wrap. Place your hand over the plastic wrap and turn the cylinder upside down. Carefully place the sealed end of the graduated cylinder into the beaker of water. Pull off the plastic wrap without losing any water from the graduated cylinder. Have a team member hold the it so that it doesn't tip over.
4. Place one end of a bendable straw in one hole of a 2-hole stopper. Insert the plastic tubing into the other hole. Place one end of the rubber tubing over the tubing.
5. Without lifting the cylinder above the water's surface, insert the free end of the long piece of tubing inside the cylinder. Have a team continue to hold the cylinder.
6. Put the stopper in the flask. Record the initial reading of the water in the graduated cylinder in your Science Journal.
7. Gently blow into the straw and watch the change in volume of the water. Continue blowing into the straw until the graduated cylinder contains 50 mL of gas (air).

Apply It

8. **Draw a diagram** of your set up, also known as a eudiometer. Label all the parts, and describe their functions.
9. **Key Concept** Describe a scenario in which a life scientist would use this instrument to measure gases.

Lesson 3 Case Study

Reading Guide

Key Concepts
ESSENTIAL QUESTIONS

- How do independent and dependent variables differ?
- How is scientific inquiry used in a real-life scientific investigation?

Vocabulary

variable p. NOS 22
dependent variable p. NOS 22
independent variable p. NOS 22
constants p. NOS 22

g Multilingual eGlossary

Academic Standards for Science

7.NS.1 Make predictions and develop testable questions based on research and prior knowledge.
7.NS.4 Incorporate variables that can be changed, measured or controlled.
7.NS.7 Keep accurate records in a notebook during investigations

Figure 8 Microalgae are plantlike organisms that can make oils.

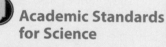

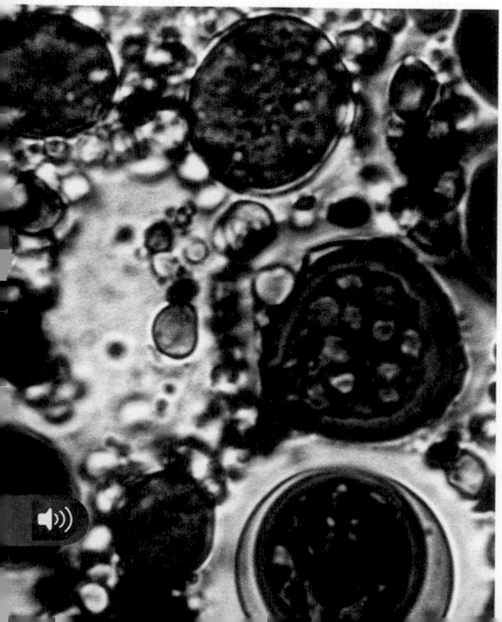

Biodiesel from Microalgae

For the last few centuries, fossil fuels have been the main sources of energy for industry and transportation. But, scientists have shown that burning fossil fuels negatively affects the environment. Also, some people are concerned about eventually using up the world's reserves of fossil fuels.

During the past few decades, scientists have explored using protists to produce biodiesel. Biodiesel is a fuel made primarily from living organisms. Protists, shown in **Figure 8,** are a group of microscopic organisms that usually live in water or moist environments. Some of these protists are plantlike because they make their own food using a process called photosynthesis. Microalgae are plantlike protists.

Designing a Controlled Experiment

Scientists use scientific inquiry to investigate the use of protists to make biodiesel. They designed controlled experiments to test their hypotheses. In the margins of this lesson are examples of how scientists in the study practiced inquiry and the skills you read about in Lesson 1. The notebook pages contain information that a scientist might write in a science journal.

A controlled experiment is a scientific investigation that tests how one variable affects another. A **variable** *is any factor in an experiment that can have more than one value.* In controlled experiments, there are two types of variables. The **dependent variable** *is the factor measured or observed during an experiment.* The **independent variable** *is the factor that you want to test. It is changed by the investigator to observe how it affects a dependent variable.* **Constants** *are the factors in an experiment that remain the same.*

Key Concept Check How do independent and dependent variables differ?

A controlled experiment has two groups—an experimental group and a control group. The experimental group is used to study how a change in the independent variable changes the dependent variable. The control group contains the same factors as the experimental group, but the independent variable is not changed. Without a control, it is difficult to know whether your experimental observations result from the variable you are testing or from another factor.

Biodiesel

The idea of engines running on fuel made from plant or plantlike sources is not entirely new. Rudolph Diesel, shown in **Figure 9,** invented the diesel engine. He used peanut oil to demonstrate how his engine worked. However, when petroleum was introduced as a diesel fuel source, it was preferred over peanut oil because it was cheaper.

Reading Check What did Rudolph Diesel use as fuel?

Oil-rich food crops, such as soybeans, can be used as a source of biodiesel. However, some people are concerned that crops grown for fuel sources will replace crops grown for food. If farmers grow more crops for fuel, then the amount of food available worldwide will be reduced. Because of food shortages in many parts of the world, replacing food crops with fuel crops is not a good solution.

Figure 9 Rudolph Diesel invented the first diesel engine in the early 1900s.

Aquatic Species Program

In the late 1970s, the U.S. Department of Energy began funding its Aquatic Species Program (ASP) to investigate ways to remove air pollutants. Coal-fueled power plants produce carbon dioxide (CO_2), a pollutant, as a by-product. In the beginning, the study examined all aquatic organisms that use CO_2 during photosynthesis—their food-making process. These included large plants, commonly know as seaweeds, plants that grow partially underwater, and microalgae. It was hoped these organisms might remove excess CO_2 from the atmosphere. During the studies, however, the project leaders noticed that some microalgae produced large amounts of oil. The program's focus soon shifted to using microalgae to produce oils that could be processed into biodiesel.

A hypothesis is a tentative explanation that can be tested by scientific investigations. A prediction is a statement of what someone expects to happen next in a sequence of events.

Scientific investigations often begin when someone observes an event in nature and wonders why or how it occurs.

Observations:
While testing microalgae to discover if they would absorb carbon pollutants, ASP project leaders saw that some species of microalgae had high oil content.

Prediction:
If the right conditions are met, then plants and plantlike organisms can be used as a source of fuel.

One way to test a hypothesis is to design an experiment and collect data.

Design an Experiment and Collect Data:
The ASP scientists developed a rapid screening test to discover which microalgae species produced the most oil.

During a long investigation, scientists form many hypotheses and conduct many tests.

Hypothesis:
Microalgae species in shallow saltwater ponds are most resistant to variations in temperature and salt content.
Prediction:
Microalgae species most resistant to variations in temperature and salt content will be the most useful species in producing biodiesel.

Hypothesis:
Microalgae grown with inadequate amounts of nitrogen alter their growth processes and produce more oil.
Independent Variable:
amount of nitrogen available
Dependent Variable:
amount of oil produced
Constants: the growing conditions of microalgae (temperature, water quality, exposure to the Sun, etc.)

Figure 10 Green microalgae and diatoms showed the most promise during testing for biodiesel production.

Which Microalgae?

Microalgae are microscopic organisms that live in marine (salty) or freshwater environments. Like many plants and other plantlike organisms, they use photosynthesis and make sugar. The process requires light energy. Microalgae make more sugar than they can use as food. They convert excess sugar to oil. Scientists focused on these microalgae because their oil then could be processed into biodiesel.

The scientists began their research by collecting and identifying promising microalgae species. The search focused on microalgae in shallow, inland, saltwater ponds. Scientists predicted that these microalgae were more resistant to changes in temperature and salt content in the water.

By 1985, a test was in place for identifying microalgae with high oil content. Two years later, 3,000 microalgae species had been collected. Scientists checked these samples for tolerance to acidity, salt levels, and temperature and selected 300 species. Of these 300 species, green microalgae and diatoms, as shown in **Figure 10**, showed the most promise. However, it was obvious that no one species was going to be perfect for all climates and water types.

Oil Production in Microalgae

Scientists also began researching how microalgae produce oil. Some studies suggested that starving microalgae of nutrients, such as nitrogen, could increase the amount of oil they produced. However, starving microalgae also caused them to be smaller, resulting in no overall increase in oil production.

Outdoor Testing v. Bioreactors

By the 1980s, the ASP scientists were growing microalgae in outdoor ponds in New Mexico. However, outdoor conditions were very different from those in the laboratory. Cooler temperatures in the outdoor ponds resulted in smaller microalgae. Native algae species also invaded the ponds, forcing out the high-oil-producing laboratory microalgae species.

The scientists continued to focus on growing microalgae in open ponds, such as the one shown in **Figure 11.** Many scientists still believe that these open ponds are better for producing large quantities of biodiesel from microalgae. But, some researchers are now growing microalgae in closed glass containers called bioreactors, also shown in **Figure 11.** Inside these bioreactors, organisms live and grow under controlled conditions. This method avoids many of the problems associated with open ponds. However, bioreactors are more expensive than open ponds.

A biofuel company in the western United States has been experimenting with a low-cost bioreactor. A scientist at the company explained that they examined the ASP program and hypothesized that they could use long plastic bags, shown in **Figure 11,** instead of closed glass containers.

Open ponds are less expensive than bioreactors for growing microalgae.

Figure 11
These three methods of growing microalgae are examples of three different hypotheses that are being tested in controlled experiments.

Microalgae grown in plastic bags are very expensive to harvest.

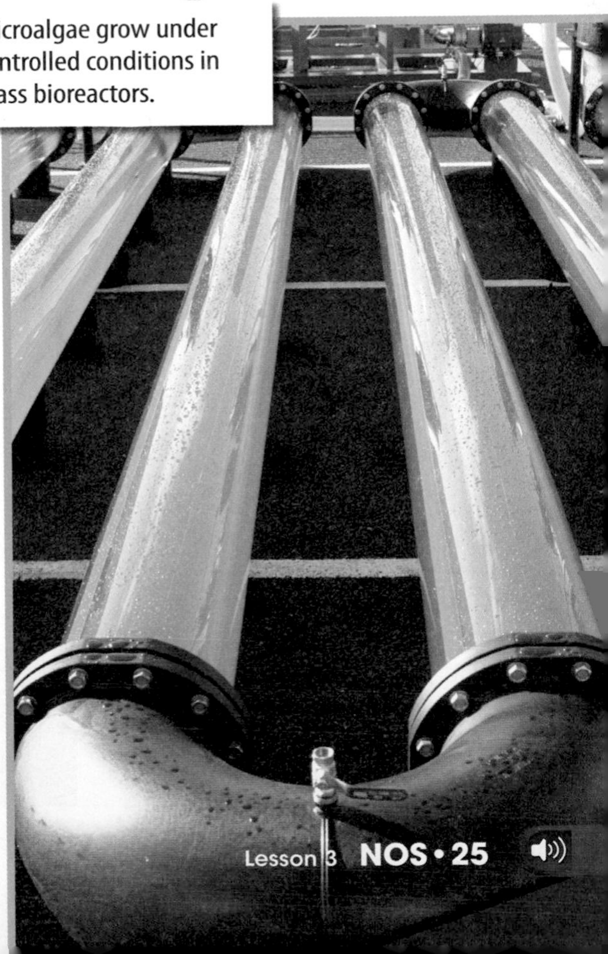

Microalgae grow under controlled conditions in glass bioreactors.

Why So Many Hypotheses?

According to Dr. Richard Sayre, a biofuel researcher, all the ASP research was based on forming hypotheses. Dr. Sayre says, "It was hypothesis-driven. You just don't go in and say 'Well, I have a feeling this is the right way to do it.' You propose a hypothesis. Then you test it."

Dr. Sayre added, "Biologists have been trained over and over again to develop research strategies based on hypotheses. It's sort of ingrained into our culture. You don't get research support by saying, 'I'm going to put together a system, and it's going to be wonderful.' You have to come up with a question. You propose some strategies for answering the question. What are your objectives? What outcomes do you expect for each objective?"

Reading Check Why is it important for a scientific researcher to develop a good hypothesis?

Scientists hypothesize that they can increase microalgae oil production by distributing light to greater depths.

Hypothesis:
If the top layer of microalgae blocks light from reaching microalgae beneath them, then they produce less oil because light is not distributed evenly to all microalgae.
Prediction:
If light is distributed more evenly, then more microalgae will grow, and more oil will be produced.

Increasing Oil Yield

Scientists from a biofuel company in Washington State thought of another way to increase oil production. Researchers knew microalgae use light energy, water, and carbon dioxide and make sugar. The microalgae eventually convert sugar into oil. The scientists wondered if they could increase microalgae oil production by distributing light to all microalgae. The experimental lab setup to test this idea is shown in **Figure 12.**

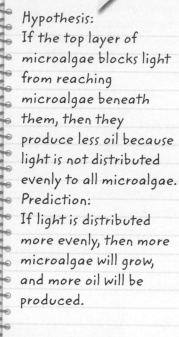

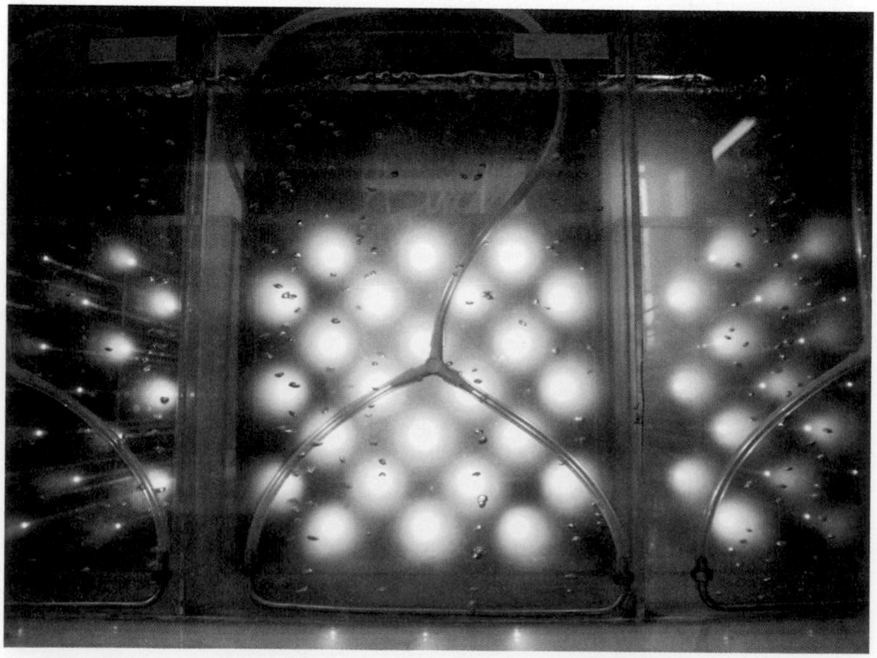

Figure 12 Acrylic rods distribute light to microalgae below the water's surface. If microalgae receive light, they can photosynthesize and eventually produce oils. Without light, microalgae are not productive.

Bringing Light to Microalgae

Normally microalgae grow near the surface of a pond. Any microalgae about 5 cm below the pond's surface will grow less. Why is this? First, water blocks light from reaching deep into a pond. Second, microalgae at the top of a pond block light from reaching microalgae below them. Only the top part of a pond is productive.

Experimental Group

Researchers decided to assemble a team of engineers to design a light-distribution system. Light rods distribute artificial light to microalgae in a bioreactor. The bioreactor controls the environmental conditions that affect how the microalgae grow. These conditions include temperature, nutrient levels, carbon dioxide level, airflow, and light.

Reading Check In the experimental group, what variables are controlled in the bioreactor?

Data from their experiments showed scientists how microalgae in well-lit environments grow compared to how microalgae grow in dimmer environments. Using solar data for various parts of the country, the scientists concluded that the light rod would significantly increase microalgae growth and oil production in outdoor ponds. These scientists next plan to use the light-rod growing method in outdoor ponds.

Field Testing

Scientists plan to take light to microalgae instead of moving microalgae to light. Dr. Jay Burns is chief microalgae scientist at a biofuel company. He said, "What we are proposing to do is to take the light from the surface of a pond and distribute it throughout the depth of the pond. Instead of only the top 5 cm being productive, the whole pond becomes productive."

Reading Check What is the benefit of the light-distribution system?

Scientists tested their hypothesis, collected data, analyzed the data, and drew conclusions.

Analyze Results:
The experimental results showed that microalgae would produce more oil using a light-rod system than by using just sunlight.
Draw a Conclusion:
The researchers concluded that the light-rod system greatly increased microalgae oil production.

Research scientists and scientists in the field rely on scientific methods and scientific inquiry to solve real-life problems. When a scientific investigation lasts for several years and involves many scientists, such as this study, many hypotheses can be tested. Some hypotheses are supported, and other hypotheses are not. However, information is gathered and lessons are learned. Hypotheses are refined and tested many times. This process of scientific inquiry results in a better understanding of the problem and possible solutions.

Figure 13 During cultivation, paddlewheels bring microalgae to the surface and expose them to light.

Another Way to Bring Light to Microalgae

Light rods are not the only way to bring light to microalgae. Paddlewheels, as shown in **Figure 13**, can be used to keep the microalgae's locations changing. Paddlewheels continuously rotate microalgae to the surface. This exposes the organisms to more light.

Key Concept Check Describe three ways in which scientific inquiry was used in this case study.

Why Grow Microalgae?

While the focus of this case study is microalgae growth for biodiesel production, there are other benefits of growing microalgae, as shown in **Figure 14**. Power plants that burn fossil fuels release carbon dioxide into the atmosphere. Evidence indicates that this contributes to global warming. During photosynthesis, microalgae use carbon dioxide and water, release oxygen, and produce sugar, which they convert to oil. Not only do microalgae produce a valuable fuel, they also remove pollutants from and add oxygen to the atmosphere.

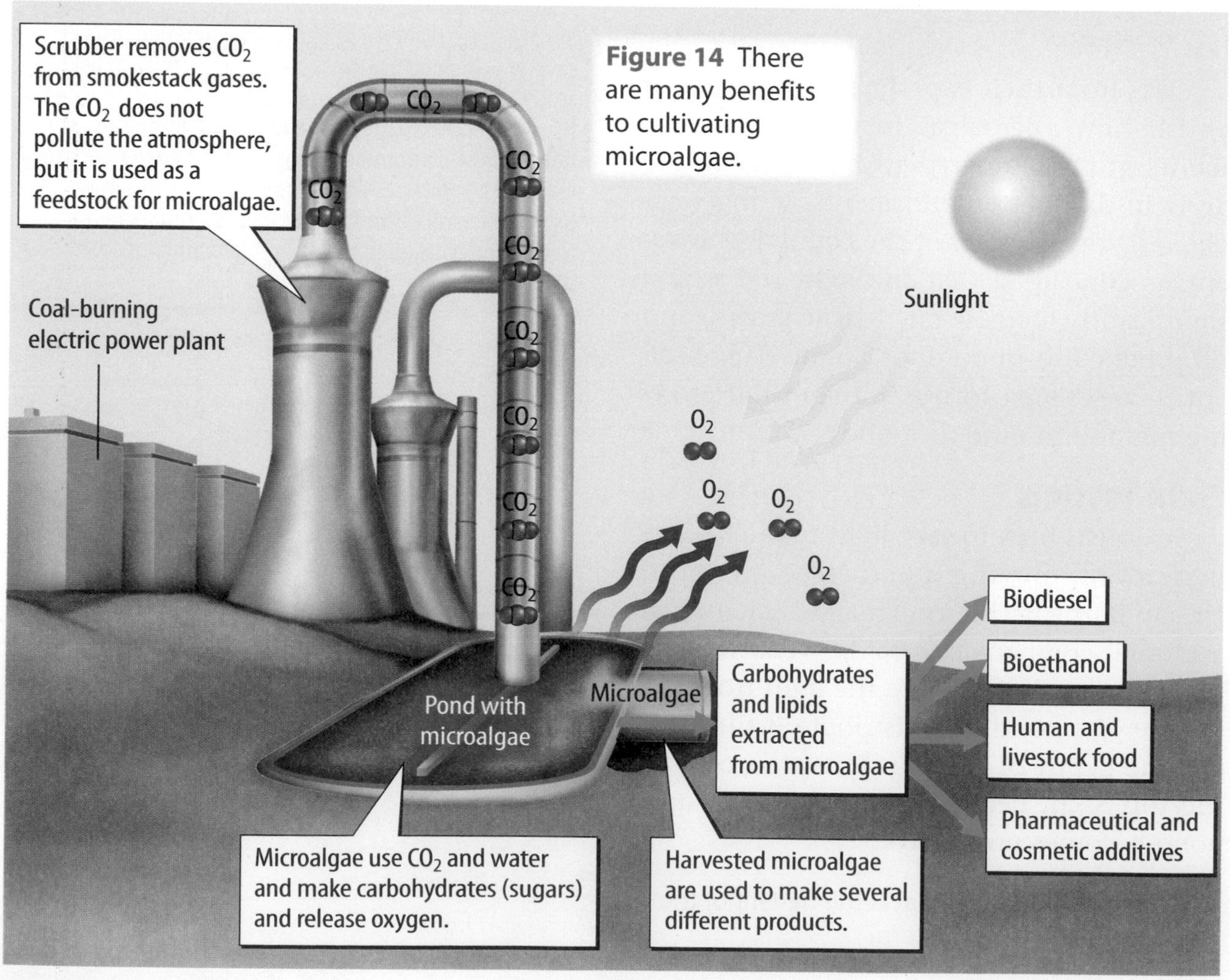

Scrubber removes CO_2 from smokestack gases. The CO_2 does not pollute the atmosphere, but it is used as a feedstock for microalgae.
CO_2
Coal-burning electric power plant
Sunlight
O_2
Biodiesel
Bioethanol
Human and livestock food
Pharmaceutical and cosmetic additives
Carbohydrates and lipids extracted from microalgae
Microalgae
Pond with microalgae
Microalgae use CO_2 and water and make carbohydrates (sugars) and release oxygen.
Harvested microalgae are used to make several different products.

Figure 14 There are many benefits to cultivating microalgae.

Are microalgae the future?

Scientists face many challenges in their quest to produce biodiesel from microalgae. For now, the costs of growing microalgae and extracting their oils are too high to compete with petroleum-based diesel. However, the combined efforts of government-funded programs and commercial biofuel companies might one day make microalgae-based biodiesel an affordable reality in the United States. In fact, a company in Israel has a successful test plant in operation, as shown in **Figure 15.** Plans are underway to build a large-scale industrial facility to convert carbon dioxide gases released from an Israeli coal-powered electrical plants into useful microalgae products. If this technology performs as expected, microalgae cultivation might occur near coal-fueled power plants in other parts of the world, too.

Figure 15 This microalgae test facility in Israel is reducing the amount of carbon dioxide pollution in the atmosphere.

Currently, scientists have no final conclusions about using microalgae as a fuel source. As long as petroleum remains relatively inexpensive and available, it probably will remain the preferred source of diesel fuel. However, if petroleum prices increase or availability decreases, new sources of fuel will be needed. Biodiesel made from microalgae oils might be one of the alternative fuel sources used.

Lesson 3 Review

Assessment Online Quiz

Use Vocabulary

1. **Define** *variable* in your own words.
2. **Contrast** the terms *dependent variable, independent variable,* and *constants.*

Understand Key Concepts

3. Which factor does the investigator change during an investigation?
   A. constant
   B. dependent variable
   C. independent variable
   D. variable
4. **Give an example** of a scientific inquiry used in a real-life scientific investigation that is not mentioned in this chapter.

Interpret Graphics

5. **Organize Information** Copy and fill in a graphic organizer like the one below with information about the three types of oil production discussed in the study.

Critical Thinking

6. **Hypothesize** other methods to either increase the oil content of microalgae or to grow greater amounts of microalgae for biodiesel production.
7. **Evaluate** scientists' efforts to increase the oil content of microalgae and to grow microalgae more quickly. What would you do differently?

How can you design a bioreactor?

Materials

500-mL Erlenmeyer flask

one-hole stopper with a short pieces of plastic tubing in the hole

500-mL beaker

Also needed: rubber tubing (15 cm), water, 100-mL graduated cylinder, plastic wrap (10 cm × 30 cm), scissors, bendable straw, yeast, sugar, triple-beam balance, stopwatch, ice, thermometer

Safety

You are part of scientific team studying how yeast grows in a bioreactor. In a bioreactor, yeast use sugar as an energy source and release carbon dioxide gas as a waste product. One way you can tell how fast yeast grow is to measure the volume of gas yeast produce.

Ask a Question

How do water temperature and sugar concentration affect yeast growth?

Make Observations

1. Read and complete a lab safety form.
2. Copy the data table shown on the next page into your Science Journal.
3. Place weighing paper or waxed paper on the triple-beam balance, and then zero the balance. Do not place solids directly on the balance. Measure 3 g of yeast. Use the paper to transport the yeast back to your lab station.
4. Repeat step 3 to measure 4 g of sugar.
5. Measure and pour 350 mL of water into both the Erlenmeyer flask and the beaker. Measure 100 mL of water in the graduated cylinder.

6. Seal the graduated cylinder with plastic wrap. Place you hand over the plastic wrap, and turn the graduated cylinder upside down. Carefully place the sealed end of the graduated cylinder into a beaker of water. Pull off the plastic wrap without losing any water from the cylinder. Have a team member hold the graduated cylinder so that it doesn't tip over.
7. Place one end of a 15-cm piece of rubber tubing over the short plastic or glass tubing in the stopper. Without lifting the cylinder above the water's surface, insert the free end of the long piece of tubing inside the graduated cylinder. Have a team continue to hold it. Record the initial reading of the water level in the graduated cylinder in your Science Journal.
8. Add the sugar and then the yeast to the Erlenmeyer flask. Place the stopper in the flask and swirl it to mix the contents. This flask is your bioreactor.
9. Record the volume of gas produced every 10 min for half an hour. To calculate the volume of gas produced for each 10 min time interval, subtract the initial volume from the final volume.

Form a Hypothesis

10. As a class, form a hypothesis that explains how a change in the amount of sugar in your bioreactor affects carbon dioxide production. Form a second hypothesis that explains how a change in temperature of the water affects carbon dioxide production.

Test Your Hypotheses

11. As a class, develop procedures to test your hypotheses. Use a range of temperatures and different amounts of sugar in your tests.
12. With your teammates, set up several bioreactors with the conditions you outlined in your procedures. Record the results from each bioreactor in a separate data table.
13. Using the class data, create two line graphs—one graph for each hypothesis.

Analyze and Conclude

14. **Analyze** What conditions resulted in the fastest growth of yeast?
15. **Compare** Which of the two variables had a greater influence on the growth of yeast? How did you draw that conclusion?
16. **The Big Idea** Which scientific processes did you use in your investigation of bioreactors?

Communicate Your Results

Present your team's results to your class. Include visual aids and at least one graph.

Inquiry Extension

As part of your presentation, propose future research that your team will conduct on bioreactors. Describe other variables or other organisms your team will investigate. Explain the goal of your future research. Will you develop a product that can be marketed? Will you provide an explanation to solve a scientific problem? Will you develop a new technology?

Gas Produced

Temperature of water ________

Amount of sugar

Time (min)	Eudiometer Reading (mL)
0	
10	
20	
30	

Lab Tips

- ☑ Make sure the graduated cylinder is not tilted when you take readings.
- ☑ If you use a recycled water bottle as your bioreactor, do not squeeze the bottle once you place the stopper in it or you can force air into the eudiometer.

Remember to use scientific methods.

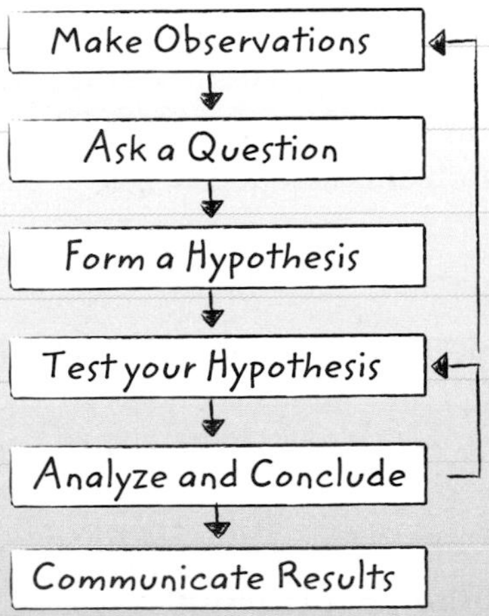

Study Guide and Review

WebQuest

THE BIG IDEA **The process of scientific inquiry and performing scientific investigations can provide answers to questions about your world.**

Key Concepts Summary	Vocabulary
Lesson 1: Understanding Science • Scientific inquiry, also known as scientific methods, is a collection of skills that scientists use in different combinations to perform scientific investigations. • Scientific investigations often result in new **technology**, new materials, newly discovered objects or events, or answers to questions. • A scientist can help prevent bias in a scientific investigation by taking random samples, doing blind studies, repeating an experiment several times, and keeping accurate and honest records.	**science** p. NOS 4 **observation** p. NOS 6 **inference** p. NOS 6 **hypothesis** p. NOS 6 **prediction** p. NOS 7 **technology** p. NOS 8 **scientific theory** p. NOS 9 **scientific law** p. NOS 9 **critical thinking** p. NOS 10
Lesson 2: Measurement and Scientific Tools • **Precision** is a description of how similar or close measurements are to each other. **Accuracy** is a description of how close a measurement is to an accepted value. • **Significant digits** communicate the precision of the tool used to make measurements. • Life scientists use many tools, such as science journals, microscopes, computers, magnifying lenses, slides, and dissecting tools.	**description** p. NOS 14 **explanation** p. NOS 14 **International System of Units (SI)** p. NOS 14 **precision** p. NOS 16 **accuracy** p. NOS 16 **significant digits** p. NOS 17
Lesson 3: Case Study: Biodiesel from Microalgae • The **independent variable** is a factor in an experiment that is manipulated or changed by the investigator to observe how it affects a dependent variable. The **dependent variable** is the factor measured or observed during an experiment. • Scientific inquiry is used to gain information and find solutions to real-life problems and questions.	**variable** p. NOS 22 **dependent variable** p. NOS 22 **independent variable** p. NOS 22 **constants** p. NOS 22

Use Vocabulary

Explain the relationship between each set of terms.

1. scientific law, scientific theory
2. observation, explanation
3. hypothesis, scientific theory
4. description, explanation
5. International System of Units (SI), significant digits
6. variable, constant

Assessment
Online Test Practice

Understand Key Concepts

7 Which is a quantitative observation?

A. 15 m long
B. red color
C. rough texture
D. strong odor

8 Which is one way scientists indicate how precise and accurate their experimental measurements are?

A. They keep accurate, honest records.
B. They make sure their experiments can be repeated.
C. They use significant figures in their measurements.
D. They record small samples of data.

9 Which is NOT a source of bias?

A. accurate records
B. equipment choice
C. funding source
D. hypothesis formation

Critical Thinking

10 **Explain** What would be the next step in the scientific inquiry process below?

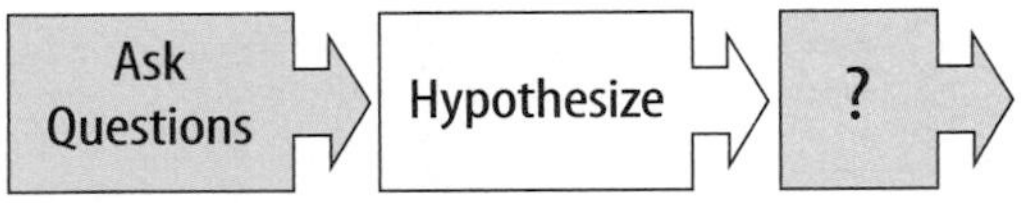

11 **Select** a science career that uses technology. Explain how that career would be different if the technology had not been invented.

12 **Identify** the experimental group, the control group, and controls in the following example. Explain your decision.

A scientist tests a new cough medicine by giving it to a group who have colds. The scientist gives another group with colds a liquid and tells them it is cough medicine. The people in both groups are women between the ages of 20 and 30 who normally are in good health.

Writing in Science

13 **Write** a five-sentence paragraph that includes examples of how bias can be intentional or unintentional and how scientists can prevent bias. Be sure to include topic and concluding sentences in your paragraph.

REVIEW THE BIG IDEA

14 What process do scientists use to perform scientific investigations? List a possible sequence of steps in a scientific inquiry and explain your reasoning.

15 What next step of scientific methods might these marine biologists perform?

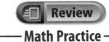

Math Skills

Review
Math Practice

Significant Digits

16 How many significant figures are in 0.00840, 15.7, and 13.040?

Unit 1

Motion & Forces

3500 B.C.
The oldest wheeled vehicle is depicted in Mesopotamia, near the Black Sea.

400 B.C.
The Greeks invent the stone-hurling catapult.

1698
English military engineer Thomas Savery invents the first crude steam engine while trying to solve the problem of pumping water out of coal mines.

1760–1850
The Industrial Revolution results in massive advances in technology and social structure in England.

1769
The first vehicle to move under its own power is designed by Nicholas Joseph Cugnot and constructed by M. Breszin. A second replica is built that weighs 3,629 kg and has a top speed of 3.2 km per hour.

1794
Eli Whitney receives a patent for the mechanical cotton gin.

1800

1900

1817
Baron von Drais invents a machine to help him quickly wander the grounds of his estate. The machine is made of two wheels on a frame with a seat and a pair of pedals. This machine is the beginning design of the modern bicycle.

1903
Wilbur and Orville Wright build their airplane, called the Flyer, and take the first successful, powered, piloted flight.

1976
The first computer for home use is invented by college dropouts Steve Wozniak and Steve Jobs, who go on to found Apple Computer, Inc.

? Inquiry
Visit ConnectED for this unit's STEM activity.

Systems

▲ **Figure 1** Whether U R A QT or a TRUE FRIEND, the candy hearts you read on Valentine's Day come to you through the interaction of many systems.

For Valentine's Day, stores display boxes of candy hearts, like in **Figure 1.** Where do the candy hearts come from? How are they made? The answers have to do with systems. A system is a collection of parts that interact with one another. Smaller systems often work together as subsystems of a larger system.

There are many kinds of systems. Social systems, such as school systems, involve interactions among people. Natural systems include ecosystems and body systems. Engineered systems, such as a manufacturing system, provide services or products to people. Power systems, such as a generator, transform various forms of energy into useful energy to provide propulsion or motion to other products or systems.

Characteristics of a System

All systems have a specific purpose. Most systems, such as the power, manufacturing, packaging, and transportation systems shown in **Figure 2,** are described in terms of the system's input, processing, output, and feedback.

Input: material, energy, or information that enters a system
Processing: the changes that the system makes to the input
Output: material, energy, or information that leaves a system
Feedback: information from a system that regulates another system's input, process, and output.

Figure 2 Follow the steps through the systems that bring candy hearts to grocery stores every February. ▼

Power System

Input: Natural sources of potential energy, such as the Sun, natural gas, coal, and wind, are harnessed as an energy source.

Processing: Energy that leaves the power system is used to drive other products or systems.

Output: An engineered device, such as a generator, transforms natural sources of potential energy into a useful form of energy, such as electricity.

Interactions Among Systems

All parts of a system interact with one another. In addition, subsystems of the same overall system interact, too. For example, as shown in **Figure 2,** the output from the power system is energy, which is an input to the other subsystems. The output from the manufacturing system is the candy hearts that become the input to the packaging system. In turn, the output from the packaging system is input to the transportation system.

Order and Change in Systems

Each subsystem provides feedback to the other subsystems. A change in one subsystem often affects the others. If a packaging machine breaks down, this information must be provided to manufacturing. After manufacturing receives the feedback, it slows production. Slowing production will also affect the transportation system, since not as many boxes will be shipped.

Inquiry MiniLab — 25 minutes

Can you design a system?

1. Select an object that you use every day.
2. List the inputs, the processing steps, and the outputs in the system that produces the object.
3. Draw a diagram of the object's manufacturing system.

Analyze and Conclude

1. **Identify** What are the inputs, the processing steps, and the outputs in your system?
2. **Predict** What feedback might be necessary to keep your system working well?
3. **Decide** With what other systems would your system interact?

Transportation System

Input: Boxes of candy hearts and trucks
Processing: Boxes of candy are tracked and shipped to stores.
Output: Boxes of candy hearts on the shelves of grocery stores

Feedback: If candy sales are low, feedback is sent to the manufacturing system for less candy to be made and to the power system signaling less energy is needed.

Manufacturing System

Input: Energy, candy ingredients, and machines
Processing: Machines mix the ingredients, process the candy, and cut sheets of the candy into hearts.
Output: Candy hearts

Packaging System

Input: Candy hearts and boxes
Processing: The candy hearts get placed into cartons, and then the cartons are boxed.
Output: Boxes of candy hearts

Chapter 1

Using Energy and Heat

THE BIG IDEA What are energy transfers and energy transformations?

Inquiry Energy Transformations?

When you look at this photo, do you think of electricity? This power plant transforms the energy stored in coal to the electric energy that people use in their homes and businesses.

- How do you use energy in your home?
- Can you think of other types of energy?
- What are energy transfers and energy transformations?

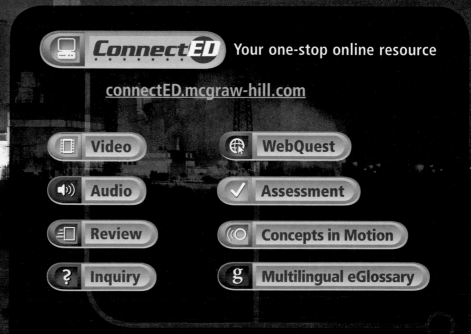

Get Ready to Read

What do you think?

Before you read, decide if you agree or disagree with each of these statements. As you read this chapter, see if you change your mind about any of the statements.

1. An object sitting on a high shelf has no energy.
2. There are many forms of energy.
3. In most systems, no energy is transferred to the environment.
4. Some forms of energy are replenished naturally.
5. Only particles that make up moving objects are in motion.
6. Thermal energy can be transferred in several ways.

ConnectED Your one-stop online resource

connectED.mcgraw-hill.com

- Video
- WebQuest
- Audio
- Assessment
- Review
- Concepts in Motion
- Inquiry
- Multilingual eGlossary

Lesson 1

Reading Guide

Key Concepts
ESSENTIAL QUESTIONS

- How do potential energy and kinetic energy differ?
- How are mechanical energy and thermal energy similar?
- What two forms of energy are carried by waves?

Vocabulary

energy p. 9
potential energy p. 9
chemical energy p. 10
nuclear energy p. 10
kinetic energy p. 11
electric energy p. 11
mechanical energy p. 12
thermal energy p. 12
wave p. 13
sound energy p. 13
radiant energy p. 14

Academic Standards for Science
Covers: 7.1.2, 7.1.4, 7.NS.1, 7.NS.2, 7.NS.4, 7.NS.7

Forms of Energy

Inquiry Got Energy?

This horse and rider need energy to move and to perform their life processes, such as breathing, digesting food, and transporting nutrients and wastes throughout their bodies. The source of energy for both the horse and the rider are the same. It comes from the foods they eat. What form of energy is found in foods? Are there other forms of energy?

Inquiry Launch Lab

15 minutes

Can you transfer energy?

You can transfer energy to a ball when you throw it. What are other ways you transfer energy?

1. Read and complete a lab safety form.
2. Hold the handle of a **tuning fork,** and gently strike one arm of the tuning fork with a **mallet.** (Use only the mallet provided for this purpose.)
3. Dip the arms of the tuning fork in a **beaker** of water. Observe what happens, and record your observations in your Science Journal.

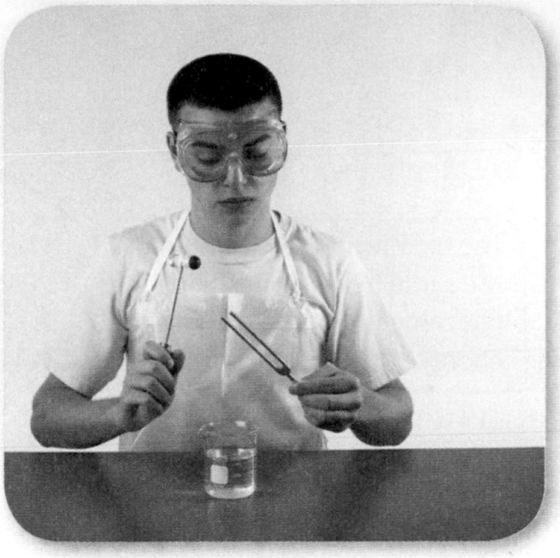

Think About This

1. What is the source of energy that produced sound from the tuning fork? How do you think the tuning fork produced the sound?
2. **Key Concept** What happened to the water when the tuning fork was placed in it? Explain what you think happened to the water, the tuning fork, and the energy.

Energy

Some breakfast cereals promise to give you enough energy to get your day off to a great start. News reports often mention the price of oil, which is an energy source that provides fuel for cars and for transporting goods around the world. Meteorologists talk about the approach of a storm system with a lot of energy. News anchors report on earthquakes and tsunamis, which carry so much energy they cause great damage. Politicians talk about the nation's energy policy and the need to conserve energy and to find new energy sources. Energy influences everything in your life, including the climate, the economy, and your body. Scientists define **energy** as *the ability to cause change.*

Potential Energy

Have you ever seen an object perched on the edge of a ledge, such as the one in **Figure 1**? The object's position could easily change, which means it has energy. **Potential energy** *is stored energy due to the interaction between objects or particles.* Objects have potential energy if they have the potential to cause change. Examples of potential energy include objects that could fall due to gravity (interactions between objects—Earth and the egg) and particles that could move because of electric or magnetic forces (interactions between particles—protons and electrons).

Figure 1 The egg has potential energy because gravitational force can pull it to the ground. A simple nudge could send it falling to the floor.

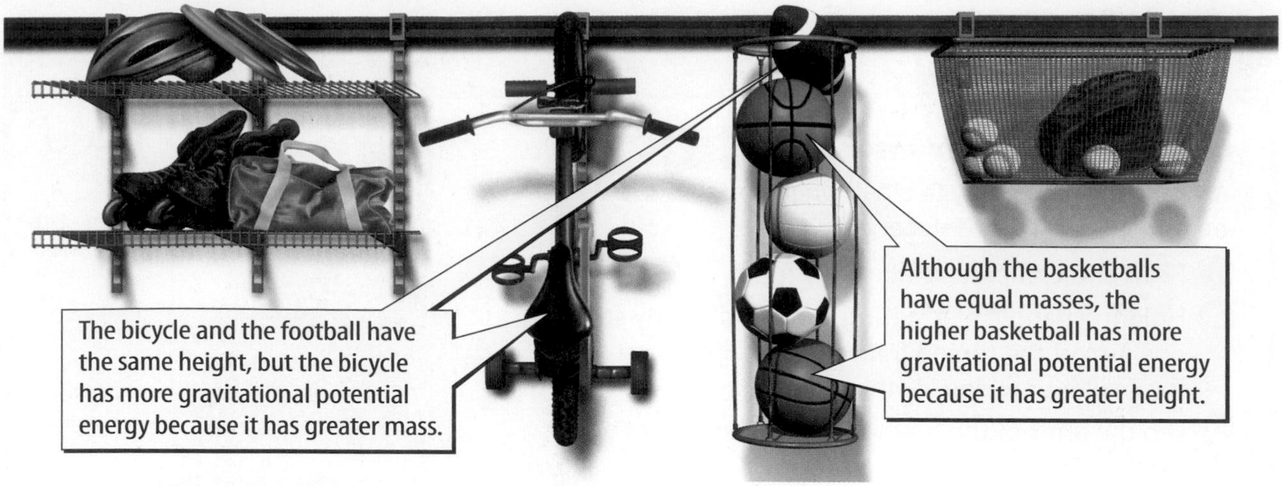

The bicycle and the football have the same height, but the bicycle has more gravitational potential energy because it has greater mass.
Although the basketballs have equal masses, the higher basketball has more gravitational potential energy because it has greater height.

▲ **Figure 2** All of these objects have gravitational potential energy because they have mass and height.

▲ **Figure 3** Your body breaks the chemical bonds in the foods you eat and uses the energy for life processes, including movement.

▲ **Figure 4** In stars, including the Sun, atoms combine or fuse together to form heavier atoms.

Gravitational Potential Energy

Do the items stored on the garage organizer in **Figure 2** have potential energy? The answer is yes, every item— including the shelves and the brackets—has gravitational potential energy. Objects have gravitational potential energy if they have mass and height above Earth's surface.

The gravitational potential of an object energy depends on two factors—the mass of an object and the distance the object is from Earth, as shown in **Figure 2.**

Chemical Energy

Suppose you take the skates from the shelf and play hockey with your friends. Where does your body get the energy it needs? Energy in your body comes from the foods you eat. All objects, including your body and the apple in **Figure 3,** are made of atoms that are joined by chemical bonds. **Chemical energy** *is the energy stored in and released from the bonds between atoms.* Your body breaks chemical bonds in foods and converts the released energy into other forms of energy that your body can use.

Nuclear Energy

The energy stored in and released from the nucleus of an atom is called **nuclear energy.** If you watch a beautiful sunset like the one in **Figure 4,** you experience nuclear energy. The Sun's energy is released through the process of nuclear fusion. During nuclear fusion, the nuclei of atoms join together and release large amounts of energy. Nuclear energy also is released when an atom breaks apart. This breaking apart of an atom is called nuclear fission. Some power plants use nuclear fission to generate, or make, electricity.

▲ **Figure 5** The kinetic energy (KE) of an object is related to the object's mass and speed.

Visual Check Which of the bowling balls has gravitational potential energy? Explain.

Concepts in Motion **Animation**

Kinetic Energy

Are you moving your hand as you take notes? Are you squirming in your chair trying to find a comfortable position? If so, you have **kinetic energy**—*energy due to motion.* All objects that have motion have kinetic energy.

Kinetic Energy of Objects

An object's kinetic energy is related to the mass and the speed of the object. For example, suppose you are bowling like the people in **Figure 5.** The girl on the left is holding a 3.6-kg bowling ball. Because the ball is not moving, it has no speed and therefore, no kinetic energy. The bowling balls shown in the other two photos have the same speed, 8.0 m/s, but the ball on the right has a greater mass. Therefore, the ball on the right has greater kinetic energy than the ball in the middle.

REVIEW VOCABULARY
speed
the distance an object moves per unit of time

Electric Energy

Even objects you can't see have kinetic energy. Recall that all materials are made of atoms. In an atom, electrons move around a nucleus. Sometimes electrons even move from one atom to another. Because electrons are moving, they have kinetic energy. When electrons move, they create an electric current. *The energy in an electric current is* **electric energy.** In **Figure 6,** electrons move from one terminal of the battery through the copper wire and bulb to the other terminal of the battery. As the electrons move, their energy is transformed into light. Your brain and the nerves in your body that tell your arm and leg muscles to move also use electric energy.

Key Concept Check How do potential energy and kinetic energy differ?

Figure 6 Electric energy is kinetic energy because the electrons have both mass and motion. ▼

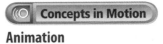

Figure 7 Mechanical energy is due to large-scale motions and object interactions. Thermal energy is due to atomic-scale motions and particle interactions.

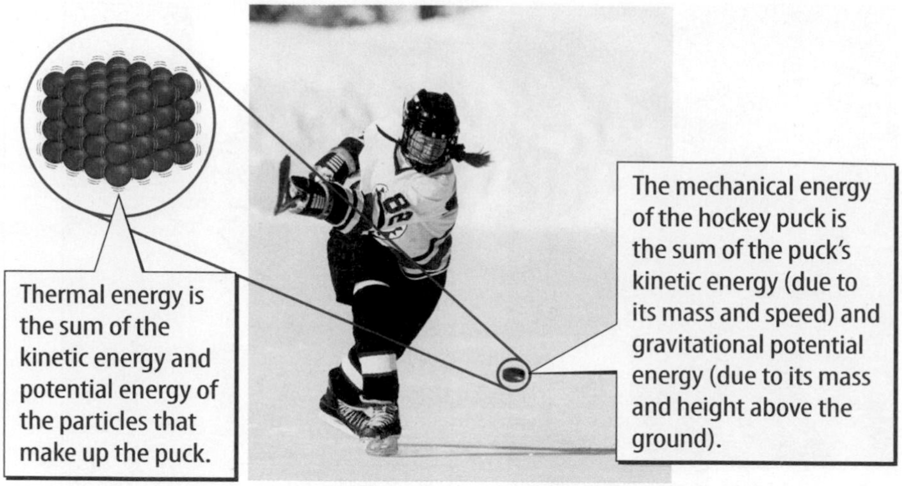

Thermal energy is the sum of the kinetic energy and potential energy of the particles that make up the puck.
The mechanical energy of the hockey puck is the sum of the puck's kinetic energy (due to its mass and speed) and gravitational potential energy (due to its mass and height above the ground).

Combined Kinetic Energy and Potential Energy

Your school part of an education system. Earth is part of the solar system. A system is a collection of parts that interact and act together as a whole. In science, everything that is not in a given system is the environment. For example, the hockey player, the hockey stick, the hockey puck, and the ice under the player in **Figure 7** can be considered a system.

WORD ORIGIN
mechanical
from Greek *mēchanē*, means "machine"

Mechanical Energy

Does the hockey puck in **Figure 7** have kinetic energy or potential energy? It has mass and motion, so it has kinetic energy. It also has height above Earth, so it has gravitational potential energy. Scientists often study the energy of systems, such as the one described above. *The sum of the potential energy and the kinetic energy in a system is* **mechanical energy.** You might think of mechanical energy as the ability to move another object. What happens when the hockey puck hits the net? The net moves. The hockey puck has mechanical energy that causes another object to move.

FOLDABLES®

Make a horizontal four-column chart book. Label it as shown. Use it to organize your notes on the different forms of energy that fall into each of the categories.

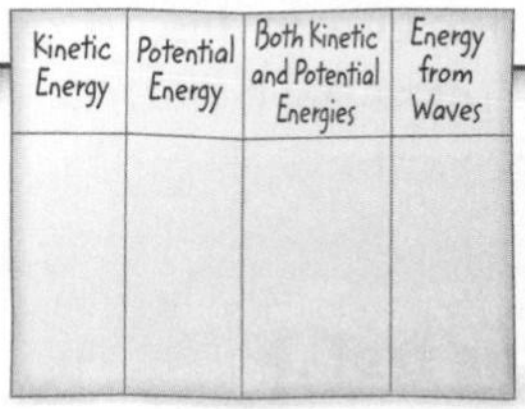

Thermal Energy

Even when the hockey puck is lying on the floor with no obvious motion, the particles that make up the solid puck are in motion—they vibrate back and forth in place. Therefore, the particles have kinetic energy. The particles also have potential energy because of attractive forces between the particles. An object's **thermal energy** *is the sum of the kinetic energy and the potential energy of the particles that make up the object.* Thermal energy of an object increases when the potential energy, the kinetic energy, or both increase.

Key Concept Check Compare mechanical energy and thermal energy.

Figure 8 When a raindrop falls into water, waves form. The waves carry energy, not matter, across the pond.

Energy Carried by Waves

Have you ever watched a raindrop fall into a still pool of water, as shown in **Figure 8**? The raindrop disturbs the surface of the water and produces waves that move away from the place where the raindrop hit. *A* **wave** *is a disturbance that transfers energy from one place to another without transferring matter.* Energy, not matter, moves outward from the point where the raindrop hits the water.

Reading Check What do waves carry?

Sound Energy

When the raindrop hits the water, you hear a splash. The raindrop not only disturbs the surface of the water, it also disturbs the air. When the raindrop hits the water, it creates a sound wave in the air similar to water waves. Sound waves are waves that move through matter. The wave travels from particle to particle as the particles bump into each other, similar to falling dominoes. **Sound energy** *is energy carried by sound waves.*

As the sound wave travels, it eventually reaches your ear. The sound energy moves tiny hairs inside your ear. This movement is transformed into an electric signal that travels to your brain. Your brain interprets the signal as the sound of a water splash.

Inquiry MiniLab 15 minutes

How do waves transfer energy?

You know that sound energy travels through matter. Does sound travel faster through a solid, a liquid, or a gas?

1. Read and complete a lab safety form.
2. Place a **ruler** on top of a sheet of **newspaper.**
3. Stand **20 dominoes** on end with the sides 1 cm apart. The narrow edges should touch the ruler.
4. Hold the ruler in place. Have your partner start a **stopwatch** as you tip the first domino toward the others. Turn the stopwatch off when the last domino falls. Record the time in your Science Journal.
5. Repeat steps 3 and 4 with the dominoes 2 cm apart. Record the time.

Analyze and Conclude

1. **Identify Relationships** Is there a relationship between how far apart the dominoes are and the time it takes them to transfer energy?
2. **Key Concept** Particles in a solid are closer together than particles in a liquid. Particles in a liquid are closer together than particles in a gas. If sound waves travel by transferring energy from particle to particle in matter, would sound waves travel faster through a solid, a liquid, or a gas? Explain.

Radiant Energy

Have you ever wondered what light is? Light is a form of energy carried by electromagnetic waves, which are electric and magnetic waves moving perpendicularly to one another, as shown in **Figure 9.** *The energy carried by electromagnetic waves is* **radiant energy.** Electromagnetic waves travel through matter and through spaces with little or no matter, such as outer space. Electromagnetic waves often are described by their wavelengths. Wavelength is the distance from one point on a wave to the nearest point just like it.

Visible light is only one form of radiant energy. Gamma rays and X-rays are electromagnetic waves with very short wavelengths. Gamma rays and X-rays often are used in medical procedures. Ultraviolet rays have wavelengths that are a little shorter than those of light. This form of radiant energy is what gives you sunburn. Infrared rays are the energy used by many television remote controls to change channels. They also provide the warmth you feel when the Sun shines on you. Radar, television, and radio waves have long wavelengths compared to visible light.

Key Concept Check What two forms of energy are carried by waves?

Figure 9 Radiant energy is carried by electromagnetic waves (also called rays) with different wavelengths.

Visual Check Determine one type of radiant energy that has a shorter wavelength than visible light and another type that has a longer wavelength.

Electromagnetic Wave

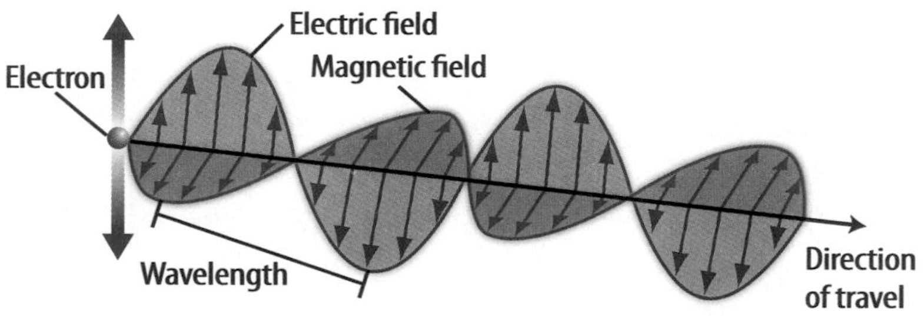

Electromagnetic Spectrum

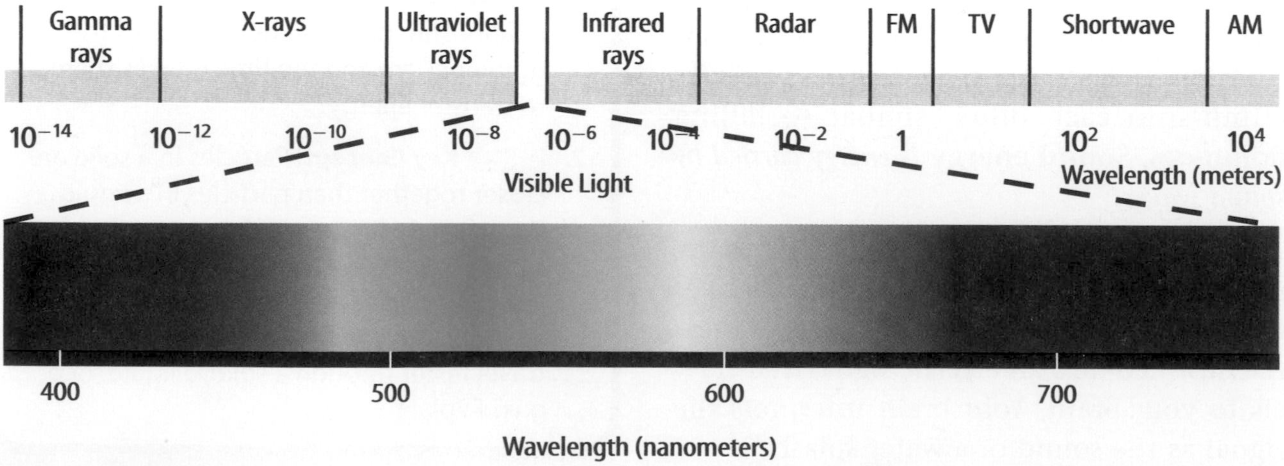

Lesson 1 Review

Assessment Online Quiz

Visual Summary

Objects can have potential energy (stored energy) and kinetic energy (energy due to movement).

Mechanical energy is due to large-scale motions and interactions in a system. Thermal energy is due to atomic-scale motions and interactions in particles.

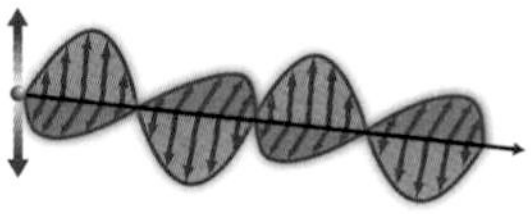

Two kinds of energy carried by waves are sound energy and radiant energy.

FOLDABLES®

Use your lesson Foldable to review the lesson. Save your Foldable for the project at the end of the chapter.

What do you think NOW?

You first read the statements below at the beginning of the chapter.

1. An object sitting on a high shelf has no energy.

2. There are many forms of energy.

Did you change your mind about whether you agree or disagree with the statements? Rewrite any false statements to make them true.

Use Vocabulary

1. The ability to cause change is ________.
2. Energy can be carried by ________, but matter cannot.

Understand Key Concepts

3. **Compare** How are thermal energy and mechanical energy similar?
4. Which form of energy does NOT involve kinetic energy?
   - **A.** chemical
   - **B.** electric
   - **C.** mechanical
   - **D.** thermal
5. **Explain** why an airplane flying from New York to Los Angeles has both kinetic energy and potential energy.
6. **Describe** How are the two forms of energy carried by waves and matter related?

Interpret Graphics

7. **Identify** Where are kinetic energy and potential energy the greatest in the loop?

8. **Summarize** Copy and fill in the following graphic organizer to show forms of potential energy.

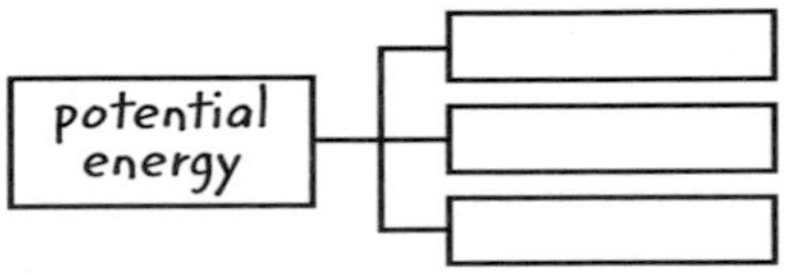

Critical Thinking

9. **List** Which has more kinetic energy: a 5-kg object moving at 5 m/s, 1 m off the ground or a 5-kg object at rest 2 m off the ground?

45 minutes

How can you classify different types of energy?

Materials

magnifying lens

musical greeting card

Safety

When you open a musical greeting card, you probably don't think about how many different forms of energy it uses. What types of energy are used in a musical greeting card?

Learn It

To **classify** means to sort objects into groups based on common features or functions. You can sort different types of energy based on the definitions of each type of energy and your experiences using them. Use this knowledge as you classify the different types of energy used in a musical greeting card.

Try It

1. Read and complete a lab safety form.
2. Carefully observe a musical greeting card before and during its operation. Ask questions such as: "What makes it start? What makes it stop? What is the energy source? What produces the sound?"
3. Write a hypothesis about how you think the greeting card works. What forms of energy are involved in its operation?
4. Carefully dismantle a second musical greeting card. Make a scientific illustration of the electronic parts. Label as many parts as you can. Use a magnifying lens if necessary.
5. Set the dismantled card in operation. Observe any motion. Gently touch parts of the card as it produces sound.
6. Using the card and your illustration, identify and label the different types of energy involved in the card's operation from the time it turns on until it turns off. Record your observations in your Science Journal.

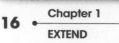

Apply It

7. **Identify Cause and Effect** What causes the card to turn on? What causes it to turn off?
8. **Classify** List all of the types of energy involved in the operation of your card.
9. **Infer** What produces the sound? How does the sound from the card reach your ear?
10. **Key Concept** What are some examples of potential energy and kinetic energy in the operation of your card? Explain.

Lesson 2 Energy Transfers and Transformations

Reading Guide

Key Concepts
ESSENTIAL QUESTIONS

- What is the law of conservation of energy?
- How is energy transformed and transferred?
- What are renewable and nonrenewable energy resources?

Vocabulary

law of conservation of energy p. 18
energy transfer p. 19
energy transformation p. 19
work p. 19
open system p. 21
closed system p. 21
renewable energy resource p. 22
nonrenewable energy resource p. 24

g Multilingual eGlossary

Academic Standards for Science

7.1.1 Explain that when energy is transferred from one system to another, the total quantity of energy does not change.

Also covers: 7.1.3, 7.4.1, 7.4.2, 7.NS.1, 7.NS.4, 7.NS.6, 7.NS.7, 7.NS.10, 7.DP.5

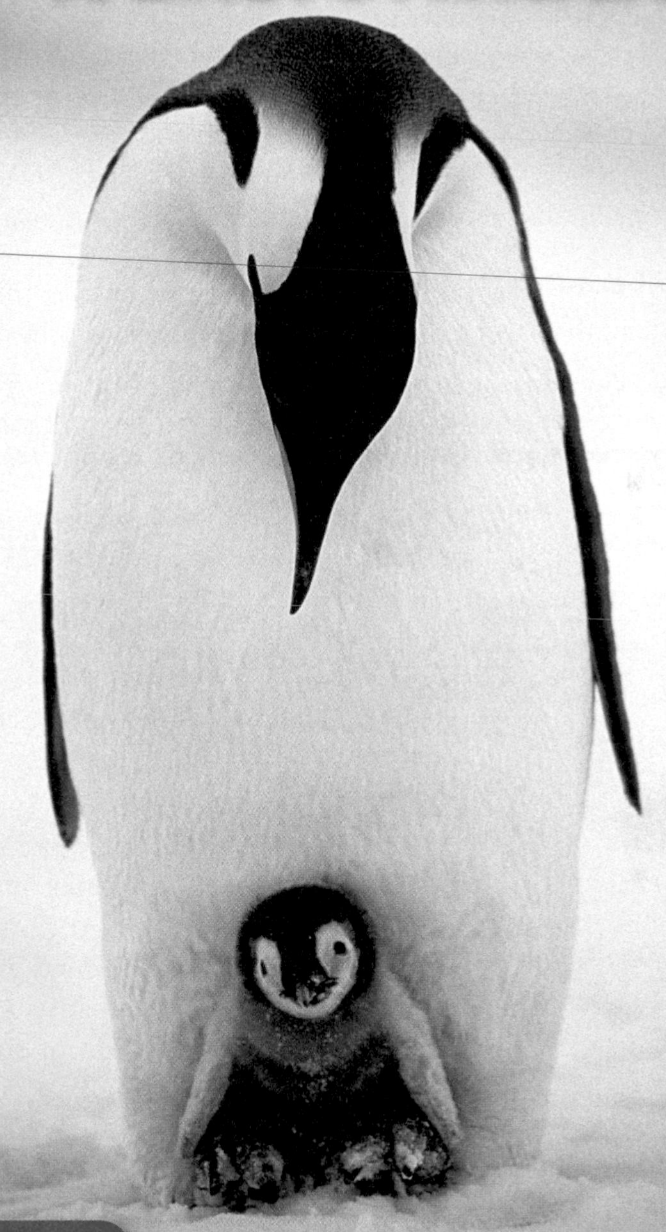

Inquiry Warm and Cozy?

This penguin chick lives in one of the coldest places on Earth—Antarctica. The chick is standing on its parent's feet to insulate its feet from the ice. This helps prevent thermal energy of the chick's body from transferring to the ice. The chick cuddles with its parent to absorb thermal energy from its parent's body. Without receiving thermal energy from the parent, the baby would quickly die.

Inquiry Launch Lab

20 minutes

How does a flashlight work?

If the lights go out, you might turn on a flashlight. You know that when you flip the switch, the light will go on. What happens? How does the flashlight work?

1. Read and complete a lab safety form.
2. Examine a **flashlight.** List the parts that you can see. Predict the types of energy involved in the operation of the flashlight.
3. Use the switch to turn the flashlight on. What do you think happened inside the flashlight to produce the light? Write your ideas in your Science Journal.
4. Take the flashlight apart. Discuss the kinds of energy involved in producing light.

Think About This

1. Was light the only type of energy produced? Why or why not?
2. **Key Concept** Describe the different types of energy involved in a flashlight. Draw a sequence diagram showing how each form of energy changes to the next form.

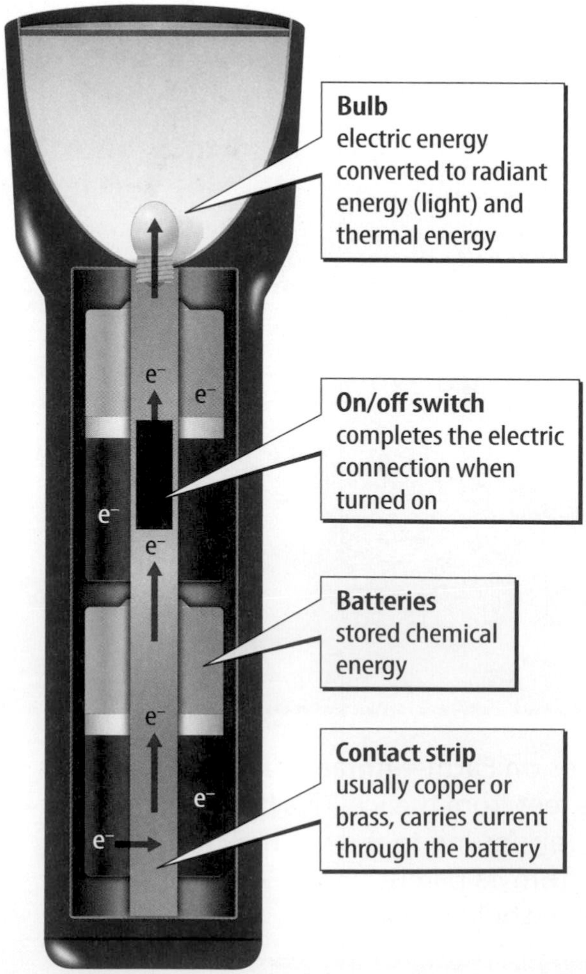

Figure 10 Several energy changes occur in a flashlight.

Law of Conservation of Energy

Think about turning on the flashlight in the Launch Lab. *The* **law of conservation of energy** *says that energy can be transformed from one form to another, but it cannot be created or destroyed.* In the flashlight shown in **Figure 10,** chemical energy of the battery is transformed to electric energy (moving electrons) that moves through the contact strip to the bulb. The electric energy is transformed into radiant energy and thermal energy in the lightbulb. The law of conservation of energy indicates that the amount of radiant energy that shines out of the flashlight cannot be greater than the chemical energy stored in the battery.

Key Concept Check What is the law of conservation of energy?

The amount of radiant energy given off by the flashlight is less than the chemical energy in the battery. Where is the missing energy? As you read this lesson, you will learn that in every energy transformation, some energy transfers to the environment.

Chemical energy is transformed to mechanical energy.
Mechancal energy is transferred to the tennis ball.

Figure 11 Energy transfers and transformations take place when the tennis player hits the ball.

Visual Check Identify at least one energy transformation that occurs as the ball moves through the air.

Energy Transfer

What happens when the tennis player in **Figure 11** hits the ball with the racket? The mechanical energy of the racket changes the movement of the ball, and the ball's mechanical energy increases. *When energy moves from one object to another without changing form, an* **energy transfer** *occurs.* The tennis racket transfers mechanical energy to the tennis ball.

Energy Transformation

Where does the mechanical energy in the tennis player's racket come from? Chemical energy stored in the player's muscles changes to mechanical energy when she swings her arm. *When one form of energy is converted to another form of energy, an* **energy transformation** *occurs.*

Key Concept Check Identify an energy transfer and an energy transformation that occurs when someone plays a guitar.

Energy and Work

You might be thinking that reading about energy is a lot of work. But to a scientist, it's not work at all. To a scientist, **work** *is the transfer of energy that occurs when a force makes an object move in the direction of the force. Work is only being done while the force is acting on the object.* As the tennis player swings the racket, the racket applies a force to the ball for about a meter. Although the ball moves 10 m, work is done by the racket only during the time the racket applies a force to the ball. When the ball separates from the racket, the racket no longer does work.

Suppose the tennis player is standing still before she serves the ball. She is using her muscles to hold the ball. Is she doing work on the ball? No; because the ball is not moving, she is not doing work. If a force does not make an object move in the direction of the force, it does no work on the object.

Math Skills

Use a Formula

The amount of work done on an object is calculated using the formula $W = F \times d$, where W = work, F = the force applied to the object, and d = the distance the force moves the object. For example, a student slides a library book across a table. The student pushed the book with a force of **8.5 newtons (N)** a distance of **0.3 m**. The book slides a total distance of 1 m. How much work is done on the book?

$W = F \times d$

$W = 8.5\ \text{N} \times 0.30\ \text{m} = 2.55\ \text{N·m} = 2.6\ \text{J}$

Recall that the distance used to calculate work is the distance the force was applied to the object.

Note: 1 N·m = 1 J, so 2.6 J of work was done on the book.

Practice

A student lifts a backpack straight up with a force of 53.5 N for a distance of 0.65 m. How much work is done on the backpack?

Review

- **Math Practice**
- **Personal Tutor**

Inefficiency of Energy Transformations

When a tennis player hits a ball with a racket, most of the mechanical energy of the racket transfers to the ball, but not all of it. You know when a ball hits a racket because you can hear a sound. Some of the mechanical energy of the racket is transformed to sound energy. In addition, some of the mechanical energy of the racket is transformed to thermal energy. The temperature of the racket, the ball, and the air surrounding both objects increases slightly. Anytime there is an energy transformation or energy transfer, some energy is transformed into thermal energy.

Reading Check Summarize the energy transformations that occur when a tennis racket hits a tennis ball.

Recall the flashlight at the beginning of the lesson. The transformation of chemical energy of the battery to radiant energy from the lightbulb is inefficient, too. As the electric energy moves through the circuit, some electric energy transforms to thermal energy. When electric energy transforms to radiant energy in the lightbulb, more energy transforms to thermal energy. In some flashlights, the bulb is warm to the touch.

Recall that the law of conservation of energy says that energy cannot be created or destroyed. When scientists say that energy transformations are inefficient, they do not mean that energy is destroyed. Energy transformations are inefficient because not all the energy that is transformed to another form of energy is usable.

Inquiry MiniLab

20 minutes

How can you transfer energy?

When you ride your bicycle, pushing the pedals with your feet makes the wheels turn. However, your feet don't touch the wheels. How can you transfer energy to another object without touching it?

1. Read and complete a lab safety form.
2. Place a **cork** at one edge of a **rectangular pan** half-filled with water.
3. Discuss with your teammates how you can make the cork move to the opposite edge of the pan without touching it. Possible tools include a **drinking straw,** a **plastic spoon,** and a **length of string,** but you can't physically touch the cork with these items. You also may use any other methods you can think of without touching the cork.
4. Try each of your ideas. Record your results in your Science Journal.

Analyze and Conclude

1. **Explain** which method that you tried was the most effective and the least effective.
2. **Hypothesize** What would make the cork easier to move? Explain.
3. **Key Concept** What form of energy did you start with to move the cork? In what ways was the energy transferred and transformed during each trial?

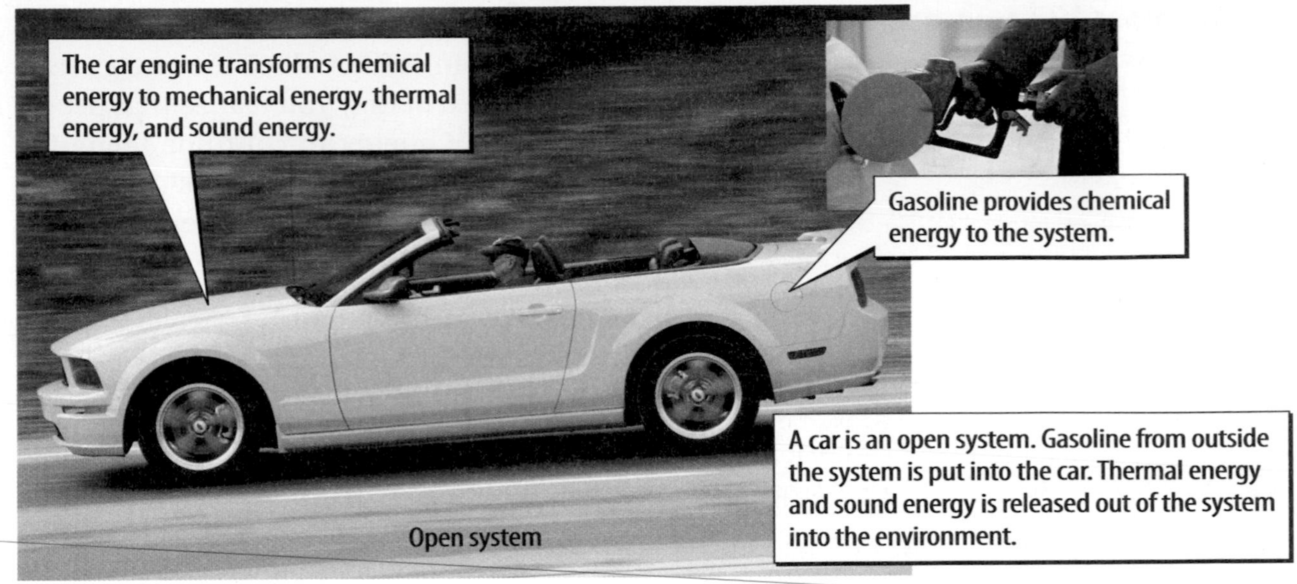

The car engine transforms chemical energy to mechanical energy, thermal energy, and sound energy.
Gasoline provides chemical energy to the system.
A car is an open system. Gasoline from outside the system is put into the car. Thermal energy and sound energy is released out of the system into the environment.
Open system

Figure 12 A car is an open system. Gasoline is an input. Thermal energy and sound energy are outputs.

Open Systems

In Lesson 1, you read that scientists often study the energy of systems. A car, as shown in **Figure 12,** is a system. Chemical energy of the fuel is transformed to mechanical energy of the moving car. Because energy transformations are inefficient, some of the chemical energy transforms to thermal energy and sound energy that are released to the environment. An **open system,** such as a car engine, *is a system that exchanges matter or energy with the environment.*

Review
Personal Tutor

Closed Systems

Can you think of a system that does not exchange energy with the environment? What about a flashlight? A flashlight releases radiant energy and thermal energy into the environment. What about your body? You eat food, which contains chemical energy and comes from the environment. Your body also releases several types of energy into the environment, including thermal energy, mechanical energy, and sound energy. *A* **closed system** *is a system that does not exchange matter or energy with the environment.* In reality, there are no closed systems. Every physical system transfers some energy to or from its environment. Scientists use the idea of a closed system to study and model the movement of energy.

WORD ORIGIN
system
from Greek *systema*, means "whole made of several parts"

Energy Transformations and Electric Energy

You probably have heard someone say, "turn off the lights, you're wasting energy." This form of energy is electric energy. Most appliances you use every day require electric energy. Where does this energy come from?

ACADEMIC VOCABULARY

resource
(noun) a stock or supply of materials, money, or other assets that can be used as needed

Renewable Energy Resources

If you think about all of the energy used in the United States, you realize that people need a lot of energy to continue living the way they do. This huge demand for energy and the desire to protect the environment has resulted in a search for renewable energy resources. *A* **renewable energy resource** *is an energy resource that is replaced as fast as, or faster than, it is used.* There are several different kinds of renewable energy resources.

▲ **Figure 13** Solar power plants transform radiant energy from the Sun to electric energy.

Solar Radiant energy from the Sun, or solar energy, is one energy resource that can be converted into electric energy. Some solar energy plants, such as the one in **Figure 13,** transform radiant energy into electric energy with photovoltaic (foh toh vohl TAY ihk), or solar, cells. Photovoltaic cells are made from thin wafers of the element silicon. When radiant energy from the Sun hits the cells, it knocks electrons away from the silicon atoms. This movement of electrons is electric energy. Some homes, businesses, and small appliances, such as calculators, use photovoltaic cells to provide electricity.

In some solar energy plants, radiant energy from the Sun is transformed into thermal energy. The thermal energy is used to convert water to steam. The steam turns a generator, which transforms mechanical energy into electric energy.

▲ **Figure 14** Wind turbines transform kinetic energy from the wind to electric energy.

Wind Have you ever driven along a highway and seen wind turbines such as those in **Figure 14?** Wind turbines are built in places where winds blow almost continuously, such as the vast open spaces of the southwestern United States. Wind moves the blades of the turbine, turning a generator that transforms kinetic energy of the wind to electric energy. One of the drawbacks of wind energy is that wind does not blow steadily at all times. This source of electric energy is not very consistent or predictable.

Hydroelectric If you ever have stood underneath a shower, you have felt the energy of falling water. In hydroelectric plants, falling water from rivers and dams is channeled through a turbine. When the turbine spins, mechanical energy is transformed to electric energy. Most of the hydroelectric energy produced in the United States comes from the western part of the country. The hydroelectric plant shown in **Figure 15** is at Shasta Lake in California.

The major drawback of hydroelectric energy is that dams and turbines can interrupt the natural movements of animals in rivers and lakes. Also, there are a limited number of places where rivers are large enough for these energy plants to be built.

▲ **Figure 15** Potential energy stored in elevated water is transformed into electric energy in some energy plants.

Geothermal Earth's temperature increases as you go deeper below the surface. But in a few places, Earth is very hot close to the surface. Geothermal plants are built where thermal energy from Earth is near Earth's surface. In these energy plants, thermal energy is transferred to water creating steam. The steam turns turbines in electric generators. The states with the most geothermal reservoirs are Alaska, Hawaii, and California. The geothermal reservoir shown in **Figure 16** has been producing geothermal power in California since 1921.

▲ **Figure 16** In geothermal energy plants such as The Geysers, thermal energy inside Earth is transformed into electric energy.

Concepts in Motion **Animation**

Biomass Biomass includes wood, plants, and even manure and garbage. All of these sources of stored chemical energy can be transformed to electric energy in energy plants like the one in **Figure 17.** Burning biomass releases carbon dioxide into the atmosphere. Some scientists believe this contributes to climate change and global warming. However, when biomass crops are grown, the plants use carbon dioxide during photosynthesis, reducing the overall amount of carbon dioxide produced in the process.

▲ **Figure 17** Chemical energy stored in biomass, such as wood, plants, manure, and garbage, is used to generate electric energy in some locations.

Reading Check Which energy plant is usually built on a lake or a river?

Electrical Energy Resources

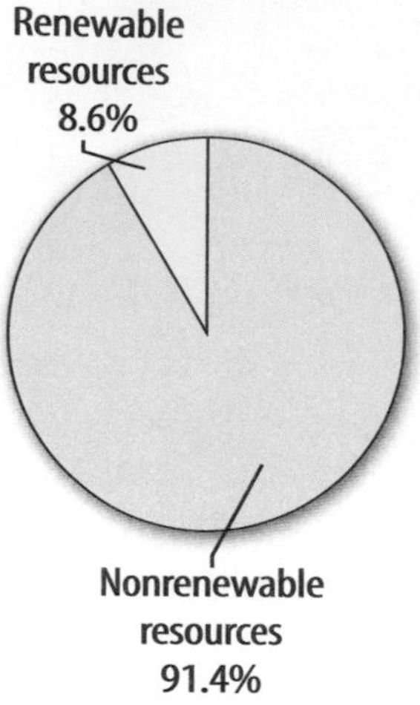

Table 1 Electric Energy Net Generation by Resources as of 2007

Nonrenewable Resources		Renewable Resources	
Resource	**Percentage**	**Resource**	**Percentage**
petroleum	1.6	biomass	about 1.0
natural gas	21.6	hydroelectric	5.8
coal	48.5	geothermal	<1.0
other gases	0.3	wind	<1.0
uranium (nuclear power)	19.4	solar and other	<1.0
Total	**91.4**	**Total**	**About 8.6**

Table 1 Most of the energy used in the United States comes from nonrenewable energy resources.

Visual Check Which resource is used to produce the most electric energy in the United States?

Nonrenewable Energy Resources

Most of the energy used in homes, schools, stores, and businesses comes from fossil fuels and nuclear energy, as shown in **Table 1.** Fossil fuels and nuclear energy are **nonrenewable energy resources**—*an energy resource that is available in limited amounts or that is used faster than it can be replaced in nature.*

Fossil Fuels Petroleum, natural gas, propane, and coal are fossil fuels. Ancient plants stored radiant energy from the Sun as chemical energy in their molecules. This chemical energy was passed on to the animals that ate the plants. Over millions of years, geological processes converted the remains of these ancient plants and animals into fossil fuels. Fossil fuels are a very concentrated form of chemical energy that easily transforms into other forms of energy. However, when fossil fuels burn, they release harmful wastes such as sulfur dioxide, nitrogen oxide, and carbon dioxide. Sulfur dioxide and nitrogen oxide contribute to acid rain. As you read, carbon dioxide is suspected of contributing to global climate change.

Nuclear Energy In nuclear energy plants, uranium atoms are split apart in a process called nuclear fission. Nuclear fission produces thermal energy, which heats water, producing steam. The steam turns turbines that produce electric energy. While nuclear energy plant emissions are not harmful, the waste from these plants is radioactive. The safe disposal of radioactive waste is a major challenge associated with nuclear energy.

Key Concept Check What are renewable and nonrenewable energy resources?

FOLDABLES®

Make a vertical two-tab book and label it as shown. Use it to explain renewable and nonrenewable resources.

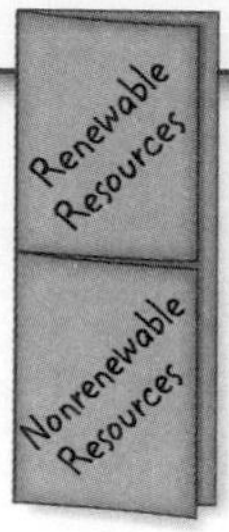

Lesson 2 Review

Visual Summary

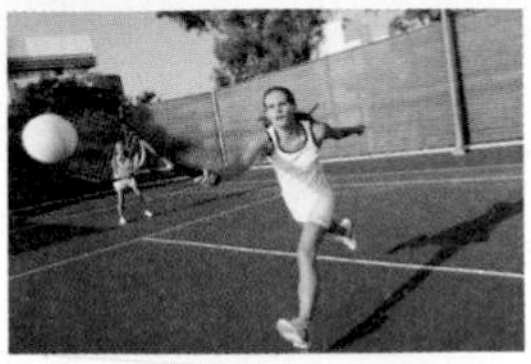

Energy can be transferred and transformed, but it cannot be created or destroyed.

Systems are classified as open systems or closed systems based on their interactions with their environment.

Energy resources are classified as renewable or nonrenewable based on their abundance and availability.

FOLDABLES

Use your lesson Foldable to review the lesson. Save your Foldable for the project at the end of the chapter.

What do you think NOW?

You first read the statements below at the beginning of the chapter.

3. In most systems, no energy is transferred to the environment.

4. Some forms of energy are replenished naturally.

Did you change your mind about whether you agree or disagree with the statements? Rewrite any false statements to make them true.

Use Vocabulary

1 **Define** *energy transformation.*

Understand Key Concepts

2 **Paraphrase** the law of conservation of energy.

3 Which of the following is NOT an example of energy transformations?
 A. A bicyclist pedals to school.
 B. A car's engine moves a car.
 C. A sound wave travels across a hall.
 D. The Sun shines on a tree, and it produces more cells.

4 **Describe** a kind of renewable energy that you could use in your home, and explain why it is a good choice.

Interpret Graphics

5 **Explain** why the object shown here is an open system.

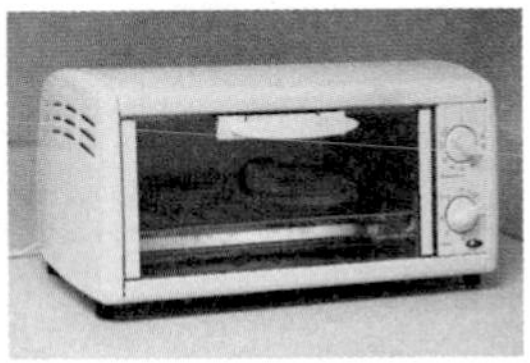

6 **Summarize** Copy and fill in the following graphic organizer to show four possible renewable resources of electric energy.

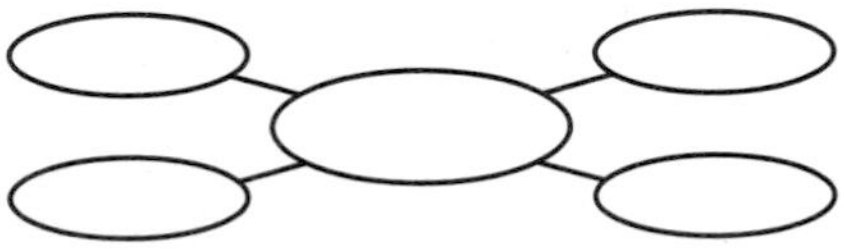

Critical Thinking

7 **Consider** A car company wants to build a wind-powered car that converts 100 percent of the mechanical energy in the wind to the mechanical energy of the moving car. Explain why the company will fail.

Math Skills　Review
Math Practice

8 A child pushes a toy truck with a force of 5.6 N a distance of 3.5 m. How much work is done on the truck?

GREEN SCIENCE

Biomass

Fresh Ideas About Not-So-Fresh Sources of Fuel

Grass clippings can be broken down to produce methane gas. The device used to convert grass clippings to methane gas is called a digester. The methane gas produced can be used in place of natural gas in appliances. It also can be used to power turbines that produce electricity.

Many people consider grass clippings, dog waste, and used cooking oil garbage. But instead of seeing these materials as garbage, some innovative thinkers see them as sources of biomass energy.

For centuries, humans have used biomass, such as wood, for energy. New technology is expanding the ways biomass can be used. Now biomass can be converted into fuel used to power automobiles, heat homes, and generate electricity.

The use of these fuel sources has several benefits. First, any fuel produced using biomass decreases dependence on nonrenewable resources such as fossil fuels. Also, use of these materials for fuel decreases the amount of waste going to landfills. Technologies to generate fuel from biomass continue to be developed and improved. Who knows what will be used for fuel in the future!

▲ **Dog waste can be converted to fuel in a methane digester. Dog waste contains a lot of energy because of the healthy, energy-rich foods fed to most dogs in the United States.**

▲ **Used cooking oil is an expensive disposal problem for restaurants. Instead, it can be collected and used on its own or combined with diesel fuel to power specially equipped vehicles.**

It's Your Turn

RESEARCH Technology has been developed that uses waste from slaughterhouses to make oil. Find out more about this process. Prepare an oral presentation to share what you have learned with other students in your class.

Lesson 3 Particles in Motion

Reading Guide

Key Concepts
ESSENTIAL QUESTIONS

- What is the kinetic molecular theory?
- In what three ways is thermal energy transferred?
- How are thermal conductors and insulators different?

Vocabulary

temperature p. 29
heat p. 30
conduction p. 31
radiation p. 31
convection p. 31
vaporization p. 33
thermal conductor p. 34
thermal insulator p. 34

g Multilingual eGlossary

Video BrainPOP®

Academic Standards for Science

7.1.1 Explain that when energy is transferred from one system to another, the total quantity of energy does not change.

7.1.2 Describe and give examples of how energy can be transferred from place to place and transformed from one form to another through radiation, convection and conduction.

Also covers: 7.NS.1, 7.NS.3, 7.NS.4, 7.NS.5, 7.NS.7, 7.NS.9, 7.NS.11

Inquiry Catchin' Some Waves?

This Agama lizard regulates its body temperature by absorbing thermal energy from its environment. Some lizards raise their body temperature well above the air temperature by absorbing radiant energy transferred by waves from the Sun.

Inquiry Launch Lab

20 minutes

Where is it the hottest?

⚠ Tie back hair and roll up sleeves.

Would your hands get just as warm if you held them at the sides of a campfire instead of directly over a campfire?

1. Read and complete a lab safety form. Copy the table into your Science Journal. .
2. Use **modeling clay** to hold a **birthday candle** upright. Use a **ring stand and clamp** to mount a **thermometer** horizontally above the candle. The thermometer bulb should be 10 cm above the top of the candle. Record the temperature on the thermometer in your table. Use a **match** to light the candle. Record the temperature every 30 seconds until the temperature reaches 70°C. Add more time columns to the table if needed. Blow out the candle.

⚠ *Do not put thermometer within 10 cm of the flame.*

3. Repeat steps 3–5 with a new candle. This time mount the thermometer 10 cm to the side of the candle flame.

Thermometer Above Flame				
Time (sec)	0	30	60	90
Temp. (°C)				
Thermometer to the Side of Flame				
Time (sec)	0	30	60	90
Temp. (°C)				

Think About This

Key Concept How do you think the energy from the flame traveled to the thermometer in each trial? Explain.

Figure 18 Particles that make up all matter, including carbonated beverages, are in constant motion. On average, solid particles move slowest, liquid particles move faster, and gas particles move the fastest.

Concepts in Motion **Animation**

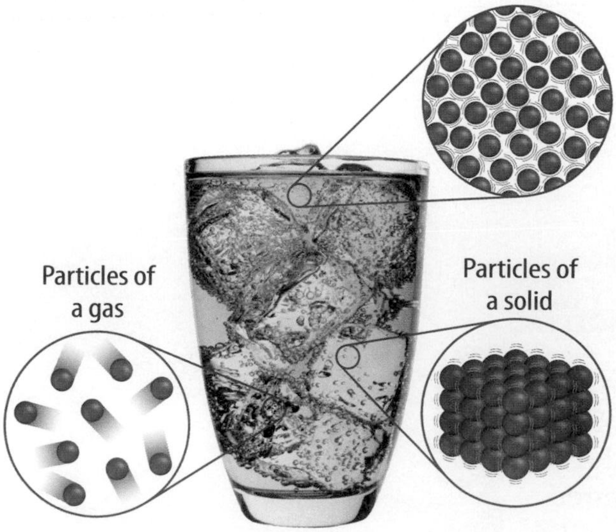

Kinetic Molecular Theory

You read in Lesson 2 that in every energy transformation some of the energy is transformed into thermal energy. Some of this thermal energy transfers to other materials. The transfer of thermal energy between materials depends on the movement of particles in the materials. The kinetic molecular theory explains how particles move. It has three major points:

- All matter is made of particles.
- Particles are in constant, random motion.
- Particles constantly collide with each other and with the walls of their container.

The kinetic molecular theory explains that the carbonated beverage in **Figure 18** is made of particles. The particles move in different directions and at different speeds. They collide with each other and with the particles that make up the ice and the glass.

Key Concept Check What are the three points of the kinetic molecular theory?

Temperature

When you pick up a glass of ice cold soda, the glass feels cold. Could you estimate its temperature? The temperature of something depends on how much kinetic energy the particles that make up the material have. *The measure of the average kinetic energy of the particles in a material is* **temperature.** If most of the drink particles have little kinetic energy, the drink has a low temperature and the glass feels cold. The SI unit for temperature is the kelvin (K). However, scientists often use the Celsius temperature scale (°C) to measure temperature.

Thermal Expansion

Suppose your teacher told everyone in your classroom to run around. There probably would not be enough space in your classroom for everyone to run as fast as they could. But, if you were in a large gymnasium, then everyone could run very quickly. When the particles that make up a material move slowly, they occupy less volume than they do at a higher temperature. As the temperature of a material increases, particles begin to move faster. They collide with each other more often and push each other farther apart. Thermal expansion is the increase in volume of a material due to a temperature increase, as shown in **Figure 19.** When the temperature of a material decreases, its volume decreases, This is thermal contraction.

Most materials contract as their temperature decreases, but water is an exception. When water is cooled to near its freezing point, interactions between water molecules push the molecules apart. Water expands as it freezes because of these molecular interactions, as shown in **Figure 20.**

Figure 19 The balloon on the top was cooled to −198°C using liquid nitrogen. As the balloon warms to room temperature, the molecules move faster and expand. The balloon undergoes thermal expansion. ▼

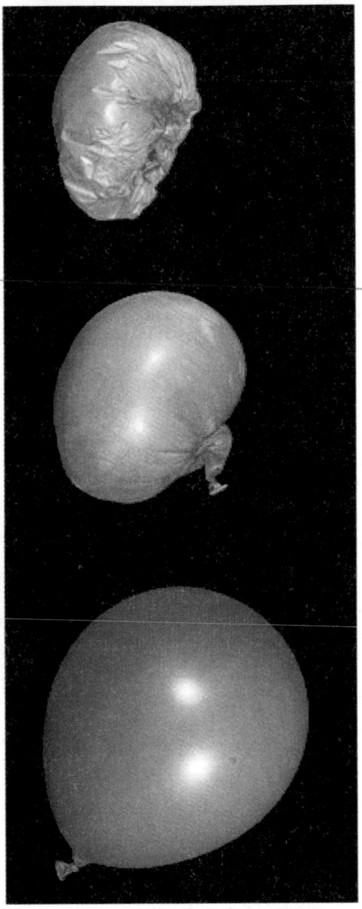

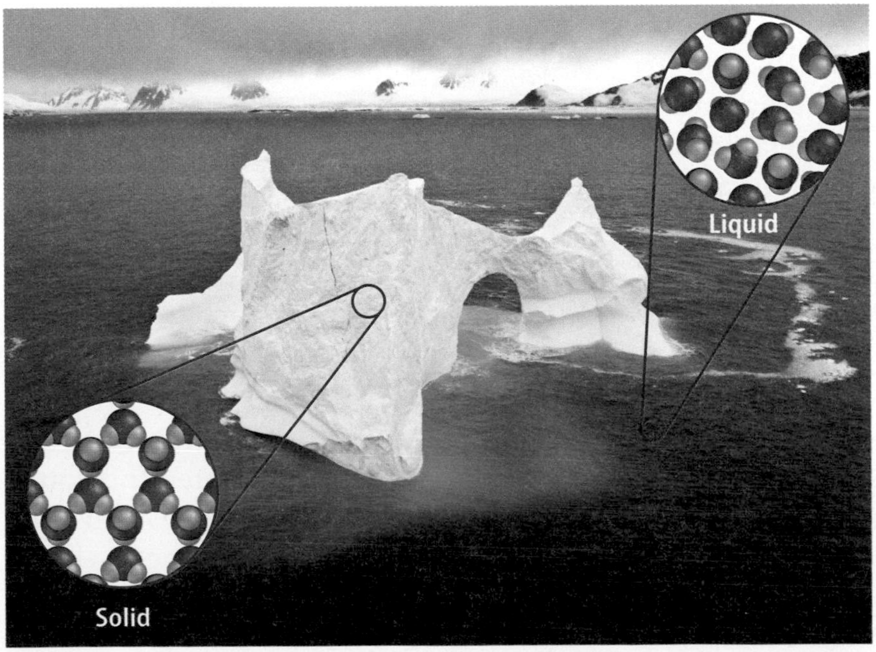

◀ **Figure 20** Because of the structure of a water molecule, as water freezes, the molecules attract in a way that creates empty spaces between them. This makes ice less dense than water. Because ice is less dense than water, ice floats on water.

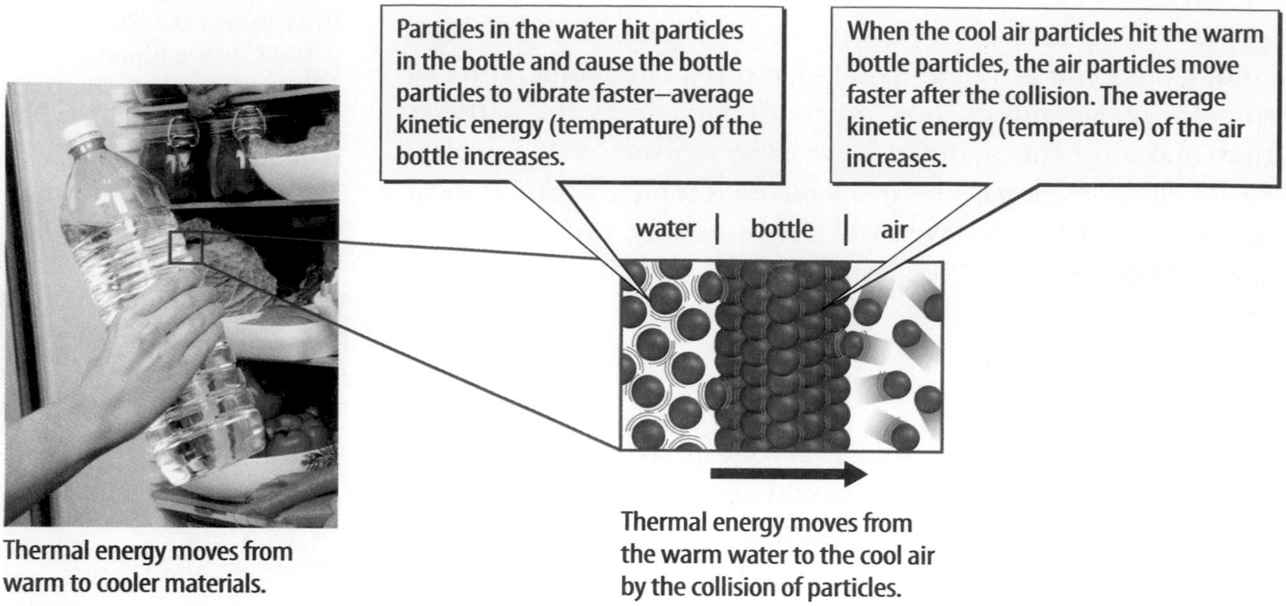

Particles in the water hit particles in the bottle and cause the bottle particles to vibrate faster—average kinetic energy (temperature) of the bottle increases.
When the cool air particles hit the warm bottle particles, the air particles move faster after the collision. The average kinetic energy (temperature) of the air increases.
water | bottle | air
Thermal energy moves from warm to cooler materials.
Thermal energy moves from the warm water to the cool air by the collision of particles.

Figure 21 Thermal energy is transferred by collisions of particles.

Transferring Thermal Energy

Suppose you put a warm bottle of water in the refrigerator. As shown in **Figure 21**, moving water molecules collide with the particles that make up the bottle. These collisions transfer kinetic energy to the particles that make up the bottle, and they vibrate faster. As the particles move faster, their average kinetic energy, or temperature, increases. The particles that make up the bottle then collide with particles that make up the air in the refrigerator.

The average kinetic energy of the particles that make up the air in the refrigerator increases. In other words, the temperature of the air in the refrigerator increases. The average kinetic energy of the particles of water decreases as thermal energy moves from the water to the bottle. Therefore, the temperature of the water decreases.

As the kinetic energy of the particles that make up a material increases, the thermal energy of the particles increases. As the kinetic energy of the particles that make up a material decreases, the thermal energy of the particles decreases. So, when particles transfer kinetic energy, they transfer thermal energy.

Thermal Energy and Heat

Thermal energy moves from warmer materials, such as the warm water in the bottle, to cooler materials, such as the cool air in the refrigerator. *The movement of thermal energy from a region of higher temperature to a region of lower temperature is called* **heat.** Because your hand is warmer than the water bottle, thermal energy moves from your hand to the bottle. When you place the warm bottle in the refrigerator, thermal energy moves from the warm bottle to the cool air in the refrigerator.

Thermal Equilibrium

What happens if you leave the water in the refrigerator for several hours? The temperature of the water, the bottle, and the air in the refrigerator become the same. When the temperatures of materials that are in contact are the same, the materials are said to be in thermal **equilibrium.** After the materials reach thermal equilibrium, the particles that make up the water, the bottle, and the air continue to collide with each other. The particles transfer kinetic energy back and forth, but the average kinetic energy of all the particles remains the same.

Heat Transfer

Suppose you want to heat water to cook pasta, as shown in **Figure 22.** You put a pan of water on the stove and turn the stove on. How is thermal energy transferred to the water?

1 Conduction Fast-moving particles of the gases in the flame collide with the particles that make up the pan. This transfers thermal energy to the pan. Then, the particles that make up the pan collide with particles of water, transferring thermal energy to the water. **Conduction** *is the transfer of thermal energy by collisions between particles in matter.*

2 Radiation If you put your hands near the side of the pan, you feel warmth. The thermal energy you feel is from **radiation**—*the transfer of thermal energy by electromagnetic waves.* All objects emit radiation, but warmer materials, such as hot water, emit more radiation than cooler ones.

3 Convection The flame, or hot gases, heats water at the bottom of the pan. The water at the bottom of the pan undergoes thermal expansion and is now less dense than the water above it. The denser water sinks and forces the less dense, warmer water upward. The water continues this cycle of warming, rising, cooling, and sinking, as thermal energy moves throughout the water. *The transfer of thermal energy by the movement of the particles from one part of a material to another is* **convection.** Convection also occurs in the atmosphere. Warm, less-dense air is forced upward by cooler, more-dense falling air. Thermal energy is transferred as the air rises and sinks.

Key Concept Check In what three ways is thermal energy transferred?

FOLDABLES®

Create a horizontal tri-fold book. Label it as shown. Use it to explain the different ways in which thermal energy is transferred.

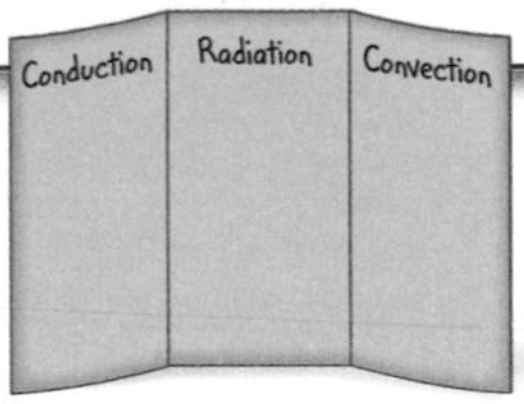

WORD ORIGIN

equilibrium
from Latin *aequus,* means "equal"; and *libra,* means "a balance or scale"

Figure 22 Conduction, radiation, and convection are ways in which thermal energy is transferred.

Review
Personal Tutor

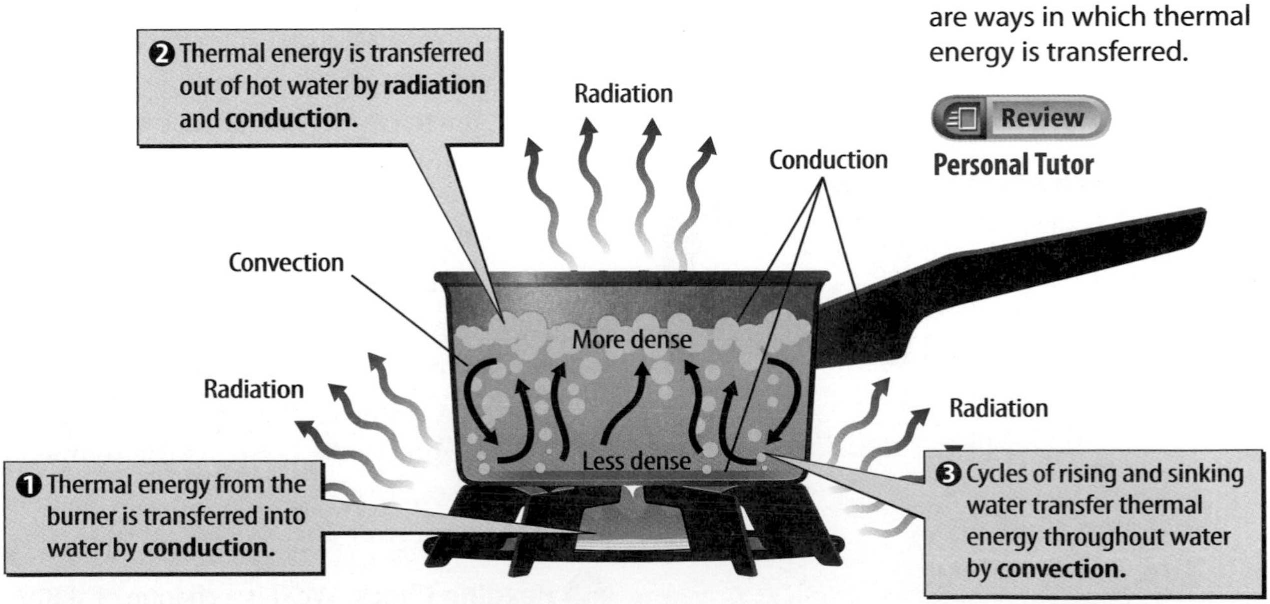

2 Thermal energy is transferred out of hot water by **radiation** and **conduction.**
Radiation
Conduction
Convection
More dense
Radiation
Less dense
Radiation
1 Thermal energy from the burner is transferred into water by **conduction.**
3 Cycles of rising and sinking water transfer thermal energy throughout water by **convection.**

Figure 23 If enough thermal energy is added to a material, it will change state.

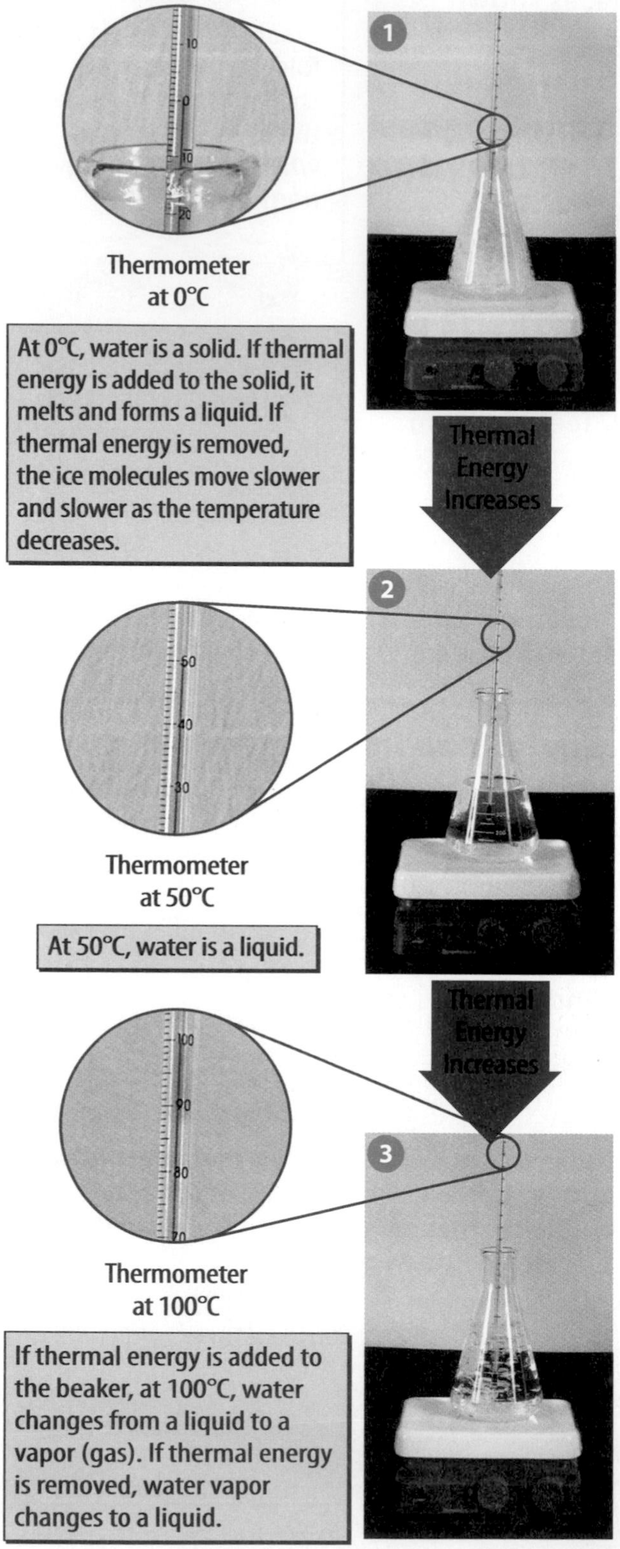

1
Thermometer at 0°C
At 0°C, water is a solid. If thermal energy is added to the solid, it melts and forms a liquid. If thermal energy is removed, the ice molecules move slower and slower as the temperature decreases.
Thermal Energy Increases
2
Thermometer at 50°C
At 50°C, water is a liquid.
Thermal Energy Increases
3
Thermometer at 100°C
If thermal energy is added to the beaker, at 100°C, water changes from a liquid to a vapor (gas). If thermal energy is removed, water vapor changes to a liquid.

Heat and Changes of State

When thermal energy is added or removed from a substance, sometimes only the temperature changes. At other times, a more dramatic change occurs—a change of state.

Changes Between Solids and Liquids

What happens if you place a flask of ice on a hot plate, as shown in **Figure 23?** Thermal energy moves from the hot plate to the flask then to the ice. The temperature of the ice increases. When the temperature of the ice reaches the melting point of ice, 0°C, the ice begins to melt. Melting is the change of state from a solid to a liquid. Although ice melts at 0°C, other materials have different melting points. For example, helium melts at −272°C, silver melts at 962°C, and diamonds melt at a temperature over 3,550°C.

As thermal energy transfers to the melting ice, the temperature (average kinetic energy) of the ice does not change. However, the potential energy of the ice increases. As the water molecules move farther apart, the potential energy between the molecules increases.

The reverse process occurs when thermal energy is removed from water. When water is placed in a freezer, thermal energy moves from the water to the colder air in the freezer. The average kinetic energy (temperature) of the water decreases. When the temperature of the water reaches 0°C, the water begins to freeze. Freezing is the change of state from a liquid to a solid. Notice that the freezing point of water is the same as the melting point of ice. Freezing is the opposite of melting.

While water is freezing, the temperature remains at 0°C until all the water is frozen. Once all the water freezes, the temperature of the ice begins to decrease. As the temperature decreases, the water molecules vibrate in place at a slower and slower rate.

Reading Check What is a change of state?

Changes Between Liquids and Gases

What happens when ice melts? As thermal energy transfers to the ice, the particles move faster and faster. The average kinetic energy of the water particles that make up ice increases and the ice melts. The temperature of the ice continues to increase until it reaches 100°C. At 100°C, water begins to vaporize. **Vaporization** *is the change of state from a liquid to a gas.* While the water is changing state—from a liquid to a gas—the kinetic energy of the particles remains constant.

Liquids vaporize in two ways—boiling and evaporation. Vaporization that occurs within a liquid is called boiling. Vaporization that occurs at the surface of a liquid is called evaporation. Have you heard the term *water vapor?* The gaseous state of a substance that is normally a liquid or a solid at room temperature is called vapor. Because water is liquid at room temperature, its gaseous state is referred to as water vapor.

The reverse process also can occur. Removing thermal energy from a gas changes it to a liquid. The change of state from a gas to a liquid is condensation. The condensation of water vapor that forms on grass overnight is called dew.

Changes Between Solids and Gases

Usually, water transforms from a solid to a liquid and then to a gas as it absorbs thermal energy. However, this is not always the case. On cold winter days, ice often changes directly to water vapor without passing through the liquid state. **Sublimation** is the change of state that occurs when a solid changes to a gas without passing through the liquid state. Dry ice, or solid carbon dioxide, sublimes as shown in **Figure 24.** Dry ice is used to keep foods frozen when they are shipped.

When thermal energy is removed from some materials, they undergo deposition. Deposition is the change of state from a gas directly to a solid without passing through the liquid state. Water vapor undergoes deposition when it freezes and forms frost, as shown in **Figure 24.**

Science Use v. Common Use

sublime

Science Use to change from a solid state to a gas state without passing through the liquid state

Common Use inspiring awe; supreme, outstanding, or lofty in thought or language

Figure 24 Not all materials go through all three states of matter when they change state. Some materials undergo sublimation (left), and other materials undergo deposition (right).

Visual Check How are sublimation and deposition related?

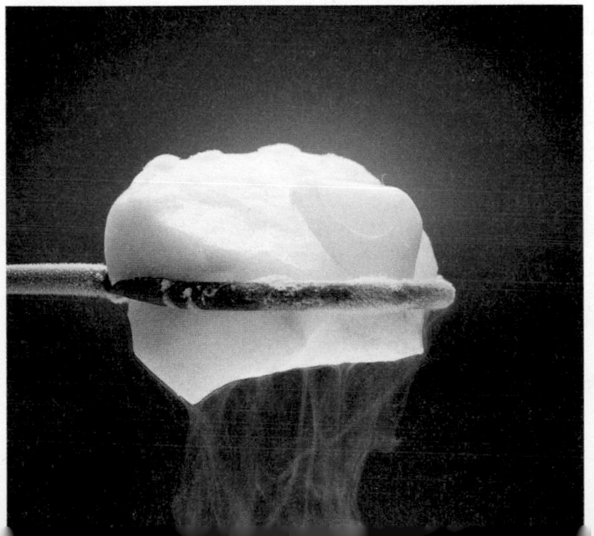

Figure 25 The color variations of this thermogram show the temperature variations in the pan and stove burner. The temperature scale is from white (warmest) through red, yellow, green, cyan, blue, and black (coolest).

Visual Check Why are the handles black?

Conductors and Insulators

When you put a metal pan on a burner, the pan gets very hot. If the pan has a handle made of wood or plastic, such as the one in **Figure 25,** the handle stays cool. Why doesn't the handle get hot like the pan as a result of thermal conduction?

The metal that makes up the pan is a **thermal conductor,** *a material in which thermal energy moves quickly.* The atoms that make up thermal conductors have electrons that are free to move, transferring thermal energy easily. The material that makes up the pan's handles is a **thermal insulator,** *a material in which thermal energy moves slowly.* The electrons in thermal insulators are held tightly in place and do not transfer thermal energy easily.

Key Concept Check How do thermal conductors differ from thermal insulators?

Inquiry MiniLab

25 minutes

What affects the transfer of thermal energy?

Ice-cold water stays cold longer in a foam cup than in a glass beaker. What other materials keep liquids cold?

1. Read and complete a lab safety form.
2. Place 75 mL of very warm water in each of three **100-mL beakers.**
3. Place a piece of **aluminum foil** over the first beaker and a piece of **cotton batting** over the second beaker. Leave the third beaker open.
4. Place **ice cubes** of equal sizes in three **petri dishes.** Place one dish on top of each beaker. Use a **stopwatch** to measure the time it takes for each ice cube to melt.
5. Make a table in your Science Journal. Label the first column of the rows *Beaker 1, Beaker 2,* and *Beaker 3.* In the second column, record the time it takes each ice cube to melt.

Analyze and Conclude

1. **Identify Cause and Effect** What caused the ice cubes over each beaker to melt? Use the kinetic molecular theory in your explanation.
2. **Identify Relationships** What role did thermal conductors and thermal insulators play in the rate at which the ice cubes melted?
3. **Key Concept** Describe the ways thermal energy transferred from the beakers to the ice.

Lesson 3 Review

Assessment Online Quiz

Visual Summary

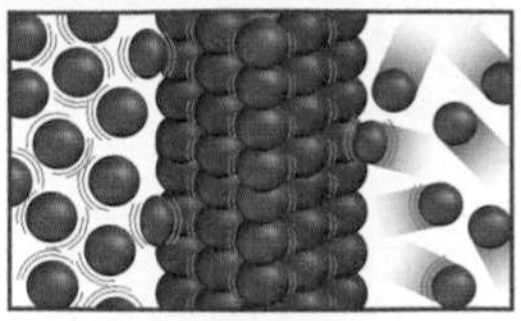

The kinetic molecular theory explains how particles move in matter.

Thermal energy is transferred in various ways by particles and waves.

Materials vary in how well they conduct thermal energy.

FOLDABLES®

Use your lesson Foldable to review the lesson. Save your Foldable for the project at the end of the chapter.

What do you think NOW?

You first read the statements below at the beginning of the chapter.

5. Only particles that make up moving objects are in motion.

6. Thermal energy can be transferred in several ways.

Did you change your mind about whether you agree or disagree with the statements? Rewrite any false statements to make them true.

Use Vocabulary

1. **Define** *temperature* in your own words.
2. **Explain** how heat is related to thermal energy.

Understand Key Concepts

3. **Summarize** the kinetic molecular theory.
4. Which of the following is NOT a way in which thermal energy is transferred?
   A. conduction
   B. convection
   C. radiation
   D. sublimation
5. **Differentiate** between a cloth safety belt and a metal buckle in terms of thermal conductors and insulators.

Interpret Graphics

6. **Explain** how the polar bear below can gain thermal energy if the temperature of the air is below freezing.

7. **Summarize** Copy and fill in the graphic organizer below showing the state-of-matter changes as thermal energy is added to ice.

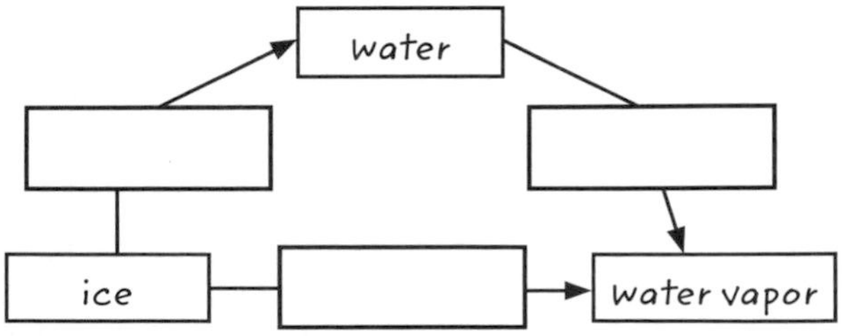

Critical Thinking

8. **Compare** You hold a 65°C cup of cocoa. Your hand is 37°C and the outside air is 6°C. Describe the flow of thermal energy.

Power a Device with a Potato

Materials

galvanized nails

pennies

LED bulb

Also needed: potato, alligator clip wires, paper plate, multimeter

Safety

In this chapter, you have learned about many types of energy and how energy can be transformed and transferred. Can a common potato transfer energy? Think about the inside of a potato. Is there anything in it that can carry an electric current?

Question

Can potatoes conduct electricity and light a bulb?

Procedure

1. Read and complete a lab safety form.
2. With your teammates, discuss what you know about electric circuits. How can you build an electric circuit using a potato as a battery? Write your ideas in your Science Journal. Draw a diagram of your circuit.
3. Use the materials provided to build the circuit shown in the picture.
4. Place half a potato on a paper plate. Push a galvanized, or zinc-coated, nail and a penny into the potato half.
5. Using two alligator clip wires, attach one end of each wire to the nail and to the penny.
6. Attach the positive probe from the multimeter to the alligator clip wire coming from the penny. Attach the negative probe to the alligator clip wire coming from the nail. Does your battery produce an electric current?
7. Push another galvanized nail and a penny into another potato half. Connect the second potato half to the first, as shown in the diagram, connecting the penny on one potato to the nail on the other. Use the meter to test your battery. Record your data in your Science Journal.

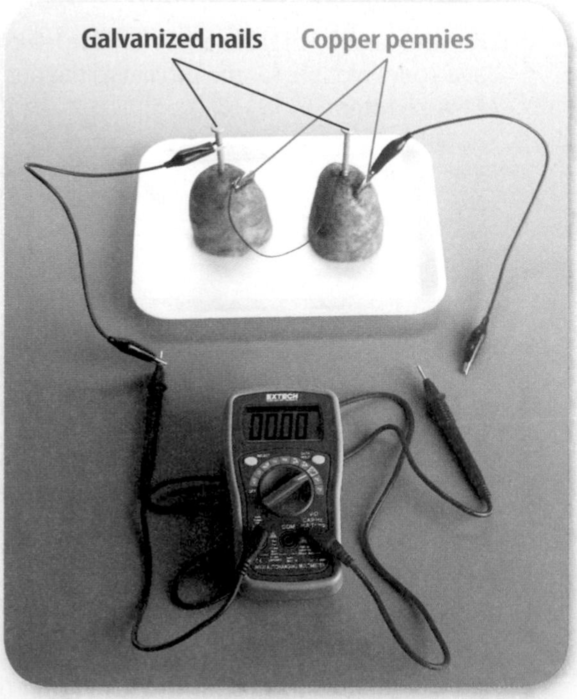

8

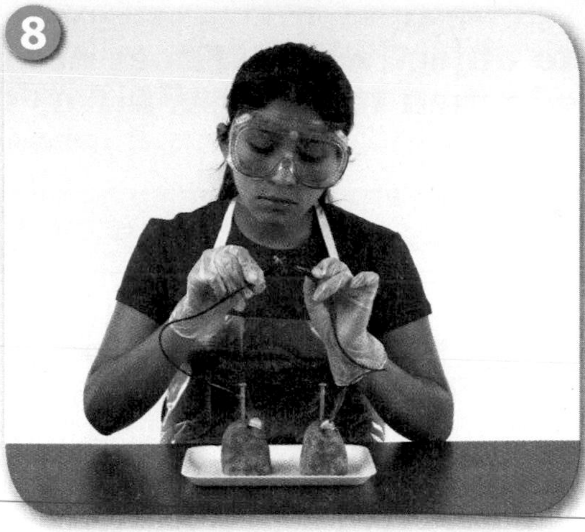

Lab Tips

☑ Check the wires in your circuit frequently to make sure they are in tight contact with the nail and the penny.

☑ Set the meter to the lowest range of DC voltage. Some meters require electricity to operate, so the voltage meter might register a lower voltage than is actually in the potato. Use a battery-operated meter, if possible, to avoid this problem.

8. Replace the meter with an LED bulb. Hook one end of the potato battery circuit to each wire coming from the bulb. Does the bulb light?
9. If necessary, redesign your battery circuit until you get the bulb to light. Review all ideas with your teacher before testing your circuit.

Analyze and Conclude

10. **Predict** What sort of devices do you think your potato battery will operate? Explain your answer.
11. **Explain** In this battery, electrons moved from the nails to the pennies. Why did this process light the bulb?
12. **The Big Idea** Describe, in order, all the energy transfers and transformations in your potato battery.

Communicate Your Results

In small groups, discuss how your battery worked and how you might improve its design. Discuss how changing the distance between the penny and the nail might affect your results.

Inquiry Extension

Try other types of food, such as a lemon or an apple. Which type of food produces the most electricity? Try other types of nails, such as a steel nail. Replace the penny with a strip of copper or aluminum. What works? What doesn't?

Remember to use scientific methods.

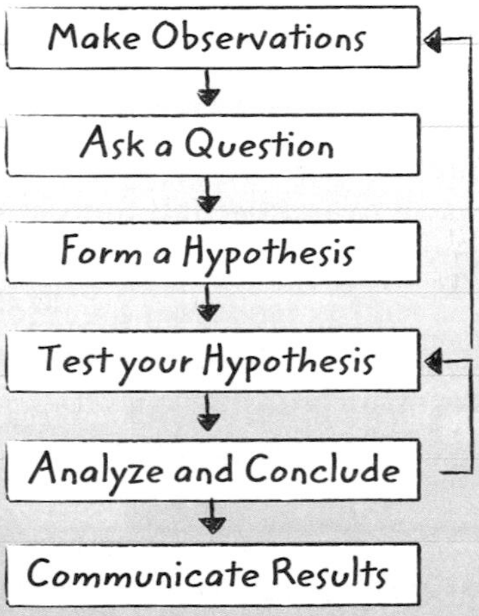

Chapter 1 Study Guide

THE BIG IDEA **Energy is transferred from object to object when it does not change form; energy is transformed when it changes form.**

Key Concepts Summary	Vocabulary

Lesson 1: Forms of Energy

- **Potential energy** is stored energy, and **kinetic energy** is energy of motion.
- Both **mechanical energy** and **thermal energy** involve kinetic energy and potential energy. Mechanical energy is the sum of the kinetic energy and the potential energy in a system of objects. Thermal energy is the sum of the kinetic energy and the potential energy in a system of particles.
- **Sound energy** and **radiant energy** are carried by waves.

Vocabulary

energy p. 9
potential energy p. 9
chemical energy p. 10
nuclear energy p. 10
kinetic energy p. 11
electric energy p. 11
mechanical energy p. 12
thermal energy p. 12
wave p. 13
sound energy p. 13
radiant energy p. 14

Lesson 2: Energy Transfers and Transformations

- The **law of conservation of energy** says that energy can be transformed from one form to another, but it cannot be created or destroyed.
- Energy is transformed when it is converted from one form to another. It is transferred when it moves from one object to another.
- **Renewable energy resources** are resources that are replaced as fast as, or faster than they are used. **Nonrenewable energy resources** are resources that are available in limited quantities or are used faster than they can be replaced.

Vocabulary

law of conservation of energy p. 18
energy transfer p. 19
energy transformation p. 19
work p. 19
open system p. 21
closed system p. 21
renewable energy resource p. 22
nonrenewable energy resource p. 24

Lesson 3: Particles in Motion

- The kinetic molecular theory says that all objects are made of particles; all particles are in constant, random motion; and the particles collide with each other and with the walls of their container.
- Thermal energy is transferred by **conduction, radiation,** and **convection.**
- A **thermal conductor** transfers thermal energy easily and a **thermal insulator** does not transfer thermal energy easily.

Vocabulary

temperature p. 29
heat p. 30
conduction p. 31
radiation p. 31
convection p. 31
vaporization p. 33
thermal conductor p. 34
thermal insulator p. 34

Review
- Personal Tutor
- Vocabulary eGames
- Vocabulary eFlashcards

FOLDABLES® Chapter Project

Assemble your lesson Foldables as shown to make a Chapter Project. Use the project to review what you have learned in this chapter.

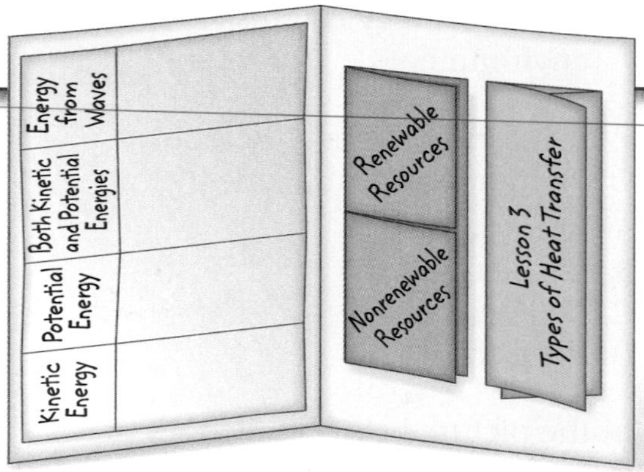

Use Vocabulary

1. Compare and contrast sound energy and radiant energy.
2. Explain why chemical energy and nuclear energy are both considered potential energy.
3. Describe how an open system differs from a closed system.
4. The energy of moving electrons is ________.
5. The energy carried by electromagnetic waves is ________.
6. Define *work* in your own words.
7. Define *conduction* in your own words.

Link Vocabulary and Key Concepts

Concepts in Motion **Interactive Concept Map**

Copy this concept map, and then use vocabulary terms from the previous page to complete the concept map.

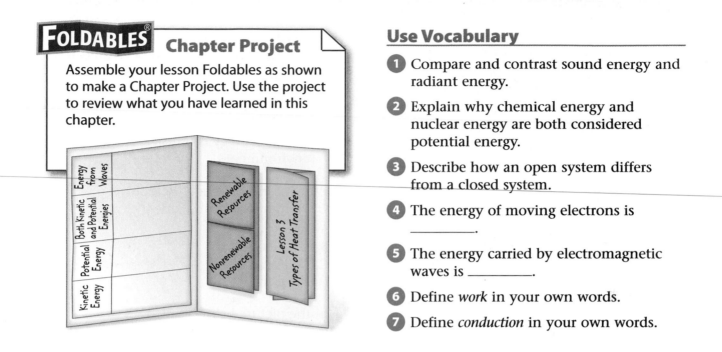

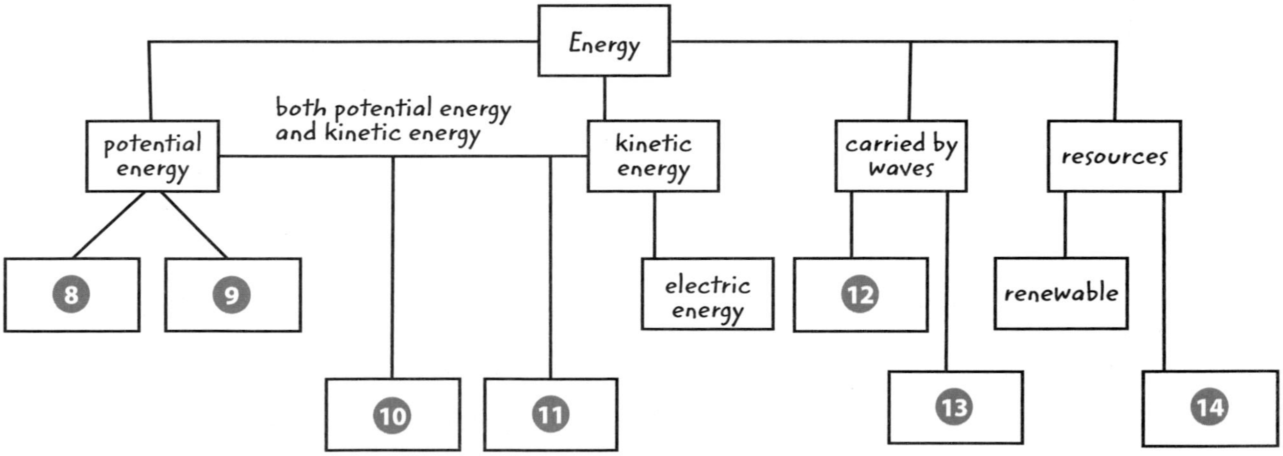

Chapter 1 Review

Understand Key Concepts

1. What type of energy does the statue have?

A. electric energy
B. mechanical energy
C. sound energy
D. thermal energy

2. Which is a form of energy that cannot be stored?
A. chemical energy
B. gravitational potential energy
C. nuclear energy
D. sound energy

3. Waves can transfer energy, but they
A. cannot carry sounds.
B. do not move matter.
C. always have the same wavelength.
D. are unable to move through empty space.

4. Which involves ONLY an energy transfer?
A. A boy turns on an electric toaster to warm a piece of bread.
B. A can of juice cools off in a cooler on a hot summer day.
C. A cat jumps down from a tree branch.
D. A truck burns gasoline and moves 20 km.

5. Which could occur in a closed system?
A. Chemical energy is transformed to electric energy in the system.
B. During a transformation of chemical energy to mechanical energy, thermal energy is released to the environment.
C. Electric energy from the environment is transferred to the system.
D. Radiant energy is transferred to the environment.

6. Which form of energy relies on gravitational potential energy?
A. fossil fuels
B. geothermal
C. hydroelectric
D. nuclear

7. In the picture below, how does the thermal energy definitely flow?

A. from the air to the dog
B. from the dog to the snow
C. from the snow to the air
D. from the snow to the dog

8. Which decreases the thermal energy of a can of soup you just took out of your pantry?
A. letting the can sit on the counter for an hour
B. opening the lid of the can of soup with a can opener
C. placing the can of soup under a bright light
D. putting the can of soup in the refrigerator

Assessment
Online Test Practice

Critical Thinking

9. **Identify** all the different forms of energy and all the energy transformations that you see in the picture below.

10. **Compare** the energy transformations that take place in the human body to the energy transformations that take place in a gasoline-powered car.

11. **Compare and contrast** each of the following terms: melting and freezing, boiling and evaporation, and sublimation and deposition.

12. **Judge** Determine whether the following statement is correct and explain your reasoning: *The amount of chemical energy in a flashlight's battery is equal to the radiant energy transferred to the environment.*

13. **Evaluate** Using what you read about thermal energy, explain why sidewalks are built as panels with space between them.

14. **Explain** Convection space heaters are small appliances that sit on the floor. Explain how they can heat an entire room.

Writing in Science

15. **Write** a short explanation to a friend explaining the following scenario: Most air-conditioned rooms are set to a temperature of about 22°C. Human body temperature is 37°C. Why don't people in an air-conditioned room come to thermal equilibrium with the room?

REVIEW THE BIG IDEA

16. Describe at least four energy transfers or energy transformations that occur in your body.

17. The photo below shows an electrical power plant that uses coal to generate electricity. What type of energy resource is coal? What are the advantages and disadvantages of using coal to generate electricity?

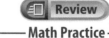

Math Skills

Review
Math Practice

Use a Formula

18. A child pulls a toy wagon with a force of 25.0 N for a distance of 8.5 m. How much work did the child do on the wagon?

19. A man pushes a box with a force of 75.0 N across a 12.0 m loading dock. How much work did he do on the box?

Standardized Test Practice

Record your answers on the answer sheet provided by your teacher or on a separate sheet of paper.

Multiple Choice

Use the figure to answer questions 1 and 2.

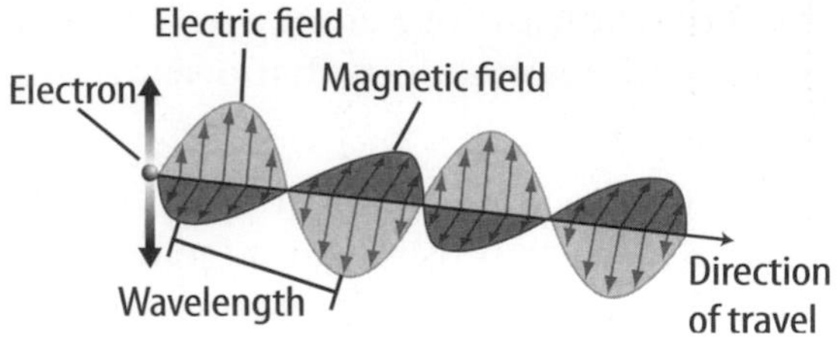

1 Which kind of energy is carried by the wave model shown?

A chemical energy
B electric energy
C radiant energy
D sound energy

2 Which property does this type of wave have that other kinds of waves do not?

A It can travel through air.
B It can travel through water.
C It can travel through a vacuum.
D It can travel through metal wires.

3 Which accurately describes potential energy and kinetic energy?

A A moving soccer ball has potential energy, while a rolling bowling ball has kinetic energy.
B A rock at the top of a cliff has potential energy, while a moving stream has kinetic energy.
C The energy stored in chemical bonds is potential energy, while the energy stored in an atom's nucleus is kinetic energy.
D The energy stored in an atom's nucleus is potential energy, while the energy stored in chemical bonds is kinetic energy.

4 Which describes the sum of potential energy and kinetic energy of objects or systems?

A nuclear energy and electric energy
B nuclear energy and mechanical energy
C thermal energy and electric energy
D thermal energy and mechanical energy

Use the figure to answer questions 5 and 6.

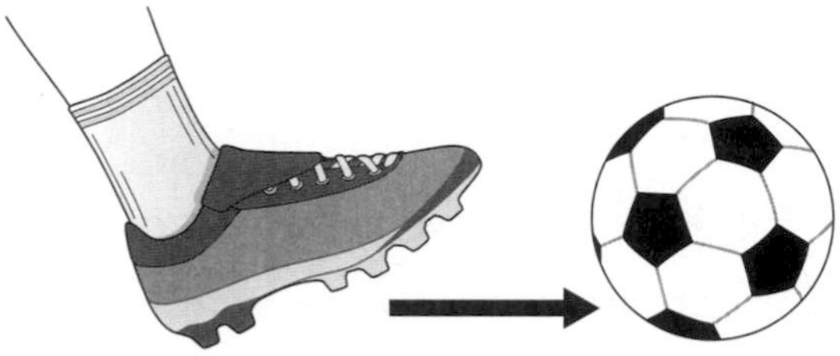

5 The figure above shows someone kicking a soccer ball. Which energy transformation occurs to make the foot move?

A chemical energy to mechanical energy
B mechanical energy to chemical energy
C mechanical energy to mechanical energy
D thermal energy to mechanical energy

6 Which energy transfer occurs to make the ball move?

A chemical energy from ball to foot
B chemical energy from foot to ball
C mechanical energy from ball to foot
D mechanical energy from foot to ball

7 Which is a renewable energy resource that is used to produce electricity?

A biomass
B coal
C natural gas
D petroleum

Assessment

Online Standardized Test Practice

8 A portable radio transforms chemical energy in batteries into electric energy and then into sound energy. However, not all of the energy from the batteries is converted to sound energy. Which describes how a portable radio still upholds the law of conservation of energy?

- **A** Some energy is destroyed due to inefficiency.
- **B** Some energy goes back into the batteries to be used later.
- **C** Some energy is lost to the surroundings as thermal energy.
- **D** Some energy is lost to the surroundings as chemical energy.

Use the figure to answer question 9.

9 The figure above shows a pan of water being heated on a stove. Which statement is true?

- **A** The pan and the flame are a closed system.
- **B** The natural gas is undergoing an energy transfer.
- **C** Thermal energy is not transferred, and the temperature remains constant.
- **D** This process results in a temperature change and possibly a change of state.

Constructed Response

Use the figure to answer question 10.

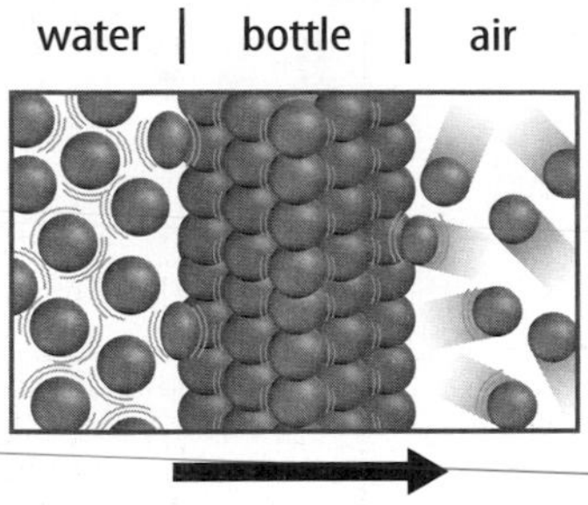

10 Imagine putting a warm bottle of water into a refrigerator. The figure models the particles that make up the water, the bottle, and the air. Explain the energy transfer between the cold refrigerator air outside the bottle and the warm water inside the bottle.

11 How does an open system differ from a closed system?

12 How does the relationship between temperature and volume of water differ from most other materials?

NEED EXTRA HELP?												
If You Missed Question...	1	2	3	4	5	6	7	8	9	10	11	12
Go to Lesson...	1	1	1	1	2	2	2	2	2	3	2	3

Chapter 2

Motion, Forces, and Newton's Laws

THE BIG IDEA

In what ways do forces affect an object's motion?

Inquiry How did they get up there?

When you stop a video of moving acrobats, they sometimes look as if they are frozen in the air. A still photo of an acrobat in midair can help you analyze exactly what is happening.

- What are some ways you could describe the motion of the acrobats in the air?
- What caused the acrobats to fly high into the air?
- In what ways do forces affect the motion of the acrobats?

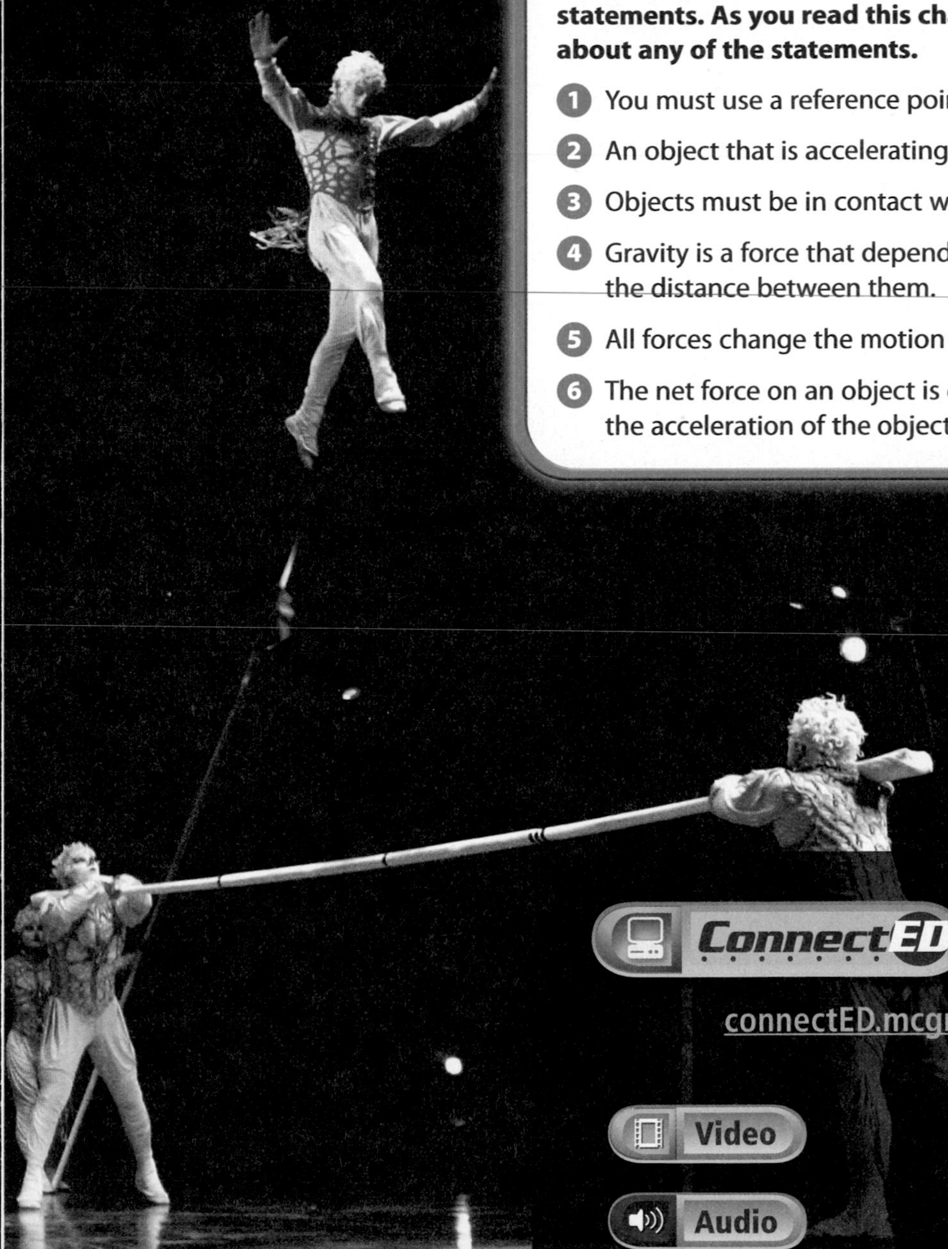

Get Ready to Read

What do you think?

Before you read, decide if you agree or disagree with each of these statements. As you read this chapter, see if you change your mind about any of the statements.

1. You must use a reference point to describe an object's motion.
2. An object that is accelerating must be speeding up.
3. Objects must be in contact with one another to exert a force.
4. Gravity is a force that depends on the masses of two objects and the distance between them.
5. All forces change the motion of objects.
6. The net force on an object is equal to the mass of the object times the acceleration of the object.

ConnectED Your one-stop online resource

connectED.mcgraw-hill.com

- Video
- WebQuest
- Audio
- Assessment
- Review
- Concepts in Motion
- Inquiry
- Multilingual eGlossary

Lesson 1

Describing Motion

Reading Guide

Key Concepts

ESSENTIAL QUESTIONS

- What information do you need to describe the motion of an object?
- How are speed, velocity, and acceleration related?
- How can a graph help you understand the motion of an object?

Vocabulary

g Multilingual eGlossary

Video BrainPOP®

Academic Standards for Science

7.1.5 Describe and investigate how forces between objects can act at a distance, such as magnetic, electrical or gravitational forces, or by means of direct contact between objects.

Also covers: 7.1.7, 7.NS.1, 7.NS.2, 7.NS.7, 7.NS.9

Inquiry Where is the white ball?

In an arcade, many games involve something moving. Objects speed up, slow down, and change direction. How would you describe the position of the white ball in this game at any moment in time? How is its motion different from the motion of the other balls? What words could you use to describe the motion of the ball?

Inquiry Launch Lab

15 minutes

How can you describe motion?

You see things move in many ways each day. You might see a train moving along a track or raindrops falling to the ground. What information do you need to describe an object's motion?

1. Read and complete a lab safety form.
2. Choose a **small object,** such as a ball or a pencil. Move the object in some way.
3. Have a partner write a short description of the movement in the Science Journal.
4. Exchange objects and descriptions with several other pairs of students. Each time, use the description to try to duplicate the original motion.

Think About This

1. **Contrast** Why were some descriptions more useful than others when you tried to duplicate the motion?
2. **Key Concept** What information do you think you need to accurately describe an object's motion?

Motion

Suppose you have been playing a shuffleboard game in an arcade. You decide to try something new, so you walk to a racing game. As you walk to the new game, your position in the room changes. **Motion** *is the process of changing position.* If the games are 5 m apart, you could say that your position changed by 5 m.

Motion and Reference Points

How would you describe your motion to a friend? You could say that you walked 5 m away from the shuffleboard game. Or you could say that you moved 5 m toward the racing game. *The starting point you use to describe the motion or the position of an object is called the* **reference point.** Motion is described differently depending on the reference point you choose. You can choose any point as a reference point. Both the racing game and the shuffleboard game can be reference points.

In addition to using a reference point to describe motion, you also need a direction. For example, the puck is moving away from the girl in **Figure 1.** Other descriptions of direction might include east or west, or up or down.

Reading Check Describe your motion as you walk from your desk to the door. Use a reference point and a direction.

Figure 1 A description of the motion of the puck depends on the reference point you choose.

Visual Check Name three different reference points you could choose in order to describe the motion of the puck.

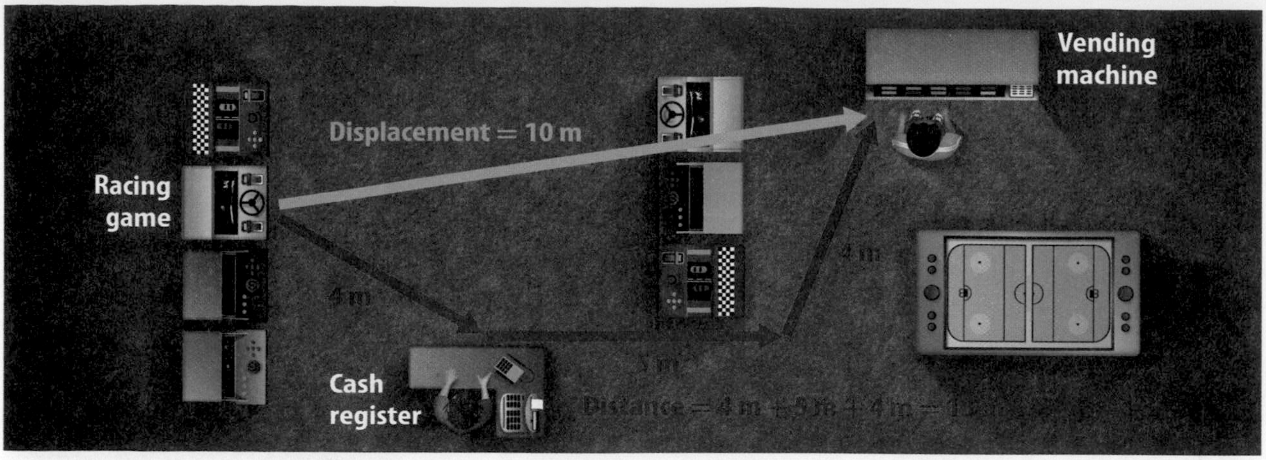

▲ **Figure 2** The distance traveled and the displacement from the game to the vending machine differ.

Distance and Displacement

Suppose you finish playing the racing game, and you go to the cash register to get more tokens. Then, you go to the vending machine for a snack. Your path is shown by the red arrows in **Figure 2.** How far did you travel? **Distance** *is the total length of your path.* The total distance you traveled is 4 m + 5 m + 4 m = 13 m.

Your **displacement** *is the distance between your initial, or starting, position and your final position.* Displacement is represented with a straight arrow extending from the starting point to the ending point. The displacement between the racing game where you started and the vending machine where you stopped is shown by the blue arrow in **Figure 2.** Your displacement is 10 m. To give a complete description of your motion, you must include a reference point, your displacement, and your direction from the reference point.

Key Concept Check What information do you need to describe an object's motion?

Speed

Suppose you run out of tokens and leave the arcade. Walking slowly, it takes a long time to get to the end of the block. When you realize that you need to meet a friend at the library in 15 minutes, you start to run. When running, you travel the distance of the next block in a shorter time. How does your motion differ in the two blocks? Since you traveled the second block in less time than the first, your speed was different. **Speed** *is the distance an object moves divided by the time it took to move that distance.*

Constant and Changing Speed

Speed can be constant or changing. Look at **Figure 3.** The stopwatches above the girl show her motion every second for 6 seconds. In the first 4 seconds, the girl moves with constant, or unchanging, speed because she travels the same distance during each second. When the girl starts running, the distance she travels each second gets larger and larger. The girl's speed changes.

▼ **Figure 3** The girl's speed begins to change between seconds 4 and 5.

Average Speed

Suppose you want to figure out how fast you ran from the arcade to the library. As you ran, your speed probably changed from second to second. Therefore, in order to describe the speed you traveled, you describe the average speed of the entire trip. Average speed is the ratio of the distance an object moves to the time it takes for the object to move that distance. If it takes you 15 minutes, or 0.25 h, to run the 1 km to the library, your average speed was 1 km/0.25 h, or 4 km/h.

FOLDABLES®

Make a horizontal three-tab concept map book. Label it as shown. Use it to organize your notes on motion as you read the lesson.

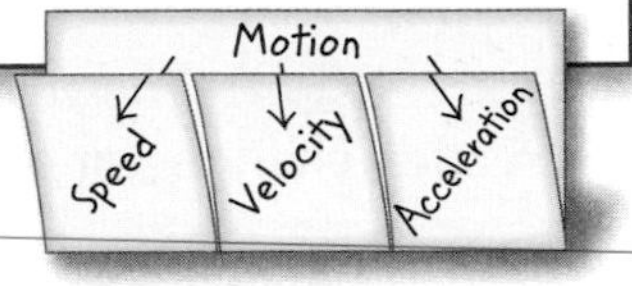

Velocity

If you tell your friend that you traveled about 4 km/h, you are describing your speed. You could give your friend a better description of your motion if you also told him or her the direction in which you are moving. **Velocity** *is the speed and direction of an object's motion.*

Often, velocity is shown by using an arrow, as shown in **Figure 4.** The length of the arrow represents the speed of an object, while the direction in which the arrow points represents the direction in which the object is moving.

WORD ORIGIN

velocity
from Latin *velocitatem,* means "swiftness or speed"

Constant Velocity

Velocity is constant, or does not change, when an object's speed and direction of movement do not change. If you use an arrow to describe velocity, you can divide the arrow into segments to show whether velocity is constant. Look at the skateboarding arrow in **Figure 4.** Each segment of the arrow shows the distance and the direction you move in a given unit of time. Because each segment is the same length, you are moving the same distance and in the same direction during each interval of time. Because both your speed and direction of movement are constant, you are moving at a constant velocity.

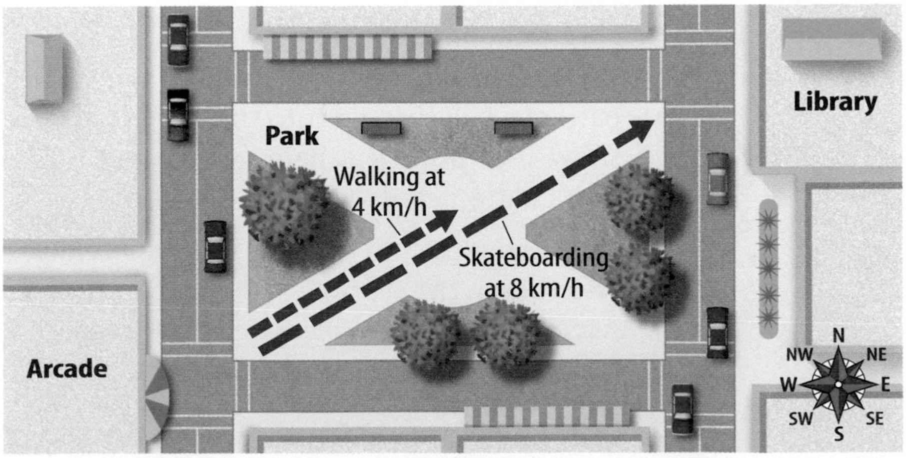

Figure 4 Your skateboarding velocity is greater than your walking velocity. Both velocities are constant because they represent a constant speed in a constant direction.

Figure 5 The velocity of an object changes if the speed changes, the direction changes, or both the speed and the direction change.

Inquiry MiniLab

15 minutes

How can velocity change?

The velocity of an object can change in two ways. Can you recognize the ways velocity changes?

1. Read and complete a lab safety form.
2. Toss a **one-hole stopper** to your partner. Observe and record the motion of the stopper.
3. Hold the stopper above a table. Release it. Record your observations in your Science Journal.
4. Tie one end of a **50-cm string** to the stopper. Gently swing the stopper at a constant speed in a horizontal circle near the floor.

Analyze and Conclude

1. **Analyze** the speed and the direction of the stopper each time you moved it. Which of these changed and which stayed the same each time?
2. **Key Concept** How were changes in the motion of the stopper related to changes in velocity?

Changing Velocity

Velocity can change even if the speed of an object remains constant. Recall that velocity includes both an object's speed and its direction of travel. **Figure 5** shows several examples of changing velocity.

In the first panel, the ball drops toward the ground in a straight line, or constant direction. The increased length of each arrow shows that the speed of the ball increases as it falls. As speed changes, velocity changes.

In the second panel, each arrow is the same length. This tells you that the Ferris-wheel cars travel around a circle at a constant speed. However, each arrow points in a different direction. This tells you that the cars are changing direction. As direction changes, velocity changes.

The third panel of **Figure 5** shows the path of a ball thrown into the air. The arrows show that both the ball's speed and direction change, so its velocity changes.

When either an object's speed or velocity changes, the object is accelerating. **Acceleration** *is the measure of the change in velocity during a period of time.*

Key Concept Check Can an object traveling at a constant speed have a changing velocity? Why or why not?

Calculating Acceleration

When a ball is dropped, as in the first panel of **Figure 5,** its speed increases as it falls toward the ground. The velocity of the ball is changing. Therefore, the ball is accelerating. You can calculate acceleration using the following equation:

$$a = \frac{v_f - v_i}{t}$$

The symbol for acceleration is *a*. In this lesson, *v* represents only the speed of an object. You do not need to consider the object's direction. The symbol v_f represents the final speed, and the symbol v_i represents the initial, or starting, speed. The symbol *t* stands for the time it takes to make that change in speed.

Key Concept Check How does acceleration differ from velocity?

Positive Acceleration

When an object, such as a falling ball, speeds up, its final speed is greater than its initial speed. If you calculate the ball's acceleration, the numerator (final speed minus initial speed) is positive, so the acceleration is positive. In other words, when an object speeds up, it has positive acceleration.

Negative Acceleration

If a ball is thrown straight up into the air, it slows down as it travels upward. The initial speed of the ball is greater than its final speed. The numerator in the equation is negative, so the acceleration is negative. In other words, as an object slows down, it has negative acceleration. Some people refer to this as deceleration.

Math Skills — Solve a One-Step Equation

Solve for Acceleration A skateboarder moving at 2 m/s starts skating down a ramp. As the skateboarder heads down the ramp, she accelerates to a speed of 6 m/s in 4 seconds. What is the skateboarder's acceleration?

1. **This is what you know:**
   final speed: $v_f = 6$ m/s
   initial speed: $v_i = 2$ m/s
   time: $t = 4$ s

2. **This is what you need to find out:** acceleration: *a*

3. **Use this formula:** $a = \frac{v_f - v_i}{t}$

4. **Substitute:**
   the values for v_f, v_i, and t: $\frac{6 \text{ m/s} - 2 \text{ m/s}}{4 \text{ s}}$
   subtract: $\frac{4 \text{ m/s}}{4 \text{ s}}$
   and divide: $= 1 \text{ m/s}^2$

Answer: The acceleration is 1 m/s^2.

Practice

As the skateboarder starts moving up the other side of the ramp, her velocity changes from 6 m/s to 0 m/s in 3 seconds. What was her acceleration?

Review
- **Math Practice**
- **Personal Tutor**

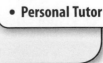

▲ **Figure 6** Tracking devices help scientists record the movement of animals, such as polar bears.

Using Graphs to Represent Motion

How can you track the motion of an animal that can move hundreds of miles without being seen by humans? In order to understand the movements of animals, such as the polar bear in **Figure 6,** biologists put tracking devices on them. These devices constantly send information about the position of the animal to **satellites.** Biologists download the data from the satellites and create graphs of motion such as those shown in **Figures 7** and **8.**

Displacement-Time Graphs

Figure 7 is a displacement-time graph of a polar bear's motion. The *x*-axis shows the time, and the *y*-axis shows the displacement of the polar bear from a reference point.

The line on a displacement-time graph represents the average speed the bear at that particular moment in time. It does not show the actual path of motion. As the average speed of the bear changes, the slope of the line on the graph changes. Because of this, you can use a displacement-time graph to describe the motion of an object.

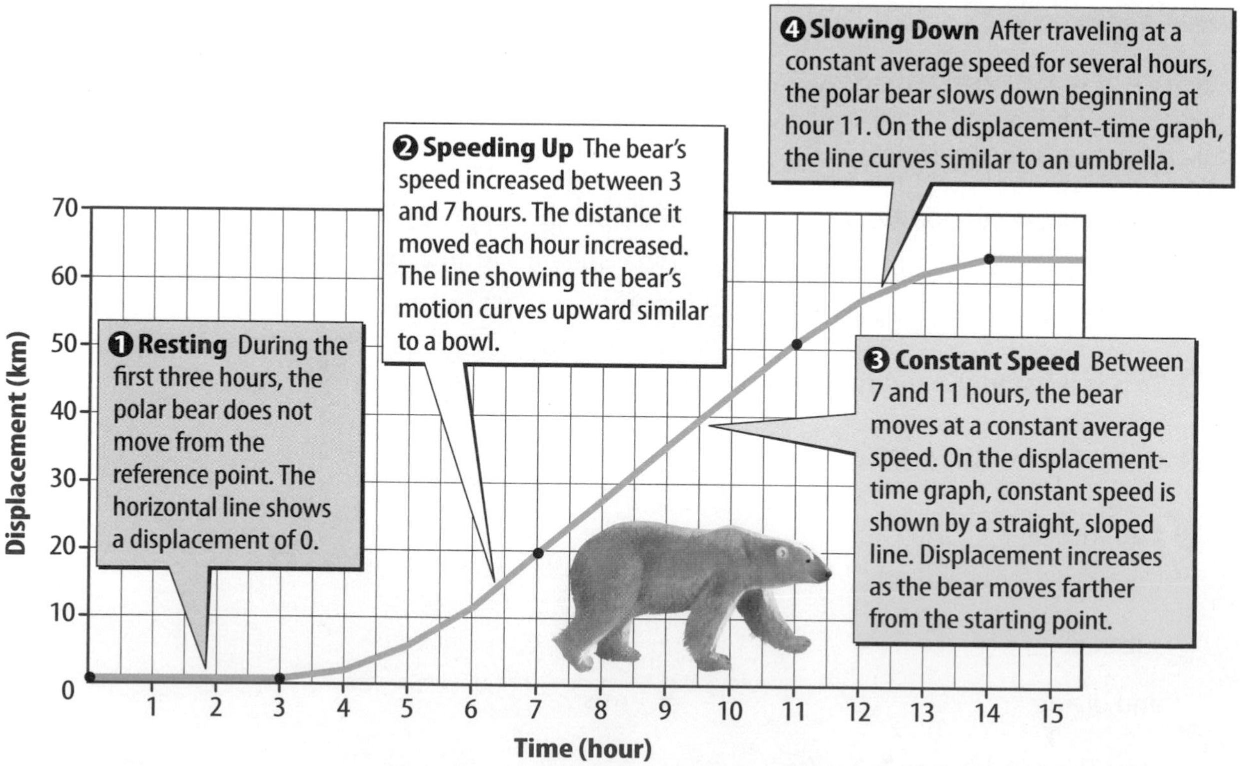

❹ Slowing Down After traveling at a constant average speed for several hours, the polar bear slows down beginning at hour 11. On the displacement-time graph, the line curves similar to an umbrella.
❷ Speeding Up The bear's speed increased between 3 and 7 hours. The distance it moved each hour increased. The line showing the bear's motion curves upward similar to a bowl.
❶ Resting During the first three hours, the polar bear does not move from the reference point. The horizontal line shows a displacement of 0.
❸ Constant Speed Between 7 and 11 hours, the bear moves at a constant average speed. On the displacement-time graph, constant speed is shown by a straight, sloped line. Displacement increases as the bear moves farther from the starting point.
Displacement (km)
0
10
20
30
40
50
60
70
1 2 3 4 5 6 7 8 9 10 11 12 13 14 15
Time (hour)

▲ **Figure 7** The displacement-time graph shows the bear's speed and distance from the reference point at any point in time.

Visual Check What was the average speed of the bear between hours 7 and 11?

Review **Personal Tutor**

Figure 8 The speed-time graph shows the speed of the bear at any given time during its journey. A horizontal line on a speed-time graph shows an object with a constant speed.

Visual Check What happened to the bear's speed between hours 5 and 6?

Concepts in Motion **Animation**

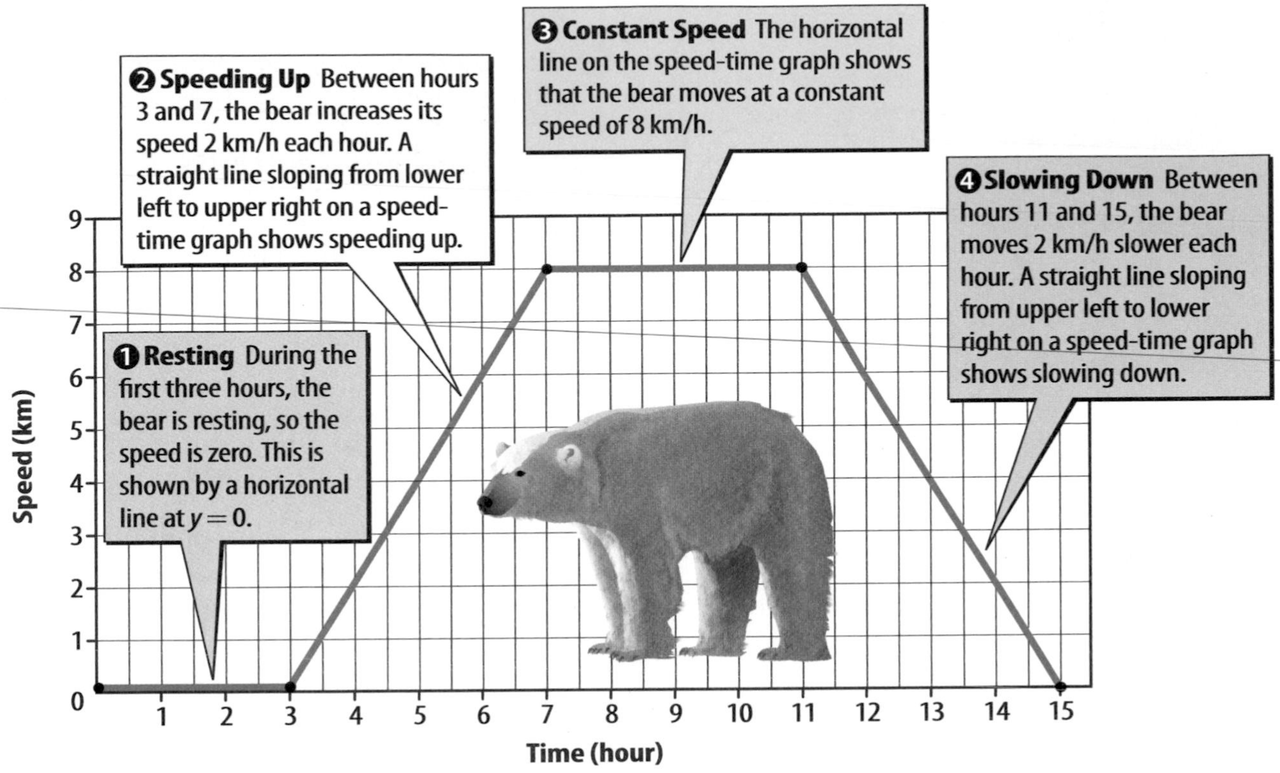

1 Resting During the first three hours, the bear is resting, so the speed is zero. This is shown by a horizontal line at $y = 0$.
2 Speeding Up Between hours 3 and 7, the bear increases its speed 2 km/h each hour. A straight line sloping from lower left to upper right on a speed-time graph shows speeding up.
3 Constant Speed The horizontal line on the speed-time graph shows that the bear moves at a constant speed of 8 km/h.
4 Slowing Down Between hours 11 and 15, the bear moves 2 km/h slower each hour. A straight line sloping from upper left to lower right on a speed-time graph shows slowing down.
Speed (km)
0
1
2
3
4
5
6
7
8
9
1
2
3
4
5
6
7
8
9
10
11
12
13
14
15
Time (hour)

Speed-Time Graphs

Figure 8 is a speed-time graph of the polar bear's motion. The x-axis shows the time, and the y-axis shows the speed of the bear. Notice that, in this case, the line shows how the speed, rather than the displacement, changes as the bear moves. A horizontal line at $y = 0$ means the bear is at rest because its speed is 0 km/hr. Notice that a horizontal line at $y = 0$ on either a displacement-time graph or a speed-time graph represents the bear at rest.

Keep in mind that *constant speed* is describing average speed. The bear might have sped up or slowed down slightly each second. But, during hours 7–11, you could describe that the bear's average speed remained constant since it covered the same distance each hour.

Interpreting the lines on graphs can provide you with a lot of information about the motion of an object.

Key Concept Check How can a graph help you understand an object's motion?

ACADEMIC VOCABULARY

satellite
(noun) an object in orbit around another object

Lesson 1 Review

Assessment — Online Quiz
Inquiry — Virtual Lab

Visual Summary

A description of an object's motion includes a reference point, a direction from the reference point, and a distance.

Speed is the distance traveled by an object in a unit of time. Velocity includes both speed and direction of motion.

Acceleration is a change in velocity. Velocity changes when either the speed, the direction, or both the speed and the direction change.

FOLDABLES®

Use your lesson Foldable to review the lesson. Save your Foldable for the project at the end of the chapter.

What do you think NOW?

You first read the statements below at the beginning of the chapter.

1. You must use a reference point to describe an object's motion.
2. An object that is accelerating must be speeding up.

Did you change your mind about whether you agree or disagree with the statements? Rewrite any false statements to make them true.

Use Vocabulary

1. **Describe** in your own words how you would choose a reference point.
2. **Distinguish** between the terms *distance* and *displacement.*

Understand Key Concepts

3. **Describe** the motion of a book as you lift it from the table and place it on a shelf.
4. Which of the following does NOT cause an object to accelerate?
   - **A.** change in direction
   - **B.** constant velocity
   - **C.** slowing down
   - **D.** speeding up
5. **Apply** Draw a speed-time graph of a parade float that accelerates from rest to 0.5 km/hr in 1 min and then moves at a constant speed for 10 min.

Interpret Graphics

6. **Draw** The table below includes information about the motion of an elevator. Draw a displacement-time graph using the data, and explain the elevator's motion.

Displacement	Time
0 m	0 s
1 m	1 s
4 m	2 s
10 m	3 s
10 m	4 s

Critical Thinking

7. **Analyze** whether you could have a vertical line on a displacement-time graph. Why or why not?

Math Skills

Review — Math Practice

8. What is the acceleration of a track star who goes from a speed of 0 m/s to a speed of 9 m/s in 3 s?

It's Moving!

HOW IT WORKS

Fooling the Eye

You know that you describe an object's motion by explaining how its position changes. Did you know that you can use this concept to make a movie that shows nonmoving objects in motion! It's called stop-motion photography. How does it work?

1. First, set an object in a scene and take a picture of it. Keep changing the position of the object in the scene, taking a picture after each change.
2. Now use software to link all the pictures into a video. When you view the video, it will appear as if the object moved on its own. Of course, it's just an illusion. The illusion works because of the way your eye works. Motion is a change of position, and that's exactly what your eyes are seeing with stop-motion photography.

It's Your Turn

EXPERIMENT Set up your own stop-motion photography studio. If you don't have a camera, make sketches of each change. When you are finished, make a flip book of your sketches or photographs.

Lesson 2

Forces

Reading Guide

Key Concepts
ESSENTIAL QUESTIONS

- How do different types of forces affect objects?
- What factors affect the way gravity acts on objects?
- How do balanced and unbalanced forces differ?

Vocabulary
force p. 57
contact force p. 58
noncontact force p. 58
friction p. 59
gravity p. 59
balanced forces p. 61
unbalanced forces p. 61

Multilingual eGlossary

Video

What's Science Got to do With It?

Academic Standards for Science

Covers: 7.1.5, 7.1.6, 7.1.7, 7.NS.3, 7.NS.4, 7.NS.5, 7.NS.7, 7.NS.8, 7.NS.11, 7.DP.2, 7.DP.4, 7.DP.5, 7.DP.9, 7.DP.11

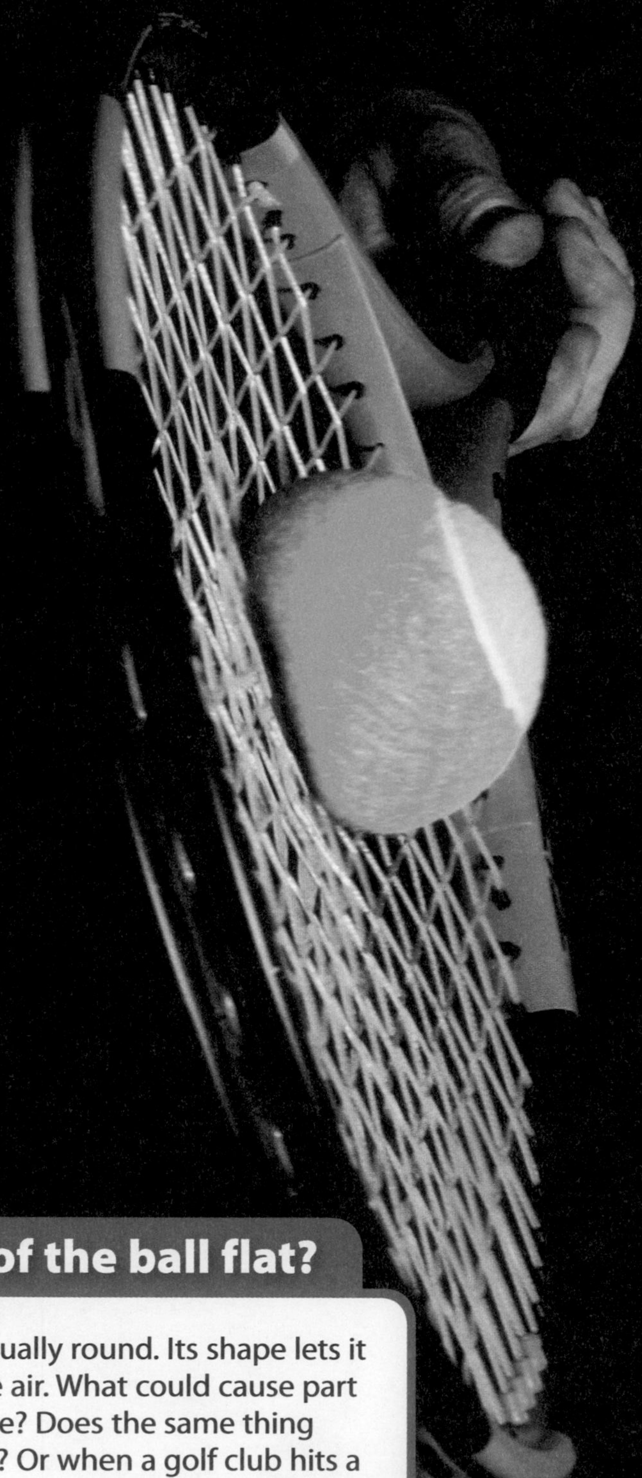

Inquiry Why is one side of the ball flat?

A ball, such as this tennis ball, is usually round. Its shape lets it roll farther and travel farther in the air. What could cause part of a ball to become flat like this one? Does the same thing happen when a baseball hits a bat? Or when a golf club hits a golf ball?

Inquiry Launch Lab

10 minutes

How can you change an object's shape and motion?

You probably can think of many ways that things change. For example, paper can change from a flat sheet to a crumpled ball. A sailboat changes its location as it moves across a lake. How can you change an object's shape and motion?

1. Read and complete a lab safety form.
2. Observe and record in your Science Journal how you make the following changes. Change the shape of a handful of **clay** several times.
3. Mold the clay into a log. Cause the log to roll, and then cause it to stop rolling.
4. Cause the log to roll so that its speed changes. Then change the log's direction of motion. Observe and record in your Science Journal how you make these changes.

Think About This

1. **Describe** what you did to change the shape of the clay.
2. **Explain** how you changed the motion of the clay.
3. **Key Concept** How was your interaction with the clay similar when you changed its shape and when you changed its motion?

What are forces?

What do typing on a computer, lifting a bike, and putting on a sweater have in common? They all involve an interaction between you and another object. You push on the keys. You push or pull on the bike. You pull on the sweater. *A push or pull on an object is a* **force.**

A force has both size and direction. In **Figure 9,** the length of the arrow represents the size of the force. The direction in which the arrow points represents the direction of the force. The unit of force is the newton (N). It takes about 4 N of force to lift a can of soda.

There are two ways a force can affect an object. A force can change an object's speed. It also can change the direction in which the object is moving. In other words, a force can cause acceleration. Recall that acceleration is a change in an object's velocity—its speed and/or its direction in a given time. When you apply a force to a tennis ball, such as the one shown in the picture on the previous page, the force first stops the motion of the ball. The force then causes the ball to accelerate in the opposite direction, changing both its speed and direction.

Reading Check In what ways can forces affect objects?

Figure 9 The arrows show forces with very different sizes acting in opposite directions.

FOLDABLES®

Make a horizontal two-tab book. Label it as shown. Use it to organize your notes on forces.

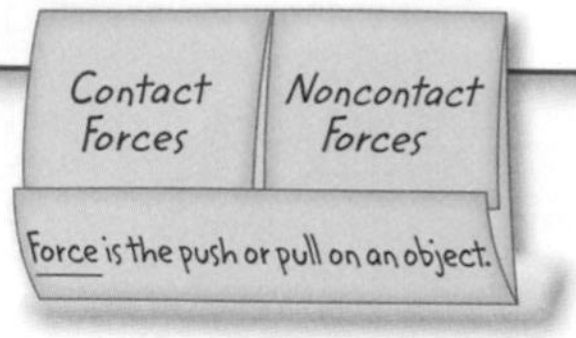

Types of Forces

Some forces are easy to recognize. You can see a hammer applies a force as it hits a nail. Other forces seem to act on objects without touching them. For example, what force causes your ice cream to fall toward the ground if it slips out of the cone?

Contact Forces

The top left image of **Figure 10** shows a baker pushing his hand into dough, causing the top of the dough to accelerate downward. You can see the baker's hand and the dough come into contact with each other. *A* **contact force** *is a push or a pull applied by one object to another object that is touching it.* Contact forces also are called mechanical forces. The top half of **Figure 10** also shows other types of contact forces.

Noncontact Forces

The bottom left image of **Figure 10** shows a girl's hair being pulled toward the slide even though it isn't touching the slide. *A force that pushes or pulls an object without touching it is a* **noncontact force.** The force that pulls the girl's hair is an electric force. The bottom half of **Figure 10** shows other noncontact forces, such as magnetism and gravity.

Key Concept Check What is the difference between the way contact and noncontact forces affect objects?

Figure 10 The pictures in the top row show examples of various types of contact forces. The ones in the bottom row show examples of several types of noncontact forces.

A **contact**, or mechanical, force is a force exerted by a physical object that touches another object.

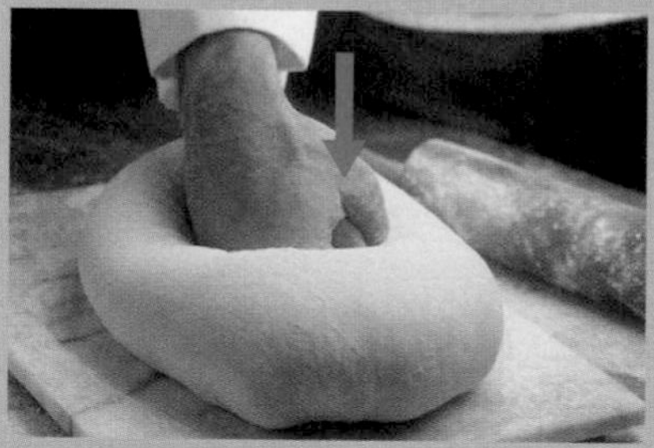

An **applied force** is a force in which one object directly pushes or pulls on another object.

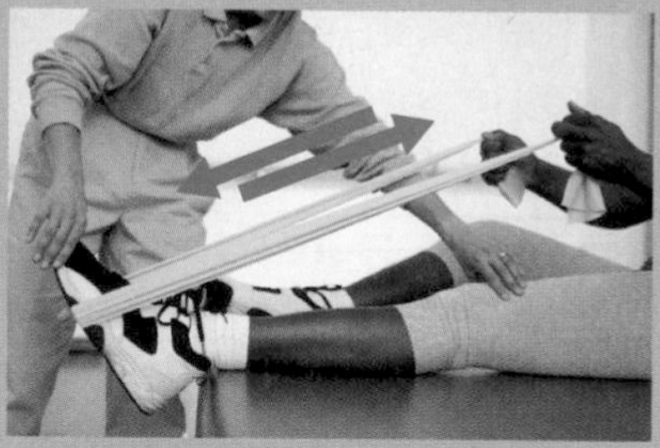

An **elastic** or spring force is the force exerted by a compressed or stretched object.

A **normal force** is the support force exerted on an object that touches another stable object.

A **noncontact**, or field, force is a force exerted when there is no visible object exerting the force.

Electric forces cause the girl's hair to stick out.

Magnetic forces hold these magnets apart.

Gravity is the force that pulls these divers toward the water.

Inquiry **MiniLab** 20 minutes

How does friction affect an object's motion?

Air resistance is a force that opposes the motion of an object moving through air.

1. Read and complete a lab safety form.
2. Make a model parachute from **tissue paper, string, tape,** and a **metal washer.**
3. Use a **meterstick** to measure heights of 1, 2, 3, and 4 m on a nearby wall. Mark them with **tape.**
4. Drop the parachute from the 4-m mark. Your partner should start a **stopwatch** as soon as you drop the parachute and should stop the stopwatch when the washer passes the 3-m mark. Repeat this step three more times stopping the stopwatch at the 2-m mark, the 1-m mark, and the ground. Record the times in your Science Journal.
5. Remove the washer from the parachute. Measure and record the time for the washer to fall from the 4-m mark to the floor without the parachute.

Think About This

1. **Graph** the motion of the parachute on a distance-time graph.
2. **Calculate** the average speed of the washer with and without the parachute.
3. **Key Concept** How did friction affect the speed of the parachute and the washer?

Friction

Why does the baseball player in **Figure 11** slow down as he slides toward the base? **Friction** *is a contact force that resists the sliding motion between two objects that are touching.* The force of friction acts in the opposite direction of the motion, as shown by the blue arrow. Rougher surfaces produce greater friction than smooth surfaces. Other factors, such as the weight of an object, also affect the force of friction.

Figure 11 The player must overcome friction or he won't reach the base.

Gravity

Is there anywhere on Earth where you could drop a pencil and not have it fall? No! **Gravity** *is a noncontact attractive force that exists between all objects that have mass.*

Mass is the amount of matter in an object. Both your pencil and Earth have mass. They exert a gravitational pull on each other. In fact, they exert the same gravitational force on each other. Why doesn't your pencil pull Earth toward it? It actually does! The pencil has very little mass, so the force of gravity causes it to rapidly accelerate downward toward Earth's surface. Earth "falls" upward toward the pencil at the same time, but because of its mass, Earth's motion is too small to see.

WORD ORIGIN
gravity
from Latin *gravitare,* means to unite, join together

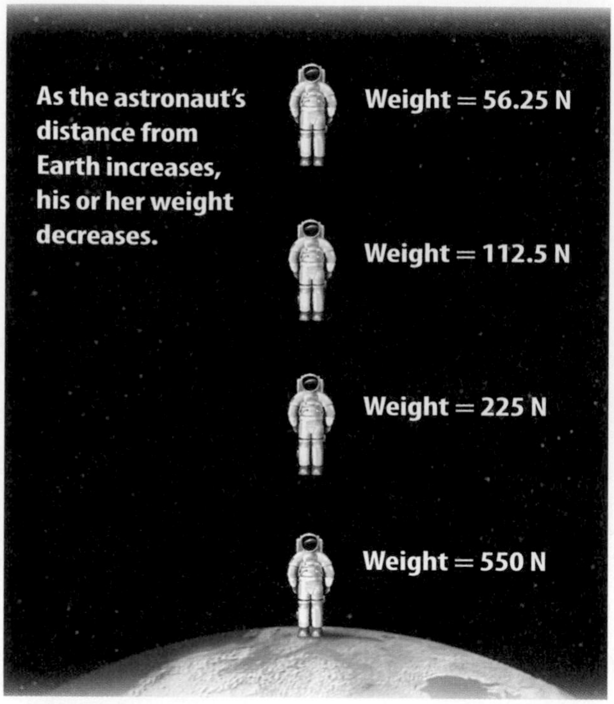

▲ **Figure 12** Gravitational force (weight) decreases as the distance between the centers of the objects increases.

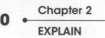

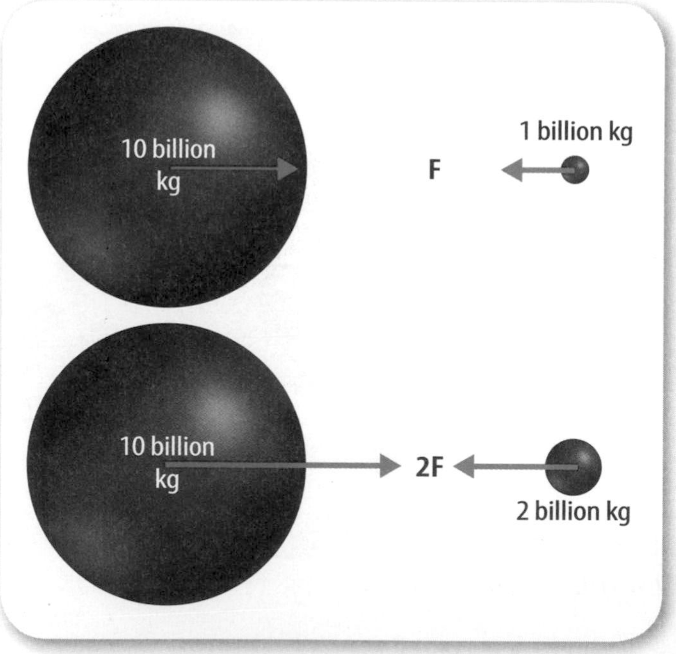

▲ **Figure 13** The force of attraction between the bottom two objects is twice as much as between the top two objects.

Visual Check Describe the acceleration of the bottom spheres due to the gravitational force between them.

Review Personal Tutor

Distance and Gravity

You may have heard that astronauts become weightless in space. This is not true. Astronauts do have some weight in space, but it is much less in space than their weight on Earth. Weight is a measure of the force of gravity acting on an object. As two objects get farther apart, the gravitational force between the objects decreases. **Figure 12** shows how the weight of an astronaut changes as he or she moves farther from Earth.

You know that all objects exert a force of gravity on all other objects. If the astronaut drops a hammer on the Moon, will it fall toward Earth? No, the attraction between the Moon and the hammer is stronger than the attraction between Earth and the hammer because the hammer is very close to the Moon and very far from Earth. The hammer will fall down toward the Moon.

Mass and Gravity

Another factor that affects the force of gravity between two objects is the mass of the objects. As the mass of one or both objects increases, the gravitational force between them increases. For example, in **Figure 13,** *F* stands for the gravitational force. As the figure shows, doubling the mass of one of the objects doubles the force of attraction.

The effect of mass on the force of gravity is most noticeable when one object is very massive, such as a planet, and the other object has much less mass, such as a person. Even though the force of gravity acts equally on both objects, the less massive object accelerates more quickly due to its smaller mass. Because the planet accelerates so slowly, all you observe is the object with less mass "falling" toward the object with greater mass.

Key Concept Check What factors affect the way gravity acts on objects?

Combining Forces

Have you ever played tug-of-war? If you alone pull against a team, you will probably be pulled over the line. However, if you are on a team, your team might pull the rope hard enough to cause the other team to move in your direction. When several forces act on an object, the forces combine to act as a single force. The sum of the forces acting on an object is called the net force.

Forces in the Same Direction

When different forces act on an object in the same direction, you can find the net force by adding the forces together. In **Figure 14,** each team member pulls in the same direction. The net force on the rope is 110 N + 90 N + 100 N = 300 N.

Forces in Opposite Directions

When forces act in opposite directions, you must include the direction of the force when you add them. Like numbers on a number line, forces in the direction to the right are normally considered to be positive values. Forces to the left are negative values. In the first panel of **Figure 15,** the team on the right pulls with a force of 300 N. The team on the left pulls with a force of –300 N. The net force is 300 N + (–300 N) = 0.

Balanced and Unbalanced Forces

The net force on the rope in the top of **Figure 15** is 0. *When the net force on an object is 0 N, the forces acting on it are* **balanced forces.** If the forces acting on an object are balanced, the object's motion does not change. *When the net force acting on an object is not 0, the forces acting on the object are* **unbalanced forces.** The forces acting on the rope in the bottom of **Figure 15** are unbalanced. Unbalanced forces cause objects to change their motion, or accelerate.

Key Concept Check How do balanced and unbalanced forces differ?

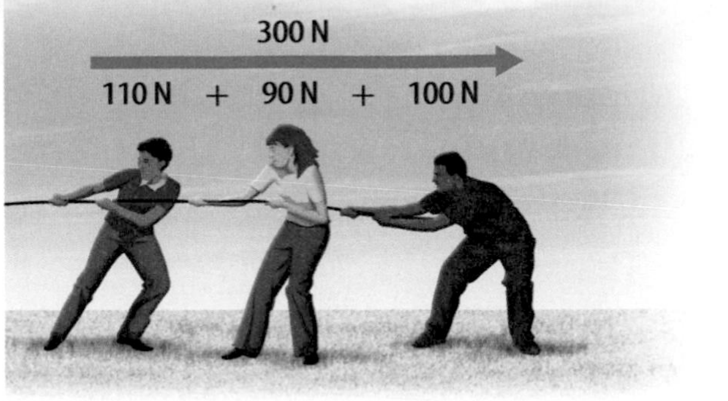

▲ **Figure 14** Forces in the same direction act as a single force.

Visual Check What would the total force be if the person on the right stopped pulling?

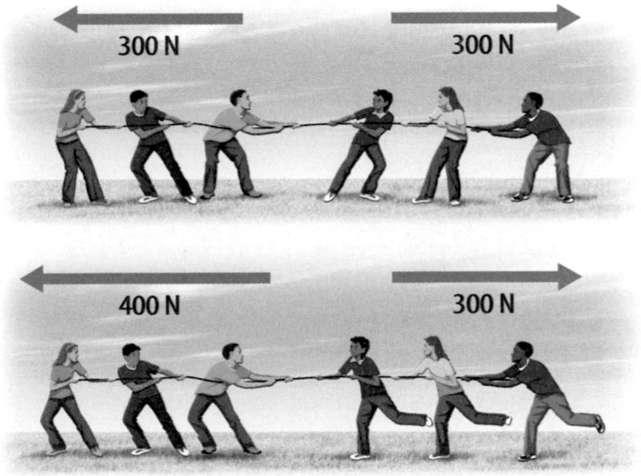

▲ **Figure 15** No change in motion takes place when forces on an object are balanced. Unbalanced forces cause the team on the right to accelerate to the left.

Review Personal Tutor

Lesson 2 Review

Assessment Online Quiz

Visual Summary

Forces are pushes and pulls exerted by objects on each other. Contact forces occur when objects are touching. Noncontact forces act from a distance.

Gravity is a force of attraction between two objects. The amount of gravitational force depends on the mass of the objects and the distance between them.

Balanced forces do not affect motion. Unbalanced forces change motion.

FOLDABLES®

Use your lesson Foldable to review the lesson. Save your Foldable for the project at the end of the chapter.

What do you think NOW?

You first read the statements below at the beginning of the chapter.

3. Objects must be in contact with one another to exert a force.

4. Gravity is a force that depends on the masses of two objects and the distance between them.

Did you change your mind about whether you agree or disagree with the statements? Rewrite any false statements to make them true.

Use Vocabulary

1. **Describe** friction in your own words.
2. Two examples of ________ are gravity and magnetism.

Understand Key Concepts

3. As the distance between two objects increases, the gravitational force between the objects
   - **A.** increases.
   - **B.** decreases.
   - **C.** creates friction.
   - **D.** stays the same.
4. **Describe** the forces acting on a cyclist who is slowing down as he or she climbs a hill.
5. **Identify** any balanced and unbalanced forces acting on a book resting on a table.

Interpret Graphics

6. **Copy and complete** the graphic organizer to explain how distance and mass affect the force of gravity.

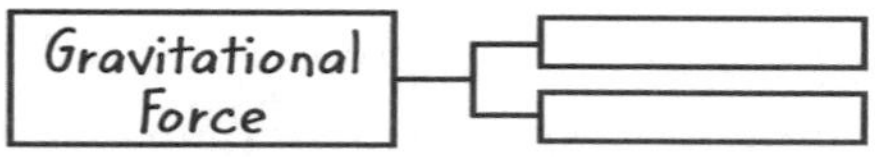

7. **Analyze** the four forces acting on the airplane flying at an altitude of 3,000 m, as shown below. How do the forces affect the plane's motion?

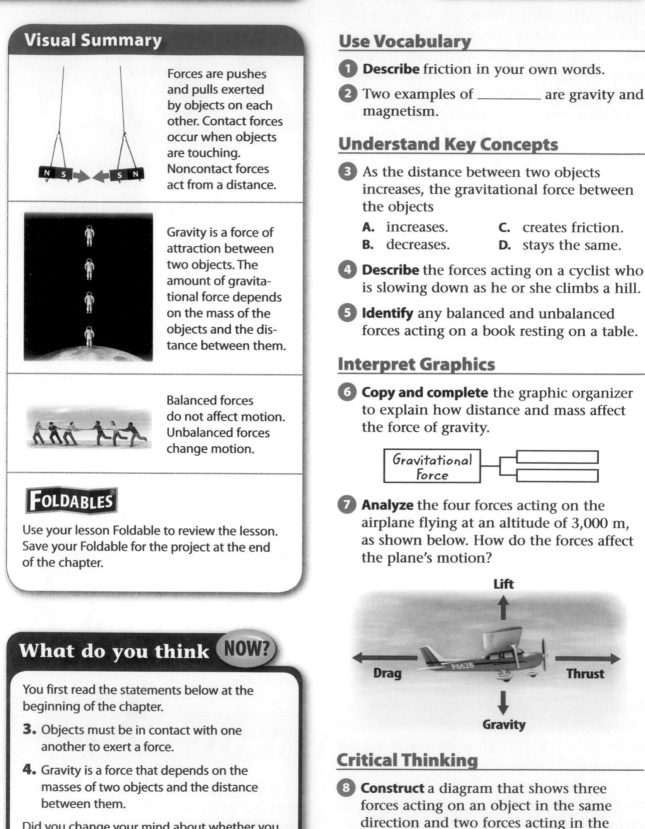

Critical Thinking

8. **Construct** a diagram that shows three forces acting on an object in the same direction and two forces acting in the opposite direction. Give the forces values that would cause no change in motion.

Inquiry **Skill Practice** **Identify and Manipulate Variables** **40 minutes**

What factors affect friction?

When you push or pull an object across a surface, the force of friction resists the object's motion. If the friction is strong, you need a greater force to move the object. How does manipulating variables, such as mass and surface texture, affect friction?.

Materials

balance

masking tape

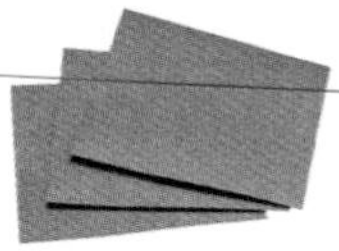
sandpaper (fine, medium, coarse)

5-N spring scale, 10-N spring scale

string

Also needed: wooden block, 250-g weight, thumbtack

Safety

Learn It

In any experiment, it is important to **identify and manipulate variables.** The independent variable is the factor that you change during the experiment. The variable that might change as a result of the independent variable is called the dependent variable. Changing only one variable at a time helps you focus clearly on what is causing the dependent variable to change.

Try It

1. Read and complete a lab safety form.
2. You will test the effect that mass, surface area, and surface texture have on the force needed to pull a block across a surface. Discuss the investigation with your partner. Predict whether each of the three variables will affect friction between a block and the surface.
3. Think about how you can test your prediction. Consider the following questions:
   - What tests will you perform? For each test, identify the independent variable and the dependent variable.
   - What materials will you use?
   - What type of data table will you construct to record your data?
4. Test several methods for moving your object that you think might work. Based on your results, write a plan for your teacher to approve.

Apply It

5. Work with your partner to carry out your experiment. Record your results in your Science Journal.
6. Describe the independent variable and the dependent variables you used for each test you performed.
7. **Key Concept** Did your tests support your prediction about the effects of mass, surface area, and surface texture on friction? Explain.

Lesson 3

Newton's Laws of Motion

Reading Guide

Key Concepts

ESSENTIAL QUESTIONS

- How do unbalanced forces affect an object's motion?
- How are the acceleration, the net force, and the mass of an object related?
- What happens to an object when another object exerts a force on it?

Vocabulary

inertia p. 65

Newton's first law of motion p. 65

Newton's second law of motion p. 68

Newton's third law of motion p. 69

force pair p. 69

Multilingual eGlossary

Video BrainPOP®

Academic Standards for Science

7.1.6 Explain that forces have magnitude and direction and those forces can be added to determine the net force acting on an object.

Also covers: 7.1.7, 7.NS.2, 7.NS.7, 7.NS.9, 7.NS.11, 7.DP.1, 7.DP.3, 7.DP.5, 7.DP.6, 7.DP.7, 7.DP.10, 7.DP.11

Inquiry How does this feel?

Rides like this are called thrill rides because the riders feel as if they are going to crash, fall, or take off into space. How do forces cause these sensations? Why are the bars that hold the riders in place so important?

Inquiry Launch Lab

15 minutes

How are forces and motion related?

In the last lesson, you read about different forces acting on objects. Sometimes forces can produce unexpected results. In this lab, you will observe the effect of forces on an object's motion.

1. Read and complete a lab safety form.
2. Place an **index card** on a **plastic jar.** Center a **nickel** on top of the card.
3. Flick the card away horizontally. Observe the motion of the nickel. Record your observations about the motion in your Science Journal.
4. Spread a sheet of **newspaper** on the table with about 10 cm hanging over the edge.
5. Place a **book,** a **pen,** and a **paper clip** on top of the paper. Then quickly pull the edge of the paper straight down. Record your observations in your Science Journal.

Think About This

1. **Identify** the forces acting on the objects in steps 3 and 5.
2. **Key Concept** How do you think forces are related to the motion of the objects?

Newton's Laws

Recall that forces are measured in a unit called a newton (N), named after English scientist Isaac Newton, who studied the motion of objects. Newton summarized his findings in three laws of motion. You demonstrate Newton's laws when you run to catch a baseball or ride your bike. How could you use Newton's laws to explain how the rides and the games at an amusement park work?

Newton's First Law

What causes the motion of amusement park rides to give riders a thrill? Without protective devices to hold you in your seat, you could fly off the ride! *The tendency of an object to resist a change in motion is called* **inertia.** Inertia acts to keep you at rest when the ride starts moving. It also keeps you moving in a straight line when the ride stops or changes direction. Your safety belt keeps you in the seat and moving with the ride.

Newton's first law of motion *states that if the net force acting on an object is zero, the motion of the object does not change.* In other words, an object remains at rest or in constant motion unless an outside, unbalanced force acts on it. Newton's first law of motion is sometimes called the law of inertia.

FOLDABLES®

Use two sheets of paper to make a layered book. Label it as shown. Use it to organize your notes on Newton's laws.

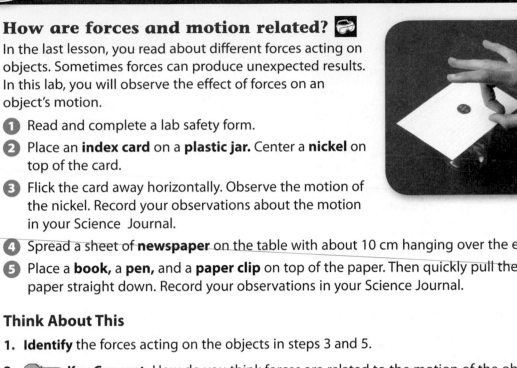

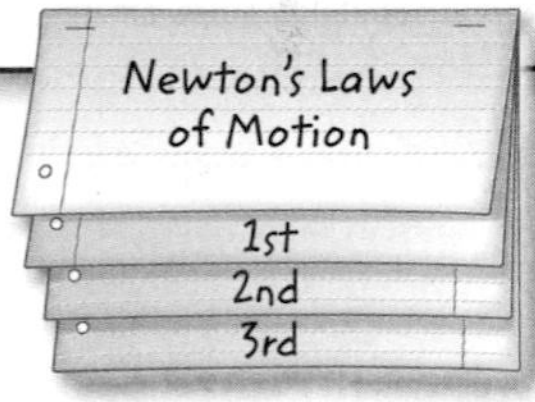

SCIENCE USE V. COMMON USE

inertia

Science Use the tendency to resist a change in motion

Common Use lack of action

Figure 16 The free-fall car's velocity is constant in both images because the forces are balanced.

Inquiry MiniLab

20 minutes

How does inertia affect an object?

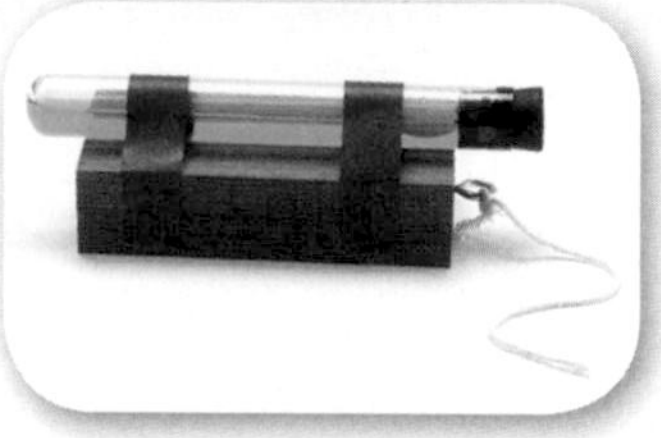

1. Read and complete a lab safety form.
2. Attach one end of a 20-cm long **string** to the **eye hook** that is attached to one end of a **wooden block.**
3. Half fill a **large test tube** with **colored water. Stopper** the tube tightly. Use **transparent tape** to attach the test tube to the block.
4. Use the string to pull the block. Observe the water when the block is at rest, as its velocity changes, and when its velocity is constant. Record your observations in your Science Journal.

Analyze and Conclude

1. **Describe** the motion of the water in the tube when the tube is at rest, accelerating, and moving at a constant velocity.
2. **Key Concept** How does Newton's first law explain your observations?

Effects of Balanced Forces

Suppose you are at an amusement park and you want to ride a free-fall car, such as the one shown in **Figure 16.** How does the ride illustrate Newton's first law of motion? Recall that when the forces acting on an object are balanced, the object is either at rest or moving with a constant velocity.

Objects at Rest At the top of the ride, the force of the cable pulling upward on the car is equal to the force of gravity pulling downward on the car. Gravity and the cables pull on the car equally, but in opposite directions, so the forces are balanced. The car is at rest, as shown in the first panel of **Figure 16.** As long as the forces remain balanced, the car remains at rest.

Objects in Motion To lift the car to the top of the ride, the cable pulls upward. After a short acceleration, the car moves upward at a constant speed. The force of the cable pulling upward is the same size as the force of gravity pulling downward. With the forces once again balanced, the car rises to the top of the ride at a constant velocity. This is shown in the second panel of **Figure 16.** Newton's first law describes the car's motion when the forces applied to it are balanced.

Balanced forces act on the car only when it is at rest or moving with a constant velocity. When the car reaches the top of the ride, it doesn't remain at rest for long. When the operator releases the upward pull on the cable, the forces become unbalanced. Gravity causes the car to accelerate toward the ground. Because inertia tends to keep you at rest, the car feels as if it falls out from under you. Your safety belt acts as an outside force to keep you attached to the car.

Reading Check What happens to the velocity of the car when the upward pull of the cable is greater than the downward pull of gravity as the car rises toward the top?

◀ Figure 17 🔑
Unbalanced forces cause the bungee jumper to speed up or slow down.

Key
→ Force
→ Acceleration

Speeding Up Slowing Down

Effects of Unbalanced Forces

You continue your visit to the amusement park with a ride on the reverse bungee jump. According to Newton's first law of motion, the motion of an object changes only when a net force acts on it. This ride gives you two chances to experience what a net force can do.

Speeding Up After the ride attendant releases you, the upward force of the bungee cord is greater than the downward force of gravity. The forces are unbalanced as shown by the blue arrows in the left image in **Figure 17.** The net force acting on you is upward, and you **accelerate** upward as shown by the green arrow.

Slowing Down As you approach the top of your bungee jump, the cords become slack, as shown on the right in **Figure 17.** The blue arrows show that the upward force becomes less than the downward force of gravity. Even though you are still are moving upward because of inertia, the net force is now due to the downward force of gravity. You slow down, or decelerate.

🔑✔ **Key Concept Check** If one force on an object is 5 N upward and the other is 10 N downward, what is the object's motion?

Changing Direction Your next stop is a swing ride such as the one shown in **Figure 18.** When the ride starts to turn, the force of the cables pulls your chair toward the center of the ride. The force of gravity acts downward. Because these forces don't act in opposite directions, the unbalanced force constantly changes your direction. You accelerate as you move in a circle.

The designers of amusement-park rides use inertia to create excitement. Much of what makes a swing ride fun is the feeling that you might fly off the ride with constant velocity if your safety belt didn't hold you in place.

WORD ORIGIN ··········
accelerate
from Latin *celer*, means "swift"

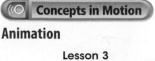

▲ Figure 18 🔑 The unbalanced force of the cable pulling toward the center causes acceleration in a circle.

Concepts in Motion
Animation

Figure 19 Using a large force to throw the ball gives you the best chance of knocking over the bottles.

Newton's Second Law of Motion

Suppose you play a carnival game in which you throw a ball to knock over wooden bottles, as shown in **Figure 19.** You throw the ball, but not all the bottles fall over. On your second throw, you use all your strength to throw the ball as fast as you can. The ball hits the bottles and they all fall over.

When you threw the ball the second time, the ball left your hand with a greater final velocity than when you threw it the first time. This means the acceleration of the second ball was greater than the acceleration of the first ball. Why is this? **Newton's second law of motion** *states that the acceleration of an object is equal to the net force applied to the object divided by the object's mass.* When you threw the ball the second time, you used your muscles and arm to push harder, or increase the force, on the ball. When you increased the force, the ball's acceleration increased. The increased acceleration resulted in a greater final velocity of the ball as it left your hand.

$$\textbf{acceleration} = \frac{\textbf{force}}{\textbf{mass}} \qquad a = \frac{F}{m}$$

Calculating Acceleration

You can use the equation to calculate the acceleration of the ball. If you apply a force of **1.5 N** to a ball with a mass of **0.3 kg**, what is the ball's acceleration?

$$\textbf{acceleration} = \frac{\textbf{force}}{\textbf{mass}} \qquad \textbf{acceleration} = \frac{\textbf{1.5 N}}{\textbf{0.3 kg}} = \frac{5 \text{ m}}{\text{s}^2}$$

What do you think would happen to the acceleration if you double the force on the ball? The equation tells you!

$$\textbf{acceleration} = \frac{\textbf{force}}{\textbf{mass}} \qquad \textbf{acceleration} = \frac{\textbf{3.0 N}}{\textbf{0.3 kg}} = \frac{10 \text{ m}}{\text{s}^2}$$

When you double the force, the acceleration also doubles.

Changing the Mass

What would happen to the acceleration if the force you apply stays the same, but the mass of the ball changes? Instead of 0.3 kg, the ball has a mass of **0.6 kg**.

$$\textbf{acceleration} = \frac{\textbf{force}}{\textbf{mass}} \qquad \textbf{acceleration} = \frac{\textbf{1.5 N}}{\textbf{0.6 kg}} = \frac{2.5 \text{ m}}{\text{s}^2}$$

A ball with twice the mass has half the acceleration. Newton's second law lets you predict what combination of force and mass you need to get the acceleration you need.

Key Concept Check How are the acceleration, the net force, and the mass of an object related?

◀ **Figure 20** Each car exerts a force of the same size on the other car. The amount that each car accelerates depends on its mass.

Newton's Third Law

Suppose you are driving bumper cars with a friend, like in **Figure 20**. What happens when you crash into each other? **Newton's third law of motion** *says that when one object exerts a force on a second object, the second object exerts a force of the same size, but in the opposite direction, on the first object.* According to Newton's third law, the bumper cars apply forces to each other that are equal but are in opposite directions.

Action and Reaction Forces

When two objects apply forces on each other, one of the forces is called the action force, and the other is called the reaction force. For example, if the left car hits the right car in **Figure 20**, then the force exerted by the left car is the action force. The force exerted by the right car is the reaction force.

Key Concept Check What happens when one object exerts a force on a second object?

Force Pairs

As you walk, your shoes push against the ground. If the ground did not push back with equal force, gravity would pull you down into the ground! *When two objects exert forces on each other, the two forces are a* **force pair.** The opposite forces of the bumper cars hitting each other in **Figure 20** are a force pair. Force pairs are not the same as balanced forces. Balanced forces combine or cancel each other out because they act on the same object. Each force in a force pair acts on a different object.

In **Figure 21**, the girl exerts a force on the ball. The ball exerts an equal but opposite force on the girl. Why does the ball's motion change more than the girl's motion? Newton's laws work together. Newton's first law explains that a force is needed to change an object's motion. His third law describes the action-reaction forces. Newton's second law explains why the effect of the force is greater on the ball. The mass of the ball is much less than the mass of the girl. A force of the same size produces a greater acceleration in an object with less mass—the ball.

Figure 21 The opposite forces of the girl's head and the ball are a force pair. ▼

Visual Check If the force of the girl's head on the ball is 1.5 N upward, what is the force of the ball on the girl's head?

Newton's Laws in Action

Newton's laws do not apply to all motion in the universe. For example, they don't correctly predict the motion of very tiny objects, such as atoms or electrons. They do not work for objects that approach the speed of light.

However, because Newton's laws apply to the moving objects you observe each day, from amusement park rides to the movement of stars and planets, they are extremely useful. Using Newton's laws, humans have traveled to other planets and invented many useful tools and machines. You can often see the effects of all three laws at the same time. **Table 1** gives you some everyday examples of Newton's laws in action. Think about Newton's laws as you move through your day.

Table 1 Newton's laws explain the motions you experience every day.

Visual Check How do you know that the table is exerting a force on the bowl of fruit?

Table 1 Newton's Laws in Action

Example	Newton's First Law	Newton's Second Law	Newton's Third Law
Resting 	The upward and downward forces on the bowl are balanced. The motion of the bowl is not changing. It is at rest.	Because the bowl is at rest, its acceleration is $0\ m/s^2$. You can use Newton's second law to calculate the net force on the bowl: $F = m \times a$ $F = 2\ kg \times 0\ m/s^2$ $F = 0\ N$	The force of gravity pulls the bowl down so it exerts a force on the table. The table pushes up on the bowl with a force that is the same size, but in the opposite direction.
Walking 	The forces acting on the man and the woman are balanced. Their inertia keeps them moving at a constant speed in a straight line.	When an object moves at a constant velocity, there is no acceleration. A net force would have to act on the people before they would speed up or slow down.	The woman's feet push against the sand as she walks. The sand pushes on the woman's feet with equal force, moving her forward. The same is true of the man.
Skateboarding 	Inertia keeps the dog and the skateboard at rest until the dog produces a net force by pushing its paw on the road.	When net forces act on the dog and the road, or Earth, the dog will accelerate at a much greater rate because its mass is much less than that of Earth.	The dog's paw exerts a backward force on the road. The road exerts an equal but opposite force on the dog's paw, pushing it forward.

Lesson 3 Review

Assessment Online Quiz

Visual Summary

Newton's first law of motion states that the motion of an object remains constant unless acted on by an outside force. This also is called the law of inertia.

Newton's second law of motion relates an object's acceleration to its mass and the net force applied to the object.

Newton's third law of motion states that for every action force, there is an equal but opposite reaction force. The two forces are called a force pair.

FOLDABLES®

Use your lesson Foldable to review the lesson. Save your Foldable for the project at the end of the chapter.

What do you think NOW?

You first read the statements below at the beginning of the chapter.

5. All forces change the motion of objects.

6. The net force on an object is equal to the mass of the object times the acceleration of the object.

Did you change your mind about whether you agree or disagree with the statements? Rewrite any false statements to make them true.

Use Vocabulary

1. **Describe** an example of Newton's third law of motion.
2. **Distinguish** between Newton's first and second laws of motion.

Understand Key Concepts

3. In order to accelerate, an object must be acted on by
   - **A.** a force pair.
   - **B.** a large mass.
   - **C.** balanced forces.
   - **D.** unbalanced forces.
4. **Interpret** A bicyclist rides with a constant velocity of 8 m/s. What would you need to know to calculate the net force on the rider?

Interpret Graphics

5. **Analyze** The diagram below shows the forces acting on a box. Describe the motion of the box.

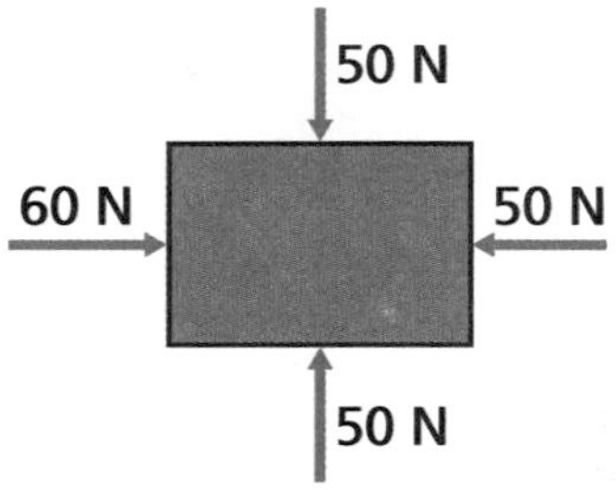

6. **Copy and complete** the graphic organizer by describing each of Newton's laws.

Critical Thinking

7. **Apply** Why does a box on the seat of a car slide around on the seat when the car speeds up, slows down, or turns a corner?
8. **Predict** what would happen if two people with equal mass standing on skateboards pushed against each other.
9. **Solve** A hockey player hits a 0.2-kg puck that accelerates at a rate of 20 m/s^2. What force did the player exert on the puck?

2–3 class periods

Design an Amusement Park Attraction Using Newton's Laws

Materials

wood board (1-m x 20-cm)

masking tape

string

tennis ball

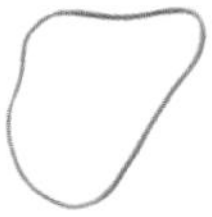

large rubber band

foam tubing

Also needed: marble

Safety

What is your favorite ride or game at an amusement park? You may think that amusement parks are just for fun, but Newton's laws are important in the design of every ride and game. Work with a group to design and build a ride or game that applies Newton's laws.

Ask a Question

How do Newton's laws describe an amusement-park ride or game?

Make Observations

1. Read and complete a lab safety form.
2. Discuss different rides and games with your group. Think about how Newton's laws explain each attraction.
3. Your model ride or game must be a working model. You will not use motors, but your ride must use several different forces to make it work. If you design a game, it must demonstrate one or more of Newton's laws. Test several ideas with your group. If one idea does not work, adjust the design or try a different idea.
4. Based on your tests, choose one model ride or game to build.
5. Decide on the materials you will use. You may use some from the list or others approved by your teacher.
6. Write a design, along with a sketch, for your ride or game. List the materials, and describe how the ride or game will work. Ask your teacher to approve your design.

Form a Hypothesis

7 Based on your observations, formulate a hypothesis that explains why your ride or game will work according to one or more of Newton's laws.

Test Your Hypothesis

8 Build your ride or game according to your approved design.

9 Use your ride or game to test your design. In your Science Journal, identify which of Newton's laws are demonstrated by each part of your model. Also record details about your tests and your results.

Analyze and Conclude

10 **Evaluate** Did your ride or game clearly model Newton's laws? Explain.

11 **Analyze** Which of Newton's laws of motion most describes the way your ride or game works? Why?

12 **Compare** your ride or game to those built by other groups. Which do you think is the best example of each of Newton's laws? Explain your opinion.

13 THE BIG IDEA **The Big Idea** Describe the relationship between the forces and the motion for the ride or the game you built.

Communicate Your Results

Demonstrate your ride or game for the class. Explain how one or more of Newton's laws influence the way the ride or game works.

Inquiry Extension

Work with others in your group to write a brochure titled *Newton's Amusement Park.* The brochure should include descriptions and illustrations of the various rides and games, along with a brief explanation of how Newton's laws affect each ride or game.

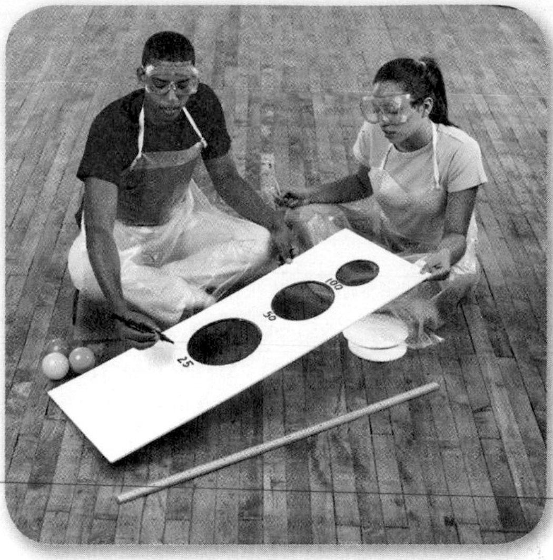

Lab Tips

☑ Test different parts of your design idea to be sure each part works before you settle on one design to build.

☑ Avoid making your ride or game too complicated. A simple ride or game might be better.

Remember to use scientific methods.

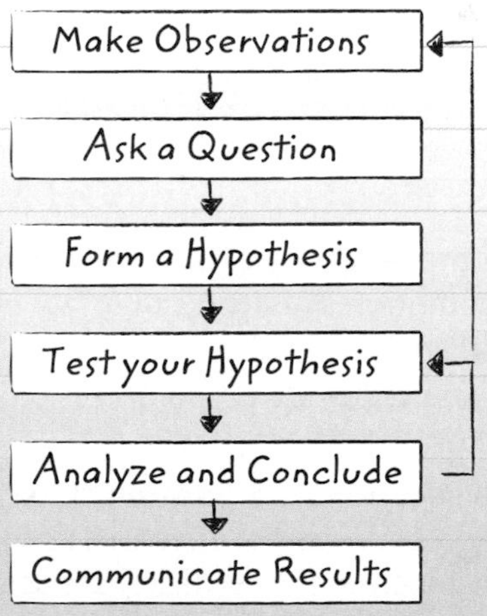

Chapter 2 Study Guide

WebQuest

THE BIG IDEA **Forces are pushes and pulls that may change the motion of an object. Balanced forces result in an object remaining at rest or moving at a constant speed. Unbalanced forces result in the acceleration of an object.**

Key Concepts Summary

Lesson 1: Describing Motion

- An object's **motion** depends on how it changes position. Motion can be described using **speed, velocity,** or **acceleration.**
- Speed is how fast an object moves. Velocity describes an object's speed and the direction it moves. Acceleration describes the rate at which an object's velocity changes.
- A graph can show you how either the displacement or the speed of an object changes over time.

Vocabulary

motion p. 47
reference point p. 47
distance p. 48
displacement p. 48
speed p. 48
velocity p. 49
acceleration p. 50

Lesson 2: Forces

- A **force** is a push or pull on an object. **Contact forces** include **friction** and applied forces. **Noncontact forces** include **gravity,** electricity, and magnetism.
- Gravity is a force of attraction between any two objects. Gravitational force increases as the masses of the objects increase and decreases as the distance between the objects increases.
- **Balanced forces** acting on an object cause no change in the motion of the object. When **unbalanced forces** act on an object, the sum of the forces is not equal to zero. Unbalanced forces cause acceleration.

Vocabulary

force p. 57
contact force p. 58
noncontact force p. 58
friction p. 59
gravity p. 59
balanced forces p. 61
unbalanced forces p. 61

Lesson 3: Newton's Laws of Motion

- **Inertia** is the tendency of an object to resist a change of motion. **Newton's first law of motion** states that an object will remain at rest or in constant straight-line motion unless unbalanced forces act on the object.
- **Newton's second law of motion** states that the acceleration of an object increases as the force acting on it increases and decreases as the mass of the object increases.
- **Newton's third law of motion** states that for every action force, there is an equal but opposite reaction force. The action-reaction forces are called a **force pair.**

Vocabulary

inertia p. 65
Newton's first law of motion p. 65
Newton's second law of motion p. 68
Newton's third law of motion p. 69
force pair p. 69

Review
- **Personal Tutor**
- **Vocabulary eGames**
- **Vocabulary eFlashcards**

FOLDABLES® **Chapter Project**

Assemble your lesson Foldables as shown to make a Chapter Project. Use the project to review what you have learned in this chapter.

Use Vocabulary

1. An object's ________ is the difference between a object's final position and its starting position.
2. Give a specific example of motion.
3. Name two forces that may act on objects at a distance.
4. Explain what must happen to an object in order for it to accelerate.
5. What kinds of things can you predict using Newton's second law of motion?
6. The law of inertia is another name for ________.
7. You can explain the forces that act when you push against a wall using ________.
8. A ________ describes two forces that act on different objects.

Link Vocabulary and Key Concepts

Concepts in Motion **Interactive Concept Map**

Copy this concept map, and then use vocabulary terms and other terms from the chapter to complete the concept map.

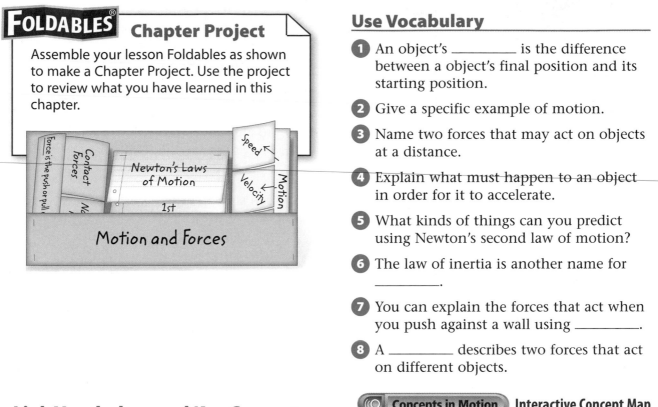

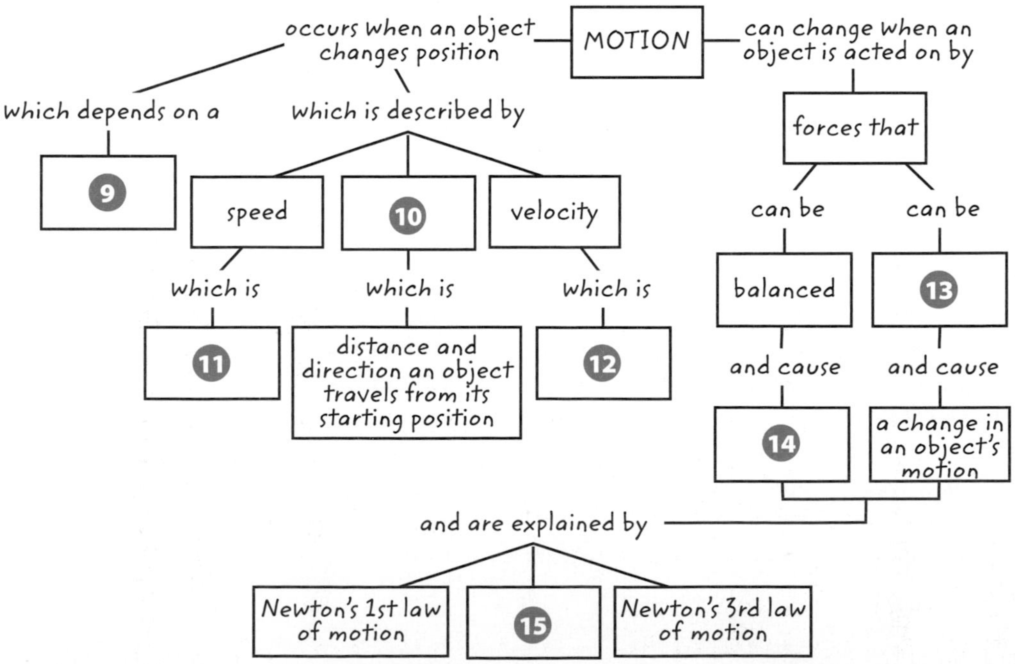

Chapter 2 Review

Understand Key Concepts

1 In which motions are the distance and the displacement the same?

A. A bird flies from its nest to the ground and back to its nest.
B. A dog chases its tail in a circle four times.
C. A fish swims all the way across a pond and then halfway back.
D. A worm moves 5 cm along a straight crack in a sidewalk.

2 The graph below represents the motion of a swimmer. Which statement best describes the swimmer's motion?

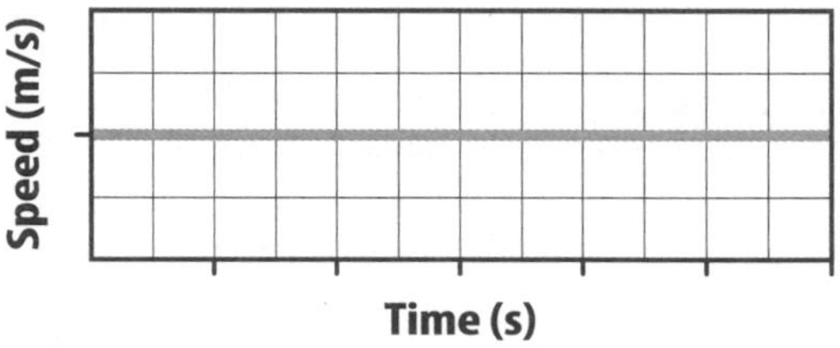

A. The swimmer is at rest.
B. The swimmer is in constant motion.
C. The swimmer's speed is changing.
D. The swimmer is accelerating.

3 An airplane travels 290 km between Austin and Dallas in 1 h 15 min. What is its average speed?

A. 160 km/h
B. 200 km/h
C. 232 km/h
D. 250 km/h

4 Which represents a force pair?

A. A book pushes down on a table, and gravity pulls the book toward the floor.
B. A boy's foot pushes down on a bicycle pedal. The pedal pushes up on his foot.
C. A golf club hits a golf ball. Gravity pulls the ball back down to Earth.
D. A person's foot pushes on the floor, and the person's weight pushes on the floor.

Use the figure below to answer questions 5–7.

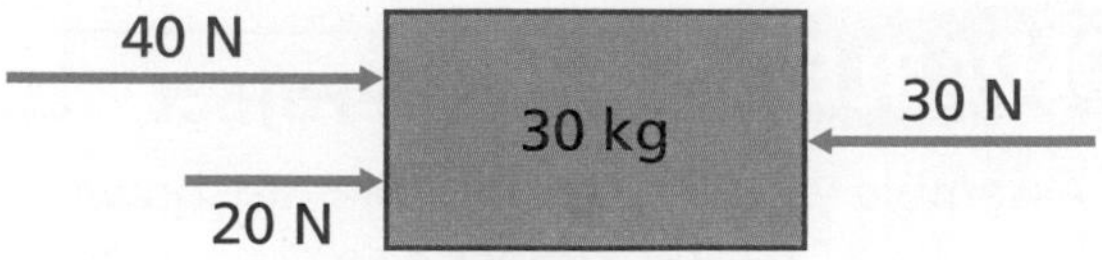

5 What is the net force on the object?

A. 30 N to the right
B. 30 N to the left
C. 60 N to the right
D. 90 N to the left

6 Which statement best describes the motion of the object?

A. It accelerates to the right.
B. It remains at rest.
C. It doesn't change speed but changes its direction of motion.
D. It moves at constant speed to the right.

7 What is the acceleration of the object?

A. 0 m/s^2
B. 1.0 m/s^2 to the right
C. 1.6 m/s^2 to the right
D. 3 m/s^2 to the left

8 Which is a contact force?

A. A girl pulls the plug of an electric hair dryer from the socket.
B. A leaf falls to the ground because of Earth's gravitational force.
C. A magnet pulls on a nail 2 cm away.
D. A small bit of paper is pulled toward an electrically charged comb.

9 Which best describes the relationship between the force acting on an object, the object's mass, and the acceleration of the object?

A. Newton's first law of motion
B. Newton's law of inertia
C. Newton's second law of motion
D. Newton's third law of motion

Assessment

Online Test Practice

Critical Thinking

10 **Contrast** the force of gravity between these pairs of objects: a 1-kg mass and a 2-kg mass that are 1 m apart; a 1-kg mass and a 2-kg mass that are 2 m apart; and two 2-kg masses that are 1 m apart.

11 **Construct** Ed rides an escalator moving at a constant speed to the second floor, which is 12 m above the first floor. The ride takes 15 s. Draw a displacement-time graph and a speed-time graph of his ride.

12 **Calculate** A marathon runner covers 42.0 km in 3 h 45 min. What was the runner's average speed?

13 **Justify** An astronomer measures the velocity of an object in space and decides that there is no net force acting on the object. Which of Newton's laws helped the astronomer make this decision?

14 **Analyze** The photo shows an astronaut tethered to a spacecraft. Use Newton's laws to describe what will happen when the astronaut pushes against the spacecraft.

Writing in Science

15 **Write** A driver followed a van with a surfboard strapped on top. The driver claims that the van stopped so quickly that the surfboard flew backward, hitting his car and causing damage. He wants the driver of the van to pay for damage to his vehicle and medical costs. You are the judge in the case. Use Newton's laws of motion to write a judgment in the case.

REVIEW THE BIG IDEA

16 While carrying a heavy box up the stairs, you set the box on a step and rest. Then you pick up the box and carry it to the top of the stairs. Describe these actions in terms of balanced and unbalanced forces acting on the box.

17 In what ways did balanced and unbalanced forces affect the motion of the acrobats in the air. What forces caused them to rise into the air? What forces are acting on them in the picture?

Math Skills

Review

Math Practice

Solve a One-Step Equation

18 A runner covers a distance of 1,500 m in 4 min. What is the runner's average speed?

19 Leaving the starting block, the runner accelerates from a speed of 0 m/s to a speed of 2 m/s in 3 s. What is the runner's acceleration?

20 What acceleration is produced when a 3,000-N force acts on a 1,200-kg car? Ignore any friction.

21 What force would a bowler have to exert on a 6-kg bowling ball to cause it to accelerate at the rate of 4 m/s^2?

Standardized Test Practice

Record your answers on the answer sheet provided by your teacher or on a sheet of paper.

Multiple Choice

1 Which is the result of an object's motion?

A a change in mass

B a change in position

C a change in reference point

D a change in volume

2 Which would be used to calculate an object's acceleration?

A change in its time divided by speed

B change in its velocity divided by time

C change in its speed divided by velocity

D change in its velocity divided by speed

Use the table below to answer questions 3 and 4.

Car	Initial Speed (m/s)	Final Speed (m/s)	Time (s)
A	0	25	10
B	25	15	10
C	15	25	20
D	10	10	25

3 Which car had a negative acceleration?

A car A

B car B

C car C

D car D

4 Which car or cars had an acceleration greater than 2 m/s^2?

A car A only

B car B only

C cars A and C

D cars A, C, and D

Use the graph to answer questions 5 and 6.

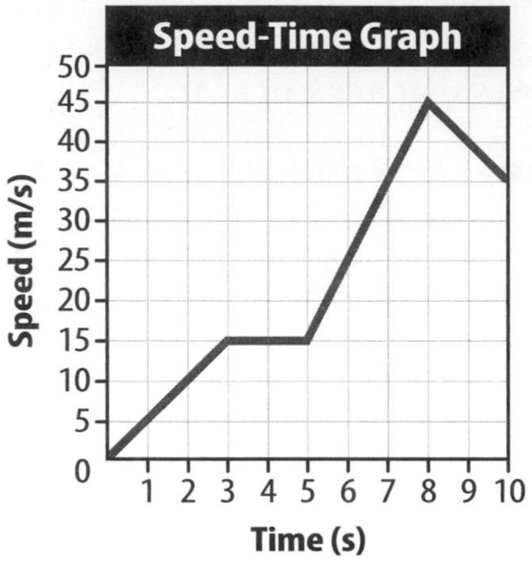

5 During which time period did the object slow down?

A 0–3 seconds

B 3–5 seconds

C 5–8 seconds

D 8–10 seconds

6 Which term describes the motion in the time period from 3 to 5 seconds?

A at rest

B constant speed

C slowing down

D speeding up

7 Which is a contact force?

A gravity

B friction

C magnetic force

D electrical force

8 Which can cause the force of gravity between two objects to increase?

A if both objects start to spin

B if one object increases in mass

C if both objects decrease in mass

D if the objects move farther apart

9 Which could be the net force acting on an object when the forces are balanced?

A −10 N

B 0 N

C 2 N

D 10 N

Use the diagram to answer question 10.

10 A skateboarder is traveling at a constant speed to the left. Suddenly the two forces shown act on him. Which describes the motion of the skateboarder when the two forces shown suddenly act on him?

A His motion stops.

B His speed increases.

C His speed decreases.

D His motion stays the same.

Constructed Response

Use the blank graph to answer questions 11 and 12.

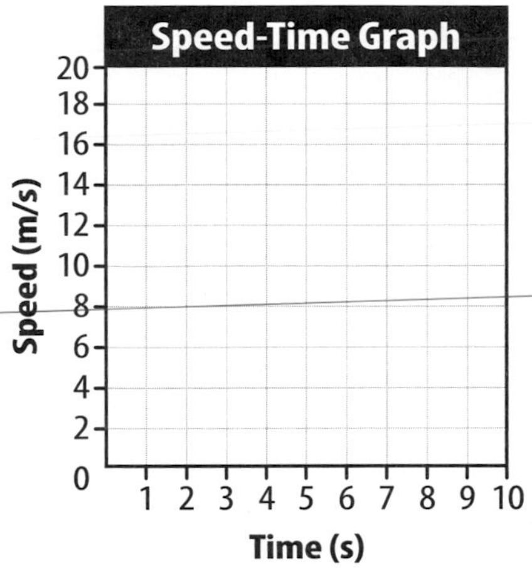

11 Describe how a period of constant acceleration would appear on a speed-time graph.

12 Describe how a period of nonconstant, positive acceleration would appear on a speed-time graph.

13 How does increasing the mass of an object affect the acceleration of an object if the forces acting on the object remain the same.? Explain.

14 According to Newton's third law of motion, what happens when you push on a sturdy wall with a force of 10 N?

NEED EXTRA HELP?														
If You Missed Question...	1	2	3	4	5	6	7	8	9	10	11	12	13	14
Go to Lesson...	1	1	1	1	1	1	2	2	2	3	1	1	3	3

Chapter 3

Work and Simple Machines

THE BIG IDEA **How do machines make doing work easier?**

Inquiry Hard Work or Not?

Digging this hole with a hand shovel would be hard work. Using an earthmover makes the task easier to do. You probably think writing an essay for English class is hard work, but is it?

- What do you think work is?
- How do you think work and energy are related?
- How do you think machines make doing work easier?

Get Ready to Read

What do you think?

Before you read, decide if you agree or disagree with each of these statements. As you read this chapter, see if you change your mind about any of the statements.

1. You do work when you push a book across a table.
2. Doing work faster requires more power.
3. Machines always decrease the force needed to do a job.
4. A well-oiled, low-friction machine can be 100 percent efficient.
5. A doorknob is a simple machine.
6. A loading ramp makes it easier to lift a load.

ConnectED Your one-stop online resource

connectED.mcgraw-hill.com

- Video
- Audio
- Review
- Inquiry
- WebQuest
- Assessment
- Concepts in Motion
- Multilingual eGlossary

Lesson 1

Reading Guide

Key Concepts
ESSENTIAL QUESTIONS

- What must happen for work to be done?
- How does doing work on an object change its energy?
- How are work and power related?

Vocabulary

work p. 83

power p. 87

Multilingual eGlossary

Academic Standards for Science

7.4.1 Understand that energy is the capacity to do work.

7.4.3 Explain that power is the rate that energy is converted from one form to another.

7.4.4 Explain that power systems are used to provide propulsion for engineered products and systems.

Also covers: 7.NS.3, 7.NS.4, 7.NS.7

Work and Power

Inquiry Enough Power?

A powerful tugboat can pull this large cargo ship. Could a much smaller boat also get this work done? As you will soon read, work and power are closely related.

Inquiry Launch Lab — 10 minutes

How do you know when work is done?

Many things that seem like hard work to you are not work at all in the scientific sense. This activity explores the scientific meaning of work.

1. Read and complete a lab safety form.
2. Tie a **string** around a **book.** Center the string on the book, and place the book on a desk.
3. Attach a **spring scale** to the string. Have a partner read the scale as you pull on the scale as shown in the photo. Pull very gently at first and then slowly increase how hard you pull.
4. Record in your Science Journal the scale reading when the book begins to move.

Think About This

1. What amount of force was needed to make the book move? How do you know?
2. **Key Concept** How do you think force and motion might be related to doing work? Explain your reasoning.

What is work?

Students might say studying and doing homework is hard **work.** To a scientist, these things take no work at all. Why? Because the scientific meaning of work includes forces and motion, not concentration. In science, **work** *is the transfer of energy to an object by a force that makes an object move in the direction of the force. Work is only being done while the force is applied to the object.*

Imagine pushing your bicycle into a bike rack. Your push (a force) makes your bicycle (an object) move. Therefore, work is done. You do no work if you push on the bicycle and it does not move. A force that does not make the object move does no work. The weight lifter shown in **Figure 1** does work in one example but not in the other.

Word Origin
work
from Old English *weorc,* means "activity"

Figure 1 The weight lifter does work only when he moves the weights.

The weight lifter does work on the weights when he exerts a force that makes the weights move.

Although the weight lifter exerts force, no work is done on the weights because the weights are not moving.

FOLDABLES®

Use two sheets of paper to make a layered book. Label it as shown. Use it to organize your notes on work.

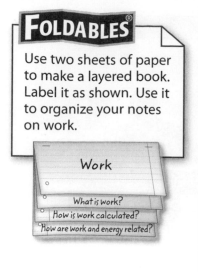

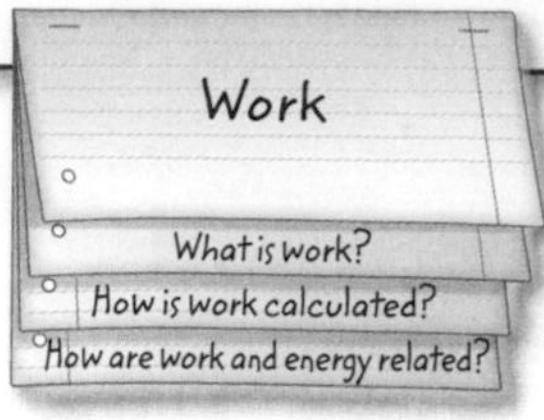

Work
What is work?
How is work calculated?
How are work and energy related?

Calculating Work

The amount of work done is easy to calculate. You must know two things to calculate work—force and distance, as shown in the following equation.

Work Equation

Work (in joules) = **force** (in newtons) × **distance** (in meters)

$$W = Fd$$

The force must be in newtons (N) and distance must be in meters (m). When you multiply force and distance together, the result has units of newton-meter (N•m). The newton-meter is also known as the joule (J). Like other types of energy, work is measured in joules. The joule is the SI unit of work and energy.

The distance in the work equation is the distance the object moves while the force is acting on it. Suppose you push on a book over a distance of 0.25 m and then the book slides 3.0 m. Which distance do you use? You calculate the work done using 0.25 m because the force was applied along that distance.

Key Concept Check How is work done?

Math Skills — Work Equation

Solve for Work A student pushes a desk 2.0 m across the floor using a constant force of 25.0 N. How much work does the student do on the desk?

1. **This is what you know:** force: $F = 25.0$ N; distance: $d = 2.0$ m
2. **This is what you need to find:** work: W
3. **Use this formula:** $W = Fd$
4. **Substitute:** values for F and d into the formula and multiply: $W = (\mathbf{25.0\ N}) \times (\mathbf{2.0\ m}) = 50.0$ N•m
5. **Convert units:** (N) × (m) = N•m = J

Answer: The amount of work done is 50.0 J.

Practice

A child pushes a toy truck 2.5 m across a floor with a constant force of 22 N. How much work does the child do on the toy truck?

Review
- Math Practice
- Personal Tutor

Figure 2 A force that acts in the direction of the motion does work.

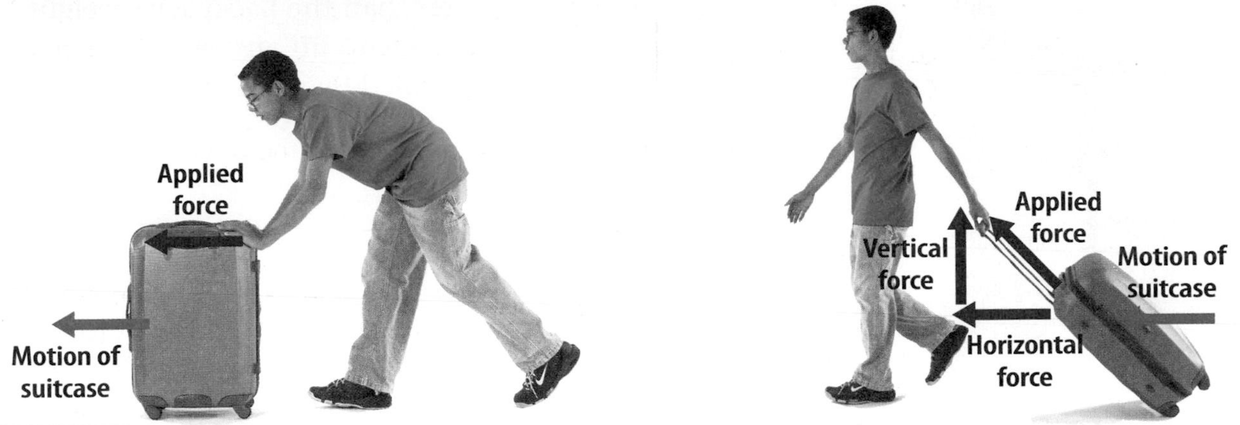

Visual Check How are the applied forces different in each example?

Factors That Affect Work

The work done on an object depends on the direction of the force applied and the direction of motion, as shown in **Figure 2.** Sometimes the force and the motion are in the same direction, such as when you push a suitcase along the floor. To calculate the work in this case, simply multiply the force and the distance.

Force at an Angle Now imagine pulling a wheeled suitcase, as shown in **Figure 2.** Note that the suitcase moves along the floor, but the force acts at an angle to the direction of the suitcase's motion. In other words, the force and the motion are not in the same direction. How do you calculate work?

Only the part of the force that acts in the direction of motion does work. Notice in **Figure 2** that the force has a horizontal part and a vertical part. Only the horizontal part of the force moves the suitcase across the floor. Therefore, only the horizontal part of the force is used in the work equation. The vertical part of the force does no work on the suitcase.

Reading Check What part of a force does work when the direction of the force and the direction of motion are not the same?

Inquiry MiniLab 20 minutes

What affects work?

Explore how different surfaces affect the work needed to pull an object across it.

1. Read and complete a lab safety form.
2. Tie a **string** around the center of a **book.** Attach a **spring scale** to the string.
3. Place the book on a desk next to a **meterstick.** Have a partner read the scale as you pull horizontally on it. Determine the least amount of force needed to slide the book 0.2 m at a constant speed. Record your data in your Science Journal in a table like the one below.
4. Repeat step 3 using the floor and other surfaces as instructed by your teacher.

Sliding Book Data		
Surface	Force (N)	Work (J)
Desk		
Floor		

Analyze and Conclude

1. **Determine** the work done in each trial.
2. **Compare** the surface requiring the least force to the one requiring the most force.
3. **Key Concept** What caused the change in work done for each surface?

Upward force
Weight

▲ **Figure 3** The amount of force needed to lift the backpack is equal to the weight of the backpack.

Lifting Objects Lifting your backpack requires you to do work. The backpack has weight because of the downward force of gravity acting on it. To lift your backpack, you must pull upward with a force equal to or greater than the backpack's weight, as shown in **Figure 3.** The work done to lift any object is equal to the weight of the object multiplied by the distance it is lifted.

Reading Check How do you calculate the work done when lifting an object?

Work and Energy

Doing work on an object transfers energy to the object. This is important to scientists because it helps them predict how an object will act when forces are applied to it. Recall that moving objects have kinetic energy. The boy in **Figure 4** does work on the tray when he applies a force that makes the tray move. This work transfers energy to the tray. The added energy is the kinetic energy of the moving tray.

Work done when you lift an object also increases the object's energy. Recall that the gravitational potential energy of an object increases as its height above the ground increases. When the girl in **Figure 4** lifts the tray the gravitational potential energy of the tray increases. The tray also gains kinetic energy as the tray moves upward. The girl did work on the tray as she lifted it. She transferred energy to the tray, increasing the tray's potential and kinetic energy.

Key Concept Check How does doing work on an object change its energy?

Figure 4 Doing work on a tray transfers energy to it. The energy change can be in the form of kinetic energy or potential energy.

Visual Check How does the tray's energy change when it is lifted?

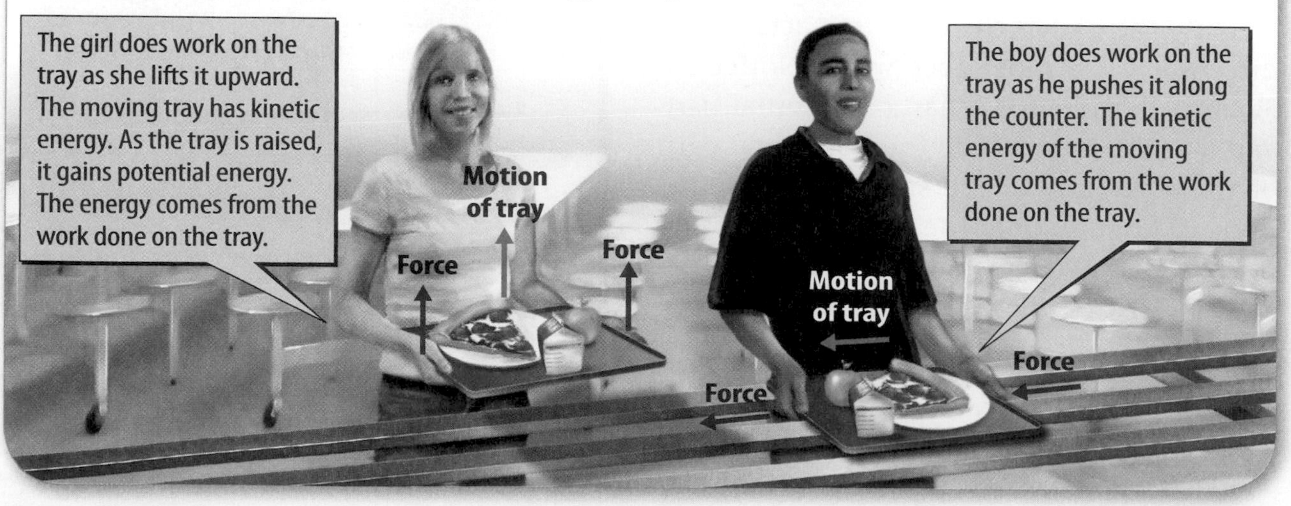
The girl does work on the tray as she lifts it upward. The moving tray has kinetic energy. As the tray is raised, it gains potential energy. The energy comes from the work done on the tray.
Motion of tray
Force
Force
Motion of tray
Force
Force
The boy does work on the tray as he pushes it along the counter. The kinetic energy of the moving tray comes from the work done on the tray.

What is power?

What does it mean to have power? If two weight lifters lift identical weights to the same height, they both do the same amount of work. How quickly a weight lifter lifts a weight does not change the amount of work done. Doing work more quickly, does affect **power**—*the rate at which work is done.* A weight lifter lifting a weight more quickly exerts more power.

Knowing the power required for a task enables engineers to properly size engines and motors. You can calculate power by dividing the work done by the time needed to do the work. In the power equation, work done is in joules (J) and time is in seconds (s). The SI unit of power is the watt (W). Note that 1 J/s = 1 W.

SCIENCE USE V. COMMON USE

power

Science Use the rate at which work is done

Common Use the ability to accomplish something or to command or control other people

Power Equation

$$\textbf{power} \text{ (in watts)} = \frac{\textbf{work} \text{ (in joules)}}{\textbf{time} \text{ (in seconds)}}$$

$$P = \frac{W}{t}$$

You know that power is the rate at which work is done. You also know that work **transfers** energy. Thus, you can think of power as the rate at which energy is transferred to an object.

ACADEMIC VOCABULARY

transfer

(verb) to move from one place to another

Key Concept Check How are work and power related?

Math Skills — Power Equation

Solve for Power A boy does 18 J of work in 2.0 s on his backpack as he lifts it from a table. How much power did the boy use on the backpack?

1. **This is what you know:** work: $W = 18$ J time: $t = 2.0$ s
2. **This is what you need to find:** power: P
3. **Use this formula:** $P = \frac{W}{t}$
4. **Substitute:** values for W and t into the formula and divide $P = \frac{18 \text{ J}}{2.0 \text{ s}} = 9.0$ J/s
5. **Convert units:** J/s = W $\frac{18 \text{ J}}{2.0 \text{ s}}$

The symbol for work, *W*, is usually italicized. However, the abbreviation for watt, W, is not italicized.

Answer: The amount of power used was 9.0 W.

Practice

A child pulls a wagon, doing 360 J of work in 8.0 s. How much power is exerted?

Review
- **Math Practice**
- **Personal Tutor**

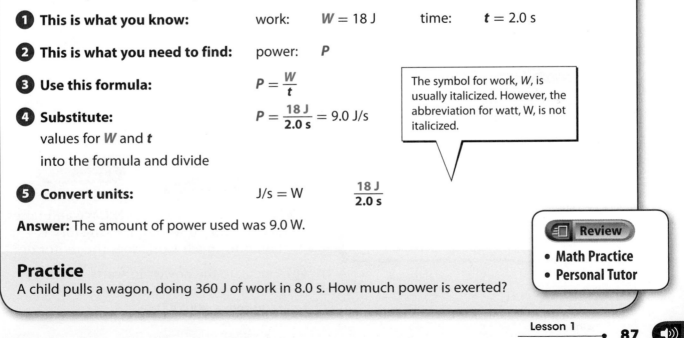

Lesson 1 Review

Assessment Online Quiz
Inquiry Virtual Lab

Visual Summary

Work is done on an object when the object moves in the direction of the applied force.

When work is done on an object, energy is transferred to the object.

To increase power, work must be done in less time.

FOLDABLES®

Use your lesson Foldable to review the lesson. Save your Foldable for the project at the end of the chapter.

Use Vocabulary

1. **Use the term** *work* in a sentence.
2. **Define** *power* in your own words.

Understand Key Concepts

3. **Explain** how work and power are related.
4. Lifting a stone block 146 m to the top of the Great Pyramid required 146,000 J of work. How much work was done to lift the block halfway to the top?
   A. 36,500 J
   B. 73,000 J
   C. 146,000 J
   D. 292,000 J
5. **Give** an example of a situation in which doing work on an object changed its energy. Explain how the energy changed.

Interpret Graphics

6. **Explain** why this motionless weight lifter is not doing work.

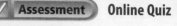

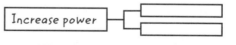

7. **Determine Cause and Effect** Copy and complete the graphic organizer below to list two ways power can be increased.

Increase power → [ ] / [ ]

Critical Thinking

8. **Explain** When you type on a computer keyboard, do you do work on the computer keys? Explain your answer.

What do you think NOW?

You first read the statements below at the beginning of the chapter.

1. Work is done when you push a book across a table.

2. Doing work faster requires more power.

Did you change your mind about whether you agree or disagree with the statements? Rewrite any false statements to make them true.

Math Skills

Review
Math Practice

9. A motor applies a 5000-N force and raises an elevator 10 stories. If each story is 4 m tall, how much work does the motor do?
10. Calculate the power, in watts, needed to mow a lawn in 50 minutes if the work required is 500,000 J.

SCIENCE & SOCIETY

What is horsepower?

You might be surprised to learn that there is a connection between a horse and a steam engine.

In the early 1700s, horses did work on farms, powered factories, and moved vehicles. When people spoke of power, they literally were referring to horsepower. It was natural, then, for James Watt to think in terms of horsepower when he set out to improve the steam engine.

▼ A draft horse powering a mill

Watt did not invent the steam engine, but he realized its potential. He also realized that he needed a way to measure the power produced by steam engines. Watt knew that fabric mills used horses to power machinery. A worker attached a horse to a power wheel. The horse turned the wheel by walking in a 24-ft diameter circle at a rate of two revolutions per minute. From this information, Watt calculated the power supplied by a horse to be about 33,000 foot-pounds per minute. This amount of power became known as 1 horsepower (1 hp).

▲ An early steam engine developed by James Watt

Watt succeeded in making better steam engines. Eventually, some steam engines produced more than 200 hp. Something unexpected happened as a result of all this power—life changed. More work was done and done faster. The mills expanded. People moved to the cities to work in the mills. Populations of cities in industrialized countries increased. The world changed because steam engines easily could produce more horsepower than horses.

▼ With cheap power came factories, jobs, and pollution.

It's Your Turn

RESEARCH Steam engines are seldom used today. Research steam engines to determine why the power source that was key to the Industrial Revolution is no longer used.

Lesson 2

Reading Guide

Key Concepts
ESSENTIAL QUESTIONS

- What are three ways a machine can make doing work easier?
- What is mechanical advantage?
- Why can't the work done by a machine be greater than the work done on the machine?

Vocabulary

mechanical advantage p. 94

efficiency p. 95

g Multilingual eGlossary

Academic Standards for Science

7.4.1 Understand that energy is the capacity to do work.

7.4.2 Explain that energy can be used to do work using many processes, for example generation of electricity by harnessing wind energy.

Also covers: 7.NS.3, 7.NS.4, 7.NS.5, 7.NS.7, 7.NS.8

Using Machines

Inquiry Could it be worse?

Have you ever shoveled snow? You probably thought it was hard work. But imagine moving all of the snow only using your hands instead of a shovel. A shovel is a simple machine that makes moving snow easier.

Inquiry Launch Lab

15 minutes

How do machines work?

Bicycles, pencil sharpeners, staplers, and doorknobs are machines that make specific tasks easier to do. How does the way a machine operates make work easier to do?

1. Read and complete a lab safety form.
2. Examine a **can opener** and answer these questions.
   - How many different ways does the can opener move?
   - Where do you apply force to the can opener?
   - Where does the can opener apply force to the can?
   - Is the amount of force you apply to the can opener different from the force the can opener applies to the can?
   - Does the can opener change the direction of the forces applied to it?
3. Use the can opener to open a **can.** Record the process step by step in your Science Journal.

Think About This

1. Why is a can opener considered a machine? What task does it make easier to do?
2. **Key Concept** Review your observations. Identify several ways the can opener makes opening a can easier.

What is a machine?

If you ride a bicycle to school, you have firsthand experience with a machine. A machine is any device that makes doing something easier. The snow shovel on the previous page is a machine that is used to move snow. The scissors and the watch shown in **Figure 5** are also machines. As these example show, some machines are simple and other machines are more complex.

Like a pair of scissors, a leaf rake, broom, screwdriver, baseball bat, shovel, and doorknob are all machines. Other machines, such as a watch, an automobile, a snowblower, and a lawn mower, are more complex. All machines make tasks easier, but they do not decrease the amount of work required. Instead, a machine changes the way in which the work is done.

Reading Check Do machines decrease the amount of work needed for a task? Explain.

Figure 5 A machine makes work easier to do regardless of whether it is simple or complex.

Inquiry MiniLab 20 minutes

Does a ramp make it easier to lift a load?

In this lab, you will use a ramp and determine why it is useful for lifting heavy loads.

1. Read and complete a lab safety form.
2. Attach a **toy car** to the hook of a **spring scale.** Slowly lift the car off the table. Record in your Science Journal the force shown on the scale.
3. Lean a 30–40-cm **wood board** against a stack of three **textbooks** as shown. Use the scale to slowly pull the car up the ramp at a constant speed. Record the force.

Analyze and Conclude

1. **Compare** How did the force needed to lift the car off the table compare with the force needed to pull the car up the ramp?
2. **Key Concept** How does a ramp make work easier? Does the ramp decrease the amount of work done? Explain.

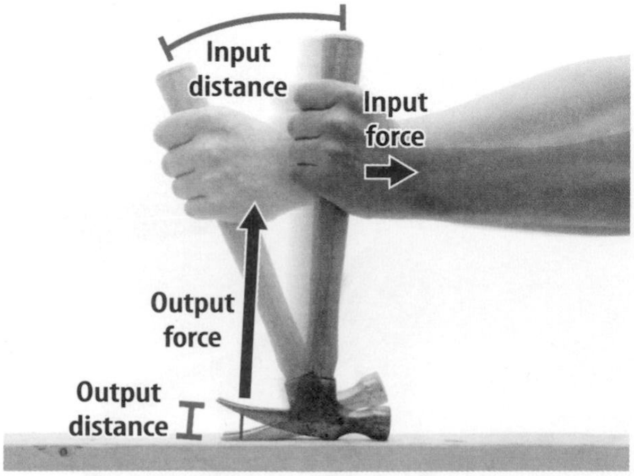

Figure 6 You exert an input force on the hammer. The hammer exerts an output force on the nail.

Input Force to Output Force

To use a machine, such as a hammer, you must apply a force to it. This force is the input force. The machine changes the input force into an output force, as shown in **Figure 6.** You apply an input force when you pull on the hammer's handle. The hammer changes the input force to an output force that pulls the nail out of the board.

Input Work to Output Work

Squeezing the handles of a pair of scissors makes the blades move. You apply an input force that moves part of the machine—the scissors—and does work. The work is called input work, W_{in}. It is the product of the input force and the distance the machine moves in the direction of the input force.

Machines convert, or change, input work to output work. They do this by applying an output force on something and making it move. The output work, W_{out}, is the product of the output force and the distance part of the machine moves in the direction of the output force. The examples in **Figure 7** on the next page show these relationships.

How do machines make work easier to do?

A machine can make work easier in three ways. It can change

- the size of a force;
- the distance the force acts;
- the direction of a force.

How hard it would be to pull a nail out of a board using your fingers? A hammer makes it easier in three ways. It changes the sizes of the forces and the distances the forces act. Notice that the person applies a smaller force over a longer distance, and the hammer exerts a greater force over a shorter distance. The hammer changes the direction of the input force. You pull back on the handle, and the hammer pulls up on the nail.

❶ Change the Size of a Force

Could you use only your hands to pull a nailed-down board from a deck? Probably not. However, a crowbar makes this task fairly easy, as shown in **Figure 7**. You would start by placing the tip of a crowbar under the edge of the board. Then you would press down on the opposite end of the crowbar. The tip of the crowbar would lift the board away from the supporting board below. Repeating this process, you could remove the length of the board from the deck.

A crowbar is a machine. It makes work easier by changing a input force into a larger output force. Note that although the output force is greater than the input force, it acts over a shorter distance.

Reading Check How does a crowbar make work easier?

❷ Change the Distance a Force Acts

Using a rake to gather leaves is an example of a machine that increases the distance over which a force acts. As shown in **Figure 7**, a person's hands move one end of the rake a short distance. The other end of the rake, however, sweeps through a greater distance making it easier to rake leaves. Note that the force applied by the rake (the output force) decreases as the distance over which the force acts (the output distance) increases. This relationship is true for all machines.

❸ Change the Direction of a Force

Machines also can make work easier by changing the direction of the input force. A machine is used in **Figure 7** to lift a load. A rope tied to an object passes through a pulley. As the free end of the rope is pulled down, the object tied to the other end of the rope is lifted up. The machine changes the direction of the applied force.

Key Concept Check In what three ways do machines make doing work easier?

Figure 7 Machines make work easier in three ways.

❶ When the output force is greater than the input force, the output force acts over a shorter distance.

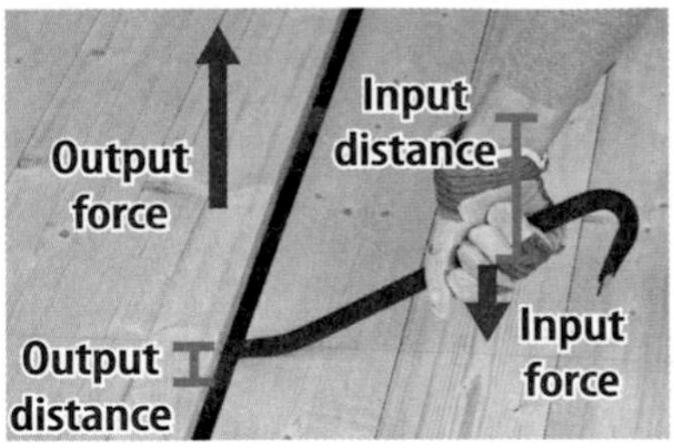

Input force × Input distance = Output force × Output distance

Input work = Output work

❷ When the output force acts over a longer distance than the input force, the output force is less than the input force.

Input force × Input distance = Output force × Output distance

Input work = Output work

❸ Equal output and input forces act over equal distances.

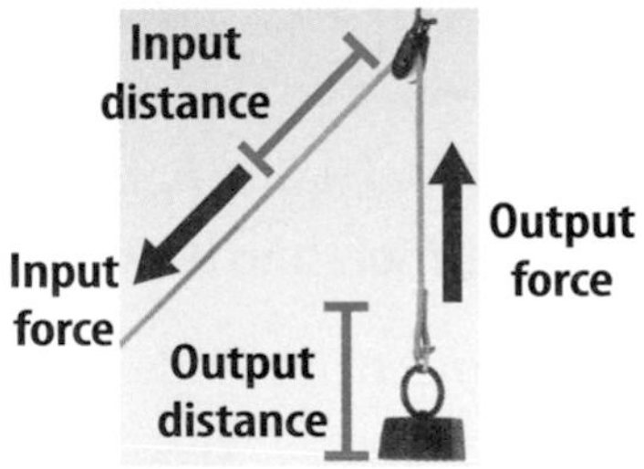

Input force × Input distance = Output force × Output distance

Input work = Output work

Word Origin

mechanical
from Greek *mechanikos,* means "machine"

What is mechanical advantage?

Most machines change the size of the force applied to them. *A machine's* **mechanical advantage** *is the ratio of a machine's output force produced to the input force applied.* The mechanical advantage, or *MA*, tells you how many times larger or smaller the output force is than the input force.

Foldables®

Make a three-tab book from a sheet of horizontal paper. Label it as shown. Use it to summarize the three ways machines make doing work easier.

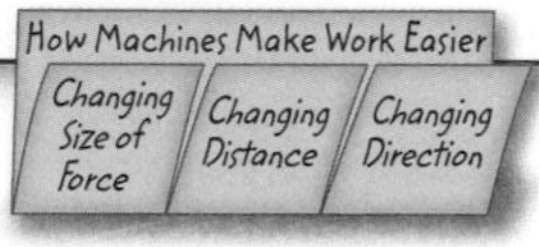

Mechanical Advantage Equation

$$\textbf{mechanical advantage} \text{ (no units)} = \frac{\textbf{output force} \text{ (in newtons)}}{\textbf{input force} \text{ (in newtons)}}$$

$$MA = \frac{F_{out}}{F_{in}}$$

Mechanical advantage can be less than 1, equal to 1, or greater than 1. A mechanical advantage greater than 1 means the output force is greater than the input force. A crowbar, for example, has a mechanical advantage much greater than 1.

The ideal mechanical advantage, or *IMA*, is the mechanical advantage if no friction existed. Machines cannot operate at ideal mechanical advantage because friction always exists.

Key Concept Check What is mechanical advantage?

Math Skills — Mechanical Advantage Equation

Solve for Mechanical Advantage A carpenter applies 525 N to the end of a crowbar. The force exerted on the board is 1,575 N. What is the mechanical advantage of the crowbar?

1. **This is what you know:** input force: $F_{in} = 525$ N; output force: $F_{out} = 1{,}575$ N
2. **This is what you need to find:** mechanical advantage: MA
3. **Use this formula:** $MA = \frac{F_{out}}{F_{in}}$
4. **Substitute:** the values for F_{in} and F_{out} into the formula and divide: $MA = \frac{1{,}575 \text{ N}}{525 \text{ N}} = 3$

Answer: The mechanical advantage is 3.

Practice

While raking leaves, a woman applies an input force of 32 N to a rake. The rake has an output force of 16 N. What is the mechanical advantage of the rake?

Review
- **Math Practice**
- **Personal Tutor**

What is efficiency?

The output work done by a machine never exceeds the input work of the machine. The reason for this is friction. Friction converts some of the input work to thermal energy. The converted energy cannot be used to do work.

The **efficiency** *of a machine is the ratio of the output work to the input work.* Efficiency is calculated using the equation below. Because output work is always less than input work, a machine's efficiency is always less than 100 percent. As shown in **Figure 8,** lubricating a machine's moving parts increases efficiency.

Efficiency Equation

$$\textbf{efficiency} \text{ (in \%)} = \frac{\textbf{output work} \text{ (in joules)}}{\textbf{input work} \text{ (in joules)}} \times 100\%$$

$$\textbf{efficiency} = \frac{W_{out}}{W_{in}} \times 100\%$$

Key Concept Check Why can't the work done by a machine be greater than the work done on the machine?

Figure 8 A lubricant reduces friction by forming a thin film between moving surfaces.

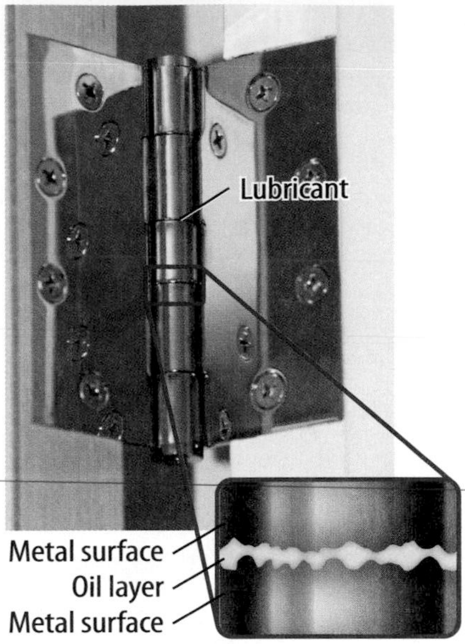

Math Skills — Efficiency Equation

Solve for Efficiency A mechanic does 78.0 J of work pulling the rope on a pulley to lift a motor. The output work of the pulley is 64.0 J. What is the efficiency of the pulley?

1. **This is what you know:** input work: $W_{in} = 78.0$ J; output work: $W_{out} = 64.0$ J
2. **This is what you need to find:** **efficiency**
3. **Use this formula:** $\textbf{efficiency} = \frac{W_{out}}{W_{in}} \times 100\%$
4. **Substitute:** the values for W_{in} and W_{out} into the formula and divide — $\textbf{efficiency} = \frac{64.0 \text{ J}}{78.0 \text{ J}} \times 100\% = 82.1\%$

Answer: The efficiency is 82.1%

Practice

A carpenter turns a handle to adjust a saw blade. The input work is 55 J and the output work is 51 J. What is the efficiency of the blade adjuster?

Review
- **Math Practice**
- **Personal Tutor**

Lesson 2 Review

Assessment Online Quiz
Inquiry Virtual Lab

Visual Summary

A machine makes a task easier and it can be simple or complex.

The mechanical advantage of a machine indicates how it changes an input force.

The efficiency of a machine is increased when a lubricant coats moving parts.

FOLDABLES®

Use your lesson Foldable to review the lesson. Save your Foldable for the project at the end of the chapter.

What do you think NOW?

You first read the statements below at the beginning of the chapter.

3. Machines always decrease the force needed to do a job.

4. A well-oiled, low-friction machine can be 100 percent efficient.

Did you change your mind about whether you agree or disagree with the statements? Rewrite any false statements to make them true.

Use Vocabulary

1. **Define** *efficiency* in your own words.
2. **Distinguish** between efficiency and mechanical advantage.

Understand Key Concepts

3. **Explain** how friction reduces the efficiency of machines.
4. Which machine efficiency is impossible?
   - **A.** 1 percent
   - **B.** 80 percent
   - **C.** 99 percent
   - **D.** 100 percent
5. **Compare and contrast** input and output forces and input and output distances for a hammer pulling a nail out of a board.

Interpret Graphics

6. **Analyze** How does a rake make gathering leaves easier? Explain in terms of distances and forces.
7. **Organize** Copy and fill in the graphic organizer below to describe three ways machines can make work easier.

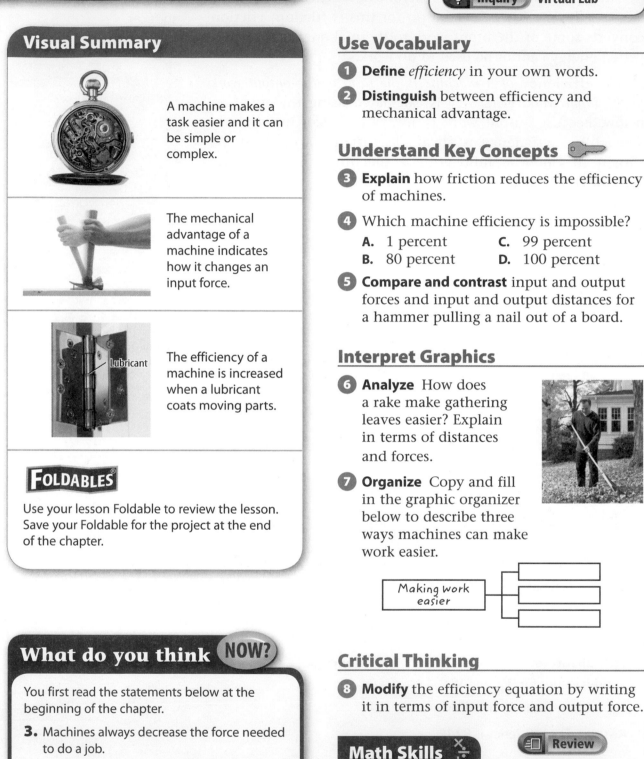

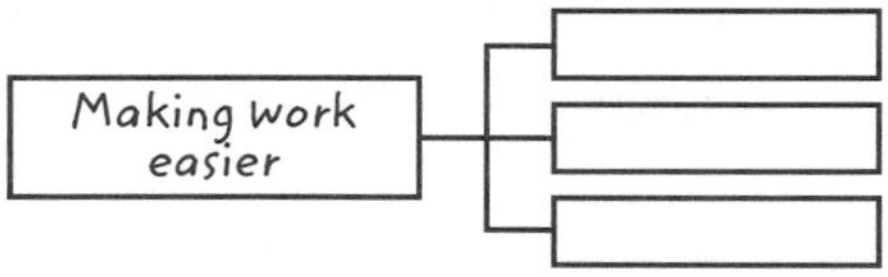

Critical Thinking

8. **Modify** the efficiency equation by writing it in terms of input force and output force.

Math Skills

Review
Math Practice

9. A pulley system uses a 250-N force to lift a 2,750-N crate. What is the mechanical advantage of the system?
10. An assembly line machine needs 150 J of input work to do 90 J of output work. What is the efficiency of the machine?

How does mechanical advantage affect a machine?

Materials

centimeter ruler

clear plastic tape

modeling clay

spring scale

Safety

Machines change forces and make work easier. In this lab, you build and use a simple machine to lift a load, and record force and distance data. You then interpret data and determine how the mechanical advantage of the machine affected the results.

Learn It

Measurements and observations are data. When you **interpret data,** you look for patterns and relationships in the data.

Try It

1. Read and complete a lab safety form.
2. Lay a metric ruler on a table so one end extends over an edge, as shown below. Tape the other end of the ruler to the table. Make sure the free end of the ruler moves up and down easily. This is your simple machine.
3. Use a spring scale to measure the mass of a handful-sized lump of clay. Use this weight as the output force (F_{out}) for your tests.
4. Push the clay onto the 15-cm mark of the ruler so that it sticks.
5. Attach a spring scale to the ruler's free end. Pull upward on the spring scale so the ruler lifts off of the table. Record the force reading as the input force (F_{in}).

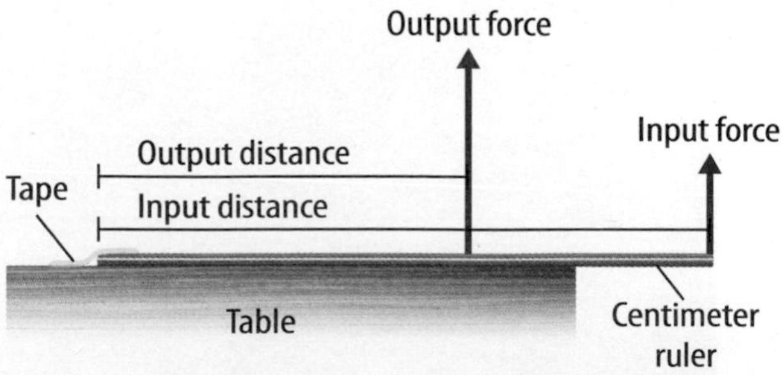

6. Make a data table in your Science Journal. Record your measurements, including the distance from the taped end to the clay (d_{out}) and from the taped end to the spring scale (d_{in}).
7. Calculate the mechanical advantage (MA) of the machine from your data. $MA = \frac{F_{out}}{F_{in}}$.

Apply It

8. Move the clay to the 27-cm mark. Repeat steps 5 through 7.
9. Move the clay to two other locations on the ruler, repeating steps 5 through 7 each time.
10. How is the machine's mechanical advantage related to d_{out}, the distance from the taped end of the ruler to the clay?
11. When the spring scale lifts the end of the ruler up, is the clay lifted the same amount? Does the amount the clay is lifted depend on its location along the ruler? Explain.
12. **Key Concept** What is the relationship between the machine's mechanical advantage and how easy it is to lift the clay?

Lesson 3

Simple Machines

Reading Guide

Key Concepts
ESSENTIAL QUESTIONS

- What is a simple machine?
- How is the ideal mechanical advantage of simple machines calculated?
- How are simple machines and compound machines different?

Vocabulary

simple machine p. 99
lever p. 100
fulcrum p. 100
wheel and axle p. 102
inclined plane p. 103
wedge p. 104
screw p. 104
pulley p. 105

Multilingual eGlossary

Video
- **BrainPOP®**
- **Science Video**

Academic Standards for Science

7.4.2 Explain that energy can be used to do work using many processes, for example generation of electricity by harnessing wind energy.

Also covers: 7.NS.1, 7.NS.3, 7.NS.4, 7.NS.5, 7.NS.7, 7.NS.8, 7.NS.9, 7.NS.10

Inquiry Hit or Miss?

A trebuchet (TRE bu shet) is a device from the Middle Ages designed to hurl large rocks. The trebuchet was effective at hurling rocks at castle walls, though it had limited accuracy. A trebuchet is a large simple machine.

Inquiry Launch Lab

15 minutes

How does a lever work?

Humans have used levers for thousands of years to make work easier. How does a lever change the force applied to it?

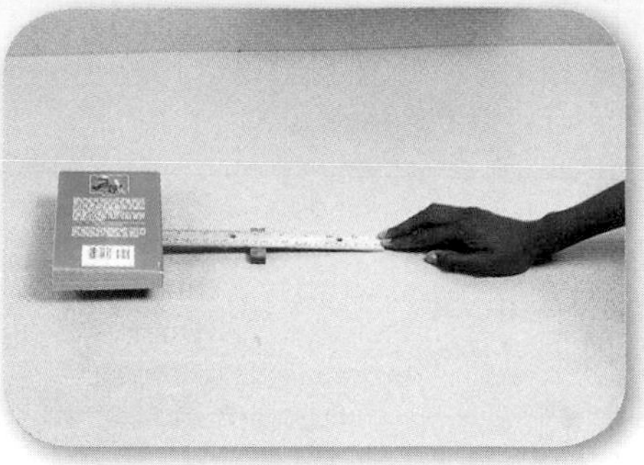

1. Read and complete a lab safety form.
2. Place a **ruler** on top of an **eraser** as shown. Place a **book** on one end of the ruler.
3. Lift the book by pushing down on the other end of the ruler. Record in your Science Journal how easy or difficult it is to lift the book.
4. Repeat steps 2 and 3 several times using different locations of the eraser along the ruler.

Think About This

1. Explain how changing the position of the eraser affected the force exerted by the lever.
2. **Key Concept** How would you describe the motion of the lever? Is the motion of the lever simple or complicated? Explain.

What is a simple machine?

Some machines, such as a trebuchet, have only a few parts. Six types of **simple machines**, shown in **Figure 9**, *do work using only one movement.* They are lever, wheel and axle, inclined plane, wedge, screw, and pulley.

Key Concept Check Describe a simple machine.

Figure 9 The six types of simple machines are shown below. Each simple machine does work with one motion.

Lever

Wheel and axle

Inclined plane

Wedge

Screw

Pulley

The Three Classes of Levers

Figure 10 The location of the input force, the output force, and the fulcrum determine the class of lever.

1 First-Class Lever

2 Second-Class Lever

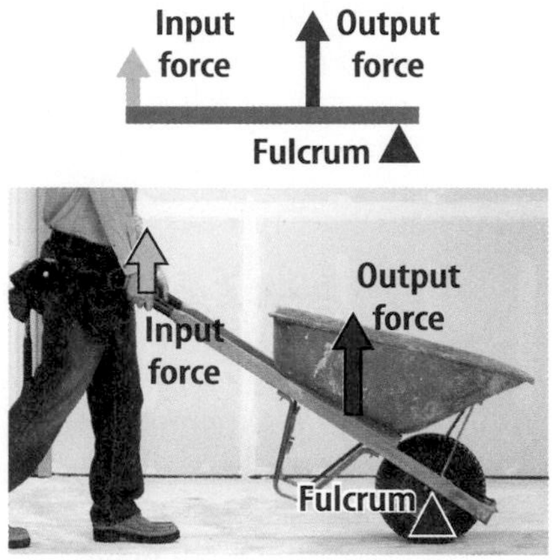

3 Third-Class Lever

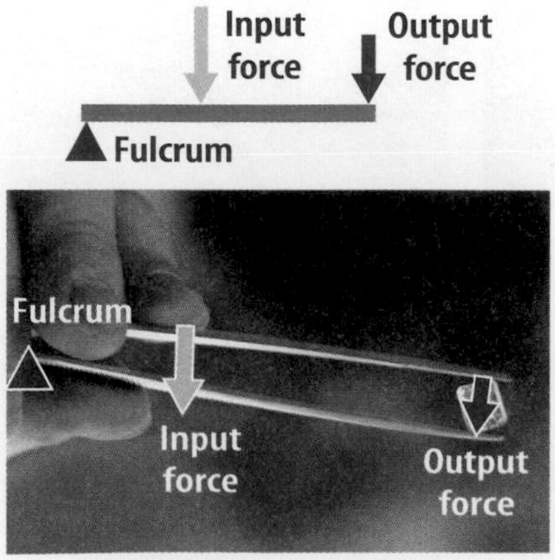

Levers

The next time you open an aluminum beverage can, watch how the finger tab works. The finger tab is a **lever**—*a simple machine made up of a bar that pivots, or rotates, about a fixed point. The point about which a lever pivots is called a* **fulcrum.** The fulcrum on the aluminum beverage can in **Figure 10** is where the finger tab attaches to the can.

Notice that the input force and the output force act on opposite ends of the finger tab. The distance from the fulcrum to the input force on the tab is the *input arm.* The distance from the fulcrum to the end of the tab that pushes down on the can is the *output arm.*

There are three types of levers, also shown in **Figure 10.** First-class, second-class, and third-class levers differ in where the input force and output force are relative to the fulcrum.

1 In a first-class lever, the fulcrum is between the input force and the output force. The direction of the input force is always different than the direction of the output force. A hammer is a first-class lever when it is used to pull a nail out of wood. A finger tab on a beverage can is also a first-class lever.

2 A second-class lever has the output force between the input force and the fulcrum. The output force and the input force act in the same direction. A second-class lever makes the output force greater than the input force. A wheelbarrow, a nut cracker, and your foot are second-class levers.

3 The input force is between the output force and the fulcrum in a third-class lever. The output force is less than the input force, though both forces act in the same direction. Tweezers, a rake, and a broom are examples of third-class levers.

Reading Check What is a lever?

Mechanical Advantage of Levers

Mechanical Advantage of a First-Class Lever

Output force

Input force

Output arm | Input arm

Fulcrum

- Fulcrum location determines mechanical advantage.
- ~~Mechanical advantage can be less~~ than 1, equal to 1, or greater than 1.

Mechanical Advantage of a Second-Class Lever

Output force

Input force

Output arm | Input arm

Fulcrum

- Input arm is longer than output arm.
- Output force is greater than input force.
- Mechanical advantage is greater than 1.

Mechanical Advantage of a Third-Class Lever

Input force

Output force

Output arm | Input arm

Fulcrum

- Input arm is shorter than output arm.
- Output force is less than input force.
- Mechanical advantage is less than 1.

Mechanical Advantage of Levers

The ideal mechanical advantage of a lever equals the length of the input arm divided by the length of the output arm.

Ideal Mechanical Advantage of a Lever

$$\text{ideal mechanical advantage} = \frac{\text{length of input arm (in meters)}}{\text{length of output arm (in meters)}}$$

$$IMA = \frac{L_{in}}{L_{out}}$$

First-Class Levers The location of the fulcrum determines the mechanical advantage in first-class levers. In **Figure 11,** the mechanical advantage of the lever is greater than 1 because the input arm is longer than the output arm. This makes the output force greater than the input force. When the mechanical advantage is equal to 1, the input and output arms and input and output forces are equal. If the mechanical advantage is less than 1, the input arm is shorter than the output arm. The output force then is less than the input force.

Second-Class Levers The input arm is longer than the output arm for all second-class levers. The mechanical advantage of a second-class lever is always greater than 1.

Third-Class Levers For third-class levers, the input arm is always shorter than the output arm. Thus, the mechanical advantage of a third-class lever is always less than 1.

 Key Concept Check How is the ideal mechanical advantage of a lever calculated?

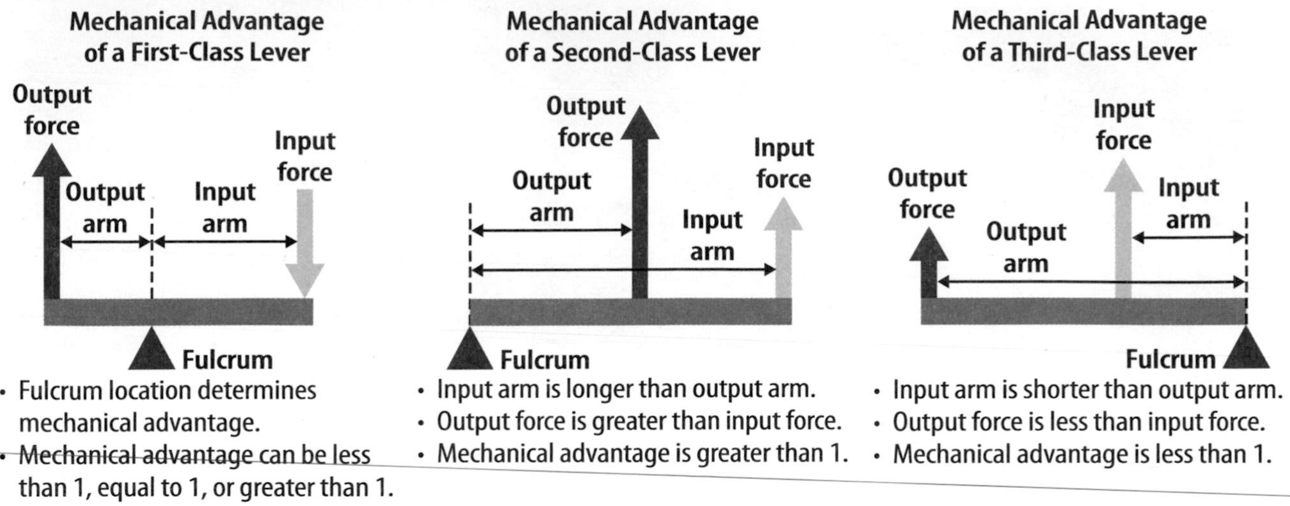

Figure 11 The mechanical advantage of a lever varies depending on the location of the fulcrum.

✓ **Visual Check** How does the input arm compare to the output arm in a second-class lever? In a third-class lever?

⬛ **Review**

Personal Tutor

Levers in the Body

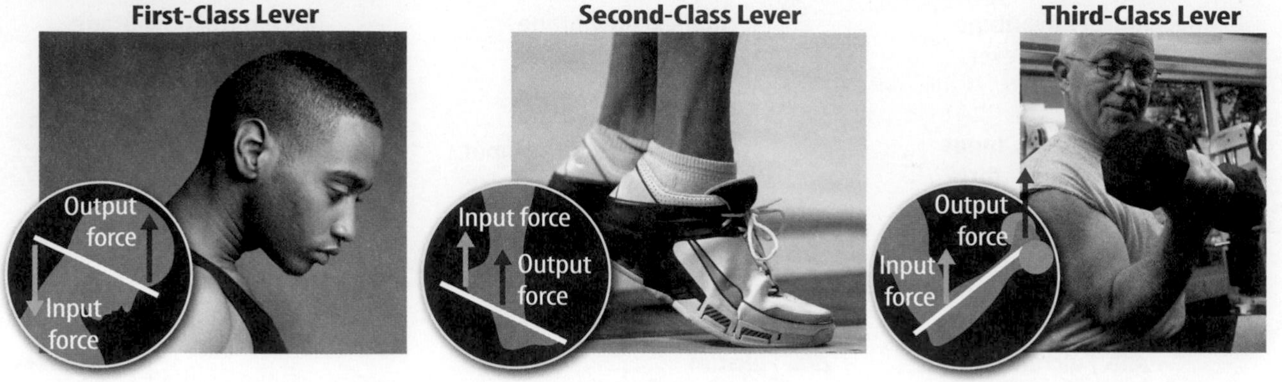

▲ **Figure 12** The neck, foot, and arm are examples of first-, second-, and third-class levers in the human body.

Levers in the Human Body

The human body uses all three classes of levers to move. Muscles provide the input force for the levers. Examples of levers in the neck, foot, and arm are shown in **Figure 12.**

The Neck Your neck acts like a first-class lever. The fulcrum is the joint connecting the skull to the spine. The neck muscles provide the input force. The output force is applied to the head and helps support your head's weight.

The Foot When standing on your toes, the foot acts like a second-class lever. The ball of the foot is the fulcrum. The input force comes from muscles on the back of the lower leg.

The Arm Your forearm works like a third-class lever. The elbow is the fulcrum and the input force comes from muscles located near the elbow.

Figure 13 A screwdriver is a wheel and axle. The handle is the wheel and the shaft is the axle. ▼

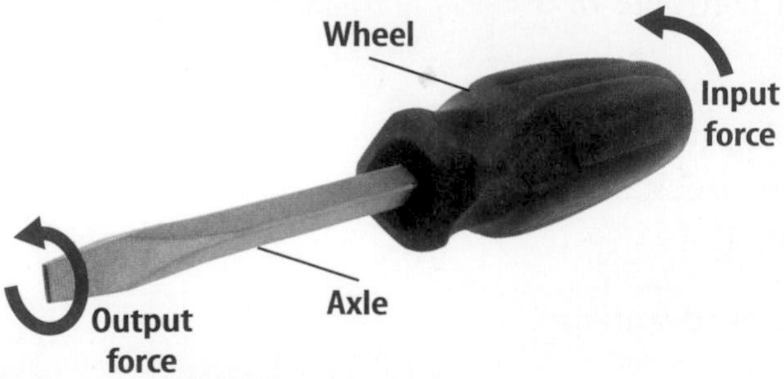

Wheel and Axle

A **wheel and axle** *is an axle attached to the center of a wheel and both rotate together.* Note that *axle* is another word for a shaft. The screwdriver shown in **Figure 13** is a wheel and axle. The handle is the wheel because it has the larger diameter. The axle is the shaft attached to the handle. Both the handle and the shaft rotate when the handle turns.

Mechanical Advantage of a Wheel and Axle

For a wheel and axle, the length of the input arm is the radius of the wheel. Likewise, the length of the output arm is the radius of the axle. These lengths give the ideal mechanical advantage as shown in the equation below.

Ideal Mechanical Advantage of Wheel and Axle

$$\text{ideal mechanical advantage} = \frac{\textbf{radius of wheel} \text{ (in meters)}}{\textbf{radius of axle} \text{ (in meters)}}$$

$$IMA = \frac{r_{wheel}}{r_{axle}}$$

FOLDABLES®

Make a six-tab book and label it as shown. Use your book to summarize information about six simple machines.

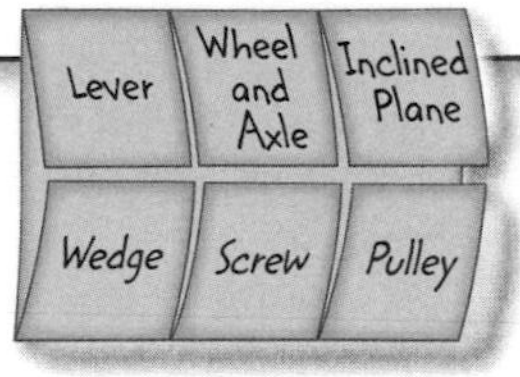

Using a Wheel and Axle

You know a screwdriver makes it easier to turn a screw. But how does a screwdriver work? Examining the mechanical advantage equation offers an explanation. When you turn a screwdriver, you apply an input force to the handle (the wheel). The output force is applied to the screw by the screwdriver's shaft (the axle). Because the wheel is larger than the axle, the mechanical advantage is greater than 1. This makes the screw easier to turn.

Inclined Planes

The ancient Egyptians built pyramids using huge stone blocks. Moving the blocks up the pyramid must have been difficult. To make the task easier, ramps were often used. *A ramp, or* **inclined plane,** *is a flat, sloped surface.* It takes less force to move an object upward along an inclined plane than it does to lift the object straight up. As shown in **Figure 14,** ramps are still useful for moving heavy loads.

Figure 14 Moving a sofa is easier using a ramp. As shown, using a ramp only requires a 100-N force to move the 500-N sofa. Because of friction, no ramp operates at its ideal mechanical advantage.

Figure 15 A wedge that splits wood is a simple machine. ▶

Concepts in Motion
Animation

Mechanical Advantage of Inclined Planes

The ideal mechanical advantage of an inclined plane equals its length divided by its height. See the equation below.

Ideal Mechanical Advantage of an Inclined Plane

$$\textbf{ideal mechanical advantage} = \frac{\textbf{length of inclined plane} \text{ (in meters)}}{\textbf{height of inclined plane} \text{ (in meters)}}$$

$$IMA = \frac{\ell}{h}$$

Note that increasing the length and decreasing the height of the inclined plane increases its ideal mechanical advantage. The longer or less-sloped an inclined plane is, the less force is needed to move an object along its surface.

Wedges

A sloped surface that moves is called a **wedge.** A wedge is really a type of inclined plane with one or two sloping sides. A doorstop is a wedge with one sloped side. The wedge shown in **Figure 15** is a wedge with two sloped sides. Notice how the shape of the wedge gives the output forces a different direction than the input force.

Your front teeth also are wedges. As you push your front teeth into food, the downward force is changed by your teeth into a sideways force that pushes the food apart.

Reading Check How are a wedge and a ramp different?

Figure 16 The groove, or thread, that wraps around a screw is an inclined plane. ▼

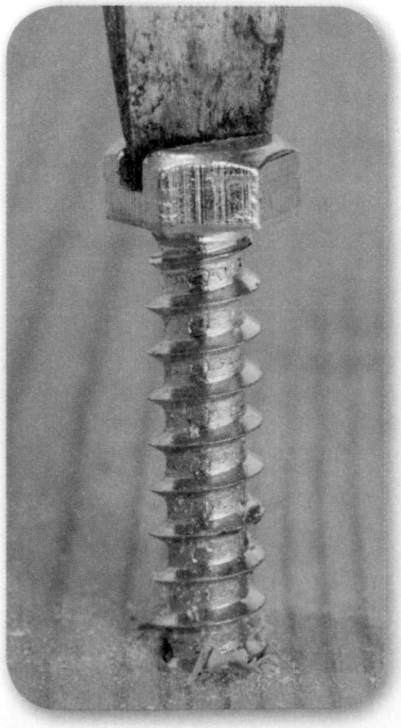

Screws

As shown in **Figure 16,** a **screw** *is an inclined plane wrapped around a cylinder.* When you turn a screw, the screw threads change the input force to an output force. The output force pulls the screw into the material.

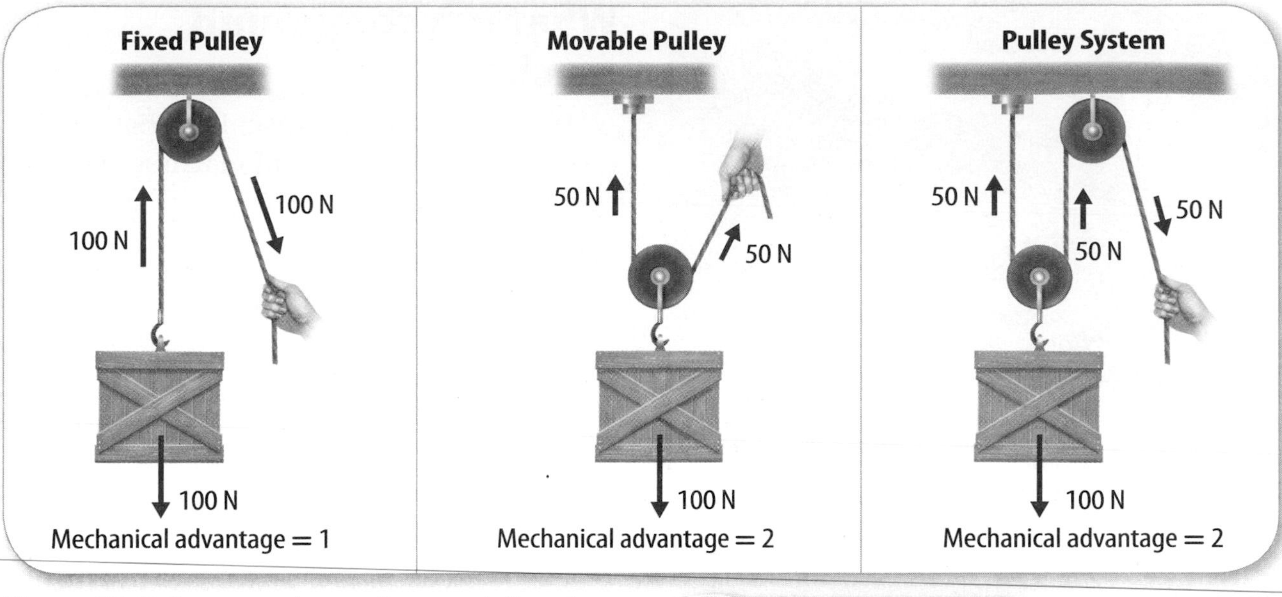

Figure 17 Pulleys can change force and direction.

Pulleys

You might have seen large cranes lifting heavy loads at construction sites. The crane uses a **pulley**—*a simple machine that is a grooved wheel with a rope or a cable wrapped around it.*

Fixed Pulleys Have you ever pulled down on a cord to raise a window blind? The cord passes through a fixed pulley mounted to the top of the window frame. A fixed pulley only changes the direction of the force, as shown **Figure 17.**

Movable Pulleys and Pulley Systems A pulley can also be attached to the object being lifted. This type of pulley, called a movable pulley, is shown in **Figure 17.** Movable pulleys decrease the force needed to lift an object. The distance over which the force acts increases.

A pulley system is a combination of fixed and movable pulleys that work together. An example of a pulley system is shown in **Figure 17.**

Mechanical Advantage of Pulleys The ideal mechanical advantage of a pulley or a pulley system is equal to the number of sections of rope pulling up on the object.

Inquiry **MiniLab** **20 minutes**

Can you increase mechanical advantage?

Pulley systems change the size and the direction of an applied force. How can you change the mechanical advantage of a pulley system?

1. Read and complete a lab safety form.
2. Use two **broomsticks** and an 8-m length of **rope** to make a pulley system as shown. Hold each broomstick waist-high. Tie the rope to one of the broomsticks and loop it around the other.
3. Have a student pull the free end of the rope as shown. Record in your Science Journal the forces acting on the broomsticks.

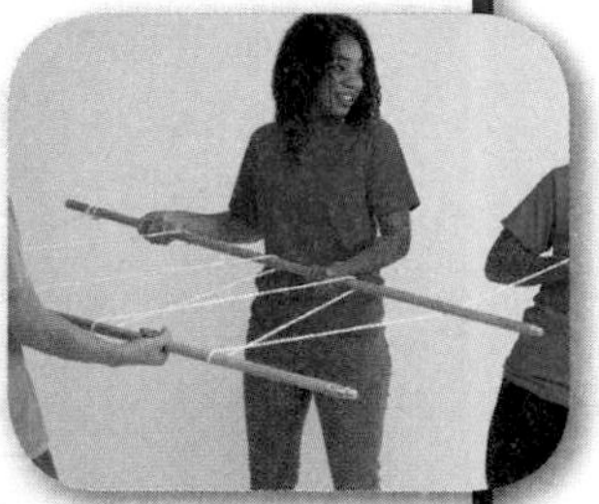

4. Take the excess rope and make two more loops around the broomsticks. Repeat step 3.

Analyze and Conclude

1. **Describe** how the forces applied on the broomsticks changed when the number of loops in the pulley system increased.
2. **Key Concept** Relate the number of rope segments in each pulley system to the mechanical advantage of each system.

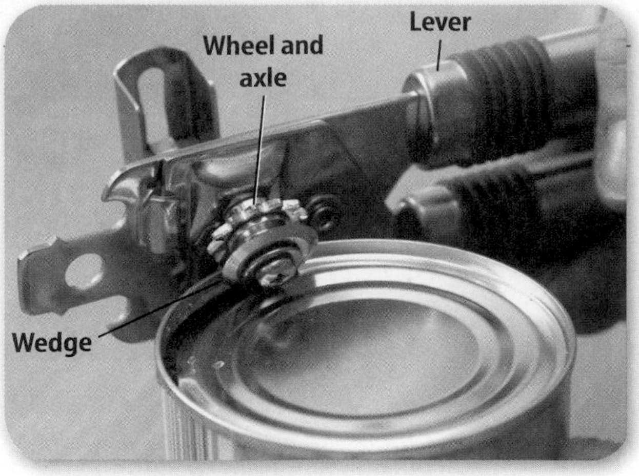

▲ **Figure 18** A can opener is a compound machine. It uses a second-class lever to move the handle, a wheel and axle to turn the blade, and a wedge to puncture the lid.

Visual Check How many simple machines are part of the can opener?

Figure 19 A system of gears is a compound machine. Notice how the direction of rotation changes from one gear to the next. ▼

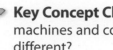

What is a compound machine?

Two or more simple machines that operate together form a compound machine. The can opener in **Figure 18** is a compound machine.

Key Concept Check How are simple machines and compound machines different?

Gears

A gear is a wheel and axle with teeth around the wheel. Two or more gears working together form a compound machine. When the teeth of two gears interlock, turning one gear causes the other to turn. The direction of motion, as shown in **Figure 19,** changes from one gear to the next.

Gears of different sizes turn at different speeds. Smaller gears rotate faster than larger gears. The amount of force transmitted through a set of gears is also affected by the size of the gears. The input force applied to a large gear is reduced when it is applied to a smaller gear.

Efficiency of Compound Machines

How can you determine the efficiency of a compound machine? The efficiency of a compound machine is calculated by multiplying the efficiencies of each simple machine together.

Consider the can opener in **Figure 18.** It is made up of three simple machines. Suppose the efficiencies are as follows:

- efficiency of lever = 95%
- efficiency of wheel and axle = 90%
- efficiency of wedge = 80%

The efficiency of the can opener is equal to the product of these efficiencies.

$$\text{efficiency of the can opener} = 95\% \times 90\% \times 80\% = 68\%$$

Each simple machine decreases the overall efficiency of the compound machine.

Lesson 3 Review

Assessment Online Quiz

Inquiry Virtual Lab

Visual Summary

Six simple machines are the lever, wheel and axle, inclined plane, wedge, screw, and pulley.

All levers rotate, or pivot, about the fulcrum.

The kind of wedge used to split logs is a simple machine.

FOLDABLES®

Use your lesson Foldable to review the lesson. Save your Foldable for the project at the end of the chapter.

What do you think NOW?

You first read the statements below at the beginning of the chapter.

5. A doorknob is a simple machine.

6. A loading ramp makes it easier to lift a load.

Did you change your mind about whether you agree or disagree with the statements? Rewrite any false statements to make them true.

Use Vocabulary

1. **Define** *wheel and axle* in your own words.

Understand Key Concepts

2. Identify the simple machine in which the fulcrum is between the input force and the output force.
   - **A.** wheel and axle
   - **B.** lever
   - **C.** inclined plane
   - **D.** pulley
3. **Determine** how the ideal mechanical advantage of a ramp changes if the ramp is made longer.
4. **Calculate** the ideal mechanical advantage of a screwdriver with a 24-mm radius handle and an 8-mm radius shaft.
5. **Explain** how simple and compound machines are different.

Interpret Graphics

6. **Observe** the scissors shown. They have a pin about which the blades rotate. Each blade has a sloped cutting surface. Identify the simple machines in a pair of scissors.

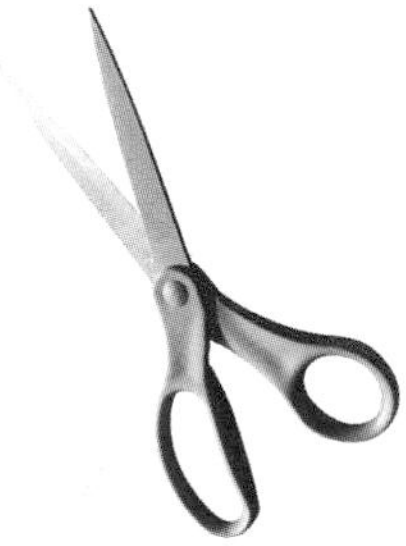

7. **Organize Information** Copy and fill in the graphic organizer below with the equations used to calculate the ideal mechanical advantage of each these simple machines.

Type of Simple Machine	Ideal Mechanical Advantage
Lever	
Wheel and axle	
Inclined plane	

Critical Thinking

8. **Suggest** a way in which a pulley could be considered a type of lever.

Comparing Two Simple Machines

Materials

250-g hanging mass

5-N spring scale

small pulley

ring stand

meterstick

Also needed: 50-cm × 15-cm board, books, 2-m length of heavy string

Safety

You will use a pulley and an inclined plane to lift a 250-g mass to a height of 20 cm. Which simple machine makes the work of lifting the load the easiest?

Question

Will the pulley or the inclined plane have a greater mechanical advantage?

Procedure

1. Read and complete a lab safety form.
2. Examine the equipment and diagrams. With your group, discuss why each simple machine has a mechanical advantage when lifting the mass.
3. Predict whether the pulley or the inclined plane will provide the greatest mechanical advantage in lifting the mass. Record your prediction in your Science Journal.
4. Also in your Science Journal, make a data table with columns for data you plan to collect to calculate mechanical advantage for each simple machine.

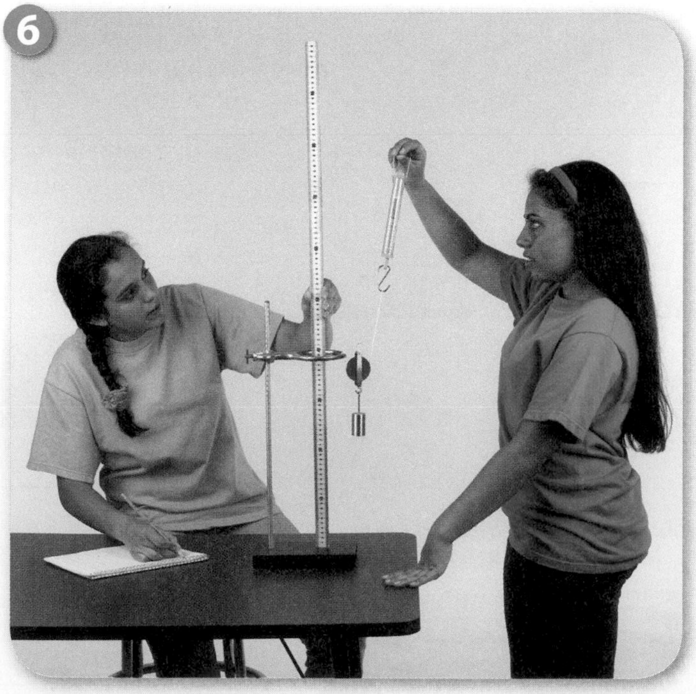

5. Use a spring scale to measure the weight of the 250-g mass. Record the weight in newtons.
6. Set up the pulley and the ring stand as shown on the previous page. Adjust the spring scale and the pulley so that the weight just clears the table. Use the spring scale as shown to slowly lift the weight to a height of 20 cm. Record the force in newtons. Repeat.
7. Set up the inclined plane as shown to the right so that the top of the ramp is 20 cm above the table. Attach the spring scale to the weight. Beginning at the bottom of the ramp, use the spring scale to pull the weight slowly up the ramp. Record the force in newtons. Repeat.

Analyze and Conclude

8. **Interpret Data** What is the mechanical advantage of the pulley and the inclined plane? Was your prediction correct? Explain.
9. **Explain** What other measurements would you need in order to calculate the efficiency of each machine?
10. **The Big Idea** Did the amount of work done on the weight to lift it to a height of 20 cm change with each machine? Explain. Did the machines make doing the work easier?

Communicate Your Results

Make a large data table on which all groups can display their data. Discuss similarities and differences between group data.

Inquiry Extension

How can you increase the mechanical advantage of your inclined plane? To investigate your question, design a controlled experiment.

Lab Tips

- ☑ A movable pulley supports part of the weight, allowing less force to be used to lift the object.
- ☑ The ideal mechanical advantage of an inclined plane is the length of the ramp divided by the height of the ramp.

Remember to use scientific methods.

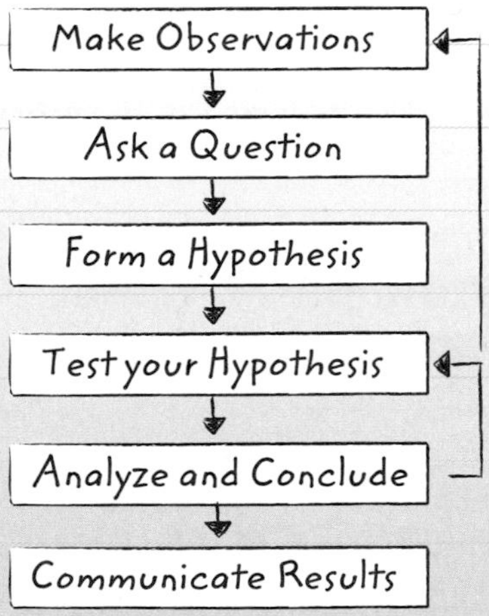

Chapter 3 Study Guide

THE BIG IDEA **A machine makes work easier by changing the size of the applied force, changing the distance over which the applied force acts, or changing the direction of the applied force.**

Key Concepts Summary

Lesson 1: Work and Power

- For **work** to be done on an object, an applied force must move the object in the direction of the force.
- When work is done on an object, the energy of the object increases.
- **Power** is the rate at which work is done.

Vocabulary

work p. 83
power p. 87

Lesson 2: Using Machines

- A machine can make work easier in three ways: changing the size of a force, changing the distance the force acts, or changing the direction of a force.
- The **mechanical advantage** of a machine is the ratio of the output force to the input force.
- Because of friction, the output work done by a machine is always less than the input work to the machine.
- Friction between moving parts converts some of the input work into thermal energy and decreases the **efficiency** of the machine.

Vocabulary

mechanical advantage p. 94
efficiency p. 95

Lesson 3: Simple Machines

- A **simple machine** does work using only one movement.
- The ideal mechanical advantage of simple machines is calculated using simple formulas.
- A compound machine is made up of two or more simple machines that operate together.

Vocabulary

simple machine p. 99
lever p. 100
fulcrum p. 100
wheel and axle p. 102
inclined plane p. 103
wedge p. 104
screw p. 104
pulley p. 105

Assessment
- Personal Tutor
- Vocabulary eGames
- Vocabulary eFlashcards

FOLDABLES® Chapter Project

Assemble your lesson Foldables as shown to make a Chapter Project. Use the project to review what you have learned in this chapter.

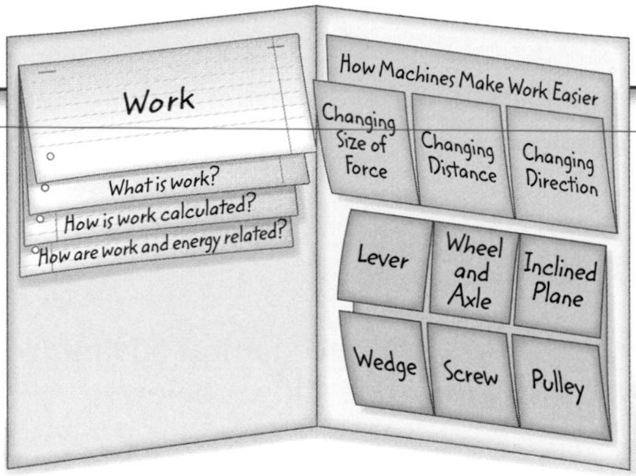

Use Vocabulary

Match each phrase with the correct vocabulary term from the Study Guide.

1. A wheel and axle is an example of a(n) ________.
2. As work is done more quickly, the ________ required increases.
3. A third-class lever has a(n) ________ that is always less than 1.
4. The ________ of a machine is always less than 100 percent.
5. A sloped road is an example of a(n) ________.
6. Your front teeth act like a(n) ________.
7. A(n) ________ is an inclined plane wrapped around a cylinder.

Concepts in Motion Interactive Concept Map

Link Vocabulary and Key Concepts

Copy this concept map, and then use vocabulary terms from the previous page and other terms in this chapter to complete the concept map.

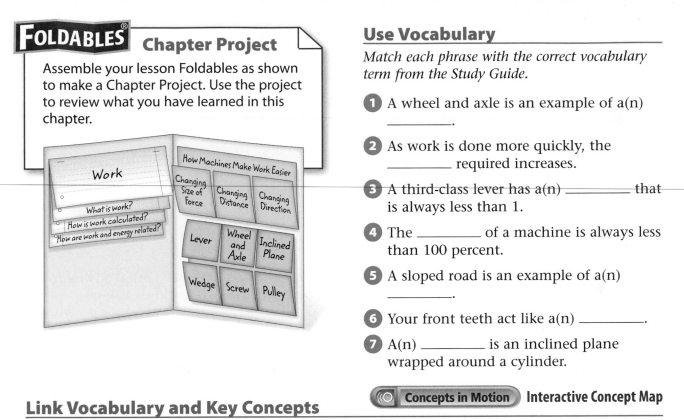

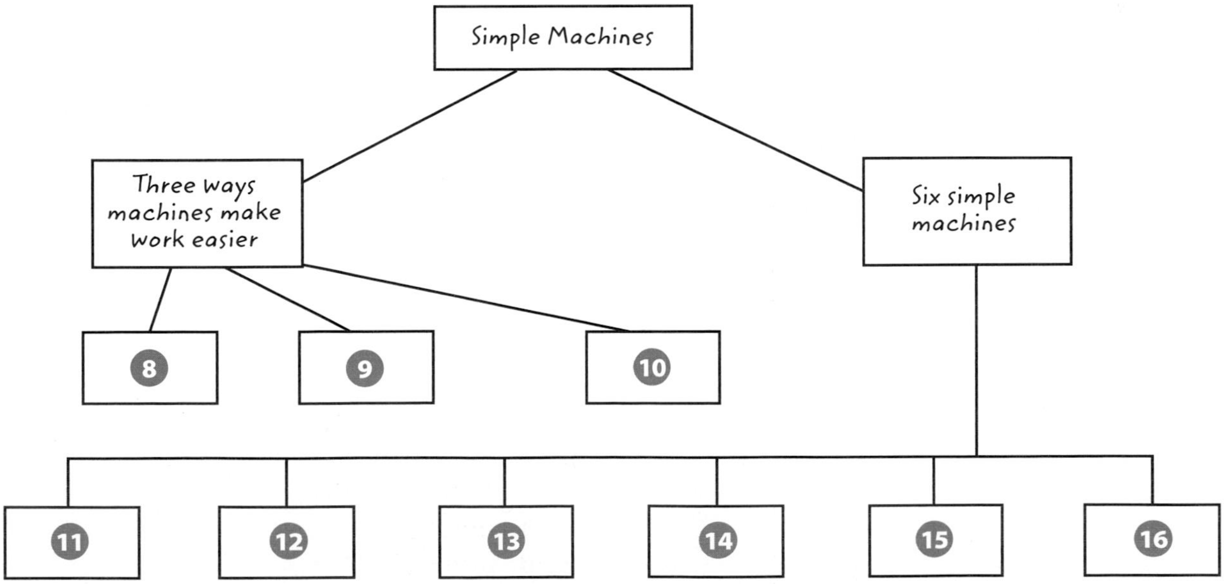

Chapter 3 Review

Understand Key Concepts

1. Which must be true when work is done?
   A. No force acts on the object.
   B. An object slows down.
   C. An object moves quickly.
   D. An object moves in the same direction as a force exerted on it.

2. Which must be true when work is done on a resting object and the object moves?
   A. The energy of the object changes.
   B. The energy of the object is constant.
   C. The force on the object is constant.
   D. The force on the object is zero.

3. Which increases the power used in lifting the backpack?
   A. lifting at a constant speed
   B. lifting at an angle
   C. lifting more quickly
   D. lifting a lighter backpack

4. Which does more work on an object?
   A. pushing a 50-N object a distance of 2 m
   B. pushing a 120-N object a distance of 7 m
   C. pushing a 150-N object a distance of 5 m
   D. pushing a 300-N object a distance of 1 m

5. Which must be true if a machine's mechanical advantage is equal to 2?
   A. Direction of force is changed.
   B. Output force equals input force.
   C. Output force is greater than input force.
   D. Output work is greater than input work.

6. Which is ideal mechanical advantage of the pulley system?
   A. 1
   B. 2
   C. 3
   D. 4

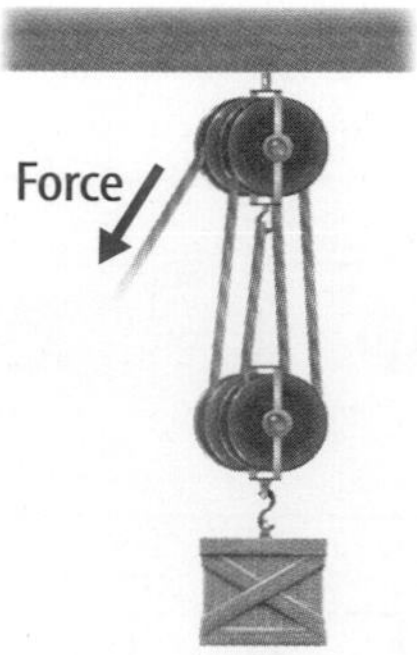

7. How does friction affect a machine?
   A. It converts input work into thermal energy.
   B. It converts output work into thermal energy.
   C. It converts thermal energy into input work.
   D. It converts thermal energy into output work.

8. Which is a simple machine?
   A. tweezers
   B. bicycle
   C. can opener
   D. car

9. What is the ideal mechanical advantage of the wheel and axle shown below?

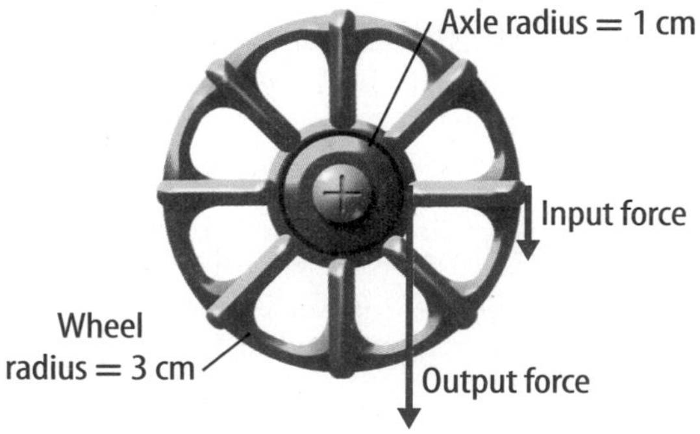

   A. 1
   B. 2
   C. 3
   D. 4

10. Which is most easily used as either a wheel and axle or as a lever?
   A. ax
   B. scissors
   C. screwdriver
   D. screw

11. Which quantity increases when a frictionless ramp is used to lift an object?
   A. input force
   B. input distance
   C. input work
   D. output work

Critical Thinking

12. **Contrast** the work done when you lift a box with the work done when you carry the box across a room.

13. **Analyze** Does a weight lifter transfer more energy, less energy, or the same amount of energy when lifting the weight faster? Explain.

14. **Decide** First you lift an object from the floor onto a shelf. Then, you move the object from the shelf back to the floor. Do you perform the same amount of work each time? Explain.

15. **Explain** why the output work done by a machine is never greater than the input work to the machine.

16. **Suggest** a reason the efficiency of a machine used in a factory might decrease over time. What could be done to increase the efficiency?

17. **Explain** Imagine using a screwdriver to drive a screw into a piece of wood. Explain why turning the handle of the screwdriver is easier than turning its shaft.

18. **Explain** Can you determine if work is being done on the backpack simply by looking at this photo? Explain why or why not.

Writing in Science

19. **Write** a paragraph about using an inclined plane on the Moon. Objects weigh less on the Moon because the force of gravity is less than on Earth. Explain whether this affects the mechanical advantage of the inclined plane or the way it is used.

REVIEW THE BIG IDEA

20. How do machines make doing work easier? Describe several examples of how machines change forces and make work easier to do.

21. Explain why the earthmover below uses more power than a person moving the same amount of dirt with a shovel.

Math Skills

Review Math Practice

Use Numbers

22. How much work is done when a force of 30 N moves an object a distance of 3 m?

23. How much power is used when 600 J of work is done in 10 s?

24. How much force would be needed to push a box weighing 30 N up a ramp that has a ideal mechanical advantage of 3? Assume there is no friction.

25. Calculate the efficiency of a machine that requires 20 J of input work to do 10 J of output work.

26. Calculate the mechanical advantage of a machine that changes an input force of 50 N into an output force of 150 N.

27. A compound machine is made up of four simple machines. If the efficiencies of the simple machines are 98%, 93%, 87%, and 92%, respectively, what is the overall efficiency of the compound machine?

Standardized Test Practice

Record your answers on the answer sheet provided by your teacher or on a sheet of paper.

Multiple Choice

1 Which is the SI unit of work?

A ampere
B joule
C newton
D watt

2 Which transfers both kinetic energy and potential energy to an object?

A lifting it
B lowering it
C pushing it
D rolling it

Use the chart below to answer questions 3 and 4.

Moving a Chair	
Force	20 newtons
Distance	5 meters
Time	2 seconds

3 How much work was involved in moving the chair?

A 4 J
B 10 J
C 40 J
D 100 J

4 How much power was used to move the chair?

A 10 W
B 20 W
C 50 W
D 200 W

5 Which is a third-class lever?

A a broom
B a hammer
C a nutcracker
D a wheelbarrow

Use the chart below to answer question 6.

Mechanical Advantage Equation
$\text{mechanical advantage} = \dfrac{\text{output force}}{?}$

6 Which correctly completes the mechanical advantage equation?

A distance
B time
C input force
D output work

7 A simple machine is NOT able to

A change the size of a force.
B decrease the amount of work required.
C exert an output force on an object.
D make work easier to perform.

8 Which MUST happen in order for work to be done?

A A force must move an object.
B A machine must transfer force.
C Force must be applied to an object.
D Output force must exceed input force.

9 Which increases the efficiency of a complex machine?

A adding more simple machines
B increasing input force
C putting more work in
D reducing friction by lubricating

Use the diagram below to answer question 10.

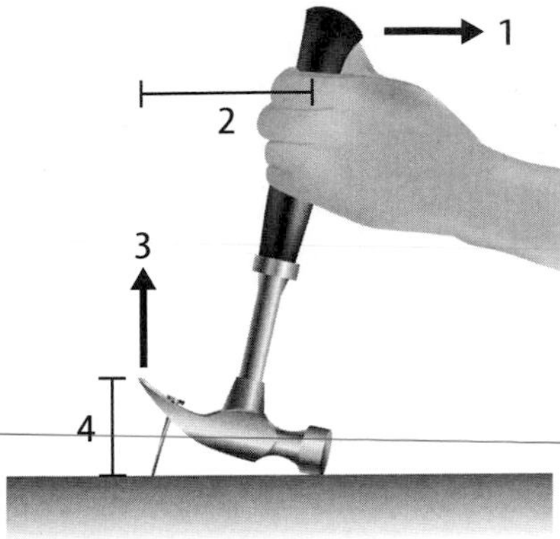

10 Which number represents the output distance in the diagram above?

A 1

B 2

C 3

D 4

11 What information is needed to calculate the ideal mechanical advantage of an inclined plane?

A its height and length

B its length and thickness

C its thickness and weight

D its weight and width

12 Which is a characteristic feature of a wedge?

A cable

B fulcrum

C slope

D thread

Constructed Response

Use the table below to answer questions 13 and 14.

Simple Machine	Example	Task
Lever		
Inclined plane		
Wheel and axle		
Pulley		
Wedge		
Screw		

13 In the table, the six types of simple machines are listed. Provide an example of each machine. Then, list an everyday task you have performed with the help of the machine.

14 How do each of the simple machines in the table above make work easier?

15 What is the difference between simple and compound machines?

16 Describe a real-life situation in which simple machines would make work easier. Identify two machines that would be helpful in the situation and explain how they would be used.

17 What two factors affect the amount of work done on an object? When does a force acting on an object NOT do work? Give an example.

NEED EXTRA HELP?																	
If You Missed Question...	1	2	3	4	5	6	7	8	9	10	11	12	13	14	15	16	17
Go to Lesson...	1	1	1	1	3	2	2	1	2	2	3	3	3	3	3	2,3	1

Chapter 4

Waves, Light, and Sound

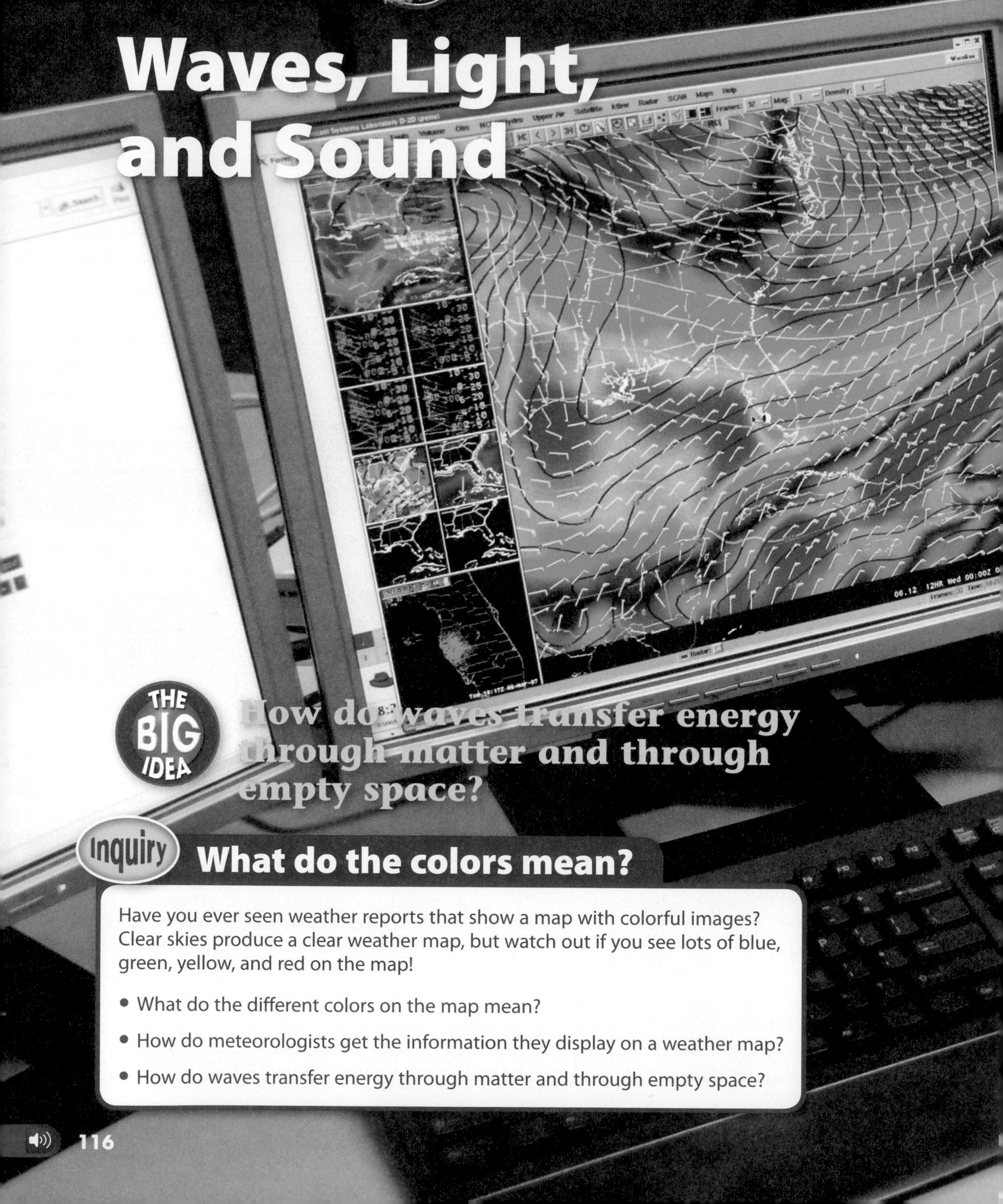

THE BIG IDEA How do waves transfer energy through matter and through empty space?

Inquiry: What do the colors mean?

Have you ever seen weather reports that show a map with colorful images? Clear skies produce a clear weather map, but watch out if you see lots of blue, green, yellow, and red on the map!

- What do the different colors on the map mean?
- How do meteorologists get the information they display on a weather map?
- How do waves transfer energy through matter and through empty space?

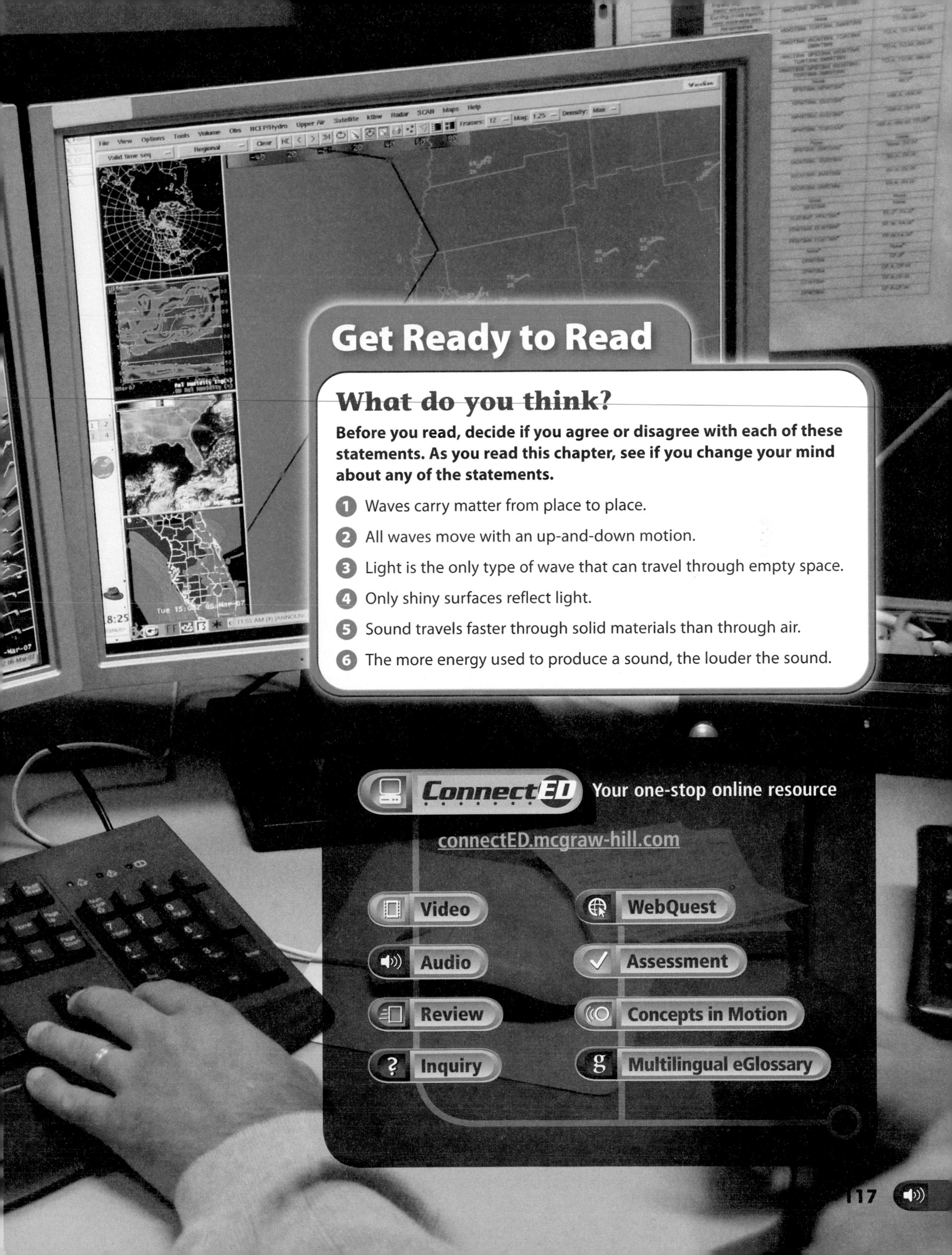

Get Ready to Read

What do you think?

Before you read, decide if you agree or disagree with each of these statements. As you read this chapter, see if you change your mind about any of the statements.

1. Waves carry matter from place to place.
2. All waves move with an up-and-down motion.
3. Light is the only type of wave that can travel through empty space.
4. Only shiny surfaces reflect light.
5. Sound travels faster through solid materials than through air.
6. The more energy used to produce a sound, the louder the sound.

ConnectED Your one-stop online resource

connectED.mcgraw-hill.com

- Video
- Audio
- Review
- Inquiry
- WebQuest
- Assessment
- Concepts in Motion
- Multilingual eGlossary

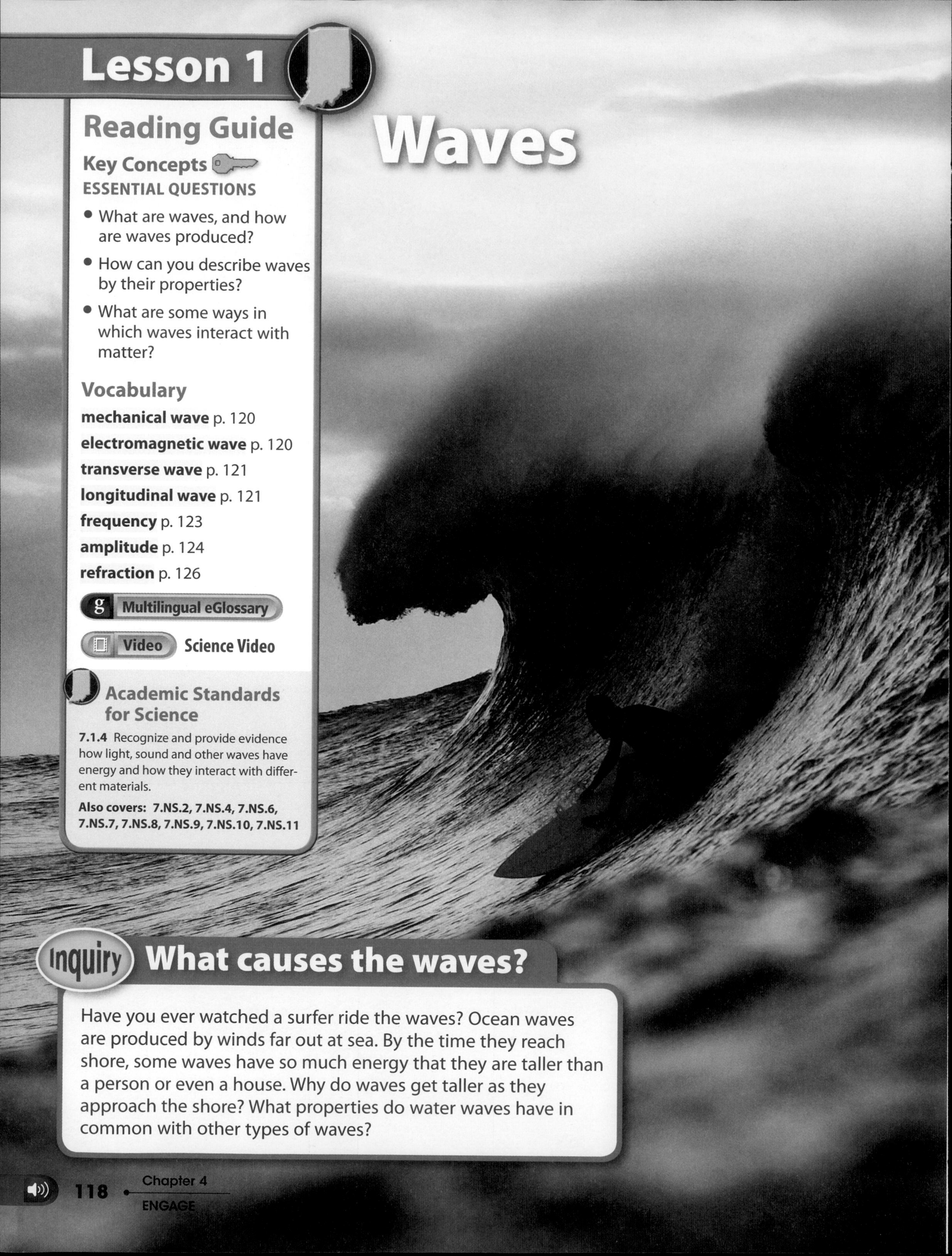

Lesson 1

Waves

Reading Guide

Key Concepts

ESSENTIAL QUESTIONS

- What are waves, and how are waves produced?
- How can you describe waves by their properties?
- What are some ways in which waves interact with matter?

Vocabulary

mechanical wave p. 120

electromagnetic wave p. 120

transverse wave p. 121

longitudinal wave p. 121

frequency p. 123

amplitude p. 124

refraction p. 126

g Multilingual eGlossary

Video Science Video

Academic Standards for Science

7.1.4 Recognize and provide evidence how light, sound and other waves have energy and how they interact with different materials.

Also covers: 7.NS.2, 7.NS.4, 7.NS.6, 7.NS.7, 7.NS.8, 7.NS.9, 7.NS.10, 7.NS.11

Inquiry What causes the waves?

Have you ever watched a surfer ride the waves? Ocean waves are produced by winds far out at sea. By the time they reach shore, some waves have so much energy that they are taller than a person or even a house. Why do waves get taller as they approach the shore? What properties do water waves have in common with other types of waves?

Inquiry Launch Lab

15 minutes

How do waves form?

You probably have seen water waves on the surface of a lake or a swimming pool. How are the waves produced?

1. Read and complete a lab safety form.
2. Place **books** under opposite edges of a **glass pan**. Add about 5 mm of water to the pan. Place a **sheet of white paper** under the pan. Wait until the water is still.
3. Place a **cork** in the water about halfway between the center and the edge of the pan. Dip your **pencil** tip into the center of the water one time. What happens to the cork? Record your observations of the water and the cork in a data table in your Science Journal.
4. Repeatedly tap your pencil tip on the surface of the water slowly. Record your observations.
5. Repeat step 4, tapping your pencil tip faster this time. Record your observations.

Think About This

1. How are the waves you produced in steps 3 and 4 alike? How are they different?
2. How does the behavior of the cork change in steps 4 and 5?
3. **Key Concept** What do you think is the source of the waves that you made?

What are waves?

A flag waves in the breeze. Ocean waves break onto a beach. You wave your hand at a friend. All of these actions have something in common. Waves always begin with a source of energy that causes a back-and-forth or up-and-down disturbance, or movement. In **Figure 1**, energy of the wind causes a disturbance in the flag. This disturbance moves along the length of the flag as a wave. A wave is a disturbance that transfers energy from one place to another without transferring matter.

Key Concept Check What are waves?

Energy Transfer

Wind transfers energy to the fabric in the flag. The flag ripples back and forth as the energy travels along the fabric. Notice that each point on the flag moves back and forth, but the fabric does not move along with the wave. Recall, waves only transfer energy, not matter, from place to place.

When you lift a pebble, you transfer energy to it. Suppose you drop the pebble into a pond. The pebble's energy transfers to the water. Waves carry the energy away from the point where the pebble hit the water. The water itself moves up and down as the wave passes, but the water does not move along with the wave.

Figure 1 The wave is a disturbance that transfers energy along the flag.

▲ **Figure 2** The energy of the falling pebble produces a mechanical wave.

Two Main Types of Waves

Some waves carry energy only through matter. Other types of waves can carry energy through matter or empty space.

Mechanical Waves *A wave that travels only through matter is a* **mechanical wave.** A medium is the matter through which a mechanical wave travels. A mechanical wave forms when a source of energy causes particles that make up a medium to vibrate. For example, a pebble falling into water transfers its kinetic energy to particles of the water, as shown in **Figure 2.** The water particles vibrate and push against nearby particles, transferring the energy outward. After each particle pushes the next particle, it returns to its original rest position. Energy is transferred, but the water particles are not.

WORD ORIGIN

mechanical
from Greek *mekhanikos,* means "like a machine"

Electromagnetic Waves *A wave that can travel through empty space or through matter is an* **electromagnetic wave.** This type of wave forms when a charged particle, such as an electron, vibrates. For example, electromagnetic waves transfer the Sun's energy to Earth through empty space. Once the waves reach Earth, they travel through matter, such as the atmosphere or a glass window of your house.

Key Concept Check How are waves produced?

REVIEW VOCABULARY

perpendicular
at right angles

Describing Wave Motion

Some waves move particles of a medium up and down or side to side, **perpendicular** to the direction the wave travels. For example, the waves in a flag move side to side, perpendicular to the direction the wind. Other wave disturbances move particles of the medium forward then backward in same direction, or parallel, to the motion of the wave. And last, some waves are a combination of both of these two types of motion. **Table 1** summarizes these three types of wave motion—transverse, longitudinal, or a combination of both.

Table 1 Electromagnetic waves are always transverse. Mechanical waves can be either transverse, longitudinal, or a combination of both. ▼

Table 1 Types of Wave Motion

Type of Wave Motion	Mechanical Waves	Electromagnetic Waves
Transverse—perpendicular to the direction the wave travels	✓ example: flag waving in a breeze	✓ example: light waves
Longitudinal—parallel to the direction the wave travels	✓ example: sound waves	
Combination—both transverse and longitudinal	✓ example: water waves	

Transverse Wave

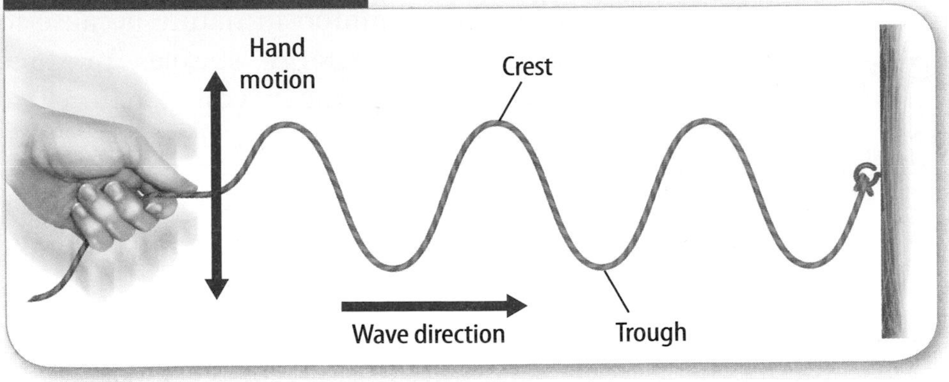

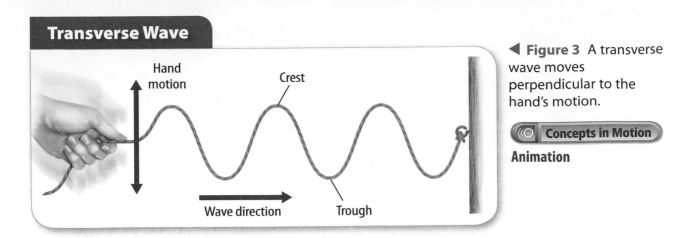

◀ **Figure 3** A transverse wave moves perpendicular to the hand's motion.

Concepts in Motion **Animation**

Transverse Waves *A wave in which the disturbance is perpendicular to the direction the wave travels is a* **transverse wave.** A breeze produces transverse waves in a flag. You can make transverse waves by attaching one end of a rope to a hook and holding the other end, as in **Figure 3.** When you move your hand up and down, transverse waves travel along the rope. High points on a wave are called crests. Low points are called troughs.

Recall that a vibrating charge, such as an electron, produces an electromagnetic wave. Electromagnetic waves are transverse waves. The electric and magnetic wave disturbances are perpendicular to the motion of the vibrating charge. You read that light is a form of energy transferred by transverse electromagnetic waves. X-rays and radio waves are two other examples.

FOLDABLES®

Make a vertical three-tab Venn book. Label it as shown. Use it to compare and contrast transverse and longitudinal waves.

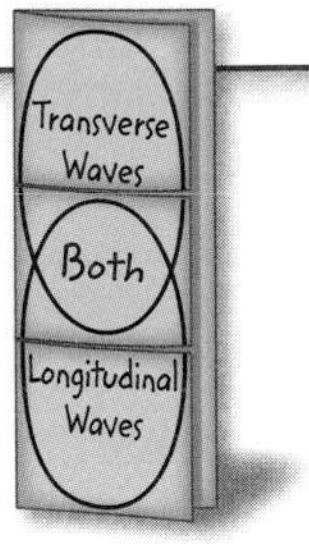

Longitudinal Waves *A wave that makes the particles of a medium move back and forth parallel to the direction the wave travels is a* **longitudinal wave.** Longitudinal waves are mechanical waves. Like a transverse wave, a longitudinal wave disturbance passes energy from particle to particle of a medium. For example, when you knock on a door, energy of your hand transfers to the particles that make up the door. The energy of the vibrating particles of the door is then transferred to the air in the next room. Also, you can make a longitudinal wave by pushing or pulling on a coiled spring toy, as in **Figure 4.** Pushing moves the coils closer together. Pulling spreads the coils apart.

Longitudinal Wave

Concepts in Motion **Animation**

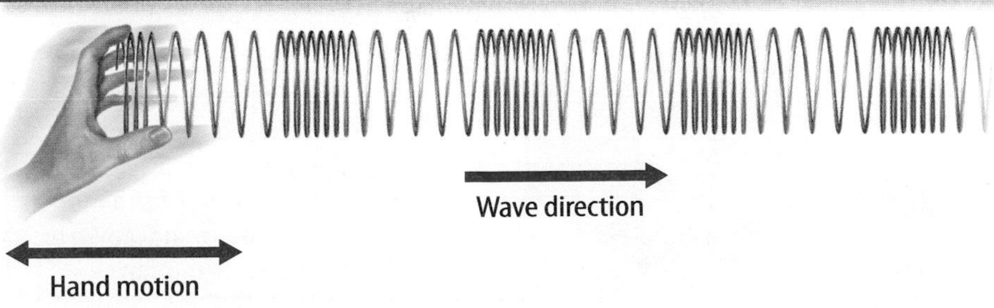

◀ **Figure 4** The back-and-forth motion of the hand causes a back-and-forth motion in the spring. The longitudinal waves move parallel to the hand's motion.

Water Waves

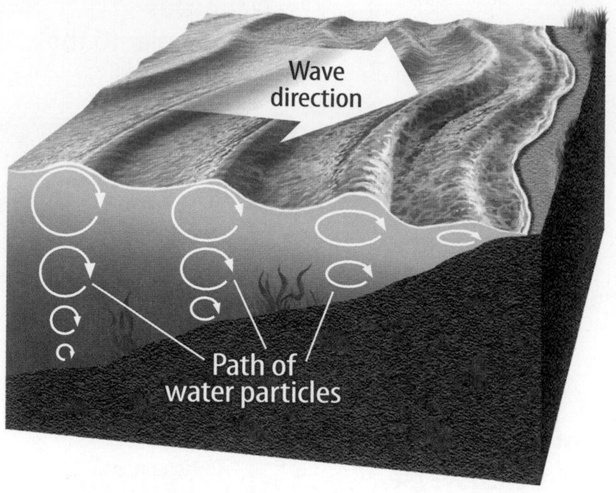

Figure 5 Waves cause water particles to move in small circles.

⊘**Visual Check** How is the path of the water particles near the water's surface different from the path near the ocean floor?

Figure 6 Seismic waves can be longitudinal, transverse, or a combination of the two. ▼

⊘**Visual Check** Which seismic wave is similar to a water wave?

((⊙)) **Concepts in Motion** Animation

Waves in Nature

Waves are common in nature because so many different energy sources produce waves. Two common waves in nature are water waves and seismic waves.

Water Waves Although water waves look like transverse waves, water particles move in circles, as shown in **Figure 5.** Water waves are a combination of transverse and longitudinal waves. Water particles move forward and backward. They also move up and down. The result is a circular path that gets smaller as the wave approaches land.

Water waves form because there is friction between the wind at sea and the water. Energy from the wind transfers to the water as the water moves toward land. Like all waves, water waves only transport energy. Because the waves move only through matter, water waves are mechanical waves.

Seismic Waves When layers of rock of Earth's crust suddenly shift, an earthquake occurs. The movement of rock sends out waves that travel to Earth's surface. An earthquake wave is called a seismic wave. As shown in **Figure 6,** there are different types of seismic waves. Seismic waves are mechanical waves because they move through matter.

Seismic Waves

P waves are longitudinal waves. They cause the ground to move back and forth, parallel to the direction the wave travels.

Particle movement

S waves are transverse waves. They cause the ground to move up and down or side to side, perpendicular to the direction the wave travels.

Particle movement

Surface waves are a combination of longitudinal and transverse waves. They have back-and-forth motion as well as up-and-down or side-to-side motion.

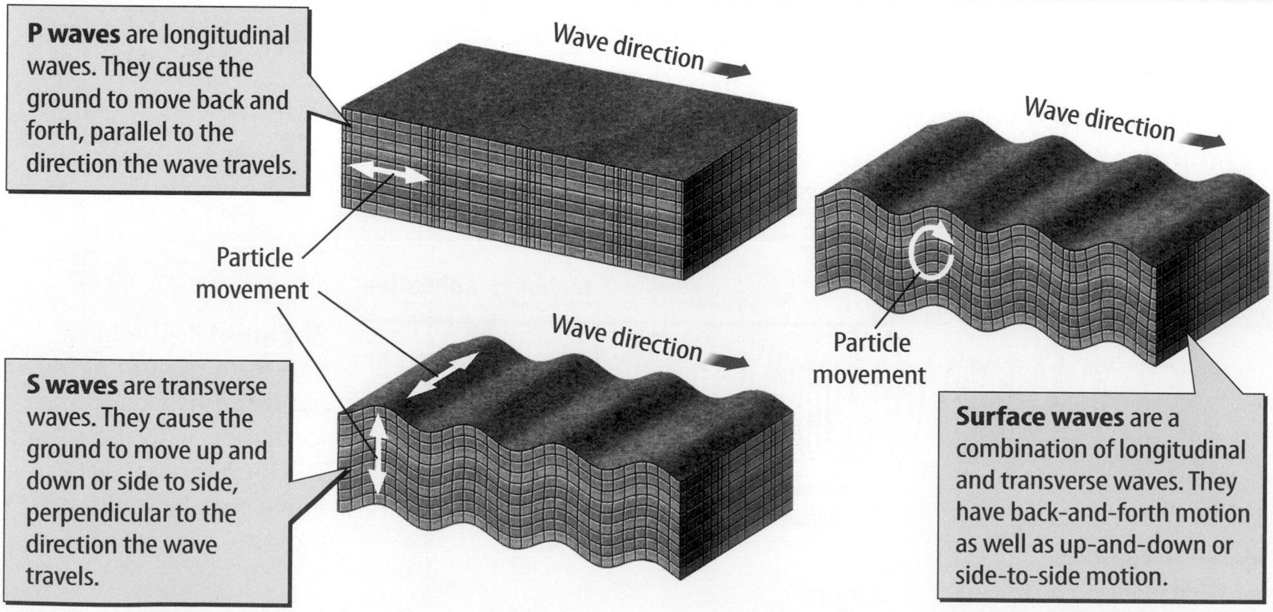

Inquiry MiniLab

15 minutes

How can you make waves with different properties?

Waves traveling through a spring can have different wavelengths and frequencies.

1. Read and complete a lab safety form.
2. Use **tape** to secure one end of a **spring toy** to your desk and the other end to the floor. Tie pieces of **string** to the spring 1/4, 1/2, and 3/4 of the way between the floor and the desk.
3. Pull a few of the lowest coils on the spring toy to the right. Release. Record your observations in your Science Journal.
4. Slowly tap the bottom of the spring toward the right. Repeat, this time doubling your rate of tapping. Record your observations.
5. Push down the bottom 5 cm of the spring toy. Release. Repeat, this time pushing down the bottom 10 cm. Record your observations.

Analyze and Conclude

1. **Compare** the movement of the pieces of string in step 4 and in step 5.
2. **Classify** the types of waves you made in steps 3–5 as transverse or longitudinal.
3. **Key Concept** What do the waves transfer up and down the spring toy?

Properties of Waves

How could you describe water waves at a beach? You might describe properties such as the height or the speed of the wave. When scientists describe waves, they describe the properties of wavelength and frequency.

Wavelength

The distance between a point on one wave, such as the crest, and the same point on the next wave is called the wavelength. Different types of waves can have wavelengths that range from thousands of kilometers to less than the size of an atom!

Frequency

The number of wavelengths that pass a point each second is a wave's **frequency.** Frequency is measured in hertz (Hz). One hertz equals one wave per second. As shown in **Figure 7,** the longer the wavelength, the lower the frequency. As the distance between the crests gets shorter, the number of waves passing a point each second increases.

Reading Check What is frequency?

Figure 7 You can describe the wavelength and the frequency of both transverse and longitudinal waves.

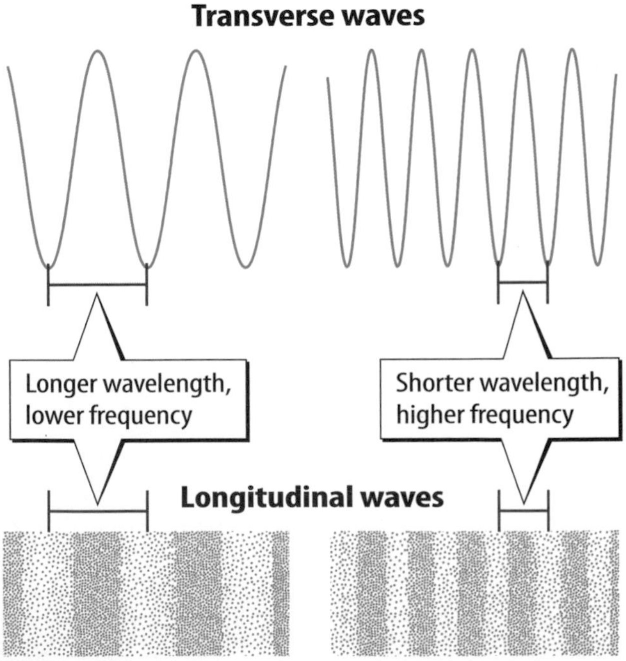

Table 2 Wave Speeds

Type of Wave	Typical wave speed (m/s)
Ocean wave	25
Sound wave in air	340
Transverse seismic wave (S wave)	1,000 to 8,000
Longitudinal seismic wave (P wave)	1,000 to 14,000
Electromagnetic wave through empty space	300,000,000

▲ **Table 2** The speed of a wave depends on the type of wave and the medium through which the wave travels.

Wave Speed

A wave's speed depends on the medium, or type of material, through which it travels. Electromagnetic waves always travel through empty space at the same speed, 3×10^8 m/s. That's 300 million meters each second! They travel slower through a medium, or matter, because they must interact with particles. Mechanical waves also travel slower through matter because the waves transfer energy from one particle to another. For example, sound waves travel about one-millionth the speed of light waves. The speed of water waves depends on the strength of the wind that produces them. **Table 2** compares the speeds of different types of waves.

Amplitude and Energy

Different waves carry different amounts of energy. Some earthquakes, for example, are catastrophic because they carry so much energy. A shift in Earth's crust can cause particles in the crust to vibrate back and forth very far from their rest positions, producing seismic waves. In January 2010, seismic waves in Haiti transferred enough energy to destroy entire cities.

A wave's **amplitude** *is the maximum distance a wave varies from its rest position.* For mechanical waves, amplitude is the maximum distance the particles of the medium move from their rest positions as a wave passes. The more energy a mechanical wave has, the larger its amplitude. The amplitude of a transverse mechanical wave is shown in **Figure 8.**

Key Concept Check How can you describe waves?

Figure 8 As more energy is used to produce a mechanical wave, particles of a medium vibrate farther from their rest positions. ▶

Amplitude and Energy

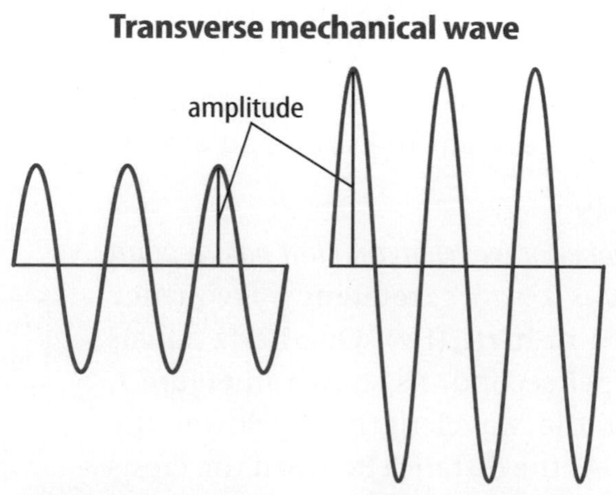

Wave Interaction with Matter

You have read that when you knock on a door, longitudinal sound waves transfer the energy of the knock through the door. However, when a person in the next room hears the knock, it is not as loud as the sound on your side of the door. The sound is weaker after it passes through the door because the waves interact with the matter that makes up the door.

Transmission

Some of the sound from your knock passes through the door. The waves transmit, or carry, the energy all the way through the door. The energy then passes into air particles, and the person on the other side hears the knock.

Absorption

Some of the sound is absorbed by the particles that make up the door. Instead of passing through the door, the energy increases the motion of the particles of the wood. The sound energy changes to thermal energy within the door. Therefore, less sound energy passes into the air in the next room.

Reflection

Some of the energy you used to knock on the door reflects, or bounces back, into the room you are in. Sound waves in the air transfer sound back to your ears. **Figure 9** shows how the energy of electromagnetic waves can also be transmitted, absorbed, or reflected.

Reading Check What are transmission, absorption, and reflection?

Transmission, Absorption, and Reflection

Figure 9 As waves travel, some of the energy they carry is transmitted, some is absorbed, and some is reflected by the particles in matter.

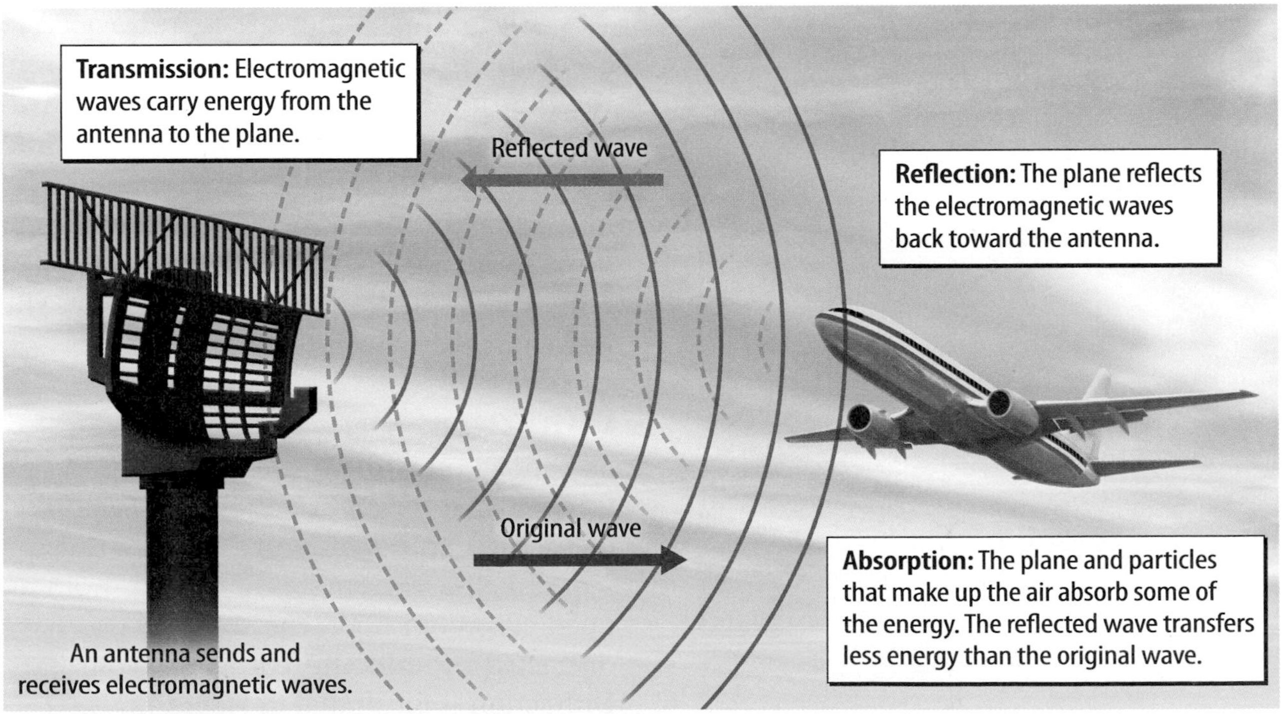

Transmission: Electromagnetic waves carry energy from the antenna to the plane.
Reflected wave
Reflection: The plane reflects the electromagnetic waves back toward the antenna.
Original wave
Absorption: The plane and particles that make up the air absorb some of the energy. The reflected wave transfers less energy than the original wave.
An antenna sends and receives electromagnetic waves.

Visual Check Does all of the energy reflected from the plane return to the antenna? Why or why not?

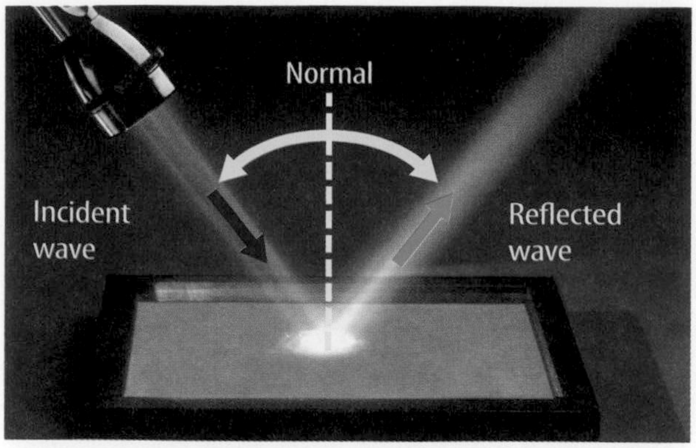

▲ **Figure 10** The law of reflection describes the direction of a reflected wave.

Concepts in Motion **Animation**

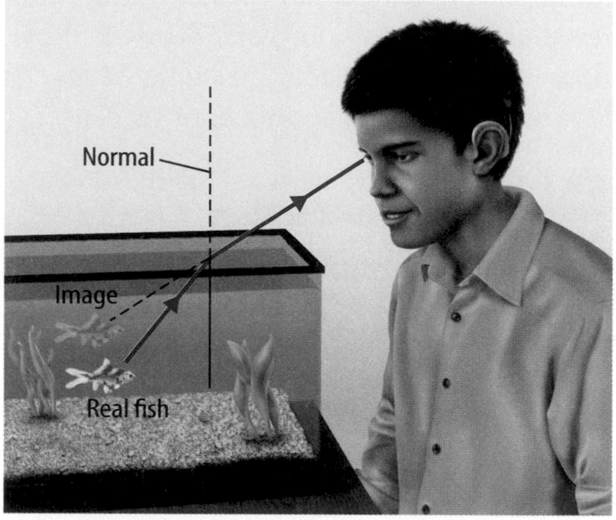

▲ **Figure 11** Refraction causes the fish to appear in a place different from its real location.

Review **Personal Tutor**

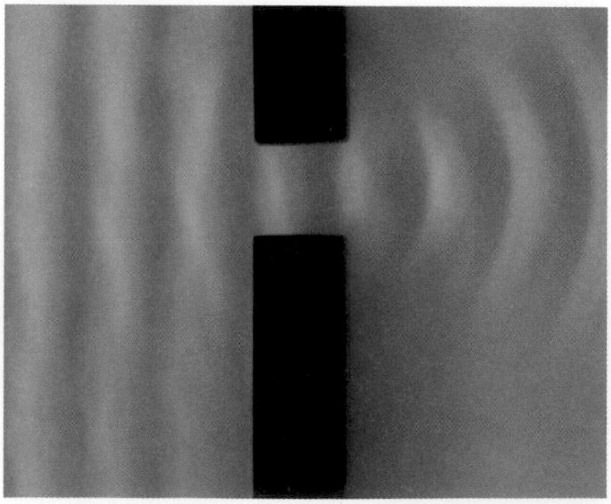

▲ **Figure 12** Diffraction causes waves to spread around barriers and through openings.

Law of Reflection

You can predict how waves will reflect from a smooth surface. The red arrow in **Figure 10** represents a light wave approaching a surface at an angle. This is called the incident wave. The blue arrow represents the reflected wave. The dotted line perpendicular to the surface at the point where the wave hits the surface is the normal. The law of reflection states that the angle between the incident wave and the normal always equals the angle between the reflected wave and the normal. If the incident angle in **Figure 10** increases, the reflected angle also increases.

Refraction

The change in direction of a wave as it changes speed, moving from one medium into another, is called **refraction.** The image of the fish in **Figure 11** is an example. Light reflects off the fish in all directions. The light speeds up as it moves from water into air. Notice that the light refracts away from the normal, or the line perpendicular to the surface at which the wave moves from one medium to other. This is the light the boy sees. His brain assumes the light traveled in a straight line. The light seems to come from the position of the image. Note that waves only refract if they move at an angle into another medium. They do not refract if they move straight into a medium. Waves refract toward the normal if they slow down when entering a medium and away from the normal if they speed up.

Diffraction

Diffraction is the change in direction of a wave when it travels past the edge of an object or through an opening. If you walk down a school hall and hear sound coming from an open classroom door, the sound waves have diffracted around the corner to your ears. Diffraction is illustrated in **Figure 12.**

Key Concept Check What are some ways in which waves interact with matter?

Lesson 1 Review

Assessment Online Quiz
Inquiry Virtual Lab

Visual Summary

A wave is a disturbance that transfers energy from one place to another without transferring matter.

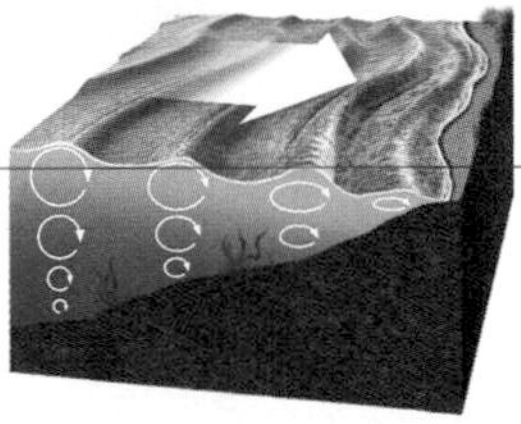

A wave can have a disturbance parallel or perpendicular to the direction the wave travels. Some waves are a combination of the two directions.

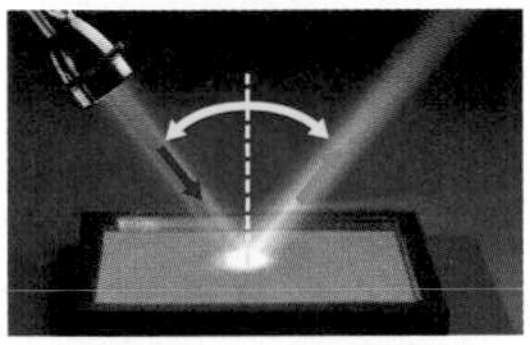

Waves can interact with matter by reflection, refraction, and diffraction.

FOLDABLES®

Use your lesson Foldable to review the lesson. Save your Foldable for the project at the end of the chapter.

What do you think NOW?

You first read the statements below at the beginning of the chapter.

1. Waves carry matter from place to place.
2. All waves move with an up-and-down motion.

Did you change your mind about whether you agree or disagree with the statements? Rewrite any false statements to make them true.

Use Vocabulary

1. **Define** *longitudinal wave* in your own words.
2. A wave that can travel through both matter and empty space is a(n) ________.

Understand Key Concepts

3. In which type of wave does the medium travel in a circular motion?
   A. electromagnetic **C.** transverse
   B. longitudinal **D.** water
4. **Identify** what produces a mechanical wave. An electromagnetic wave?
5. **Compare and contrast** how transmission, reflection, and absorption affect a wave.

Interpret Graphics

6. **Identify** The picture below shows a light ray bouncing off a flat surface. What is the correct scientific term for this interaction?

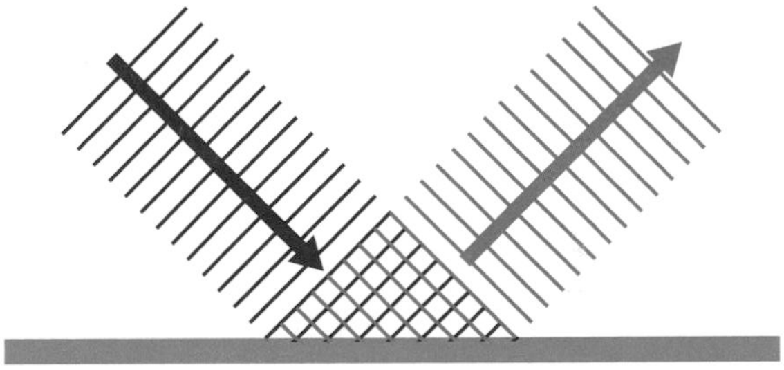

7. **Organize** Copy and fill in the graphic organizer below. In each oval, list a way in which waves can interact with matter.

Critical Thinking

8. **Decide** A forest fire makes a loud roaring sound. The explosive processes that release energy from the Sun occur at a much higher temperature. Why don't you hear a roaring sound from the Sun?

Inquiry **Skill Practice** **Observe** 30 minutes

How do water waves interact with matter?

Materials

9-in. × 13-in. glass pan

sponges cut into thin strips

plastic snap-together blocks

adhesive putty

2-cm wooden dowel

Also needed: 2 books, white paper

Safety

You can use a ripple tank to observe waves with different properties. Think about how waves interact with matter and with each other. How can you change the properties of the waves?

Learn It

Scientists **observe** items and events and then record what they see. When you make observations, you should carefully look for details and then record your observations accurately and completely.

Try It

1. Read and complete a lab safety form.
2. Make a ripple tank by placing books under opposite edges of a glass pan. Secure the edges with putty. Pour water into the pan until it is about 5 mm deep. Place a sheet of white paper under the pan. Lay strips of sponge inside the short ends of the pan to absorb wave energy. Lay a dowel in the opposite end of the pan.
3. Tap the dowel with your finger to make a series of waves. Observe properties of the waves. Increase and decrease the wavelength of your waves. Explain in your Science Journal how you changed the wavelength.
4. Make barriers from snap-together blocks. Place the barriers end-to-end in your ripple tank at an angle to the dowel, as shown in the photo. What will happen to waves that hit against the barrier? Try it, and then change the angle of the barrier and repeat. Record your observations.
5. Place the barrier in the middle of the pan, parallel to the dowel, with a small space between the two parts. Demonstrate diffraction by making waves with different frequencies move through the space between the barriers. Observe how the waves change when they move through the space. Repeat, increasing the distance between the barriers. Record your observations.

Apply It

6. **Describe** How does changing the barrier's angle change the waves?
7. **Draw a diagram** of the waves passing between the two barriers.
8. **Predict** Place the barriers in a new formation in your tank. Predict the behavior of the waves. Draw a diagram of your setup and your prediction. How well were you able to foresee what the waves were going to do?
9. **Key Concept** Summarize your observations of wave reflection and diffraction in your investigation.

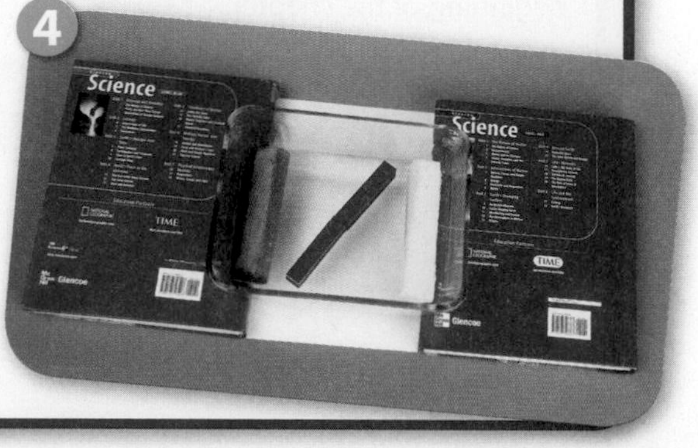

Lesson 2

Light

Reading Guide

Key Concepts
ESSENTIAL QUESTIONS

- How does light differ from other forms of electromagnetic waves?
- What are some ways in which light interacts with matter?
- How do eyes change light waves into the images you see?

Vocabulary

radio wave p. 131
infrared wave p. 132
ultraviolet wave p. 132
transparent p. 134
translucent p. 134
opaque p. 134
intensity p. 136

g Multilingual eGlossary

Video
- **BrainPOP®**
- **Science Video**
- **What's Science Got to do With It?**

Academic Standards for Science

7.1.4 Recognize and provide evidence how light, sound and other waves have energy and how they interact with different materials.

Also covers: 7.NS.4, 7.NS.7, 7.NS.11, 7.DP.5, 7.DP.7, 7.DP.11

Inquiry Spreading Light?

Thick trees in a forest can block much of the sunlight, but some light still shines through. Why do you see bands of dim and bright light? Like all electromagnetic waves, light travels in straight lines. But light that moves past the trees can scatter and spread out.

Inquiry Launch Lab

15 minutes

Can you see the light?

When light travels through a medium, it interacts with the particles of the medium. Each material affects light differently.

1. Read and complete a lab safety form.
2. Obtain a **collection of materials** from your teacher. Make a two-column data table in your Science Journal. Write the headings *Material* above the left column and *Estimated Percentage of Light That Passes Through* above the right column. List each of your materials in the left column.
3. Shine a **flashlight** through one of the materials. Observe how much of the light passes through.
4. Estimate the percentage of light that passes through the material. Record your estimate in the data table.
5. Repeat steps 3 and 4 for each of the remaining materials.
6. Rank each material in order from the one that allows the most light to pass through to the one that allows the least amount of light to pass through.

Think About This

1. Which material allows the most light to pass through? Why?
2. What happens to the light when you shine your flashlight on the material you ranked number 3?
3. **Key Concept** Summarize ways in which you think the materials affect the light.

What are light waves?

You have read that there are two main types of waves—mechanical and electromagnetic. Mechanical waves move only through matter, but electromagnetic waves can move through matter and through empty space. Now you will read about different types of electromagnetic waves. The most familiar type of electromagnetic wave is light.

Recall that vibrating charged particles produce electromagnetic waves with many different wavelengths. Only a narrow **range** of these wavelengths are detected by most people's eyes. This small range of electromagnetic waves is what is known as light. Light waves and other forms of electromagnetic waves differ in wavelength and frequency.

ACADEMIC VOCABULARY
range
(noun) a set of values from least to greatest

An object that produces light is a luminous object. The Sun is Earth's major source of visible light. Almost half the Sun's energy that reaches Earth is visible light. Other luminous objects include lightbulbs and objects that produce light as they burn, such as a campfire.

Key Concept Check How does light differ from other forms of electromagnetic waves?

The Electromagnetic Spectrum

Light is just a one type of electromagnetic wave. There is a wide range of electromagnetic waves that make up the electromagnetic spectrum, shown in **Figure 13.** Besides light, you encounter several other types of electromagnetic waves every day, and they probably play an important role in your life.

Types of Electromagnetic Waves

The electromagnetic spectrum consists of seven main types of waves. These waves range from low-energy, long-wavelength radio waves to very high-energy, short-wavelength gamma rays. Notice the relationship between wavelength, frequency, and energy indicated by the arrows in **Figure 13.** As the wavelength of electromagnetic waves decreases, the wave frequency increases. Low-frequency electromagnetic waves carry low amounts of energy, and high-frequency waves carry high amounts of energy.

Radio Waves *A low-frequency, low-energy electromagnetic wave that has a wavelength longer than about 30 cm is called a* **radio wave.** Radio waves have the least amount of energy of any electromagnetic wave. On Earth, radio and television transmitters produce radio waves that carry radio and television signals.

Microwaves You might use microwaves to cook your food. Microwaves also carry cell phone signals. Wavelengths of microwaves range from about 1 mm to 30 cm. Microwaves easily pass through smoke, light rain, and clouds, which makes them useful for transmitting information by satellites. Weather radar systems reflect microwaves off rain or storm clouds to detect and calculate the storm's distance and motion. Then, these calculations are used to make weather maps like the one shown on the first page of this chapter.

The Electromagnetic Spectrum

Review Personal Tutor

Figure 13 Electromagnetic waves have different wavelengths, frequencies, and energy.

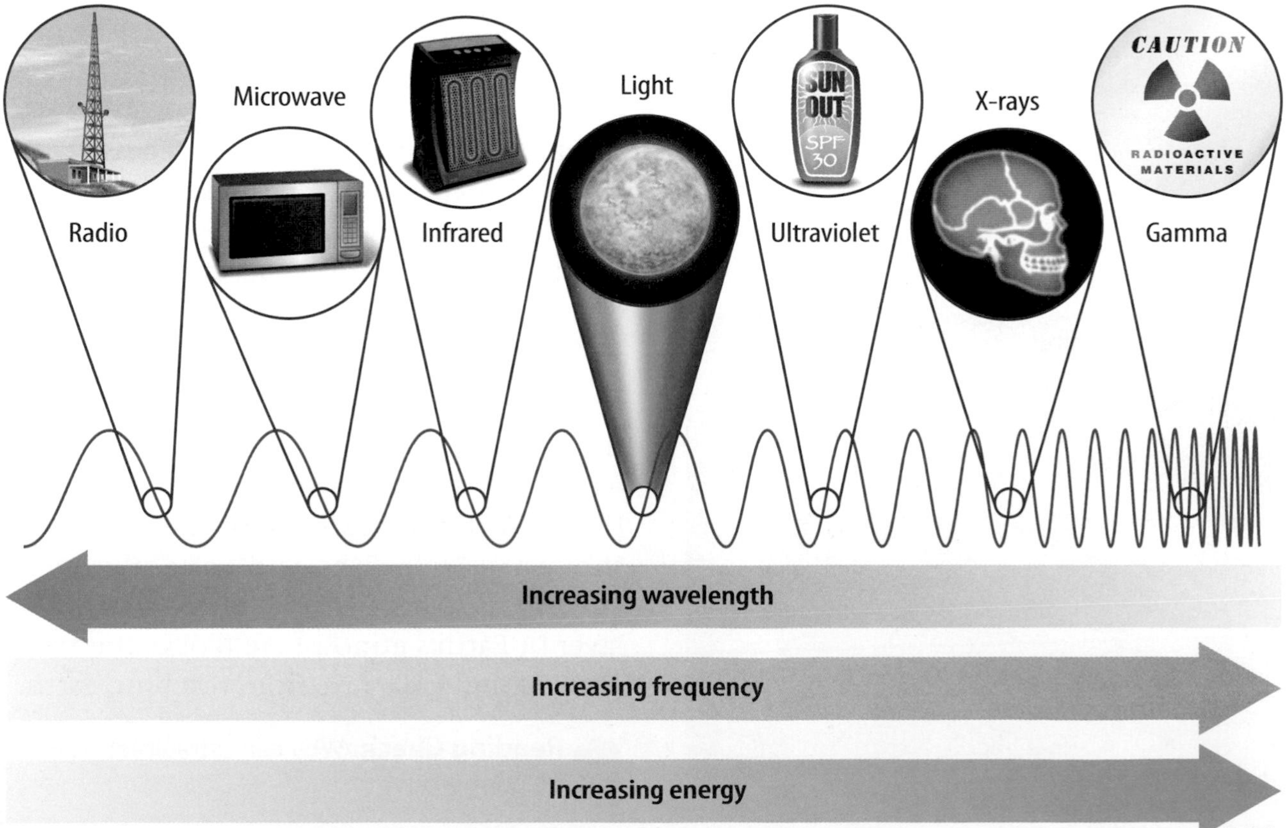

▲ **Figure 14** Infrared waves travel outward in all directions from the campfire.

Word Origin

infrared
from Latin *infra*, means "below"; and *ruber*, means "red"

ultraviolet
from Latin *ultra*, means "beyond"; and *viola*, means "violet"

Figure 15 The ozone layer protects Earth from the most dangerous ultraviolet waves from the Sun. ▼

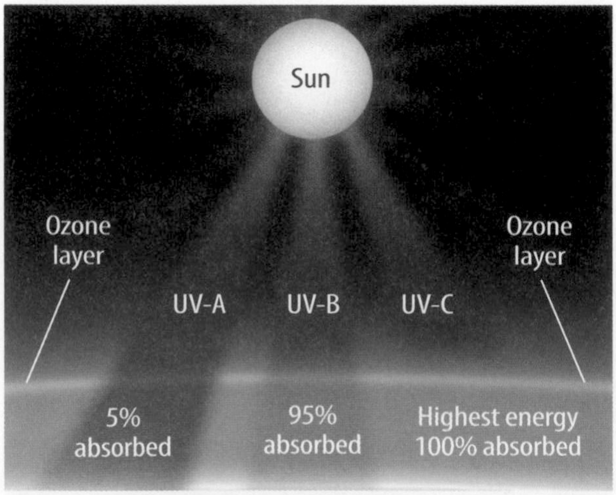

Light When you turn on a lamp or stand in sunshine, you probably don't think about waves entering your eyes. However, as you have read, light is a type of electromagnetic wave that the eyes detect. Light includes a range of wavelengths. You will read later in this lesson how this range of wavelengths relates to various properties of light.

Infrared Waves *An electromagnetic wave with a wavelength shorter than a microwave but longer than light is an* **infrared wave.** When you sit near a heater or a campfire, as in **Figure 14,** infrared waves transfer energy to your skin, and you feel warm. The Sun is Earth's major source of infrared waves. However, vibrating molecules in any type of matter, including your body, emit infrared waves.

Reading Check How do infrared waves and microwaves differ?

Ultraviolet Waves *An electromagnetic wave with a slightly shorter wavelength and higher frequency than light is an* **ultraviolet wave.** Electromagnetic waves with shorter wavelengths carry more energy than those with longer wavelengths and, therefore, can be harmful to living things. You might have heard that ultraviolet waves, or UV rays, from the Sun can be dangerous. These waves carry enough energy to cause particles of matter to combine or break apart and form other types of matter. Exposure to high levels of these waves can damage your skin.

Ultraviolet waves from the Sun are sometimes labeled UV-A, UV-B, or UV-C based on their wavelengths. UV-A have the longest wavelengths and the least energy. UV-C are the most dangerous because they have the shortest wavelengths and carry the most energy. As shown in **Figure 15,** the ozone layer in Earth's atmosphere blocks the Sun's most harmful UV rays from reaching Earth.

Reading Check Why can ultraviolet waves be dangerous?

▲ **Figure 16** X-rays are useful for security scans because they have enough energy to pass through soft parts of luggage.

Visual Check How do the views of hard parts and soft parts of luggage differ in this X-ray image?

X-rays High-energy electromagnetic waves that have slightly shorter wavelengths and higher frequencies than ultraviolet waves are X-rays. These waves can be very powerful. They have enough energy to pass through skin and muscle, but denser bone can stop them. This makes them useful for taking pictures of the inside of the body. Airport scanners, as in **Figure 16,** sometimes use X-rays to take pictures of the contents of luggage.

Gamma Rays Electromagnetic waves produced by vibrations within the nucleus of an atom are called gamma rays. They have shorter wavelengths and higher frequencies than any other form of electromagnetic wave. Gamma rays carry so much energy that they can penetrate about 10 cm of lead, one of the densest elements. On Earth, gamma rays are produced by radioactive elements and nuclear reactions.

Reading Check Why do you think gamma rays cannot be used for communication in the same way radio waves are used?

Electromagnetic Waves from the Sun

The Sun produces an enormous amount of energy that is carried outward in all directions as electromagnetic waves. Because Earth is so far from the Sun, Earth receives less than one-billionth of the Sun's energy. However, if all the Sun's energy that reaches Earth in a 20-minute period could be transformed to useful energy, it could power the entire Earth for a year!

As shown in **Figure 17,** about 44 percent of the Sun's energy that reaches Earth is carried by light waves, and about 49 percent is carried by infrared waves. About 7 percent is carried by ultraviolet waves. Radio waves, microwaves, X-rays, and gamma rays carry less than 1 percent of the Sun's energy.

Figure 17 Infrared waves, light, and ultraviolet waves carry almost all of the Sun's energy. ▼

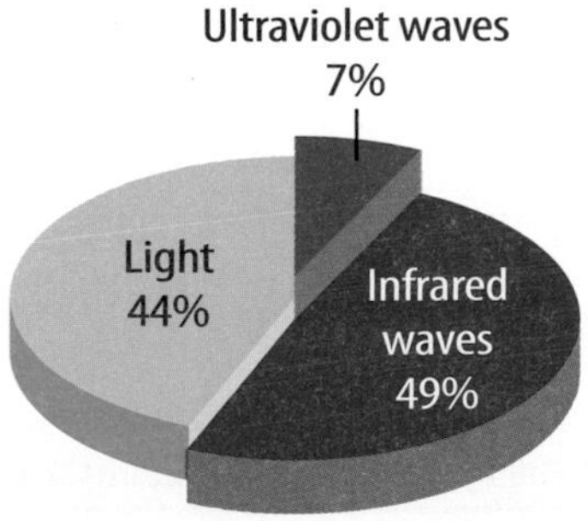

Speed, Wavelength, and Frequency

How could you describe the light from stars or the lights in a city at night? You might use words like *bright* or *dim*, or you might describe the color of the lights. You also could say how easily the light moves through a material. People use properties to describe light and to distinguish one color of light from another.

Like all types of electromagnetic waves, light travels at a speed of 3×10^8 m/s in empty space. When light enters a medium, or matter, it slows down. This is because of the interaction between the waves and the particles that make up the matter.

The wavelength and the frequency of a light wave determine the color of the light. The average human eye can distinguish among millions of wavelengths, or colors. Reds have the longest wavelengths and the lowest frequencies of light. Colors at the violet end of the visible light spectrum have the shortest wavelengths and the highest frequencies.

Light and Matter Interact

In Lesson 1, you read that matter can transmit, absorb, or reflect waves. How do these interactions affect light that travels from a source to your eyes?

Transmission

Air and clear glass, as shown in **Figure 18,** transmit light with little or no distortion. *A material that allows almost all of the light striking it to pass through, and through which objects can be seen clearly is* **transparent.**

Materials such as waxed paper or frosted glass also transmit light, but you cannot see through them clearly. *A material that allows most of the light that strikes it to pass through, but through which objects appear blurry is* **translucent.**

Absorption

Some materials absorb most of the light that strikes them. They transmit no light. Therefore, you cannot see objects through them. *A material through which light does not pass is* **opaque.**

Interactions of Light and Matter

Figure 18 Materials transmit, absorb, and reflect different amounts of light. This determines whether the material is transparent, translucent, or opaque.

Translucent
The upper part of this window contains panes of translucent frosted glass. Light that moves through the glass is scattered. Sometimes you can see colors and vague images through translucent materials, but it is difficult to determine what the shapes are.

Opaque
You cannot see through the window frame because the material is opaque. All of the light that strikes the material is either absorbed or reflected. The color of the frame is brown because it contains pigments that reflect wavelengths of brown light and absorb all other wavelengths of light.

Transparent
You can see clearly through a material such as this window glass because it is transparent. Light moves through the material without being scattered.

Reflection

Why can you see your reflection clearly in a mirror, but not in the wall of your room? Recall that waves reflect off surfaces according to the law of reflection. Parallel rays that reflect from a smooth surface remain parallel and form a clear image. Light that reflects from a bumpy surface scatters in many directions. A wall seems smooth, but up close it is too bumpy to form a clear image.

Different types of matter interact with light in different ways. For example, the window in **Figure 18** both transmits and reflects light. Some of the light that strikes an opaque object, such as a book, is absorbed and reflected at the same time. Reflected light allows an object to be seen.

Key Concept Check How does light interact with matter?

Color

The colors of an object depends on the wavelengths of light that enters the eye. A luminous object, such as a campfire, is the color of light that it emits. If an object is not luminous, its perceived color depends on other factors.

Opaque Objects Suppose white light strikes an American flag. The blue background absorbs all wavelengths of light except blue. The blue wavelengths reflect back to your eye. The red stripes absorb all colors but red, and red reflects to your eye. The white stars and stripes reflect all colors. You see white. An opaque object is the color it reflects, as shown in **Figure 19.**

Transparent and Translucent Objects If you look at a white lightbulb through a filter of red plastic wrap, only red wavelengths are transmitted through the plastic. The red plastic absorbs other wavelengths. Therefore, the lightbulb appears to be red. .

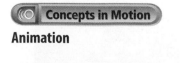

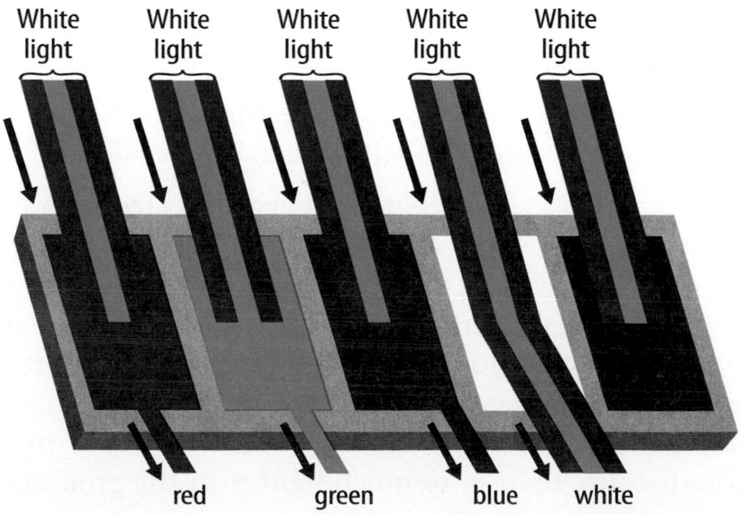

Figure 19 The color of an opaque object is the color of the light that reflects off the object. White objects reflect all colors of light. Black objects absorb all colors. Common black objects are visible because they actually reflect a small amount of light.

Concepts in Motion

Animation

Inquiry MiniLab

20 minutes

What color is the puppet?

An object's color depends on the materials it is made of. Does the color of light shining on an object have any effect?

1. Read and complete a lab safety form.
2. Copy the data table into your Science Journal.
3. Make a red filter by adding three drops of **red food coloring** to 100 mL of water in a **beaker.** Make blue and green filters using **blue and green food coloring.** With **scissors,** cut puppets out of **white and green paper.**
4. Turn off the lights. Shine a **flashlight** through the red water filter onto the white puppet. Record the puppet's color in the table.
5. Repeat step 4 using the colored filters listed in the table. When using more than one color of light, align the beakers so light moves through both and onto the puppet. Record your observations in the data table.

Light	Original Puppet Color	Observed Puppet Color
Red	White	
Green	White	
Blue	White	
Red	Green	
Green	Green	
Blue	Green	
Red and blue	White	
Red and blue	Green	
Red and green	White	
Red and green	Green	

Analyze and Conclude

1. **Model** Draw a picture showing whether each color of light was reflected or absorbed by the green puppet.
2. **Key Concept** How does the interaction of light and matter affect the puppet colors?

Figure 20 Light from nearby buildings and other sources can prevent you from seeing stars in the sky.

Intensity of Light

Another property you can use to describe light is intensity. **Intensity** *is the amount of energy that passes through a square meter of space in one second.* Intensity depends on the amount of energy a source emits. Light from a flashlight, for example, has a much lower intensity than light from the Sun. Intensity also depends on the light's distance from the source. When near a lamp, you probably notice that the intensity of the light is greater closer to the lamp than it is farther away. Many of the stars in **Figure 20** emit as much energy as the Sun. However, the light from the stars is less intense than light from the Sun, because the stars are so much farther away than the Sun.

The brightness of a light is a person's perception of intensity. One person's eyes might be more sensitive to light than someone else's eyes. As a result, different people might describe the intensity of a light differently. In addition, eyes are more sensitive to some colors than others. The environment also can affect the brightness of a light. Many stars are visible in the bottom photo of **Figure 20.** Few stars are visible in the top photo because there is so much light near the ground.

Interaction of Sunlight and Matter

Have you ever wondered why the sky is blue or the Sun is yellow? The interaction of light and matter causes interesting effects such as these when sunlight travels through air.

Scattering of Sunlight

As sunlight moves through Earth's atmosphere, most of the light reaches the ground. However, blue wavelengths are shorter than red wavelengths. The particles that make up the air scatter the shorter blue wavelengths more than they scatter longer wavelengths. The sky appears blue because the blue wavelengths spread out in every direction. They eventually reach the eye from all parts of the sky.

A light source, such as the Sun, that emits all colors of light should appear white. Why does the Sun often appear yellow instead of white? As shown in **Figure 21,** after the blue wavelengths of light scatter, the remaining colors appear yellow.

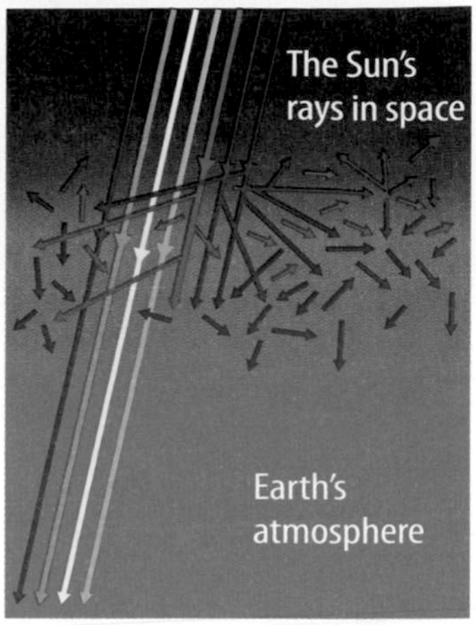

▲ **Figure 21** The Sun appears yellow because only longer wavelengths of light travel through the air in a straight line.

Reading Check Why is the sky blue? Why is the Sun yellow?

Refraction of Sunlight

Another interesting effect of sunlight occurs because of refraction. Recall that light changes speed as it travels from one medium into another. If light enters a new medium at an angle, the light wave refracts, or changes direction.

As shown in **Figure 22,** the refraction of light can affect the appearance of the setting Sun. The Sun's rays slow down when they enter Earth's atmosphere. The light rays refract toward Earth's surface. The brain assumes the rays that reach your eyes have traveled in a straight line, and the Sun seems to be higher in the sky than it actually is. This refraction causes you to see the Sun even after it has set below Earth's horizon.

FOLDABLES®

Make a vertical two-tab book using the labels shown. Use it to organize your notes on scattering and refraction.

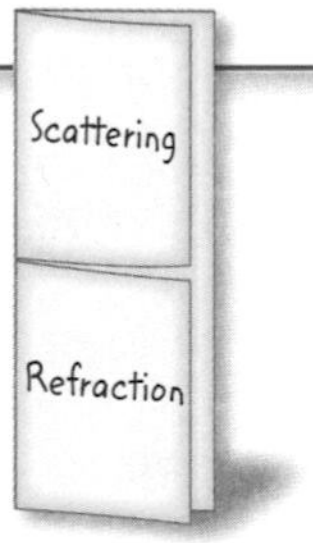

Figure 22 After the Sun actually sets, its light rays refract, and you see the Sun above the horizon.

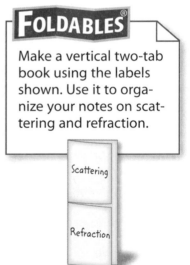

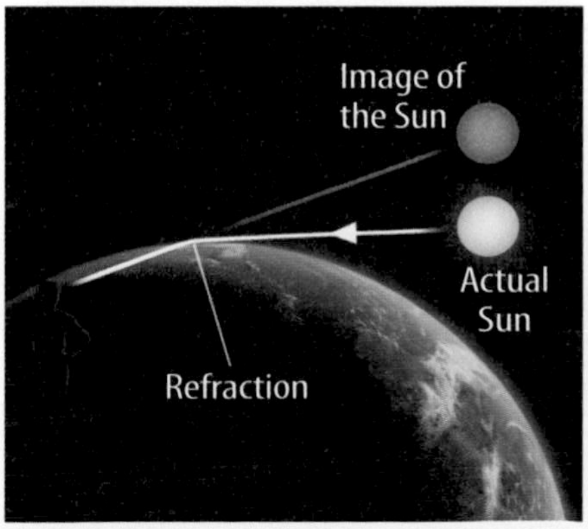

Vision and the Eye

Light enables objects to be seen. Light from luminous objects travels directly from the object to the viewer. Objects also are seen when they reflect light to the eyes. What happens to light after it enters the eyes? How do eyes and the brain transform light waves into information about people, places, and things?

As shown in **Figure 23,** light enters the eye through the cornea. The cornea and the lens focus light onto the retina. Cells in the retina absorb the light and send signals about the light to the brain. Follow the steps in **Figure 23** to learn more about how the eye works.

Key Concept Check How do eyes change light waves into the images you see?

The Eye

Concepts in Motion Animation

Figure 23 The parts of the eye work together to change light waves into signals your brain interprets as images.

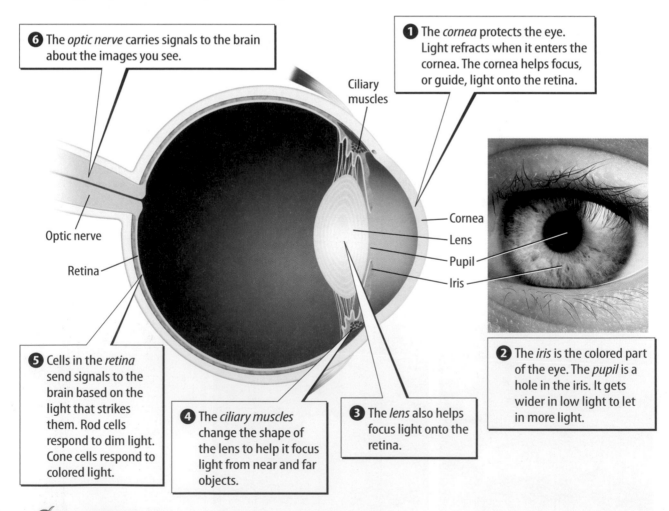

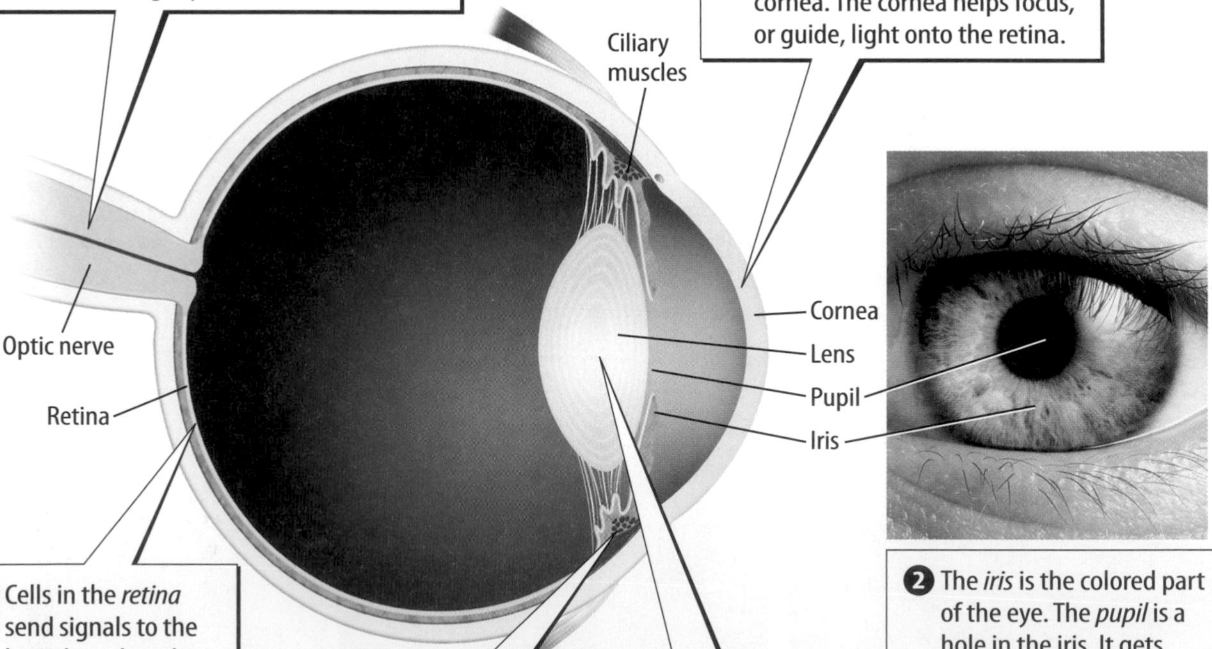

❶ The *cornea* protects the eye. Light refracts when it enters the cornea. The cornea helps focus, or guide, light onto the retina.

❷ The *iris* is the colored part of the eye. The *pupil* is a hole in the iris. It gets wider in low light to let in more light.

❸ The *lens* also helps focus light onto the retina.

❹ The *ciliary muscles* change the shape of the lens to help it focus light from near and far objects.

❺ Cells in the *retina* send signals to the brain based on the light that strikes them. Rod cells respond to dim light. Cone cells respond to colored light.

❻ The *optic nerve* carries signals to the brain about the images you see.

Visual Check What part of the eye responds to color?

Lesson 2 Review

✓ Assessment Online Quiz

Visual Summary

The different types of electromagnetic waves play important roles in your life.

Materials transmit, absorb, and reflect different amounts of light.

Interaction with matter produces interesting effects in sunlight. You can see the Sun even after it sets below the horizon.

FOLDABLES®

Use your lesson Foldable to review the lesson. Save your Foldable for the project at the end of the chapter.

What do you think NOW?

You first read the statements below at the beginning of the chapter.

3. Light is the only type of wave that can travel through empty space.

4. Only shiny surfaces reflect light.

Did you change your mind about whether you agree or disagree with the statements? Rewrite any false statements to make them true.

Use Vocabulary

1 **Contrast** radio waves, infrared waves, and ultraviolet waves.

2 **Explain** the difference between a transparent and a translucent material.

Understand Key Concepts

3 Which eye part responds to colored light?

A. cones **C.** iris

B. cornea **D.** lens

4 **Compare** the ways light interacts with a red book and a red stained-glass window.

5 **Describe** how light waves and ultraviolet waves differ.

Interpret Graphics

6 **Explain** the diagram below in terms of the interaction of light waves with matter.

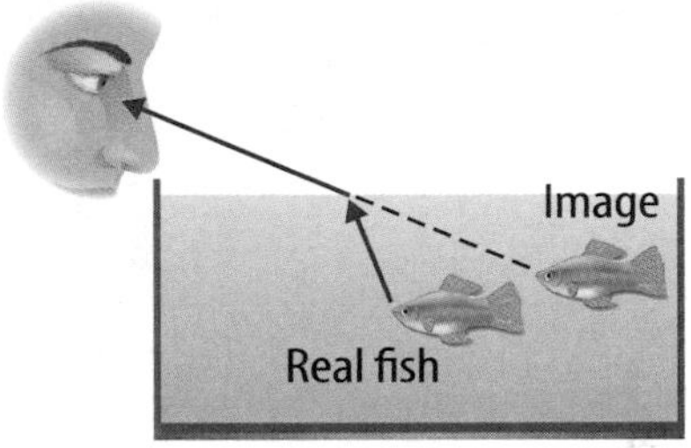

7 **Sequence** Copy and fill in a graphic organizer like the one below that shows the sequence of wave types in the electromagnetic spectrum. Add boxes as necessary.

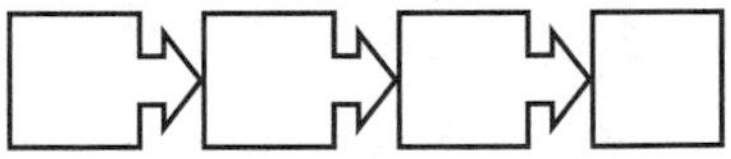

Critical Thinking

8 **Decide** If you turn on an electric stove and stand to the side of it, what type of electromagnetic wave causes you to feel heat from the burner?

9 **Construct** a drawing of the major parts of the eye and describe how each part helps turn light waves into visual information.

GREEN SCIENCE

Light

Is it keeping you from sleeping at night?

This image was created using data gathered by satellites. It shows light pollution generated by human populations around the world.

◀ The lights used to keep this road safe contribute to light pollution.

Imagine trying to sleep in this house! Light shining in bedroom windows at night is a form of light pollution. ▶

Trash on the sidewalk, automobile exhaust in the air, and fertilizer in a river's water are all types of pollution. But did you know that light also can be considered pollution? Light pollution is a serious problem in many urban areas worldwide.

Artificial lighting can be very useful. It can help keep areas free from crime and allow people to work and drive safely after dark. However, the lights people use often shine out into surrounding areas or up into the night sky. This is called light pollution.

Light pollution is a term that refers to the negative effects of artificial lighting. For example, light pollution can disrupt the daily cycles of nocturnal animals. Also, light that escapes into the atmosphere is wasted energy. In some areas, observing the night sky is very

Awareness of light pollution is increasing. Groups such as the American Medical Association (AMA) have recognized the negative impact of light pollution. The AMA has passed resolutions advocating energy-efficient, fully shielded streetlight design. Individuals can take steps to decrease light pollution by carefully choosing outdoor lights with light-pollution reduction in mind.

It's Your Turn

OBSERVE AND DRAW Observe the night sky near your home, and make a drawing of what you observe. Then, discuss how light pollution in your area might compare with light pollution in other parts of the country.

Lesson 3

Sound

Reading Guide

Key Concepts
ESSENTIAL QUESTIONS

- What are some properties of sound waves?
- How do your ears enable you to hear sounds?

Vocabulary

compression p. 143

rarefaction p. 143

pitch p. 143

decibel p. 145

g Multilingual eGlossary

Video Science Video

Academic Standards for Science

7.1.4 Recognize and provide evidence how light, sound and other waves have energy and how they interact with different materials.

Also covers: 7.NS.2, 7.NS.5, 7.NS.7, 7.NS.9, 7.NS.11, 7.DP.1, 7.DP.3, 7.DP.5, 7.DP.6, 7.DP.7, 7.DP.10, 7.DP.11

Inquiry How does it make sounds?

Have you ever stood nearby as a marching band plays or carefully watched musicians during a concert? The notes they play can be high or low, loud or soft, or anything in between. Why are the sounds so different? How are sounds perceived?

Inquiry Launch Lab

10 minutes

How can you change the sound of a straw?

Sounds are longitudinal waves that travel through matter. If you blow across a straw, you can make different wavelengths of sound. How do different wavelengths change the sounds you hear?

1. Read and complete a lab safety form.
2. Using **scissors,** cut a **straw** in half. Cut one of the halves into two equal parts. Cut one of those parts into two equal parts.
3. Blow across the top of each straw. How do the sounds differ? Make a data table in your Science Journal, and then record your observations in your data table.
4. Repeat step 3, this time covering the bottom of each straw with your finger.

Think About This

1. What is the source of energy that creates the sound waves?
2. How does covering the bottom of the straw change the sound?
3. **Key Concept** How do the sounds made by a long straw and a short straw differ? Why do you think this is?

What are sound waves?

Just as light is a type of wave that can be seen, sounds are a type of wave that can be heard. Sound waves are longitudinal mechanical waves. Unlike light waves, sound waves must travel through a medium.

Figure 24 People and animals hear different ranges of sound frequencies.

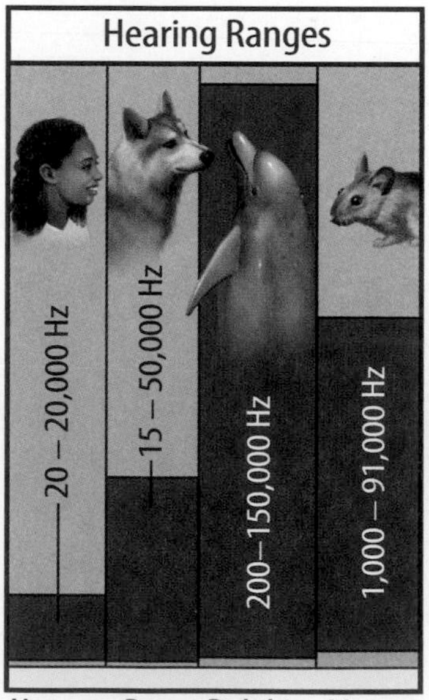

Audible Vibrations

Suppose you strike two metal pans together. Now, suppose you strike two pillows together. How would the two sounds differ? Sound waves are vibrations the ear can detect. You hear a loud sound when you hit the pans together because they vibrate so much. You barely hear the pillows because they vibrate so little. Healthy, young humans can hear sound waves produced by vibrations with frequencies between about 20 Hz and 20,000 Hz. As people age, their ability to hear the higher and lower frequencies of sound decreases. The human ear is most sensitive to frequencies between 1,000 Hz and 4,000 Hz.

Animals have ranges of hearing that help them catch prey or avoid predators. For example, elephants hear sounds as low as 15 Hz. Chickens hear sounds between 125 Hz and 2,000 Hz. Porpoises can hear sounds between 75 Hz and 150,000 Hz! Ranges for other animals are listed in **Figure 24.**

Sound Waves

Concepts in Motion Animation

Figure 25 A sound wave produces compressions and rarefactions as it passes through matter.

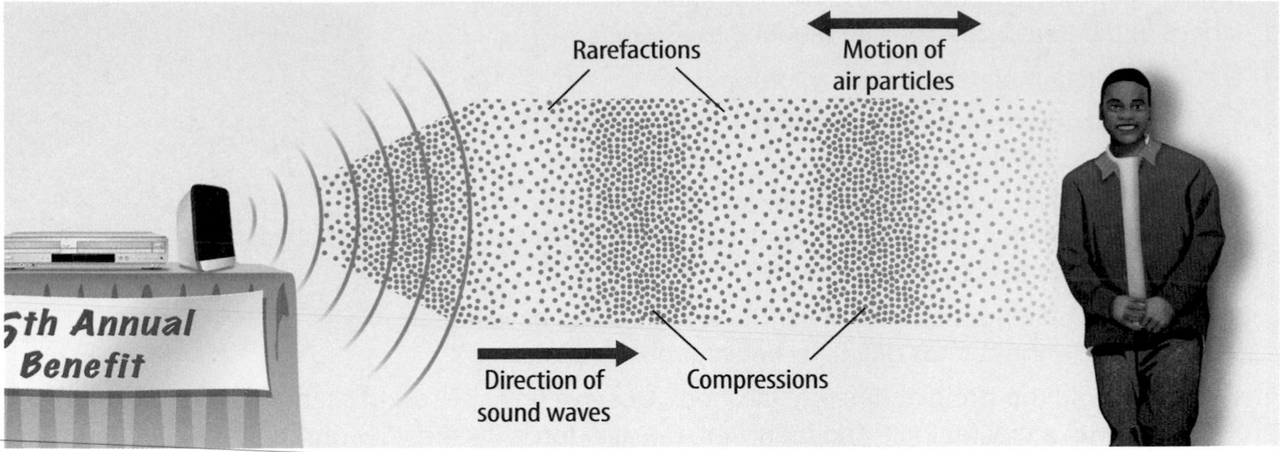

Compressions and Rarefactions

Sound waves usually travel to your ears through air. Air particles are in constant motion. As the particles bounce off objects, they exert a force, or pressure. **Figure 25** shows how sound waves moving through air change the air pressure by causing air particles to move toward and then away from each other.

Suppose you pluck a guitar string. As the string springs back, it pushes air particles forward, forcing them closer together. This increases the air pressure near the string. *A* **compression** *is the region of a longitudinal wave where the particles of the medium are closest together.* As the string vibrates, it moves in the other direction. This leaves behind a region with lower pressure. *A* **rarefaction** *is the region of a longitudinal wave where the particles are farthest apart.*

Reading Check How do compressions and rarefactions differ?

Properties of Sound Waves

A sound wave is described by its wavelength, frequency, amplitude, and speed. These properties of sound waves depend on the compressions and rarefactions of the sound waves.

Wavelength, Frequency, and Pitch

Recall that the wavelength of a wave becomes shorter as the wave's frequency increases. How does the frequency of a sound wave affect what is heard?

The perception of how high or low a sound seems is called **pitch.** The higher the frequency, the higher the pitch of the sound. For example, a female voice generally produces higher-pitched sounds than a male voice. This is because the female voice has a higher range of frequencies. **Figure 26** shows the range of frequencies produced by several instruments and voices.

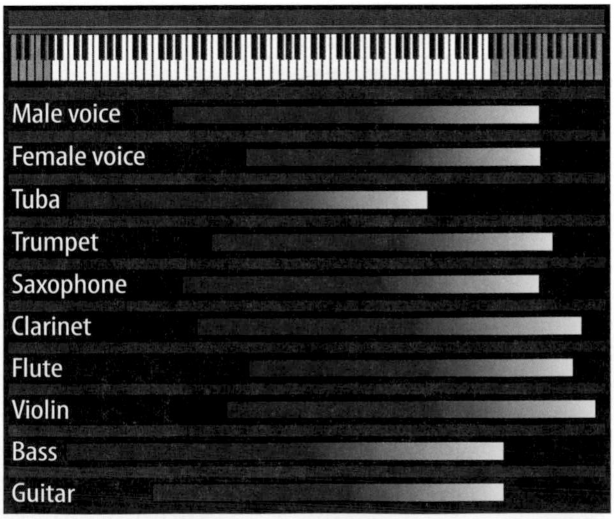

▲ **Figure 26** People and instruments have different ranges of sound frequencies.

Inquiry MiniLab

10 minutes

Can you make different sounds with string?

A guitar player makes different sounds by holding and plucking the strings in different ways. You can model these sounds.

1. Read and complete a lab safety form.
2. Use **scissors** to cut a piece of **string** 1 m long. Attach one end securely to the leg of a desk.
3. Hold the other end, and stretch the string horizontally. Pluck the string several times, and observe the sound. Record your observations in your Science Journal.
4. Continue holding the string at various locations and plucking it. Notice how the sounds differ. Record your observations.
5. Again, hold the string at different locations. Observe how the sound changes as you pull the string with a greater force and then with a weaker force. Record your observations.

Analyze and Conclude

1. **Interpret** How does pulling the string tighter or changing its length affect the string's sound?
2. **Key Concept** Explain how you changed the frequency, wavelength, pitch, amplitude, and energy of the sound you made with the string.

Science Use v. Common Use

rest position

Science Use position of an undisturbed particle; particles are still in motion here

Common Use the state of something not moving

Amplitude and Energy

You use more energy to shout than to whisper. The more energy you put into your voice, the farther the particles of air move as they vibrate. The distance a vibrating particle moves from its **rest position** is the amplitude. The more energy used to produce the sound wave, the greater the amplitude.

Speed

Sound waves travel much slower than electromagnetic waves. With sound, the transmitted energy must pass from particle to particle. The type of medium and the temperature affect the speed of sound.

Type of Medium Gas particles are far apart and collide less often than particles in a liquid or a solid. As shown in **Table 3,** a gas takes longer to transfer sound energy between particles.

Temperature Particles move faster and collide more often as the temperature of a gas increases. This increase in the number of collisions transfers more energy in less time. Temperature has the opposite effect on liquids and sounds. As liquids and solids cool, the molecules move closer together. They collide more often and transfer energy faster.

Key Concept Check What are some properties of sound waves?

Table 3 The Speed of Sound

Material	Speed (m/s)
Air (0°C)	331
Air (20°C)	343
Water (20°C)	1,481
Water (0°C)	1,500
Seawater (25°C)	1,533
Ice (0°C)	3,500
Iron	5,130
Glass	5,640

Intensity and Loudness

Generally, the greater the amplitude of a sound wave, the louder the sound seems. But what happens if you move away from a sound source? As you move away, the wave's amplitude decreases and the sound seems quieter. This is because as a sound wave moves farther from the source, more and more particles collide, and the energy from the wave spreads out among more particles. Therefore, the farther you move from the source, the less energy present in the same area of space. Recall that the amount of energy that passes through a square meter of space in one second is the intensity of a wave. Loudness is your ear's perception of intensity.

The Decibel Scale

The unit used to measure sound intensity, or loudness, is the **decibel (dB).** The decibel levels of common sounds are shown in **Figure 27.** Each increase of 10 dB causes a sound about twice as loud. As the decibel level goes up, the amount of time you can listen to the sound without risking hearing loss gets shorter and shorter. People who work around loud sounds wear protective hearing devices to prevent hearing loss.

Decibel Levels

Figure 27 The decibel scale helps you understand safe limits of different types of sounds.

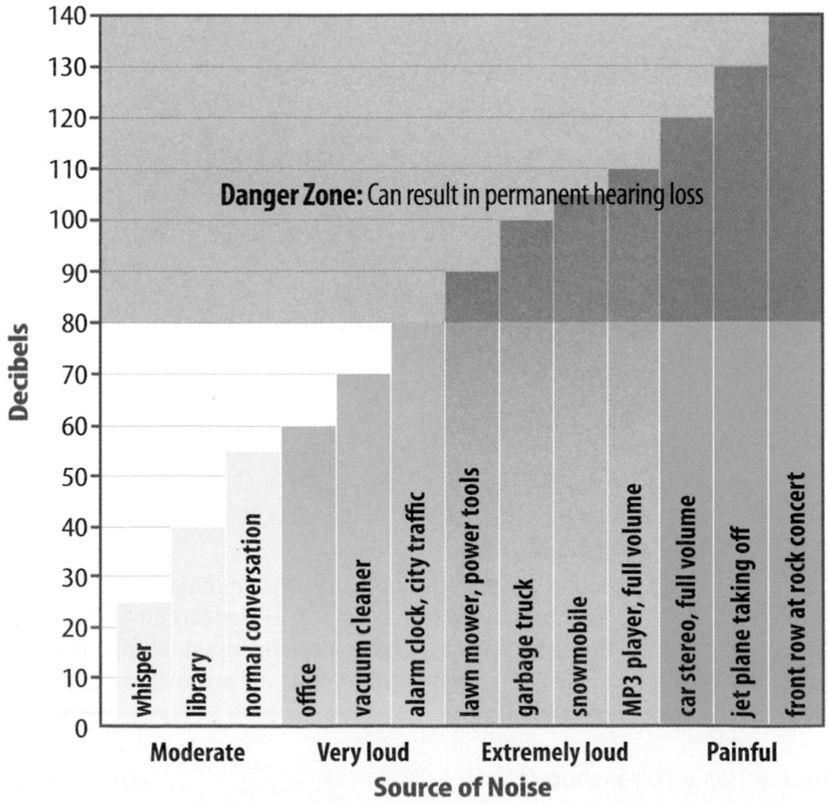

Math Skills

Use a Fraction

Because sound energy travels out in all directions from the source, the intensity of the sound decreases as you move away. You can calculate the fraction by which the sound intensity changes. The fraction $= \left(\frac{r_1}{r_2}\right)^2$, where r_1 is the starting distance and r_2 is the ending distance from the source. For example, by what fraction does sound intensity decrease if you move from **3 m** to **6 m** from a source?

1. Replace the variables with given values.
   fraction $= \left(\frac{3}{6}\right)^2$
2. Solve the problem.
   $\left(\frac{3}{6}\right)^2 = \left(\frac{1}{2}\right)^2 = \frac{1}{4}$, so the intensity decreases to $\frac{1}{4}$ of its original value.

Practice

You are standing at a distance of 2 m from a sound source. How does the sound intensity change if you move to a distance of 6 m?

Review

- **Math Practice**
- **Personal Tutor**

WORD ORIGIN

decibel
from Latin *decibus,* means "tenth"

Hearing and the Ear

FOLDABLES®

Make a horizontal four-tab book, and label it as shown. Use it to review properties of sound waves.

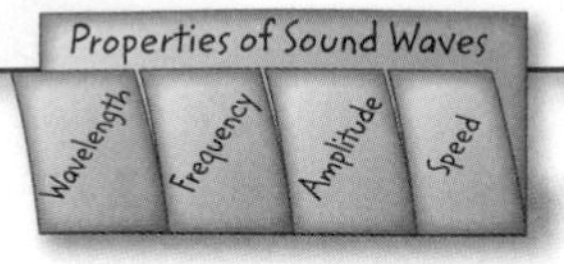

Typically, objects are seen when light enters the eyes. Similarly, sound waves enter the ears with information about the environment. The human ear has three main parts, as shown in **Figure 28.** First, the external outer ear collects sound waves. Next, the middle ear amplifies, or intensifies, the sound waves. The middle ear includes the ear drum and three small bones—the hammer, the anvil, and the stirrup, Finally, the inner ear contains the cochlea (KOH klee uh). The cochlea converts sound waves to nerve signals. These nerve signals are typically processed by the brain, creating the perception of sound.

Key Concept Check How do your ears enable you to hear sounds?

Parts of the Human Ear

Concepts in Motion **Animation**

Figure 28 The different parts of the ear work together to gather and interpret sound waves.

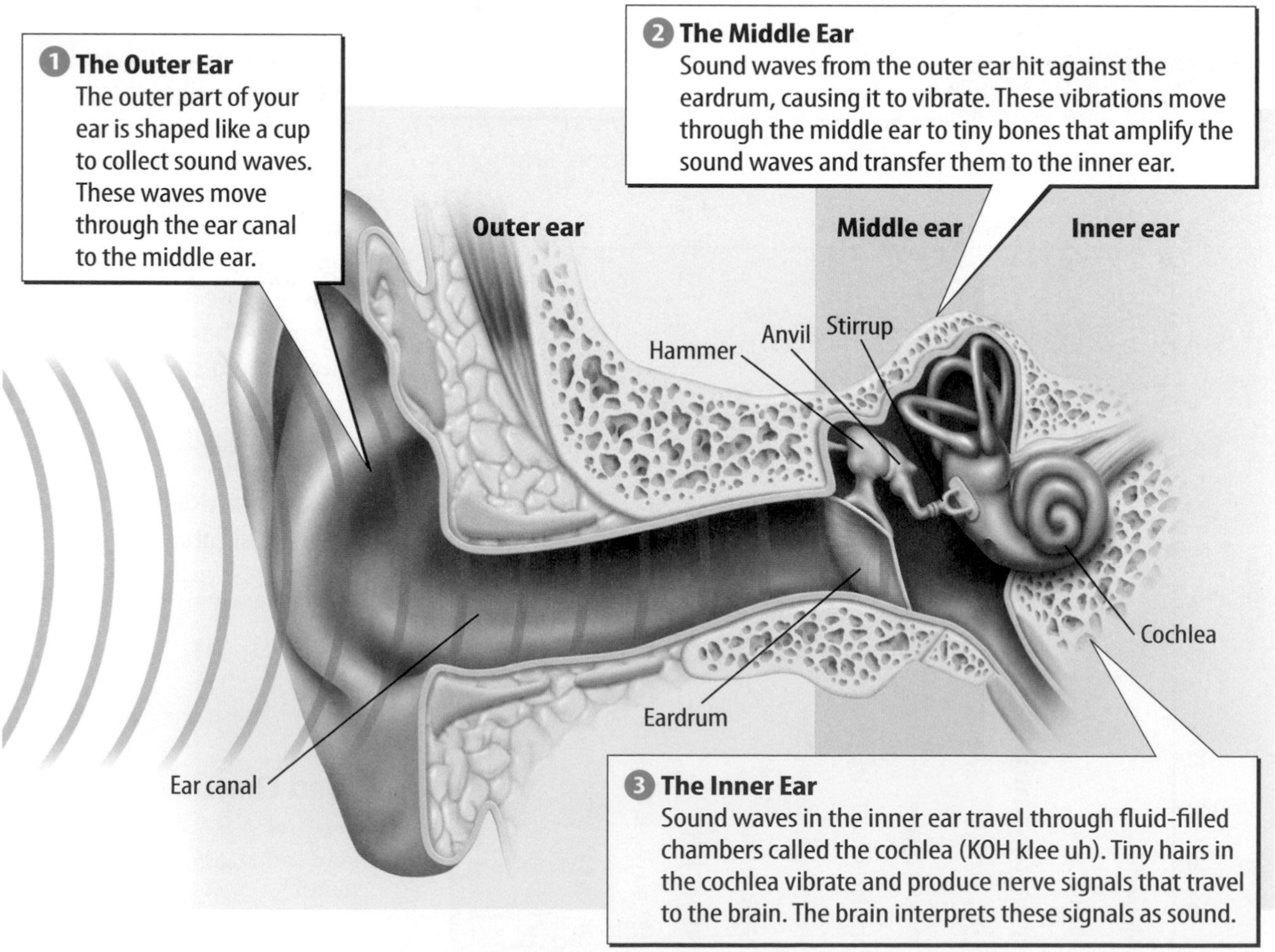

1 The Outer Ear
The outer part of your ear is shaped like a cup to collect sound waves. These waves move through the ear canal to the middle ear.
2 The Middle Ear
Sound waves from the outer ear hit against the eardrum, causing it to vibrate. These vibrations move through the middle ear to tiny bones that amplify the sound waves and transfer them to the inner ear.
Outer ear
Middle ear
Inner ear
Hammer
Anvil
Stirrup
Cochlea
Eardrum
Ear canal
3 The Inner Ear
Sound waves in the inner ear travel through fluid-filled chambers called the cochlea (KOH klee uh). Tiny hairs in the cochlea vibrate and produce nerve signals that travel to the brain. The brain interprets these signals as sound.

Visual Check Which part of the ear has a spiral shape?

Lesson 3 Review

Assessment Online Quiz

Visual Summary

Sound waves are produced when an energy source causes matter to vibrate.

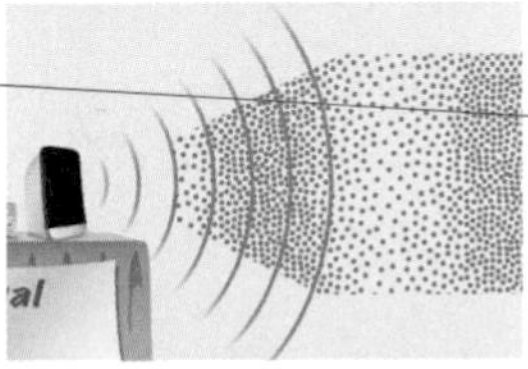

Sound waves are compressions and rarefactions that move away from a sound source.

You hear sounds when your ears capture sound waves and produce signals that travel to your brain.

FOLDABLES®

Use your lesson Foldable to review the lesson. Save your Foldable for the project at the end of the chapter.

What do you think NOW?

You first read the statements below at the beginning of the chapter.

5. Sound travels faster through solid materials than through air.

6. The more energy used to produce a sound, the louder the sound.

Did you change your mind about whether you agree or disagree with the statements? Rewrite any false statements to make them true.

Use Vocabulary

1. The property of a sound wave that relates to a high or low musical note is the sound's ________.
2. **Explain** the difference between a compression and a rarefaction in a sound wave.

Understand Key Concepts

3. Which property of a sound wave describes the amount of energy that passes through a square meter of space each second?
   - **A.** amplitude
   - **B.** frequency
   - **C.** intensity
   - **D.** wavelength
4. **Describe** how the three main parts of the ear enable people to hear.

Interpret Graphics

5. **Sequence** Copy and fill in a graphic organizer like the one below to describe the path of a sound wave from when it is produced by a source until is interpreted by the brain. Describe the function of each part of the path.

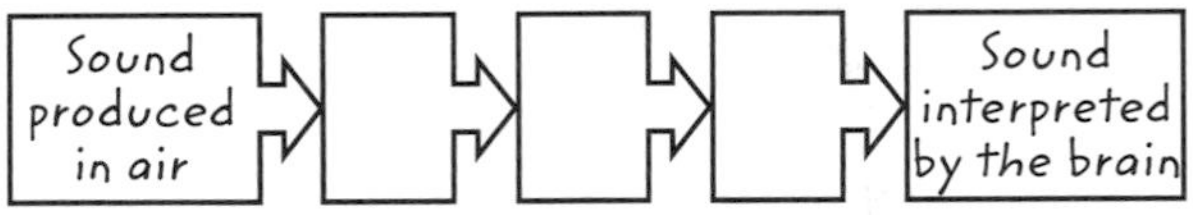

Critical Thinking

6. **Construct** a diagram of four sound waves. Two of the waves should have the same amplitude but different frequencies. The other two waves should have the same wavelength but different amplitudes. Label the properties of the waves.

Math Skills

Review — Math Practice

7. A student is standing a distance of 4 m from the school bell. If the student moves to a distance 20 m away, what fraction of the original intensity of the bell's sound will the student hear?

Inquiry **Lab**

2–3 class periods

Check the sound! Cue the lights!

Materials

coiled spring toy

snap-together plastic blocks

food coloring

flashlights

string

scissors

Also needed: variety of beakers, dowel, large glass pan, colored paper, sponge, water, white paper, office supplies

Safety

You are part of an entertainment firm that creates sound and light shows like the kind you see during a music concert or at halftime of a sports event. You have been asked to produce an exciting and entertaining wave show that is between 2 and 4 minutes long. The show must use at least three types of waves, and you must be able to identify at least three properties or behaviors of waves. Unfortunately, you do not have a big budget or high-tech equipment like professional show designers. You can use only the materials you have used in other labs in this chapter, as well as any materials your teacher approves.

Question

How can you use different waves to build an exciting and entertaining show?

Procedure

1. Read and complete a lab safety form.
2. As a group, decide on a concept or idea around which you will focus your show.
3. Develop a script for the show. Assign the different roles to the members of your group.
4. Make a table of the different waves in your show, as shown below. Consider the source of the wave and the medium through which the wave travels.
5. Create a list of the different physical concepts related to waves that you will include in your show.
6. Build all the instruments and lighting equipment required for your show. Practice your show so that everyone in your group is able to smoothly perform the different parts together for the class.

Title of the show: ____________________

Wave	Source	Medium
1.		
2.		
3.		
4.		
5.		

7 Show the script of your show to another group. Ask the group to evaluate how well you use different waves and wave properties. Get feedback on ways to make your show even more entertaining.

8 As a group, think about how you can use the suggestions you received from the other group. Consider what supplies you will need and how you will make the changes.

9 Record these suggestions and your ideas about how to make modifications to your setup in your Science Journal.

10 Make modifications to your show based on your ideas. You might need to test different parts to see how ideas work. When you have made all the changes, perform your entire show.

Analyze and Conclude

11 **Explain** How did you incorporate three types of waves into your show?

12 **Assess** What are some benefits and some challenges of using waves to create a show?

13 THE BIG IDEA **The Big Idea** How did you use the physical properties of waves in your show?

Communicate Your Results

Perform your show for your class. After your show, have your class give you feedback on how well you used different types of waves and different properties of waves to create an exciting and entertaining show.

Inquiry Extension

What were some of the problems you encountered because of the limited materials that were available for making your show? What kind of equipment would you have liked to use? Write a proposal that you might submit to a client to explain why you would like to have the funds to purchase improved sound and light equipment. Explain how a larger budget might improve the show and make people pay to see your show.

Lab Tips

- ☑ Be sure to decide on a theme around which to focus your show. For example, will it be a music concert? A sideshow at a sports event? A display at a theme park?
- ☑ Look back at the labs for this chapter for ideas on how to use waves.
- ☑ Try to make your show as creative as possible. How can you make your show exciting?

Remember to use scientific methods.

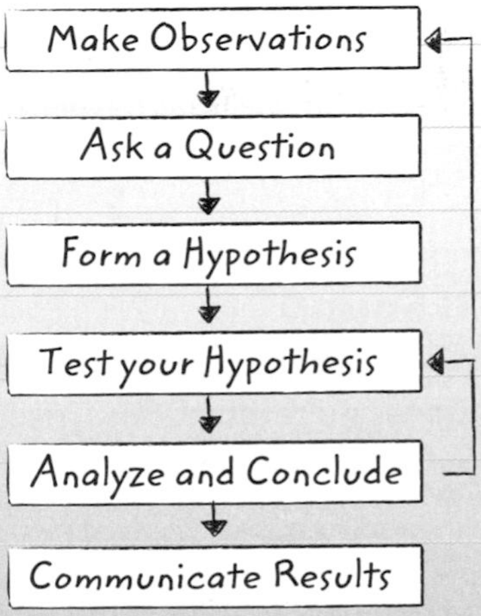

Chapter 4 Study Guide

THE BIG IDEA **Mechanical waves transfer energy from particle to particle in matter. Electromagnetic waves transfer energy through either matter or empty space.**

Key Concepts Summary

Lesson 1: Waves

- Waves are disturbances that transfer energy from place to place. A **mechanical wave** forms when a source of energy causes particles of a medium to vibrate. A vibrating electric charge produces an **electromagnetic wave.**
- You can describe wavelength, **frequency,** speed, **amplitude,** and energy of waves.
- Matter can transmit, absorb, or reflect a wave. It also can change a wave's direction by **refraction** or diffraction.

Vocabulary

mechanical wave p. 120
electromagnetic wave p. 120
transverse wave p. 121
longitudinal wave p. 121
frequency p. 123
amplitude p. 124
refraction p. 126

Lesson 2: Light

- Light differs from other forms of electromagnetic waves by its frequency, wavelength, and energy. Light is the type of electromagnetic wave that is visible with the human eye.
- Matter can transmit, absorb, and reflect light. These interactions differ in how much light the matter transmits and how it changes the direction of light.
- Cells in the retina of the eyes change light into electric signals that travel to the brain.

Vocabulary

radio wave p. 131
infrared wave p. 132
ultraviolet wave p. 132
transparent p. 134
translucent p. 134
opaque p. 134
intensity p. 136

Lesson 3: Sound

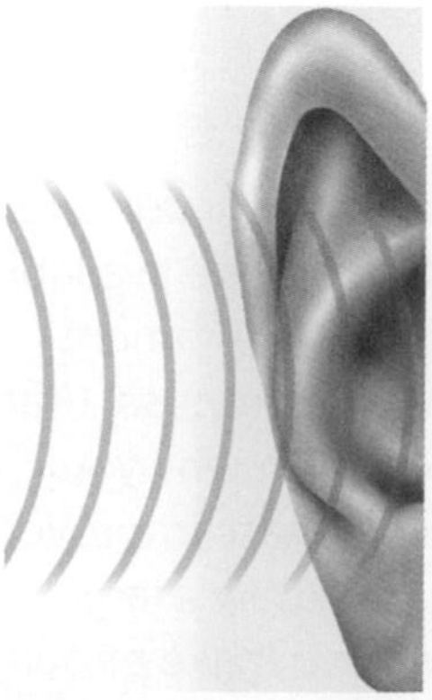

- Sound waves travel through matter as a series of **compressions** and **rarefactions.** The frequency and wavelength of a sound wave determines the **pitch.** Sound waves with greater amplitude sound louder.
- Ears collect and amplify sound and then convert it to signals the brain can interpret.

Vocabulary

compression p. 143
rarefaction p. 143
pitch p. 143
decibel p. 145

Review
- Personal Tutor
- Vocabulary eGames
- Vocabulary eFlashcards

FOLDABLES® Chapter Project

Assemble your lesson Foldables as shown to make a Chapter Project. Use the project to review what you have learned in this chapter.

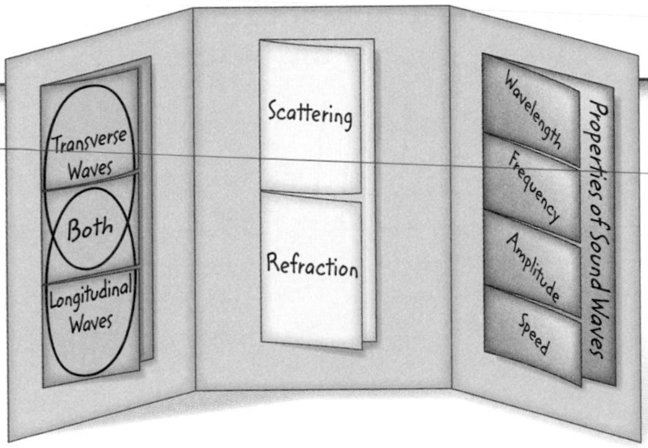

Use Vocabulary

1. The property of waves that is measured in hertz (Hz) is ________.
2. A change in direction, or ________, can occur as a wave moves into a medium.
3. A material that transmits light but through which objects appear blurry is ________.
4. An object that does not allow light to pass through it is ________.
5. The portion of a sound wave with higher-than-normal pressure is called a(n) ________.
6. A unit that describes the intensity or loudness of sound is the ________.

Link Vocabulary and Key Concepts

Concepts in Motion Interactive Concept Map

Copy this concept map, and then use vocabulary terms from the previous page to complete the concept map.

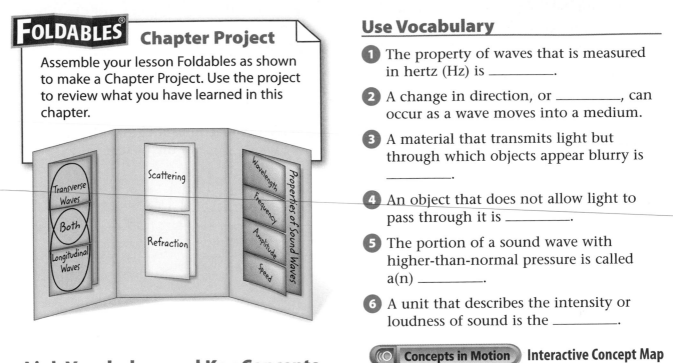

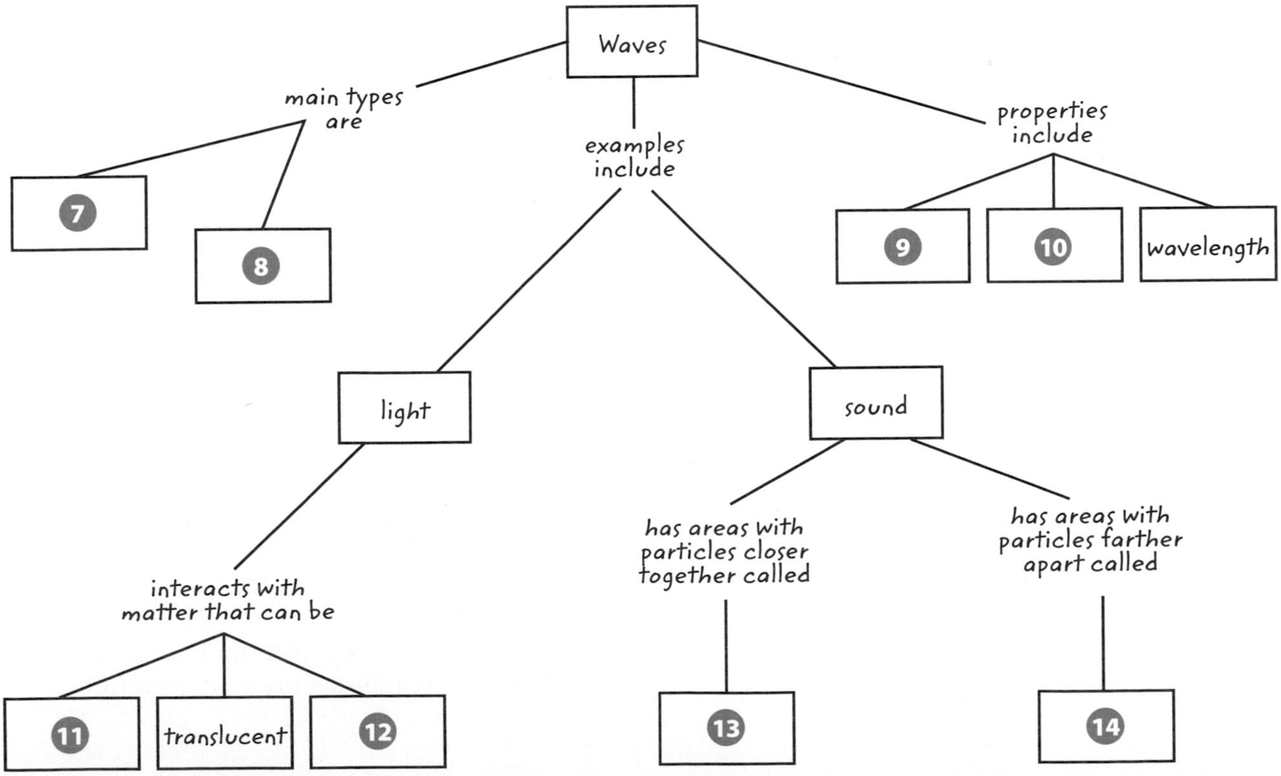

Chapter 4 Review

Understand Key Concepts

1. As a water wave passes, the particles that make up the water move
   - A. back and forth, parallel to the wave.
   - B. in circles around the same point.
   - C. up and down at right angles to the wave.
   - D. whichever direction the wave moves.

2. The refraction of a wave is caused by a change in
   - A. amplitude.
   - B. frequency.
   - C. speed.
   - D. wavelength.

3. Which is always a transverse wave?
   - A. microwave
   - B. seismic wave
   - C. sound wave
   - D. water wave

4. Wave frequency is measured in
   - A. decibels.
   - B. hertz.
   - C. meters.
   - D. seconds.

5. The arrow in the diagram below shows a point on a light wave that stops as it interacts with matter. Which type of interaction does the arrow represent?

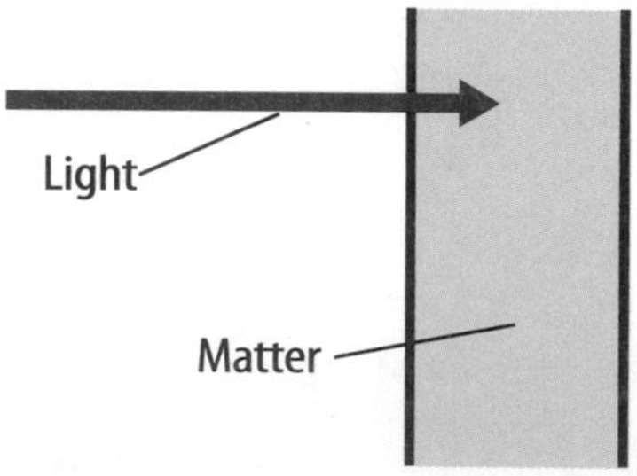

   - A. absorption
   - B. reflection
   - C. refraction
   - D. transmission

6. The distance between one point on a wave and the nearest point just like it is the
   - A. amplitude.
   - B. frequency.
   - C. pitch.
   - D. wavelength.

7. Which interactions of light with matter are taking place in the picture below?

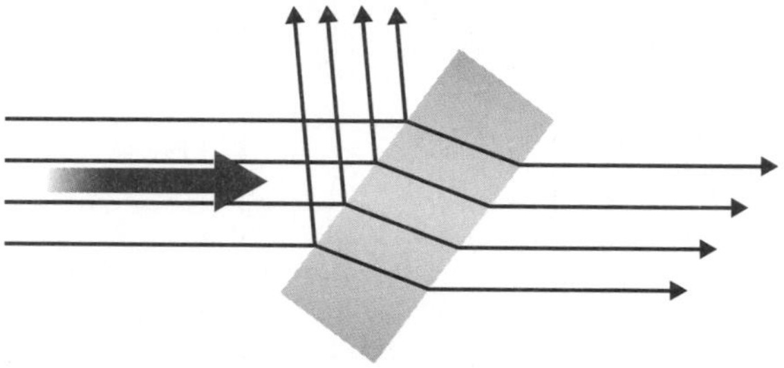

   - A. diffraction, reflection, and absorption
   - B. reflection, refraction, and transmission
   - C. reflection, scattering, and diffraction
   - D. translucent, transparent, and opaque

8. Which of the following colors of light has the longest wavelength?
   - A. red
   - B. green
   - C. violet
   - D. yellow

9. You turn up the volume on the car radio. Which of the following properties of the sound changes?
   - A. amplitude
   - B. frequency
   - C. speed
   - D. wavelength

10. If a sound is loud and low-pitched, the sound wave also has which of the following properties?
    - A. low frequency and high amplitude
    - B. low frequency and low amplitude
    - C. high frequency and high amplitude
    - D. high frequency and low amplitude

Assessment
Online Test Practice

Critical Thinking

11 **Construct** Make a diagram that shows how interactions of light waves with matter cause a flower to appear orange.

12 **Synthesize** An MP3 player at maximum volume produces sound at 110 dB. The table shows the time exposure before a risk of hearing damage. How many hours a day could you listen to your MP3 player at full volume before a hearing loss risk? Explain.

Recommended Noise Exposure Limits

Sound Level (dB)	Time Permitted (h)
90	8
95	4
100	2
105	1

13 **Summarize** What is the process by which an object can be seen and recognized? Be sure to include the interactions of light waves and matter in your summary.

14 **Hypothesize** Why does a 200-W lightbulb appear brighter than a 100-W lightbulb? Mention properties of light in your explanation.

15 **Apply** The passage of lightning through air produces thunder. Why is lightning seen before thunder is heard?

16 **Compare and Contrast** How does the motion of the medium in transverse mechanical waves, longitudinal waves, water waves, and seismic waves differ?

Writing in Science

17 **Write** a paragraph describing an example of sound waves and an example of light most people use each day. Identify a way you could change the properties of each wave.

REVIEW THE BIG IDEA

18 Explain various ways in which waves transfer energy through matter and empty space. Include correct terms to describe the various interactions of waves with matter.

19 Using the picture below, describe how the transfer of energy through matter and empty space helps a meteorologist predict the weather.

Math Skills

Review
Math Practice

Use a Fraction

20 By what fraction does the sound intensity change if you move from 2 m away from a source to 10 m away from the source?

21 You are standing 3 m from someone who is using a lawn mower. How will the sound intensity change if the person moves the mower to a distance 12 m from you?

22 A car 5 m away from you beeps its horn. How would the intensity of the beep change if you moved to a distance 40 m from the car?

Standardized Test Practice

Record your answers on the answer sheet provided by your teacher or on a sheet of paper.

Multiple Choice

Use the figure to answer questions 1–3.

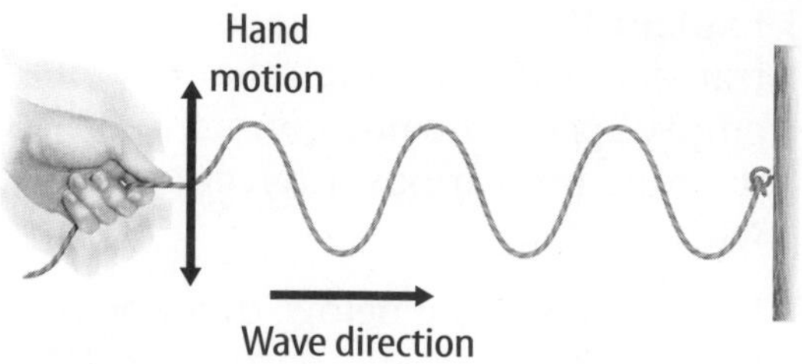

1 The figure above shows waves generated on a rope. Which type of waves are shown in the figure?

A combination

B electromagnetic

C longitudinal

D mechanical

2 Which statement best describes the correct relationship for the wave shown in the figure?

A The disturbance is parallel to the direction the wave travels.

B The disturbance is perpendicular to the direction the wave travels.

C The disturbance carries matter and energy in the same direction along the wave.

D The disturbance has both back-and-forth and up-and-down motion.

3 Which describes how the wave would change if the person's hand moved at a faster rate?

A The amplitude would decrease.

B The amplitude would increase.

C The frequency would decrease.

D The frequency would increase.

4 If two waves are traveling at the same speed, which description is most accurate?

A The wave with the longer wavelength has the higher frequency.

B The wave with the shorter wavelength has the higher frequency.

C Both waves must have equal wavelengths.

D Both waves must have equal frequencies.

5 Wood is opaque. Which describes how light waves can interact with wood?

A absorption and reflection

B diffraction and transmission

C reflection and refraction

D transmission and refraction

6 Which property is unique to electromagnetic waves?

A the ability to interact with matter

B the ability to travel through matter

C the ability to have different intensities

D the ability to travel through empty space

Use the table to answer question 7.

Incoming Light	Color of Filter	Outgoing Light
white	red	red
red	blue	none
white	blue	blue
green	green	?

7 The table above shows the interactions of different colors of light with different colors of filters. Which is the correct color to complete the table?

A green

B none

C red

D white

8 Which must be true of the cornea for the eye to work properly in sending a message to the brain?

A It must absorb light.

B It must block out light.

C It must reflect light.

D It must transmit light.

Use the table to answer question 9.

Material	Speed of Sound (m/s)
Air (0°C)	331
Air (20°C)	343
Water (0°C)	1,500
Water (20°C)	1,481
Ice (0°C)	3,500
Iron	5,130

9 Based on the data in the table, which of the following statements is most likely true?

A Sound travels fastest through gases because they are less dense.

B Sound travels fastest through liquids because they are most fluid.

C Sound travels fastest through solids because they are most dense.

D Sound travels fastest through materials that have higher temperatures.

10 Which color of light could you shine on a green object to make it appear black?

A green

B red

C white

D yellow

Constructed Response

11 You are standing outside and hear a jet flying overhead. You look up toward the direction of the sound, but you notice that the jet is far ahead of where the sound seems to come from. Explain why you can hear a jet only after it passes overhead.

Use the figure to answer question 12.

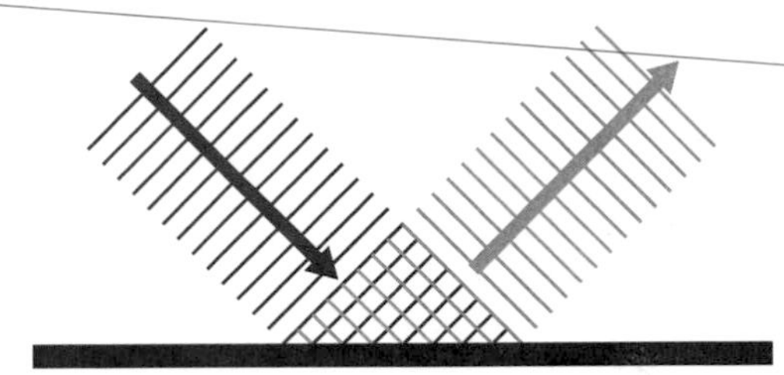

12 The figure above shows light rays striking a flat surface. Describe how the figure would change if the surface the light rays hit against were bumpy instead of flat.

13 People sometimes confuse the pitch of a sound with the sound's intensity. How would you explain the difference between these two properties to a classmate?

14 What roles do the outer ear, the middle ear, and the inner ear play in hearing?

NEED EXTRA HELP?														
If You Missed Question...	1	2	3	4	5	6	7	8	9	10	11	12	13	14
Go to Lesson...	1	1	1	1	2	2	2	2	3	2	3	2	3	3

Unit 2

Earth and Geologic Changes

5 Billion B.C. — 1700 — 1800

4.57 billion years ago
The Sun forms.

4.54 billion years ago
Earth forms.

1778
French naturalist Comte du Buffon creates a small globe resembling Earth and measures its cooling rate to estimate Earth's age. He concludes that Earth is approximately 75,000 years old.

1830
Geologist Charles Lyell begins publishing *The Principles of Geology*; his work popularizes the concept that the features of Earth are perpetually changing, eroding, and reforming.

1862
Physicist William Thomson publishes calculations that Earth is approximately 20 million years old. He claims that Earth had formed as a completely molten object, and he calculates the amount of time it would take for the surface to cool to its present temperature.

1900

2000

1899–1900
John Joly releases his findings from calculating the age of Earth using the rate of oceanic salt accumulation. He determines that the oceans are about 80–100 million years old.

1905
Ernest Rutherford and Bertrand Boltwood use radiometric dating to determine the age of rock samples. This technique would later be used to determine the age of Earth.

1956
Today's accepted age of Earth is determined by C.C. Patterson using uranium-lead isotope dating on several meteorites.

Inquiry
Visit ConnectED for this unit's **STEM** activity.

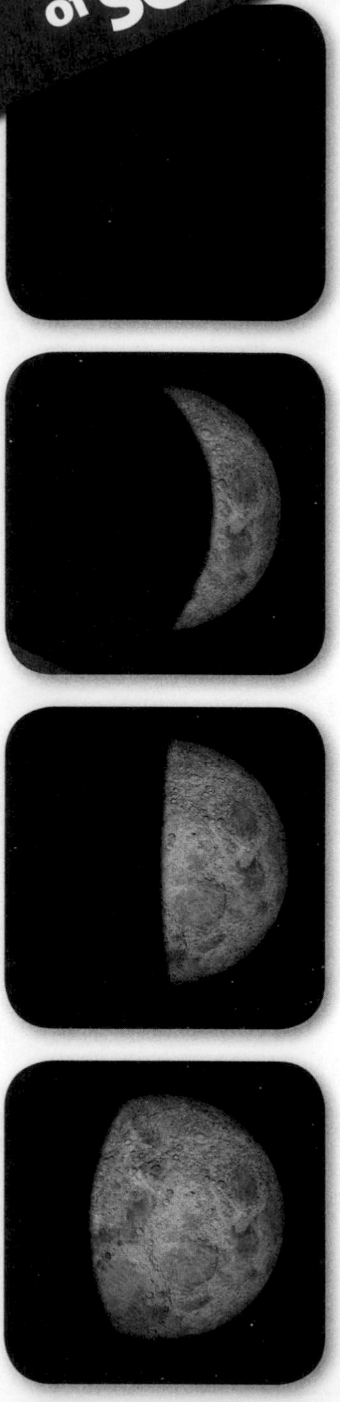

Patterns

You might sometimes see the Moon as a large, glowing disk in the night sky. At other times, the Moon appears as different shapes. These shapes are the Moon's phases, or the changing portions of the Moon that are seen from Earth. The Moon's phases occur as a repeating pattern about every 28 days. A **pattern** is a consistent plan or model used as a guide for understanding and predicting things. You can predict the next phase of the Moon or you can determine the previous phase of the Moon if you know the pattern.

Patterns in Earth Science

Patterns help scientists understand observations. This allows them to predict future events or understand past events. For instance, geologists are Earth scientists who measure the chemical composition, age, and location of rocks. They look for patterns in these measurements. The patterns allow geologists to propose what processes formed the rocks millions or billions of years ago. Geologists also use patterns to draw conclusions about how Earth has changed over time and to estimate how it will change in the future.

Meteorologists are scientists who study weather and climate. They study patterns of fronts, winds, cloud formation, precipitation, and ocean temperatures to make weather forecasts. For example, meteorologists track patterns in hurricanes, such as wind speed, movements, and rotation velocity. These patterns help meteorologists understand the conditions under which a hurricane can form. Predicting the strength and the path of a storm can help save lives, buildings, and property. When meteorologists see weather patterns similar to those of past hurricanes, they can predict the severity of the storm and when and where it will hit. Then meteorologists can send advance warnings for people to safely prepare.

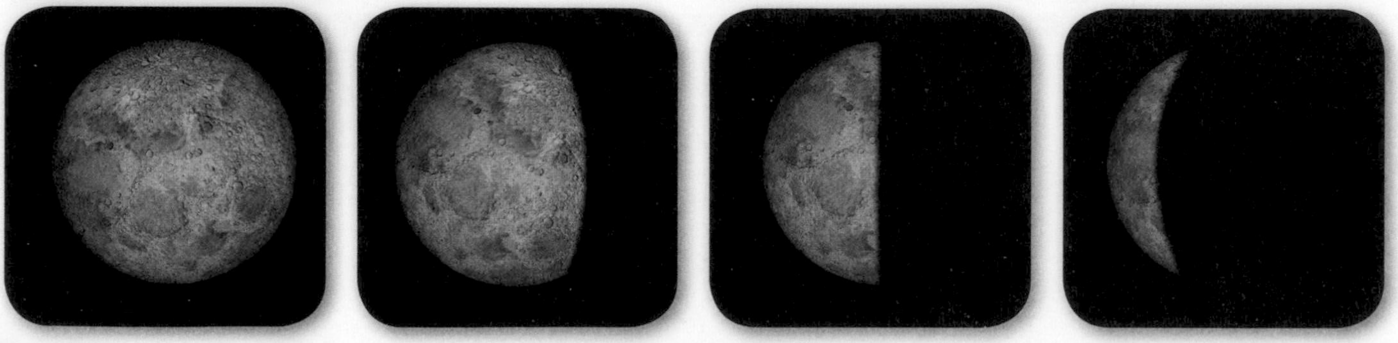

Types of Patterns

Physical Patterns

A pattern you observe using your eyes or other instruments is a physical pattern. Earthquake uplift and erosion reveal physical patterns in layers of rock, as shown in the photo. Patterns in exposed rock layers tell geologists many things, including the order in which the rocks formed, the different minerals and fossils the rocks contain, and the age and movement of landforms.

Patterns in Graphs

Scientists plot data on graphs and then analyze the graphs for patterns. Patterns on graphs can appear as straight lines, curved lines, or waves. The graph to the right shows a pattern in sea level as it increased between 1994 and 2010. Scientists analyze graphic patterns to predict events in the future. For example, a scientist might predict that in 2018, the sea level will be 20–25 mm higher than it was in 2010.

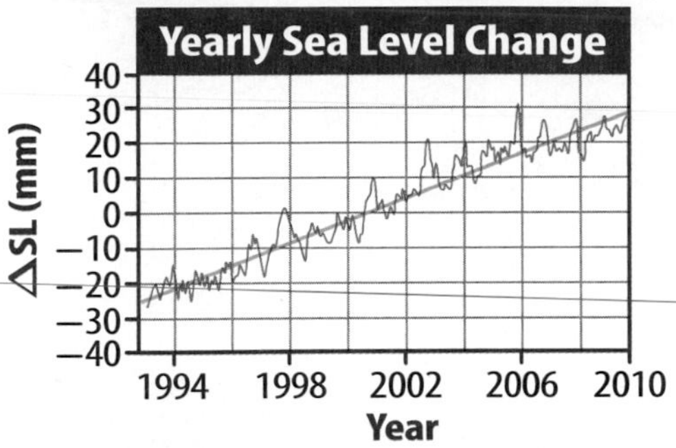

Cyclic Patterns

An event that repeats many times in a predictable order, such as the phases of the Moon, has a cyclic pattern. As shown in the graph, water temperatures in both the North and South Atlantic Ocean rise and fall equally each year. The annual changes in the water temperature follow a cyclic pattern. How do the temperature patterns in the two oceans differ?

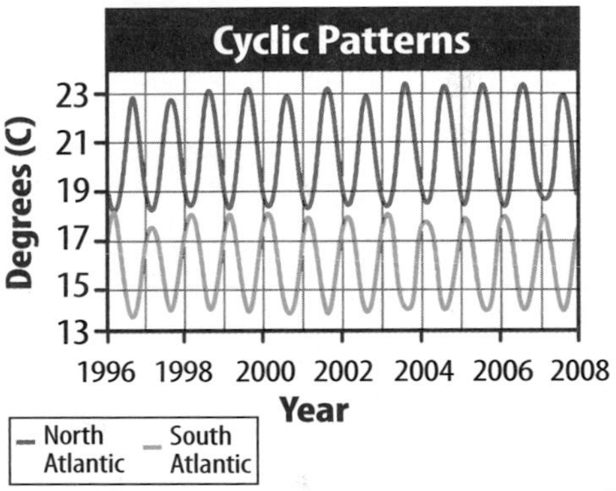

Inquiry MiniLab

15 minutes

What patterns are in your year?

What are some of the cyclic patterns in your life?

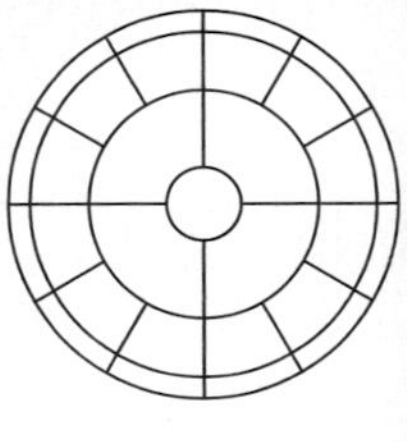

1. On a sheet of **notebook paper,** draw four concentric circles with diameters of 20 cm, 18 cm, 10 cm, and 4 cm. Write your name in the innermost circle.
2. Divide the two outermost circles into 12 equal sections. Write each month of the year (one month per section) in each section of the outermost circle. In the next circle, write personal events or activities that take place in each corresponding month.
3. Divide the 10-cm circle into four sections. Write the weather conditions and the plant patterns that correspond to the months in the outermost circle.

Analyze and Conclude

Observe If you start at one month and move inward through the rings, what patterns do you observe? How do these observations fit into the yearly cycle?

Earth's Structure

THE BIG IDEA

How is Earth structured?

Inquiry What is in the sky?

These dancing lights in the night sky are called an aurora. Interactions between Earth's atmosphere and charged particles from the Sun cause an aurora. Conditions deep in Earth's interior structure create a magnetic field that attracts the charged particles to Earth's North Pole and South Pole.

- How is Earth structured?
- How does Earth's core create Earth's magnetic field?

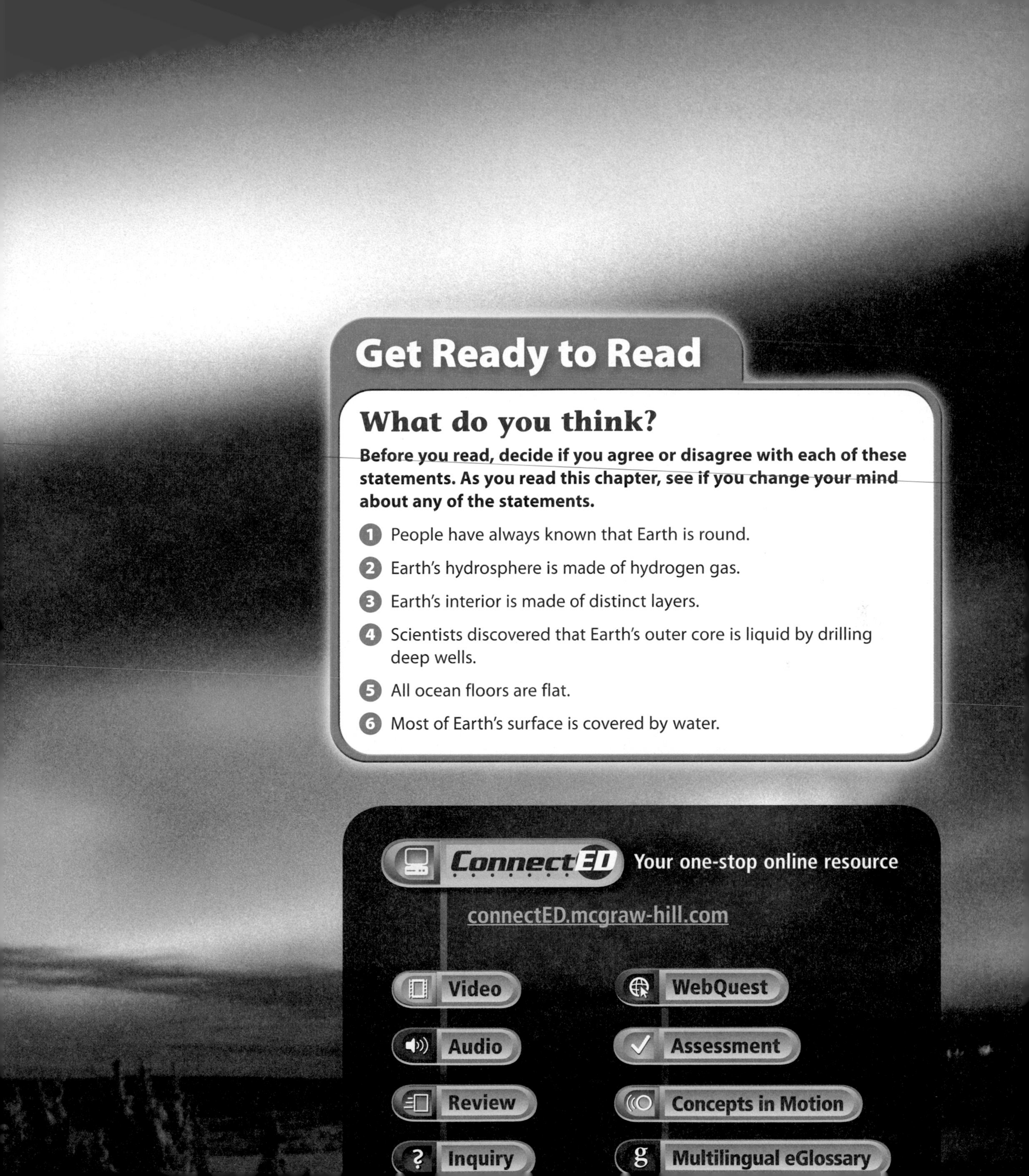

Get Ready to Read

What do you think?

Before you read, decide if you agree or disagree with each of these statements. As you read this chapter, see if you change your mind about any of the statements.

1. People have always known that Earth is round.
2. Earth's hydrosphere is made of hydrogen gas.
3. Earth's interior is made of distinct layers.
4. Scientists discovered that Earth's outer core is liquid by drilling deep wells.
5. All ocean floors are flat.
6. Most of Earth's surface is covered by water.

ConnectED Your one-stop online resource

connectED.mcgraw-hill.com

- Video
- Audio
- Review
- Inquiry
- WebQuest
- Assessment
- Concepts in Motion
- Multilingual eGlossary

Lesson 1

Spherical Earth

Reading Guide

Key Concepts
ESSENTIAL QUESTIONS

- What are Earth's major systems and how do they interact?
- Why does Earth have a spherical shape?

Vocabulary
sphere p. 163

geosphere p. 164

gravity p. 165

density p. 167

g Multilingual eGlossary

Video Science Video

Academic Standards for Science

7.1.3 Recognize and explain how different ways of obtaining, transforming, and distributing energy have different environmental consequences.

7.2.1 Describe how the earth is a layered structure composed of lithospheric plates, a mantle and a dense core.

Also covers: 7.NS.4, 7.NS.7

Inquiry Why is Earth spherical?

This image of Earth was taken from space. Notice Earth's shape and the wispy clouds that surround part of the planet. What else do you notice about Earth?

Inquiry Launch Lab

10 minutes

How can you model Earth's spheres?

Earth has different spheres made of water, solid materials, air, and life. Each sphere has unique characteristics.

1. Read and complete a lab safety form.
2. Set a **clear plastic container** on your table, and add **gravel** to a depth of about 2 cm.
3. Pour equal volumes of **corn syrup** and **colored water** into the container.
4. Observe the container for 2 minutes. Record your observations in your Science Journal.

Think About This

1. What happened to the materials?
2. **Key Concept** Which Earth sphere did each material represent?

Describing Earth

Imagine standing on a mountaintop. You can probably see that the land stretches out beneath you for miles. But you cannot see all of Earth—it is far too large. People have tried to determine the shape and size of Earth for centuries. They have done so by examining the parts they can see.

Many years ago, people believed that Earth was a flat disk with land in the center and water at the edges. Later they used clues to determine Earth's true shape, such as studying Earth's shadow on the Moon during an eclipse.

The Size and Shape of Earth

Now there are better ways to get a view of our planet. Using satellites and other technology, scientists know that Earth is a sphere. *A* **sphere** *is shaped like a ball, with all points on the surface at an equal distance from the center.* But Earth is not a perfect sphere. As illustrated in **Figure 1,** Earth is somewhat flattened at the poles with a slight bulge around the equator. Earth has a diameter of almost 13,000 km. It is the largest of the four rocky planets closest to the Sun.

Figure 1 Earth is shaped like a sphere that is somewhat flattened.

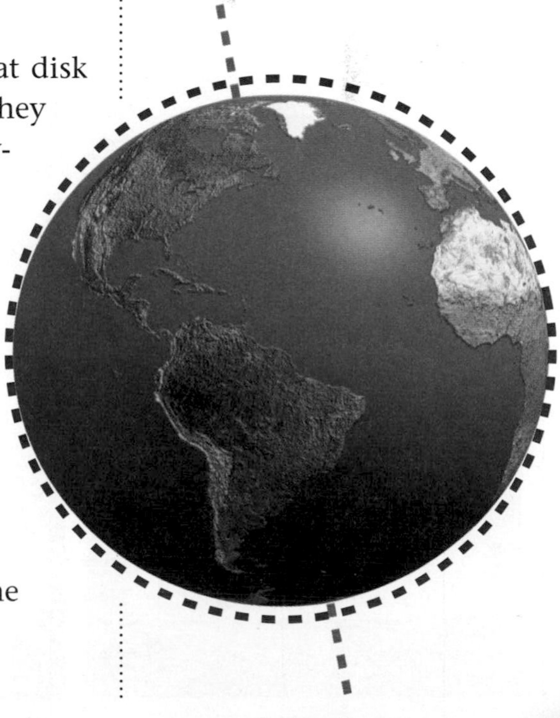

Earth Systems

Earth is large and complex. To simplify the task of studying Earth, scientists describe Earth systems, as shown in **Figure 2.** All of these systems interact by exchanging matter and energy. For example, water from the ocean evaporates and enters the atmosphere. Later, the water precipitates onto land and washes salts into the ocean.

The hydrosphere is water on Earth's surface, underground, and liquid water in the atmosphere. Most of the water in the hydrosphere is in salty oceans. Freshwater is in most rivers and lakes and underground. Frozen water, such as glaciers, is part of the cryosphere which overlaps with the hydropsphere.

The Atmosphere, the Hydrosphere, and the Cryosphere The atmosphere is the layer of gases surrounding Earth. It is Earth's outermost system. This layer is about 100 km thick. It is a mixture of nitrogen, oxygen, carbon dioxide, and traces of other gases.

The Geosphere and the Biosphere *The* **geosphere** *is Earth's entire solid body.* It contains a thin layer of soil and sediments covering a rocky center. It is the largest Earth system. The biosphere includes all living things on Earth. Organisms in the biosphere live within and interact with the atmosphere, hydrosphere, and even the geosphere.

Key Concept Check Identify Earth's major systems.

Earth's Systems

Figure 2 Earth's systems interact. A change in one Earth system affects all other Earth systems. They exchange energy and matter, making Earth suitable for life.

How did Earth form?

Earth formed about 4.6 billion years ago (bya), along with the Sun and the rest of our solar system. Materials from a large cloud of gas and dust came together, forming the Sun and all the planets. In order to understand how this happened, you first need to know how gravity works.

The Influence of Gravity

Gravity *is the force that every object exerts on every other object because of their masses.* The force of gravity between two objects depends on the objects' masses and the distance between them. The more mass either object has, or the closer together they are, the stronger the gravitational force. You can see an example of this in **Figure 3.**

FOLDABLES®

Make a half book from a sheet of paper. Label it as shown. Use it to organize your notes about Earth's formation.

Force of Gravity

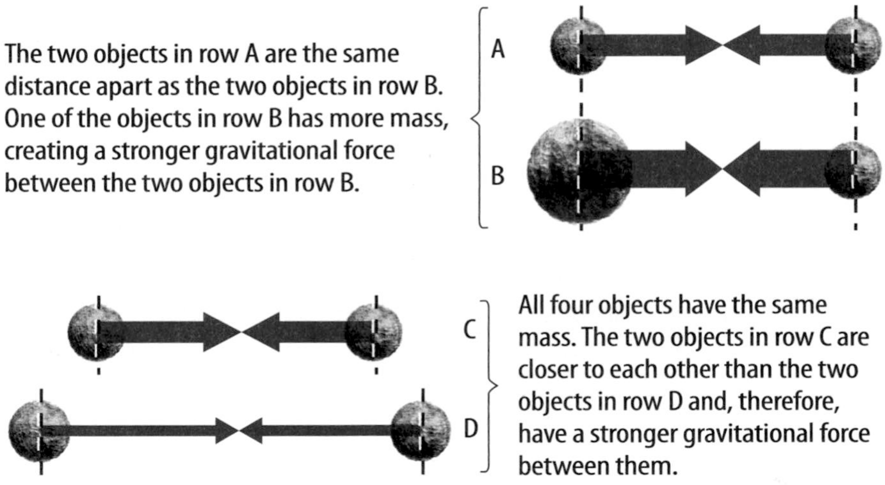

The two objects in row A are the same distance apart as the two objects in row B. One of the objects in row B has more mass, creating a stronger gravitational force between the two objects in row B.
A
B
C
D
All four objects have the same mass. The two objects in row C are closer to each other than the two objects in row D and, therefore, have a stronger gravitational force between them.

Figure 3 Mass and distance affect the strength of the gravitational force between objects.

Visual Check Why does Earth exert a greater gravitational force on you than other objects do?

The force of gravity is strongest between the objects in row B. Even though the objects in row A are the same distance apart as those in row B, the force of gravity between them is weaker because they have less mass. The force of gravity is weakest between the objects in row D.

Reading Check What factors affect the strength of the gravitational force between objects?

As illustrated in **Figure 4,** all objects on or near Earth are pulled toward Earth's center by gravity. Earth's gravity holds us to Earth's surface. Since Earth has more mass than any object near you, it exerts a greater gravitational force on you than other objects do. You don't notice the gravitational force between less massive objects.

Figure 4 Earth's gravity pulls objects toward the center of Earth.

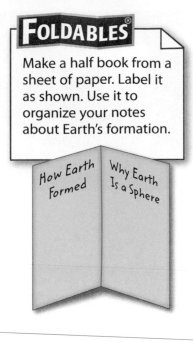

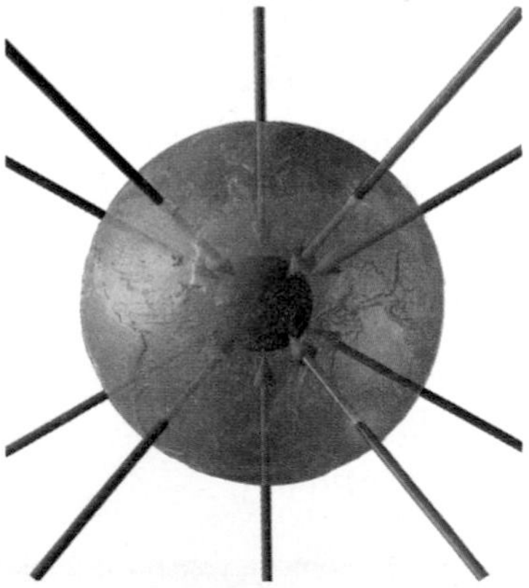

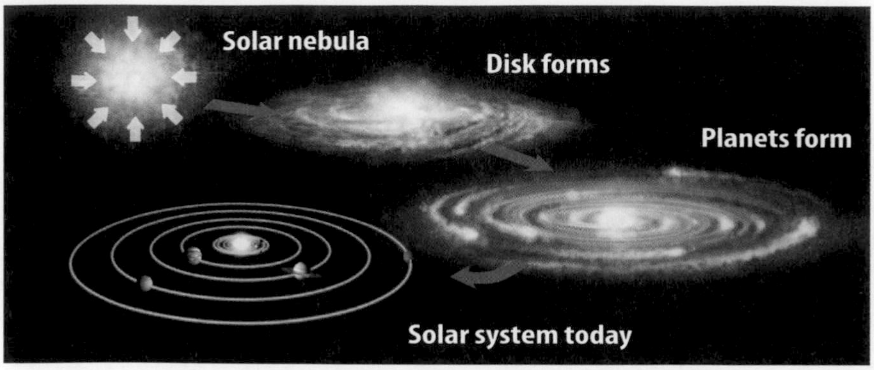

Figure 5 Gravity helped change a cloud of dust, gas, and ice, called a nebula, into our solar system. The Sun formed first, and the planets formed from the swirling disk of particles that remained.

Visual Check Our solar system formed from what type of cloud?

Review **Personal Tutor**

Inquiry MiniLab 15 minutes

Which materials will sink?

You can investigate the density of a material by comparing it to the density of water.

1. Read and complete a lab safety form.
2. Add water to a **clear, glass bowl** until it is about three-quarters full.
3. Hold a piece of **balsa wood** just under the surface of the water, then release it. Record your observations in your Science Journal. Remove the wood from the bowl.
4. Repeat step 2, using a piece of **granite, pumice,** and then **ironwood.**

Analyze and Conclude

1. **Summarize** Which materials sank? Which materials floated? Hypothesize why this happened.
2. **Key Concept** Use the concept of density to infer why the hydrosphere is above the geosphere but below the atmosphere.

The Solar Nebula

The force of gravity played a major role in the formation of our solar system. As shown in **Figure 5**, the solar system formed from a cloud of gas, ice, and dust called a nebula. Gravity pulled the materials closer together. The nebula shrank and flattened into a disk. The disk began to rotate. The materials in the center of the disk became denser, forming a star—our Sun.

Next, the planets began to take shape from the remaining bits of material. Earth formed as gravity pulled these small particles together. As they collided, they stuck to each other and formed larger, unevenly shaped objects. These larger objects had more mass and attracted more particles. Eventually enough matter collected and formed Earth. But how did the unevenly shaped, young planet become spherical?

Early Earth

Eventually the newly formed Earth grew massive and generated thermal energy, commonly called heat, in its interior. The rocks of the planet softened and began to flow.

Gravity pulled in the irregular bumps on the surface of the newly formed planet. As a result, Earth developed a relatively even spherical surface.

Key Concept Check How did Earth develop its spherical shape?

The Formation of Earth's Layers

Thermal energy from Earth's interior affected Earth in other ways, as well. Before heating up, Earth was a mixture of solid particles. The thermal energy melted some of this material and it began to flow. As it flowed, Earth developed distinct layers of different materials.

The different materials formed layers according to their densities. **Density** *is the amount of mass in a material per unit volume.* Density can be described mathematically as

$$D = m/V$$

where D is the density of the material, m is the material's mass, and V is its volume. If two materials have the same volume, the denser material will have more mass.

Reading Check Can a small object have more mass than a larger object? Explain your answer.

There is a stronger gravitational force between Earth and a denser object than there is between Earth and a less dense object. You can see this if you put an iron block and a pinewood block with the same volumes in a pan of water. The wooden block, which is less dense than water, will float on the water's surface. The iron block, which is denser than water, will be pulled through the water to the bottom of the pan.

When ancient Earth started melting, something much like this happened. The densest materials sank and formed the innermost layer of Earth. The least dense materials stayed at the surface, and formed a separate layer. The materials with intermediate densities formed layers in between the top layer and the bottom layer. Earth's three major layers are shown in **Figure 6.**

Math Skills

Solve One-Step Equations

Comparing the masses of substances is useful only if the same volume of each substance is used. To calculate density, divide the mass by the volume. The unit for density is a unit of mass, such as g, divided by a unit of volume, such as cm^3. For example, an aluminum cube has a mass of 27 g and a volume of 10 cm^3. The density of aluminum is 27 g / 10 cm^3 = 2.7 g/cm^3.

Practice

A chunk of gold with a volume of 5.00 cm^3 has a mass of 96.5 g. What is the density of gold?

Review

- **Math Practice**
- **Personal Tutor**

WORD ORIGIN

density
from Latin *densus,* means "thick, crowded"

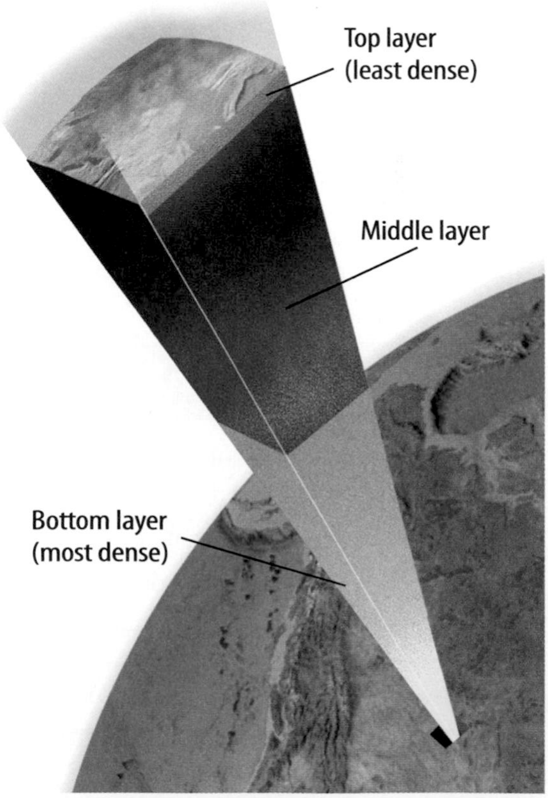

Figure 6 Earth's geosphere is divided into three major layers.

Lesson 1 Review

Assessment Online Quiz

Visual Summary

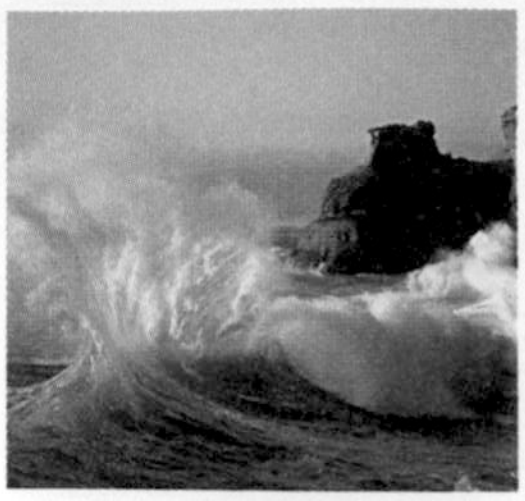

Earth's systems, including the atmosphere, hydrosphere, biosphere, and geosphere, interact with one another.

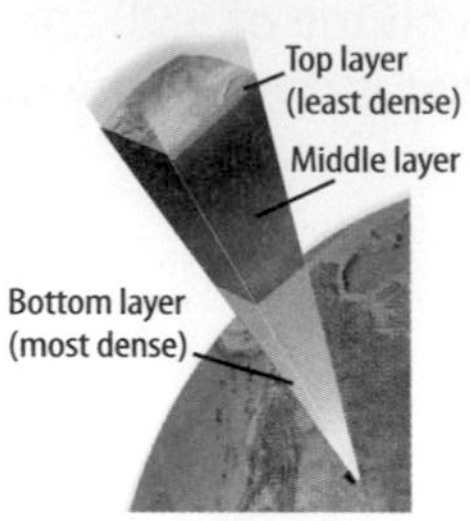

The geosphere is the solid body of Earth.

The solar system, including Earth, formed about 4.6 bya. Gravity caused particles to come together and formed a spherical Earth.

FOLDABLES®

Use your lesson Foldable to review the lesson. Save your Foldable for the project at the end of the chapter.

What do you think NOW?

You first read the statements below at the beginning of the chapter.

1. People have always known that Earth is round.
2. Earth's hydrosphere is made of hydrogen gas.

Did you change your mind about whether you agree or disagree with the statements? Rewrite any false statements to make them true.

Use Vocabulary

1 The Earth system made mainly of surface water is called the ________.

2 **Use the term** *density* in a sentence.

Understand Key Concepts

3 Which is part of the atmosphere?
- **A.** a rock
- **B.** a tree
- **C.** oxygen gas
- **D.** the ocean

4 **Describe** how gravity affected Earth's shape during Earth's formation.

Interpret Graphics

5 **Organize** Copy and complete the graphic organizer below. In each oval, list one of the following terms: *geosphere, hydrosphere, cryosphere, Earth, atmosphere,* and *biosphere.*

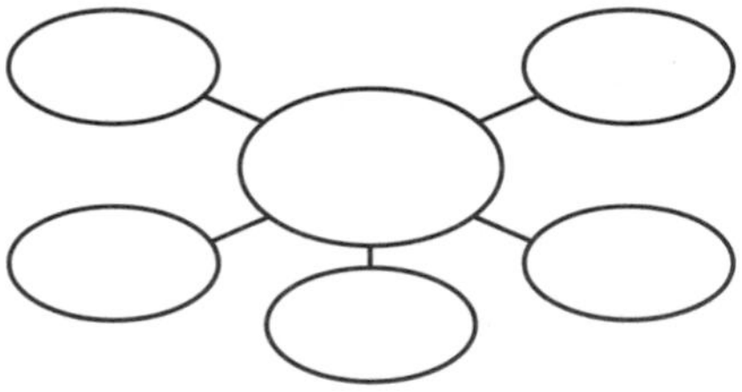

Critical Thinking

6 **Combine** your understanding of how Earth became spherical and observations of the Moon. Then form a hypothesis about the formation of the Moon.

7 **Explain** As Earth formed, did it grow larger or become smaller? Explain your answer.

Math Skills

Review — Math Practice

8 At a given temperature, 3.00 m^3 of carbon dioxide has a mass of 5.94 kg. What is the density of carbon dioxide at this temperature?

AMERICAN MUSEUM of NATURAL HISTORY

CAREERS in SCIENCE

◄ George Harlow studies diamonds to learn more about Earth's interior.

Time Capsules

Formed billions of years ago in Earth's mantle, diamonds hold important clues about our planet's mysterious interior.

George Harlow is fascinated by diamonds. Not because of their dazzling shine or their value, but because of what they can reveal about Earth. He considers diamonds to be tiny time capsules that capture a picture of the ancient mantle, where they became crystals.

Most diamonds we find today formed billions of years ago deep within Earth's mantle, over 161 km below Earth's surface. Tiny bits of mantle, called inclusions, were trapped inside these extremely hard crystals as they formed. Millions of years later, the inclusions' diamond cases still protect them.

Harlow collects these diamonds from places such as Australia, Africa, and Thailand. Back in the lab, Harlow and his colleagues remove inclusions from diamonds. First, they break open a diamond with a tool similar to a nutcracker. Then they use a microscope and a pinlike tool to sift through the diamond rubble. They look for an inclusion, which is about the size of a grain of sand. When they find one, they use an electron microprobe and a laser to analyze the inclusion's composition, or chemical makeup. The sample might be tiny, but it's enough for scientists to learn the temperature, pressure, and composition of the mantle in which the diamond formed.

Next time you see a diamond, you might wonder if it too has a tiny bit of ancient mantle from deep inside Earth.

Going Up?

Diamond crystals form deep within the mantle under intense pressures and temperatures. They come to Earth's surface in molten rock, or magma. The magma pulls diamonds from rock deep underground and rapidly carries them to the surface. The magma erupts onto Earth's surface in small, explosive volcanoes. Diamonds and other crystals and rocks from the mantle are in deep, carrot-shaped cones called kimberlite pipes that are part of these rare volcanoes.

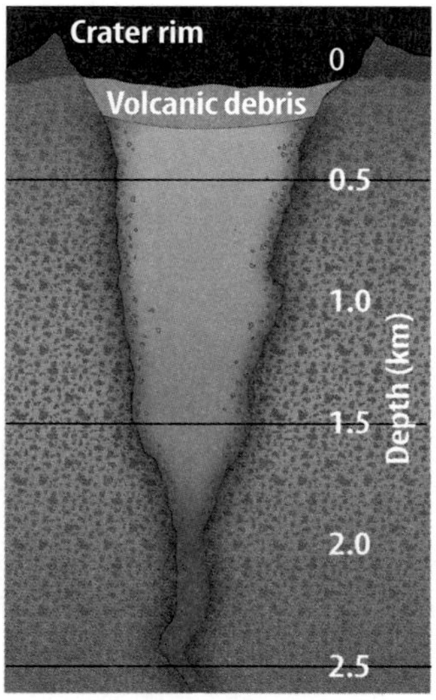

It's Your Turn

RESEARCH Diamonds are the world's most popular gemstone. What other uses do diamonds have? Research the properties of diamonds and how they are used in industry. Report your findings to your class.

Lesson 2

Earth's Interior

Reading Guide

Key Concepts
ESSENTIAL QUESTIONS

- What are the interior layers of Earth?
- What evidence indicates that Earth has a solid inner core and a liquid outer core?

Vocabulary

crust p. 173
mantle p. 174
lithosphere p. 174
asthenosphere p. 174
core p. 176
magnetosphere p. 177

g Multilingual eGlossary

Video Science Video

Academic Standards for Science

7.2.1 Describe how the earth is a layered structure composed of lithospheric plates, a mantle and a dense core.

7.2.2 Recognize that the earth possesses a magnetic field that is detectable at the surface with a compass.

Also covers: 7.NS.3, 7.NS.5, 7.NS.7, 7.NS.8, 7.NS.9

Inquiry What is inside Earth?

Earth is thousands of kilometers thick. The deepest mines and wells in the world barely scratch Earth's surface. How do you think scientists learn about Earth's interior?

Inquiry Launch Lab

10 minutes

How can you model Earth's layers?

Earth is made of three main layers: the thin outer crust, the thick mantle, and the central core. You can use different objects to model these layers.

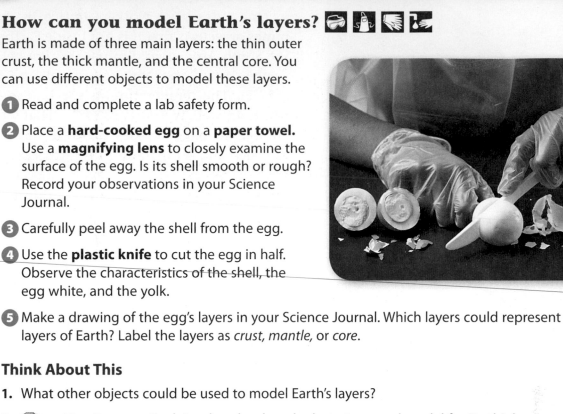

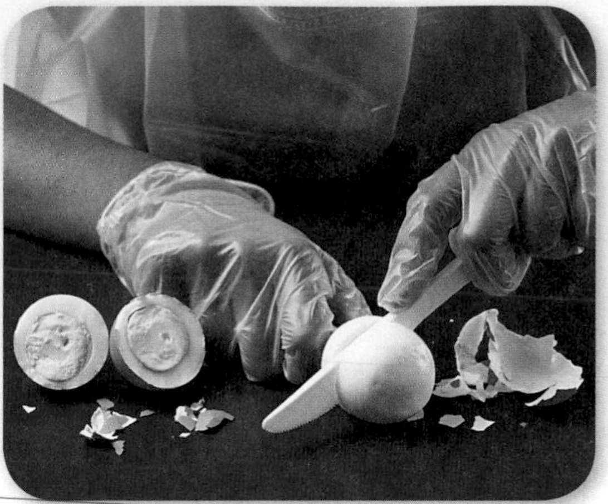

1. Read and complete a lab safety form.
2. Place a **hard-cooked egg** on a **paper towel.** Use a **magnifying lens** to closely examine the surface of the egg. Is its shell smooth or rough? Record your observations in your Science Journal.
3. Carefully peel away the shell from the egg.
4. Use the **plastic knife** to cut the egg in half. Observe the characteristics of the shell, the egg white, and the yolk.
5. Make a drawing of the egg's layers in your Science Journal. Which layers could represent layers of Earth? Label the layers as *crust, mantle,* or *core.*

Think About This

1. What other objects could be used to model Earth's layers?
2. **Key Concept** Explain why a hard-cooked egg is a good model for Earth's layers.

Clues to Earth's Interior

Were you ever given a gift and had to wait to open it? Maybe you tried to figure out what was inside by tapping on it or shaking it. Using methods such as these, you might have been able to determine the gift's contents. Scientists can't see what is inside Earth, either. But they can use indirect methods to discover what Earth's interior is like.

What's below Earth's surface?

Deep mines and wells give scientists hints about Earth's interior. The deepest mine ever constructed is a gold mine in South Africa. It is more than 3 km deep. People can go down the mine to explore the geosphere.

Drilled wells are even deeper. The deepest well is on the Kola Peninsula in Russia. It is more than 12 km deep. Drilling to such great depths is extremely difficult—it took more than 20 years to drill the Kola well. Even though people cannot go down in the well, they can send instruments down to make **observations** and bring samples to the surface. What have scientists learned about Earth's interior by studying mines and wells like the two mentioned above?

Review Vocabulary
observation
an act of recognizing and noting a fact or an occurrence

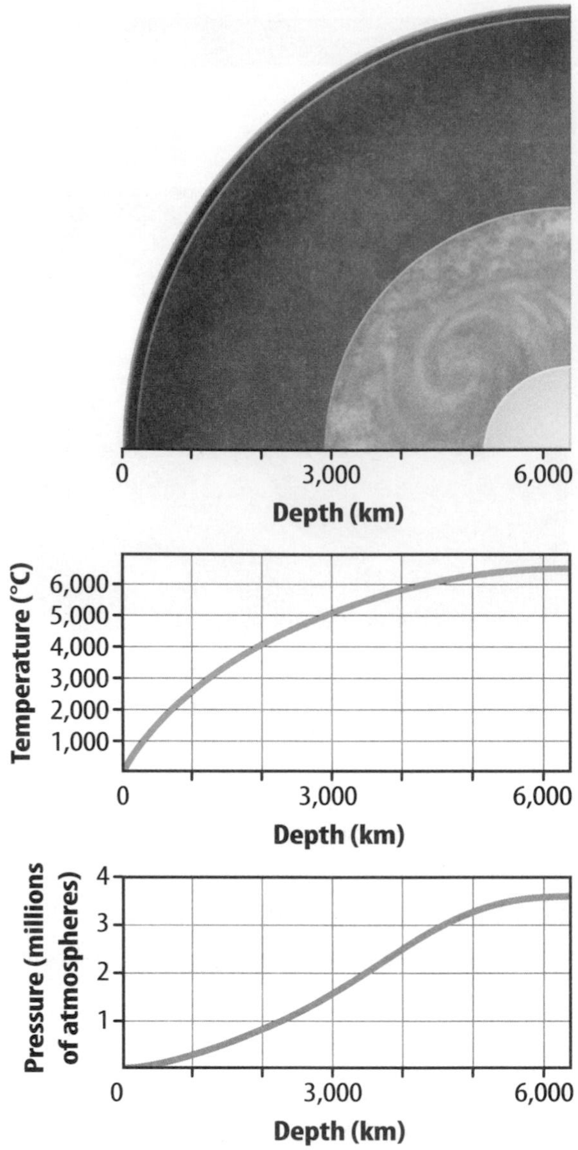

Figure 7 Temperature and pressure increase with depth in the geosphere.

Temperature and Pressure Increase with Depth

One thing that workers notice in deep mines or wells is that it is hot inside Earth. In the South African gold mines, 3.5 km below Earth's surface, the temperature is about 53°C (127°F). The temperature at the bottom of the Kola well is 190°C (374°F). That's hot enough to bake cookies! No one has ever recorded the temperature of Earth's center, but it is estimated to be about 6,000°C. As shown in **Figure 7,** temperature within Earth increases with increasing depth.

Not only does temperature increase, but pressure also increases as depth increases inside Earth. This is due to the weight of the overlying rocks. The high pressure squeezes the rocks and makes them much denser than surface rocks.

Reading Check Describe how pressure changes with depth within Earth.

High temperatures and pressures make it difficult to drill deep wells. The depth of the Kola well is less than 1 percent of the distance to Earth's center. Therefore, only a small part of the geosphere has been sampled. How can scientists learn about what is below the deepest wells?

Using Earthquake Waves

As you read earlier, scientists use indirect methods to study Earth's interior. They get most of their evidence by analyzing earthquake waves. Earthquakes release energy in the form of three types of waves. As these waves move through Earth, they are affected by the different materials they travel through. Some waves cannot travel through certain materials. Other waves change direction when they reach certain materials. By studying how the waves move, scientists are able to infer the density and composition of materials within Earth.

FOLDABLES®

Make a layered book from two sheets of paper. Use your book to organize information about Earth's crust, mantle, outer core, and inner core.

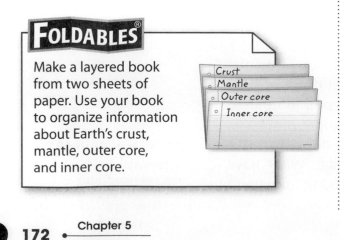

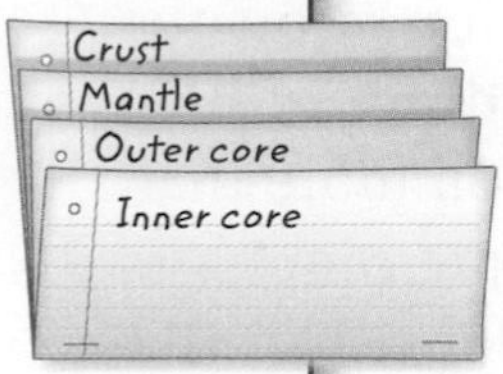

Earth's Layers

Differences in density resulted in materials within Earth, forming layers. Each layer has a different composition, with the densest material in the center of Earth.

Crust

The brittle, rocky outer layer of Earth is called the **crust.** It is much thinner than the other layers, like the shell on a hard-cooked egg. It is the least dense layer of the geosphere. It is made mostly of elements of low mass, such as silicon and oxygen.

Crustal rocks are under oceans and on land. The crust under oceans is called oceanic crust. It is made of dense rocks that contain iron and magnesium. The crust on land is called continental crust. It is about four times thicker than oceanic crust. Continental crust is thickest under tall mountains. **Figure 8** shows a comparison of the two types of crust.

There is a distinct boundary between the crust and the layer beneath it. When earthquake waves cross this boundary, they speed up. This indicates that the lower layer is denser than the crust.

Reading Check How does oceanic crust differ from continental crust?

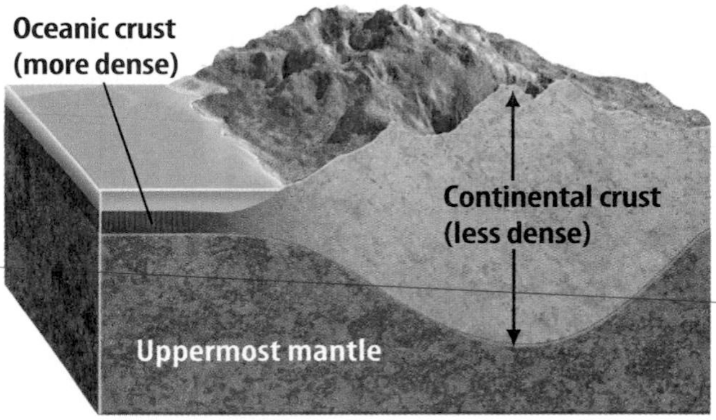

Figure 8 Oceanic crust is thin and dense compared to continental crust.

Review Personal Tutor

Inquiry MiniLab

Which liquid is densest?

Earth's layers were determined by density. The iron in the inner core makes up Earth's densest layer. The silicon and oxygen in Earth's crust are much less dense.

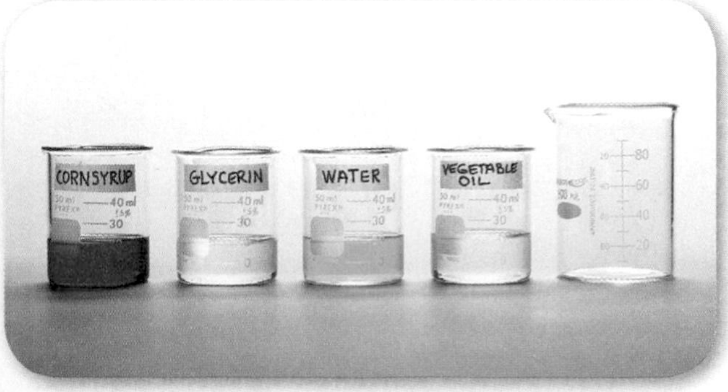

1. Read and complete a lab safety form.
2. Pour 50 mL of **corn syrup** into a **100-mL beaker.** Label the beaker.
3. Fill the remaining three beakers with 50 mL of **glycerin, water,** and **vegetable oil,** respectively. Label them.
4. Stir a few drops of **blue food coloring** into the water using a **spoon.**
5. Rinse the spoon. Then stir a few drops of **red food coloring** into the corn syrup.
6. Pour the corn syrup into a **250-mL beaker.**
7. Use a **funnel** to gently pour the glycerin on top of the corn syrup. Hold the funnel along the side of the beaker.
8. Repeat step 7 using the vegetable oil, then the water.

Analyze and Conclude

1. **Describe** what happened to the liquids. Why did this occur?
2. **Key Concept** How are the layers of liquid in the beaker similar to Earth's layers?

Mantle

Earth's mantle is immediately below the crust. *The* **mantle** *is the thick middle layer in the solid part of Earth.* It contains more iron and magnesium than oceanic crust does. This makes it denser than either type of crust. Like the crust, the mantle is made of rock. The iron-rich rocks of this layer are peridotite and eclogite. Scientists group the mantle into four layers according to the way rocks react when forces push or pull on them. **Figure 9** shows the mantle and other layers.

Uppermost Mantle The rocks in the uppermost layer of the mantle are brittle and rigid, like the rocks in the crust. Because of this, *scientists group the crust and the uppermost mantle into a rigid layer called the* **lithosphere** (LIH thuh sfihr).

Asthenosphere Below the lithosphere, rocks are so hot that tiny bits melt. When this happens, the rocks are no longer brittle. They begin to flow. Scientists use the term *plastic* to describe rocks that flow in this way. *This plastic layer within the mantle is called the* **asthenosphere** (as THE nuh sfihr).

✓ **Reading Check** Compare the lithosphere and the asthenosphere.

The asthenosphere does not resemble the plastics used to make everyday products. The word *plastic* refers to materials that are soft enough to flow. The asthenosphere flows very slowly. Even if it were possible to visit the mantle, you could never see this flow. Rocks in the asthenosphere move about as slowly as your fingernails grow.

WORD ORIGIN

asthenosphere
from Greek *asthenes,* means "weak"; and *spharia,* means "sphere"

Upper Mantle and Lower Mantle The rock below the asthenosphere is solid, but it is hotter than the rock in the asthenosphere. How can this be? The pressure at this depth is so great that no melting occurs. While increased temperature tends to melt rock, high pressure tends to prevent melting. High pressure squeezes the rock into a solid. This solid rock of the upper mantle and the lower mantle forms the largest layer of Earth.

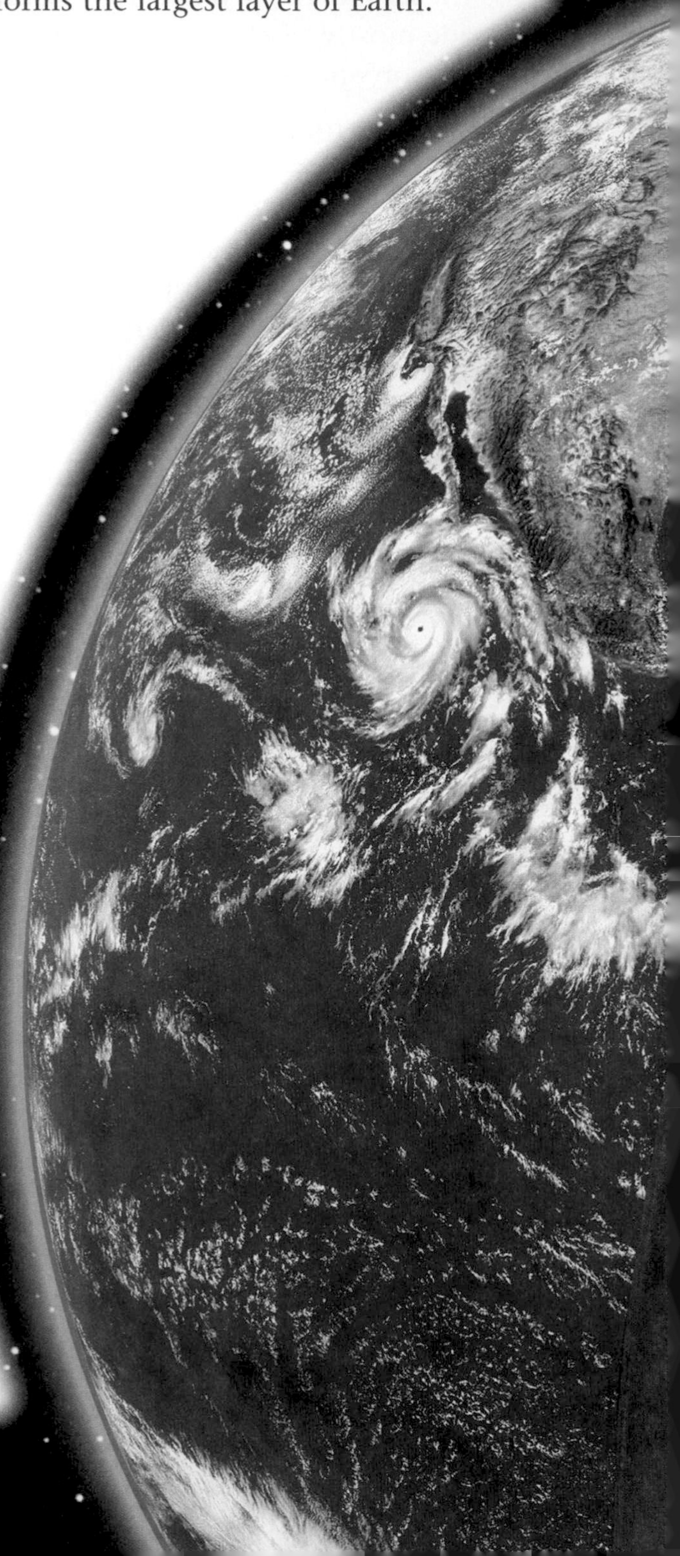

Figure 9 Earth's main layers include the crust, mantle, and core. The layers are subdivided according to chemical and physical characteristics.

Visual Check Which of Earth's layers is the most dense?

Concepts in Motion

Animation

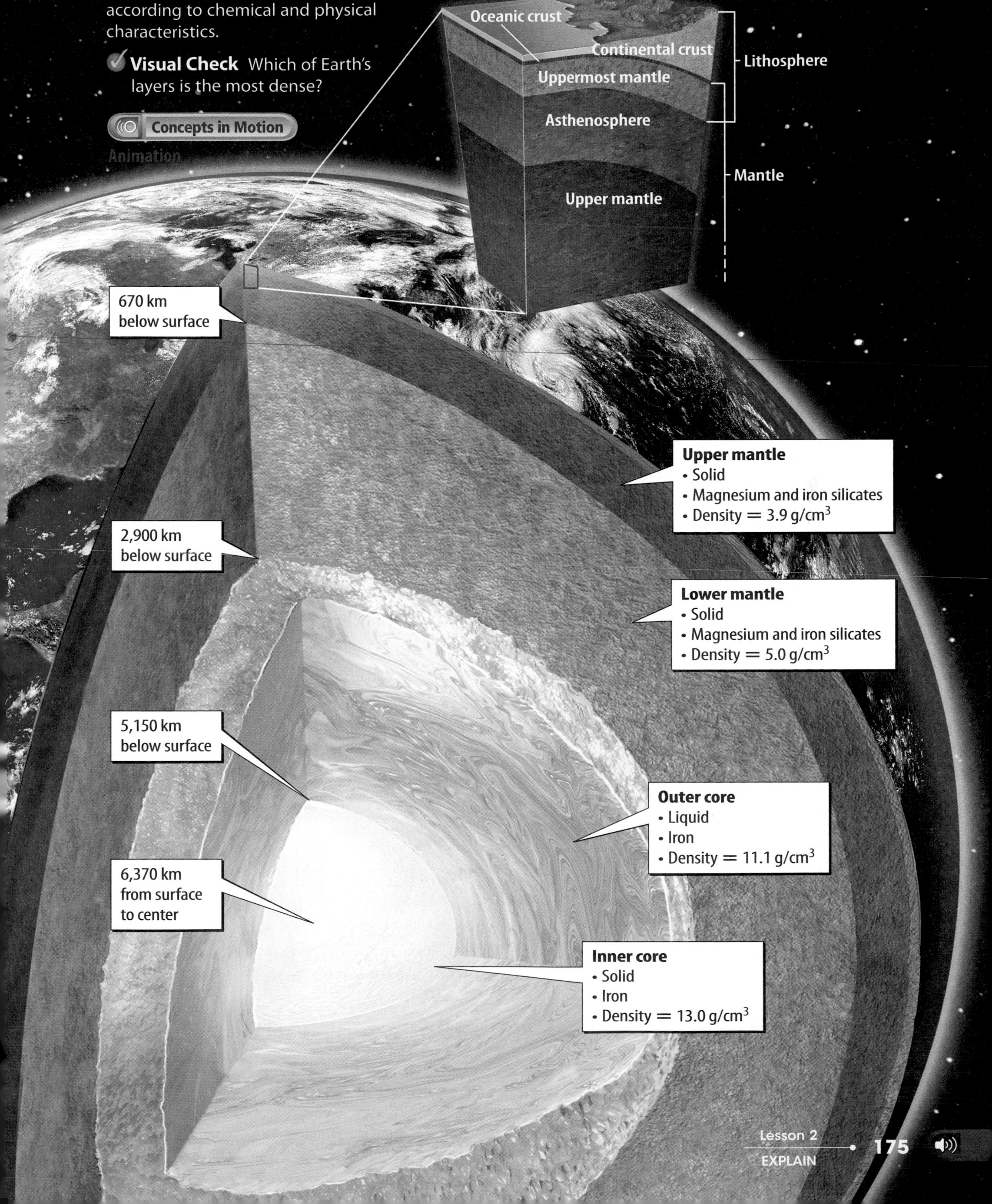

Earth's Core

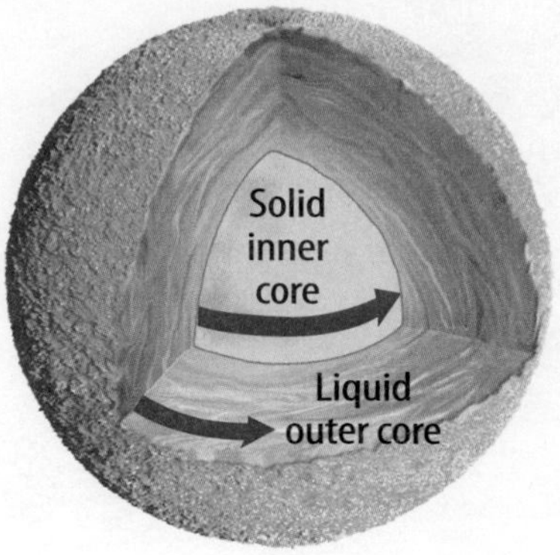

Figure 10 Earth's core has a liquid outer layer surrounding a solid inner layer of iron. The inner core spins a little faster than the outer core.

Visual Check How do the arrows in this figure indicate that the inner core spins faster than the outer core?

Core

The dense metallic center of Earth is the **core,** as shown in **Figure 10.** If you imagine Earth as a hard-cooked egg, the core is the yolk. Earth's crust and mantle are made of rock. Why is the core made of metal? Recall that in Earth's early history, the planet was much hotter than it is now. Earth materials flowed, like they do in the asthenosphere today. Scientists don't know how much of Earth melted. But they do know that it was soft enough for gravity to pull the densest material down to the center. This dense material is metal. It is mostly iron with small amounts of **nickel** and other elements. The core has a liquid outer core and a solid inner core.

Science Use v. Common Use
nickel
Science Use a specific type of metal
Common Use a coin worth five cents

Key Concept Check What are the interior layers of Earth?

Outer Core If pressure is great enough to keep the lower mantle in a solid state, how can the outer core be liquid? The mantle and core are made of different materials, and have different melting temperatures. Just like in the asthenosphere, the effects of temperature outweigh the effects of pressure in the outer core. Scientists learned that the outer core is liquid by analyzing earthquake waves, as you read about in Lesson 1.

Key Concept Check What evidence indicates that the outer core is liquid?

Inner Core The inner core is a dense ball of solid iron crystals. The pressure in the center of Earth is so high that even at temperatures of about 6,000°C, the iron is in a solid state. Because the outer core is liquid, it is not rigidly attached to the inner core. The inner core spins a little faster than the rest of Earth.

Earth's Core and Geomagnetism

Why does a compass needle point north? This happens because the metallic needle lines up with a force field surrounding Earth. This force field is caused by Earth's core.

Earth's Magnetic Field

Recall that Earth's inner core spins faster than the outer core. This produces streams of flowing, molten iron in the outer core. Earth's magnetic field is a region of magnetism produced in part by the flow of molten materials in the outer core. The magnetic field acts much like a giant bar magnet. It has opposite poles, as shown in **Figure 11.**

For centuries, people have used compasses and Earth's magnetic field to navigate. But, the magnetic field is not completely stable. Over geologic time, its strength and direction vary. At several times in Earth's history, the direction has even reversed.

Figure 11 Earth's magnetic field is produced by the movement of molten materials in the outer core.

Magnetosphere

Earth's magnetic field protects Earth from cosmic rays and charged particles coming from the Sun. It pushes away some charged particles and traps others. *The outer part of the magnetic field that interacts with these particles is called the* **magnetosphere.** Examine **Figure 12** to see how the shape of the magnetosphere is produced by the flow of these charged particles.

WORD ORIGIN

magnetosphere
from Latin *magnes,* means "lodestone"; and *spharia,* means "sphere"

The Magnetosphere

Figure 12 Trapped particles and Earth's magnetic field form a shield around Earth.

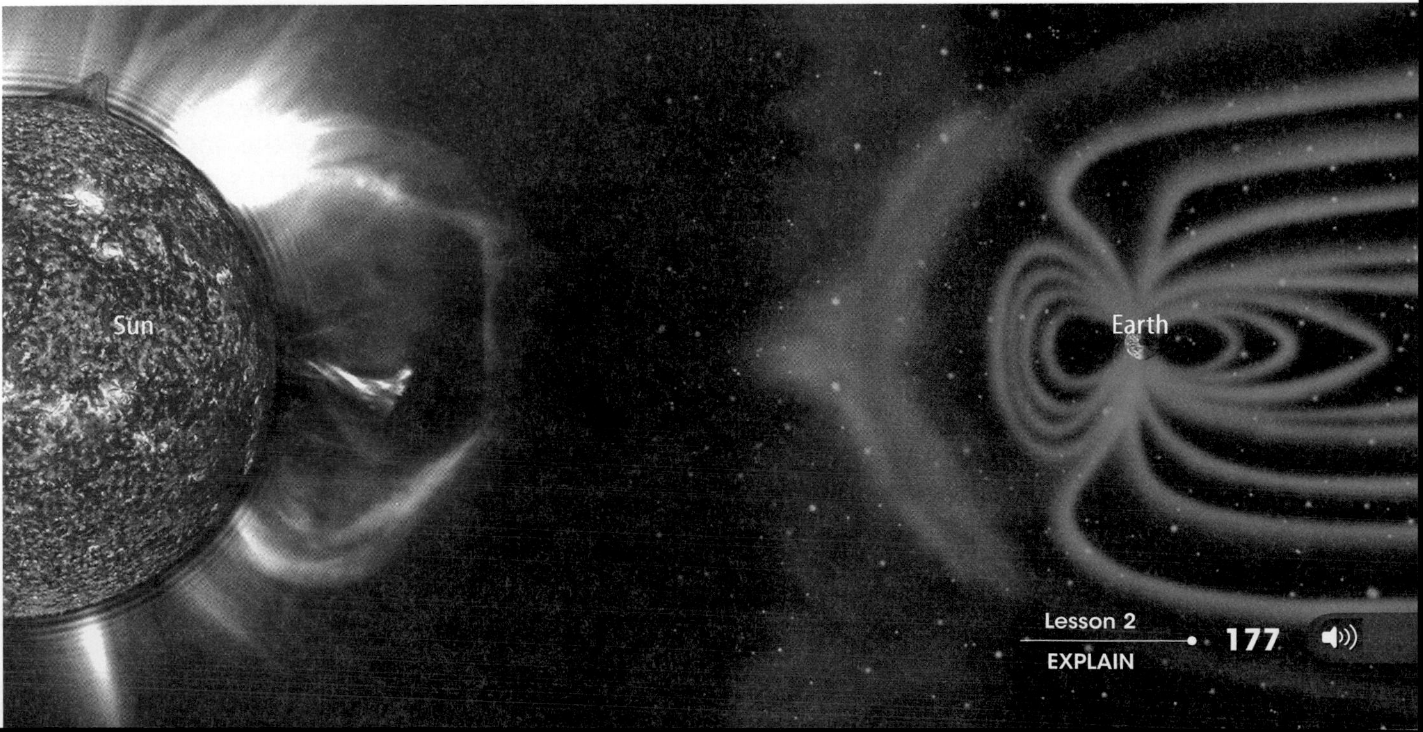

Lesson 2 Review

Assessment Online Quiz

Visual Summary

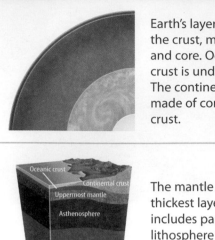

Earth's layers include the crust, mantle, and core. Oceanic crust is under oceans. The continents are made of continental crust.

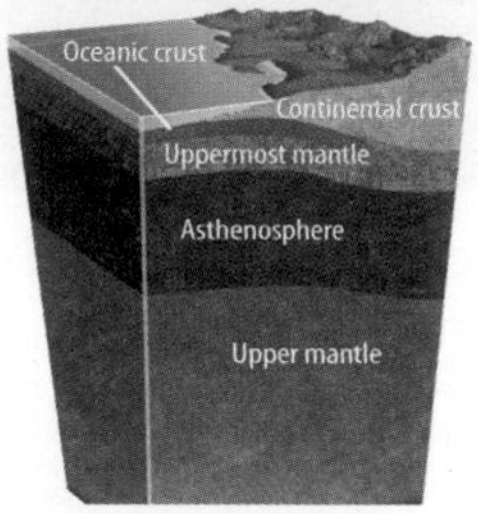

The mantle is Earth's thickest layer. It includes part of the lithosphere and the asthenosphere.

Earth's core has a liquid outer core and a solid inner core.

FOLDABLES®

Use your lesson Foldable to review the lesson. Save your Foldable for the project at the end of the chapter.

What do you think NOW?

You first read the statements below at the beginning of the chapter.

3. Earth's interior is made of distinct layers.

4. Scientists discovered that Earth's outer core is liquid by drilling deep wells.

Did you change your mind about whether you agree or disagree with the statements? Rewrite any false statements to make them true.

Use Vocabulary

1. The layer of Earth made of metal is the __________.

2. **Distinguish** between the crust and the lithosphere.

3. **Use the terms** *core* and *mantle* in a complete sentence.

Understand Key Concepts

4. Which of Earth's layers is made of melted materials?
   - **A.** the crust
   - **B.** the inner core
   - **C.** the lithosphere
   - **D.** the outer core

5. **Design** a model of Earth's layers. List the materials needed to make your model.

6. **Classify** Earth's layers based on their physical properties.

Interpret Graphics

7. **Identify** and compare the two types of crust shown below.

8. **Determine Cause and Effect** Draw a graphic organizer like the one below and list two facts about Earth's magnetic field.

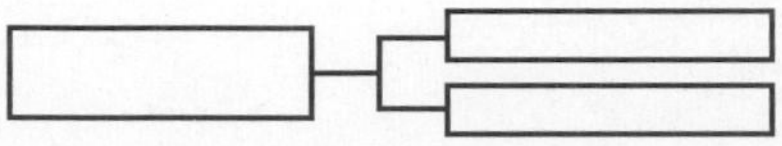

Critical Thinking

9. **Reflect** Earthquakes produce waves that help scientists understand what Earth's interior looks like, but they also harm people. Reflect on whether earthquake waves are good or bad.

How can you find the density of a liquid?

Earth's interior is made of solids and liquids that have different densities. You can measure volume and mass and then calculate density using the equation:

$$\text{Density} = \frac{\text{Mass}}{\text{Volume}}$$

Materials

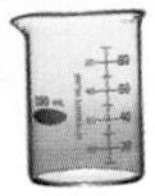
beaker

balance

graduated cylinder

vegetable oil

corn syrup

isoprophyl alcohol

Safety

Learn It

Scientists **measure** to learn how much they have of a particular type of matter. Recall that matter is anything that has mass and volume. You can measure mass using a triple-beam balance. The unit of mass you will use most often is the gram (g). You can measure liquid volume using a graduated cylinder. Millimeter (mL) is the unit of volume you will use most often.

Try It

1. Read and complete a lab safety form.
2. Measure the mass of a 50-mL graduated cylinder. Record the mass in your Science Journal.
3. Pour about 15 mL of alcohol into a clean beaker.
4. Slowly pour the alcohol into the graduated cylinder until the alcohol measures 10 mL.
5. Measure and record the mass of the alcohol and the graduated cylinder.
6. In your Science Journal, subtract the mass recorded in step 2 from the mass recorded in step 5.
7. Empty and clean the graduated cylinder as instructed by your teacher.
8. Repeat steps 3–7 using the corn syrup and then the vegetable oil.

Apply It

9. Calculate and record the density of each liquid using your mass and volume measurements and the equation shown above.
10. Which fluid has the greatest density? Which has the least? Explain your answer.
11. **Key Concept** Based on what you have learned, describe the relative density of Earth's layers.

Lesson 3

Reading Guide

Key Concepts
ESSENTIAL QUESTIONS

- What are Earth's major landforms and how do they compare?
- What are the major landform regions of the United States?

Vocabulary

landform p. 182

plain p. 184

plateau p. 185

mountain p. 185

g Multilingual eGlossary

Video BrainPOP®

Academic Standards for Science

7.2.1 Describe how the earth is a layered structure composed of lithospheric plates, a mantle and a dense core.

7.2.7 Use geological features such as karst topography and glaciation to explain how large-scale physical processes have shaped the land.

Also covers: 7.NS.3, 7.NS.5, 7.NS.11, 7.DP.4, 7.DP.6

Earth's Surface

Inquiry What do you see?

Some features on Earth's surface are flat and low. Other features are steep and high. What else is different about these features?

Inquiry Launch Lab

15 minutes

How can you measure topographic relief?

Relief describes differences in elevation for a given area. The area might have tall mountains or deep valleys. In this lab, you will use simple materials to measure relief on a model landscape.

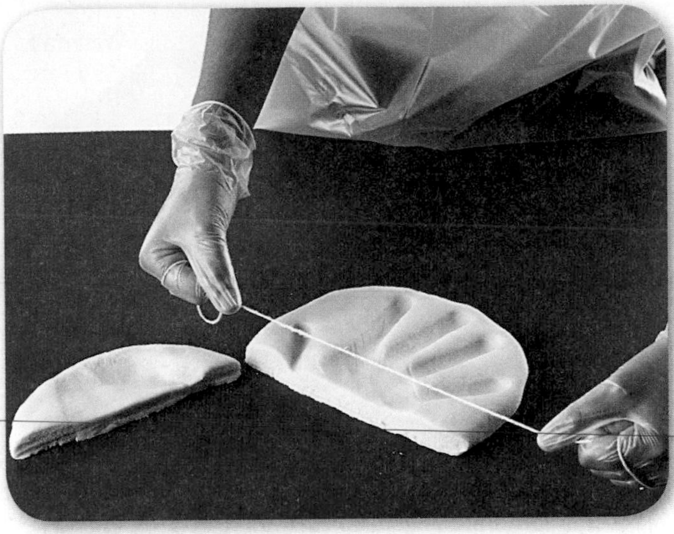

1. Read and complete a lab safety form.
2. Form some **salt dough** into a thick disk slightly larger than your hand.
3. With your fingers spread apart, press your hand firmly into the dough so that some of the dough squeezes up between your fingers.
4. Stretch **dental floss** across the finger impressions in the dough. Slice off a section of the dough model by pressing the dental floss down through the dough.
5. Also make a slice through the palm section of your dough model.
6. Observe the profiles of your two cross sections. Use a **ruler** to measure the difference between the highest and lowest points within the palm section.
7. Measure the difference between the highest and lowest points within the fingers section.

Think About This

1. What is the difference in elevation between the highest and lowest points of your hand print?
2. **Key Concept** Compare and contrast your model features. How are they similar to features on Earth?

Oceans and Continents

Earth has a variety of features, such as mountains and valleys. The surface of the ocean, however, is relatively smooth. But what is below the water's surface? Imagine that you can explore the ocean floor as easily as you travel on dry land. What do you think you would see there?

Earth's surface is made of oceans and continents. Oceans cover more than 70 percent of Earth's surface. Many of the features that appear on dry land also appear on the ocean floor. For example, the longest mountain ranges on Earth are near the centers of the oceans. Monterey Canyon, illustrated in **Figure 13**, is a submarine canyon which is comparable in size to the Grand Canyon on land.

Figure 13 From its rim to the canyon floor, Monterey Canyon reaches a maximum depth of about 1,920 m, making it slightly deeper than the Grand Canyon.

Common Landforms

Figure 14 Earth's common landforms are characterized by size, shape, slope, elevation, and relief.

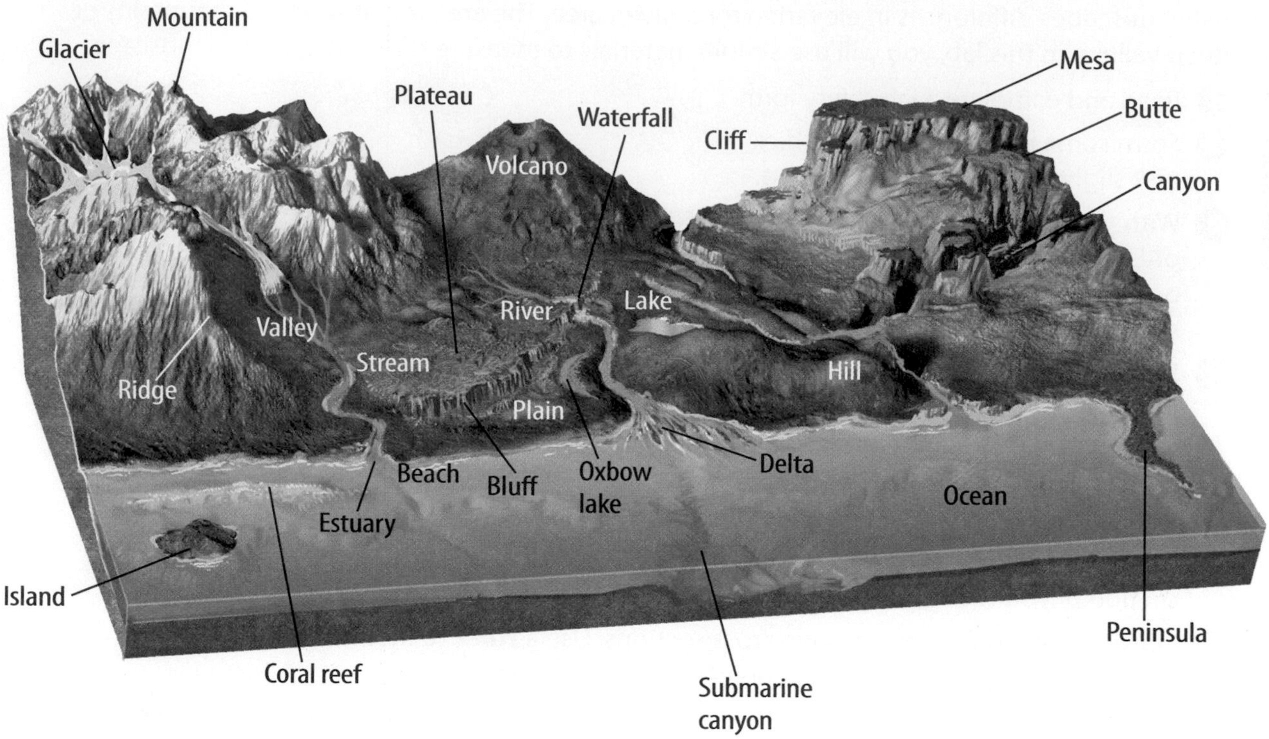

Visual Check Which landforms are most familiar to you?

ACADEMIC VOCABULARY
feature
(noun) the structure, form, or appearance of something

Landforms

Mountains, plains, plateaus, canyons, and other **features** are called landforms. Some examples of Earth's landforms are shown in **Figure 14**. **Landforms** *are topographic features formed by processes that shape Earth's surface.* They can be as big as mountains or as small as ant hills. Characteristics such as size, shape, slope, elevation, relief, and orientation to the surrounding landscape are often used to describe landforms. A landform is usually identified by its surface form and location.

Key Concept Check What are landforms?

Landforms are not permanent. Their characteristics change over time. Many factors such as erosion or uplift of Earth's surface can create and affect landforms.

Elevation

Scientists use the term *elevation* to describe the height above sea level of a particular feature. Some landforms have high elevation. Other landforms have low elevation. For example, elevation is one of the major characteristics that is used to distinguish a plain from a plateau.

Relief

Do you recall how you measured relief in the Launch Lab at the beginning of this lesson? *Relief* is a term that scientists use to describe differences in elevation. Some landforms or geographic areas are described as having low relief. This means that there is a relatively small difference between the lowest elevation and the highest elevation in an area. Landforms or areas with high relief have a relatively large difference between the lowest elevation and the highest elevation. For example, if you were to climb out of the Grand Canyon, you would probably say it has high relief.

Topography

Scientists use the term *topography* to describe the shape of a geographic area. You can describe the topography of a small location or you can think about the general topography of a large region. Relief and topography can be used to describe features on continents and on the ocean floor. Next, you will read how relief and elevation are used to describe the most common landforms on Earth—plains, plateaus, and mountains.

Inquiry MiniLab

20 minutes

How do landforms compare?

The terms *gully, ravine,* and *canyon* all describe an elongated depression formed by erosion from water. But how do these landforms differ?

1. Read and complete a lab safety form.
2. Working with a partner, use a **dictionary** to find the definition of the landforms in one of the lists below.

List 1	List 2	List 3	List 4
butte	hill	bay	channel
mesa	knoll	cove	strait
plateau	mountain	gulf	sound

3. Use **modeling clay** to represent the landforms in the list you chose.
4. Use **scissors** to cut different colors of **construction paper** and make scenes with your landforms.
5. Label each part of the scene.

Analyze and Conclude

Key Concept Compare and contrast the model landforms.

Figure 15 Plains, plateaus, and mountains differ in terms of elevation and relief. ▶

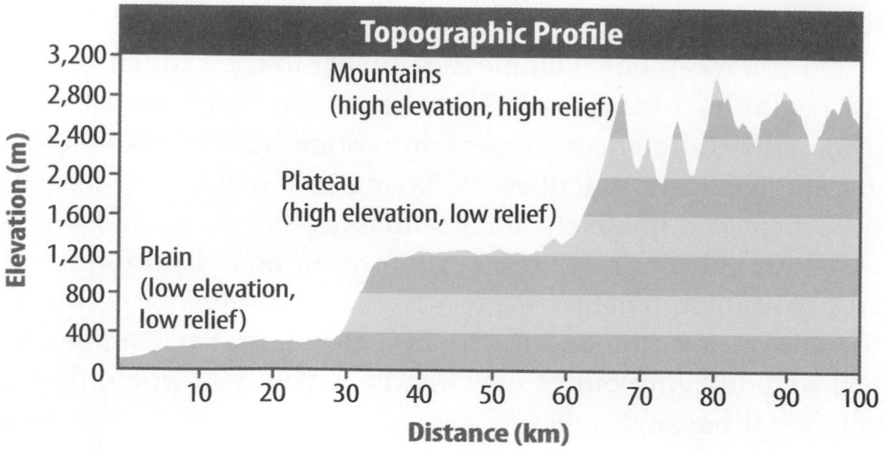

Plains

Word Origin

plain
from Latin *planus*, means "flat, level"

The features that cover most of Earth's surface are plains. **Plains** *are landforms with low relief and low elevation,* as illustrated in **Figure 15.** The broad, flat area in the center of North America is called the interior plains, as shown in **Figure 16.**

Plains can form when sediments are deposited by water or wind. Their soil is often rich. For this reason, many plains are used for growing crops or grazing animals.

Major Landform Regions

Figure 16 This map shows the major landform regions on Earth—plains, plateaus, and mountains.

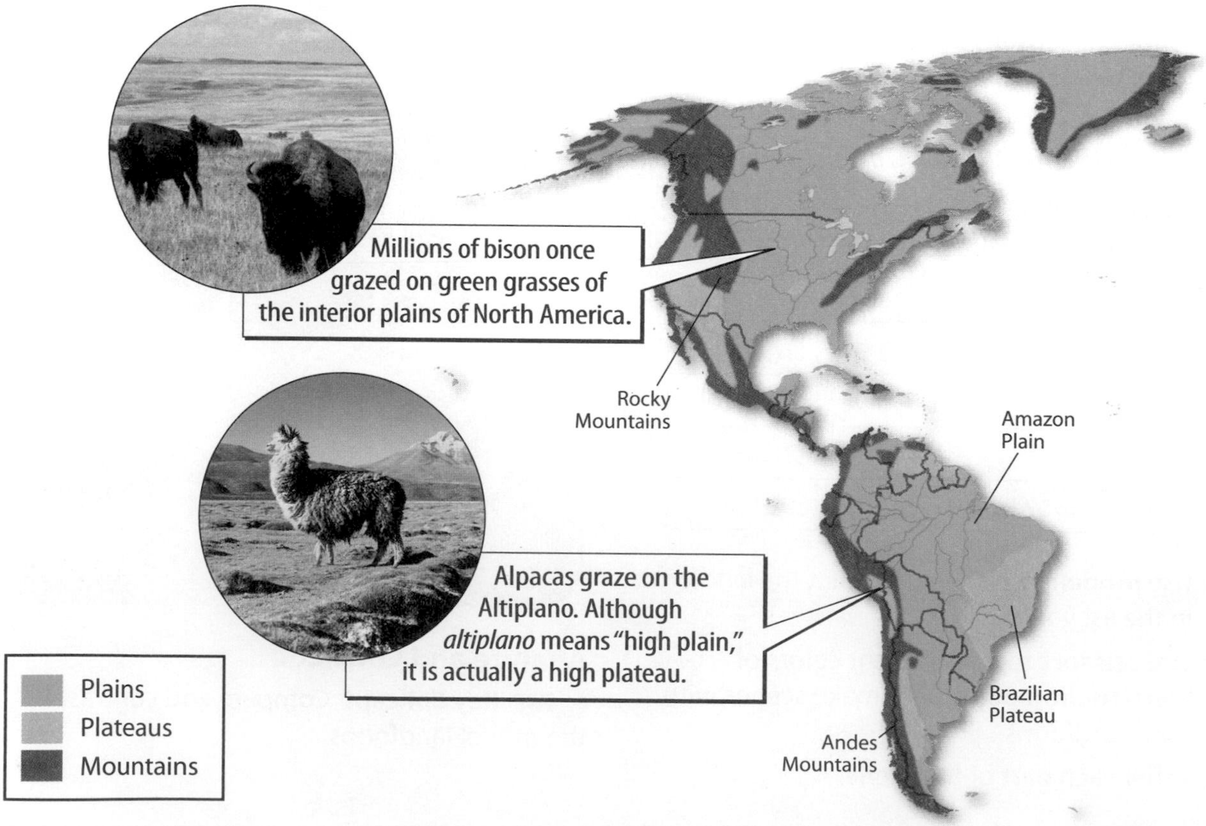

Millions of bison once grazed on green grasses of the interior plains of North America.
Rocky Mountains
Amazon Plain
Alpacas graze on the Altiplano. Although *altiplano* means "high plain," it is actually a high plateau.
Brazilian Plateau
Andes Mountains
Plains
Plateaus
Mountains

Plateaus

As you just read, plains are relatively flat and low. In contrast, plateaus are flat and high. **Plateaus** *are areas with low relief and high elevation.* Look again at **Figure 15** to see how a plateau differs from a plain.

Plateaus are much higher than the surrounding land and often have steep, rugged sides. They are less common than plains, but they are on every continent. Find some plateaus in different parts of the world in **Figure 16.**

Reading Check Describe a plateau.

Plateaus can form when forces within Earth uplift rock layers or cause collisions between sections of Earth's crust. For example, the highest plateau in the world is the Tibetan Plateau, called the "roof of the world." It is still being formed by collisions between India and Asia.

Plateaus also can be formed by volcanic activity. For example, the Columbia Plateau in the western United States is the result of the buildup of many successive lava flows.

Mountains

The tallest landforms of all are mountains. **Mountains** *are landforms with high relief and high elevation.* Look again at the world map in **Figure 16.** How many of Earth's well-know mountains can you find?

Mountains can form in several different ways. Some mountains form from the buildup of lava on the ocean floor. Eventually, the mountain grows tall enough to rise above the ocean's surface. The Hawaiian Islands are mountains that formed this way. Other mountains form when forces inside Earth fold, push, or uplift huge blocks of rocks. The Himalayas, the Rocky Mountains, and the Appalachian Mountains all formed from tremendous forces within Earth.

Visual Check Which of Earth's three major types of landforms—plains, plateaus, or mountains—covers most of Earth's land surface?

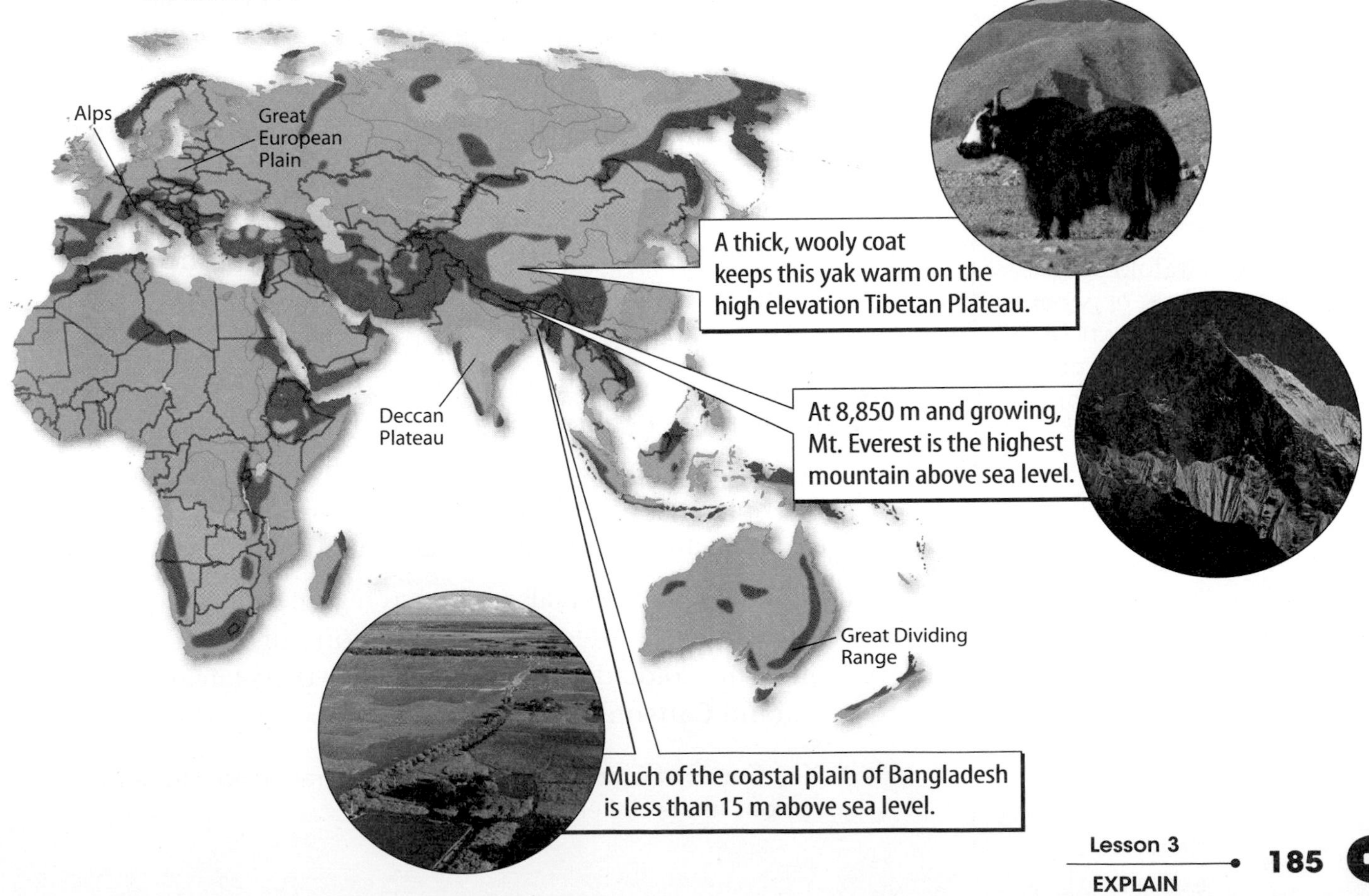

Alps
Great European Plain
Deccan Plateau
Great Dividing Range
A thick, wooly coat keeps this yak warm on the high elevation Tibetan Plateau.
At 8,850 m and growing, Mt. Everest is the highest mountain above sea level.
Much of the coastal plain of Bangladesh is less than 15 m above sea level.

Major U.S. Landform Regions

Concepts in Motion Animation

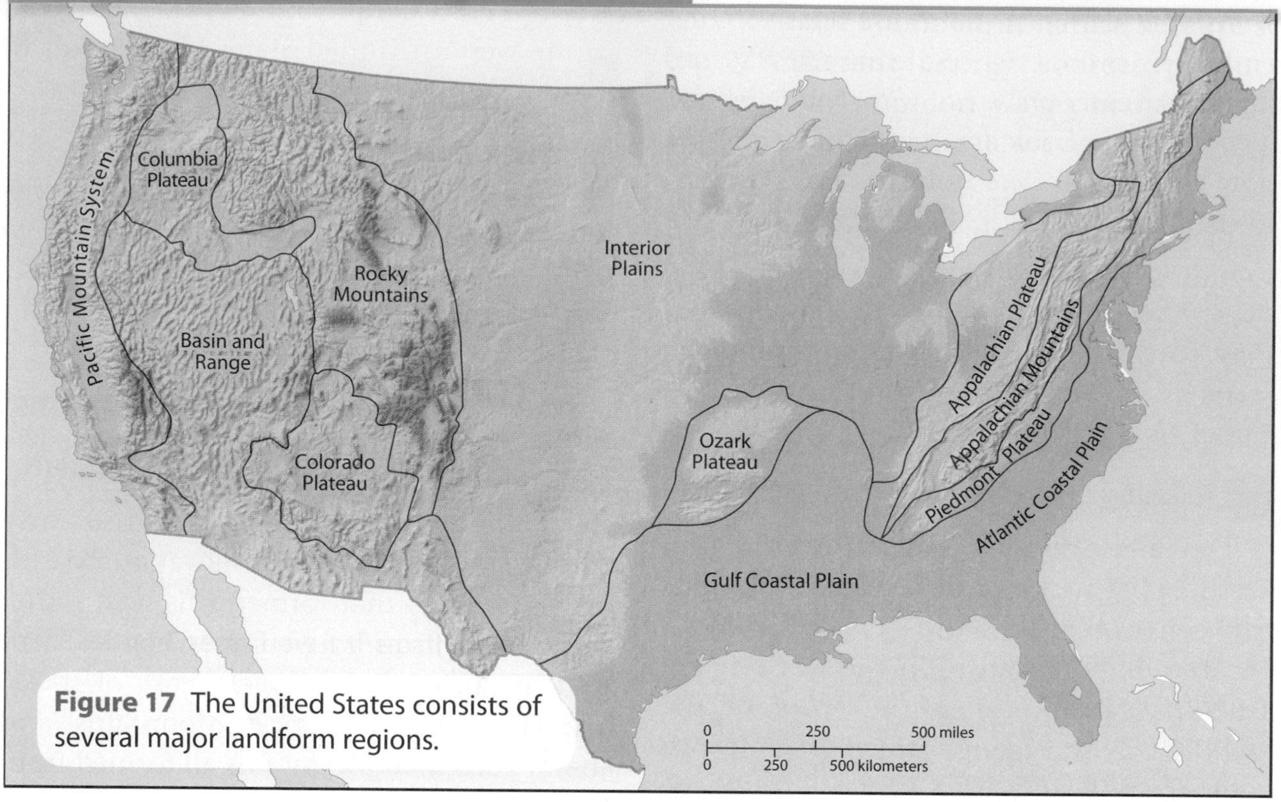

Figure 17 The United States consists of several major landform regions.

Visual Check Which landform region do you live in?

Major Landform Regions in the United States

From flat plains to towering mountains, the United States has a variety of landforms. The major landform regions in the United States are shown in **Figure 17.**

Coastal plains are along much of the East Coast and the Gulf Coast. These plains formed millions of years ago when sediments were deposited on the ocean floor.

The interior plains make up much of the central part of the United States. This flat, grassy area has thick soils and is well suited for growing crops and grazing animals.

The Appalachian Mountains, in the eastern United States, began forming about 480 million years ago (mya). They were once much taller than they are today. Erosion has reduced their average elevation to about 2,000 m. The Rocky Mountains are in the western United States and western Canada. They are younger, taller, and more rugged than the Appalachians.

The Colorado Plateau is also a rugged region. It formed when forces within Earth lifted up huge sections of Earth's crust. Over time, the Colorado River cut through the plateau, forming the Grand Canyon.

Key Concept Check Describe at least three major landform regions in the United States.

FOLDABLES®

Make a tri-fold book from a sheet of paper. Label it as shown. Use it to organize your notes about Earth's major landforms.

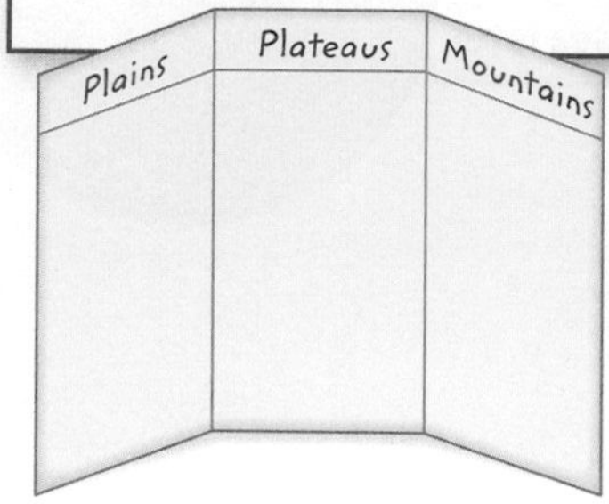

Lesson 3 Review

Assessment Online Quiz
Inquiry Virtual Lab

Visual Summary

Landforms are topographic features formed by processes that shape Earth's surface.

Major landforms include flat plains, high plateaus, and rugged mountains.

Major landform regions in the United States include the Appalachian Mountains, the Great Plains, the Colorado Plateau, and the Rocky Mountains.

FOLDABLES®

Use your lesson Foldable to review the lesson. Save your Foldable for the project at the end of the chapter.

What do you think NOW?

You first read the statements below at the beginning of the chapter.

5. All ocean floors are flat.

6. Most of Earth's surface is covered by water.

Did you change your mind about whether you agree or disagree with the statements? Rewrite any false statements to make them true.

Use Vocabulary

1. Plains and mountains are examples of ________ formed by processes that shape Earth's surface.
2. A(n) ________ is a landform with high relief and high elevation.
3. **Distinguish** between a plain and a plateau.

Understand Key Concepts

4. A landform with low relief and high elevation is a
   - **A.** mountain.
   - **B.** plain.
   - **C.** plateau.
   - **D.** topography.
5. **Describe** any landforms that are near your school.

Interpret Graphics

6. **Compare** Study the illustration below. How do plains compare to plateaus in terms of relief?

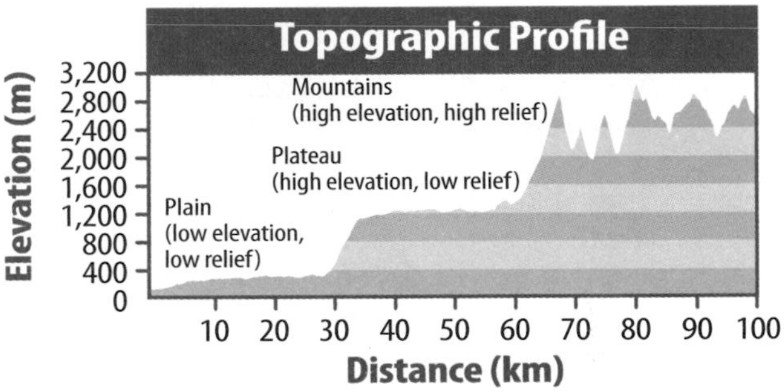

7. **Summarize** Copy and fill in the graphic organizer below to identify the major types of landforms.

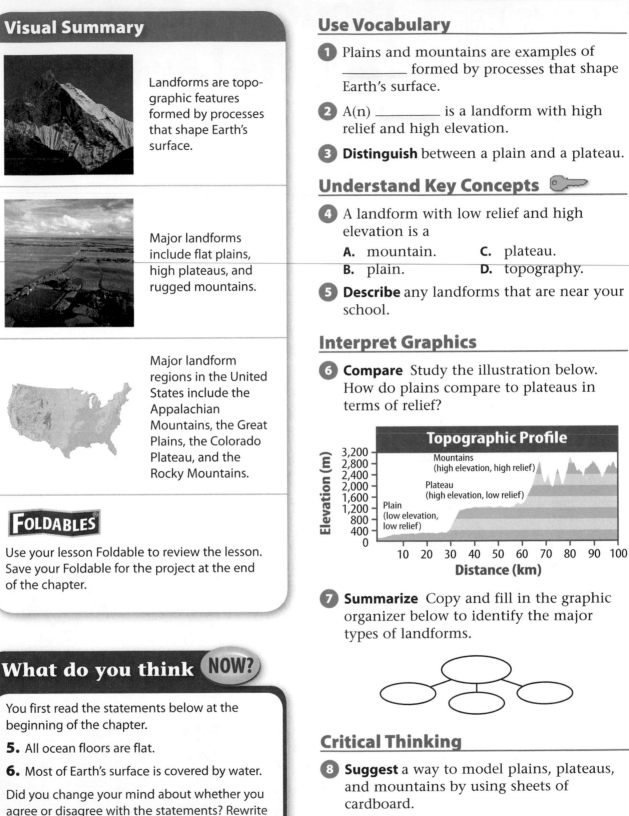

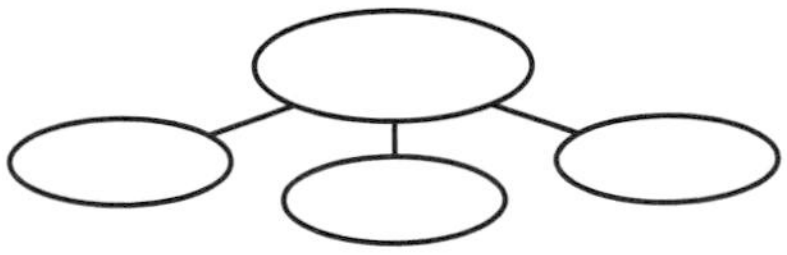

Critical Thinking

8. **Suggest** a way to model plains, plateaus, and mountains by using sheets of cardboard.
9. **Evaluate** the drawbacks and benefits of living in the mountains.

Inquiry Lab

40 minutes

Modeling Earth and Its Layers

Materials

salt dough

food coloring

waxed paper

centimeter ruler

plastic knife

rolling pin or can

Safety

Earth has distinct layers. Each layer has a specific relative volume. You can use those volumes to build a model of Earth with each of the layers in proportion.

Question

Knowing the relative volume of Earth's inner core, outer core, mantle, and crust, how can you build an accurate scale model of these layers?

Procedure

1. Read and complete a lab safety form.
2. Obtain a piece of salt dough from your teacher. Study the chart below showing the relative volume of each layer of Earth. How can you use that data to turn your lump of dough into a model of Earth's layers?

The Relative Volumes of Each Layer of Earth

Layer	Relative Volume (%)
Inner core	0.7
Outer core	15.7
Mantle	82.0
Crust	1.6

3. You might have lots of ideas about how to divide your dough into the correct proportions to build your model. Here is one way you could try:
   - Work on a sheet of waxed paper so the dough won't stick. Roll your dough into a cylinder that measures 10 cm long. The cylinder represents 100 percent of the volume.
   - Now use your centimeter ruler to measure and mark off each of the percentages listed in the chart.
   - Cut off each piece and roll it into a sphere.

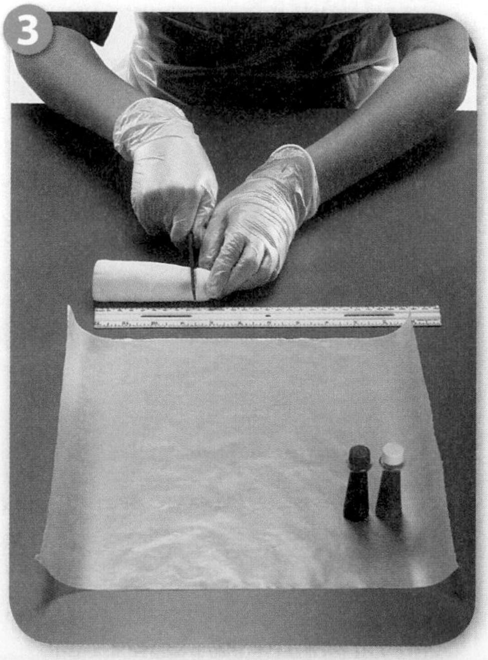

4 Use the data from the chart to figure out how you can build an accurate model.

5 Make a model of Earth's layers using the spheres that represent the relative volume of each layer. Add some food coloring to make each of the four spheres a different color. Work the salt dough so that the color is evenly distributed. Form each lump of dough into a sphere again. Your spheres should look similar to the ones shown in the photo below.

6 Cut in half the sphere representing the outer core.

7 Gently make a small depression in the flat side of each half of the outer core. Then place the inner core inside the outer core and seal the sphere.

8 Cut in half the sphere representing the mantle.

9 Gently make a small depression in the flat side of each half of the mantle. Fit the sphere representing the inner and outer cores into the mantle.

10 The last sphere represents Earth's crust. Put it on a piece of waxed paper and use a rolling pin (or a can) to spread out the sphere enough to make it fit onto the outside of the mantle.

11 Cut your model in half.

Analyze and Conclude

12 **The Big Idea** Describe how each layer of Earth is represented on your model.

13 **Think Critically** Do you think your model accurately shows the volumes of the different layers? Why or why not?

14 **Draw a Conclusion** What can you conclude about the relative volumes of the different layers? Why couldn't you stretch the crust out far enough to cover the mantle? Why couldn't you just add more dough to the crust?

Communicate Your Results

Draw and label Earth's layers. Display the drawing next to your model and use both to explain what you have discovered about Earth's layers.

Inquiry Extension

How could you make an edible model of Earth's layers? Hint: Think about using ice cream or gelatin molds.

Remember to use scientific methods.

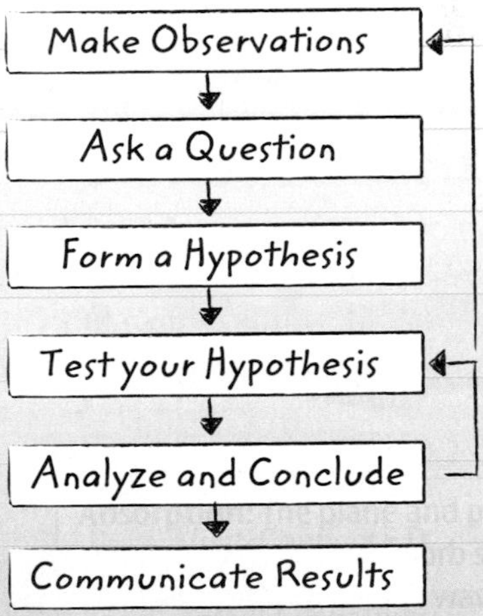

Chapter 5 Study Guide

THE BIG IDEA **Earth's three major layers are the crust, the mantle, and the core.**

Key Concepts Summary

Lesson 1: Spherical Earth

- Earth's major systems include the atmosphere, hydrosphere, cryosphere, biosphere, and **geosphere.**
- All major Earth systems interact by exchanging matter and energy. A change in one Earth system affects all other Earth systems.
- **Gravity** caused particles to come together to form a spherical Earth.

Vocabulary

sphere p. 163
geosphere p. 164
gravity p. 165
density p. 167

Lesson 2: Earth's Interior

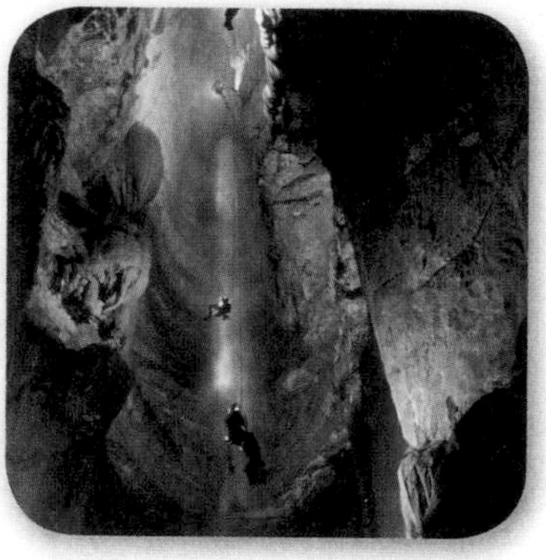

- Earth's interior layers include the **crust, mantle,** and **core.**
- By analyzing earthquake waves, scientists have determined that the outer core is liquid and the inner core is solid.

Vocabulary

crust p. 173
mantle p. 174
lithosphere p. 174
asthenosphere p. 174
core p. 176
magnetosphere p. 177

Lesson 3: Earth's Surface

- Earth's major **landforms** include **plains, plateaus,** and **mountains.** Plains have low relief and low elevation. Plateaus have low relief and high elevation. Mountains have high relief and high elevation.
- Plains, plateaus, and mountains are all found in the United States.

Vocabulary

landform p. 182
plain p. 184
plateau p. 185
mountain p. 185

Review
- Personal Tutor
- Vocabulary eGames
- Vocabulary eFlashcards

FOLDABLES® Chapter Project

Assemble your lesson Foldables as shown to make a Chapter Project. Use the project to review what you have learned in this chapter.

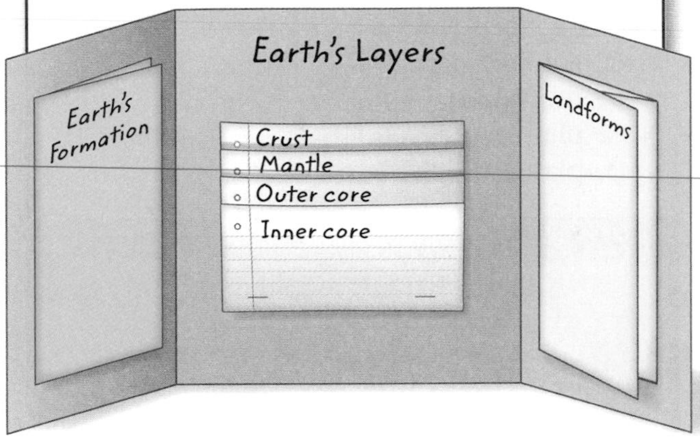

Use Vocabulary

1. Earth formed when ________ pulled together gas and dust that was spinning around the Sun.
2. The gravitational force is greater between similar-sized objects that have a higher ________.
3. The ________ is the largest of Earth's systems.
4. Small amounts of melted material in the ________ produce flow in the mantle.
5. The least dense rocks on Earth are in the ________.
6. Liquid in the ________ produces Earth's magnetic field.
7. A topographic feature formed by processes that shape Earth's surface is a ________.
8. A(n) ________ has low relief and low elevation.
9. A landform that is high and flat is a(n) ________.

Link Vocabulary and Key Concepts

Concepts in Motion Interactive Concept Map

Copy this concept map, and then use vocabulary terms from the previous page to complete the concept map.

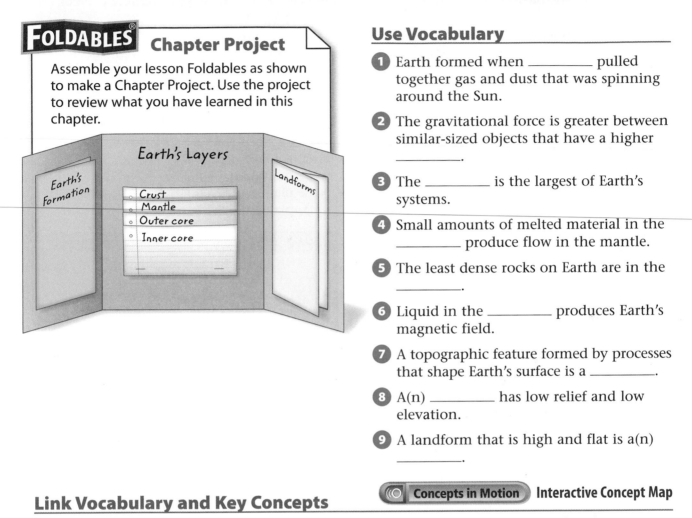

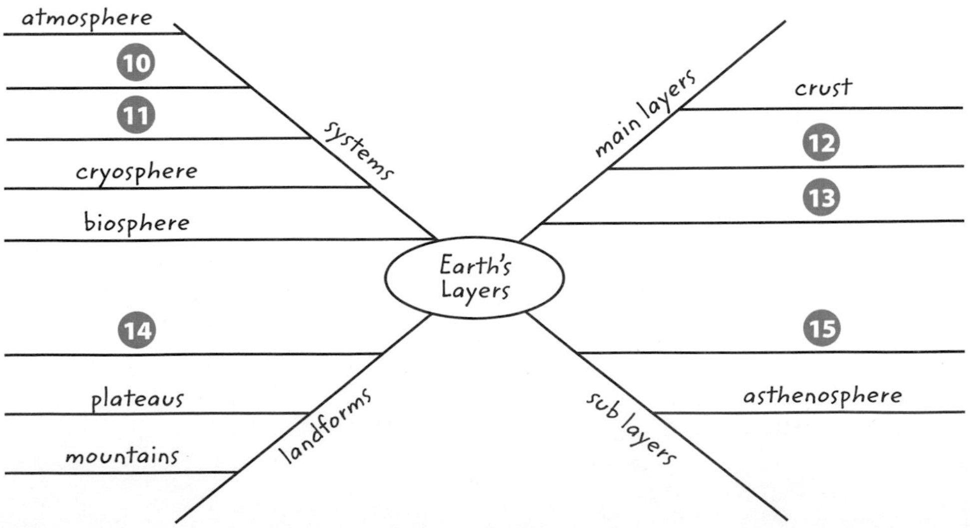

Chapter 5 Review

Understand Key Concepts

1. What does the biosphere contain?
   A. air
   B. living things
   C. rocks
   D. water

2. What affects the strength of gravity between two objects?
   A. the density of the objects
   B. the mass of the objects
   C. the distance between the objects
   D. both the mass and the distance between the objects

3. The figure below shows Earth's layers. What does the red layer represent?
   A. asthenosphere
   B. crust
   C. lithosphere
   D. mantle

4. What is the shape of Earth?
   A. disklike
   B. slightly flattened sphere
   C. sphere
   D. sphere that bulges at the poles

5. Which do scientists use to learn about Earth's core?
   A. earthquake waves
   B. mines
   C. temperature measurements
   D. wells

6. What does the magnetosphere protect people from?
   A. asteroids
   B. cosmic rays
   C. global warming
   D. sun spots

7. In the figure below, what feature is the arrow pointing to?
   A. core
   B. mountain
   C. plain
   D. plateau

8. What does topography describe?
   A. depth of an ocean feature
   B. height of a landform
   C. shape of a given area
   D. width of an area

9. What is true of landforms?
   A. They are all flat.
   B. They are permanent.
   C. They change over time.
   D. They are only on continents.

10. A box sitting on the floor models what type of landform?
    A. mountain
    B. plain
    C. plateau
    D. relief

Assessment
Online Test Practice

Critical Thinking

11 **Explain** how gravity would affect you differently on a planet with less mass than Earth, such as Mercury.

12 **Compare** materials in the geosphere to materials in the atmosphere.

13 **Consider** How would Earth's layers be affected if all the materials that make up Earth had the same density?

14 **Relate** How do Earth's systems interact?

15 **Explain** why everything on or near Earth is pulled toward Earth's center.

16 **State** how the crust and the upper mantle are similar.

17 **Summarize** Earth's crust, mantle, and core on the basis of relative position, density, and composition.

18 **Create** a model of Earth's magnetosphere.

19 **Explain** how a plateau differs from a plain.

20 **Summarize** the characteristics of the landform regions labeled in the map below.

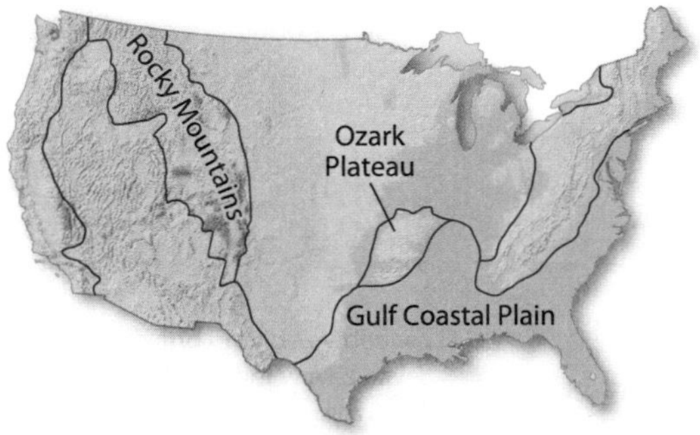

21 **Evaluate** which type of landform is best suited for agriculture.

Writing in Science

22 A song includes lyrics that usually rhyme. Write the lyrics to a song about the elevation of landforms.

REVIEW THE BIG IDEA

23 Identify and describe the different layers of Earth.

24 How does Earth's core create Earth's magnetic field?

25 Hypothesize what might happen to life on Earth if Earth did not have a magnetosphere.

Math Skills

Review
Math Practice

Solve One-Step Equations

26 A large weather balloon holds 3.00 m^3 of air. The air in the balloon has a mass of 3.75 kg. What is the density of the air in the balloon?

27 A pine board has a volume of 18 cm^3. The mass of the board is 9.0 g. What is the density of the pine board?

28 100 cm^3 of water has a mass of 100g. Will the pine board in the previous question float or sink in the water?

Standardized Test Practice

Record your answers on the answer sheet provided by your teacher or on a sheet of paper.

Multiple Choice

1 Density equals

A mass divided by volume.

B mass times volume.

C volume divided by mass.

D volume times mass.

2 Which force gave Earth its spherical shape?

A electricity

B friction

C gravity

D magnetism

Use the diagram below to answer question 3.

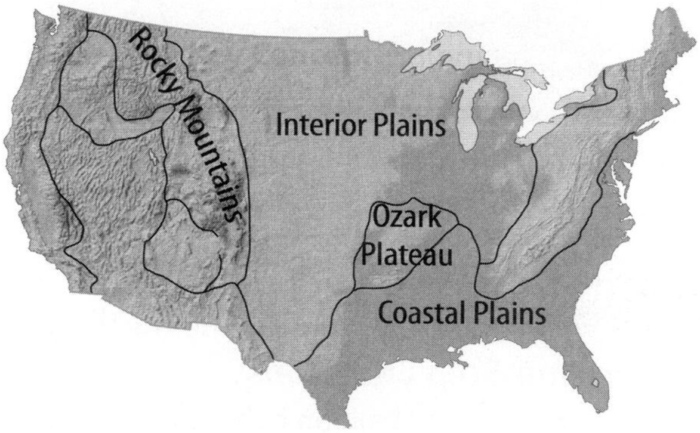

3 Which landform covers the largest area of the central United States?

A Coastal Plains

B Interior Plains

C Ozark Plateau

D Rocky Mountains

4 Which describes Earth's asthenosphere?

A brittle

B fast-moving

C freeze-dried

D plastic

Use the diagram and the graphs below to answer question 5.

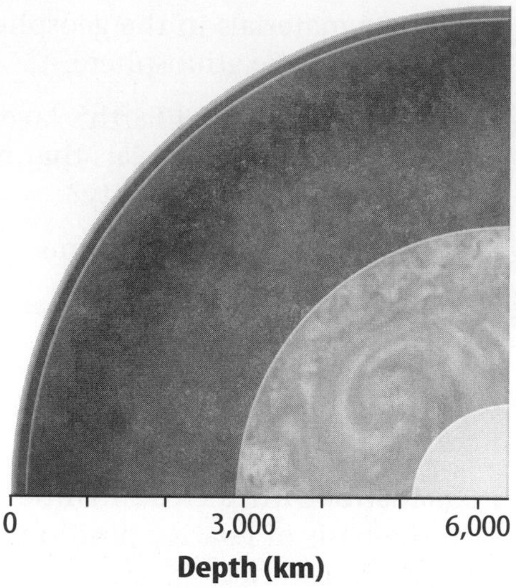

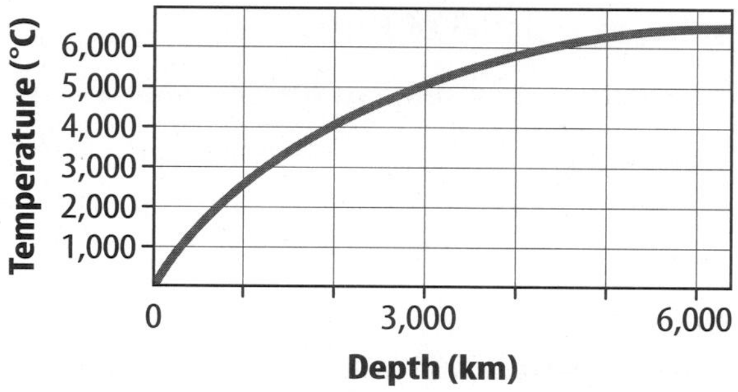

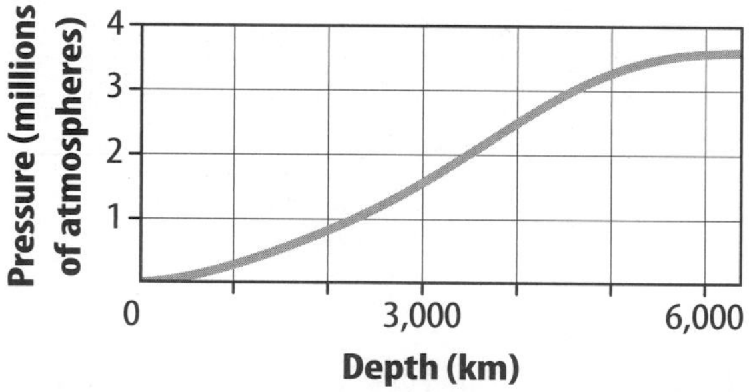

5 Which describes temperature and pressure at Earth's center?

A high pressure and high temperature

B high pressure and low temperature

C low pressure and high temperature

D low pressure and low temperature

Assessment

Online Standardized Test Practice

6 Which explains the term *topography*?

- **A** the geological ages of features
- **B** the heights and locations of features
- **C** the seasonal variation of features
- **D** the travel routes between features

7 Which is the correct order of Earth's layers from the surface to the center?

- **A** crust, core, mantle
- **B** crust, mantle, core
- **C** mantle, core, crust
- **D** mantle, crust, core

Use the diagram below to answer question 8.

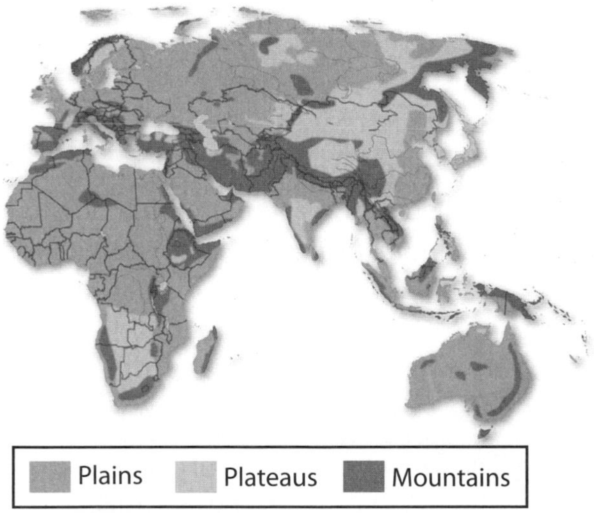

8 Which continent has the greatest area of plateaus?

- **A** Africa
- **B** Asia
- **C** Australia
- **D** Europe

Constructed Response

9 Compare and contrast plateaus and plains.

Use the diagrams below to answer questions 10–12.

10 Three Earth systems are shown above. Name each system and describe its features.

11 Describe how these three systems interact.

12 Draw a diagram of the fourth major Earth system. Describe its features.

NEED EXTRA HELP?												
If You Missed Question...	1	2	3	4	5	6	7	8	9	10	11	12
Go to Lesson...	1	1	3	2	2	3	2	3	3	1	1	1

Chapter 6

Plate Tectonics

THE BIG IDEA **What is the theory of plate tectonics?**

Inquiry Is this a volcano?

Iceland is home to many active volcanoes like this one. This eruption is called a fissure eruption. This occurs when lava erupts from a long crack, or fissure, in Earth's crust.

- Why is the crust breaking apart here?
- What factors determine where a volcano will form?
- How are volcanoes associated with plate tectonics?

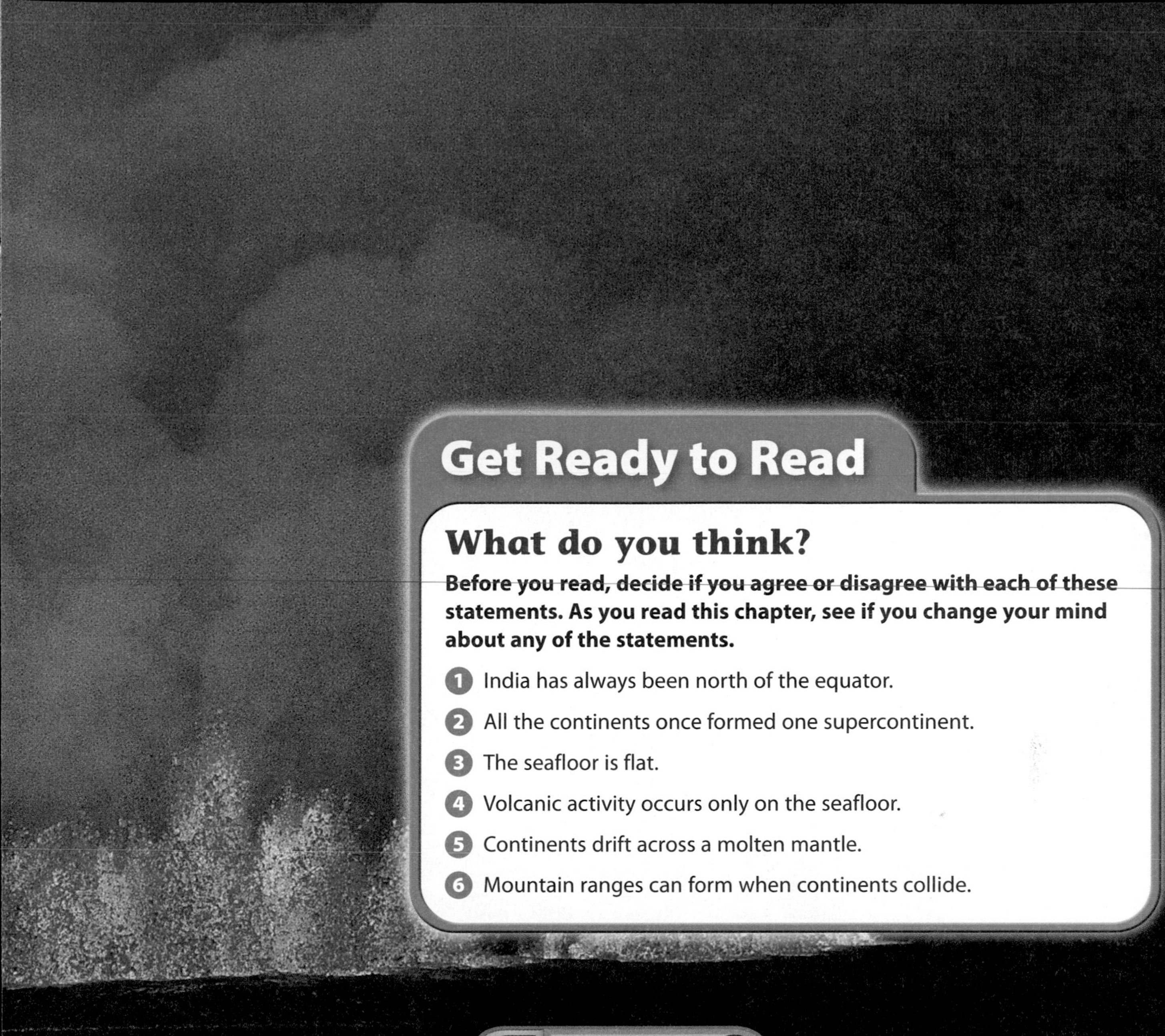

Get Ready to Read

What do you think?

Before you read, decide if you agree or disagree with each of these statements. As you read this chapter, see if you change your mind about any of the statements.

1. India has always been north of the equator.
2. All the continents once formed one supercontinent.
3. The seafloor is flat.
4. Volcanic activity occurs only on the seafloor.
5. Continents drift across a molten mantle.
6. Mountain ranges can form when continents collide.

Lesson 1

The Continental Drift Hypothesis

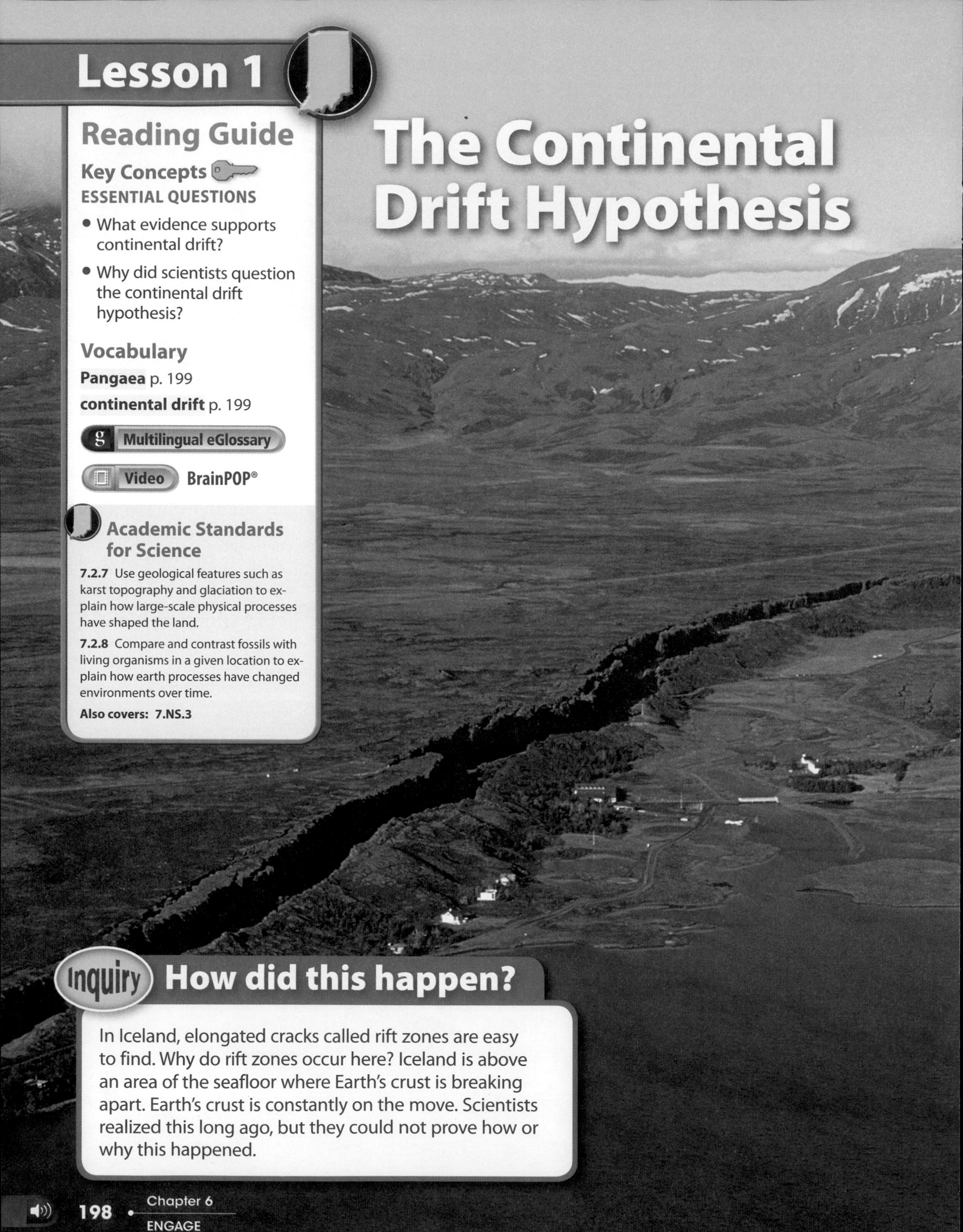

Reading Guide

Key Concepts

ESSENTIAL QUESTIONS

- What evidence supports continental drift?
- Why did scientists question the continental drift hypothesis?

Vocabulary

Pangaea p. 199

continental drift p. 199

g Multilingual eGlossary

Video BrainPOP®

Academic Standards for Science

7.2.7 Use geological features such as karst topography and glaciation to explain how large-scale physical processes have shaped the land.

7.2.8 Compare and contrast fossils with living organisms in a given location to explain how earth processes have changed environments over time.

Also covers: 7.NS.3

Inquiry How did this happen?

In Iceland, elongated cracks called rift zones are easy to find. Why do rift zones occur here? Iceland is above an area of the seafloor where Earth's crust is breaking apart. Earth's crust is constantly on the move. Scientists realized this long ago, but they could not prove how or why this happened.

Inquiry Launch Lab

20 minutes

Can you put together a peel puzzle?

Early map makers observed that the coastlines of Africa and South America appeared as if they could fit together like pieces of a puzzle. Scientists eventually discovered that these continents were once part of a large landmass. Can you use an orange peel to illustrate how continents may have fit together?

1. Read and complete a lab safety form.
2. Carefully peel an **orange,** keeping the orange-peel pieces as large as possible.
3. Set the orange aside.
4. Refit the orange-peel pieces back together in the shape of a sphere.
5. After successfully reconstructing the orange peel, disassemble your pieces.
6. Trade the entire orange peel with a classmate and try to reconstruct his or her orange peel.

Think About This

1. Which orange peel was easier for you to reconstruct? Why?
2. Look at a world map. Do the coastlines of any other continents appear to fit together?
3. **Key Concept** What additional evidence would you need to prove that all the continents might have once fit together?

Pangaea

Did you know that Earth's surface is on the move? Can you feel it? Each year, North America moves a few centimeters farther away from Europe and closer to Asia. That is several centimeters, or about the thickness of this book. Even though you don't necessarily feel this motion, Earth's surface moves slowly every day.

Nearly 100 years ago Alfred Wegener (VAY guh nuhr), a German scientist, began an important investigation that continues today. Wegener wanted to know whether Earth's continents were fixed in their positions. He proposed that *all the continents were once part of a supercontinent called* **Pangaea** (pan JEE uh). Over time Pangaea began breaking apart, and the continents slowly moved to their present positions. Wegener proposed the hypothesis of **continental drift,** *which suggested that continents are in constant motion on the surface of Earth.*

Alfred Wegener observed the similarities of continental coastlines now separated by oceans. Look at the outlines of Africa and South America in **Figure 1.** Notice how they could fit together like pieces of a puzzle. Hundreds of years ago mapmakers noticed this jigsaw-puzzle pattern as they made the first maps of the continents.

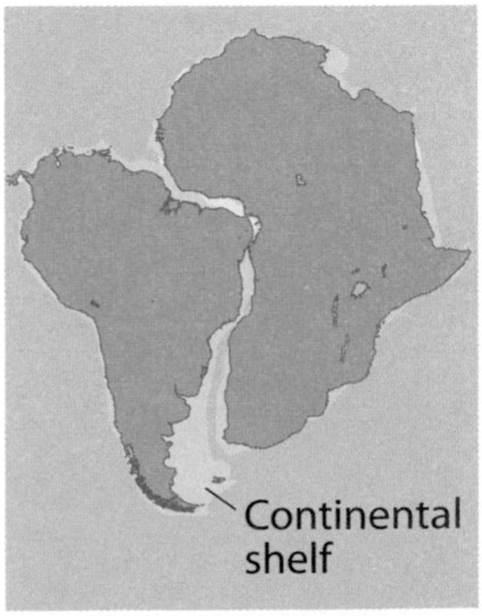

Figure 1 The eastern coast of South America mirrors the shape of the west coast of Africa.

Evidence That Continents Move

If you had discovered continental drift, how would you have tested your hypothesis? The most obvious evidence for continental drift is that the continents appear to fit together like pieces of a puzzle. But scientists were skeptical, and Wegener needed additional evidence to help support his hypothesis.

Climate Clues

When Wegener pieced Pangaea together, he proposed that South America, Africa, India, and Australia were located closer to Antarctica 280 million years ago. He suggested that the climate of the Southern Hemisphere was much cooler at the time. Glaciers covered large areas that are now parts of these continents. These glaciers would have been similar to the ice sheet that covers much of Antarctica today.

Wegener used climate clues to support his continental drift hypothesis. He studied the sediments deposited by glaciers in South America and Africa, as well as in India and Australia. Beneath these sediments, Wegener discovered glacial grooves, or deep scratches in rocks made as the glaciers moved across land. **Figure 2** shows where these glacial features are found on neighboring continents today. These continents were once part of the supercontinent Pangaea, when the climate in the Southern Hemisphere was cooler.

Climate Clues

Concepts in Motion **Animation**

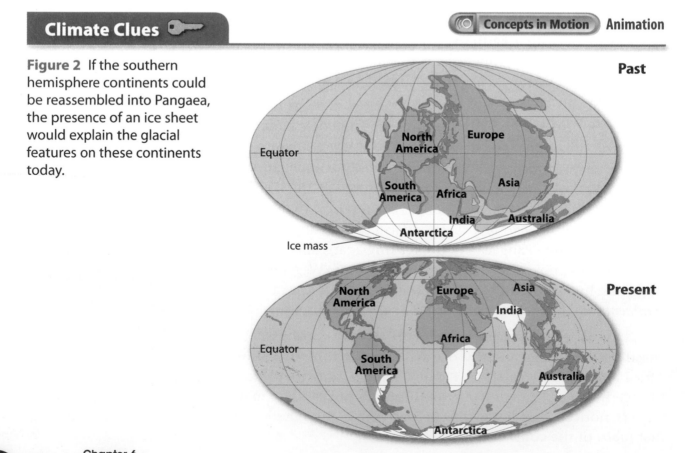

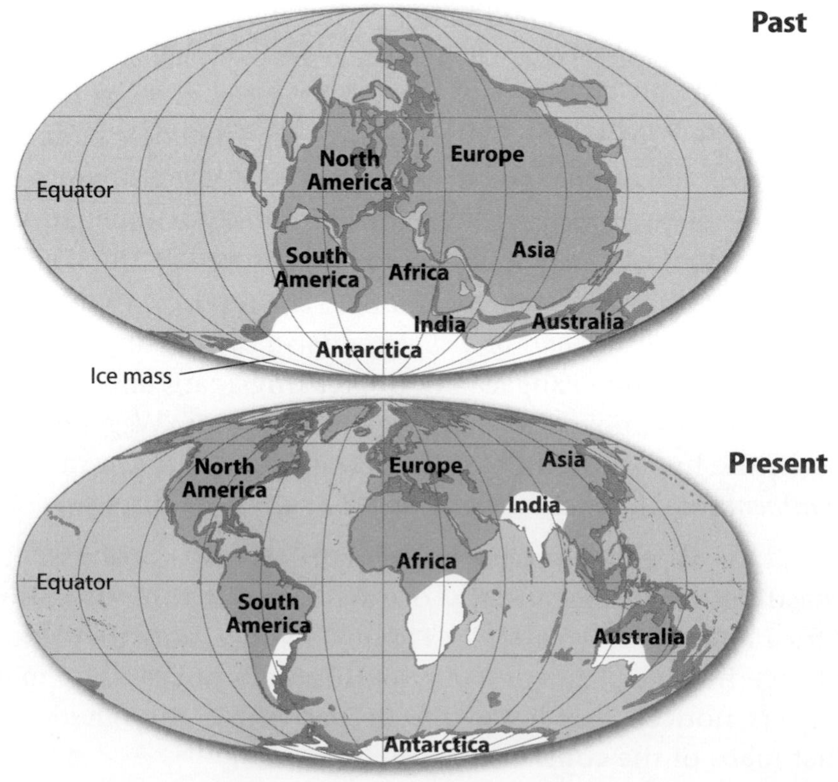

Figure 2 If the southern hemisphere continents could be reassembled into Pangaea, the presence of an ice sheet would explain the glacial features on these continents today.

Fossil Clues

Animals and plants that live on different continents can be unique to that continent alone. Lions live in Africa but not in South America. Kangaroos live in Australia but not on any other continent. Because oceans separate continents, these animals cannot travel from one continent to another by natural means. However, **fossils** of similar organisms have been found on several continents separated by oceans. How did this happen? Wegener argued that these continents must have been connected some time in the past.

REVIEW VOCABULARY

fossil
the naturally preserved remains, imprints, or traces of organisms that lived long ago

Fossils of a plant called *Glossopteris* (glahs AHP tur us) have been discovered in rocks from South America, Africa, India, Australia, and Antarctica. These continents are far apart today. The plant's seeds could not have traveled across the vast oceans that separate them. **Figure 3** shows that when these continents were part of Pangaea 225 million years ago, *Glossopteris* lived in one region. Evidence suggests these plants grew in a swampy environment. Therefore, the climate of this region, including Antarctica, was different than it is today. Antarctica had a warm and wet climate. The climate had changed drastically from what it was 55 million years earlier when glaciers existed.

Reading Check How did climate in Antarctica change between 280 and 225 million years ago?

Fossil Clues

Figure 3 Fossils of *Glossopteris* have been found on many continents that are now separated by oceans. The orange area in the image on the right represents where *Glossopteris* fossils have been found.

Visual Check Which of the continents would not support *Glossopteris* growth today?

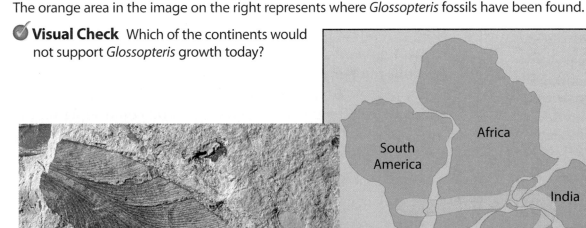

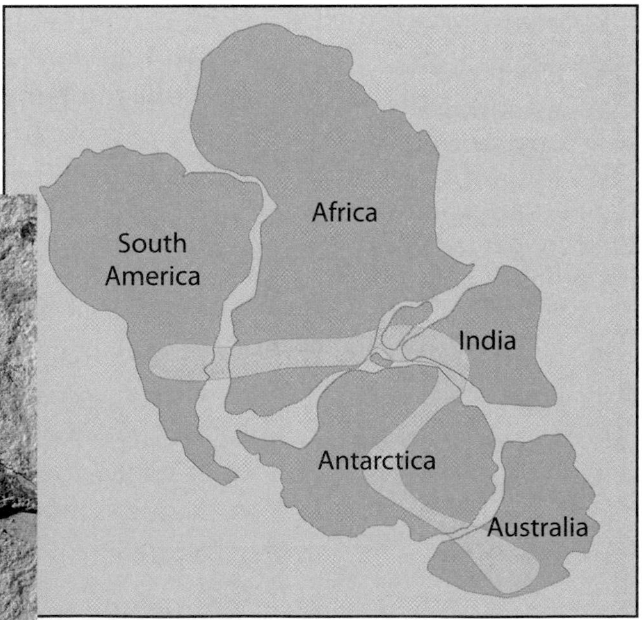

Rock Clues

Figure 4 If you could move North America and Europe next to each other, the Appalachian Mountains and the Caledonian mountains would appear to form one continuous mountain range with similar formations.

Rock Clues

Wegener realized he needed more evidence to support the continental drift hypothesis. He observed that mountain ranges like the ones shown in **Figure 4** and rock formations on different continents had common origins. Today, geologists can determine when these rocks formed. For example, geologists suggest that large-scale volcanic eruptions occurred on the western coast of Africa and the eastern coast of South America at about the same time hundreds of millions of years ago. The volcanic rocks from the eruptions are identical in both chemistry and age. Refer back to **Figure 1.** If you could superimpose similar rock types onto the maps, these rocks would be in the area where Africa and South America fit together.

The Caledonian mountain range in northern Europe and the Appalachian Mountains in eastern North America are similar in age and structure. They are also composed of the same rock types. If you placed North America and Europe next to each other, these mountains would meet and form one long, continuous mountain belt. **Figure 4** illustrates where this mountain range would be.

Key Concept Check How were similar rock types used to support the continental drift hypothesis?

FOLDABLES®

Make a horizontal half-book and write the title as shown. Use it to organize your notes on the continental drift hypothesis.

What was missing?

Wegener continued to support the continental drift hypothesis until his death in 1930. Wegener's ideas were not widely accepted until nearly four decades later. Why were scientists skeptical of Wegener's hypothesis? Although Wegener had evidence to suggest that continents were on the move, he could not explain how they moved.

One reason scientists questioned continental drift was because it is a slow process. It was not possible for Wegener to measure how fast the continents moved. The main objection to the continental drift hypothesis, however, was that Wegener could not explain what forces caused the continents to move. The mantle beneath the continents and the seafloor is made of solid rock. How could continents push their way through solid rock? Wegener needed more scientific evidence to prove his hypothesis. However, this evidence was hidden on the seafloor between the drifting continents. The evidence necessary to prove continental drift was not discovered until long after Wegener's death.

Key Concept Check Why did scientists argue against Wegener's continental drift hypothesis?

SCIENCE USE V. COMMON USE

mantle

Science Use the middle layer of Earth, situated between the crust above and the core below

Common Use a loose, sleeveless garment worn over other clothes

Inquiry MiniLab

20 minutes

How do you use clues to put puzzle pieces together?

When you put a puzzle together, you use clues to figure out which pieces fit next to each other. How did Wegener use a similar technique to piece together Pangaea?

1. Read and complete a lab safety form.
2. Using **scissors,** cut a piece of **newspaper** or a page from a **magazine** into an irregular shape with a diameter of about 25 cm.
3. Cut the piece of paper into at least 12 but not more than 20 pieces.
4. Exchange your puzzle with a partner and try to fit the new puzzle pieces together.
5. Reclaim your puzzle and remove any three pieces. Exchange your incomplete puzzle with a different partner. Try to put the incomplete puzzles back together.

Analyze and Conclude

1. **Summarize** Make a list of the clues you used to put together your partner's puzzle.
2. **Describe** How was putting together a complete puzzle different from putting together an incomplete puzzle?
3. **Key Concept** What clues did Wegener use to hypothesize the existence of Pangaea? What clues were missing from Wegener's puzzle?

Lesson 1 Review

✓ Assessment Online Quiz

Visual Summary

Past

All continents were once part of a supercontinent called Pangaea.

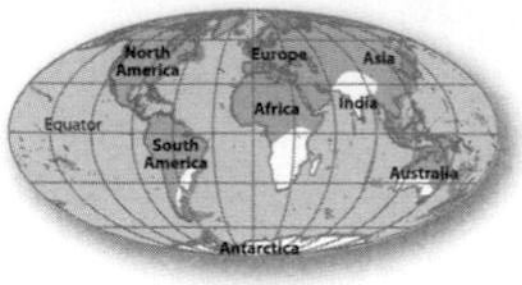

Present

Alfred Wegener proposed that continents move around on Earth's surface.

FOLDABLES®

Use your lesson Foldable to review the lesson. Save your Foldable for the project at the end of the chapter.

What do you think NOW?

You first read the statements below at the beginning of the chapter.

1. India has always been north of the equator.

2. All the continents once formed one supercontinent.

Did you change your mind about whether you agree or disagree with the statements? Rewrite any false statements to make them true.

Use Vocabulary

1. **Define** *Pangaea.*
2. **Explain** the continental drift hypothesis and the evidence used to support it.

Understand Key Concepts

3. **Identify** the scientist who first proposed that the continents move away from or toward each other.
4. Which can be used as an indicator of past climate?
   - **A.** fossils
   - **B.** lava flows
   - **C.** mountain ranges
   - **D.** tides

Interpret Graphics

5. **Interpret** Look at the map of the continents below. What direction has South America moved relative to Africa?

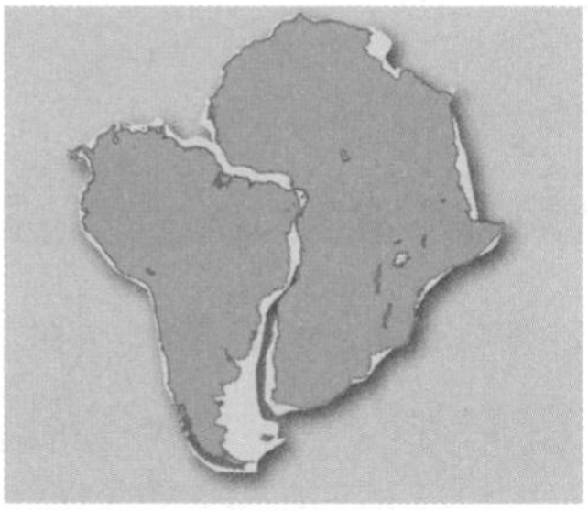

6. **Summarize** Copy and fill in the graphic organizer below to show the evidence Alfred Wegener used to support his continental drift hypothesis.

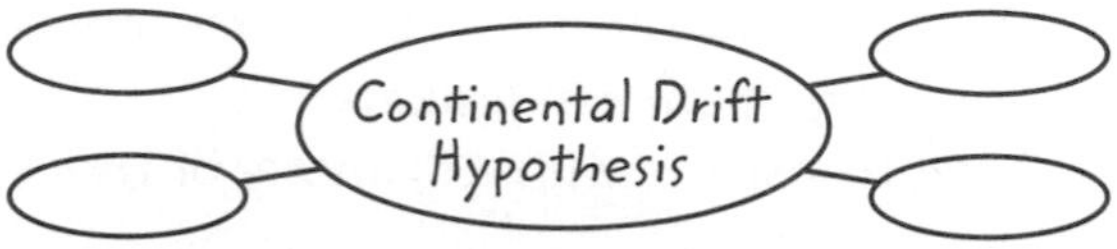

Critical Thinking

7. **Recognize** The shape and age of the Appalachian Mountains are similar to the Caledonian mountains in northern Europe. What else could be similar?
8. **Explain** If continents continue to drift, is it possible that a new supercontinent will form? Which continents might be next to each other 200 million years from now?

▼ This small mammal is a close living relative of an animal that once roamed Antarctica.

▲ Ross MacPhee is a paleontologist working for the American Museum of Natural History in New York City. Here, he is searching for fossils in Antarctica.

Gondwana

A Fossil Clue from the Giant Landmass that Once Dominated the Southern Hemisphere

If you could travel back in time 120 million years, you would probably discover that Earth looked very different than it does today. Scientists believe that instead of seven continents, there were two giant landmasses, or supercontinents, on Earth at that time. Scientists named the landmass in the northern hemisphere *Laurasia*. The landmass in the southern hemisphere was named *Gondwana*. It included the present-day continents of Antarctica, South America, Australia, and Africa.

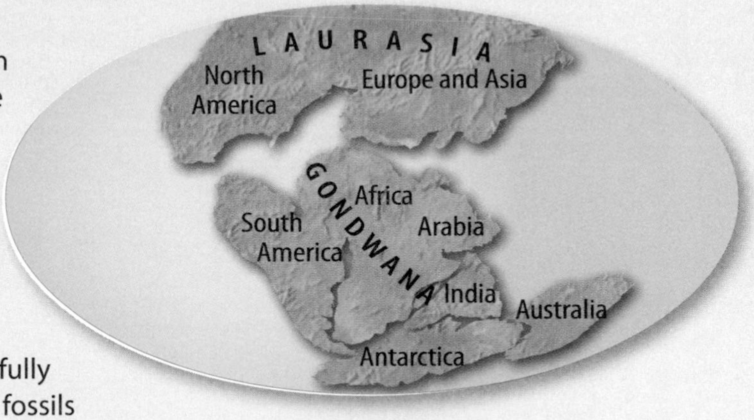

▲ *Gondwana* and *Laurasia* formed as the supercontinent Pangaea broke apart.

How do scientists know that Gondwana existed? Ross MacPhee is a paleontologist—a scientist who studies fossils. MacPhee recently traveled to Antarctica where he discovered the fossilized tooth of a small land mammal. After carefully examining the tooth, he realized that it resembled fossils from ancient land mammals found in Africa and North America. MacPhee believes that these mammals are the ancient relatives of a mammal living today on the African island-nation of Madagascar.

How did the fossil remains and their present-day relatives become separated by kilometers of ocean? MacPhee hypothesizes that the mammal migrated across land bridges that once connected parts of Gondwana. Over millions of years, the movement of Earth's tectonic plates broke up this supercontinent. New ocean basins formed between the continents, resulting in the arrangement of landmasses that we see today.

It's Your Turn

RESEARCH Millions of years ago, the island of Madagascar separated from the continent of Gondwana. In this environment, the animals of Madagascar changed and adapted. Research and report on one animal. Describe some of its unique adaptations.

Lesson 2

Development of a Theory

Reading Guide

Key Concepts

ESSENTIAL QUESTIONS

- What is seafloor spreading?
- What evidence is used to support seafloor spreading?

Vocabulary

mid-ocean ridge p. 207
seafloor spreading p. 208
normal polarity p. 210
magnetic reversal p. 210
reversed polarity p. 210

g Multilingual eGlossary

Academic Standards for Science

7.2.7 Use geological features such as karst topography and glaciation to explain how large-scale physical processes have shaped the land.

Also covers: 7.NS.3, 7.NS.4, 7.NS.5, 7.NS.7, 7.NS.8

Inquiry What do the colors represent?

The colors in this satellite image show topography. The warm colors, red, pink, and yellow, represent landforms above sea level. The greens and blues indicate changes in topography below sea level. Deep in the Atlantic Ocean there is a mountain range, shown here as a linear feature in green. Is there a connection between this landform and the continental drift hypothesis?

Inquiry Launch Lab

15 minutes

Can you guess the age of the glue?

The age of the seafloor can be determined by measuring magnetic patterns in rocks from the bottom of the ocean. How can similar patterns in drying glue be used to show age relationships between rocks exposed on the seafloor?

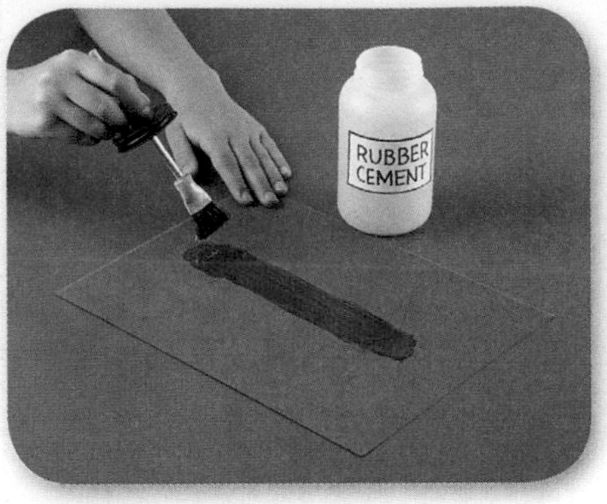

1. Read and complete a lab safety form.
2. Carefully spread a thin layer of **rubber cement** on a sheet of **paper.**
3. Observe for 3 minutes. Record the pattern of how the glue dries in your Science Journal.
4. Repeat step 2. After 1 minute, exchange papers with a classmate.
5. Ask the classmate to observe and tell you which part of the glue dried first.

Think About This

1. What evidence helped you to determine the oldest and youngest glue layers?
2. How is this similar to a geologist trying to estimate the age of rocks on the seafloor?
3. **Key Concept** How could magnetic patterns in rock help predict a rock's age?

Mapping the Ocean Floor

During the late 1940s after World War II, scientists began exploring the seafloor in greater detail. They were able to determine the depth of the ocean using a device called an echo sounder, as shown in **Figure 5.** Once ocean depths were determined, scientists used these data to create a topographic map of the seafloor. These new topographic maps of the seafloor revealed that vast mountain ranges stretched for many miles deep below the ocean's surface. *The mountain ranges in the middle of the oceans are called* **mid-ocean ridges.** Mid-ocean ridges, shown in **Figure 5,** are much longer than any mountain range on land.

Figure 5 An echo sounder produces sound waves that travel from a ship to the seafloor and back. The deeper the ocean, the longer the time this takes. Depth can be used to determine seafloor topography.

Seafloor Topography

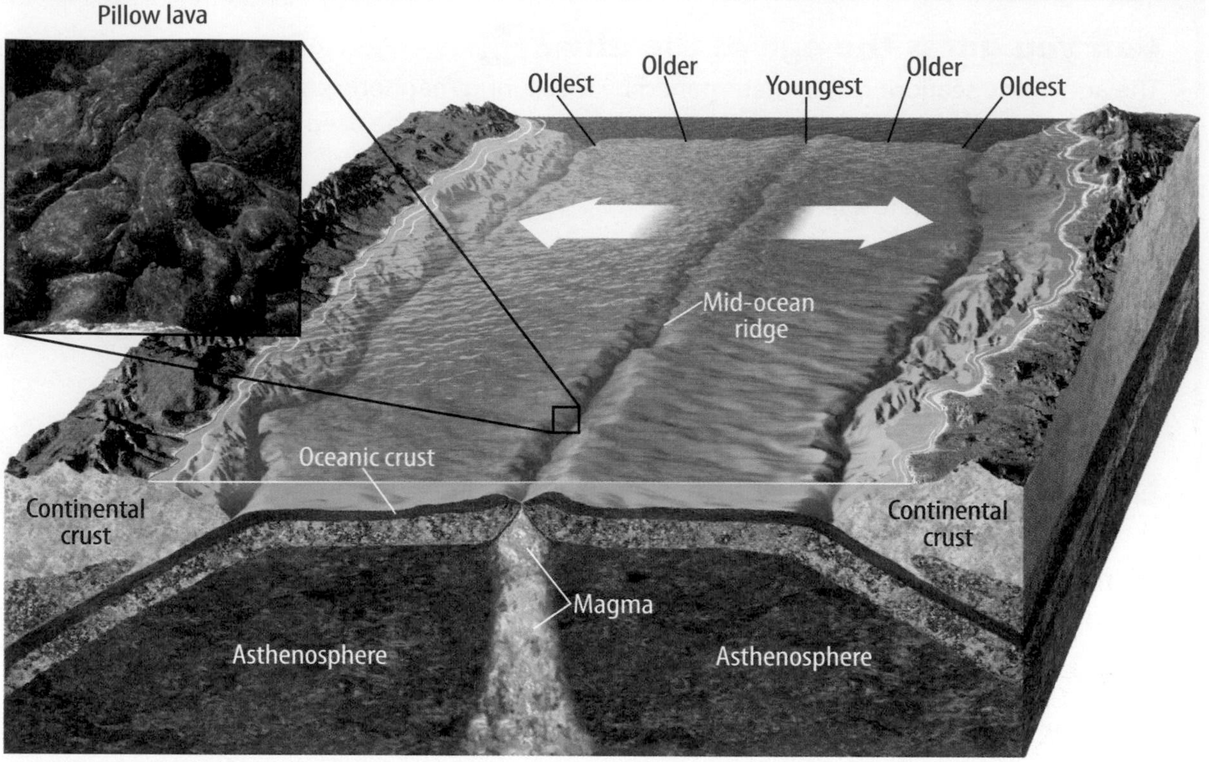

Figure 6 When lava erupts along a mid-ocean ridge, it cools and crystallizes, forming a type of rock called basalt. Basalt is the dominant rock on the seafloor. The youngest basalt is closest to the ridge. The oldest basalt is farther away from the ridge.

Visual Check Looking at the image above, can you propose a pattern that exists in rocks on either side of the mid-ocean ridge?

Seafloor Spreading

By the 1960s scientists discovered a new process that helped explain continental drift. This process, shown in **Figure 6,** is called seafloor spreading. **Seafloor spreading** *is the process by which new oceanic crust forms along a mid-ocean ridge and older oceanic crust moves away from the ridge.*

When the seafloor spreads, the mantle below melts and forms magma. Because magma is less dense than solid mantle material, it rises through cracks in the crust along the mid-ocean ridge. When magma erupts on Earth's surface, it is called lava. As this lava cools and crystallizes on the seafloor, it forms a type of rock called basalt. Because the lava erupts into water, it cools rapidly and forms rounded structures called pillow lavas. Notice the shape of the pillow lava shown in **Figure 6.**

As the seafloor continues to spread apart, the older oceanic crust moves away from the mid-ocean ridge. The closer the crust is to a mid-ocean ridge, the younger the oceanic crust is. Scientists argued that if the seafloor spreads, the continents must also be moving. A mechanism to explain continental drift was finally discovered long after Wegener proposed his hypothesis.

Key Concept Check What is seafloor spreading?

Topography of the Seafloor

The rugged mountains that make up the mid-ocean ridge system can form in two different ways. For example, large amounts of lava can erupt from the center of the ridge, cool and build up around the ridge. Or, as the lava cools and forms new crust, it cracks. The rocks move up or down along these cracks in the seafloor, forming jagged mountain ranges.

Reading Check How do mountains form along the mid-ocean ridge?

Over time, sediment accumulates on top of the oceanic crust. Close to the mid-ocean ridge there is almost no sediment. Far from the mid-ocean ridge, the layer of sediment becomes thick enough to make the seafloor smooth. This part of the seafloor, shown in **Figure 7,** is called the abyssal (uh BIH sul) plain.

Moving Continents Around

The theory of seafloor spreading provides a way to explain how continents move. Continents do not move through the solid mantle or the seafloor. Instead, continents move as the seafloor spreads along a mid-ocean ridge.

Inquiry MiniLab — 20 minutes

How old is the Atlantic Ocean?

If you measure the width of the Atlantic Ocean and you know the rate of seafloor spreading, you can calculate the age of the Atlantic.

1. Use a **ruler** to measure the horizontal distance between a point on the eastern coast of South America and a point on the western coast of Africa on a **world map.** Repeat three times and calculate the average distance in your Science Journal.
2. Use the map's legend to convert the average distance from centimeters to kilometers.
3. If Africa and South America have been moving away from each other at a rate of 2.5 cm per year, calculate the age of the Atlantic Ocean.

Analyze and Conclude

1. **Measure** Did your measurements vary?
2. **Key Concept** How does the age you calculated compare to the breakup of Pangaea 200 million years ago?

Abyssal Plain

Figure 7 The abyssal plain is flat due to an accumulation of sediments far from the ridge.

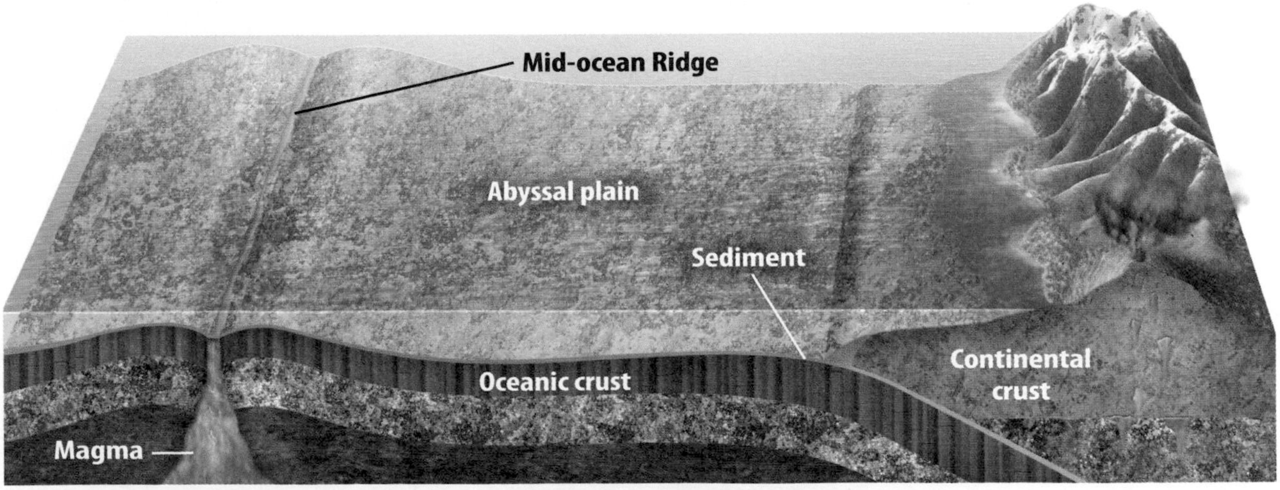

Visual Check Compare and contrast the topography of a mid-ocean ridge to an abyssal plain.

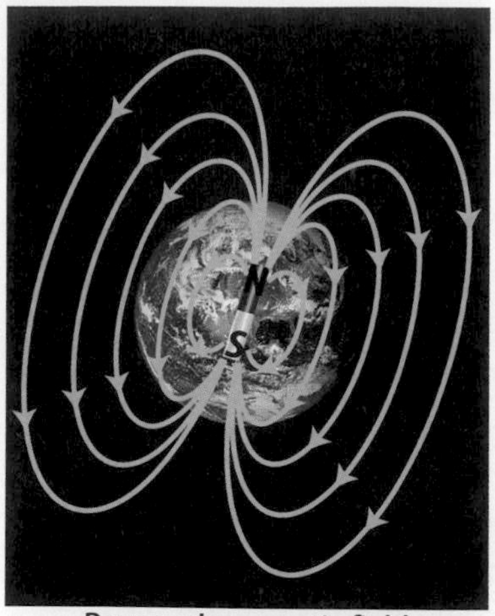

Reversed magnetic field

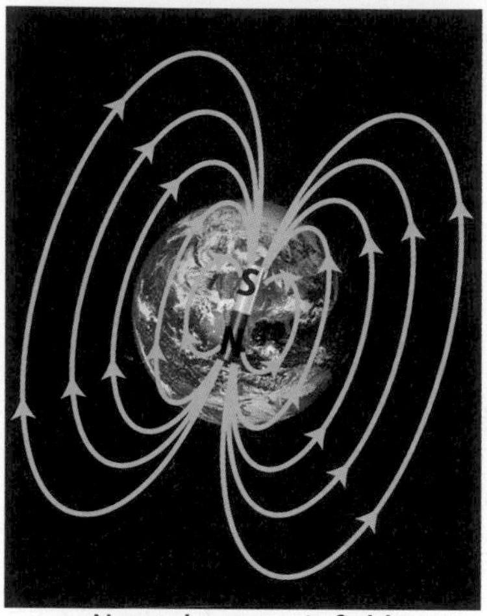

Normal magnetic field

▲ **Figure 8** Earth's magnetic field is like a large bar magnet. It has reversed direction hundreds of times throughout history.

Development of a Theory

The first evidence used to support seafloor spreading was discovered in rocks on the seafloor. Scientists studied the magnetic signature of minerals in these rocks. To understand this, you need to understand the direction and orientation of Earth's magnetic field and how rocks record magnetic information.

Magnetic Reversals

Recall that the iron-rich, liquid outer core is like a giant magnet that creates Earth's magnetic field. The direction of the magnetic field is not constant. Today's magnetic field, shown in **Figure 8,** is described as having **normal polarity**—*a state in which magnetized objects, such as compass needles, will orient themselves to point north.* Sometimes a **magnetic reversal** *occurs and the magnetic field reverses direction.* The opposite of normal polarity is **reversed polarity**—*a state in which magnetized objects would reverse direction and orient themselves to point south,* as shown in **Figure 8.** Magnetic reversals occur every few hundred thousand to every few million years.

Reading Check Is Earth's magnetic field currently normal or reversed polarity?

Rocks Reveal Magnetic Signature

Basalt on the seafloor contains iron-rich minerals that are magnetic. Each mineral acts like a small magnet. **Figure 9** shows how magnetic minerals align themselves with Earth's magnetic field. When lava erupts from a vent along a mid-ocean ridge, it cools and crystallizes. This permanently records the direction and orientation of Earth's magnetic field at the time of the eruption. Scientists have discovered parallel patterns in the magnetic signature of rocks on either side of a mid-ocean ridge.

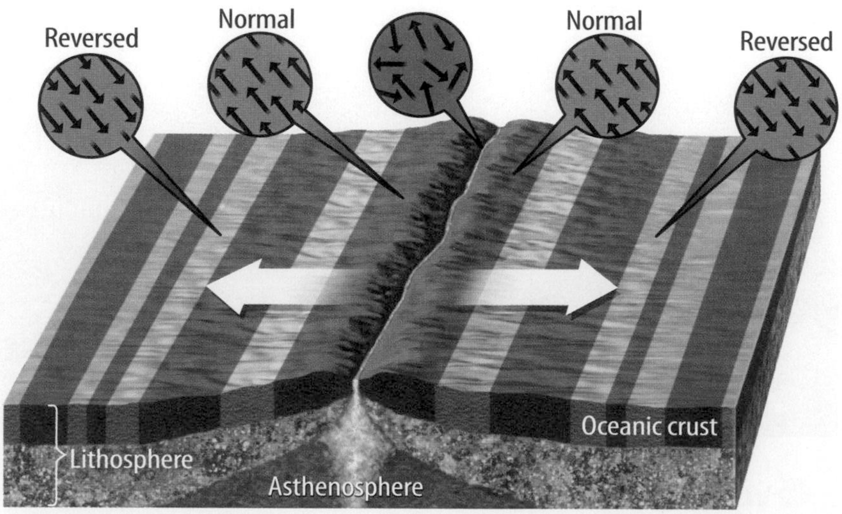

Figure 9 Iron-rich minerals in cooling lava align with Earth's magnetic field. When Earth's magnetic field changes direction, minerals in fresh lava record a new magnetic signature. ▶

Visual Check Describe the pattern in the magnetic stripes shown in the image to the right.

Seafloor Spreading Theory

Figure 10 A mirror image in the magnetic stripes on either side of the mid-ocean ridge shows that the crust formed at the ridge is carried away in opposite directions.

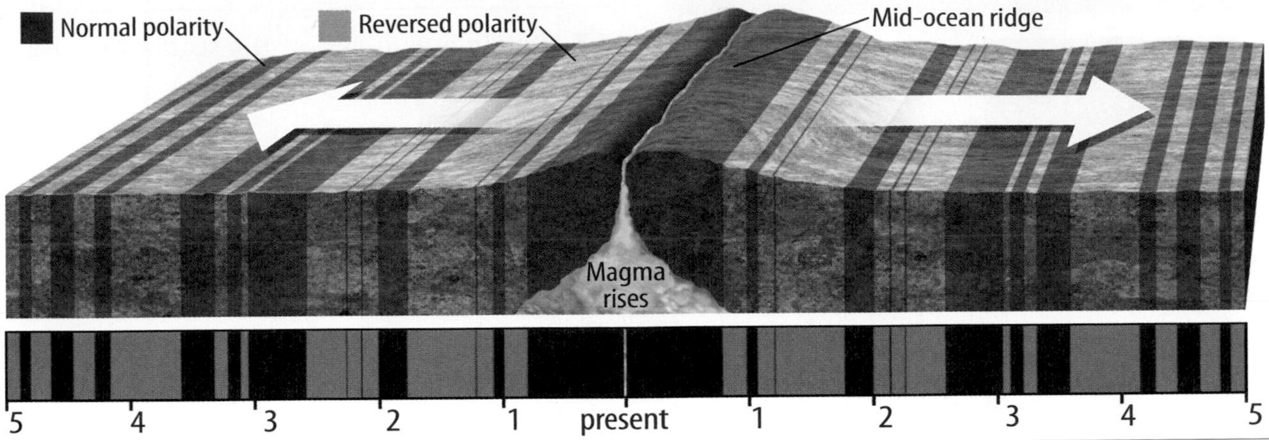

Evidence to Support the Theory

How did scientists prove the theory of seafloor spreading? Scientists studied magnetic minerals in rocks from the seafloor. They used a magnetometer (mag nuh TAH muh tur) to measure and record the magnetic signature of these rocks. These measurements revealed a surprising pattern. Scientists have discovered parallel magnetic stripes on either side of the mid-ocean ridge. Each pair of stripes has a similar composition, age, and magnetic character. Each magnetic stripe in **Figure 10** represents crust that formed and magnetized at a mid-ocean ridge during a period of either **normal** or reversed polarity. The pairs of magnetic stripes confirm that the ocean crust formed at mid-ocean ridges is carried away from the center of the ridges in opposite directions.

Reading Check How do magnetic minerals help support the theory of seafloor spreading?

Other measurements made on the seafloor confirm seafloor spreading. By drilling a hole into the seafloor and measuring the temperature beneath the surface, scientists can measure the amount of thermal energy leaving Earth. The measurements show that more thermal energy leaves Earth near mid-ocean ridges than is released from beneath the abyssal plains.

Additionally, sediment collected from the seafloor can be dated. Results show that the sediment closest to the mid-ocean ridge is younger than the sediment farther away from the ridge. Sediment thickness also increases with distance away from the mid-ocean ridge.

ACADEMIC VOCABULARY

normal
(adjective) conforming to a type, standard, or regular pattern

FOLDABLES®

Make a layered book using two sheets of notebook paper. Use the two pages to record your notes and the inside to illustrate seafloor spreading.

Lesson 2 Review

Assessment Online Quiz

Visual Summary

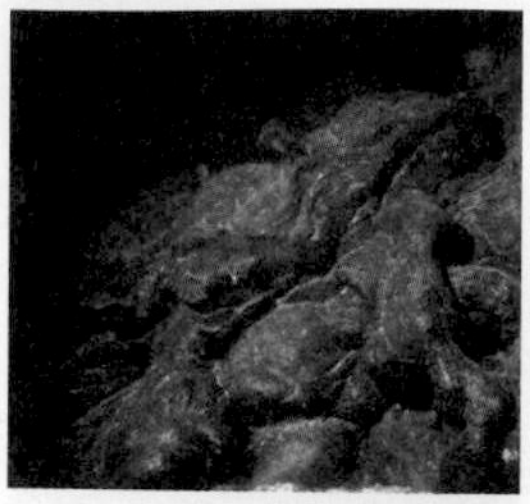

New ocean crust forms along mid-ocean ridges.

Mid-ocean ridges are large mountain ranges that extend throughout Earth's oceans.

A magnetic reversal occurs when Earth's magnetic field changes direction.

FOLDABLES®

Use your lesson Foldable to review the lesson. Save your Foldable for the project at the end of the chapter.

What do you think NOW?

You first read the statements below at the beginning of the chapter.

3. The seafloor is flat.

4. Volcanic activity occurs only on the seafloor.

Did you change your mind about whether you agree or disagree with the statements? Rewrite any false statements to make them true.

Use Vocabulary

1. **Explain** how rocks on the seafloor record magnetic reversals over time.
2. **Diagram** the process of seafloor spreading.
3. **Use the term** *seafloor spreading* to explain how a mid-ocean ridge forms.

Understand Key Concepts

4. Oceanic crust forms
   - **A.** at mid-ocean ridges.
   - **B.** everywhere on the seafloor.
   - **C.** on the abyssal plains.
   - **D.** by magnetic reversals.
5. **Explain** why magnetic stripes on the seafloor are parallel to the mid-ocean ridge.
6. **Describe** how scientists can measure the depth to the seafloor.

Interpret Graphics

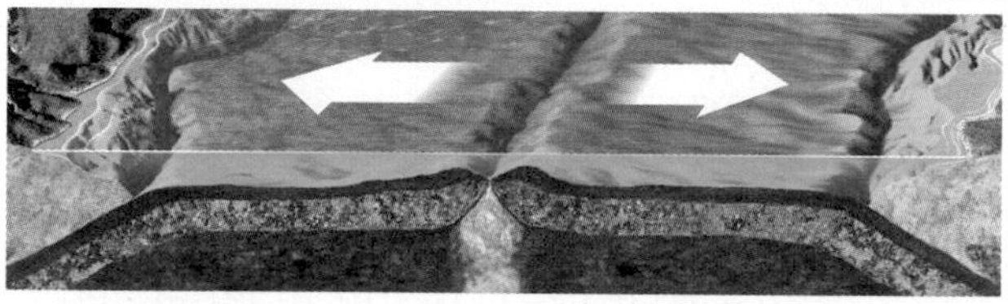

7. **Determine** Refer to the image above. Where is the youngest crust? Where is the oldest crust?
8. **Describe** how seafloor spreading helps to explain the continental drift hypothesis.
9. **Sequence Information** Copy and fill in the graphic organizer below to explain the steps in the formation of a mid-ocean ridge.

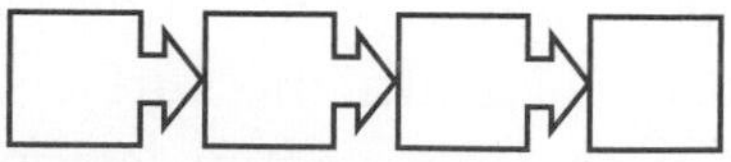

Critical Thinking

10. **Infer** why magnetic stripes in the Pacific Ocean are wider than in the Atlantic Ocean.
11. **Explain** why the thickness of seafloor sediments increases with increasing distance from the ocean ridge.

Inquiry Skill Lab **Model** 30 minutes

How do rocks on the seafloor vary with age away from a mid-ocean ridge?

Scientists discovered that new ocean crust forms at a mid-ocean ridge and spreads away from the ridge slowly over time. This process is called seafloor spreading. The age of the seafloor is one component that supports this theory.

Materials

vanilla yogurt
berry yogurt

foam board
(10 cm × 4 cm)

waxed paper

plastic spoon

Safety

Do not eat anything used in this lab.

Learn It

Scientists use **models** to represent real-world science. By creating a three-dimensional model of volcanic activity along the Mid-Atlantic Ridge, scientists can model the seafloor spreading process. They can then compare this process to the actual age of the seafloor. In this skill lab, you will investigate how the age of rocks on the seafloor changes with distance away from the ridge.

6

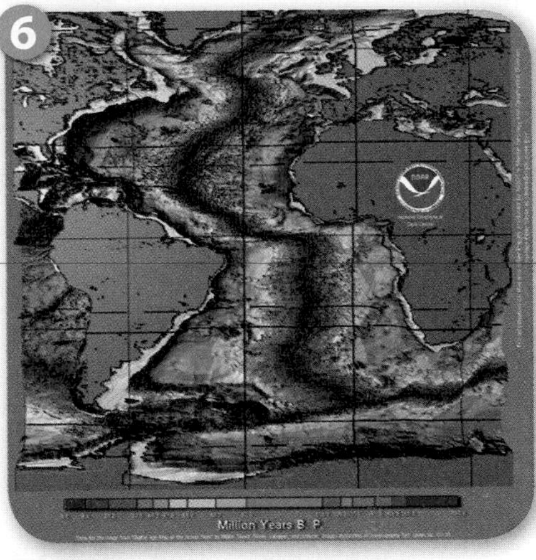

Try It

1. Read and complete a lab safety form.
2. Lay the sheet of waxed paper flat on the lab table. Place two spoonfuls of vanilla yogurt in a straight line near the center of the waxed paper, leaving it lumpy and full.
3. Lay the two pieces of foam board over the yogurt, leaving a small opening in the middle. Push the foam boards together and down, so the yogurt oozes up and over each of the foam boards.
4. Pull the foam boards apart and add a new row of two spoonfuls of berry yogurt down the middle. Lift the boards and place them partly over the new row. Push them together gently. Observe the outer edges of the new yogurt while you are moving the foam boards together.
5. Repeat step 4 with one more spoonful of vanilla yogurt. Then repeat again with one more spoonful of berry yogurt.

Apply It

6. Compare the map and the model. Where is the Mid-Atlantic Ridge on the map? Where is it represented in your model?
7. Which of your yogurt strips matches today on this map? And millions of years ago?
8. How do scientists determine the ages of different parts of the ocean floor?
9. **Conclude** What happened to the yogurt when you added more?
10. **Key Concept** What happens to the material already on the ocean floor when magma erupts along a mid-ocean ridge?

Lesson 3

The Theory of Plate Tectonics

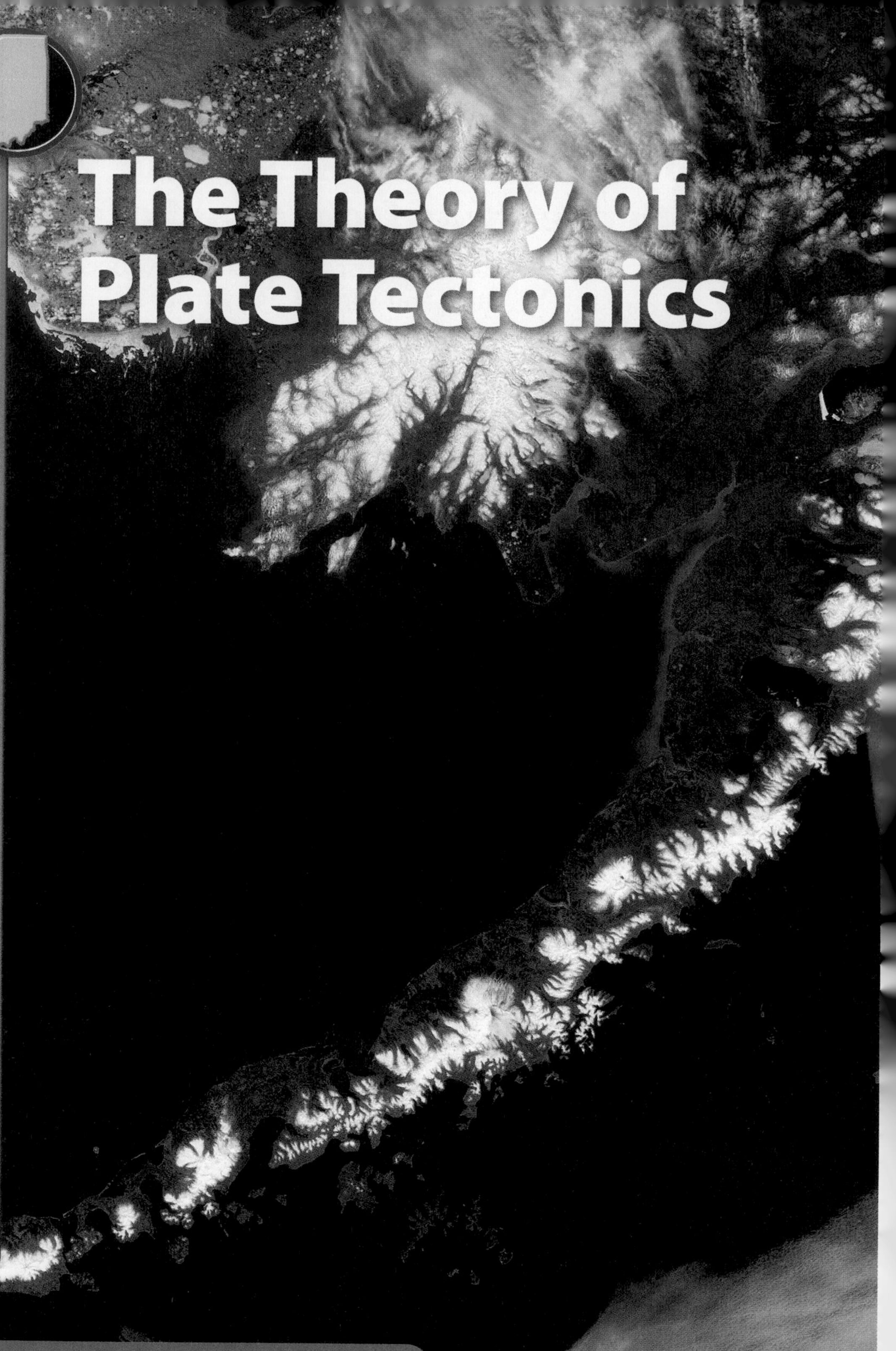

Reading Guide

Key Concepts
ESSENTIAL QUESTIONS

- What is the theory of plate tectonics?
- What are the three types of plate boundaries?
- Why do tectonic plates move?

Vocabulary
plate tectonics p. 215
lithosphere p. 216
divergent plate boundary p. 217
transform plate boundary p. 217
convergent plate boundary p. 217
subduction p. 217
convection p. 220
ridge push p. 221
slab pull p. 221

g Multilingual eGlossary

Academic Standards for Science

7.2.4 Explain how convection currents in the mantle cause lithospheric plates to move causing fast changes like earthquakes and volcanic eruptions, and slow changes like creation of mountains and formation of new ocean floor.

Also covers: 7.NS.3, 7.NS.4, 7.NS.5, 7.NS.7, 7.NS.11

Inquiry How did these islands form?

The photograph shows a chain of active volcanoes. These volcanoes make up the Aleutian Islands of Alaska. Just south of these volcanic islands is a 6 km deep ocean trench. Why did these volcanic mountains form in a line? Can you predict where volcanoes are? Are they related to plate tectonics?

Inquiry Launch Lab

15 minutes

Can you determine density by observing buoyancy?

Density is the measure of an object's mass relative to its volume. Buoyancy is the upward force a liquid places on objects that are immersed in it. If you immerse objects with equal densities into liquids that have different densities, the buoyant forces will be different. An object will sink or float depending on the density of the liquid compared to the object. Earth's layers differ in density. These layers float or sink depending on density and buoyant force.

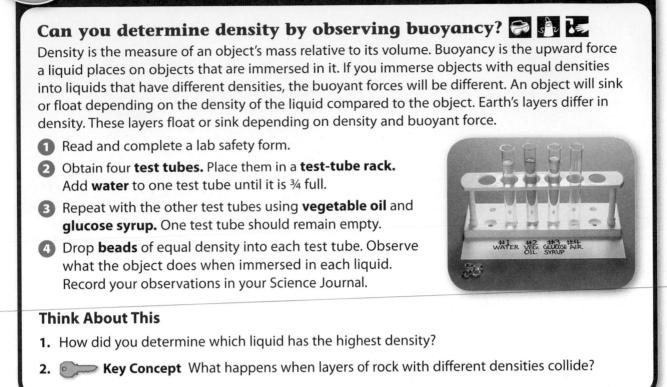

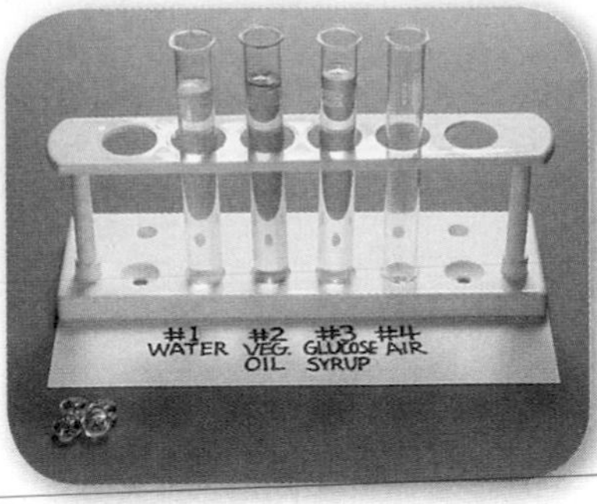

1. Read and complete a lab safety form.
2. Obtain four **test tubes.** Place them in a **test-tube rack.** Add **water** to one test tube until it is ¾ full.
3. Repeat with the other test tubes using **vegetable oil** and **glucose syrup.** One test tube should remain empty.
4. Drop **beads** of equal density into each test tube. Observe what the object does when immersed in each liquid. Record your observations in your Science Journal.

Think About This

1. How did you determine which liquid has the highest density?
2. **Key Concept** What happens when layers of rock with different densities collide?

The Plate Tectonics Theory

When you blow into a balloon, the balloon expands and its surface area also increases. Similarly, if oceanic crust continues to form at mid-ocean ridges and is never destroyed, Earth's surface area should increase. However, this is not the case. The older crust must be destroyed somewhere—but where?

By the late 1960s a more complete theory, called plate tectonics, was proposed. The theory of **plate tectonics** states that *Earth's surface is made of rigid slabs of rock, or plates, that move with respect to each other.* This new theory suggested that Earth's surface is divided into large plates of rigid rock. Each plate moves over Earth's hot and semi-plastic mantle.

Key Concept Check What is plate tectonics?

Geologists use the word *tectonic* to describe the forces that shape Earth's surface and the rock structures that form as a result. Plate tectonics provides an explanation for the occurrence of earthquakes and volcanic eruptions. When plates separate on the seafloor, earthquakes result and a mid-ocean ridge forms. When plates come together, one plate can dive under the other, causing earthquakes and creating a chain of volcanoes. When plates slide past each other, earthquakes can result.

Earth's Tectonic Plates

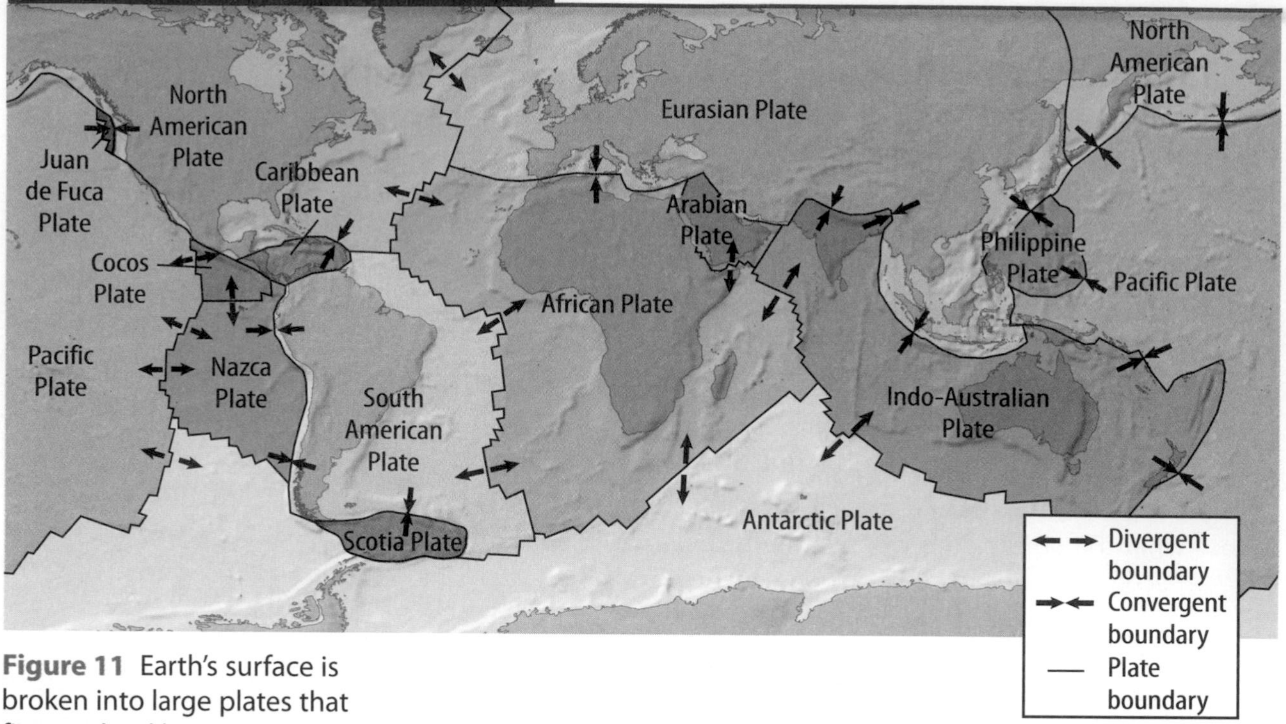

Figure 11 Earth's surface is broken into large plates that fit together like pieces of a giant jigsaw puzzle. The arrows show the general direction of movement of each plate.

Tectonic Plates

You read on the previous page that the theory of plate tectonics states that Earth's surface is divided into rigid plates that move relative to one another. These plates are "floating" on top of a hot and semi-plastic mantle. The map in **Figure 11** illustrates Earth's major plates and the boundaries that define them. The Pacific Plate is the largest plate. The Juan de Fuca Plate is one of the smallest plates. It is between the North American and Pacific Plates. Notice the boundaries that run through the oceans. Many of these boundaries mark the positions of the mid-ocean ridges.

Earth's outermost layers are cold and rigid compared to the layers within Earth's interior. *The cold and rigid outermost rock layer is called the* **lithosphere.** It is made up of the crust and the solid, uppermost mantle. The lithosphere is thin below mid-ocean ridges and thick below continents. Earth's tectonic plates are large pieces of lithosphere. These lithospheric plates fit together like the pieces of a giant jigsaw puzzle.

The layer of Earth below the lithosphere is called the asthenosphere (as THEE nuh sfihr). This layer is so hot that it behaves like a **plastic** material. This enables Earth's plates to move because the hotter, plastic mantle material beneath them can flow. The interactions between lithosphere and asthenosphere help to explain plate tectonics.

Reading Check What are Earth's outermost layers called?

SCIENCE USE V. COMMON USE

plastic

Science Use capable of being molded or changing shape without breaking

Common Use any of numerous organic, synthetic, or processed materials made into objects

Plate Boundaries

Place two books side by side and imagine each book represents a tectonic plate. A plate boundary exists where the books meet. How many different ways can you move the books with respect to each other? You can pull the books apart, you can push the books together, and you can slide the books past one another. Earth's tectonic plates move in much the same way.

Divergent Plate Boundaries

Mid-ocean ridges are located along divergent plate boundaries. *A* **divergent plate boundary** *forms where two plates separate.* When the seafloor spreads at a mid-ocean ridge, lava erupts, cools, and forms new oceanic crust. Divergent plate boundaries can also exist in the middle of a continent. They pull continents apart and form rift valleys. The East African Rift is an example of a continental rift.

Transform Plate Boundaries

The famous San Andreas Fault in California is an example of a transform plate boundary. *A* **transform plate boundary** *forms where two plates slide past each other.* As they move past each other, the plates can get stuck and stop moving. Stress builds up where the plates are "stuck." Eventually, the stress is too great and the rocks break, suddenly moving apart. This results in a rapid release of energy as earthquakes.

Convergent Plate Boundaries

Convergent plate boundaries *form where two plates collide. The denser plate sinks below the more buoyant plate in a process called* **subduction.** The area where a denser plate descends into Earth along a convergent plate boundary is called a **subduction** zone.

When an oceanic plate and a continental plate collide, the denser oceanic plate subducts under the edge of the continent. This creates a deep ocean trench. A line of volcanoes forms above the subducting plate on the edge of the continent. This process can also occur when two oceanic plates collide. The older and denser oceanic plate will subduct beneath the younger oceanic plate. This creates a deep ocean trench and a line of volcanoes called an island arc.

When two continental plates collide, neither plate is subducted, and mountains such as the Himalayas in southern Asia form from uplifted rock. **Table 1** on the next page summarizes the interactions of Earth's tectonic plates.

Key Concept Check What are the three types of plate boundaries?

FOLDABLES®

Make a layered book using two sheets of notebook paper. Use it to organize information about the different types of plate boundaries and the features that form there.

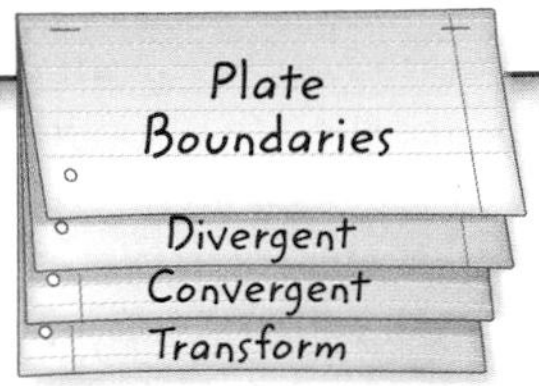

WORD ORIGIN

subduction
from Latin *subductus,* means "to lead under, removal"

Table 1 The direction of motion of Earth's plates creates a variety of features at the boundaries between the plates.

Concepts in Motion **Animation**

Table 1 Interactions of Earth's Tectonic Plates

Plate Boundary	Relative Motion	Example
Divergent plate boundary When two plates separate and create new oceanic crust, a divergent plate boundary forms. This process occurs where the seafloor spreads along a mid-ocean ridge, as shown to the right. This process can also occur in the middle of continents and is referred to as a continental rifting.	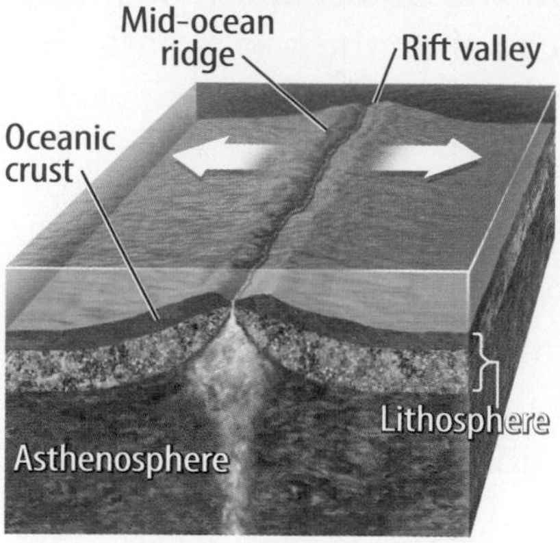	
Transform plate boundary Two plates slide horizontally past one another along a transform plate boundary. Earthquakes are common along this type of plate boundary. The San Andreas Fault, shown to the right, is part of the transform plate boundary that extends along the coast of California.	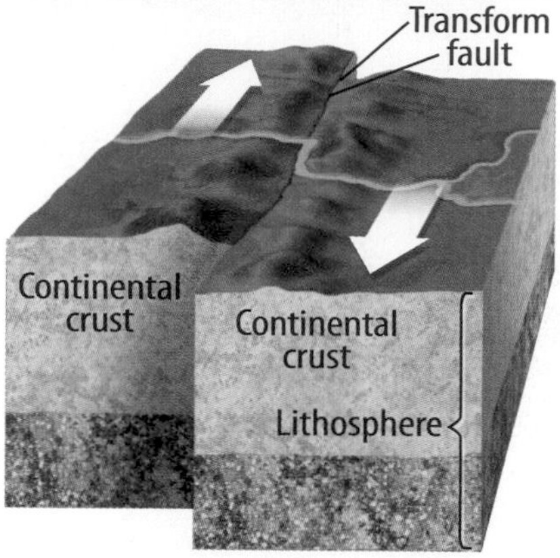	
Convergent plate boundary (ocean-to-continent) When an oceanic and a continental plate collide, they form a convergent plate boundary. The denser plate will subduct. A volcanic mountain, such as Mount Rainier in the Cascade Mountains, forms along the edge of the continent. This process can also occur where two oceanic plates collide, and the denser plate is subducted.	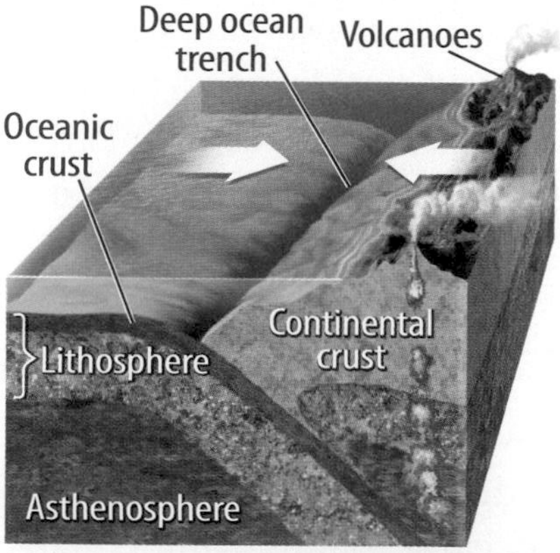	
Convergent plate boundary (continent-to-continent) Convergent plate boundaries can also occur where two continental plates collide. Because both plates are equally dense, neither plate will subduct. Both plates uplift and deform. This creates huge mountains like the Himalayas, shown to the right.	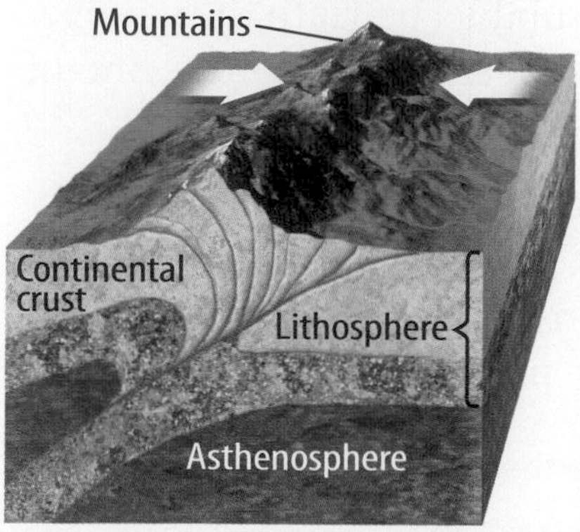	

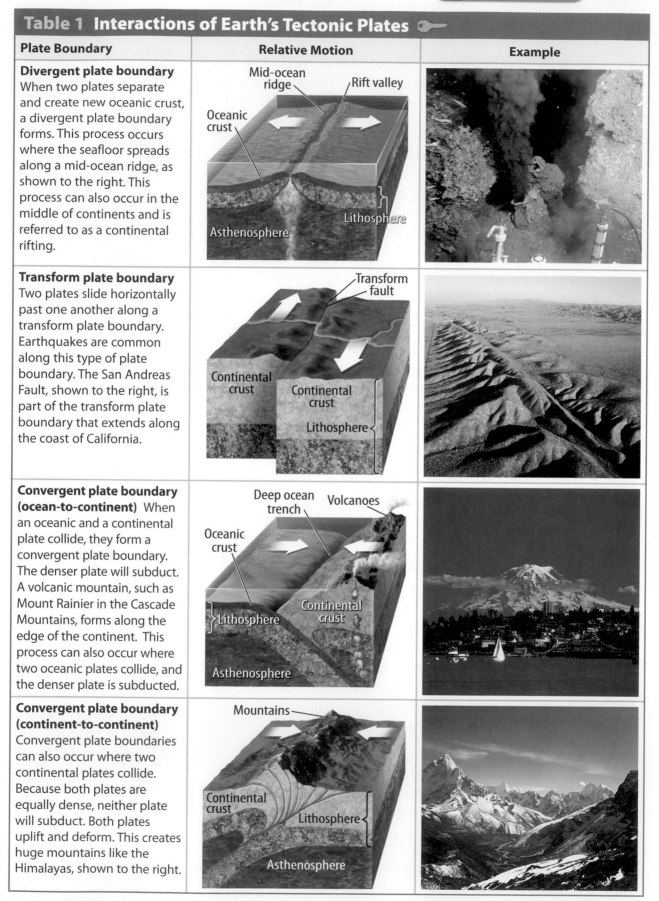

Evidence for Plate Tectonics

When Wegener proposed the continental drift hypothesis, the technology used to measure how fast the continents move today wasn't yet available. Recall that continents move apart or come together at speeds of a few centimeters per year. This is about the length of a small paperclip.

Today, scientists can measure how fast continents move. A network of satellites orbiting Earth monitors plate motion. By keeping track of the distance between these satellites and Earth, it is possible to locate and determine how fast a tectonic plate moves. This network of satellites is called the Global Positioning System (GPS).

The theory of plate tectonics also provides an explanation for why earthquakes and volcanoes occur in certain places. Because plates are rigid, tectonic activity occurs where plates meet. When plates separate, collide, or slide past each other along a plate boundary, stress builds. A rapid release of energy can result in earthquakes. Volcanoes form where plates separate along a mid-ocean ridge or a continental rift or collide along a subduction zone. Mountains can form where two continents collide. **Figure 12** illustrates the relationship between plate boundaries and the occurrence of earthquakes and volcanoes. Refer back to the lesson opener photo. Find these islands on the map. Are they located near a plate boundary?

Key Concept Check How are earthquakes and volcanoes related to the theory of plate tectonics?

Figure 12 Notice that most earthquakes and volcanoes occur near plate boundaries.

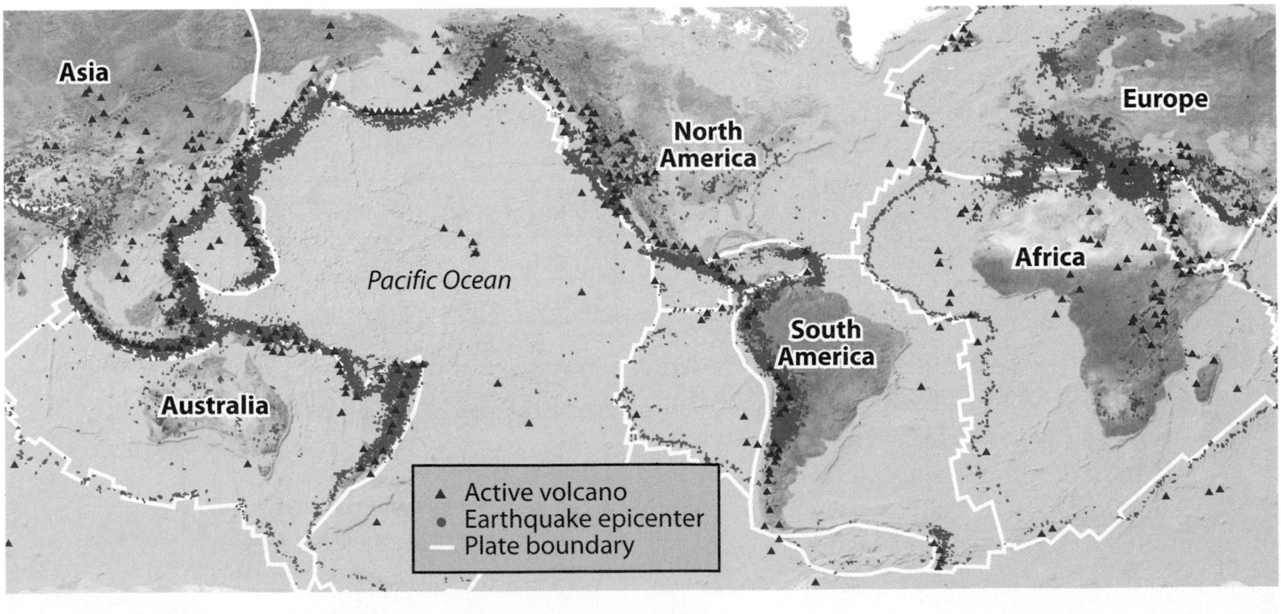

Visual Check Do earthquakes and volcanoes occur anywhere away from plate boundaries?

Figure 13 When water is heated, it expands. Less dense heated water rises because the colder water sinks, forming convection currents.

Review

Personal Tutor

Plate Motion

The main objection to Wegener's continental drift hypothesis was that he could not explain why or how continents move. Scientists now understand that continents move because the asthenosphere moves underneath the lithosphere.

Convection Currents

You are probably already familiar with the process of **convection,** *the circulation of material caused by differences in temperature and density.* For example, the upstairs floors of homes and buildings are often warmer. This is because hot air rises while dense, cold air sinks. Look at **Figure 13** to see convection in action.

Reading Check What causes convection?

Plate tectonic activity is related to convection in the mantle, as shown in **Figure 14.** Radioactive elements, such as uranium, thorium, and potassium, heat Earth's interior. When materials such as solid rock are heated, they expand and become less dense. Hot mantle material rises upward and comes in contact with Earth's crust. Thermal energy is transferred from hot mantle material to the colder surface above. As the mantle cools, it becomes denser and then sinks, forming a convection current. These currents in the asthenosphere act like a conveyor belt moving the lithosphere above.

Key Concept Check Why do tectonic plates move?

Inquiry MiniLab

20 minutes

How do changes in density cause motion?

Convection currents drive plate motion. Material near the base of the mantle is heated, which decreases its density. This material then rises to the base of the crust, where it cools, increasing in density and sinking.

1. Read and complete a lab safety form.
2. Copy the table to the right into your Science Journal and add a row for each minute. Record your observations.
3. Pour 100 mL of **carbonated water** or **clear soda** into a **beaker** or a **clear glass.**
4. Drop five **raisins** into the water. Observe the path that the raisins follow for 5 minutes.

Time Interval	Observations
First minute	
Second minute	
Third minute	

Analyze and Conclude

1. **Observe** Describe each raisin's motion.
2. **Key Concept** How does the behavior of the raisin model compare to the motion in Earth's mantle?

Convection Currents

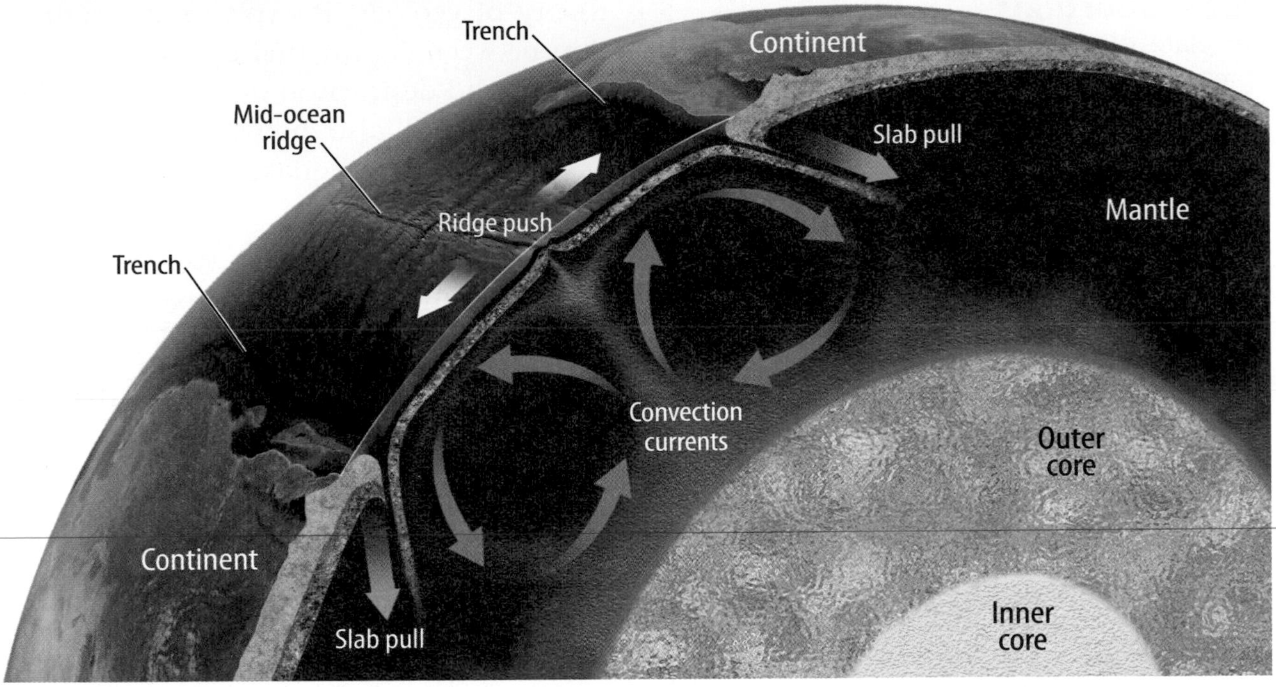

Forces Causing Plate Motion

How can something as massive as the Pacific Plate move? **Figure 14** shows the three forces that interact to cause plate motion. Scientists still debate over which of these forces has the greatest effect on plate motion.

Basal Drag Convection currents in the mantle produce a force that causes motion called basal drag. Notice in **Figure 14** how convection currents in the asthenosphere circulate and drag the lithosphere similar to the way a conveyor belt moves items along at a supermarket checkout.

Ridge Push Recall that mid-ocean ridges have greater elevation than the surrounding seafloor. Because mid-ocean ridges are higher, gravity pulls the surrounding rocks down and away from the ridge. *Rising mantle material at mid-ocean ridges creates the potential for plates to move away from the ridge with a force called* **ridge push.** Ridge push moves lithosphere in opposite directions away from the mid-ocean ridge.

Slab Pull As you read earlier in this lesson, when tectonic plates collide, the denser plate will sink into the mantle along a subduction zone. This plate is called a slab. Because the slab is old and cold, it is denser than the surrounding mantle and will sink. *As a slab sinks, it pulls on the rest of the plate with a force called* **slab pull.** Scientists are still uncertain about which force has the greatest influence on plate motion.

Figure 14 Convection occurs in the mantle underneath Earth's tectonic plates. Three forces act on plates to make them move: basal drag from convection currents, ridge push at mid-ocean ridges, and slab pull from subducting plates.

Visual Check What is happening to a plate that is undergoing slab pull?

Math Skills

Use Proportions

The plates along the Mid-Atlantic Ridge spread at an average rate of 2.5 cm/y. How long will it take the plates to spread 1 m? Use proportions to find the answer.

1. **Convert the distance to the same unit.**

$$1 \text{ m} = 100 \text{ cm}$$

2. **Set up a proportion:**

$$\frac{2.5 \text{ cm}}{1 \text{ y}} = \frac{100 \text{ cm}}{x \text{ y}}$$

3. **Cross multiply and solve for *x* as follows:**

$$2.5 \text{ cm} \times x \text{y} = 100 \text{ cm} \times 1 \text{ y}$$

4. **Divide both sides by 2.5 cm.**

$$x = \frac{100 \text{ cm y}}{2.5 \text{ cm}}$$

$$x = 40 \text{ y}$$

Practice

The Eurasian plate travels the slowest, at about 0.7 cm/y. How long would it take the plate to travel 3 m?

(1 m = 100 cm)

Review

- **Math Practice**
- **Personal Tutor**

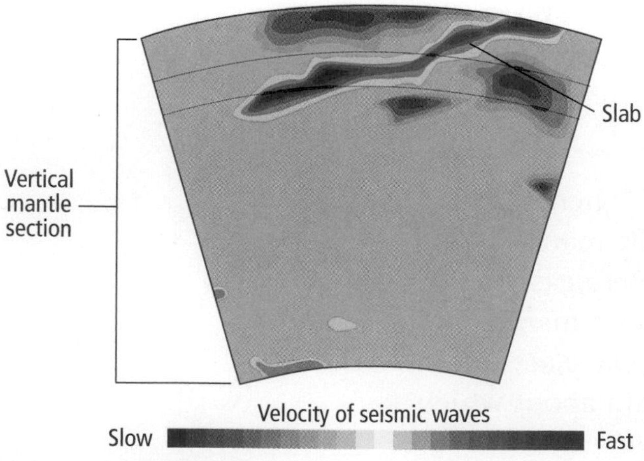

A Theory in Progress

Plate tectonics has become the unifying theory of geology. It explains the connection between continental drift and the formation and destruction of crust along plate boundaries. It also helps to explain the occurrence of earthquakes, volcanoes, and mountains.

The investigation that Wegener began nearly a century ago is still being revised. Several unanswered questions remain.

- Why is Earth the only planet in the solar system that has plate tectonic activity? Different hypotheses have been proposed to explain this. Extrasolar planets outside our solar system are also being studied.
- Why do some earthquakes and volcanoes occur far away from plate boundaries? Perhaps it is because the plates are not perfectly rigid. Different thicknesses and weaknesses exist within the plates. Also, the mantle is much more active than scientists originally understood.
- What forces dominate plate motion? Currently accepted models suggest that convection currents occur in the mantle. However, there is no way to measure or observe them.
- What will scientists investigate next? **Figure 15** shows an image produced by a new technique called anisotropy that creates a 3-D image of seismic wave velocities in a subduction zone. This developing technology might help scientists better understand the processes that occur within the mantle and along plate boundaries.

Reading Check Why does the theory of plate tectonics continue to change?

Figure 15 Seismic waves were used to produce this tomography scan. These colors show a subducting plate. The blue colors represent rigid materials with faster seismic wave velocities.

Lesson 3 Review

Assessment Online Quiz
Inquiry Virtual Lab

Visual Summary

Tectonic plates are made of cold and rigid slabs of rock.

Mantle convection—the circulation of mantle material due to density differences—drives plate motion.

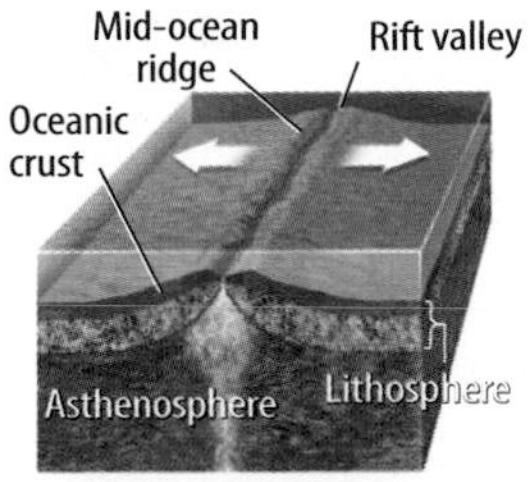

The three types of plate boundaries are divergent, convergent, and transform boundaries.

FOLDABLES®

Use your lesson Foldable to review the lesson. Save your Foldable for the project at the end of the chapter.

What do you think NOW?

You first read the statements below at the beginning of the chapter.

5. Continents drift across a molten mantle.

6. Mountain ranges can form when continents collide.

Did you change your mind about whether you agree or disagree with the statements? Rewrite any false statements to make them true.

Use Vocabulary

1. The theory that proposes that Earth's surface is broken into moving, rigid plates is called ________.

Understand Key Concepts

2. **Compare and contrast** the geological activity that occurs along the three types of plate boundaries.

3. **Explain** why mantle convection occurs.

4. Tectonic plates move because of
   A. convection currents.
   B. Earth's increasing size.
   C. magnetic reversals.
   D. volcanic activity.

Interpret Graphics

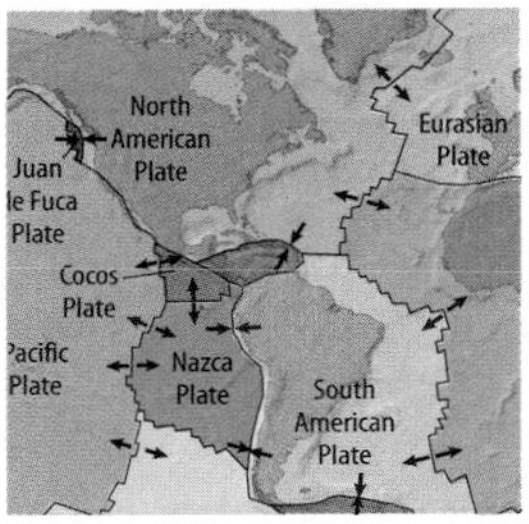

5. **Identify** Name the type of boundary between the Eurasian Plate and the North American Plate and between the Nazca Plate and South American Plate.

6. **Determine Cause and Effect** Copy and fill in the graphic organizer below to list the cause and effects of convection currents.

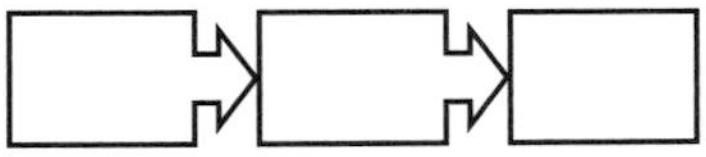

Critical Thinking

7. **Explain** why earthquakes occur at greater depths along convergent plate boundaries.

Math Skills

Review — Math Practice

8. Two plates in the South Pacific separate at an average rate of 15 cm/y. How far will they have separated after 5,000 years?

Inquiry Lab 45 minutes

Movement of Plate Boundaries

Materials

graham crackers

waxed paper (four 10×10-cm squares)

dropper

frosting

plastic spoon

Safety

Earth's surface is broken into 12 major tectonic plates. Wherever these plates touch, one of four events occurs. The plates may collide and crumple or fold to make mountains. One plate may subduct under another, forming volcanoes. They may move apart and form a mid-ocean ridge, or they may slide past each other causing an earthquake. This investigation models plate movements.

Question

What happens where two plates come together?

Procedure

Part I

1. Read and complete a lab safety form.
2. Obtain the materials from your teacher.
3. Break a graham cracker along the perforation line into two pieces.
4. Lay the pieces side by side on a piece of waxed paper.
5. Slide crackers in opposite directions so that the edges of the crackers rub together.

Part II

6. Place two new graham crackers side by side but not touching.
7. In the space between the crackers, add several drops of water.
8. Slide the crackers toward each other and observe what happens.

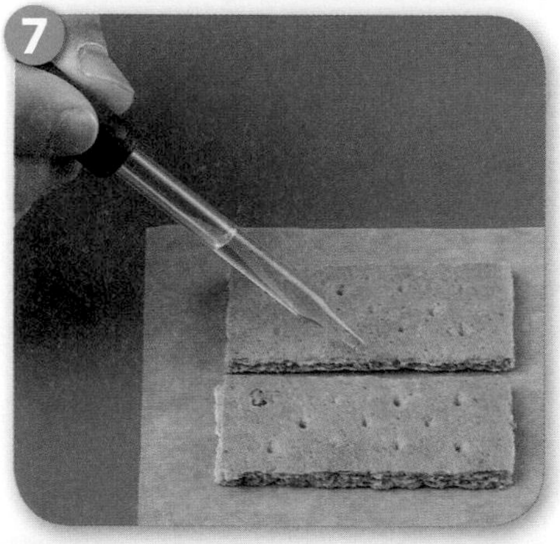

Part III

9. Place a spoonful of frosting on the waxed-paper square.
10. Place two graham crackers on top of the frosting so that they touch.
11. Push the crackers down and spread them apart in one motion.

Analyze and Conclude

12 Analyze the movement of the crackers in each of your models.

Part I

13 What type of plate boundary do the graham crackers in this model represent?

14 What do the crumbs in the model represent?

15 Did you feel or hear anything when the crackers moved past each other? Explain.

16 How does this model simulate an earthquake?

Part II

17 What does the water in this model represent?

18 What type of plate boundary do the graham crackers in this model represent?

19 Why didn't one graham cracker slide beneath the other in this model?

Part III

20 What type of plate boundary do the graham crackers in this model represent?

21 What does the frosting represent?

22 What shape does the frosting create when the crackers move?

23 What is the formation formed from the crackers and frosting?

Communicate Your Results

Create a flip book of one of the boundaries to show a classmate who was absent. Show how each boundary plate moves and the results of those movements.

Inquiry Extension

Place a graham cracker and a piece of cardboard side by side. Slide the two pieces toward each other. What type of plate boundary does this model represent? How is this model different from the three that you observed in the lab?

Lab Tips

- ☑ Use fresh graham crackers.
- ☑ Slightly heat frosting to make it more fluid for experiments.

Remember to use scientific methods.

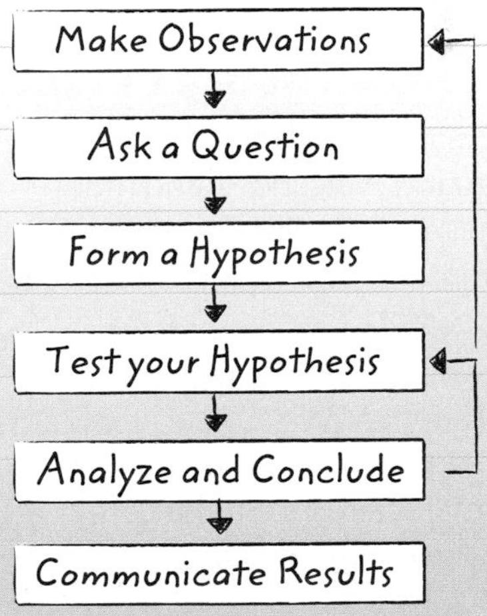

Chapter 6 Study Guide

WebQuest

THE BIG IDEA **The theory of plate tectonics states that Earth's lithosphere is broken up into rigid plates that move over Earth's surface.**

Key Concepts Summary

Lesson 1: The Continental Drift Hypothesis

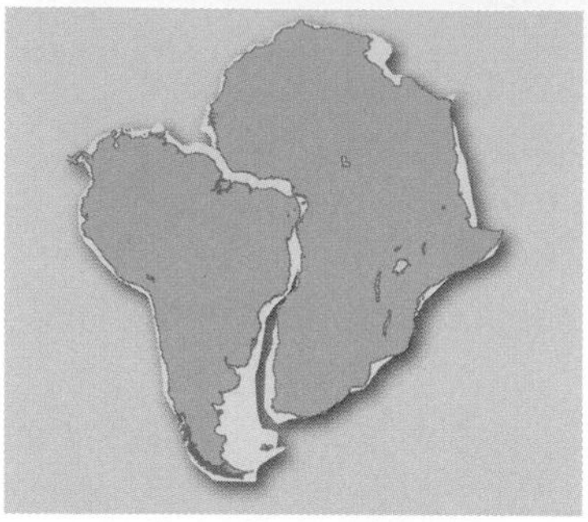

- The puzzle piece fit of continents, fossil evidence, climate, rocks, and mountain ranges supports the hypothesis of **continental drift.**
- Scientists were skeptical of continental drift because Wegener could not explain the mechanism for movement.

Vocabulary

Pangaea p. 199
continental drift p. 199

Lesson 2: Development of a Theory

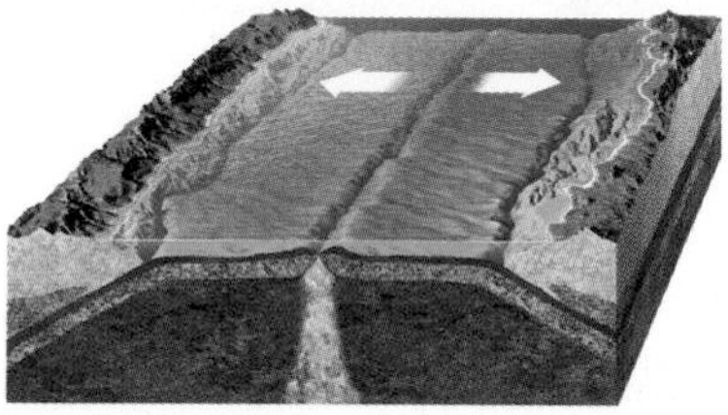

- **Seafloor spreading** provides a mechanism for continental drift.
- Seafloor spreading occurs at **mid-ocean ridges.**
- Evidence of **magnetic reversal** in rock, thermal energy trends, and the discovery of seafloor spreading all contributed to the development of the theory of plate tectonics.

Vocabulary

mid-ocean ridge p. 207
seafloor spreading p. 208
normal polarity p. 210
magnetic reversal p. 210
reversed polarity p. 210

Lesson 3: The Theory of Plate Tectonics

- Types of plate boundaries, the location of earthquakes, volcanoes, and mountain ranges, and satellite measurement of plate motion support the theory of **plate tectonics.**
- Mantle **convection, ridge push,** and **slab pull** are the forces that cause plate motion. Radioactivity in the mantle and thermal energy from the core produce the energy for convection.

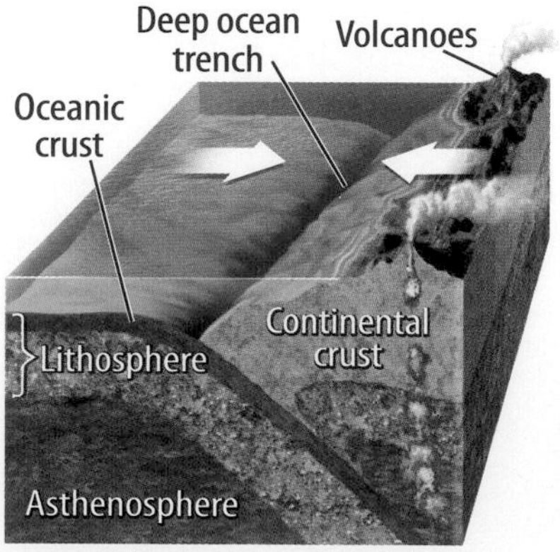

Vocabulary

plate tectonics p. 215
lithosphere p. 216
divergent plate boundary p. 217
transform plate boundary p. 217
convergent plate boundary p. 217
subduction p. 217
convection p. 220
ridge push p. 221
slab pull p. 221

Review
- Personal Tutor
- Vocabulary eGames
- Vocabulary eFlashcards

FOLDABLES® Chapter Project

Assemble your lesson Foldables as shown to make a Chapter Project. Use the project to review what you have learned in this chapter.

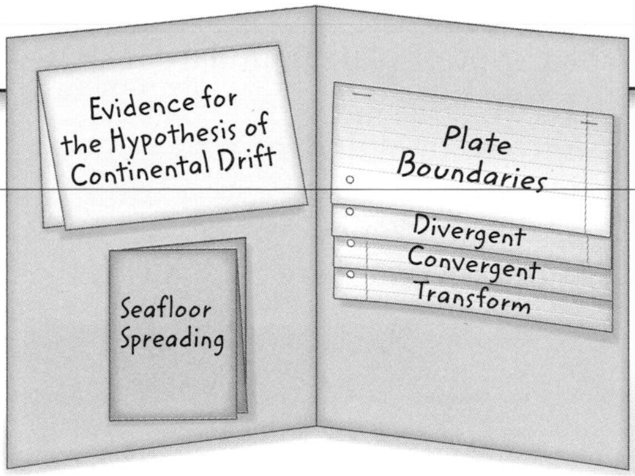

Use Vocabulary

1. The process in which hot mantle rises and cold mantle sinks is called ________.
2. What is the plate tectonics theory?
3. What was Pangaea?
4. Identify the three types of plate boundaries and the relative motion associated with each type.
5. Magnetic reversals occur when ________.
6. Explain seafloor spreading in your own words.

Link Vocabulary and Key Concepts

Concepts in Motion Interactive Concept Map

Copy this concept map, and then use vocabulary terms from the previous page to complete the concept map.

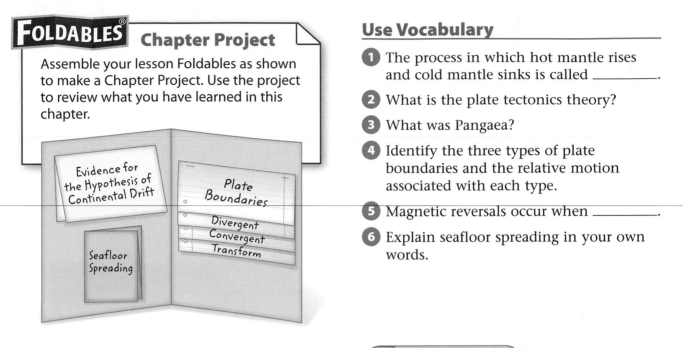

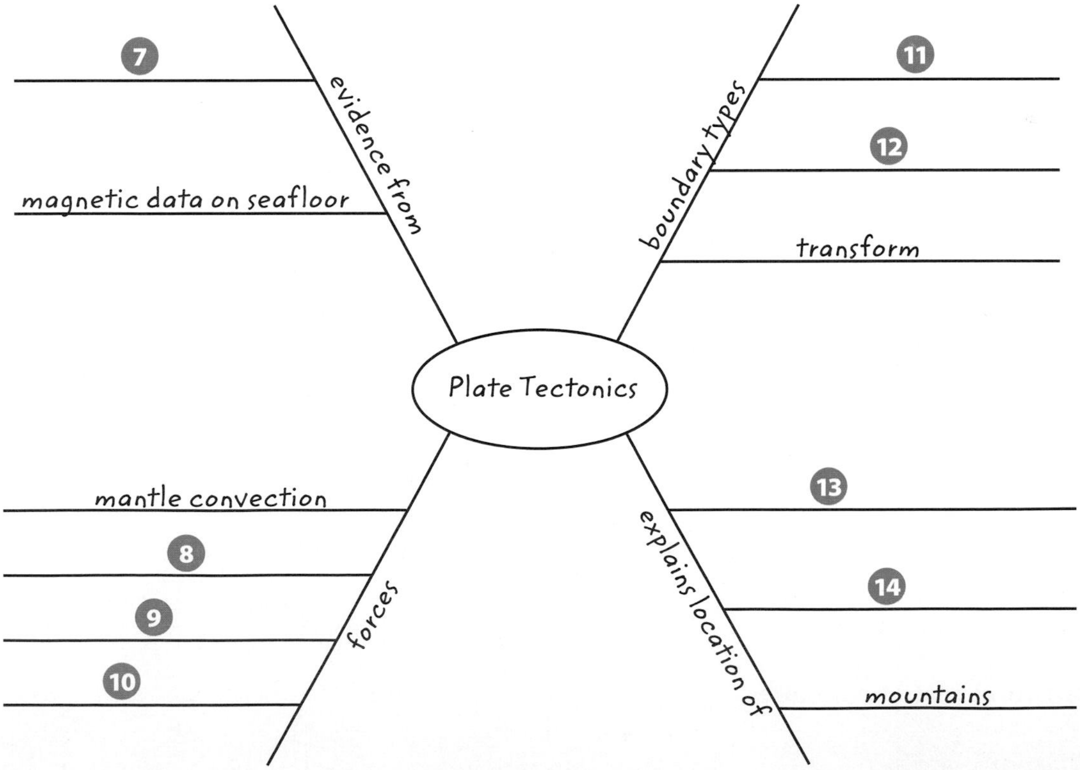

Chapter 6 Review

Understand Key Concepts

1. Alfred Wegener proposed the ________ hypothesis.
   A. continental drift
   B. plate tectonics
   C. ridge push
   D. seafloor spreading

2. Ocean crust is
   A. made from submerged continents.
   B. magnetically produced crust.
   C. produced at the mid-ocean ridge.
   D. produced at all plate boundaries.

3. What technologies did scientists NOT use to develop the theory of seafloor spreading?
   A. echo-sounding measurements
   B. GPS (global positioning system)
   C. magnetometer measurements
   D. seafloor thickness measurements

4. The picture below shows Pangaea's position on Earth approximately 280 million years ago. Where did geologists discover glacial features associated with a cooler climate?
   A. Antarctica
   B. Asia
   C. North America
   D. South America

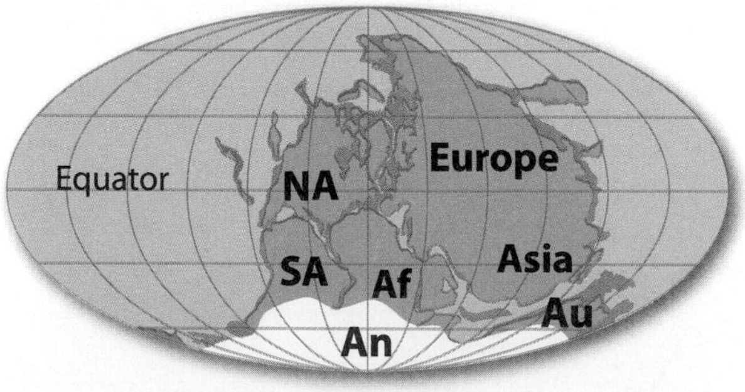

Pangaea

5. Mid-ocean ridges are associated with
   A. convergent plate boundaries.
   B. divergent plate boundaries.
   C. hotspots.
   D. transform plate boundaries.

6. Two plates of equal density form mountain ranges along
   A. continent-to-continent convergent boundaries.
   B. ocean-to-continent convergent boundaries.
   C. divergent boundaries.
   D. transform boundaries.

7. Which type of plate boundary is shown in the figure below?
   A. convergent boundary
   B. divergent boundary
   C. subduction zone
   D. transform boundary

8. What happens to Earth's magnetic field over time?
   A. It changes polarity.
   B. It continually strengthens.
   C. It stays the same.
   D. It weakens and eventually disappears.

9. Which of Earth's outermost layers includes the crust and the upper mantle?
   A. asthenosphere
   B. lithosphere
   C. mantle
   D. outer core

Critical Thinking

10 **Evaluate** The oldest seafloor in the Atlantic Ocean is located closest to the edge of continents, as shown in the image below. Explain how this age can be used to figure out when North America first began to separate from Europe.

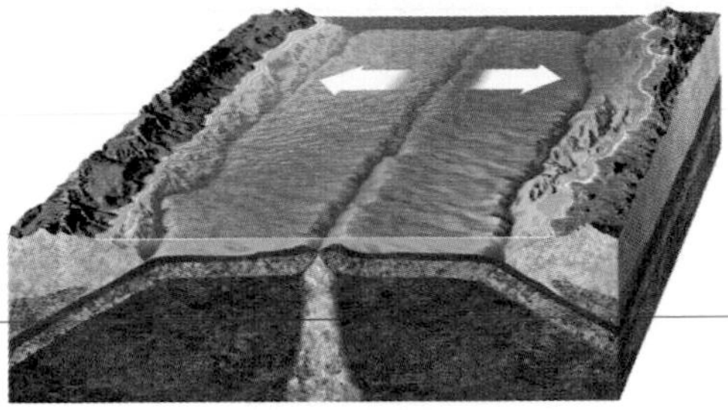

11 **Examine** the evidence used to develop the theory of plate tectonics. How has new technology strengthened the theory?

12 **Explain** Sediments deposited by glaciers in Africa are surprising because Africa is now warm. How does the hypothesis of continental drift explain these deposits?

13 **Draw** a diagram to show subduction of an oceanic plate beneath a continental plate along a convergent plate boundary. Explain why volcanoes form along this type of plate boundary.

14 **Infer** Warm peanut butter is easier to spread than cold peanut butter. How does knowing this help you understand why the mantle is able to deform in a plastic manner?

Writing in Science

15 **Predict** If continents continue to move in the same direction over the next 200 million years, how might the appearance of landmasses change? Write a paragraph to explain the possible positions of landmasses in the future. Based on your understanding of the plate tectonic theory, is it possible that new supercontinents will form in the future?

REVIEW THE BIG IDEA

16 What is the theory of plate tectonics? Distinguish between continental drift, seafloor spreading, and plate tectonics. What evidence was used to support the theory of plate tectonics?

17 Use the image below to interpret how the theory of plate tectonics helps to explain formation of huge mountains like the Himalaya.

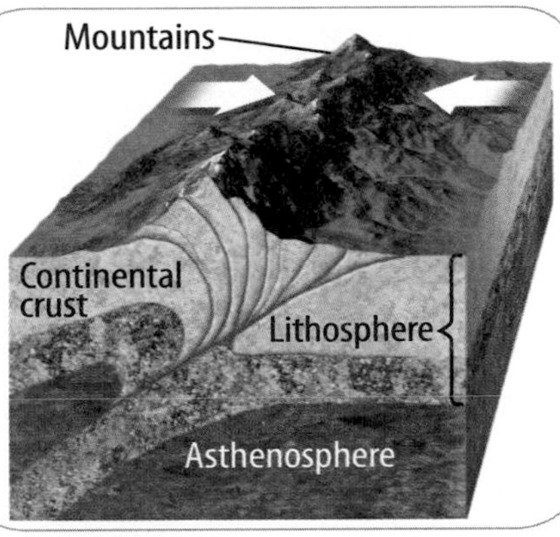

Math Skills

Review

Math Practice

Use Proportions

18 Mountains on a convergent plate boundary may grow at a rate of 3 mm/y. How long would it take a mountain to grow to a height of 3,000 m? (1 m = 1,000 mm)

19 The North American Plate and the Pacific Plate have been sliding horizontally past each other along the San Andreas fault zone for about 10 million years. The plates move at an average rate of about 5 cm/y.

- **a.** How far have the plates traveled, assuming a constant rate, during this time?
- **b.** How far has the plate traveled in kilometers? (1 km = 100,000 cm)

Standardized Test Practice

Record your answers on the answer sheet provided by your teacher or on a sheet of paper.

Multiple Choice

Use the diagram below to answer questions 1 and 2.

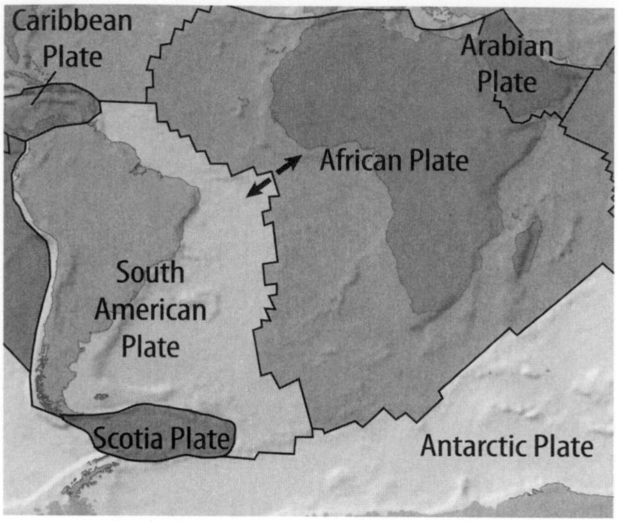

1 In the diagram above, what does the irregular line between tectonic plates represent?

A abyssal plain
B island chain
C mid-ocean ridge
D polar axis

2 What do the arrows indicate?

A magnetic polarity
B ocean flow
C plate movement
D volcanic eruption

3 What evidence helped to support the theory of seafloor spreading?

A magnetic equality
B magnetic interference
C magnetic north
D magnetic polarity

4 Which plate tectonic process creates a deep ocean trench?

A conduction
B deduction
C induction
D subduction

5 What causes plate motion?

A convection in Earth's mantle
B currents in Earth's oceans
C reversal of Earth's polarity
D rotation on Earth's axis

6 New oceanic crust forms and old oceanic crust moves away from a mid-ocean ridge during

A continental drift.
B magnetic reversal.
C normal polarity.
D seafloor spreading.

Use the diagram below to answer question 7.

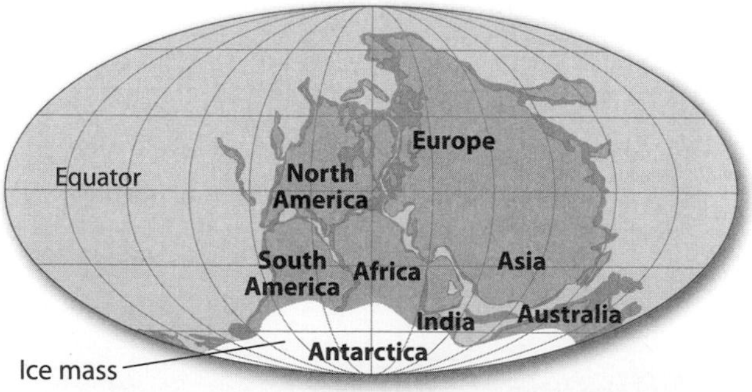

7 What is the name of Alfred Wegener's ancient supercontinent pictured in the diagram above?

A Caledonia
B continental drift
C *Glossopteris*
D Pangaea

Use the diagram below to answer question 8.

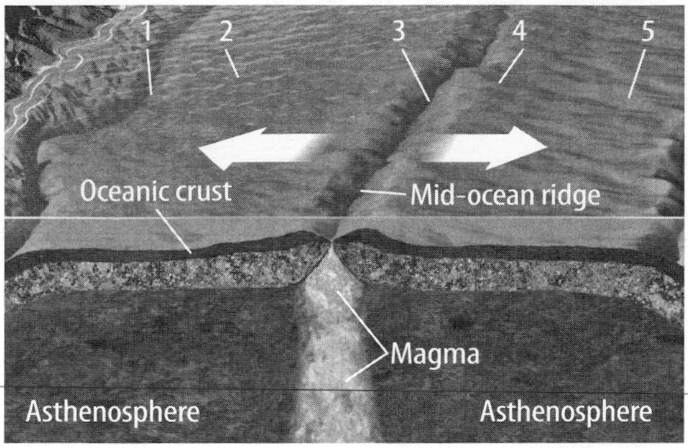

8 The numbers in the diagram represent seafloor rock. Which represent the oldest rock?

A 1 and 5

B 2 and 4

C 3 and 4

D 4 and 5

9 Which part of the seafloor contains the thickest sediment layer?

A abyssal plain

B deposition band

C mid-ocean ridge

D tectonic zone

10 What type of rock forms when lava cools and crystallizes on the seafloor?

A a fossil

B a glacier

C basalt

D magma

Constructed Response

Use the table below to answer questions 11 and 12.

Plate Boundary	Location

11 In the table above, identify the three types of plate boundaries. Then describe a real-world location for each type.

12 Create a diagram to show plate motion along one type of plate boundary. Label the diagram and draw arrows to indicate the direction of plate motion.

13 Identify and explain all the evidence that Wegener used to help support his continental drift hypothesis.

14 Why was continental drift so controversial during Alfred Wegener's time? What explanation was necessary to support his hypothesis?

15 How did scientists prove the theory of seafloor spreading?

16 If new oceanic crust constantly forms along mid-ocean ridges, why isn't Earth's total surface area increasing?

NEED EXTRA HELP?																
If You Missed Question...	1	2	3	4	5	6	7	8	9	10	11	12	13	14	15	16
Go to Lesson...	3	3	2	3	3	2	1	2	2	2	3	3	1	1	2	3

Chapter 7

Geologic Time

THE BIG IDEA What have scientists learned about Earth's past by studying rocks and fossils?

Inquiry What happened to the dinosaurs?

This Triceratops lived millions of years ago. Hundreds of other kinds of dinosaurs lived at the same time. Some were as big as houses; others were as small as chickens. Scientists learn about dinosaurs by studying their fossils. Like many organisms that have lived on Earth, dinosaurs disappeared suddenly. Why did the dinosaurs disappear?

- How has Earth changed over geologic time?
- How do geologic events affect life on Earth?
- What have scientists learned about Earth's past by studying rocks and fossils?

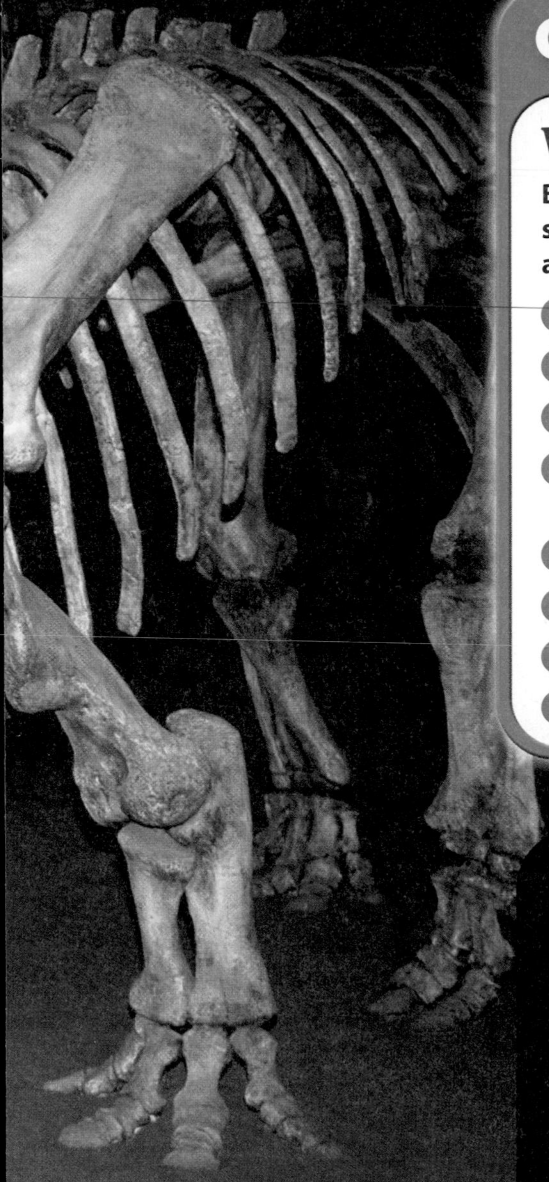

Get Ready to Read

What do you think?

Before you read, decide if you agree or disagree with each of these statements. As you read this chapter, see if you change your mind about any of the statements.

1. All geologic eras are the same length of time.
2. Meteorite impacts cause all extinction events.
3. North America was once on the equator.
4. All of Earth's continents were part of a huge supercontinent 250 million years ago.
5. All large Mesozoic vertebrates were dinosaurs.
6. Dinosaurs disappeared in a large mass extinction event.
7. Mammals evolved after dinosaurs became extinct.
8. Ice covered nearly one-third of Earth's land surface 10,000 years ago.

ConnectED Your one-stop online resource

connectED.mcgraw-hill.com

- Video
- Audio
- Review
- Inquiry
- WebQuest
- Assessment
- Concepts in Motion
- Multilingual eGlossary

Lesson 1

Reading Guide

Key Concepts
ESSENTIAL QUESTIONS

- How was the geologic time scale developed?
- What are some causes of mass extinctions?
- How is evolution affected by environmental change?

Vocabulary

eon p. 235

era p. 235

period p. 235

epoch p. 235

mass extinction p. 237

land bridge p. 238

geographic isolation p. 238

g Multilingual eGlossary

Video

- BrainPOP®
- Science Video

Academic Standards for Science

7.2.3 Characterize the immensity of geologic time and recognize that it is measured in eras and epochs.

7.2.8 Compare and contrast fossils with living organisms in a given location to explain how earth processes have changed environments over time.

Geologic History and the Evolution of Life

Inquiry What happened here?

A meteorite 50 m in diameter crashed into Earth 50,000 years ago. The force of the impact created this crater in Arizona and threw massive amounts of dust and debris into the atmosphere. Scientists hypothesize that a meteorite 200 times this size—the size of a small city—struck Earth 65 million years ago. How might it have affected life on Earth?

Inquiry Launch Lab

20 minutes

Can you make a time line of your life?

How would you organize a time line of your life? You might include regular events, such as birthdays. But you might also include special events, such as a weekend camping trip or a summer vacation.

1. Read and complete a lab safety form.
2. Use **scissors** to cut two pieces of **graph paper** in half. **Tape** them together to make one long piece of paper. Write down the years of your life in horizontal sequence, marked off at regular intervals.
3. Choose up to 12 important events or periods of time in your life. Mark those events on your time line.

Think About This

1. Do the events on your time line appear at regular intervals?
2. **Key Concept** How do you think the geologic time scale is like a time line of your life?

Developing a Geologic Time Line

Think about what you did over the last year. Maybe you went on vacation during the summer or visited relatives in the fall. To organize events in your life, you use different units of time, such as weeks, months, and years. Geologists organize Earth's past in a similar way. They developed a time line of Earth's past called the geologic time scale. As shown in **Figure 1,** time units on the geologic time scale are thousands and millions of years long—much longer than the units you use to organize events in your life.

Units in the Geologic Time Scale

Eons *are the longest units of geologic time.* Earth's current eon, the Phanerozoic (fan er oh ZOH ihk) eon, began 542 million years ago (mya). *Eons are subdivided into smaller units of time called* **eras.** *Eras are subdivided into* **periods.** *Periods are subdivided into* **epochs** (EH pocks). Epochs are not shown on the time line in **Figure 1.** Notice that the time units are not equal. For example, the Paleozoic era is longer than the Mesozoic and Cenozoic eras combined.

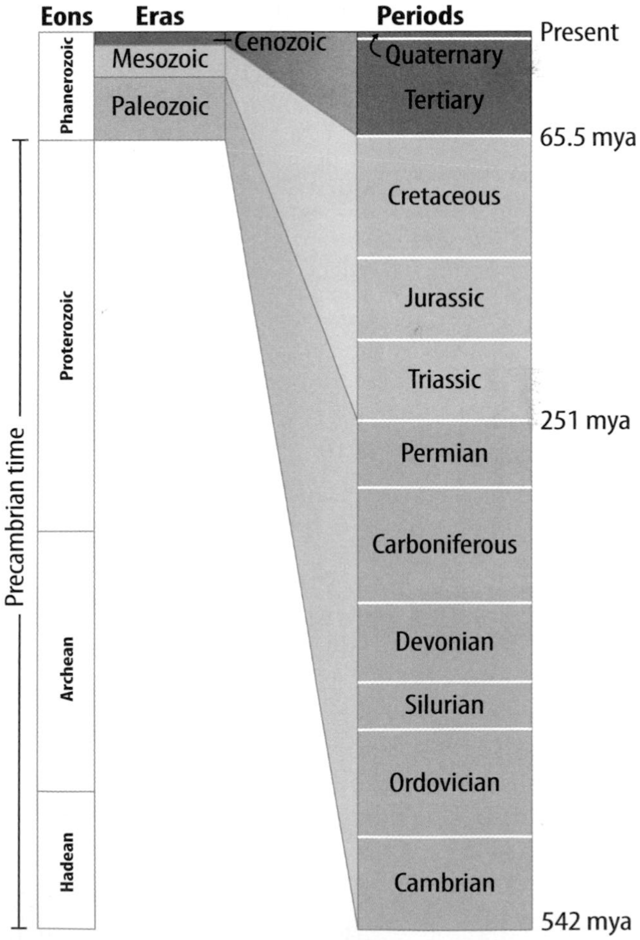

Figure 1 In the geologic time scale, the 4.6 billion years of Earth's history are divided into time units of unequal length.

Fossils in Rock Layers

Concepts in Motion Animation

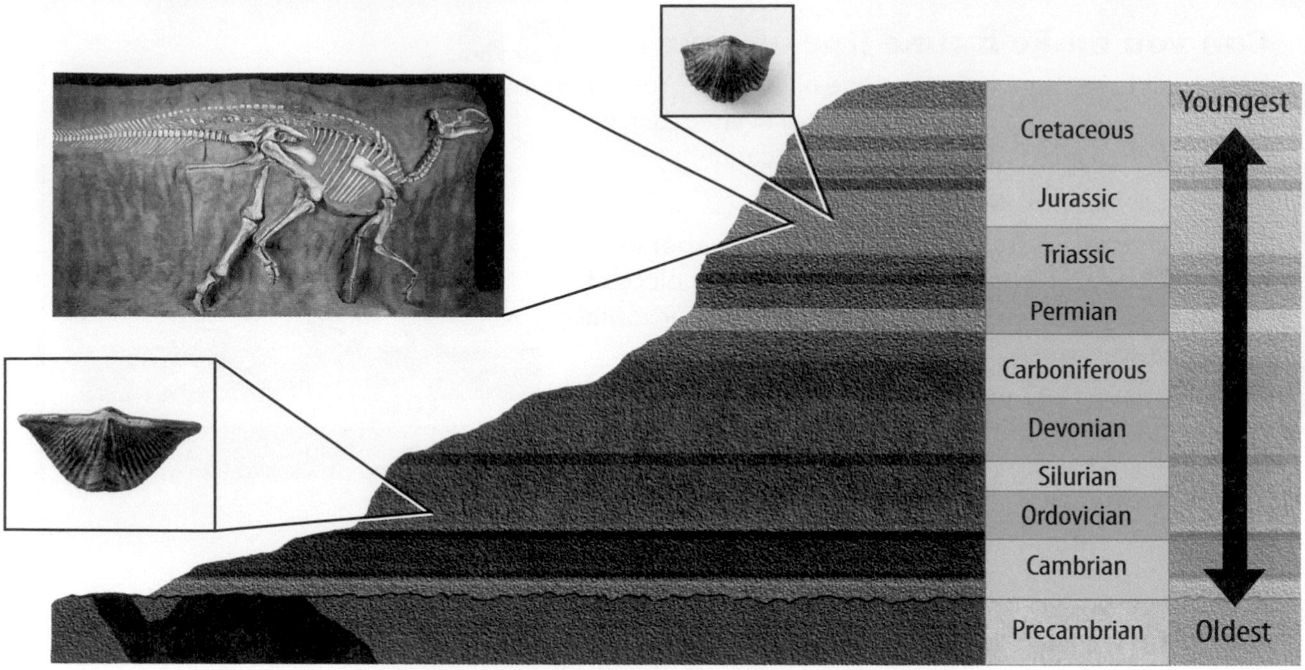

Figure 2 Both older and younger rocks contain fossils of small, relatively simple life-forms. Only younger rocks contain larger, more complex fossils.

SCIENCE USE V. COMMON USE

scale

Science Use a series of marks or points at known intervals

Common Use an instrument used for measuring the weight of an object

The Time Scale and Fossils

Hundreds of years ago, when geologists began developing the geologic time **scale,** they chose the time boundaries based on what they observed in Earth's rock layers. Different layers contained different fossils. For example, older rocks contained only fossils of small, relatively simple life-forms. Younger rocks contained these fossils as well as fossils of other, more complex organisms, such as dinosaurs, as illustrated in **Figure 2.**

Major Divisions in the Geologic Time Scale

While studying the fossils in rock layers, geologists often saw abrupt changes in the types of fossils within the layers. Sometimes, fossils in one rock layer did not appear in the rock layers right above it. It seemed as though the organisms that lived during that period of time had disappeared suddenly. Geologists used these sudden changes in the fossil record to mark divisions in geologic time. Because the changes did not occur at regular intervals, the boundaries between the units of time in the geologic time scale are irregular. This means the time units are of unequal length.

The time scale is a work in progress. Scientists debate the placement of the boundaries as they make new discoveries.

FOLDABLES®

Make a four-door book from a vertical sheet of paper. Use it to organize information about the units of geologic time.

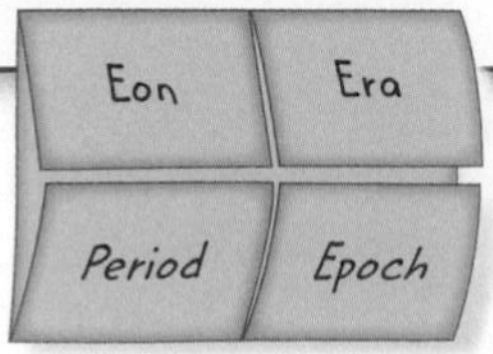

Key Concept Check Why are fossils important in the development of the geologic time scale?

Responses to Change

Sudden changes in the fossil record represent times when large populations of organisms died or became extinct. *A* **mass extinction** *is the extinction of many species on Earth within a short period of time.* As shown in **Figure 3,** there have been several mass extinction events in Earth's history.

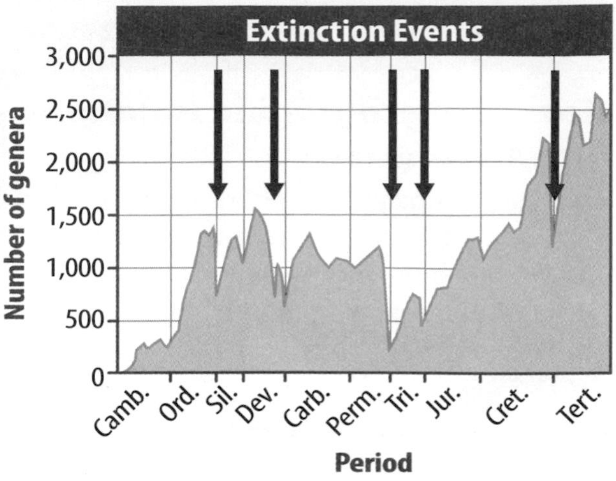

Figure 3 There have been five major mass extinctions in Earth's history. In each one, the number of genera—groups of species—decreased sharply.

Visual Check When was Earth's greatest mass-extinction event?

Changes in Climate

What could cause a mass extinction? All species of organisms depend on the environment for their survival. If the environment changes quickly and species do not adapt to the change, they die.

Many things can cause a climate change. For example, gas and dust from volcanoes can block sunlight and reduce temperatures. As you read on the first page of this lesson, the results of a meteorite crashing into Earth would block sunlight and change climate.

Scientists hypothesize that a meteorite impact might have caused the mass extinction that occurred when dinosaurs became **extinct.** Evidence for this impact is in a clay layer containing the element iridium in rocks around the world. Iridium is rare in Earth rocks but common in meteorites. No dinosaur fossils have been found in rocks above the iridium layer. A sample of rock containing this layer is shown in **Figure 4.**

Word Origin

extinct
from Latin *extinctus,* means "dying out"

Key Concept Check Describe a possible event that could cause a mass extinction.

Meteorite Impact

Nearly all fossils below the iridium layer in Earth's rocks are different from those above, indicating that a mass extinction occurred.

Figure 4 An iridium-enriched clay layer in Earth's rocks is evidence that a large meteorite crashed into Earth 65 million years ago. A meteorite impact can contribute to a mass extinction event.

Inquiry MiniLab

10 minutes

How does geographic isolation affect evolution?

Have you ever played the phone game? How is this game similar to what happens when populations of organisms are separated?

1. Form two groups.
2. One person in each group should whisper a sentence—provided by your teacher—into the ear of his or her neighbor. Each person in turn will whisper the sentence to his or her neighbor until it returns to the first person.

Analyze and Conclude

1. **Observe** Did the sentence change? Did it change in the same way in each group?
2. **Key Concept** How is this activity similar to organisms that are geographically isolated?

Geography and Evolution

When environments change, some species of organisms are unable to adapt. They become extinct. However, other species do adapt to environmental changes. Evolution is the change in species over time as they adapt to their environments. Sudden, catastrophic changes in the environment can affect evolution. So can the slow movement of Earth's tectonic plates.

Land Bridges When continents collide or when sea level drops, landmasses can join together. *A* **land bridge** *connects two continents that were previously separated.* Over time, organisms move across land bridges and evolve as they adapt to new environments.

Geographic Isolation The movement of tectonic plates or other slow geologic events can cause geographic areas to move apart. When this happens, populations of organisms can become isolated. **Geographic isolation** *is the separation of a population of organisms from the rest of its species due to some physical barrier, such as a mountain range or an ocean.* Separated populations of species evolve in different ways as they adapt to different environments. Even slight differences in environments can affect evolution, as shown in **Figure 5.**

Key Concept Check How can geographic isolation affect evolution?

Geographic Isolation

Concepts in Motion **Animation**

Figure 5 A population of squirrels was gradually separated as the Grand Canyon developed. Each group adapted to a slightly different environment and evolved in a different way.

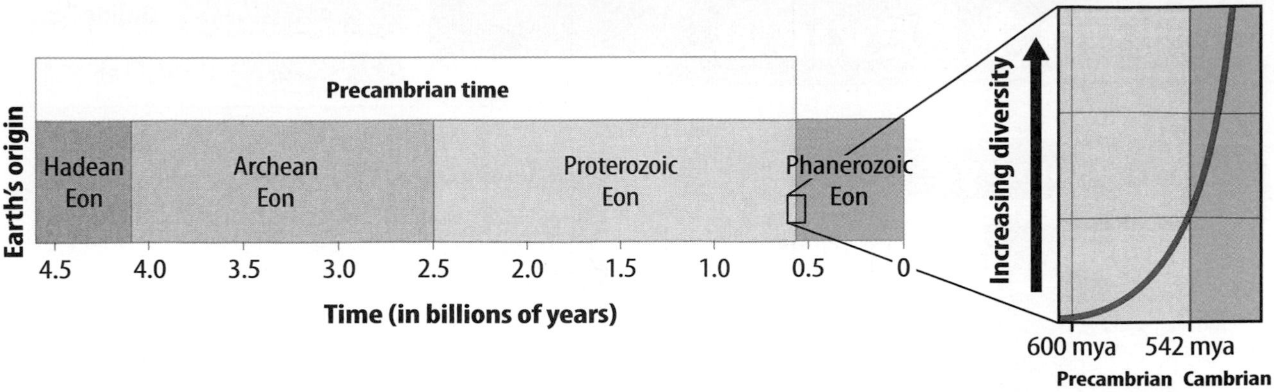

Figure 6 Precambrian time is nearly 90 percent of Earth's history. An explosion of life-forms appeared at the beginning of the Phanerozoic eon, during the Cambrian period.

Review
Personal Tutor

Precambrian Time

Life has been evolving on Earth for billions of years. The oldest fossil evidence of life on Earth is in rocks that are about 3.5 billion years old. These ancient life-forms were simple, unicellular organisms, much like present-day bacteria. The oldest fossils of multicellular organisms are about 600 million years old. These fossils are rare, and early geologists did not know about them. They hypothesized that multicellular life first appeared in the Cambrian (KAM bree un) period, at the beginning of the Phanerozoic eon 542 mya. Time before the Cambrian was called Precambrian time. Scientists have determined that Precambrian time is nearly 90 percent of Earth's history, as shown in **Figure 6.**

Precambrian Life

The rare fossils of multicellular life-forms in Precambrian rocks are from soft-bodied organisms different from organisms on Earth today. A drawing of what they might have looked like is shown in **Figure 7.** Many of these species became extinct at the end of the Precambrian.

Figure 7 Precambrian life-forms lived 600 mya at the bottom of the sea.

Cambrian Explosion

Precambrian life led to a sudden appearance of new types of multicellular life-forms in the Cambrian period. This sudden appearance of new, complex life-forms, indicated on the right in **Figure 6,** is often referred to as the Cambrian explosion. Some Cambrian life-forms, such as trilobites, were the first to have hard body parts. Because of their hard body parts, trilobites were more easily preserved. More evidence of trilobites is in the fossil record. Scientists hypothesize that some of them are distant ancestors of organisms alive today.

Reading Check What is the Cambrian explosion?

Lesson 1 Review

✓ Assessment Online Quiz

? Inquiry Virtual Lab

Visual Summary

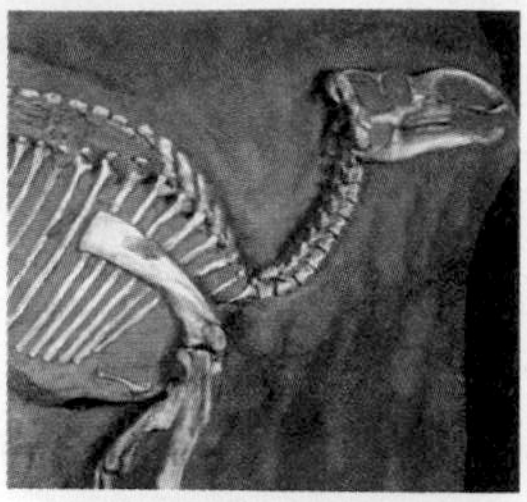

Earth's history is organized into eons, eras, periods, and epochs.

Climate change caused by the results of a meteorite impact could contribute to a mass extinction event.

Slow changes in geography affect evolution.

FOLDABLES®

Use your lesson Foldable to review the lesson. Save your Foldable for the project at the end of the chapter.

What do you think NOW?

You first read the statements below at the beginning of the chapter.

1. All geologic eras are the same length of time.
2. Meteorite impacts cause all extinction events.

Did you change your mind about whether you agree or disagree with the statements? Rewrite any false statements to make them true.

Use Vocabulary

1. **Distinguish** between an eon and an era.
2. A(n) ________ might form when continents move close together.
3. A(n) ________ might occur if an environment changes suddenly.

Understand Key Concepts

4. Which could contribute to a mass-extinction event?
   - **A.** an earthquake
   - **B.** a hot summer
   - **C.** a hurricane
   - **D.** a volcanic eruption
5. **Explain** how geographic isolation can affect evolution.
6. **Distinguish** between a calendar and the geologic time scale.

Interpret Graphics

7. **Explain** what the graph below represents. What happened at this time in Earth's past?

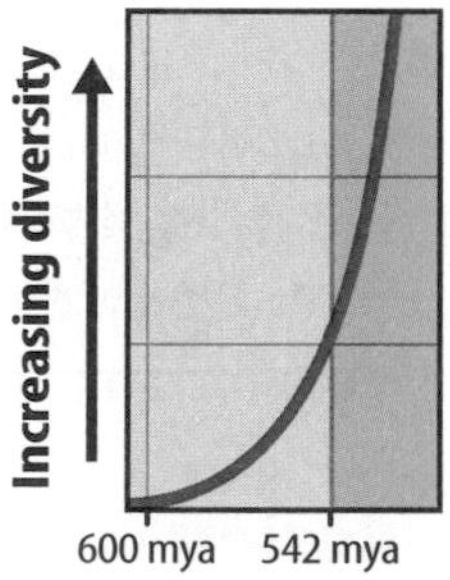

8. **Organize Information** Copy and fill in the graphic organizer below to show units of the geologic time scale from longest to shortest.

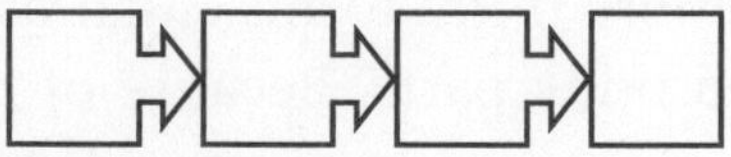

Critical Thinking

9. **Suggest** how humans might contribute to a mass extinction event.
10. **Propose** why Precambrian rocks contain few fossils.

Inquiry Skill Practice — Interpret Data

30 minutes

How has life changed over time?

Fossil evidence indicates that there have been wide fluctuations in the types, or diversity, of organisms that have lived on Earth over geologic time.

Learn It

Line graphs compare two variables and show how one variable changes in response to another variable. Line graphs are particularly useful in presenting data that change over time. The first line graph below shows how the diversity of genera has changed over time. The second graph shows how extinction rates, presented as percentages of genera, have changed over time. **Interpret data** in these graphs to learn how they relate to each another.

Try It

1. Carefully study each graph. Note that time, the independent variable, is plotted on the *x*-axis of each graph. The dependent variable of each graph—the diversity, or number of genera, in one graph and the extinction rate in the other graph—are plotted on the *y*-axes.
2. Use the graphs to answer questions 3–7.

Apply It

3. According to the graph on the left, at what time in Earth's past was diversity the lowest? At what time was diversity the highest?
4. Approximately what percentage of genera became extinct 250 million years ago?
5. Approximately when did each of Earth's major mass extinctions take place?
6. What is the relationship between diversity and extinction rate?
7. **Key Concept** How have mass extinctions helped scientists develop the geologic time scale?

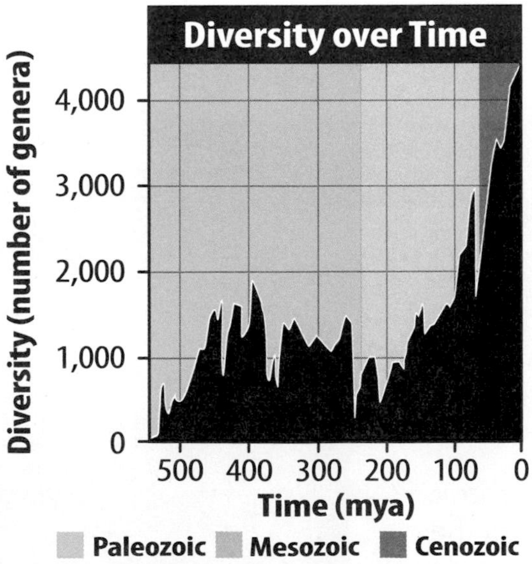

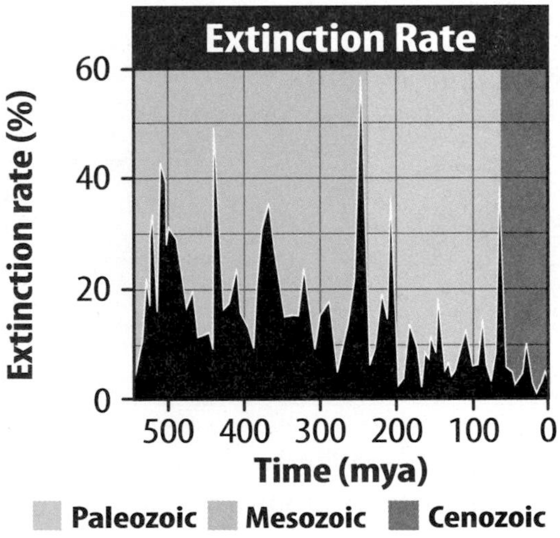

Lesson 2

The Paleozoic Era

Reading Guide

Key Concepts
ESSENTIAL QUESTIONS

- What major geologic events occurred during the Paleozoic era?
- What does fossil evidence reveal about the Paleozoic era?

Vocabulary

Paleozoic era p. 243
Mesozoic era p. 243
Cenozoic era p. 243
inland sea p. 244
coal swamp p. 246
supercontinent p. 247

g Multilingual eGlossary

Academic Standards for Science

7.2.3 Characterize the immensity of geologic time and recognize that it is measured in eras and epochs.

Inquiry What animal was this?

Imagine going for a swim and meeting up with this Paleozoic monster. *Dunkleosteus* (duhn kuhl AHS tee us) was one of the largest and fiercest fish that ever lived. Its head was covered in bony armor 5 cm thick—even its eyes had bony armor. It had razor-sharp teethlike plates that bit with a force like that of present-day alligators.

Inquiry Launch Lab

20 minutes

What can you learn about your ancestors?

Scientists use fossils and rocks to learn about Earth's history. What could you use to research your past?

1. Write as many facts as you can about one of your grandparents or other older adult family members or friends.
2. What items, such as photos, do you have that can help you?

Think About This

1. If you wanted to know about a great-great-great grandparent, what clues do you think you could find?
2. How does knowledge about past generations in your family benefit you today?
3. **Key Concept** How do you think learning about distant relatives is like studying Earth's past?

Early Paleozoic

In many families, three generations—grandparents, parents, and children—live closely together. You could call them the old generation, the middle generation, and the young generation. These generations are much like the three eras of the Phanerozoic eon. *The* **Paleozoic** (pay lee uh ZOH ihk) **era** *is the oldest era of the Phanerozoic eon. The* **Mesozoic** (mez uh ZOH ihk) **era** *is the middle era of the Phanerozoic eon. The* **Cenozoic** (sen uh ZOH ihk) **era** *is the youngest era of the Phanerozoic eon.*

Word Origin

Paleozoic
from Greek *palai,* means "ancient"; and Greek *zoe,* means "life"

As shown in **Figure 8,** the Paleozoic era lasted for more than half the Phanerozoic eon. Because it was so long, it is often divided into three parts: early, middle, and late. The Cambrian and Ordovician periods make up the Early Paleozoic.

The Age of Invertebrates

The organisms from the Cambrian explosion were invertebrates (ihn VUR tuh brayts) that lived only in the oceans. Invertebrates are animals without backbones. So many kinds of invertebrates lived in Early Paleozoic oceans that this time is often called the age of invertebrates.

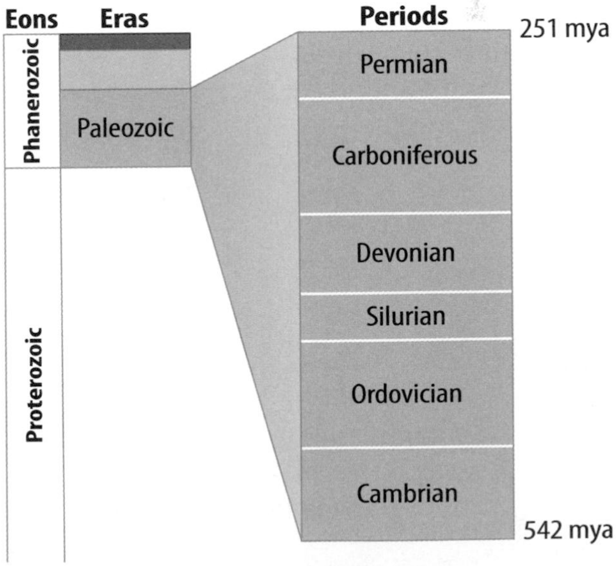

Figure 8 The Paleozoic era lasted for 291 million years. It is divided into six periods.

Figure 9 Earth's continents and life-forms changed dramatically during the Paleozoic era.

Visual Check In what period did life first appear on land?

Geology of the Early Paleozoic

If you could have visited Earth during the Early Paleozoic, it would have seemed unfamiliar to you. As shown in **Figure 9,** there was no life on land. All life was in the oceans. The shapes and locations of Earth's continents also would have been unfamiliar, as shown in **Figure 10.** Notice that the landmass that would become North America was on the equator.

Earth's climate was warm during the Early Paleozoic. Rising seas flooded the continents and formed many shallow inland seas. *An* **inland sea** *is a body of water formed when ocean water floods continents.* Most of North America was covered by an inland sea.

Reading Check How do inland seas form?

FOLDABLES®

Make a horizontal, three-tab book. Label it as shown. Use your book to record information about changes during the Paleozoic Era.

Early Paleozoic | Middle Paleozoic | Late Paleozoic

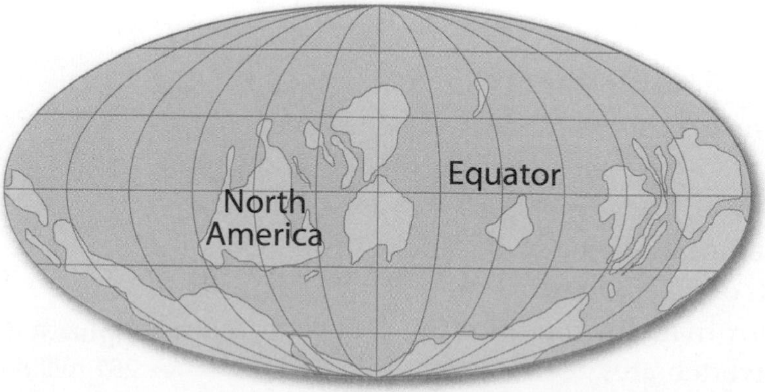

Figure 10 During the Early Paleozoic, North America straddled the equator.

Middle Paleozoic

The Early Paleozoic ended with a mass extinction event, but many invertebrates survived. New forms of life lived in huge coral reefs along the edges of the continents. Soon, animals with backbones, called vertebrates, evolved.

The Age of Fishes

Some of the earliest vertebrates were fishes. So many types of fishes lived during the Silurian (suh LOOR ee un) and Devonian (dih VOH nee un) periods that the Middle Paleozoic is often called the age of fishes. Some fishes, such as the *Dunkleosteus* pictured at the beginning of this lesson, were heavily armored. **Figure 11** also shows what a *Dunkleosteus* might have looked like. On land, cockroaches, dragonflies, and other insects evolved. Earth's first plants appeared. They were small and lived in water.

Geology of the Middle Paleozoic

Middle Paleozoic rocks contain evidence of major collisions between moving continents. These collisions created mountain ranges. When several landmasses collided with the eastern coast of North America, the Appalachian (ap uh LAY chun) Mountains began to form. By the end of the Paleozoic era, the Appalachians were probably as high as the Himalayas are today.

Key Concept Check How did the Appalachian Mountains form?

Figure 11 *Dunkleosteus* was a top Devonian predator.

Late Paleozoic

Like the Early Paleozoic, the Middle Paleozoic ended with a mass extinction event. Many marine invertebrates and some land animals disappeared.

The Age of Amphibians

In the Late Paleozoic, some fishlike organisms spent part of their lives on land. *Tiktaalik* (tihk TAH lihk) was an organism that had lungs and could breathe air. It was one of the earliest amphibians. Amphibians were so common in the Late Paleozoic that this time is known as the age of amphibians.

Ancient amphibian species adapted to land in several ways. As you read, they had lungs and could breathe air. Their skins were thick, which slowed moisture loss. Their strong limbs enabled them to move around on land. However, all amphibians, even those living today, must return to the water to mate and lay eggs.

Reptile species evolved toward the end of the Paleozoic era. Reptiles were the first animals that did not require water for reproduction. Reptile eggs have tough, leathery shells that protect them from drying out.

Key Concept Check How did different species adapt to land?

Coal Swamps

During the Late Paleozoic, dense, tropical forests grew in swamps along shallow inland seas. When trees and other plants died, they sank into the swamps, such as the one illustrated in **Figure 12.** *A* **coal swamp** *is an oxygen-poor environment where, over time, plant material changes into coal.* The coal swamps of the Carboniferous (car buhn IF er us) and Permian periods eventually became major sources of coal that we use today.

Figure 12 Plants buried in ancient coal swamps became coal.

Formation of Pangaea

Geologic evidence indicates that many continental collisions occurred during the Late Paleozoic. As continents moved closer together, new mountain ranges formed. By the end of the Paleozoic era, Earth's continents had formed a giant supercontinent—Pangaea. *A* **supercontinent** *is an ancient landmass which separated into present-day continents.* Pangaea formed close to Earth's equator, as shown in **Figure 13.** As Pangaea formed, coal swamps dried up and Earth's climate became cooler and drier.

The Permian Mass Extinction

The largest mass extinction in Earth's history occurred at the end of the Paleozoic era. Fossil evidence indicates that 95 percent of marine life-forms and 70 percent of all life on land became extinct. This extinction event is called the Permian mass extinction.

Key Concept Check What does fossil evidence reveal about the end of the Paleozoic era?

Scientists debate what caused this mass extinction. The formation of Pangaea likely decreased the amount of space where marine organisms could live. It would have contributed to changes in ocean currents, making the center of Pangaea drier. But Pangaea formed over many millions of years. The extinction event occurred more suddenly.

Some scientists hypothesize that a large meteorite impact caused drastic climate change. Others propose that massive volcanic eruptions changed the global climate. Both a meteorite impact and large-scale eruptions would have ejected ash and rock into the atmosphere, blocking out sunlight, reducing temperatures, and causing a collapse of food webs.

Whatever caused it, Earth had fewer species after the Permian mass extinction. Only species that could adapt to the changes survived.

Pangaea

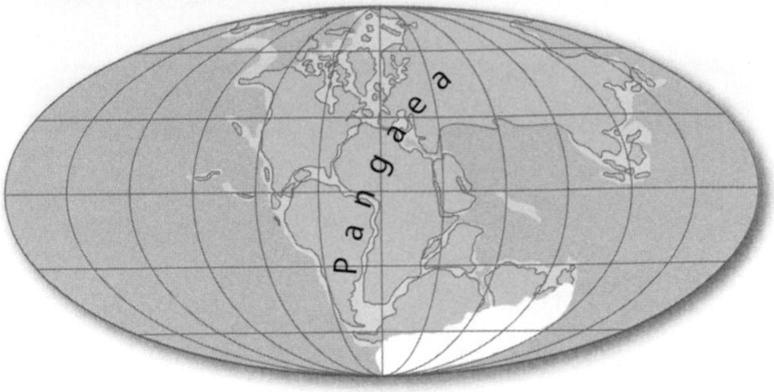

Figure 13 The supercontinent Pangaea formed at the end of the Paleozoic era.

Concepts in Motion **Animation**

Inquiry MiniLab — 20 minutes

What would happen if a supercontinent formed?

Many organisms live along continental coastlines. What happens to coastlines when continents combine and form a supercontinent?

1. Read and complete a lab safety form.
2. Form a stick of **modeling clay** into a flat pancake shape. Form three pancake shapes from an identical stick of clay. Make all four shapes equal thicknesses.
3. With a **flexible tape measure,** measure the perimeter of each shape.

Analyze and Conclude

1. **Compare** Is the perimeter of the larger shape more or less than the combined perimeters of the three smaller shapes?
2. **Key Concept** How might the formation of Pangaea have affected life on Earth?

Lesson 2 Review

✓ Assessment **Online Quiz**

Visual Summary

Life slowly moved to land during the Paleozoic era as amphibians and reptiles evolved.

In the Late Paleozoic, massive coal swamps formed along inland seas.

At the end of the Paleozoic era, a mass extinction event coincided with the final stages of the formation of Pangaea.

FOLDABLES®

Use your lesson Foldable to review the lesson. Save your Foldable for the project at the end of the chapter.

What do you think NOW?

You first read the statements below at the beginning of the chapter.

3. North America was once on the equator.

4. All of Earth's continents were part of a huge supercontinent 250 million years ago.

Did you change your mind about whether you agree or disagree with the statements? Rewrite any false statements to make them true.

Use Vocabulary

1 **Distinguish** between the Paleozoic era and the Mesozoic era.

2 When ocean water covers part of a continent, a(n) ________ forms.

3 **Use the term** *supercontinent* in a complete sentence.

Understand Key Concepts

4 Which was true of North America during the Early Paleozoic?

A. It had many glaciers.
B. It was at the equator.
C. It was part of a supercontinent.
D. It was populated by reptiles.

5 **Compare** ancient amphibians and reptiles and explain how each group adapted to live on land.

6 **Draw** a cartoon that shows how the Appalachian Mountains formed.

Interpret Graphics

7 **Organize** A time line of the Paleozoic era is pictured below. Copy the time line and fill in the missing periods.

Paleozoic					
	Ordovician	Silurian	Devonian	Carboniferous	

8 **Sequence** Copy and fill in the graphic organizer below. Start with Precambrian time, then list the eras in order.

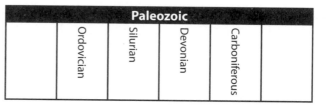

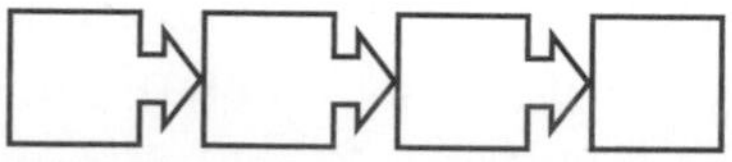

Critical Thinking

9 **Consider** What if 100 percent of organisms had become extinct at the end of the Paleozoic era?

10 **Evaluate** the possible effects of climate change on present-day organisms.

When did coal form?

Coal is fossilized plant material. When swamp plants die, they become covered by oxygen-poor water and change to peat. Over time, high temperatures and pressure from sediments transform the peat into coal. When did the plants live that formed the coal we use today?

Learn It

A bar graph can display the same type of information as a line graph. However, instead of data points and a line that connects them, a bar graph uses rectangular bars to show how values compare. **Interpret the data** below to learn when most coal formed.

Try It

1. Carefully study the bar graph. Notice that time is plotted on the *x*-axis (as geologic periods), and that coal deposits (as tons accumulated per year) are plotted on the *y*-axis.
2. Use the graph and what you know about coal formation to answer the following questions.

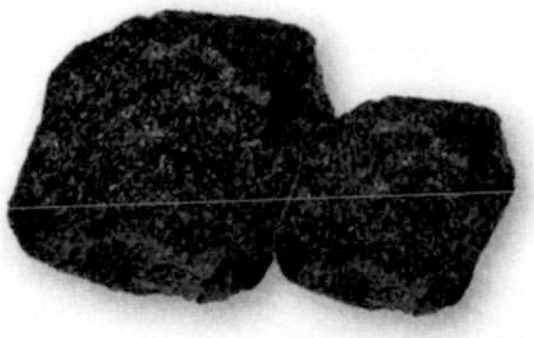

Apply It

3. Which coal deposits are oldest? Which are youngest?
4. During which geologic period did most of the coal form?
5. Approximately how much coal accumulated during the Paleozoic era? The Mesozoic era?
6. Why are there no data on the graph for the Cambrian, Ordovician, and Silurian periods of geologic time?
7. **Key Concept** What does fossil evidence reveal about the Paleozoic era?

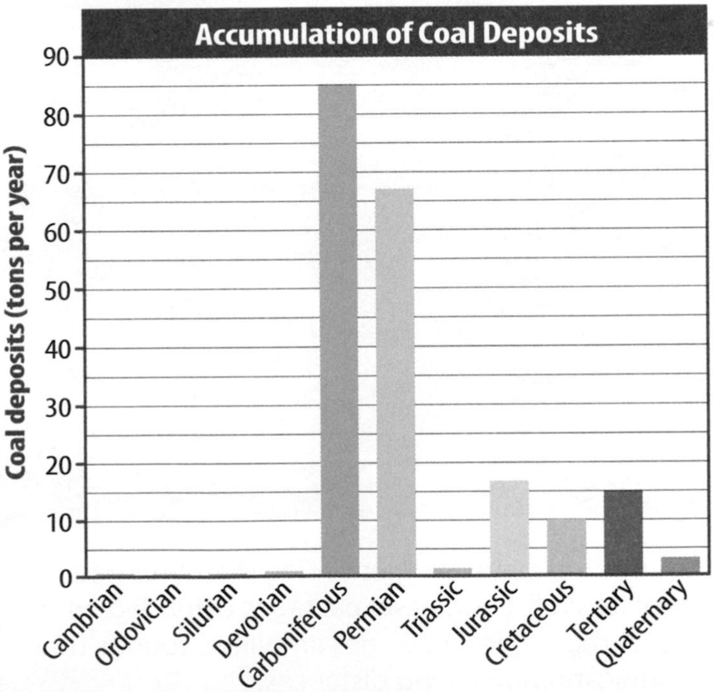

Lesson 3

Reading Guide

Key Concepts
ESSENTIAL QUESTIONS

- What major geologic events occurred during the Mesozoic era?
- What does fossil evidence reveal about the Mesozoic era?

Vocabulary
dinosaur p. 254
plesiosaur p. 255
pterosaur p. 255

g Multilingual eGlossary

Academic Standards for Science

7.2.3 Characterize the immensity of geologic time and recognize that it is measured in eras and epochs.

7.2.8 Compare and contrast fossils with living organisms in a given location to explain how earth processes have changed environments over time.

Also covers: 7.DP.2, 7.DP.6, 7.DP.7, 7.DP.8, 7.DP.9

The Mesozoic Era

nquiry Mesozoic Thunder?

Can you imagine the sounds this dinosaur made? *Corythosaurus* had a tall, bony crest on top of its skull. Long nasal passages extended into the crest. Scientists suspect these nasal passages amplified sounds that could be used for communicating over long distances.

Inquiry Launch Lab

20 minutes

How diverse were dinosaurs?

How many different dinosaurs were there?

1. Read and complete a lab safety form.
2. Your teacher will give you an **index card** listing a species name of a dinosaur, the dinosaur's dimensions, and the time when it lived.
3. Draw a picture of what you imagine your dinosaur looked like. Before you begin, decide with your classmates what common scale you should use.
4. **Tape** your dinosaur drawing to the Mesozoic time line your teacher provides.

Think About This

1. What was the biggest dinosaur? The smallest? Can you see any trends in size on the time line?
2. Did all the dinosaurs live at the same time?
3. **Key Concept** Dinosaurs were numerous and diverse. Do you think any dinosaurs could swim or fly?

Geology of the Mesozoic Era

When people imagine what Earth looked like millions of years ago, they often picture a scene with dinosaurs, such as the *Corythosaurus* shown on the opposite page. Dinosaurs lived during the Mesozoic era. The Mesozoic era lasted from 251 mya to 65.5 mya. As shown in **Figure 14,** it is divided into three periods: the Triassic (tri A sihk), the Jurassic (joo RA sihk), and the Cretaceous (krih TAY shus).

Breakup of Pangaea

Recall that the supercontinent Pangaea formed at the end of the Paleozoic era. The breakup of Pangaea was the dominant geologic event of the Mesozoic era. Pangaea began to break apart in the Late Triassic. Eventually, Pangaea split into two separate landmasses—Gondwanaland (gahn DWAH nuh land) and Laurasia (la RAY SHZah). Gondwanaland was the southern continent. It included the future continents of Africa, Antarctica, Australia, and South America. Laurasia, the northern continent, included the future continents of North America, Europe, and Asia.

FOLDABLES®

Make a shutter-fold book from a vertical sheet of paper. Label it as shown. Use it to record information about changes during the Mesozoic era.

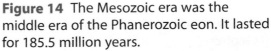

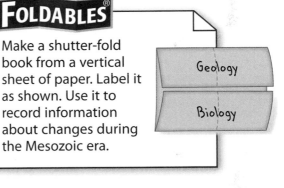

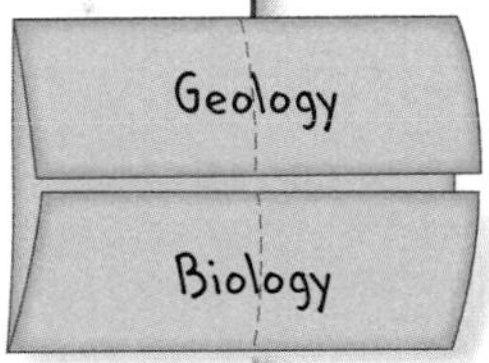

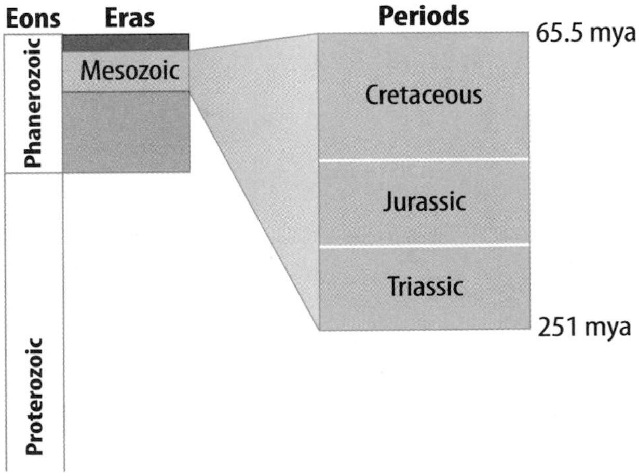

Figure 14 The Mesozoic era was the middle era of the Phanerozoic eon. It lasted for 185.5 million years.

Figure 15 Dinosaurs dominated the Mesozoic era, but many other species also lived during this time in Earth's history.

Return of Shallow Seas

The type of species represented in **Figure 15** adapted to an environment of lush tropical forests and warm ocean waters. That is because the climate of the Mesozoic era was warmer than the climate of the Paleozoic era. It was so warm that, for most of the era, there were no ice caps, even at the poles. With no glaciers, the oceans had more water. Some of this water flowed onto the continents as Pangaea split apart. This created narrow channels that grew larger as the continents moved apart. Eventually, the channels became oceans. The Atlantic Ocean began to form at this time.

Key Concept Check When did the Atlantic Ocean begin to form?

Sea level rose during most of the Mesozoic era, as shown in **Figure 16.** Toward the end of the era, sea level was so high that inland seas covered much of Earth's continents. This provided environments for the evolution of new organisms.

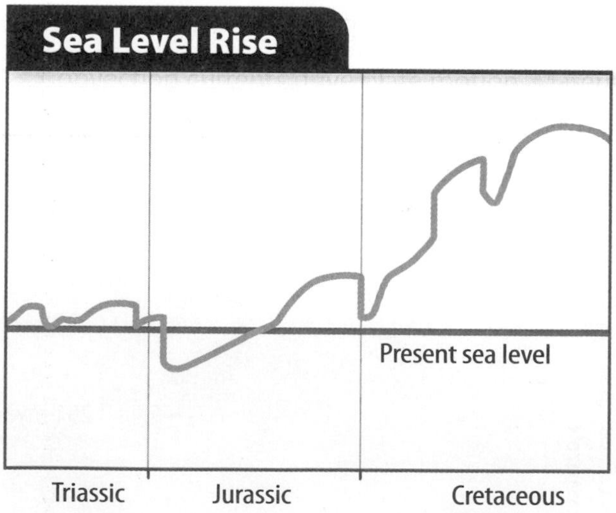

Figure 16 Earth's sea level rose during the Mesozoic era.

Visual Check In which period was sea level at its highest?

Mesozoic North America

Along North America's eastern coast and the Gulf of Mexico, sea level rose and receded over millions of years. As this happened, seawater **evaporated,** leaving massive salt deposits behind. Some of these salt deposits are sources of salt that are mined today. Other salt deposits later became traps for oil. Today, salt traps in the Gulf of Mexico are an important source of oil.

Throughout the Mesozoic era, the North American continent moved slowly and steadily westward. Its western edge collided with several small landmasses carried on an ancient oceanic plate. As this plate subducted beneath the North American continent, the crust buckled inland, slowly pushing up the Rocky Mountains, shown on the map in **Figure 17.** In the dry southwest, windblown sand formed huge dunes. In the middle of the continent, a warm inland sea formed.

Key Concept Check How did the Rocky Mountains form?

REVIEW VOCABULARY

evaporated
changed from liquid to gas

Figure 17 The Rocky Mountains began forming during the Mesozoic era. By the end of the era, an inland sea covered much of the central part of North America.

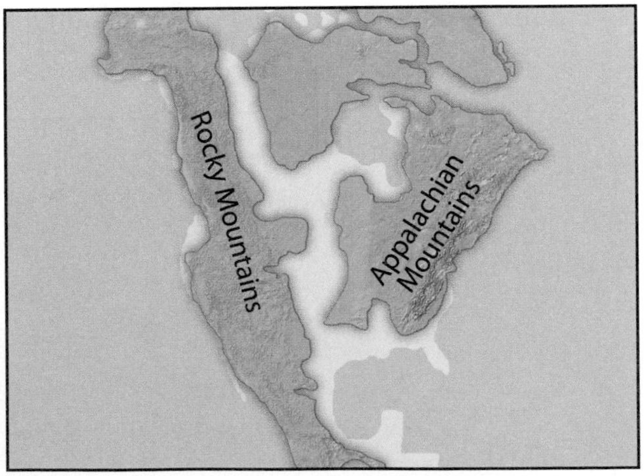

Inquiry MiniLab 20 minutes

Can you run like a reptile?

Unlike the limbs of crocodiles and other modern reptiles, dinosaur limbs were positioned directly under their bodies. What did this mean?

1. Pick a partner. One of you—the dinosaur—will run on all fours with arms held straight directly below the shoulders. The other—the crocodile—will run with arms bent and positioned out from the body.
2. Race each other, then reverse positions.

Analyze and Conclude

1. **Compare** Which could move faster—the dinosaur or the crocodile?
2. **Infer** Which posture do you think could support more weight?
3. **Key Concept** How might their posture have enabled dinosaurs to become so successful? How might it have helped them become so large?

Mesozoic Life

The species of organisms that survived the Permian mass extinction event lived in a world with few species. Vast amounts of unoccupied space were open for organisms to inhabit. New types of cone-bearing trees, such as pines and cycads, began to appear. Toward the end of the era, the first flowering plants evolved. Dominant among vertebrates living on land were the dinosaurs. Hundreds of species of many sizes existed.

Dinosaurs

Though dinosaurs have long been considered reptiles, scientists today actively debate dinosaur classification. Dinosaurs share a common ancestor with present-day reptiles, such as crocodiles. However, dinosaurs differ from present-day reptiles in their unique hip structure, as shown in **Figure 18.** **Dinosaurs** *were dominant Mesozoic land vertebrates that walked with legs positioned directly below their hips.* This meant that many walked upright. In contrast, the legs of a crocodile stick out sideways from its body. It appears to drag itself along the ground.

Scientists hypothesize that some dinosaurs are more closely related to present-day birds than they are to present-day reptiles. Dinosaur fossils with evidence of feathery exteriors have been found. For example, *Archaeopteryx* (ar kee AHP tuh rihks), a small bird the size of a pigeon, had wings and feathers but also claws and teeth. Many scientists suggest it was an ancestor to birds.

Figure 18 Fossils provide evidence that the hip structure of a dinosaur enabled it to walk upright.

Other Mesozoic Vertebrates

Other Mesozoic Vertebrates

Dinosaurs dominated land. But, fossils indicate that other large vertebrates swam in the seas and flew in the air, as shown in **Figure 19.** **Plesiosaurs** (PLY zee oh sorz) *were Mesozoic marine reptiles with small heads, long necks, and flippers.* Through much of the Mesozoic, these reptiles dominated the oceans. Some were as long as 14 m.

Other Mesozoic reptiles could fly. **Pterosaurs** (TER oh sorz) *were Mesozoic flying reptiles with large, batlike wings.* One of the largest pterosaurs, the *Quetzalcoatlus* (kwetz oh koh AHT lus), had a wingspread of nearly 12 m. Though they could fly, pterosaurs were not birds. As you have read, birds are more closely related to dinosaurs.

Key Concept Check How could you distinguish fossils of plesiosaurs and pterosaurs from fossils of dinosaurs?

Figure 19 Not all large Mesozoic vertebrates were dinosaurs.

Visual Check How did the limbs of these reptiles compare to the limbs of dinosaurs?

WORD ORIGIN

pterosaur
from Greek *pteron,* means "wing"; and *sauros,* means "lizard"

Appearance of Mammals

Dinosaurs and reptiles dominated the Mesozoic era, but another kind of animal also lived during this time—mammals. Mammals evolved early in the Mesozoic and remained small in size throughout the era. Few were larger than present-day cats.

Cretaceous Extinction Event

The Mesozoic era ended 65.5 mya with a mass extinction called the Cretaceous extinction event. You read in Lesson 1 that scientists propose a large meteorite impact contributed to this extinction. This crash would have produced enough dust to block sunlight for a long time. There is evidence that volcanic eruptions also occurred at the same time. These eruptions would have added more dust to the atmosphere. Without light, plants died. Without plants, animals died. Dinosaur species and other large Mesozoic vertebrate species could not adapt to the changes. They became extinct.

Lesson 3 Review

Assessment Online Quiz

Visual Summary

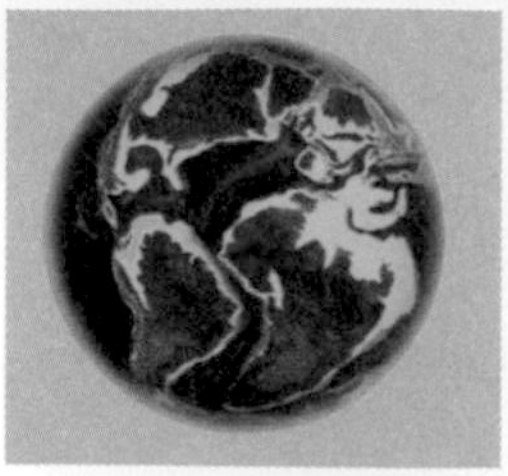

As Pangaea broke up, the continents began to move into their present-day positions.

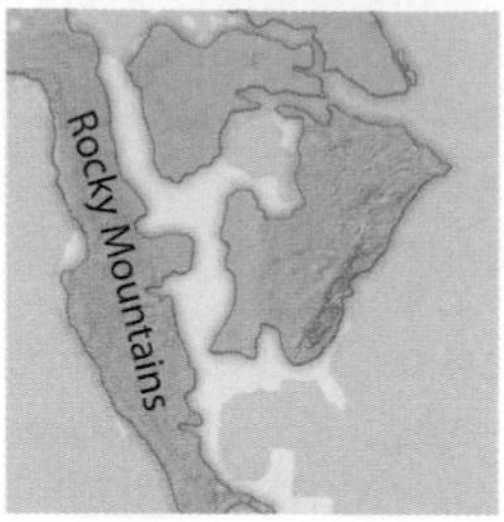

The Mesozoic climate was warm and sea level was high.

Dinosaurs were not the only large vertebrates that lived during the Mesozoic era.

FOLDABLES®

Use your lesson Foldable to review the lesson. Save your Foldable for the project at the end of the chapter.

What do you think NOW?

You first read the statements below at the beginning of the chapter.

5. All large Mesozoic vertebrates were dinosaurs.

6. Dinosaurs disappeared in a large mass extinction event.

Did you change your mind about whether you agree or disagree with the statements? Rewrite any false statements to make them true.

Use Vocabulary

1. A ________ was a marine Mesozoic reptile.
2. A ________ was a Mesozoic reptile that could fly.

Understand Key Concepts

3. Which major event happened during the Mesozoic era?
   A. Humans evolved.
   B. Life moved onto land.
   C. The Appalachian Mountains formed.
   D. The Atlantic Ocean formed.
4. **Compare** the sizes of reptiles and mammals during the Mesozoic era.
5. **Explain** how the Rocky Mountains formed.

Interpret Graphics

6. **Identify** Which type of vertebrate does each skeletal figure below represent?

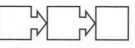

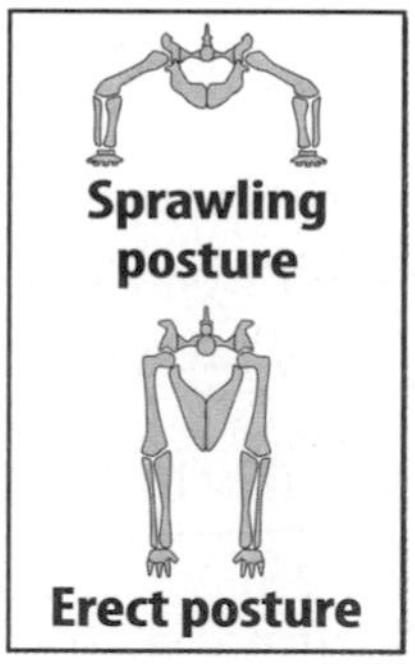

7. **Sequence** Copy and fill in the graphic organizer below to list the periods of the Mesozoic era in order.

Critical Thinking

8. **Infer** how Earth might be different if there had been no extinction event at the end of the Mesozoic era.
9. **Propose** how the breakup of Pangaea might have affected evolution.

AMERICAN MUSEUM of NATURAL HISTORY

CAREERS in SCIENCE

Digging Up a Surprise

A fossil discovery in China reveals some unexpected clues about early mammals.

The Mesozoic era, 251 to 65.5 million years ago, was the age of the dinosaurs. Many different species of dinosaurs roamed Earth, from the ferocious tyrannosaurs to the giant, long-necked brachiosaurs. What other animals lived among the dinosaurs? For years, paleontologists assumed that the only mammals that lived at that time were no bigger than mice. They were no match for the dinosaurs.

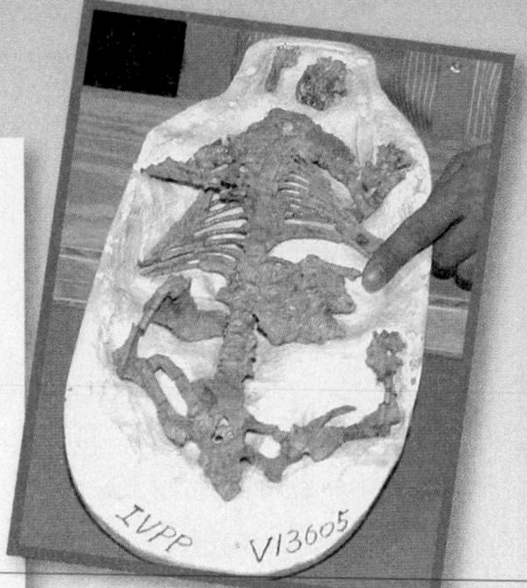

▲ **Paleontologists studying a fossil of the mammal *Repenomamus robustus* found tiny *Psittacosaurus* bones in its stomach.**

Recent fossil discoveries revealed new information about these early mammals. Jin Meng is a paleontologist at the American Museum of Natural History in New York City. In northern China, Meng and other paleontologists discovered fossils of animals that probably died in volcanic eruptions 130 million years ago. Among these fossils were the remains of a mammal over 1 foot long—about the size of a small dog. A representation of the mammal, *Repenomamus robustus* (reh peh noh MA muhs • roh BUS tus), is shown to the right.

This fossil would reveal an even bigger surprise. When examined under microscopes in the lab, scientists discovered small bones in the fossil's rib cage where its stomach had been. The bones were the tiny limbs, fingers, and teeth of a young plant-eating dinosaur. The mammal's last meal had been a young dinosaur!

This was an exciting discovery. Meng and his team learned that early mammals were larger than they thought and were meat eaters, too. Those tiny bones proved to be a huge find. Paleontologists now have a new picture of how animals interacted during the age of dinosaurs.

This is a representation of a young *Psittacosaurus*—only 12 cm long. ►

It's Your Turn

DIAGRAM With a group, research the plants and the animals that lived in the same environment as *Repenomamus*. Create a drawing showing the relationships among the organisms. Compare your drawing to those of other groups.

Lesson 4

Reading Guide

Key Concepts
ESSENTIAL QUESTIONS

- What major geologic events occurred during the Cenozoic era?
- What does fossil evidence reveal about the Cenozoic era?

Vocabulary

Holocene epoch p. 259
Pleistocene epoch p. 261
ice age p. 261
glacial groove p. 261
mega-mammal p. 262

g Multilingual eGlossary

Academic Standards for Science

7.2.3 Characterize the immensity of geologic time and recognize that it is measured in eras and epochs.

Also covers: 7.NS.7, 7.NS.11, 7.DP.9

The Cenozoic Era

Inquiry Is this animal alive?

No, this is a statue in a Los Angeles, California, pond that has been oozing tar for thousands of years. It shows how a mammoth might have become stuck in a tar pit. Mammoths lived at the same time as early humans. What do you think it was like to live alongside these animals?

Inquiry Launch Lab

10 minutes

What evidence do you have that you went to kindergarten?

Rocks and fossils provide evidence about Earth's past. The more recent the era, the more evidence exists. Is this true for you, too?

1. Make a list of items you have, such as a diploma, that could provide evidence about what you did and what you learned in kindergarten.
2. Make another list of items that could provide evidence about your school experience during the past year.

Think About This

1. Which list is longer? Why?
2. **Key Concept** How do you think the items on your lists are like evidence from the first and last eras of the Phanerozoic eon?

Geology of the Cenozoic Era

Have you ever experienced a severe storm? What did your neighborhood look like afterward? Piles of snow, rushing water, or broken trees might have made your neighborhood seem like a different place. In a similar way, the landscapes and organisms of the Paleozoic and Mesozoic eras might have been strange and unfamiliar to you. Though some unusual animals lived during the Cenozoic era, this era is more familiar. People know more about the Cenozoic than they know about any other era because we live in the Cenozoic era. Its fossils and its rock record are better preserved.

As shown in **Figure 20,** the Cenozoic era spans the time from the end of the Cretaceous period, 65.5 mya, to present day. Geologists divide it into two periods—the Tertiary (TUR shee ayr ee) period and the Quaternary (KWAH tur nayr ee) period. These periods are further subdivided into epochs. *The most recent epoch, the* **Holocene** (HOH luh seen) **epoch,** *began 10,000 years ago.* You live in the Holocene epoch.

FOLDABLES®

Make a shutter-fold book from a vertical sheet of paper. Label it as shown. Use it to record information about changes during the Cenozoic era.

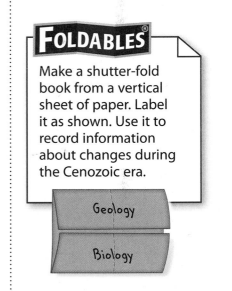

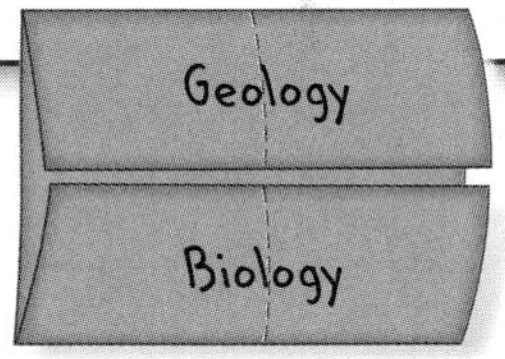

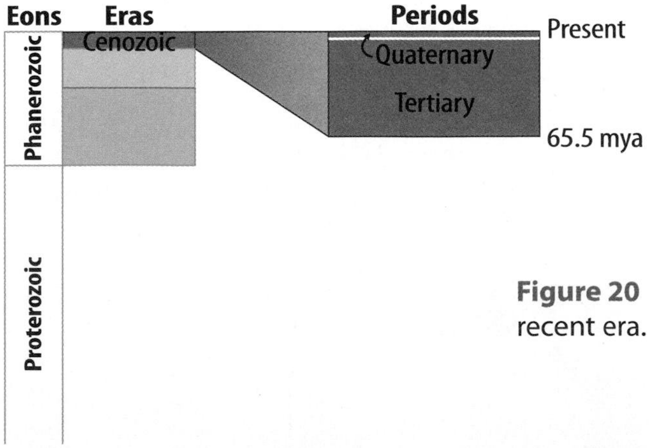

Figure 20 The Cenozoic era is Earth's most recent era. It began 65.5 mya.

Figure 21 Mammals dominated the landscapes of the Cenozoic era.

WORD ORIGIN

Cenozoic
From Greek *kainos,* means "new"; and *zoic,* means "life"

Review
Math Practice
Personal Tutor

Math Skills

Use Percentages

The Cenozoic era began 65.5 mya. What percentage of the Cenozoic era is taken up by the Quaternary period, which began 2.6 mya? To calculate the percentage of a part to the whole, perform the following steps:

a. Express the problem as a fraction.

$$\frac{2.6 \text{ mya}}{65.5 \text{ mya}}$$

b. Convert the fraction to a decimal. 2.6 mya divided by 65.5 mya = 0.040

c. Multiply by 100 and add %.
$0.040 \times 100 = 4.0\%$

Practice

What percent of the Cenozoic era is represented by the Tertiary period, which lasted from 65.5 mya to 2.6 mya? [Hint: Subtract to find the length of the Tertiary period.]

Cenozoic Mountain Building

As shown in the globes in **Figure 21,** Earth's continents continued to move apart during the Cenozoic era, and the Atlantic Ocean continued to widen. As the continents moved, some landmasses collided. Early in the Tertiary period, India crashed into Asia. This collision began to push up the Himalayas—the highest mountains on Earth today. At about the same time, Africa began to push into Europe, forming the Alps. These mountains continue to get higher today.

In North America, the western coast continued to push against the seafloor next to it, and the Rocky Mountains continued to grow in height. New mountain ranges—the Cascades and the Sierra Nevadas—began to form along the western coast. On the eastern coast, there was little tectonic activity. The Appalachian Mountains, which formed during the Paleozoic era, continue to erode today.

Reading Check Why are the Appalachian Mountains relatively small today?

Pleistocene Ice Age

Like the Mesozoic era, the early part of the Cenozoic era was warm. In the middle of the Tertiary period, the climate began to cool. By the Pliocene (PLY oh seen) epoch, ice covered the poles as well as many mountaintops. It was even colder during the next epoch—the Pleistocene (PLY stoh seen).

The **Pleistocene epoch** *was the first epoch of the Quaternary period.* During this time, glaciers advanced and retreated many times. They covered as much as 30 percent of Earth's land surface. *An* **ice age** *is a time when a large proportion of Earth's surface is covered by glaciers.* Sometimes, rocks carried by glaciers created deep gouges or grooves, as shown in **Figure 22. Glacial grooves** *are grooves made by rocks carried in glaciers.*

The glaciers contained huge amounts of water. This water originated in the oceans. With so much water in glaciers, sea level dropped. As sea level dropped, inland seas drained away, exposing dry land. When sea level was at its lowest, the Florida peninsula was about twice as wide as it is today.

Pleistocene Ice Age

Figure 22 Glacial grooves in Ohio are evidence that glaciers extended far into North America during the Pleistocene ice age.

Visual Check Approximately what percentage of the United States was covered with ice?

Figure 23 These mega-mammals lived at different times during the Cenozoic era. They are all extinct today. The human is included for reference.

Cenozoic Life—The Age of Mammals

The mass extinction event at the end of the Mesozoic era meant that there was more space for each surviving species. Flowering plants, including grasses, evolved and began to dominate the land. These plants provided new food sources. This enabled the evolution of many types of animal species, including mammals. Mammals were so successful that the Cenozoic era is sometimes called the age of mammals.

Mega-Mammals

Recall that mammals were small during the Mesozoic era. Many new types of mammals appeared during the Cenozoic era. Some were very large, such as those shown in **Figure 23.** *The large mammals of the Cenozoic era are called* **mega-mammals.** Some of the largest lived during the Oligocene and Miocene periods, from 34 mya to 5 mya. Others, such as woolly mammoths, giant sloths, and saber-toothed cats, lived during the cool climate of the Pliocene and Pleistocene periods, from 5 mya to 10,000 years ago. Many fossils of these animals have been discovered. The saber-toothed cat skull in **Figure 24** was discovered in the Los Angeles tar pits pictured at the beginning of this lesson. A few mummified mammoth bodies also have been discovered preserved for thousands of years in glacial ice.

Figure 24 The saber-toothed cat was a fierce Pleistocene predator.

Key Concept Check How do scientists know that mega-mammals lived during the Cenozoic era?

Isolated Continents and Land Bridges

The mammals depicted in **Figure 23** lived in North America, South America, Europe, and Asia. Different mammal species evolved in Australia. This is mostly because of the movement of Earth's tectonic plates. You read earlier that land bridges can connect continents that were once separated. You also read that when continents are separated, species that once lived together can become geographically isolated.

Most of the mammals that live in Australia today are marsupials (mar SOO pee ulz). These mammals, like kangaroos, carry their young in pouches. Some scientists suggest that marsupials did not evolve in Australia. Instead, they **hypothesize** that marsupial ancestors migrated to Australia from South America when South America and Australia were connected to Antarctica by land bridges, as shown in **Figure 25.** After ancestral marsupials arrived in Australia, Australia moved away from Antarctica, and water covered the land bridges between South America, Antarctica, and Australia. Over time, the ancestral marsupials evolved into the types of marsupials that live in Australia today.

Reading Check What major geologic events affected the evolution of marsupials in Australia?

ACADEMIC VOCABULARY

hypothesize
(verb) To make an assumption about something that is not positively known

Land Bridges

Figure 25 At the beginning of the Cenozoic era, Australia was linked to South America via Antarctica, which was then warm. This provided a route for animal migration.

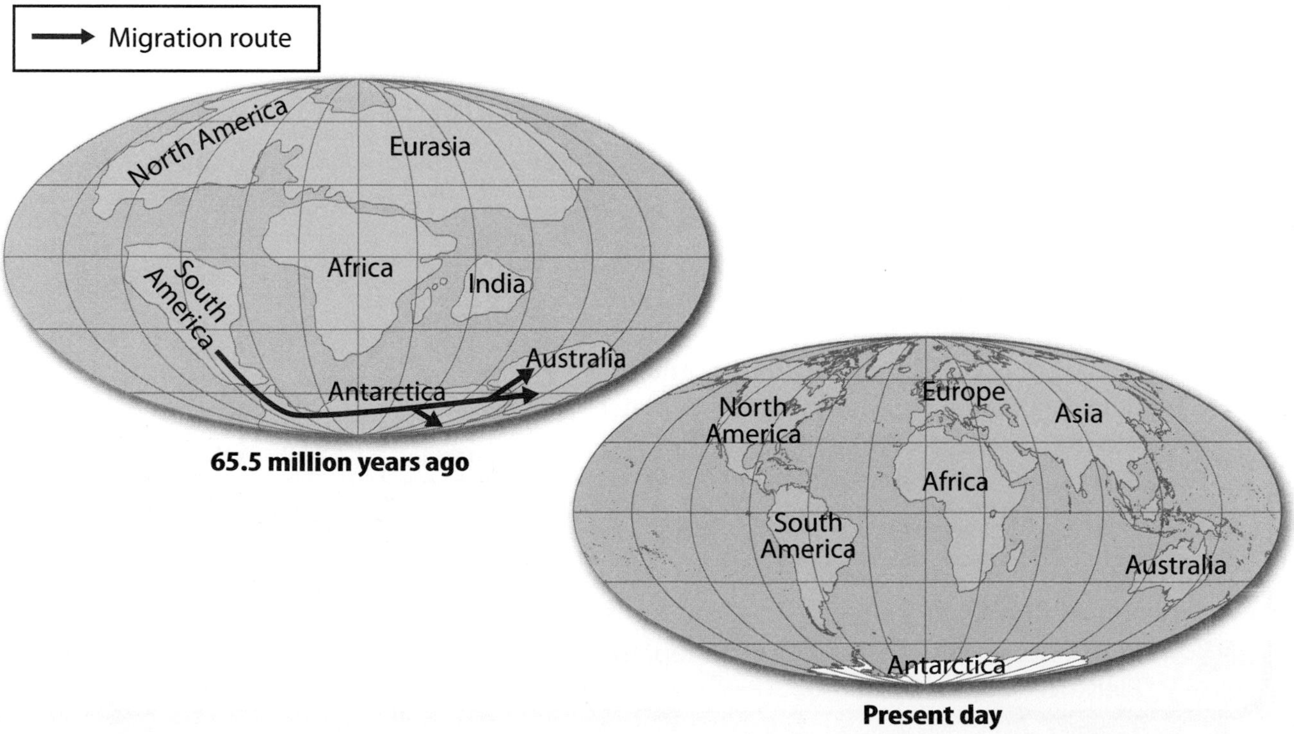

Rise of Humans

The oldest fossil remains of human ancestors have been found in Africa, where scientists think humans first evolved. These fossils are nearly 6 million years old. A skeleton of a 3.2-million-year-old human ancestor is shown in **Figure 26.**

Modern humans—called *Homo sapiens*—didn't evolve until the Pleistocene epoch. Early *Homo sapiens* migrated to Europe, Asia, and eventually North America. Early humans likely migrated to North America from Asia using a land bridge that connected the continents during the Pleistocene ice age. This land bridge is now covered with water.

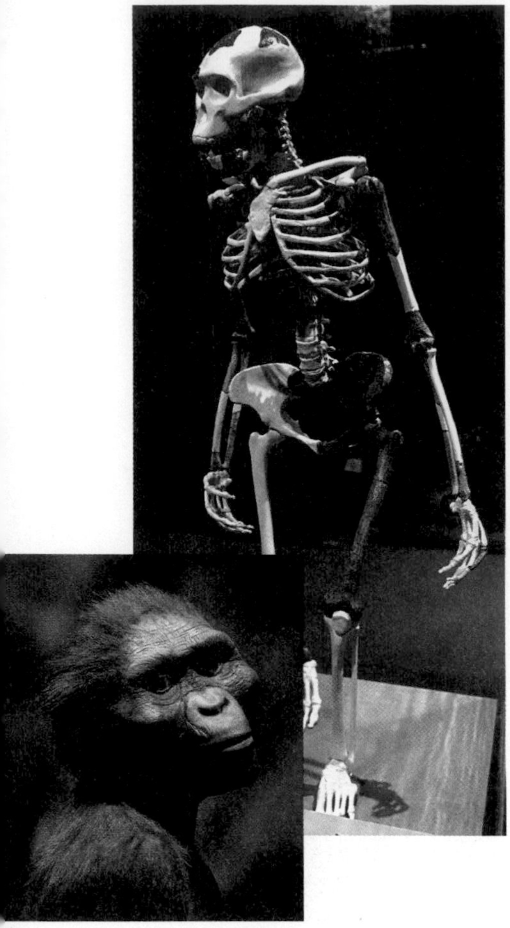

Figure 26 *Lucy* is the name scientists have given this 3.2-million-year-old human ancestor.

Pleistocene Extinctions

Climate changed at the close of the Pleistocene epoch 10,000 years ago. The Holocene epoch was warmer and drier. Forests replaced grasses. The mega-mammals that lived during the Pleistocene became extinct. Some scientists suggest that mega-mammal species could not adapt fast enough to survive the environmental changes.

Key Concept Check How did climate change at the end of the Pleistocene epoch?

Future Changes

There is evidence that present-day Earth is undergoing a global-warming climate change. Many scientists suggest that humans have contributed to this change because of their use of coal, oil, and other fossil fuels over the past few centuries.

Inquiry MiniLab

20 minutes

What happened to the Bering land bridge?

Pleistocene animals and humans likely crossed into North America from Asia using the Bering land bridge. Why did this bridge disappear?

1. Read and complete a lab safety form
2. Form two pieces of **modeling clay** into continents, each with a continental shelf.
3. Place the clay models into a **watertight container** with the continental shelves touching. Add water, leaving the continental shelves exposed. Place a dozen or more **ice cubes** on the continents.
4. During your next science class, observe the container and record your observations.

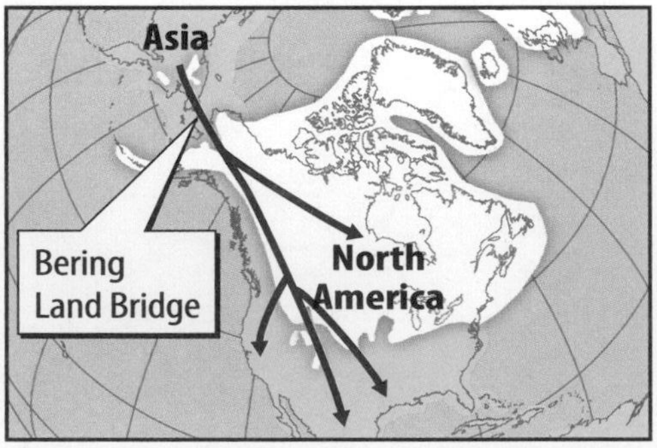

Analyze and Conclude

Key Concept How does your model represent what happened at the end of the Pleistocene epoch?

Lesson 4 Review

Assessment Online Quiz

Visual Summary

The mega-mammals that lived during most of the Cenozoic era are extinct.

Glaciers extended well into North America during the Pleistocene ice age.

Lucy is a 3.2-million-year-old human ancestor.

FOLDABLES®

Use your lesson Foldable to review the lesson. Save your Foldable for the project at the end of the chapter.

What do you think NOW?

You first read the statements below at the beginning of the chapter.

7. Mammals evolved after dinosaurs became extinct.

8. Ice covered nearly one-third of Earth's land surface 10,000 years ago.

Did you change your mind about whether you agree or disagree with the statements? Rewrite any false statements to make them true.

Use Vocabulary

1. Gouges made by ice sheets are ________.
2. You live in the ________ epoch.

Understand Key Concepts

3. Which organism lived during the Cenozoic era?

   A. *Brachiosaurus*
   B. *Dunkleosteus*
   C. saber-toothed cats
   D. trilobites

4. **Classify** Which terms are associated with the Cenozoic era: *Homo sapiens*, mammoth, dinosaur, grass?

Interpret Graphics

5. **Determine** The map below shows coastlines of the southeastern U.S. at three times during the Cenozoic era. Which choice represents the coastline at the height of the Pleistocene ice age?

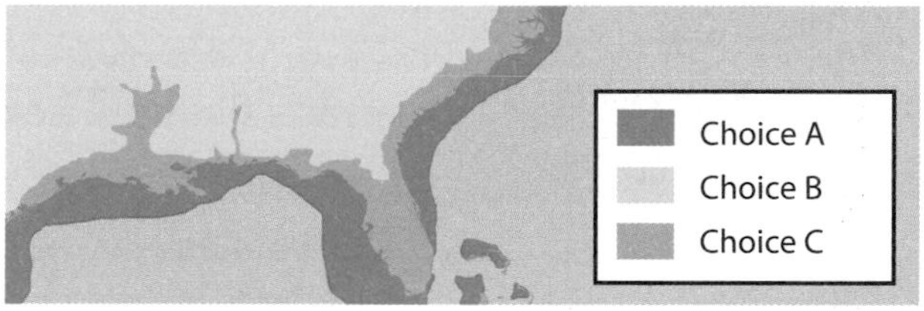

6. **Summarize** Copy and fill in the graphic organizer below to list living mammals that might be considered mega-mammals today.

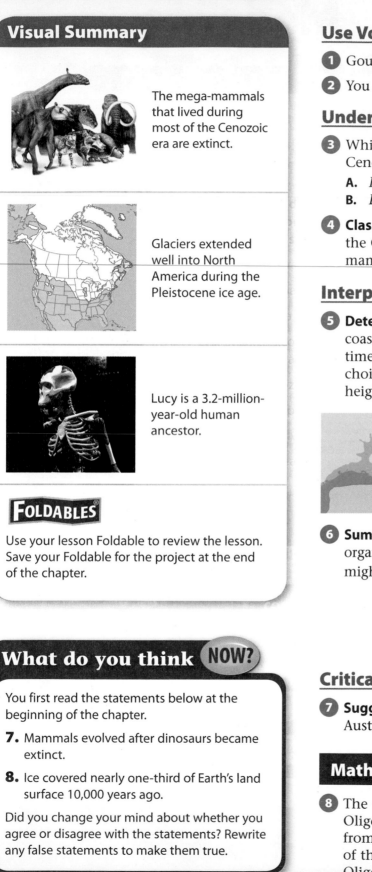

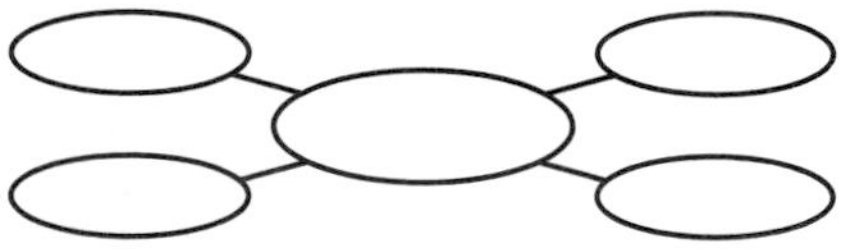

Critical Thinking

7. **Suggest** what might happen if the Australian continent crashed into Asia.

Math Skills

Review **Math Practice**

8. The Cenozoic era began 65.5 mya. The Oligocene and Miocene epochs extended from 34 mya to 5 mya. What percentage of the Cenozoic era is represented by the Oligocene and Miocene epochs?

Modeling Geologic Time

Materials

meterstick

tape measure

poster board

colored markers

colored paper

string

maps

Evidence suggests that Earth formed approximately 4.6 billion years ago. But how long is 4,600,000,000 years? It is difficult to comprehend time that extends so far into the past unless you can relate it to your own experience. In this activity, you will develop a metaphor for geologic time using a scale that is familiar to you. Then, you will create a model to share with your class.

Question

How can you model geologic time using a familiar scale?

Procedure

1. Think of something you are familiar with that can model a long period of time. For example, you might choose the length of a football field or the distance between two U.S. cities on a map—one on the east coast and one on the west coast.
2. Make a model of your metaphor using a metric scale. On your model, display the events listed in the table on the next page. Use the equation below to generate true-to-scale dates in your model.

$$\frac{\textbf{Known age of past event (years before present)}}{\textbf{Known age of Earth (years before present)}} = \frac{\boldsymbol{X}\textbf{ time scale unit location}}{\textbf{Maximum distance or extent of metaphor}}$$

Example: To find where "first fish" would be placed on your model if you used a meterstick (100 cm), set up your equation as follows:

$$\frac{\textbf{500,000,000 years}}{\textbf{4,600,000,000 years}} = \frac{\boldsymbol{X}\textbf{ (location on meterstick)}}{\textbf{100 cm}}$$

3. In your Science Journal, keep a record of all the math equations you used. You can use a calculator, but show all equations.

Analyze and Conclude

4. **Calculate** What percentage of geologic time have modern humans occupied? Set up your equation as follows:

$$\frac{100{,}000}{4{,}600{,}000{,}000} \times 100 = \text{\% of time occupied by } \textit{H. sapiens}$$

5. **Estimate** Where does the Precambrian end on your model? Estimate how much of geologic time falls within the Precambrian.
6. **Evaluate** What other milestone events in Earth's history, other than those listed in the table, could you include on your model?
7. **Appraise** the following sentence as it relates to your life: "Time is relative."
8. THE BIG IDEA **The Big Idea** The Earth events on your model are based mostly on fossil evidence. How are fossils useful in understanding Earth's history? How are they useful in the development of the geologic time scale?

Communicate Your Results

Share your model with the class. Explain why you chose the model you did, and demonstrate how you calculated the scale on your model.

Inquiry Extension

Imagine that you were asked to teach a class of kindergartners about Earth's time. How would you do it? What metaphor would you use? Why?

Some Important Approximate Dates in the History of Earth:

MYA	Event
4,600	Origin of Earth
3,500	Oldest evidence of life
500	First fish
375	*Tiktaalik* appears
320	First reptiles
250	Permian extinction event
220	Mammals and dinosaurs appear
155	Archaeopteryx appears
145	Atlantic Ocean forms
65	Cretaceous extinction event
6	Human ancestors appear
2	Pleistocene Ice Age begins
0.1	*Homo sapiens* appear
0.00052	Columbus lands in New World
??	Your birth date

Remember to use scientific methods.

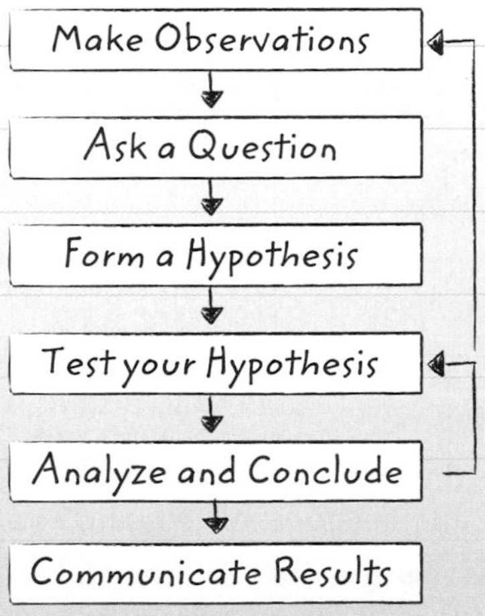

Chapter 7 Study Guide

WebQuest

THE BIG IDEA **The geologic changes that have occurred during the billions of years of Earth's history have strongly affected the evolution of life.**

Key Concepts Summary

Lesson 1: Geologic History and the Evolution of Life

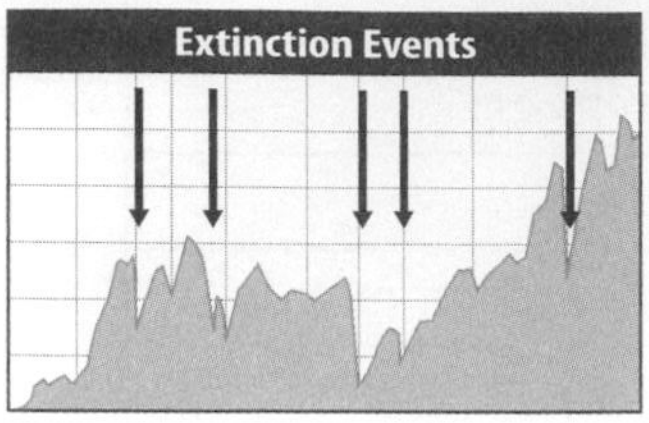

- Geologists organize Earth's history into **eons, eras, periods,** and **epochs.**
- Life evolves over time as Earth's continents move, forming **land bridges** and causing **geographic isolation.**
- **Mass extinctions** occur if many species of organisms cannot adapt to sudden environmental change.

Vocabulary

eon p. 235
era p. 235
period p. 235
epoch p. 235
mass extinction p. 237
land bridge p. 238
geographic isolation p. 238

Lesson 2: The Paleozoic Era

- Life diversified during the **Paleozoic era** as organisms moved from water to land.
- **Coal swamps** formed along **inland seas.** Later, land became drier as the **supercontinent** Pangaea formed.
- The largest mass extinction in Earth's history occurred at the end of the Permian period.

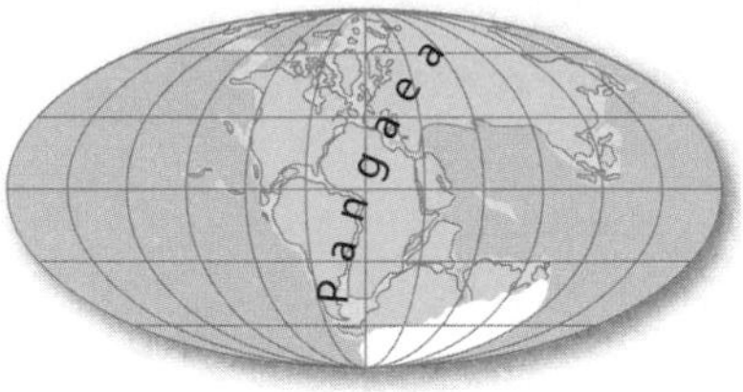

Vocabulary

Paleozoic era p. 243
Mesozoic era p. 243
Cenozoic era p. 243
inland sea p. 244
coal swamp p. 246
supercontinent p. 247

Lesson 3: The Mesozoic Era

- Sea level rose as the climate warmed.
- The Atlantic Ocean and the Rocky Mountains began to form as Pangaea broke apart.
- **Dinosaurs, plesiosaurs, pterosaurs,** and other large Mesozoic vertebrates became extinct at the end of the era.

Vocabulary

dinosaur p. 254
plesiosaur p. 255
pterosaur p. 255

Lesson 4: The Cenozoic Era

- The large, extinct mammals of the Cenozoic were **mega-mammals.**
- Ice covered nearly one-third of Earth's land at the height of the Pleistocene **ice age.**
- The **Pleistocene epoch** and the **Holocene epoch** are the two most recent epochs of the geologic time scale.

Vocabulary

Holocene epoch p. 259
Pleistocene epoch p. 261
ice age p. 261
glacial groove p. 261
mega-mammal p. 262

Review
- Personal Tutor
- Vocabulary eGames
- Vocabulary eFlashcards

FOLDABLES® Chapter Project

Assemble your lesson Foldables as shown to make a Chapter Project. Use the project to review what you have learned in this chapter.

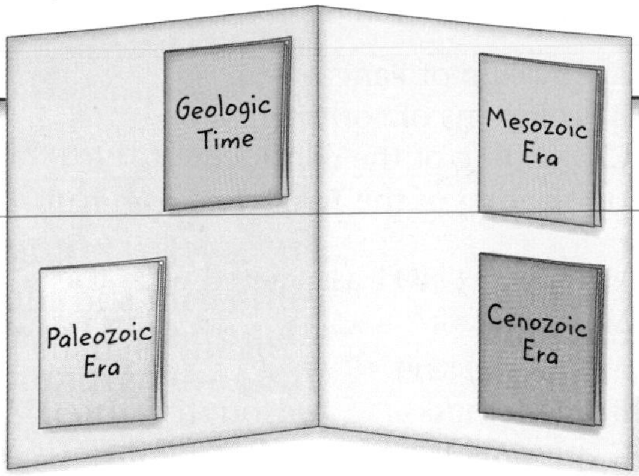

Use Vocabulary

1. The longest time unit in the geologic time scale is the ________.
2. Eras are subdivided into ________.
3. Many boundaries in the geologic time scale are marked by the occurrence of ________.
4. When glaciers melt, shallow ________ form in the interiors of continents.
5. The ________ was the first era of the Phanerozoic eon.
6. A ________ can form when plants are buried in an oxygen-poor environment.
7. Marine Mesozoic reptiles included ________.
8. Modern humans evolved during the ________.

Link Vocabulary and Key Concepts

Concepts in Motion **Interactive Concept Map**

Copy this concept map, and then use vocabulary terms from the previous page and other terms from the chapter to complete the concept map.

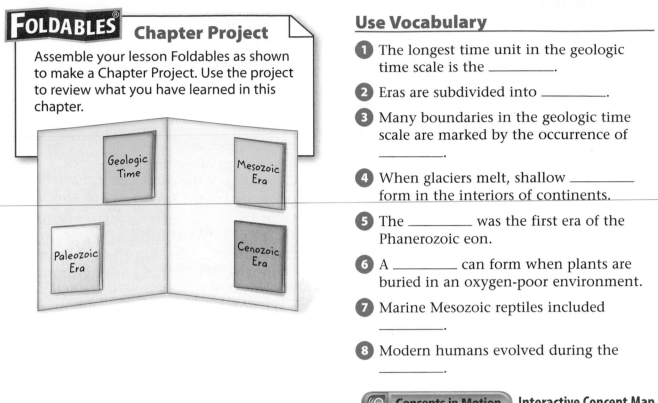

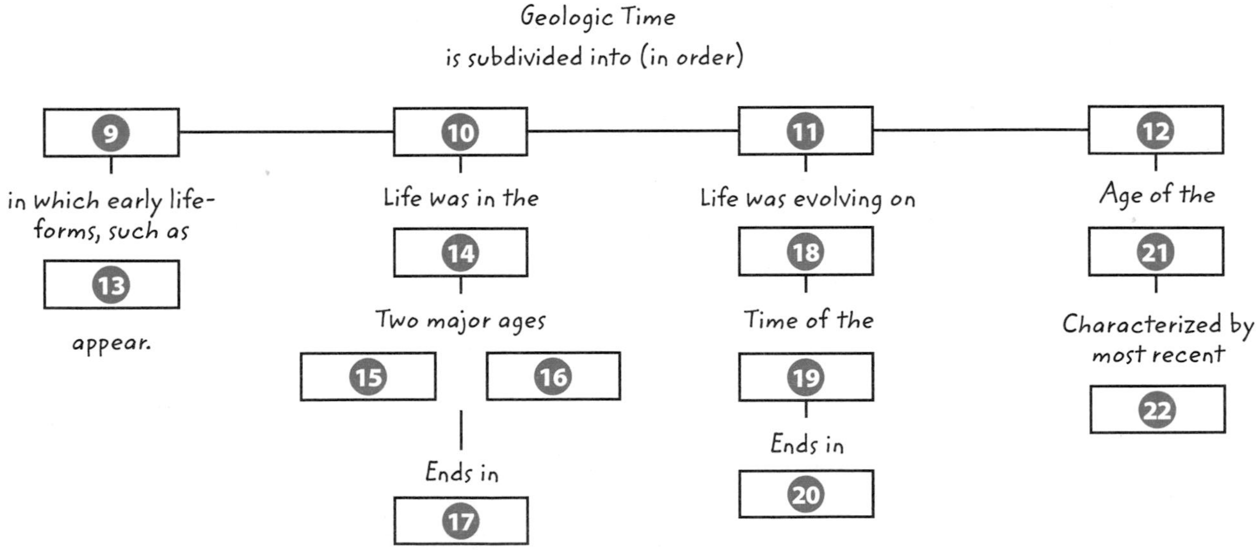

Chapter 7 Review

Understand Key Concepts

1. The trilobite fossil below represents an organism that lived during the Cambrian period.

What distinguished this organism from organisms that lived earlier in time?
   - A. It had hard parts.
   - B. It lived on land.
   - C. It was a reptile.
   - D. It was multicellular.

2. What are the many divisions in the geologic time scale based on?
   - A. changes in the fossil record every billion years
   - B. changes in the fossil record every million years
   - C. gradual changes in the fossil record
   - D. sudden changes in the fossil record

3. Which is NOT a of cause a mass extinction event?
   - A. meteorite collision
   - B. severe hurricane
   - C. tectonic activity
   - D. volcanic activity

4. Which is the correct order of eras, from oldest to youngest?
   - A. Cenozoic, Mesozoic, Paleozoic
   - B. Mesozoic, Cenozoic, Paleozoic
   - C. Paleozoic, Cenozoic, Mesozoic
   - D. Paleozoic, Mesozoic, Cenozoic

5. Which were the first organisms to inhabit land environments?
   - A. amphibians
   - B. plants
   - C. reptiles
   - D. trilobites

6. Which event(s) produced the Appalachian Mountains?
   - A. breakup of Pangaea
   - B. collisions of continents
   - C. flooding of the continent
   - D. opening of the Atlantic Ocean

7. Which was NOT associated with the Mesozoic era?
   - A. *Archaeopteryx*
   - B. plesiosaurs
   - C. pterosaurs
   - D. *Tiktaalik*

8. Which is true for the beginning of the Cenozoic era?
   - A. Mammals and dinosaurs lived together.
   - B. Mammals first evolved.
   - C. Dinosaurs had killed all mammals.
   - D. Dinosaurs were extinct.

9. What is unrealistic about the picture on this stamp?

   - A. Dinosaurs were not this large.
   - B. Dinosaurs did not have long necks.
   - C. Humans did not live with dinosaurs.
   - D. Early humans did not use stone tools.

Assessment
Online Test Practice

Critical Thinking

10 **Hypothesize** how a major change in global climate could lead to a mass extinction.

11 **Evaluate** how the Permian-Triassic mass extinction affected the evolution of life.

12 **Predict** what Earth's climate might be like if sea level were very low.

13 **Differentiate** between amphibians and reptiles. What feature enabled reptiles—but not amphibians—to be successful on land?

14 **Hypothesize** how the bone structure of dinosaur limbs might have contributed to the success of dinosaurs during the Mesozoic era.

15 **Debate** Some scientists argue that humans have changed Earth so much that a new epoch—the Anthropocene epoch—should be added to the geologic time scale. Explain whether you think this is a good idea and, if so, when it should begin.

16 **Interpret Graphics** What is wrong with the geologic time line shown below?

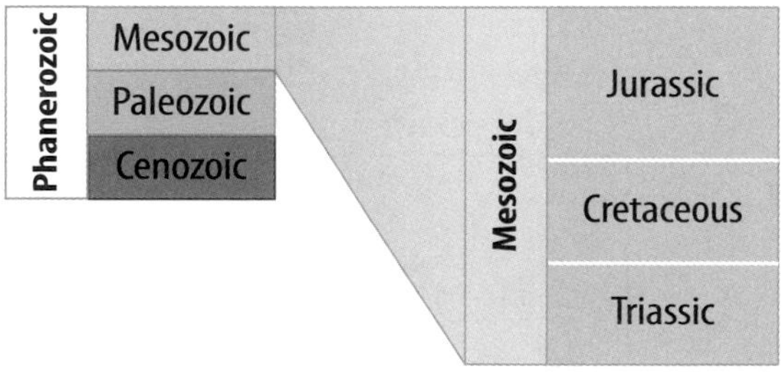

Writing in Science

17 **Decide** which period of Earth's history you would want to visit if you could travel back in time. Write a letter to a friend about your visit, describing the climate, the organisms, and the positions of Earth's continents at the time of your visit. Include a main idea, supporting details and examples, and a concluding sentence.

REVIEW THE BIG IDEA

18 What have scientists learned about Earth's past by studying rocks and fossils? How is the evolution of Earth's life-forms affected by geologic events? Provide examples.

19 The photo below shows an extinct dinosaur. What changes on Earth can cause organisms to become extinct?

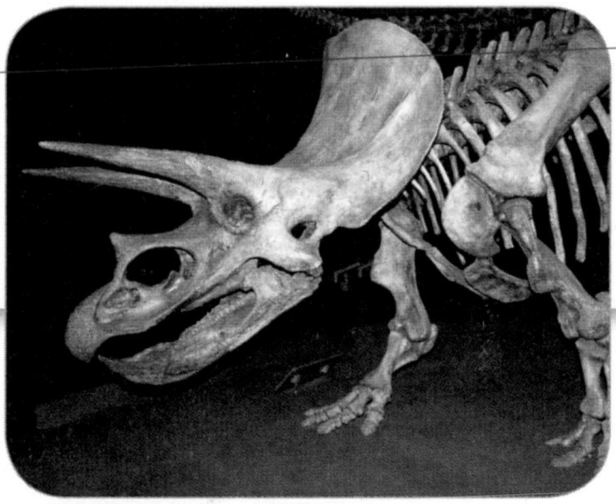

Math Skills

Review
Math Practice

Use Percentages

Use the table to answer the questions.

Era	Period	Epoch	Time Scale
Cenozoic	Quaternary	Holocene	10,000 years ago
		Pleistocene	1.8 mya
	Tertiary	Pliocene	5.3 mya
		Miocene	23.8 mya
		Oligocene	33.7 mya
		Eocene	54.8 mya
		Paleocene	65.5 mya

20 What percentage of the Quaternary period is represented by the Holocene epoch?

21 What percentage of the Tertiary period is represented by the Pliocene epoch?

Standardized Test Practice

Record your answers on the answer sheet provided by your teacher or on a sheet of paper.

Multiple Choice

Use the figure below to answer question 1.

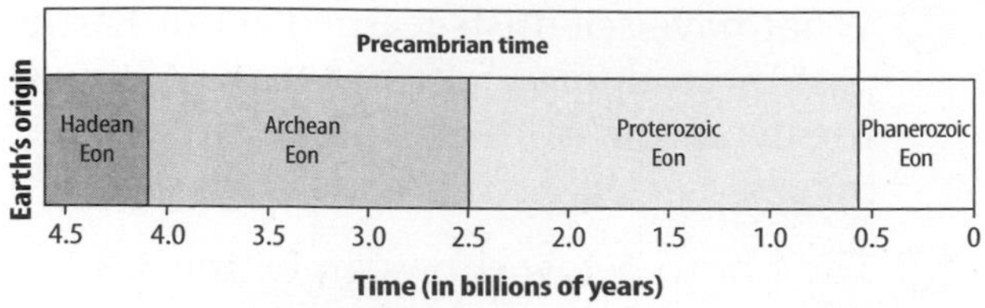

1 Approximately how long did Precambrian time last?

A 0.5 billion years
B 3.5 billion years
C 4.0 billion years
D 4.25 billion years

2 Which is the smallest unit of geologic time?

A eon
B epoch
C era
D period

3 Which is known as the age of invertebrates?

A Early Cenozoic
B Early Paleozoic
C Late Mesozoic
D Late Precambrian

4 Which made dinosaurs different from modern-day reptiles?

A head shape
B hip structure
C jaw alignment
D tail length

5 What is the approximate age of the oldest fossils of early human ancestors?

A 10,000 years
B 6 million years
C 65 million years
D 1.5 billion years

6 Which was NOT an adaptation that enabled amphibians to live on land?

A ability to breathe oxygen
B ability to lay eggs on land
C strong limbs
D thick skin

7 Which is considered a mega-mammal?

A Archaeopteryx
B plesiosaur
C Tiktaalik
D woolly mammoth

Use the figure below to answer question 8.

North America During the Pleistocene Ice Age

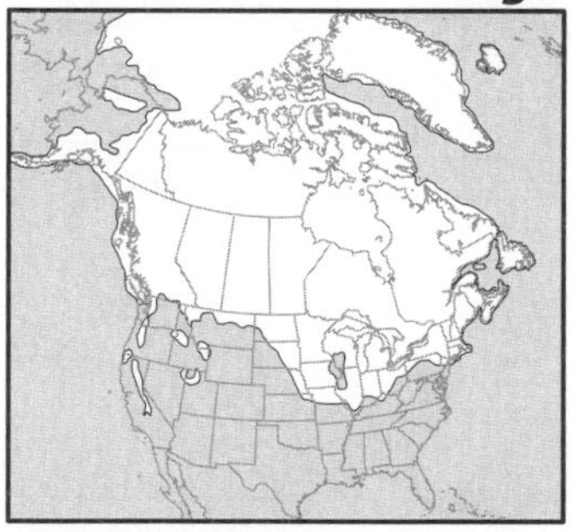

8 The figure above is a map of glacial coverage in North America. Which section of the United States would most likely have the greatest number of glacial grooves?

A the Northeast
B the Northwest
C the Southeast
D the Southwest

Assessment
Online Standardized Test Practice

Use the graph below to answer question 9.

Sea Level Rise During Mesozoic

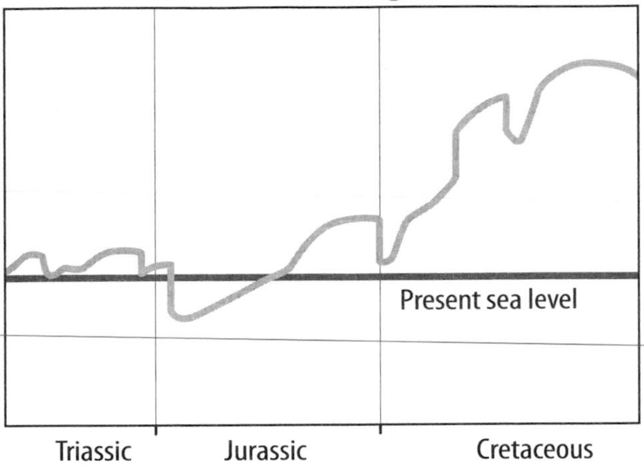

9 Based on the graph above, when might inland seas have covered much of Earth's continents?

A Early Cretaceous

B Early Jurassic

C Middle Triassic

D Late Cretaceous

10 Which did NOT occur in the Paleozoic era?

A appearance of mammals

B development of coal swamps

C evolution of invertebrates

D formation of Pangaea

11 What do geologists use to mark divisions in geologic time?

A abrupt changes in the fossil record

B frequent episodes of climate change

C movements of Earth's tectonic plates

D rates of radioactive mineral decay

Constructed Response

Use the graph below to answer questions 12 and 13.

Extinction Events

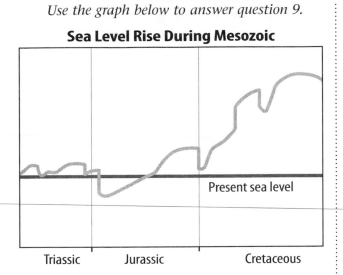

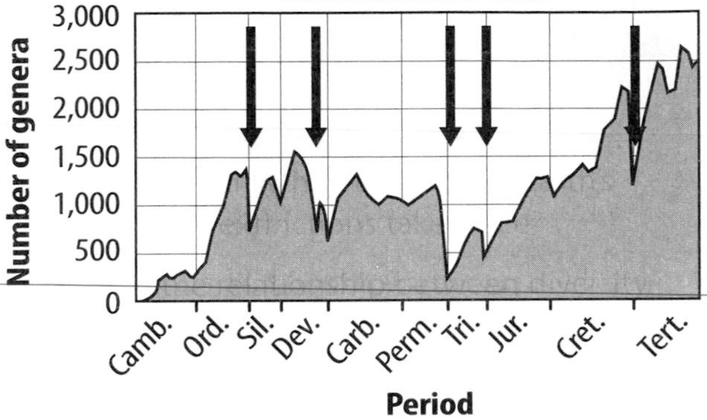

12 In the graph above, what events do the arrows mark? What happens during these events?

13 What event appears to have had the greatest impact? Explain your answer in terms of the graph.

14 What are two possible reasons why large populations of organisms die?

15 What is the relationship between the evolution of marsupials and the movement of Earth's tectonic plates?

16 Why did new and existing aquatic organisms flourish during the Mesozoic era? Use the terms glaciers, Pangaea, and sea level in your explanation.

17 What is the link between iridium and the mass extinction of dinosaurs?

NEED EXTRA HELP?																	
If You Missed Question...	1	2	3	4	5	6	7	8	9	10	11	12	13	14	15	16	17
Go to Lesson...	1	1	2	3	4	2	4	4	3	2	1	1	1	1-3	4	3	1

Unit 3

EXPLORING EARTH

10000 B.C. — 1500 — 1900

12000 B.C.
A map scratched into a mammoth jawbone, the oldest surviving map, depicts a group of settlements and the surrounding countryside in what is now Mehirich, Ukraine.

2300 B.C.
The oldest surviving city map, a map of the Mesopotamian city of Lagash that includes the layout of the city, is created.

150 A.D.
Ptolemy illustrates a world map with Earth as a sphere from 60°N to 30°S latitudes.

1506
Francesco Rosselli produces the first map to show the "New World."

1930s
Maps become increasingly accurate and factual due to the widespread use of aerial photography after World War I.

1950

2000

1960s
Geographic Information Systems (GIS) are developed. GIS displays large amounts of information and includes computer software and hardware as well as digital data and storage.

1993
The space-based Global Positioning System achieves initial operational capability.

2005
An internet mapping tool displays satellite images of Earth's surface.

? Inquiry
Visit ConnectED for this unit's **STEM** activity.

Technology

Figure 1 Lightweight, flexible solar cells developed for spacecraft help to conserve Earth's resources.

It may sound strange, but some of the greatest benefits of the space program are benefits to life here on Earth. Devices ranging from hand-held computers to electric socks rely on technologies first developed for space exploration. **Technology** is the practical application of science to commerce or industry. Space technologies have increased our understanding of Earth and our ability to locate and conserve resources.

Problems, such as how best to explore the solar system and outer space, often send scientists on searches for new knowledge. Engineers use scientific knowledge to develop new technologies for space. Then, some of those technologies are modified to solve problems on Earth. For example, lightweight solar panels on the outside of a spacecraft convert the Sun's energy into electricity that powers the spacecraft for long space voyages. Similar but smaller, flexible solar panels, as shown in **Figure 1** are now available for consumers to purchase. They can be used to power small electronics when traveling. **Figure 2** shows how other technologies from space help conserve natural resources.

This image was taken by the *Terra* satellite and shows fires burning in California. The image helps firefighters see the size and the location of the fires. It also helps scientists study the effect of fires on Earth's atmosphere. ▼

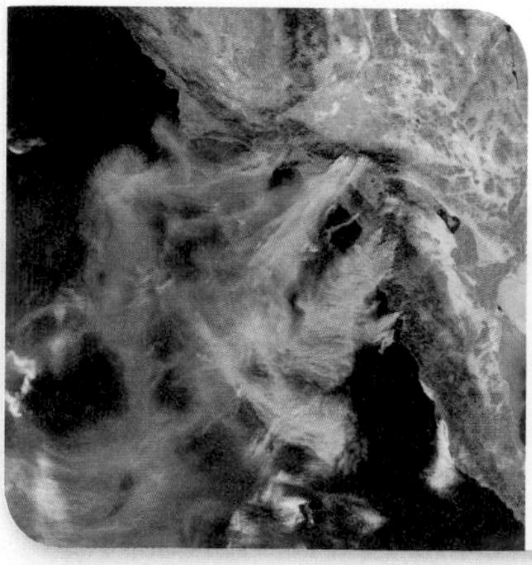

Some portable water purification kits use technologies developed to provide safe, clean drinking water for astronauts. This kit can provide clean, safe drinking water for an entire village in a remote area or supply drinking water after a natural disaster.

Engineers developed glass spheres about the size of a grain of flour to insulate super-cold spacecraft fuel lines. Similar microspheres act as insulators when mixed with paints. This technology can help reduce the energy needed to heat and cool buildings. ▼

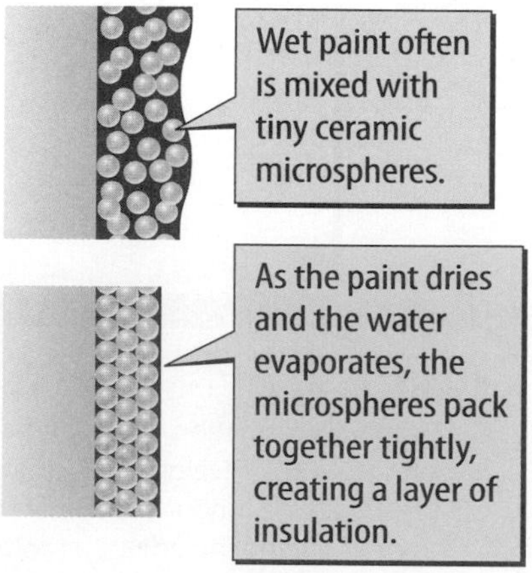

Wet paint often is mixed with tiny ceramic microspheres.
As the paint dries and the water evaporates, the microspheres pack together tightly, creating a layer of insulation.

Figure 2 Some technologies developed as part of the space program have greatly benefited life on Earth.

Figure 3 The satellite image on the left is similar to what you would see with your eyes from space. A satellite sensor that detects other wavelengths of light produced the colored satellite image on the right. It shows the locations of nearly a dozen different minerals.

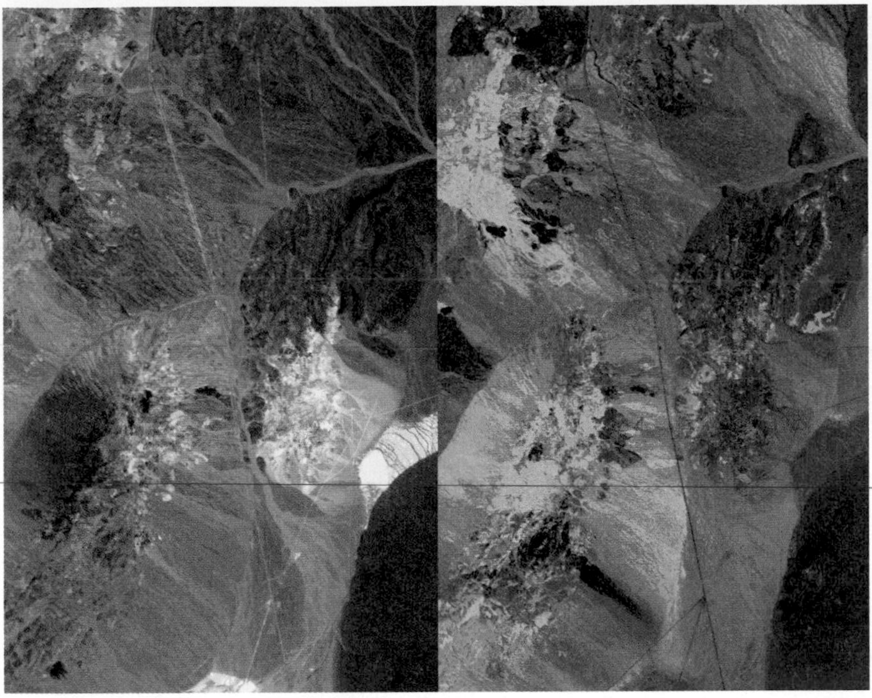

Solving Problems and Improving Abilities

Science and technology depend on each other. For example, images from space greatly improve our understanding of Earth. **Figure 3** above shows a satellite image of a Nevada mine. The satellite is equipped with sensors that detect visible light, much like your eyes do. The image on the right shows a satellite image of the same site taken with a sensor that detects wavelengths of light your eyes cannot see. This image provides information about the types of minerals in the mine. Each color in the image on the right shows the location of a different mineral, reducing the time it takes geologists to locate mineral deposits.

Scientists use other kinds of satellite sensors for different purposes. Engineers have modified space technology to produce satellite images of cloud cover over Earth's surface, as shown in **Figure 4.** Images like this one improve global weather forecasting and help scientists understand changes in Earth's atmosphere. Of course, science can answer only some of society's questions, and technology cannot solve all problems. But together, they can improve the quality of life for all.

Inquiry MiniLab 25 minutes

How would you use space technology?

Many uses for space technology haven't been discovered yet. Can you develop one?

1. Identify a problem locating, protecting, or preserving resources that could be solved using space technology.
2. Prepare a short oral presentation explaining your technology.

Analyze and Conclude

1. **Describe** How is your technology used in space?
2. **Explain** How do you use technology to solve a problem on Earth?

Figure 4 This satellite image shows reflection of sunlight (yellow), deep clouds (white), low clouds (pale yellow), high clouds (blue), vegetation (green), and sea (dark).

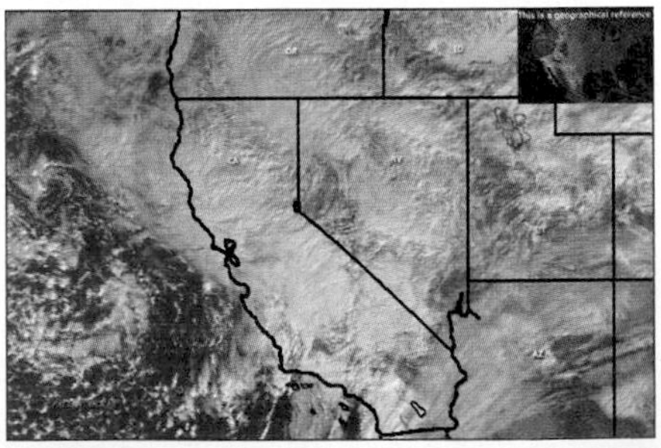

Chapter 8

Rocks

THE BIG IDEA

How do the three main types of rocks form?

Inquiry How did these rocks form?

The rocks that make up the mountains and the valley in this photo are very different from each other. They are different because different processes formed them. The sand in the foreground will someday become rocks, too.

- Why don't all rocks look the same?
- Why are rocks different colors?
- What is happening on Earth that causes different rocks to form?

Get Ready to Read

What do you think?

Before you read, decide if you agree or disagree with each of these statements. As you read this chapter, see if you change your mind about any of the statements.

1. Once a rock forms as part of a mountain, it does not change.
2. Some rocks, when exposed on Earth's surface, undergo weathering and erosion.
3. Large crystals form when lava cools quickly on Earth's surface.
4. Igneous rocks form when cooling magma crystallizes.
5. Water can dissolve rock.
6. All sedimentary rocks on Earth formed from the remains of organisms that lived in oceans.
7. With the right pressure and temperature conditions, minerals in a rock can change shape without breaking or melting.
8. Metamorphic rocks have layers that form as minerals melt and then recrystallize.

ConnectED Your one-stop online resource

connectED.mcgraw-hill.com

- Video
- Audio
- Review
- Inquiry
- WebQuest
- Assessment
- Concepts in Motion
- Multilingual eGlossary

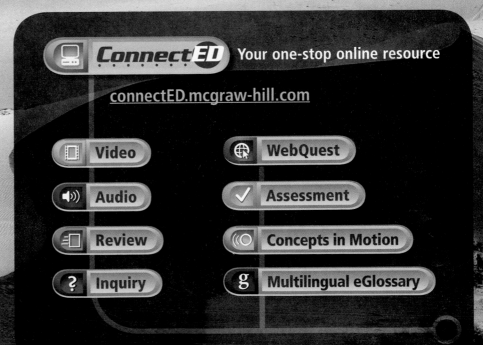

Lesson 1

Reading Guide

Key Concepts
ESSENTIAL QUESTIONS

- How are rocks classified?
- What is the rock cycle?

Vocabulary

rock p. 281
grain p. 281
texture p. 282
magma p. 283
lava p. 283
sediment p. 283
rock cycle p. 284

g Multilingual eGlossary

Video

- **BrainPOP®**
- **Science Video**

Academic Standards for Science

7.2.5 Describe the origin and physical properties of igneous, metamorphic and sedimentary rocks and how they are related through the rock cycle.

Also covers: 7.NS.7

Rocks and the Rock Cycle

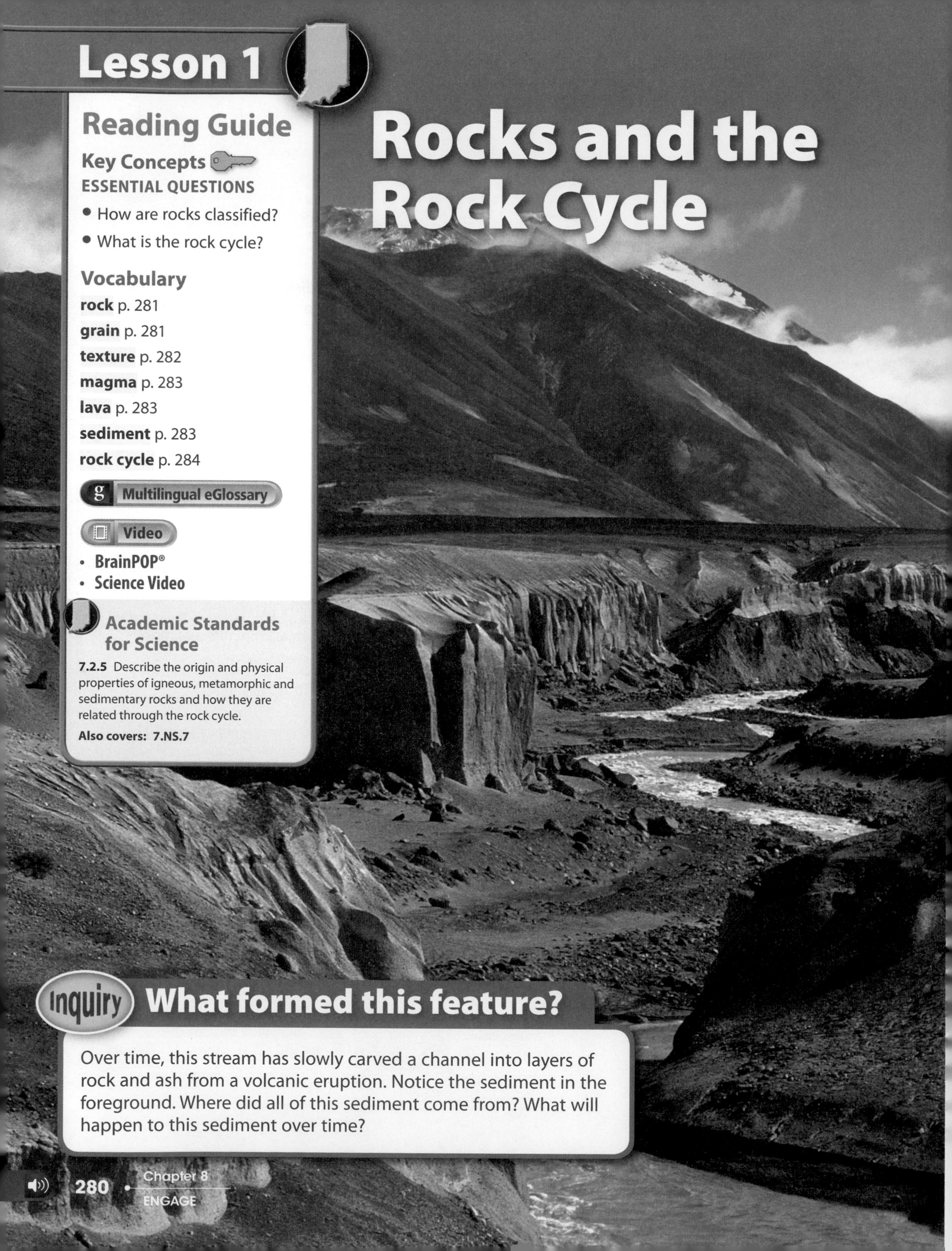

Inquiry What formed this feature?

Over time, this stream has slowly carved a channel into layers of rock and ash from a volcanic eruption. Notice the sediment in the foreground. Where did all of this sediment come from? What will happen to this sediment over time?

Inquiry Launch Lab

20 minutes

What's in a rock?

You've probably seen different types of rock, either outside or in photographs. Rocks have different colors and textures, and they can contain a combination of minerals, shells, or grains. In this activity, you will observe differences among rock samples.

1. Read and complete a lab safety form.
2. Obtain a few **rock samples** from your teacher.
3. Examine each rock, both with and without a **magnifying lens.**
4. Describe each rock sample in detail. Record the color and texture, and describe the minerals or grains in the rock for each sample in your Science Journal.

Think About This

1. Write a brief description for each rock sample in your Science Journal. Identify the ways in which your samples are similar and different.
2. **Key Concept** Do you think all rocks form in the same way? Explain.

Rocks

Rocks are everywhere. Mountains, valleys, and the seafloor are made of rocks. Rock and mineral resources even make up parts of your home. Today it is common for floors, countertops, and even tabletops to be made of some type of rock.

A **rock** *is a natural, solid mixture of minerals or grains.* Individual **mineral** crystals, broken bits of minerals, or rock fragments make up these grains. Sometimes a rock contains the remains of an organism or volcanic glass. Processes on Earth's surface can cause rocks to break apart into many different-sized fragments, as shown in **Figure 1.** *Geologists call the fragments that make up a rock* **grains.** They use a grain's size, shape, and chemical composition to classify rocks.

REVIEW VOCABULARY

mineral
a naturally occurring, inorganic solid, with a definite chemical composition, and an orderly arrangement of atoms

Figure 1 Rocks are everywhere on Earth. By studying rocks, geologists can gain a better understanding of the processes that create different rock types and the environments in which they form.

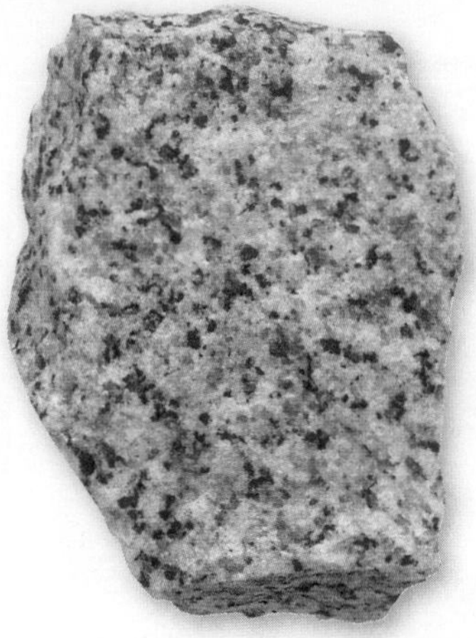

Granite

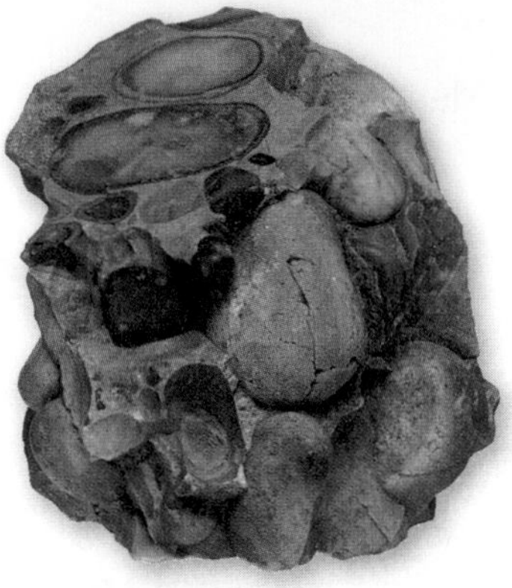

Conglomerate

Figure 2 Geologists use texture and composition to classify these rocks as granite and conglomerate.

Visual Check Compare and contrast the grain shape and size in each of these rocks.

Texture

Geologists use two important observations to classify rocks: texture and composition. *The grain size and the way grains fit together in a rock are called* **texture.** When a geologist classifies a rock by its texture, he or she looks at the size of minerals or grains in the rock, the arrangement of these individual grains, and the overall feel of the rock.

Texture also can be used to determine the environment in which a rock formed. The granite shown in **Figure 2** has large mineral crystals. This colorful, crystalline texture helps a geologist classify this rock as an igneous rock. The conglomerate (kun GLAHM rut) shown in **Figure 2** has rounded rock fragments. Well-rounded rock fragments imply that strong forces, such as water or ice, carved the individual clasts and produced smooth surfaces. This is a sedimentary rock. You will learn more about igneous, sedimentary, and a third rock type—metamorphic rocks—in the lessons that follow.

Composition

The minerals or grains present in a rock help geologists classify the rock's composition. This information can be used to determine where the rock formed, such as inside a volcano or alongside a river. Geologists conduct fieldwork using maps, a field journal, a compass, a rock hammer, and other tools to help classify a rock's composition and texture, as shown in **Figure 3.** These tools also help geologists to interpret the specific conditions under which the rock formed. For example, the presence of certain minerals might suggest that the rock formed under extreme temperature and pressure. Other minerals indicate that the rock formed from molten material deep beneath Earth's surface.

Key Concept Check How are rocks classified?

Figure 3 A geologist in the field uses tools such as a field journal, a rock hammer, and maps to interpret the conditions of rock formation.

Three Major Rock Types

Geologists classify rocks, or place them into groups, based on how they form. The three major groups of rocks are igneous, sedimentary, and metamorphic rocks. Geologists can interpret the environment where these rocks formed based on the physical and chemical characteristics of each rock type.

Igneous Rocks

You might remember that when **magma**, *molten or liquid rock underground,* cools, mineral crystals form. *Molten rock that erupts on Earth's surface is called* **lava.** When magma or lava cools and crystallizes, it creates igneous rock. As mineral crystals grow, they connect much like pieces of a jigsaw puzzle. These crystals become the grains in an igneous rock.

The texture and composition of these grains help geologists to classify the type of igneous rock and the environment where this rock may have formed. Igneous rocks form in a variety of environments including subduction zones, mid-ocean ridges, and hot spots where volcanoes are common.

Sedimentary Rocks

When rocks are exposed on Earth's surface, they can break down and be transported to new environments. Forces such as wind, running water, ice, and even gravity cause rocks on Earth's surface to break down. **Sediment** *is rock material that forms where rocks are broken down into smaller pieces or dissolved in water as rocks erode.* These materials, which include rock fragments, mineral crystals, or the remains of certain plants and animals, are the building blocks of sedimentary rocks.

Sedimentary rocks form where sediment is **deposited.** Sedimentary environments include rivers and streams, deserts, and valleys like the one shown in **Figure 4.** Even the loose sediment in the picture at the beginning of this lesson will someday turn into rock. Sedimentary rocks can be found in mountain valleys, along river banks, on the beach, or even in your backyard.

SCIENCE USE V. COMMON USE

deposit

Science Use sediment or rock added to a landform

Common Use to put money in a bank

Figure 4 Wind, water, ice, and the force of gravity can deposit sediments in environments like the mountain valley shown here.

Metamorphic Rocks

Figure 5 Metamorphic rocks form from preexisting rocks that react to changes in temperature and pressure or the addition of chemical fluids.

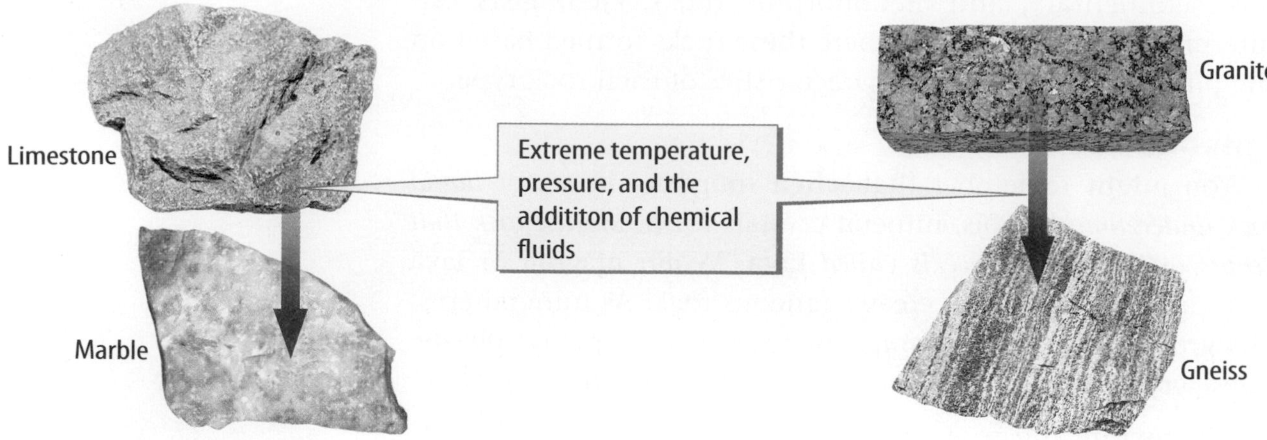

Visual Check What type of rock results when granite is subjected to extreme temperature and pressure?

Metamorphic Rocks

When rocks are exposed to extreme temperature and pressure, such as along plate boundaries, they can change to metamorphic rocks. The addition of chemical fluids can also cause rocks to become metamorphic rocks. The minerals that make up the rock's composition change as well as the texture, or arrangement of the individual mineral grains. In many cases, the change is so intense that the arrangement of the grains appears as bent or twisted layers, as shown in the gneiss in **Figure 5.** Metamorphic rocks can form from any igneous or sedimentary rock or even another metamorphic rock. For example, the igneous rock granite metamorphoses into a gneiss and the sedimentary rock limestone metamorphoses into a marble, as shown in **Figure 5.**

FOLDABLES®

Use a sheet of paper to make a horizontal half-book to illustrate and explain the rock cycle.

The Rock Cycle

When you look at a mountain of rock, it is hard to imagine it can ever change. But rocks are changing all the time. You usually don't see this change because it happens so slowly. *The series of processes that change one type of rock into another type of rock is called the* **rock cycle.** Forces on Earth's surface and deep within Earth drive this cycle. This cycle describes how one rock type can change into another rock type through natural processes. Imagine an igneous rock that begins as lava. The lava cools and crystallizes. Over time, the igneous rock is exposed on Earth's surface. Water can erode this rock and form sediments that eventually cement together and become sedimentary rock.

Key Concept Check What is the rock cycle?

Rocks in Action

Figure 6 shows how igneous, sedimentary, and metamorphic rocks originate and change throughout the rock cycle. The rectangles represent different Earth materials: magma, sediment, and the three rock types. The ovals represent natural processes that change one type of rock into another. The arrows indicate the many different pathways within the cycle both above and below the ground.

Some rock cycle processes occur only beneath Earth's surface, such as those that involve extreme temperature, pressure, and melting. Uplift is a tectonic process that forces these rocks onto Earth's surface. On the surface, rocks can change due to natural processes, such as weathering, erosion, deposition, compaction, and cementation.

Can you trace a complete pathway through the rock cycle using rock types and processes? Start anywhere on the cycle and see how many different pathways you can make.

Figure 6 There are other possible pathways on the rock cycle. Where would you draw additional arrows?

Concepts in Motion Animation

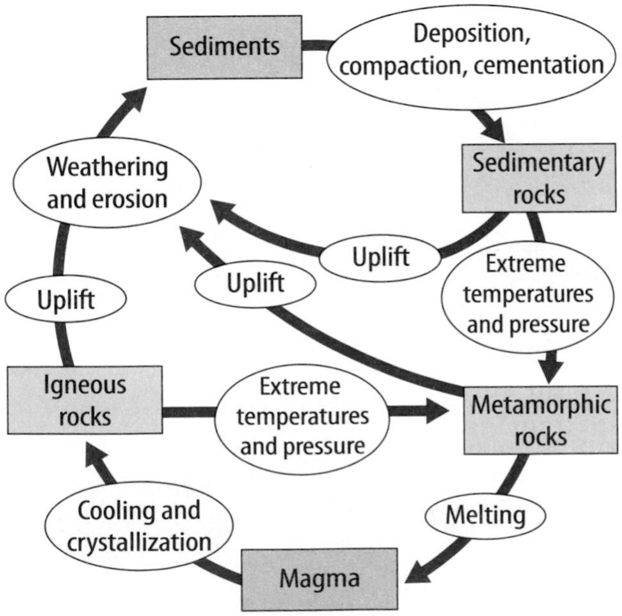

Inquiry MiniLab — 20 minutes

Can you model the rock cycle?

The rock cycle includes all the changes that can occur in rocks. You can use a crayon model of a rock to learn about some of these changes.

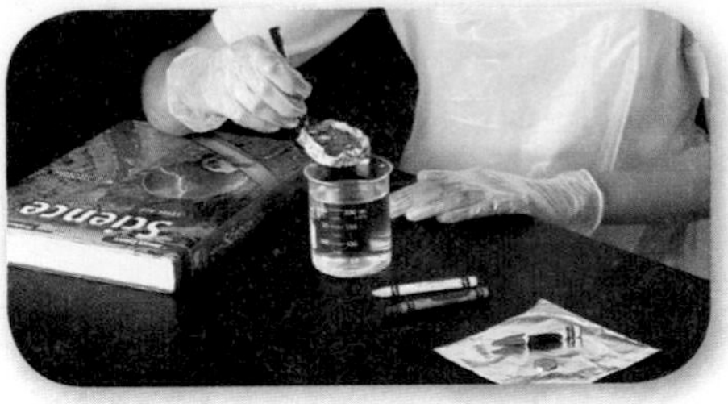

1. Read and complete a lab safety form.
2. Scrape a **coin** against the side of two or three different colors of **crayons.** Layer your scrapings on a piece of **aluminum foil.**
3. Fold the foil around the scrapings and press down hard on it with your hands. Open the package. Record your observations of the crayon rock in your Science Journal. Try to fold your crayon rock in half. It might break. Repackage your crayon rock.
4. Get a **beaker** of **hot water** from your teacher. Using **tongs,** put the foil package in the water for about 10 s. Remove it and dry it on a **paper towel.** Press your **textbook** down on top of the foil package. Open it and record your observations in your Science Journal.
5. Repackage your crayon rock. Give it to your teacher to **iron.** Allow your package to cool, then open it. Record your observations in your Science Journal.

Analyze and Conclude

1. **Recognize Cause and Effect** What part of the rock cycle did ironing your crayon rock represent?
2. **Model** What type of rock did you model in steps 3, 4, and 5?
3. **Key Concept** How could you continue the rock cycle using the crayon rock you created in step 4?

Lesson 1 Review

Assessment Online Quiz
Inquiry Virtual Lab

Visual Summary

Rocks are a natural solid mixture of minerals or grains.

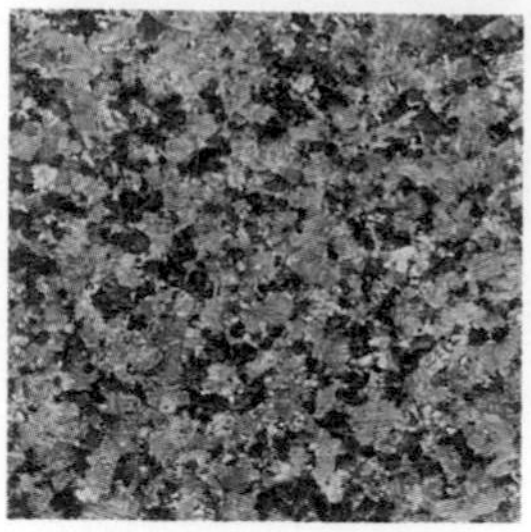

Texture describes the size and arrangement of minerals or grains in a rock.

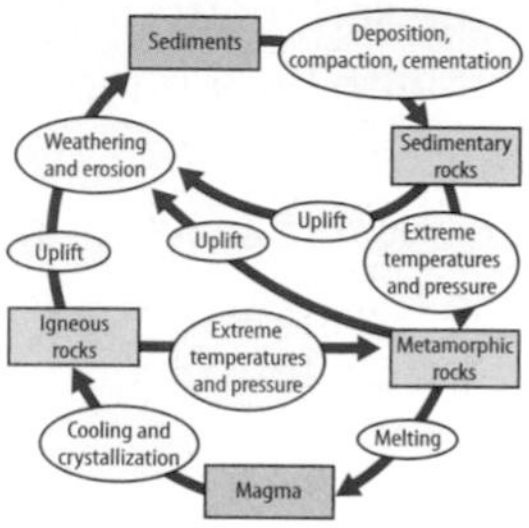

The rock cycle represents a series of processes that change one rock type into another.

FOLDABLES®

Use your lesson Foldable to review the lesson. Save your Foldable for the project at the end of the chapter.

What do you think NOW?

You first read the statements below at the beginning of the chapter.

1. Once a rock forms as part of a mountain, it does not change.
2. Some rocks, when exposed on Earth's surface, undergo weathering and erosion.

Did you change your mind about whether you agree or disagree with the statements? Rewrite any false statements to make them true.

Use Vocabulary

1. **Use the terms** *grain* and *sediment* in a sentence.
2. **Distinguish** A rock that forms as magma solidifies is a(n) ________ rock.
3. **Use the term** *metamorphic rock* in a complete sentence.

Understand Key Concepts

4. What type of rock forms on Earth's surface from pieces of other rocks?
   A. extrusive rock
   B. intrusive rock
   C. metamorphic rock
   D. sedimentary rock
5. **Explain** why there is no beginning or end to the rock cycle.
6. **Explain** how texture provides information about where a rock formed.

Interpret Graphics

7. **Analyze** the illustration of the rock cycle. Describe what processes of the rock cycle can cause a sedimentary rock to become an igneous rock.
8. **Interpret** Refer to the diagram of the lithosphere below. What rock type makes up a major part of Earth's oceanic crust?

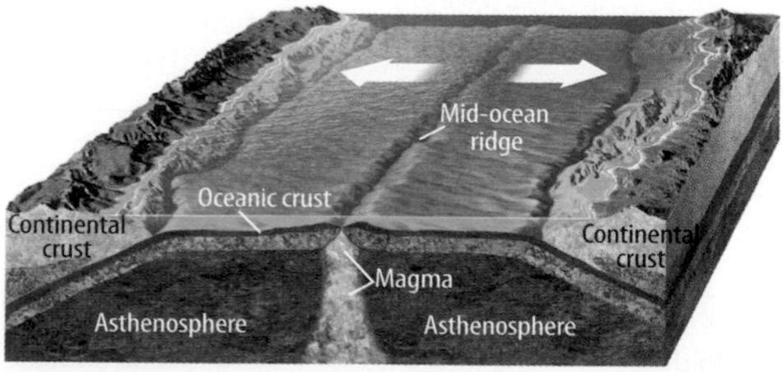

Critical Thinking

9. **Critique** the following statement: When igneous, sedimentary, or metamorphic rock is exposed to high temperatures and pressures, metamorphic rock forms.

AMERICAN MUSEUM of NATURAL HISTORY

CAREERS in SCIENCE

A supervolcano quietly simmers.

Volcanic rocks tell a story about a supervolcano's explosive past and provide clues about future eruptions.

Yellowstone National Park in Wyoming is home to thousands of natural wonders such as erupting geysers, simmering steam vents, gurgling mud pots, and colorful hot springs. Their source—superheated magma—is stored in a magma chamber that simmers a few kilometers below the park. Yellowstone is home to the largest active volcanic area in North America. Some of its past eruptions were so explosive that ash spread across the North American continent earning Yellowstone the title of supervolcano.

How do supervolcanoes form? Sarah Fowler, a geologist with the American Museum of Natural History, is searching for clues. She studies magma chambers under supervolcanoes such as Yellowstone to determine the cause of explosive eruptions. Since she can't sample the magma chamber directly, she analyzes rocks that erupted from the supervolcano in the past.

Pumice

Tuff

What do the rocks tell her? Fowler studies pumice, a lightweight volcanic rock filled with tiny holes. These holes were left behind as gas escaped from molten material during cooling and crystallization. Lava and ash that contain trapped gas erupt explosively, so Fowler knows the presence of pumice indicates an explosive past. Fowler also studies a volcanic rock called tuff. During a gas-rich eruption, a volcano ejects ash into the atmosphere. The ash settles and eventually accumulates in layers, fusing together to form tuff. Fowler examines the size of the ash to determine where the blast originated. Larger fragments fall closer to the source. Smaller ones are carried by wind and fall farther away. When Fowler finds rocks such as pumice and tuff, she records their location and studies their texture and composition. With these data, she can produce computer models that simulate past eruptions.

It is unlikely that Yellowstone will erupt any time soon; however, geologists monitor earthquake activity and other indicators for signs of a future eruption.

It's Your Turn

WRITE Imagine you are a geologist, and you discover an igneous rock, such as basalt or granite. Describe the rock in your Science Journal. Conduct some research to explain where this rock formed and the processes that led to its formation.

Lesson 2

Igneous Rocks

Reading Guide

Key Concepts
ESSENTIAL QUESTIONS

- How do igneous rocks form?
- What are the common types of igneous rocks?

Vocabulary

extrusive rock p. 290
volcanic glass p. 290
intrusive rock p. 291

g Multilingual eGlossary

Video BrainPOP®

Academic Standards for Science

7.2.5 Describe the origin and physical properties of igneous, metamorphic and sedimentary rocks and how they are related through the rock cycle.

Also covers: 7.NS.4, 7.NS.5, 7.NS.6, 7.NS.7, 7.NS.9, 7.NS.10

Inquiry Can rock be liquid?

The composition and temperature of lava influence whether it will be thick and pasty or thin and fluid, like water. How did this lava form? When it cools and crystallizes, what type of rock will it become? Where does this type of rock commonly form?

Inquiry **Launch Lab** 15 minutes

How does igneous rock form?

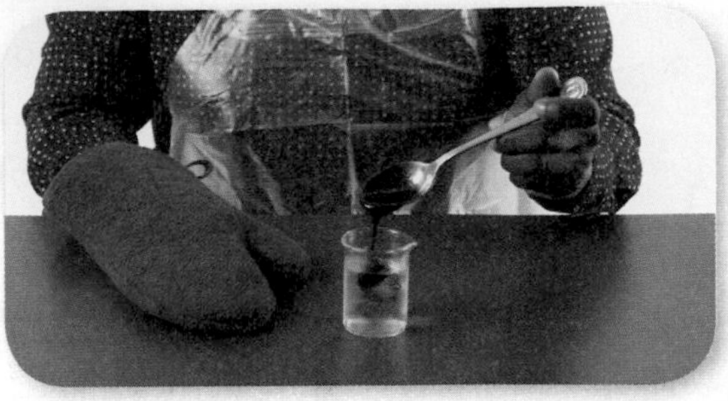

One way igneous rock forms is through the cooling and crystallization of lava. You might have seen video of molten lava flowing into the ocean. What do you think happens when the lava hits the cool ocean water?

1. Read and complete a lab safety form.
2. Observe as your teacher drips **hot, melted sugar** slowly into a **beaker** of cold water. Record what happens in your Science Journal.
3. Observe as your teacher quickly pours hot, melted sugar into a beaker of cold water. Record what happens in your Science Journal.
4. Examine each of the "candy rocks" that formed in the cold water.

Think About This

1. What is the difference between the candy rocks that formed in step 2 and the candy rocks that formed in step 3?
2. **Key Concept** How does this activity model the formation of igneous rocks?

Igneous Rock Formation

Do you remember what the difference is between magma and lava? Lava is magma that erupted onto Earth's surface during a volcanic eruption. When you hear the word lava, you might picture a hot, gooey liquid that flows easily. When lava cools and crystallizes, it becomes igneous rock. The lava shown in the picture on the previous page is already on its way to becoming solid igneous rock. It cools quickly after coming in contact with the cooler air around it. You can see where the lava has started to crystallize. It is the darker material on top of the red-hot, molten material below.

Not all magma makes it on to Earth's surface. Large volumes of magma cool and crystallize beneath Earth's surface. Under these conditions, cooling and crystallization takes a long time. The rock that results from subsurface cooling is different from the rock that results from lava cooling on Earth's surface. Over time wind, rain, and other factors can wear away materials on Earth's surface. The rock that was once deep underground may now be exposed on Earth's surface. Stone Mountain, shown in **Figure 7,** is an example of igneous rock that formed from magma cooling slowly underground.

Key Concept Check How do igneous rocks form?

Figure 7 Stone Mountain in Georgia is made of igneous rocks that formed underground and are now exposed on Earth's surface.

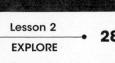

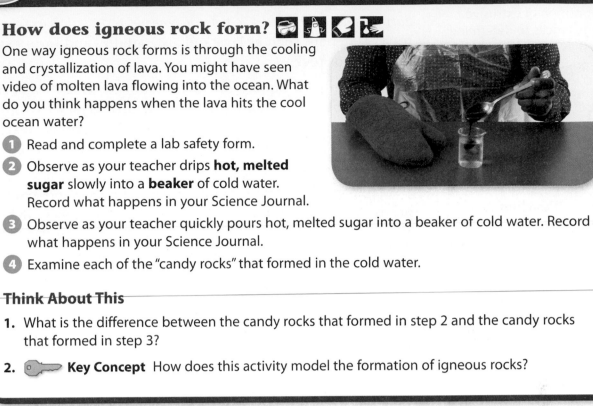

Figure 8 Geologists study the texture and composition of extrusive igneous rocks to determine how they formed.

Obsidian

Pumice

Extrusive Rocks

When volcanic material erupts and cools and crystallizes on Earth's surface, it forms a type of igneous rock called **extrusive rock.** Materials, such as lava and ash, solidify and form extrusive igneous rocks.

Lava can cool rapidly on Earth's surface. This means that there might not be enough time for any crystals to grow. Extrusive igneous rocks, therefore, have fine-grained texture. **Volcanic glass** *is rock that forms when lava cools too quickly to form crystals,* such as the obsidian shown in **Figure 8.**

Magma stored underground can contain dissolved gases. As magma moves toward the surface, pressure decreases, and the gases separate from the molten mixture. This is similar to the carbon dioxide that escapes when you open a carbonated beverage. When gas-rich lava erupts from a volcano, gases escape. Among the most noticeable features of some extrusive igneous rocks, such as pumice (PUH mus), are holes that are left after gas escapes, shown in **Figure 8.**

Reading Check Why are there holes in some igneous rocks?

Inquiry MiniLab

20 minutes

How are cooling rate and crystal size related?

Crystal size is directly related to the crystallization rate. In this lab, you will model crystal formation under different temperature conditions.

1. Read and complete a lab safety form.
2. Mix 10 mL of warm water with 10 mg of **Epsom salt** ($MgSO_4$). Dissolve completely.
3. Completely fill three **beakers** with hot, warm, or cold water. Label the beakers.
4. Place a **watch glass** on top of each beaker so its bottom is touching the water.
5. Measure 3 mL of the Epsom salt solution in a **graduated cylinder.** Pour this amount into each watch glass.
6. Leave overnight. Record your observations in your Science Journal.

Analyze and Conclude

1. **Describe** the crystals in each watch glass.
2. **Infer** In which watch glass did crystals form first?
3. **Hypothesize** How does your answer to question 2 relate to the cooling rate and crystal size of igneous rocks?
4. **Key Concept** Which watch glass represented the type of crystals found in extrusive igneous rocks? Which one represented intrusive igneous rocks?

Intrusive and Extrusive Rocks

Figure 9 Magma that cools and crystallizes beneath Earth's surface forms intrusive igneous rock. Lava or ash that erupts and cools on Earth's surface forms extrusive igneous rock.

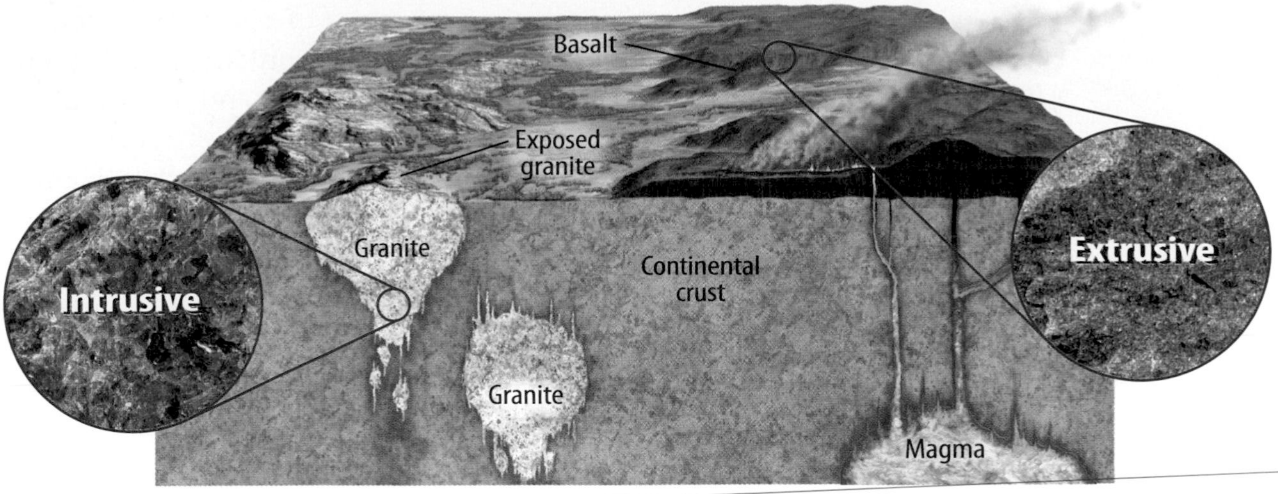

Visual Check Where is magma cooling slowly? Where is lava cooling quickly?

Intrusive Rocks

Igneous rocks that form as magma cools underground are called **intrusive rocks.** Because magma within Earth is insulated by solid rock, it cools more slowly than lava on Earth's surface. When magma cools slowly, large well-defined crystals form.

Figure 9 shows a cross section of Earth's crust where a magma chamber has solidified and formed **intrusive** rock. The arrangement of crystals in intrusive rocks is random. Crystals interlock like jigsaw puzzle pieces. A random arrangement and large crystals are typical of intrusive igneous rocks.

Reading Check Where do intrusive rocks form?

WORD ORIGIN

intrusive
from Latin *intrudere,* means "to push in"

Igneous Rock Identification

As you read in Lesson 1, two characteristics can help to identify all rocks: texture and composition. Geologists identify an igneous rock using the arrangement and size of mineral crystals in the rock. Chemical composition can also be used for igneous rock identification.

Texture

Geologists determine whether an igneous rock is extrusive or intrusive by studying the rock's texture. If the crystals are small or impossible to see without a magnifying lens, the rock is extrusive. If all the crystals are large enough to see and have an interlocking texture, the rock is intrusive.

FOLDABLES®

Use a sheet of paper to make a horizontal two-tab book. Collect information on extrusive and intrusive igneous rocks.

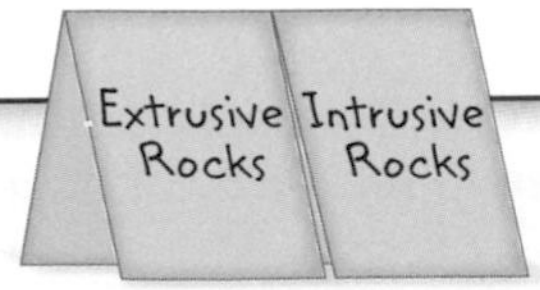

Composition

In addition to texture, geologists study the mineral composition of igneous rocks. Igneous rocks are classified, in part, based on their silica content. Light-colored minerals such as quartz and feldspar contain greater amounts of silica. Dark-colored minerals such as olivine and pyroxene contain less silica and greater amounts of elements like magnesium and iron. If minerals are difficult to identify, you can sometimes estimate the composition by observing how dark in color the rock is. Lighter-colored rocks are similar to granite in mineral composition. Darker-colored rocks are similar to basalt in composition.

Magma composition, the location where the lava or magma cools and crystallizes, and the cooling rate determine the type of igneous rock that forms. For example, granite is high in silica, and it cooled slowly beneath Earth's surface. Granite is an intrusive igneous rock. Basalt is an extrusive igneous rock that has low silica content. It formed as lava rapidly cooled on Earth's surface.

Table 1 organizes common igneous rocks according to their texture and mineral composition. Notice that an extrusive igneous rock can have the same mineral composition as an intrusive igneous rock, but their textures differ. Also notice that the minerals present in the rock affect the rock color.

Key Concept Check How are extrusive and intrusive rocks different?

Table 1 Geologists classify igneous rocks into two main groups according to texture and mineral composition.

Concepts in Motion

Interactive Table

Table 1 Common Igneous Rocks

Important Rock-Forming Minerals Present	Intrusive Texture *(all crystals visible with unaided eye)*	Extrusive Texture *(some or no crystals visible with unaided eye)*
quartz, feldspar, mica, amphibole	granite 	rhyolite 
pyroxene, feldspar, mica, amphibole, some quartz	diorite 	andesite 
olivine, pyroxene, feldspar, mica, amphibole, little or no quartz	gabbro 	basalt 

Assessment Online Quiz

Visual Summary

An extrusive igneous rock cools and crystallizes from volcanic material erupted on Earth's surface.

When lava cools fast, volcanic glass forms.

An intrusive igneous rock forms as magma cools and crystallizes deep inside Earth.

FOLDABLES®

Use your lesson Foldable to review the lesson. Save your Foldable for the project at the end of the chapter.

What do you think NOW?

You first read the statements below at the beginning of the chapter.

3. Large crystals form when lava cools quickly on Earth's surface.

4. Igneous rocks form when cooling magma crystallizes.

Did you change your mind about whether you agree or disagree with the statements? Rewrite any false statements to make them true.

Use Vocabulary

1. **Use the terms** *intrusive rock* and *extrusive rock* in a sentence.
2. **Recall** which type of igneous rock has the largest crystals.
3. **Describe** the formation of volcanic glass.

Understand Key Concepts

4. What causes holes to form in extrusive igneous rock?
   - **A.** crystals
   - **B.** gases
   - **C.** magma
   - **D.** water
5. Compare the texture of igneous rocks that crystallize deep inside Earth with those that crystallize on Earth's surface.
6. What process is required for minerals to crystallize from magma?
   - **A.** cooling
   - **B.** eruption
   - **C.** evaporation
   - **D.** melting
7. Which igneous rock contains the greatest amount of quartz?
   - **A.** basalt
   - **B.** gabbro
   - **C.** granite
   - **D.** scoria

Interpret Graphics

8. **Analyze** Which intrusive igneous rock has the same mineral composition as basalt?

9. **Organize** Draw a graphic organizer similar to the one below to identify different textures in igneous rocks.

Critical Thinking

10. **Predict** the texture of an igneous rock formed from an explosive volcanic eruption.

Inquiry **Skill Practice** **Compare and Contrast** 30 minutes

How do you identify igneous rocks?

Igneous rocks can be classified based on texture and mineral composition. The texture is dependent upon cooling environment. When magma cools slowly beneath Earth's surface, large crystals form. When lava cools quickly on Earth's surface, tiny crystals form. Color can be used to determine whether a rock is rich in silica. Geologists compare and contrast the texture and mineral composition of igneous rocks to determine the processes that formed them.

Materials

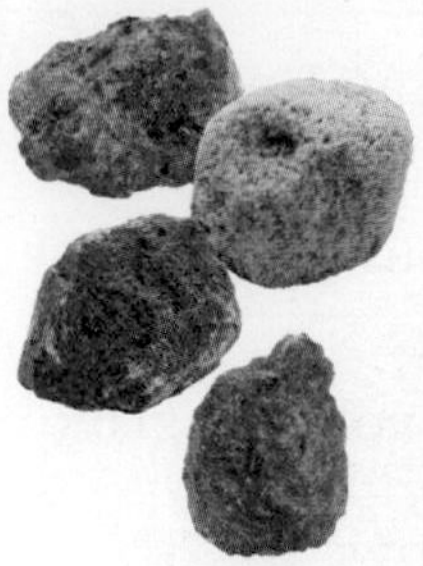

Igneous rocks (granite, pumice, basalt, gabbro, rhyolite, obsidian)

magnifying lens

Safety

Learn It

Comparisons help scientists to classify unknowns when given only a description of their properties. In this activity, you will **compare and contrast** a variety of igneous rocks and classify these rocks based on detailed descriptions of their texture and mineral composition.

Try It

1. Read and complete a lab safety form.
2. Copy the data table below in your Science Journal.
3. Obtain samples of granite and gabbro. These are both intrusive igneous rocks.
4. Describe the crystal size and color of granite and gabbro and record observations in your data table.
5. Now, obtain samples of pumice, basalt, and rhyolite. These are all extrusive igneous rocks.
6. Describe the crystal size and color of the extrusive rocks and record observations in your data table.
7. Finally, examine a sample of obsidian. Describe how this rock is different from other extrusive rocks.

Apply It

8. **Think Critically** Why do you think that obsidian (volcanic glass) differs from the other extrusive igneous rocks?
9. **Infer** Is pumice less dense than rhyolite? Explain your answer.
10. **Key Concept Check** How do the intrusive and extrusive igneous rocks differ?

Igneous Rock Characteristics

Rock	Texture: Crystal Size	Color
Granite		
Gabbro		
Pumice		
Basalt		
Rhyolite		
Obsidian		

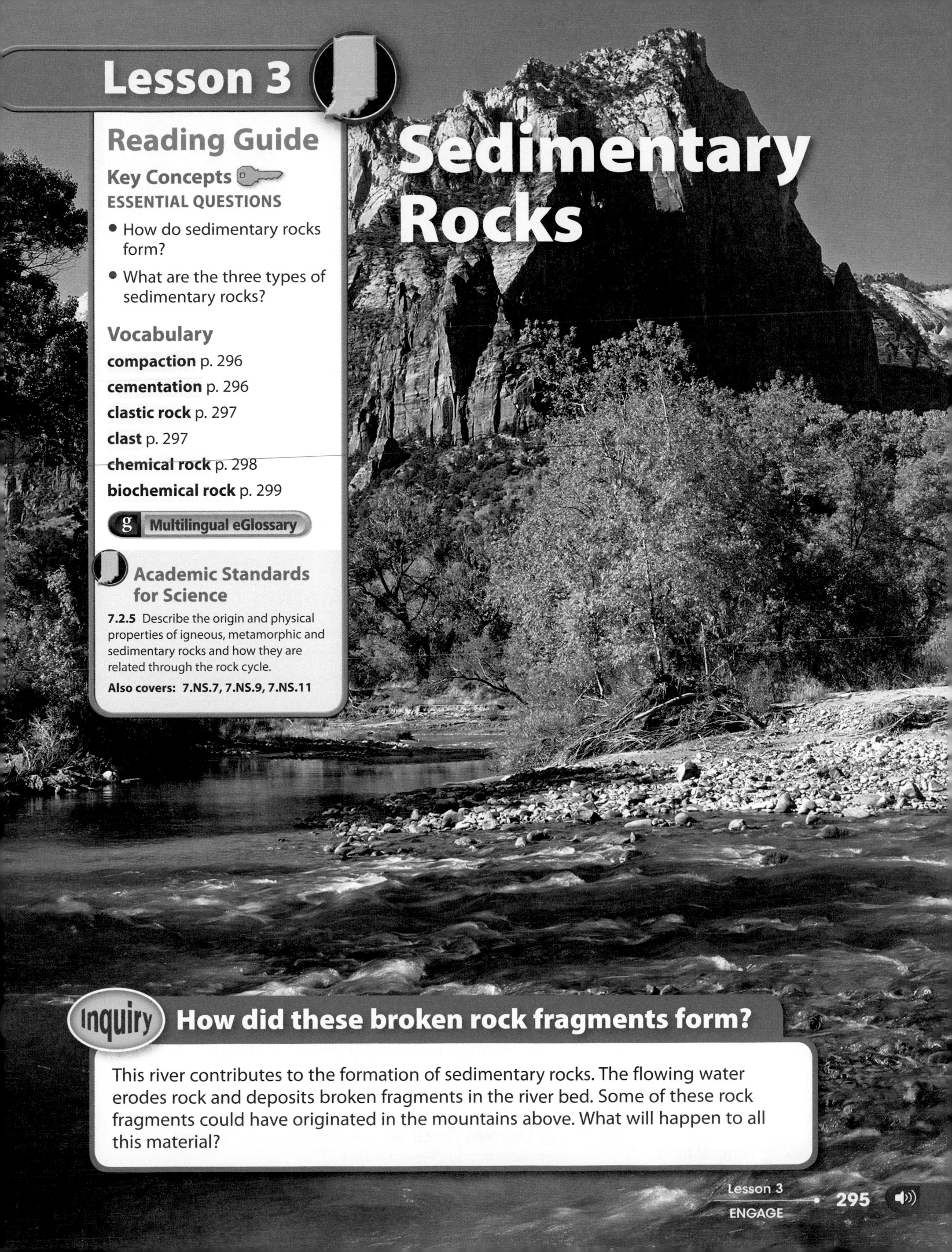

Lesson 3

Sedimentary Rocks

Reading Guide

Key Concepts
ESSENTIAL QUESTIONS

- How do sedimentary rocks form?
- What are the three types of sedimentary rocks?

Vocabulary
compaction p. 296
cementation p. 296
clastic rock p. 297
clast p. 297
chemical rock p. 298
biochemical rock p. 299

g Multilingual eGlossary

Academic Standards for Science

7.2.5 Describe the origin and physical properties of igneous, metamorphic and sedimentary rocks and how they are related through the rock cycle.

Also covers: 7.NS.7, 7.NS.9, 7.NS.11

Inquiry How did these broken rock fragments form?

This river contributes to the formation of sedimentary rocks. The flowing water erodes rock and deposits broken fragments in the river bed. Some of these rock fragments could have originated in the mountains above. What will happen to all this material?

Inquiry **Launch Lab** **20 minutes**

How do sedimentary rocks differ?

Sedimentary rocks are made from mixtures of mineral grains, rock fragments, and sometimes organic material. Can you compare grain sizes and determine types of sedimentary rock?

1. Read and complete a lab safety form.
2. Obtain a set of **labeled samples** from your teacher.
3. Use a **hand lense** to closely examine the sediment that makes up rock sample A. Record your observations in your Science Journal.
4. Repeat step 3 with the other samples in your set.
5. Review your notes and determine how many different types of sedimentary rocks you have. Check with your teacher to see if you are correct.

Think About This

1. What characteristics did you use to distinguish between the rock samples?
2. **Key Concept** Why do you think sedimentary rocks are so common on Earth's surface?

Figure 10 After sediments are deposited, the process of compaction and cementation begins.

Review **Personal Tutor**

Sedimentary Rock Formation

Like igneous rocks, sedimentary rocks can form in different environments through a series of natural steps. Water and air can change the physical or chemical properties of rock. This change can cause rock to break apart, to dissolve, or to form new minerals. When water travels through rock, some of the elements in the rock can dissolve and be transported to new locations. Mineral and rock fragments can also be transported by water, glacial ice, gravity, or wind. The sediments eventually are deposited, or laid down, where they can then accumulate in layers.

Imagine sediment deposits becoming thicker over time. Younger sediment layers bury older sediment layers. Eventually, the old and young layers of sediment can be buried by even younger sediment deposits. *The weight from the layers of sediment forces out fluids and decreases the space between grains during a process called* **compaction.** Compaction can lead to a process called cementation. *When minerals dissolved in water crystallize between sediment grains, the process is called* **cementation.** Mineral cement holds the grains together, as shown in **Figure 10.** Common minerals that cement sediment together include quartz, calcite, and clay.

Key Concept Check What is the difference between compaction and cementation?

Sedimentary Rock Identification

Like igneous rocks, sedimentary rocks are classified according to how they form. Sedimentary rocks form when sediments, rock fragments, minerals, or organic materials are deposited, compacted, and then cemented together. They also form during evaporation when minerals crystallize from water or when organisms remove minerals from the water to make their shells or skeletons.

Clastic Sedimentary Rocks

Some rocks, such as sandstone, have a gritty texture that is similar to sugar. Sandstone is a common clastic sedimentary rock. *Sedimentary rocks that are made up of broken pieces of minerals and rock fragments are known as* **clastic (KLAH stik) rocks.** *The broken pieces and fragments are called* **clasts.**

Geologists identify clastic rocks according to clast size and shape. The conglomerate in **Figure 11** is an example of a rock that was deposited in a river channel. The large sediment pieces were polished and rounded as they bounced along the bottom of the channel. However, the angular fragments in the breccia in **Figure 11** probably weren't transported far, because their sharp edges were not worn away.

Sediment size alone cannot be used to determine the environment where a clastic rock formed. For example, sediment deposited by a glacier can be the size of a car or as small as grains of flour. That's because ice can move both large and small clasts. Geologists study the shape of clasts to help determine the environment where a rock formed. For example, a fast-flowing river and ocean waves tend to move large sediment. Small, gritty sediment is typically deposited in calm environments such as the seafloor or the bottom of a lake.

Reading Check Why can't sediment size alone be used to identify a sedimentary rock environment?

FOLDABLES®

Use a sheet of paper to make a vertical two-tab book. Collect information on clastic and chemical sedimentary rocks.

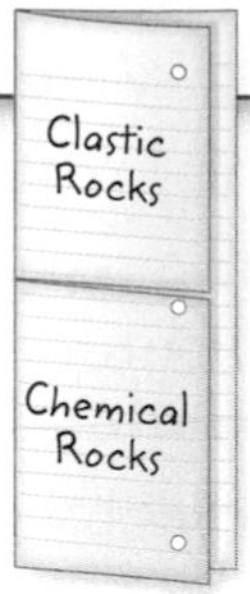

WORD ORIGIN

clastic
from Greek *klastos,* means "broken"

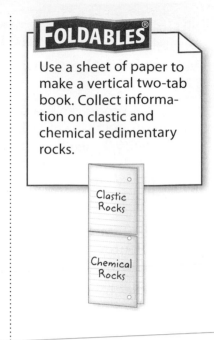

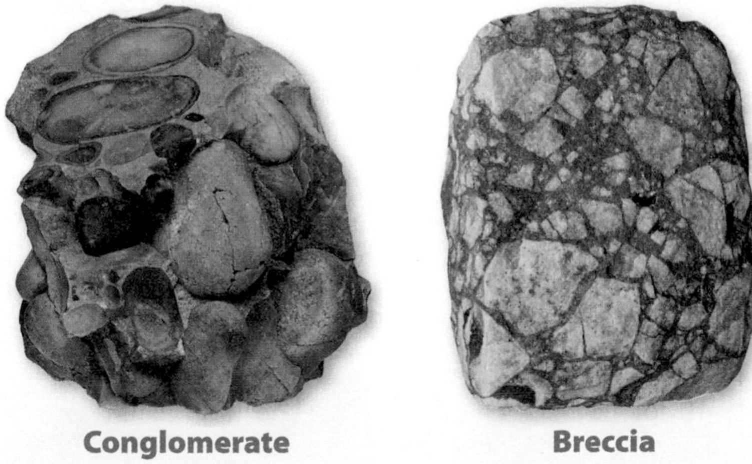

Figure 11 The clasts in this conglomerate were rounded by a fast flowing river. The forces that created the angular fragments may not have been as strong or as long-lived.

Inquiry MiniLab — 15 minutes

Where did these rocks form?

Sedimentary rocks can be classified based on the size and shape of their grains. In this activity, you will identify sedimentary rocks and use their grains to infer the environment in which they likely formed.

1. Read and complete a lab safety form.
2. Obtain a set of **rock samples** from your teacher.
3. For each rock, think about where you have seen a similar rock or the grains that this rock is made of.
4. Copy the table below in your Science Journal. Estimate and record the relative grain size and shape for each sample. Then, propose a possible environment where each rock may have formed.

	Grain Size/Shape	Environment
A		
B		
C		

Analyze and Conclude

1. **Organize** Imagine yourself standing on the beach. Arrange your samples according to the place they might have formed, from shoreline outward.
2. **Describe** the grain size for each sample.
3. **Key Concept** What types of sedimentary rocks are in your sample set?

Chemical Sedimentary Rocks

Remember that as water flows through cracks or empty spaces in rock, it can dissolve minerals in the rock. Eventually rivers carry these dissolved minerals to the oceans. Dissolved minerals entering the ocean contribute to the saltiness of seawater.

Water can become saturated with dissolved minerals. When this occurs, particles can crystallize out of the water and form minerals, as shown in **Figure 12. Chemical rocks** *form when minerals crystallize directly from water.* Rock salt, rock gypsum, and limestone are examples of common chemical sedimentary rocks.

Reading Check How do chemical rocks form?

Chemical sedimentary rocks often have an interlocking crystalline texture, similar to the textures of many igneous rocks. One difference between intrusive igneous rocks and chemical sedimentary rocks is that igneous rocks are composed of a variety of minerals and they appear multicolored. Chemical sedimentary rocks are generally composed of one dominant mineral and are uniform in color. For example, granite is made of quartz, feldspar, and mica, but rock salt is composed only of the mineral halite.

Figure 12 The water that once filled this lake bed was saturated, or filled with, dissolved halite. The water evaporated and crystalline rock salt formed.

Table 2 Common Chemical and Biochemical Rocks

Rock Name	chemical limestone	rock gypsum	rock salt	fossiliferous limestone	chert	coal
Mineral Composition	calcite	gypsum	halite	aragonite or calcite	quartz	carbon**
Type	chemical	chemical	chemical	biochemical	biochemical*	biochemical
Example	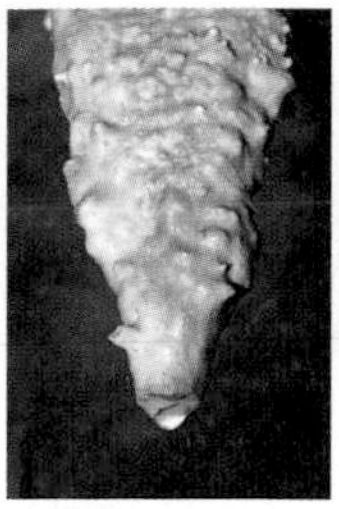					

*Some chert is not biochemical. **Carbon in coal is not a mineral.

Table 2 Chemical and biochemical sedimentary rocks are common on Earth's surface.

Concepts in Motion

Interactive Table

Biochemical Sedimentary Rocks

Biochemical rock *is a sedimentary rock that was formed by organisms or contains the remains of organisms.* The most common biochemical sedimentary rock is limestone. Marine organisms make their hard parts from dissolved minerals in the ocean. When these organisms die, their hard parts settle onto the seafloor. This sediment is compacted and cemented and forms limestone. Sometimes the remains or traces of these organisms are preserved as fossils in sedimentary rock. Geologists call limestone that contains fossils fossiliferous (FAH suh LIH fuh rus) limestone, shown in **Table 2.** Limestone is classified as a type of carbonate rock because it contains the elements carbon and oxygen. Carbonate rocks will fizz in the presence of hydrochloric acid. Geologists use this chemical property to help identify different varieties of limestone.

Not all biochemical sedimentary rocks are carbonates. Some microscopic ocean organisms make their shells by removing silicon and oxygen from seawater. When these organisms die and settle on the ocean floor, compaction and cementation turns this sediment into the sedimentary rock chert.

Coal is another type of biochemical sedimentary rock. It is composed of the remains of plants and animals from prehistoric swamps. Over time, these organic remains were buried. Burial led to compression, which eventually changed the remains into a sedimentary rock.

Key Concept Check How do chemical and biochemical sedimentary rocks form?

Lesson 3 Review

Assessment Online Quiz

Visual Summary

A clastic sedimentary rock is made of clasts of minerals or rock fragments.

When minerals crystallize directly from water, a chemical sedimentary rock results.

A biochemical sedimentary rock contains the remains living organisms or was formed by organisms.

FOLDABLES®

Use your lesson Foldable to review the lesson. Save your Foldable for the project at the end of the chapter.

What do you think NOW?

You first read the statements below at the beginning of the chapter.

5. Water can dissolve rock.

6. All sedimentary rocks on Earth formed from the remains of organisms that lived in oceans.

Did you change your mind about whether you agree or disagree with the statements? Rewrite any false statements to make them true.

Use Vocabulary

1. **Use the term** *compaction* in a sentence.
2. Coal is an example of a type of sedimentary rock called a(n) ________.
3. **Distinguish** among clastic, chemical, and biochemical sedimentary rock.

Understand Key Concepts

4. Which is a clastic rock?
   - **A.** coal
   - **B.** limestone
   - **C.** rock gypsum
   - **D.** sandstone
5. **Classify** the following sedimentary rocks as clastic, chemical, or biochemical: conglomerate, rock gypsum, fossiliferous limestone, and rock salt.
6. Identify a factor that is NOT responsible for the formation of sedimentary rocks.
   - **A.** glacier
   - **B.** magma
   - **C.** river
   - **D.** wind

Interpret Graphics

7. **Compare and contrast** the textures of conglomerate and breccia.
8. **Organize** Describe the formation of clastic sedimentary rocks from the first step to the last step. Rearrange the following terms in the correct order: transportation, cementation, deposition, erosion.

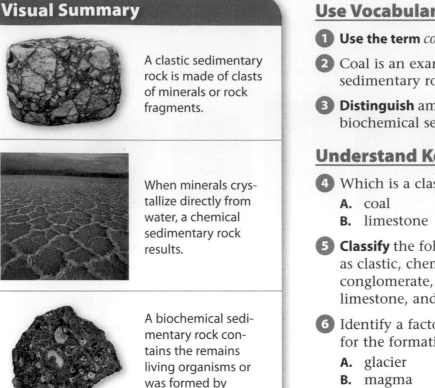

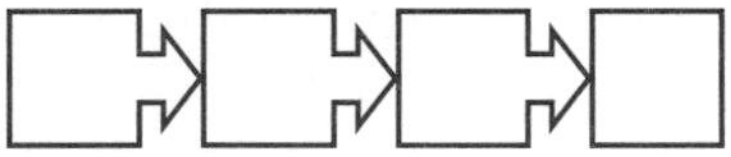

Critical Thinking

9. **Hypothesize** Over time, limestone dissolves in the presence of acid rain on Earth's surface. Relate this chemical property to the use of limestone for the construction of buildings and monuments.
10. **Analyze** this statement: As rock erodes, rivers carry dissolved minerals to the ocean, increasing the saltiness of seawater.

Inquiry **Skill Practice** **Observe** 30 minutes

How are sedimentary rocks classified?

For millions of years, rocks on Earth's surface have eroded with the help of water, wind, ice, and gravity. Sediments are transported and deposited, settling to the bottom of rivers, lakes, and oceans. Layers of sediment accumulate and undergo compaction and cementation and become a sedimentary rock. In this activity, you will use a flow chart to identify different sedimentary rocks.

Materials

sedimentary rocks (limestone, sandstone, shale, conglomerate)

vinegar

dropper

magnifying lens

Safety

Learn It

Scientists make observations to help develop hypotheses. In this activity, you will **observe** the chemical and physical properties of sedimentary rocks to identify different rock types.

Try It

1. Read and complete a lab safety form.
2. Obtain a sample set of sedimentary rocks.
3. Copy the flowchart in your Science Journal.
4. Start at the top of the flowchart. If there are particles present, determine the size of the particles, and identify the sample.
5. If the rock is smooth to the touch, test the sample with vinegar. If the sample fizzes with vinegar, it is limestone. If it does not fizz, the sample is shale.
6. Repeat steps 4-5 for four different sedimentary rock samples.

Apply It

7. **Infer** Why was vinegar used in the lab?
8. **Identify** Are the samples you identified clastic, chemical, or biochemical?
9. **Key Concept Check** What characteristics can be used to organize sedimentary rocks for identification?

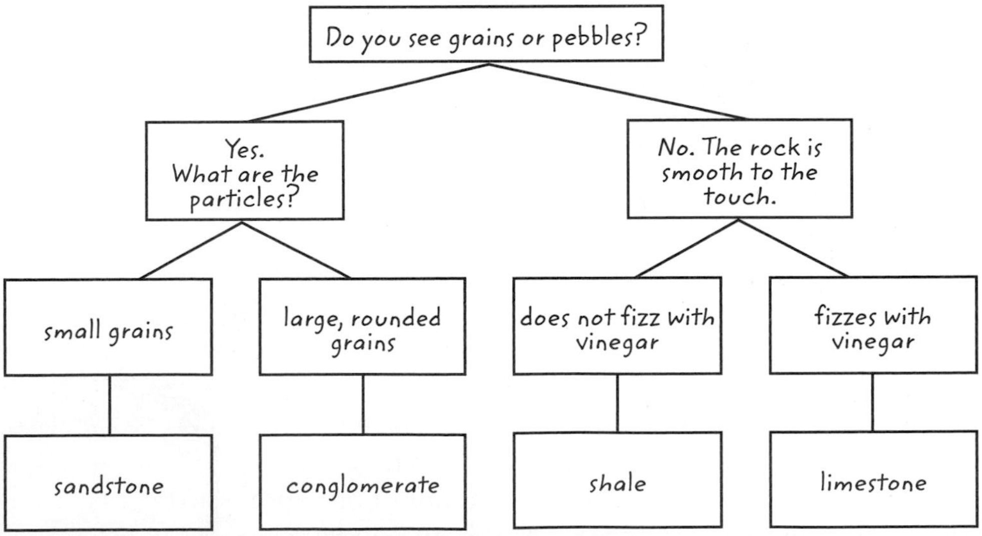

Sedimentary Rock Identification Chart

Lesson 4

Reading Guide

Key Concepts

ESSENTIAL QUESTIONS

- How do metamorphic rocks form?
- How do types of metamorphic rock differ?

Vocabulary

metamorphism p. 303
plastic deformation p. 304
foliated rock p. 305
nonfoliated rock p. 305
contact metamorphism p. 306
regional metamorphism p. 306

g Multilingual eGlossary

Academic Standards for Science

7.2.5 Describe the origin and physical properties of igneous, metamorphic and sedimentary rocks and how they are related through the rock cycle.

Also covers: 7.NS.6, 7.NS.7, 7.NS.9, 7.NS.10, 7.NS.11

Metamorphic Rocks

Inquiry How did this wrinkle?

Sediment is usually deposited in horizontal layers. Under the right conditions, those layers can be bent and twisted. Imagine the incredible amount of pressure required to cause solid rock, such as this, to bend!

Inquiry Launch Lab

20 minutes

How does pressure affect rock formation?

How does pressure affect the minerals in a rock? The arrangement of minerals in a metamorphic rock can be used to help classify the rock.

1. Read and complete a lab safety form.
2. Place some rice grains on the table.
3. Roll a **ball of clay** on top of the **rice**. Knead the ball until the rice is evenly mixed in the clay.
4. Use a **rolling pin** or a **round can** to roll the clay to a thickness of about 0.5 cm. Draw and label a picture of the sheet of clay and the rice grains in your Science Journal.
5. Fold the edge of the clay closest to you toward the edge away from you. Roll the clay in the direction you folded it. Repeat and flatten the clay to a thickness of 0.5 cm again. Draw and label a picture of the sheet of clay and the rice grains in your Science Journal.

Think About This

1. Describe the differences you observed in the orientation of rice grains between steps 4 and 5.
2. **Key Concept** What force caused the orientation of rice grains in the clay to change? How might this process be similar to the formation of metamorphic rocks?

Metamorphic Rock Formation

Imagine you left a cheese sandwich in your backpack on a hot day and then threw your backpack into your locker. Would the sandwich look the same after school? Changes in the temperature during the day would likely cause the cheese to soften. Pressure from the weight of your backpack would squish the sandwich. Like the sandwich, rocks are also affected by changes in temperatures and pressure. These rocks are called metamorphic rocks. **Metamorphism** *is any process that affects the structure or composition of a rock in a solid state as a result of changes in temperature, pressure, or the addition of chemical fluids.*

Most metamorphic rocks form deep within Earth's crust. Like igneous rocks, metamorphic rocks form under high temperature and pressure conditions. But unlike igneous rocks, metamorphic rocks do not crystallize from magma. Unlike sedimentary rocks, metamorphic rocks do not result from erosion and deposition. The metamorphic rocks shown on the facing page have changed shape. **Exposed** to extreme temperatures and pressure, the rocks were bent and twisted into wrinkly layers and are classified as metamorphic rocks.

Academic Vocabulary
expose
(verb) to appear visible

Reading Check What is metamorphism?

Inquiry MiniLab — 20 minutes

Can you model metamorphism?

Extreme temperatures and pressure can cause metamorphism. In this activity, you will model the formation of a metamorphic rock using bread and cheese spread.

1. Read and complete a lab safety form.
2. Get two pieces of **white bread**, two pieces of **wheat bread**, some **cheese spread**, and a **plastic knife** from your teacher.
3. Place a **paper towel** on the lab table.
4. Stack the bread on the paper towel in this order: white bread, wheat bread, cheese spread, white bread, wheat bread.

5. Place another paper towel on top of your stack and press down on your stack with a heavy **book.**
6. Remove the book and slowly fold your stack in half.
7. Place a paper towel on top and push down on your sandwich layers again.
8. Heat the layers in an **oven** or a **microwave oven** for about 2 minutes.

Analyze and Conclude

1. **Describe** What is the parent rock in your model of metamorphism?
2. **Interpret** In which step did you model plastic deformation? Explain.
3. **Think Critically** In what ways is your model different from metamorphism?
4. **Key Concept** Explain how changes in temperature and pressure play a role in the formation of a metamorphic rock.

Temperature and Pressure

When rocks experience an increase in temperature and pressure, they behave like a bendable plastic. Without melting, the rocks bend or fold. This *permanent change in shape by bending and folding is called* **plastic deformation.** It's one way the texture of a rock changes during metamorphism. Plastic deformation occurs during uplift events when tectonic plates collide and form mountains, such as the Himalayas in Asia. Changes in composition and structure are clues that a rock has been metamorphosed.

The rock that changes during metamorphism is called the parent rock. The temperatures required to metamorphose rock depend on the parent rock's composition. The lower limit of the temperature range for metamorphic rock formation is between 150°C and 200°C. In addition to temperature, pressure also increases with depth in Earth's crust and mantle, as shown in **Figure 13.** Pressure is measured in kilobars (kb).

Key Concept Check Under what conditions do metamorphic rocks form?

Figure 13 Pressure increases with depth in Earth.

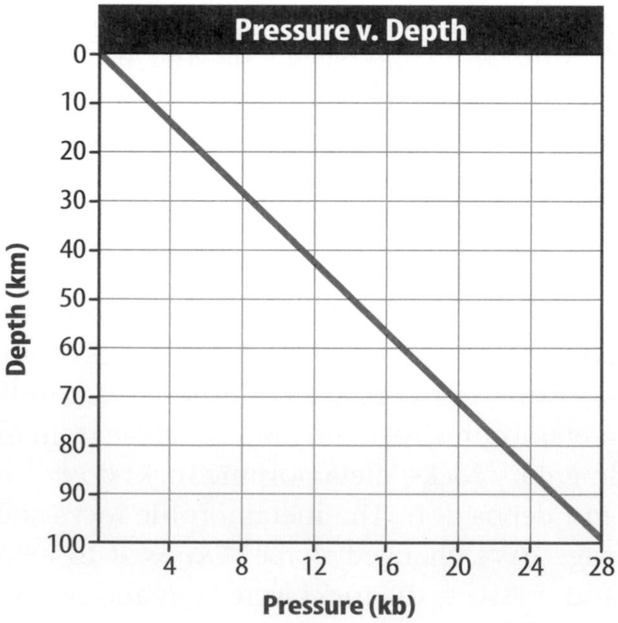

Metamorphic Rock Identification

Changes in temperature, pressure, or the addition of chemical fluids can result in the rearrangement of minerals or the formation of new minerals in a metamorphic rock. Geologists study the texture and composition of minerals to identify metamorphic rocks.

Metamorphic rocks are classified into two groups based on texture. In many cases, changes in pressure cause minerals to align and form layers in metamorphic rocks. This layering can appear similar to the layers associated with clastic sedimentary rocks. However, the crystalline minerals present in a metamorphic rock distinguish it from a clastic sedimentary rock. In other cases, the rock can have blocky, interlocking crystals that appear uniform in color.

Foliated Rocks

The metamorphic rock schist, shown in **Figure 14,** is an example of a foliated rock. **Foliated rocks** *contain parallel layers of flat and elongated minerals.* Look closely at the layers of dark and light minerals in the schist. This layering results from an an uneven distribution of pressure during metamorphism. Foliation is a common feature in metamorphic rocks.

Reading Check What type of metamorphic rock has layers?

Nonfoliated Rocks

Metamorphic rocks that have mineral grains with a random, interlocking texture are **nonfoliated rocks.** There is no obvious alignment of the mineral crystals in a nonfoliated metamorphic rock. Instead, the individual crystals are blocky and approximately equal in size. This crystalline texture differs from an igneous rock in that the minerals are generally uniform in color as opposed to multicolored, as in igneous rocks such as granite.

Math Skills

Use Graphs

The line graph in **Figure 13** represents pressure below Earth's surface. What is the pressure at a depth of 50 km?

a. Read the title of the graph to determine what data are represented.

b. Read the labels on the *x*- and *y*-axis to determine the units.

c. Move horizontally from 50 km to the orange line. Move vertically from the orange line to the *x*-axis. The pressure is 14 kb.

Practice

At what depth is the pressure 20 kb?

Review

- **Math Practice**
- **Personal Tutor**

WORD ORIGIN

foliate
from Latin *foliatus,* means "consisting of thin, leaf-like layers"

Figure 14 Elongated or flat minerals in foliated rocks line up in response to pressure.

Visual Check Can you determine the direction that pressure was applied?

Figure 15 Nonfoliated rocks don't show obvious orientation of minerals.

Contact and Regional Metamorphism

One way a nonfoliated metamorphic rock can form is when magma intrudes rock. *During* **contact metamorphism**, *magma comes in contact with existing rock, and its thermal energy and gases interact with the surrounding rock and forms new metamorphic rock.* Contact metamorphism can increase crystal size or form new minerals and change rock. A common example of a nonfoliated rock, marble, is shown in **Figure 15.** Notice the uniform color and crystal size in this specimen. **Table 3** illustrates other examples of nonfoliated and foliated metamorphic rocks.

Regional metamorphism *is the formation of metamorphic rock bodies that are hundreds of square kilometers in size.* This process can create an entire mountain range of metamorphic rock. Changes in temperature and pressure and the presence of chemical fluids act on large volumes of rock and produce metamorphic textures. These textures can help unravel the mysteries of a mountain-building event. The Himalayas in Asia and the Appalachian Mountains of the eastern United States exhibit structures associated with regional metamorphism.

Key Concept Check Compare and contrast contact metamorphism and regional metamorphism.

Table 3 Metamorphic rocks are classified into two groups based on texture and mineral composition.

Concepts in Motion
Interactive Table

Table 3 Metamorphic Rocks

Texture		Composition	Rock Name	Example
Foliated	layered	quartz, mica, clay minerals	slate	
	layered	quartz, mica, clay minerals	phyllite	
	color bands	quartz, feldspar, amphibole, mica	schist	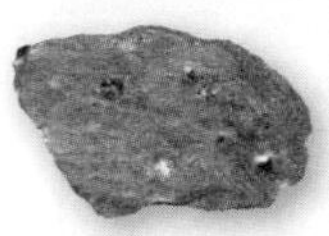
	color bands	quartz, feldspar, amphibole, pyroxene	gneiss	
Nonfoliated	blocky crystals	quartz	quartzite	
	blocky crystals	calcite	marble	

FOLDABLES®

Make a vertical two-tab book. Use it to organize your notes on contact and regional metamorphism.

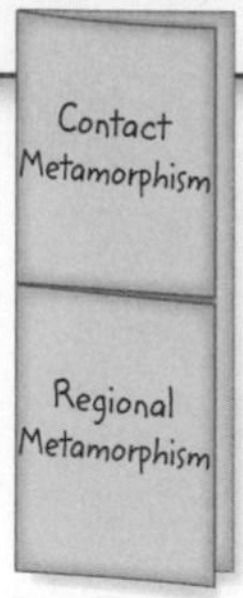

Lesson 4 Review

Assessment Online Quiz

Visual Summary

Foliated metamorphic rocks have distinct layers of flat and elongated minerals.

A nonfoliated metamorphic rock has minerals arranged in a random, interlocking texture.

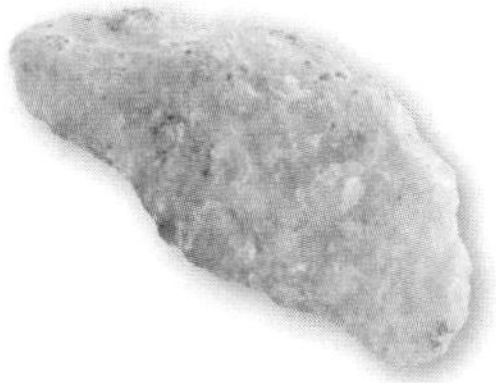

Contact metamorphism occurs when rocks come in contact with magma without melting.

FOLDABLES®

Use your lesson Foldable to review the lesson. Save your Foldable for the project at the end of the chapter.

What do you think NOW?

You first read the statements below at the beginning of the chapter.

7. With the right pressure and temperature conditions, minerals in a rock can change shape without breaking or melting.

8. Metamorphic rocks have layers that form as minerals melt and then recrystallize.

Did you change your mind about whether you agree or disagree with the statements? Rewrite any false statements to make them true.

Use Vocabulary

1. **Use the term** *plastic deformation* in a sentence.
2. Stacks of paper resemble ________ texture in metamorphic rocks.
3. Crystals in a ________ metamorphic rock are blocky and equal in size.

Understand Key Concepts

4. Which force contributes to the formation of metamorphic rocks?
   A. compaction
   B. cementation
   C. crystallization
   D. pressure
5. **Classify** the following rocks as either foliated or nonfoliated: quartzite, schist.

Interpret Graphics

6. **Identify** Create a graphic organizer to identify the three possible causes of metamorphism.

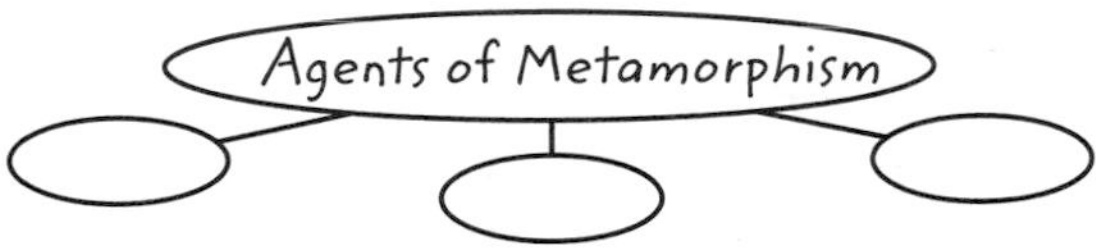

Critical Thinking

7. **Explain** how to differentiate between the igneous rock granite and the metamorphic rock gneiss.

Math Skills

Review Math Practice

8. **Based** on the graph below, what is the pressure at a depth of 40 km? At what depth would the pressure be 30 kb?

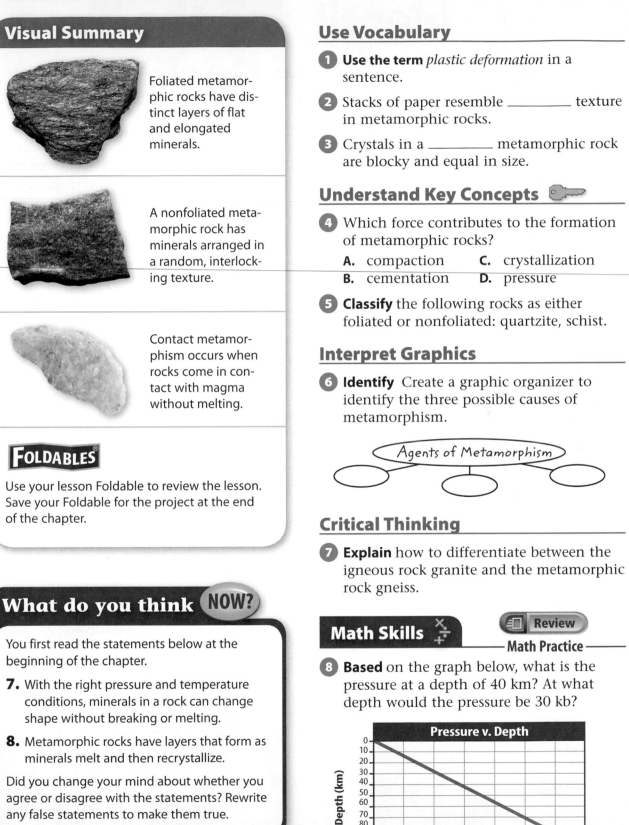

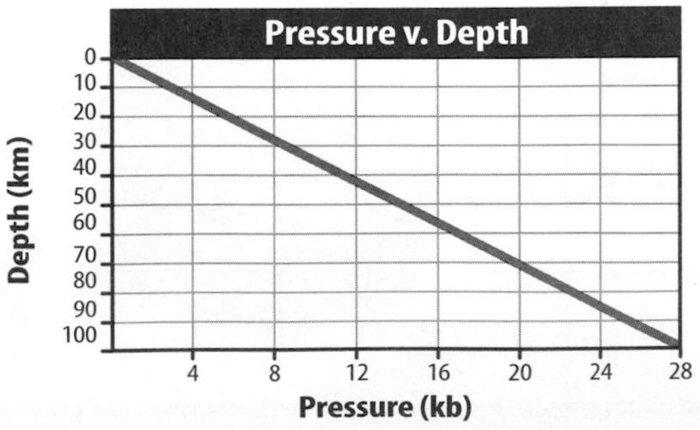

Identifying the Type of Rock

Materials

metamorphic rocks (marble, gneiss, schist)

vinegar

dropper

magnifying lens

rocks

Safety

Rocks can be classified into three major groups: igneous, sedimentary, and metamorphic. Geologists examine rock texture and mineral composition to classify rocks. Igneous rocks can be coarse or fine crystalline and multicolored or glassy. Sedimentary rocks are often layered and contain a mix of rock fragments, shells, minerals, and fossils. Metamorphic rocks can reflect a change in shape due to an increase in temperature and pressure or the addition of chemical fluids. Foliation is common in metamorphic rocks. In this activity, you will be given a variety of rock samples to try and classify based on physical and chemical properties.

Question

How can the texture and mineral composition of a rock be used to classify the rock as igneous, sedimentary, or metamorphic?

Procedure

1. Read and complete a lab safety form.
2. Obtain a metamorphic rock and examine its texture and grain size.
3. Record your observations in your Science Journal.
4. Does the rock have distinct, parallel layers? If so, it is a foliated metamorphic rock. If not, it is nonfoliated.
5. Use a dropper to place 1–2 drops of vinegar on the rock. If it fizzes, the rock contains the mineral calcite.
6. Repeat the classification steps with another metamorphic rock.

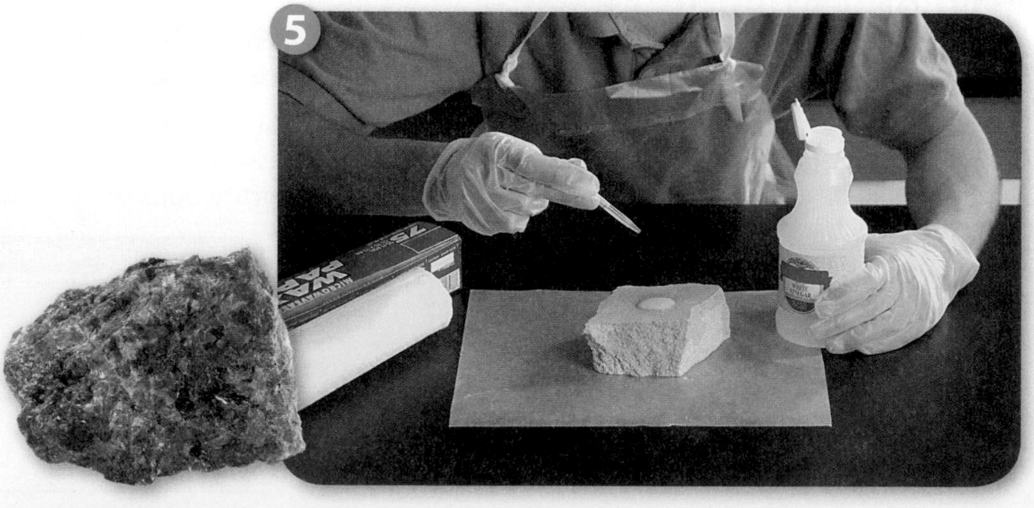

7 Design a flowchart for rock identification that incorporates the three rock types and all of the characteristics that you examined in each rock identification lab. Draw the flowchart in your Science Journal.

8 Experiment with your flowchart as you classify several unknown rock samples.

9 Refine the classification flowchart as needed so that it works for all samples that you are given.

10 Identify the unknown samples and incorporate their names into the flowchart that you created.

Analyze and Conclude

11 **Describe** why some samples were more difficult to classify than others.

12 **Explain** which characteristic was the least helpful in your classification scheme?

13 **The Big Idea** What characteristics made it easier to classify rock samples?

Communicate Your Results

Construct a poster of your final flowchart to share with your class. Be sure to label the characteristics and the choices at each step in the chart so that it is easy to follow.

Inquiry Extension

Research the rocks you identified in this activity. Explain how each rock formed, and describe the similarities and differences among the rock types.

Lab Tips

- ☑ Remember that the light or dark colors of a rock can lead to the identification of minerals in the rock.
- ☑ Rocks that fizz when acid, such as vinegar, is added to them contain the mineral calcite. Examples of such rocks include limestone and marble.

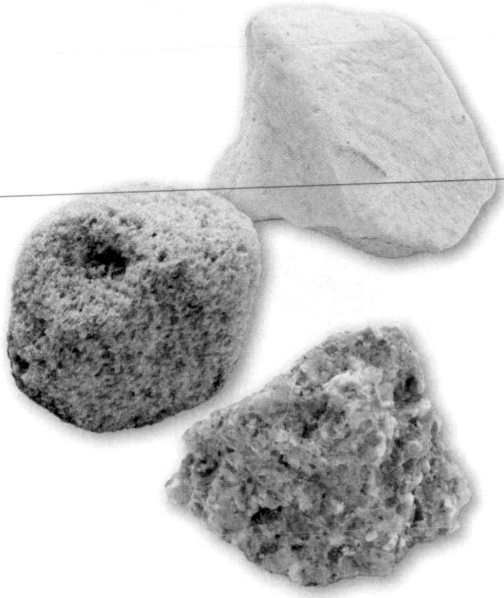

Remember to use scientific methods.

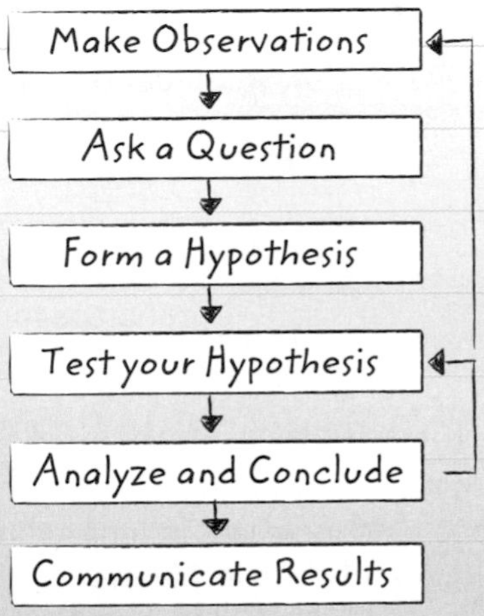

Chapter 8 Study Guide

WebQuest

THE BIG IDEA **Igneous rocks form from molten rock that cools and crystallizes. Sedimentary rocks form from compaction and cementation of sediments or evaporation and crystallization of minerals dissolved in water. Metamorphic rocks form from exposure of existing rocks to high pressures, temperatures, or the addition of chemical fluids.**

Key Concepts Summary

Lesson 1: Rocks and the Rock Cycle

- There are three major **rock** types—igneous, sedimentary, and metamorphic. Geologists study rock **texture** and mineral composition to identify rocks of each type.
- Rocks can melt or recrystallize. Rocks exposed on Earth's surface can break down due to forces such as water, ice, wind, and gravity. New rocks form under changing temperature and pressure conditions or the addition of chemical fluids.

Vocabulary

rock p. 281
grain p. 281
texture p. 282
magma p. 283
lava p. 283
sediment p. 283
rock cycle p. 284

Lesson 2: Igneous Rocks

- Igneous rocks form when volcanic material cools and crystallizes.
- Crystal size is dependent on how quickly the magma or lava cools.
- Igneous rocks range in color from light to dark, depending on their mineral composition.

Vocabulary

extrusive rock p. 290
volcanic glass p. 290
intrusive rock p. 291

Lesson 3: Sedimentary Rocks

- Weathering, erosion, transportation, deposition, **compaction, cementation,** and crystallization are the important processes in the formation of sedimentary rocks.
- A sedimentary rock's texture and mineral composition depends on where it formed and the forces that created it.

Vocabulary

compaction p. 296
cementation p. 296
clastic rock p. 297
clast p. 297
chemical rock p. 298
biochemical rock p. 299

Lesson 4: Metamorphic Rocks

- Metamorphic rocks form from a parent rock that has been exposed to increases in temperature, pressure, or the addition of chemical fluids.
- Some metamorphic rocks have **foliated** textures and are deformed. Others are composed of coarse and blocky crystals that are uniform in color.

Vocabulary

metamorphism p. 303
plastic deformation p. 304
foliated rock p. 305
nonfoliated rock p. 305
contact metamorphism p. 306
regional metamorphism p. 306

Review

- **Personal Tutor**
- **Vocabulary eGames**
- **Vocabulary eFlashcards**

FOLDABLES® Chapter Project

Assemble your lesson Foldables as shown to make a Chapter Project. Use the project to review what you have learned in this chapter.

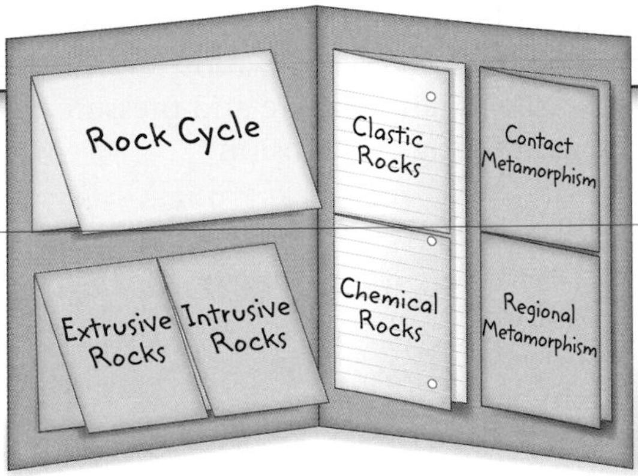

Use Vocabulary

1. Define *igneous rock.*
2. Use the word *sediment* in a sentence.
3. While remaining solid, a ________ forms at high pressure or temperatures.
4. Define *intrusive rock.*
5. Use the phrase *extrusive rock* in a sentence.
6. Identify two textures common in metamorphic rocks.
7. During ________, minerals such as calcite or quartz crystallize between grains of clastic rock.
8. A ________ texture gives a sedimentary rock a grainy appearance.
9. Use the term *chemical rock* in a sentence.
10. Describe a *nonfoliated rock.*
11. Folded layers are examples of ________ in a metamorphic rock.
12. Use the term *regional metamorphism* in a sentence.

Link Vocabulary and Key Concepts

Concepts in Motion **Interactive Concept Map**

Copy this concept map, and then use vocabulary terms from the previous page to complete the concept map.

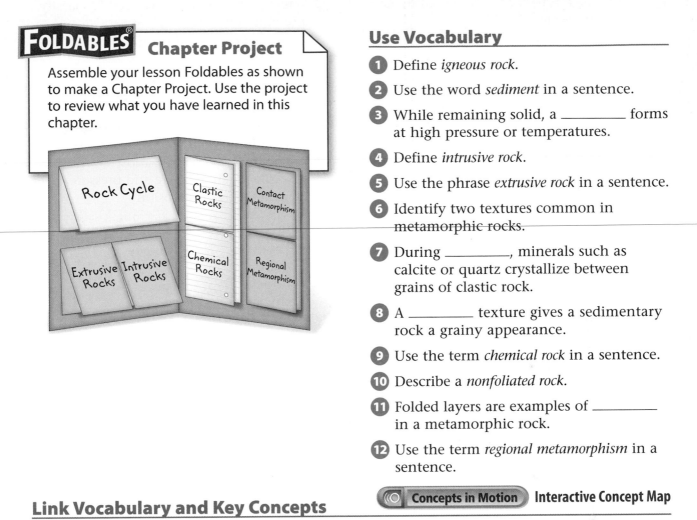

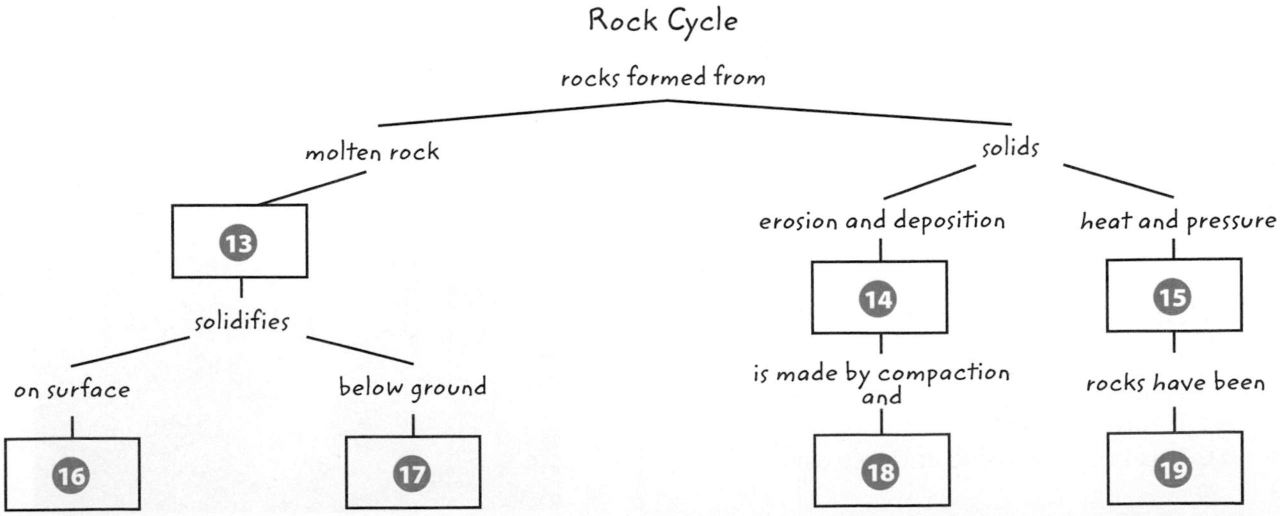

Chapter 8 Review

Understand Key Concepts

1. Which rock type forms from cooling lava on Earth's surface?
   A. extrusive igneous
   B. intrusive igneous
   C. granite
   D. limestone

2. Which process squeezes fluids from between individual grains?
   A. cementation
   B. compaction
   C. erosion
   D. transportation

3. Basalt is an example of a(n)
   A. extrusive igneous rock.
   B. intrusive igneous rock.
   C. metamorphic rock.
   D. sedimentary rock.

4. What can be determined by studying the shape of clastic grains?
   A. distance they have been transported
   B. how they were eroded
   C. mineral content of the parent rock
   D. what the parent rock was

5. Examine the rock above. Which type of rock contains fossils?
   A. basalt
   B. gneiss
   C. limestone
   D. rock gypsum

6. What is true about volcanic glass?
   A. It contains no crystals.
   B. It cools slowly.
   C. It fractures easily.
   D. It is both intrusive and extrusive.

7. Which characteristics are used to classify a sedimentary rock such as sandstone?
   A. glass content and texture
   B. grain size
   C. luster and hardness
   D. texture and mineral composition

8. How do metamorphic rocks form?
   A. compaction and cementation
   B. cooling and crystallization
   C. extreme temperature and pressure
   D. weathering and erosion

9. Which igneous rock cooled slowly?
   A. basalt
   B. granite
   C. obsidian
   D. rhyolite

10. What is the general term for a rock fragment present in a sedimentary rock?
    A. clast
    B. glass
    C. mineral
    D. pore

11. What process is occurring in this photo?
    A. cementation
    B. condensation
    C. crystallization
    D. evaporation

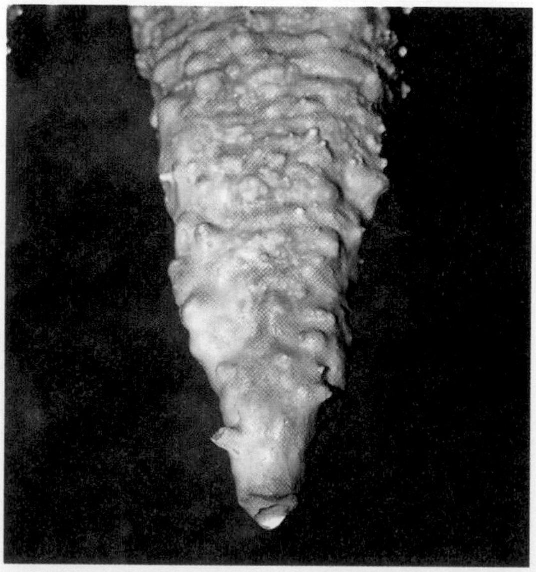

Assessment
Online Test Practice

Critical Thinking

12 **Decide** which of the three types of sedimentary rocks forms when water in a shallow sea evaporates.

13 **Complete** the chart below with at least three common rock names for each major rock type.

Rock Type	Rock Name
Igneous	
Sedimentary	
Metamorphic	

14 **Relate** What rock cycle process is the opposite of crystallization of magma?

15 **Compare** a rock cycle process on Earth's surface with a process that occurs below the surface.

16 **Hypothesize** Imagine the temperature inside Earth was no longer hot. How might this affect the rock cycle?

17 **Deduce** how a rock formed from an explosive volcanic eruption could resemble a clastic sedimentary rock.

18 **Hypothesize** how the direction of stress applied affects the arrangement of minerals in a metamorphic rock.

19 **Relate** the presence of the holes to the ability of pumice to float in water.

20 **Compare and contrast** the formation of gneiss to the formation of its parent rock, granite.

Writing in Science

21 **Write** a paragraph that distinguishes among the rock cycle processes that form metamorphic rocks and igneous rocks deep beneath Earth's surface.

REVIEW THE BIG IDEA

22 Use the rock cycle to explain how each rock type forms.

23 What might happen to the sand in the valley if more sand is deposited on top of it?

Math Skills

Review
Math Practice

Use the graph to answer the following questions.

24 At about what depth does the pressure reach 20 kb?

25 Use the trend on the graph to predict the approximate pressure at a depth of 200 km.

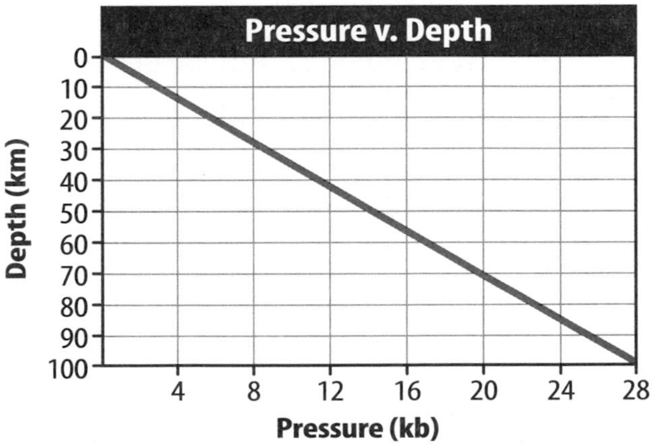

Standardized Test Practice

Record your answers on the answer sheet provided by your teacher or on a sheet of paper.

Multiple Choice

1 Light-colored minerals, such as quartz, contain greater amounts of

A iron.

B magnesium.

C manganese.

D silica.

Use the diagram below to answer question 2.

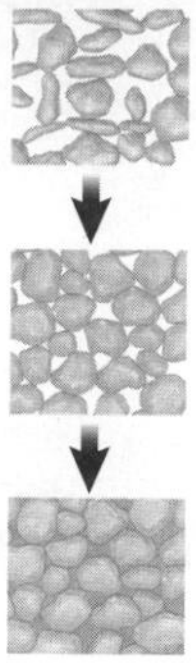

2 Which process is illustrated in the last part of the diagram above?

A cementation

B compaction

C metamorphism

D transport

3 Why don't crystals form in volcanic glass?

A The lava contained dissolved gases.

B The lava cooled deep within Earth.

C The lava cooled too quickly.

D The lava failed to erupt.

4 Marine organisms extract dissolved minerals from seawater to form ________ parts.

A basalt

B granite

C limestone

D marble

Use the graph below to answer question 5.

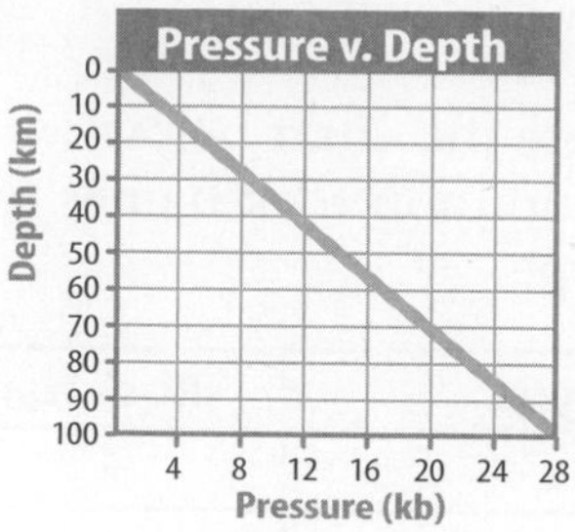

5 According to the graph above, how much greater is the pressure in Earth's interior at a depth of 100 km compared to a depth of 50 km?

A 12 kb

B 14 kb

C 16 kb

D 20 kb

6 Solid rocks exposed to changes in thermal energy, pressure, or the addition of chemical fluids form metamorphic rocks. Igneous, NOT metamorphic, rocks will form if

A the heat is withdrawn.

B the pressure decreases.

C the rock contains minerals.

D the rock melts.

7 A rock permanently changes shape by bending or folding during

A contact metamorphism.

B foliation.

C plastic deformation.

D sedimentation.

8 What is the term for broken pieces of rock?

A clasts

B crystals

C glass

D layers

Assessment

Online Standardized Test Practice

Use the diagram below to answer question 9.

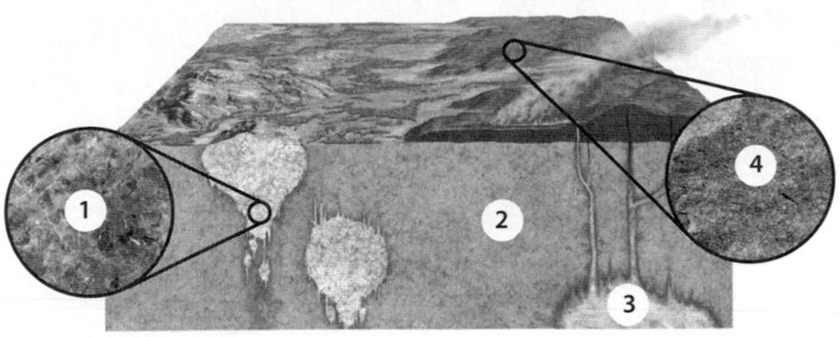

9 In the diagram above, which number represents extrusive igneous rock?

A 1
B 2
C 3
D 4

10 On what basis are rocks classified into three main groups?

A their texture
B the way they form
C their age
D their color

11 What condition produces the distinct layers of flat and elongated minerals in foliated metamorphic rocks?

A drastic changes in temperature
B random, interlocking texture
C uneven distribution of pressure
D uniformity of mineral colors

Constructed Response

Use the diagram below to answer questions 12 and 13.

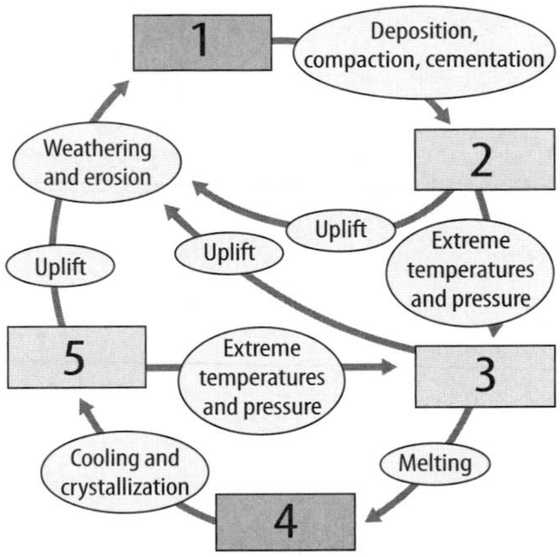

12 What do the numbers in the rock cycle above represent? Explain your reasoning.

13 Use the diagram above to identify and describe at least three processes that change rock as it travels through the rock cycle.

Use the table below to answer question 14.

Type of Rock	Process of Formation

14 What three main types of sedimentary rocks belong in column 1 of the table above? How does each type form?

NEED EXTRA HELP?														
If You Missed Question...	1	2	3	4	5	6	7	8	9	10	11	12	13	14
Go to Lesson...	2	3	2	3	4	1	4	3	2	1	4	1	1	3

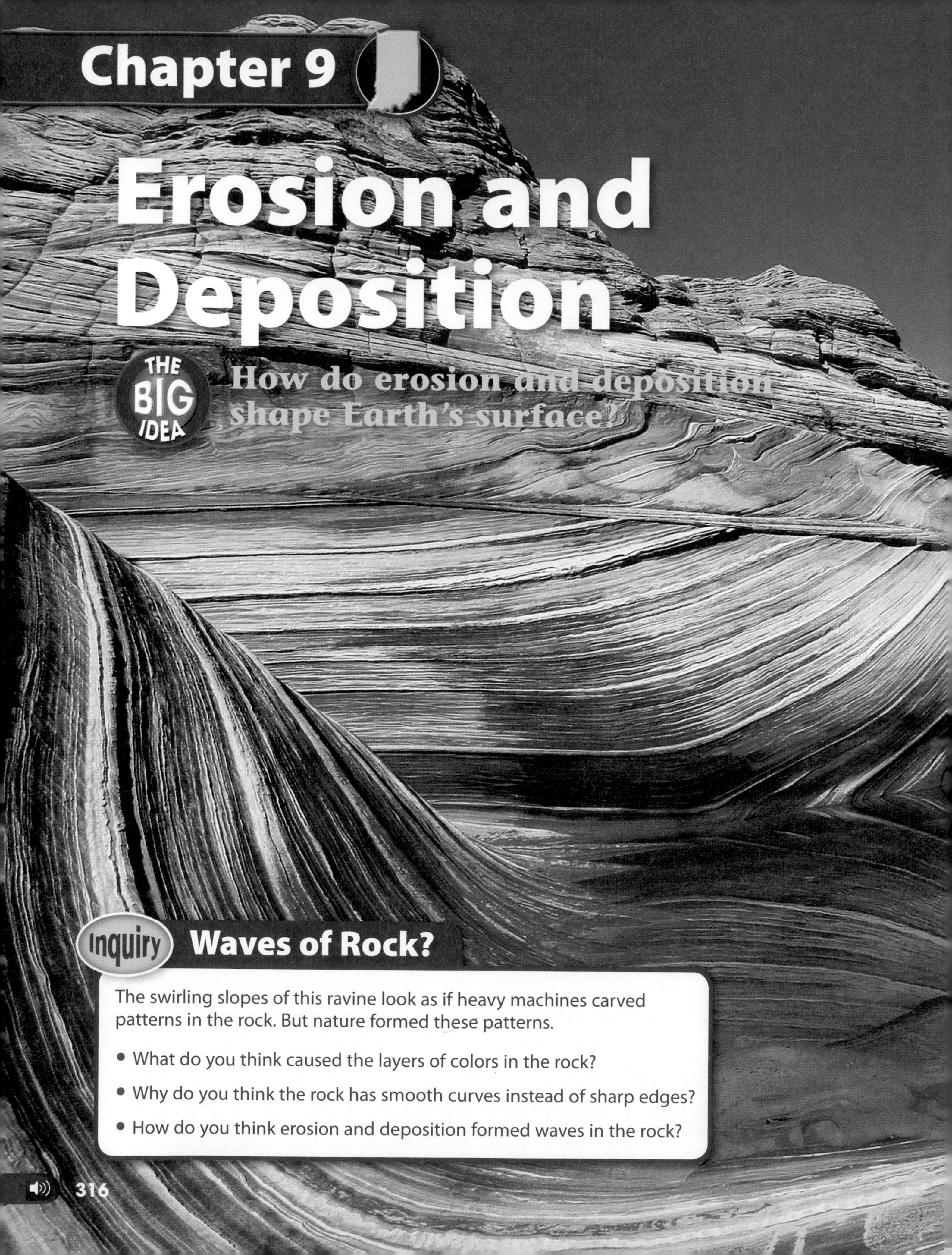

Chapter 9

Erosion and Deposition

THE BIG IDEA **How do erosion and deposition shape Earth's surface?**

Inquiry Waves of Rock?

The swirling slopes of this ravine look as if heavy machines carved patterns in the rock. But nature formed these patterns.

- What do you think caused the layers of colors in the rock?
- Why do you think the rock has smooth curves instead of sharp edges?
- How do you think erosion and deposition formed waves in the rock?

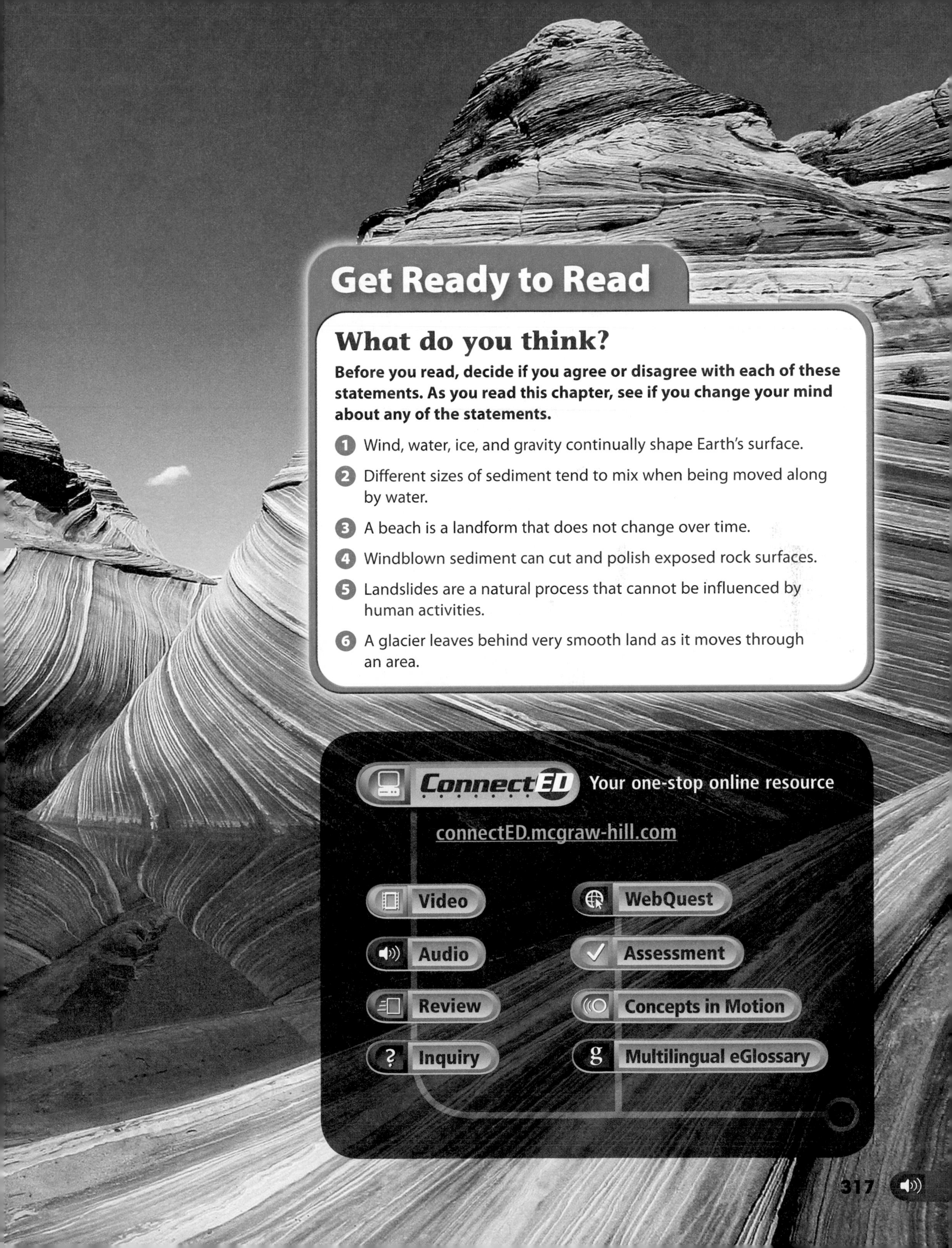

Get Ready to Read

What do you think?

Before you read, decide if you agree or disagree with each of these statements. As you read this chapter, see if you change your mind about any of the statements.

1. Wind, water, ice, and gravity continually shape Earth's surface.
2. Different sizes of sediment tend to mix when being moved along by water.
3. A beach is a landform that does not change over time.
4. Windblown sediment can cut and polish exposed rock surfaces.
5. Landslides are a natural process that cannot be influenced by human activities.
6. A glacier leaves behind very smooth land as it moves through an area.

ConnectED Your one-stop online resource

connectED.mcgraw-hill.com

- Video
- Audio
- Review
- Inquiry
- WebQuest
- Assessment
- Concepts in Motion
- Multilingual eGlossary

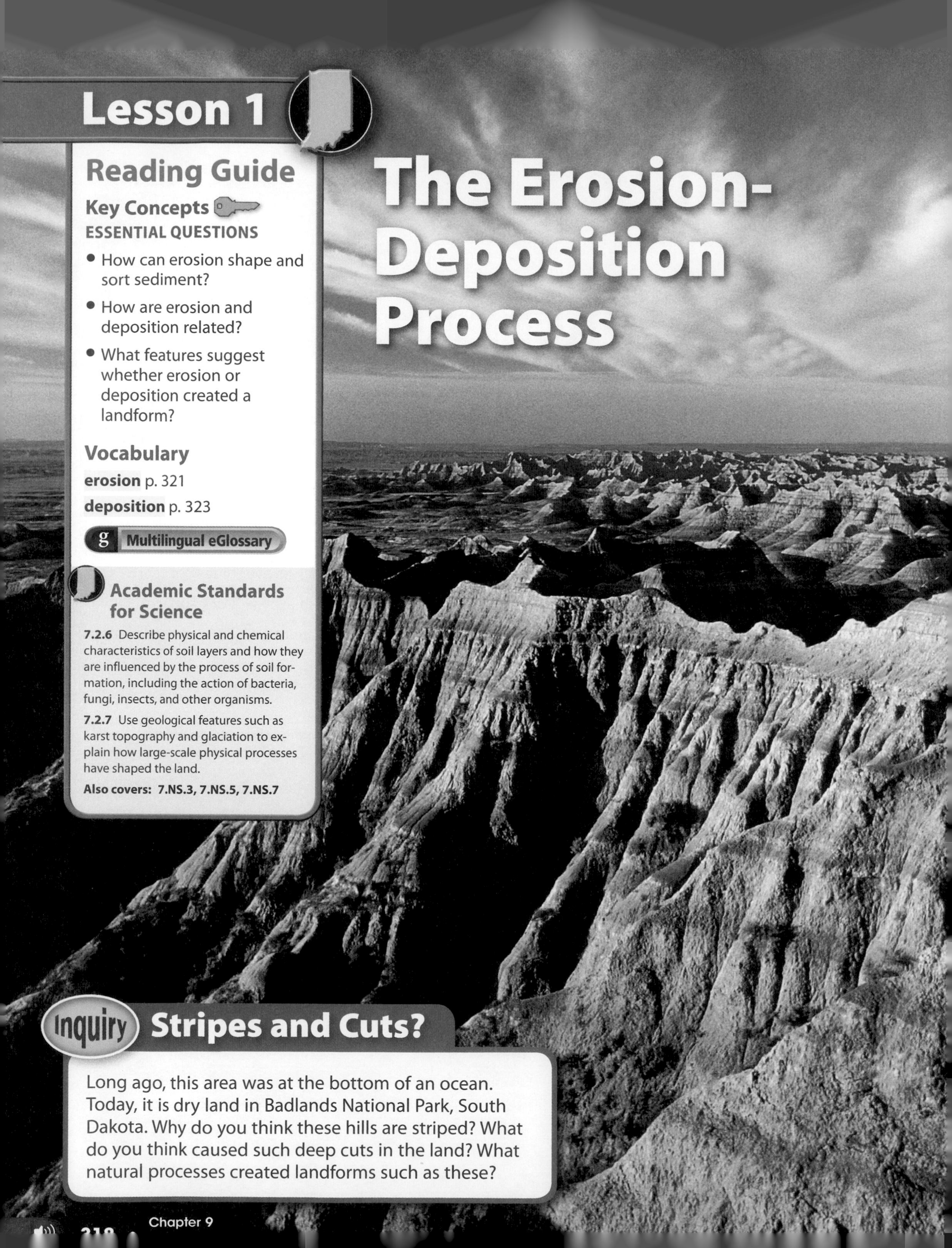

Lesson 1

The Erosion-Deposition Process

Reading Guide

Key Concepts

ESSENTIAL QUESTIONS

- How can erosion shape and sort sediment?
- How are erosion and deposition related?
- What features suggest whether erosion or deposition created a landform?

Vocabulary

erosion p. 321

deposition p. 323

g Multilingual eGlossary

Academic Standards for Science

7.2.6 Describe physical and chemical characteristics of soil layers and how they are influenced by the process of soil formation, including the action of bacteria, fungi, insects, and other organisms.

7.2.7 Use geological features such as karst topography and glaciation to explain how large-scale physical processes have shaped the land.

Also covers: 7.NS.3, 7.NS.5, 7.NS.7

Inquiry Stripes and Cuts?

Long ago, this area was at the bottom of an ocean. Today, it is dry land in Badlands National Park, South Dakota. Why do you think these hills are striped? What do you think caused such deep cuts in the land? What natural processes created landforms such as these?

Inquiry Launch Lab

10 minutes

How do the shape and size of sediment differ?

Sediment forms when rocks break apart. Wind, water, and other factors move the sediment from place to place. As the sediment moves, its shape and size can change. In this activity, you will observe the different shapes and sizes of sediment.

1. Read and complete a lab safety form.
2. Obtain a **bag of sediment** from your teacher. Pour the sediment onto a sheet of **paper.**
3. Use a **magnifying lens** to observe the differences in shape and size of the sediment.
4. Divide the sediment into groups according to its size and whether it has rounded or sharp edges.

Think About This

1. What were the different groups you used to sort the sediment?
2. **Key Concept** How do you think movement by wind and water might affect the shape and size of the sediment?

Reshaping Earth's Surface

Have you ever seen bulldozers, backhoes, and dump trucks at the construction site of a building project? You might have seen a bulldozer smoothing the land and making a flat surface or pushing soil around and forming hills. A backhoe might have been digging deep trenches for water or sewer lines. The dump trucks might have been dumping gravel or other building materials into small piles. The changes that people make to a landscape at a construction site are small examples of those that happen naturally to Earth's surface.

A combination of constructive **processes** and destructive processes produce landforms. Constructive processes build up features on Earth's surface. For example, lava erupting from a volcano hardens and forms new land on the area where the lava falls. Destructive processes tear down features on Earth's surface. A strong hurricane, for example, can wash part of a shoreline into the sea. Constructive and destructive processes continually shape and reshape Earth's surface.

Academic Vocabulary
process
(noun) an ongoing event or a series of related events

Figure 1 The continual weathering, erosion, and deposition of sediment occurs from the top of a mountain and across Earth's surface to the distant ocean.

Weathering is the breakdown of rock. Chemical weathering changes the mineral composition of rock. Physical weathering breaks rock into smaller pieces without changing its composition.

Visual Check How do you think weathering and erosion will affect the mountains over the next thousand years?

A Continual Process of Change

Imagine standing on a mountain, such as one shown in **Figure 1.** In the distance you might see a river or an ocean. What was this area like thousands of years ago? Will the mountains still be here thousands of years from now? Landforms on Earth are constantly changing, but the changes often happen so slowly that you do not notice them. What causes these changes?

Weathering

One type of a destructive process that changes Earth's surface is weathering, the breakdown of rock. Chemical weathering changes the chemical composition of rock. Physical weathering breaks rock into pieces, called sediment, but it does not change the chemical composition of rock. Gravel, sand, silt, and clay are different sizes of sediment.

Weathering Agents Water, wind, and ice are called agents, or causes, of weathering. Water, for example, can dissolve minerals in rock. Wind can grind and polish rocks by blowing particles against them. Also, a rock can break apart as ice expands or plant roots grow within cracks in the rock.

Different Rates of Weathering The mineral composition of some rocks makes them more resistant to weathering than other rocks. The differences in weathering rates can produce unusual landforms, as shown in **Figure 2.** Weathering can break away less resistant parts of the rock and leave behind the more resistant parts.

Figure 2 Different rates of weathering of rock can produce unusual rock formations.

Erosion is the wearing away of landforms and the transportation of rock fragments. This river is muddy because of the sediment it carries.
Deposition is the laying down of sediment by water, wind, glaciers, or gravity.

Erosion

What happens to weathered material? This material is often transported away from its source rock. **Erosion** *is the removal of weathered material from one location to another.* Agents of erosion include water, wind, glaciers, and gravity. The muddy water shown in **Figure 1,** for example, is evidence of erosion.

The Rate of Erosion Like weathering, erosion occurs at different rates. For example, a rushing stream can erode a large quantity of material quickly. However, a gentle stream might erode a small amount of material slowly. Factors that affect the rate of erosion include weather, climate, topography, and type of rock. For example, strong wind transports weathered rock more easily than a gentle breeze does. Weathered rock moves faster down a steep hill than across a flat area. The presence of plants and the way humans use the land also affect the rate of erosion. Erosion occurs faster on barren land than on land covered with vegetation.

Reading Check What are some factors that affect the rate of erosion?

Inquiry MiniLab — 15 minutes

Can weathering be measured?

You can measure the weathering of rocks.

1. Read and complete a lab safety form.
2. Obtain **pieces of broken rock.** Rinse the rocks and pat completely dry with **paper towels.**
3. Measure the rocks' mass using a **balance.** Record your data in your Science Journal.
4. Place the rocks in a **plastic bottle.** Cover the rocks with water, and seal the bottle. Shake the bottle vigorously for 5 minutes.
5. Rinse the rocks and pat completely dry with paper towels. Record the mass again.

Analyze and Conclude

1. **Compare and contrast** the mass of the rocks before and after rinsing.
2. **Key Concept** What evidence suggests that weathering has occurred?

Figure 3 Erosion can change poorly rounded rocks (top) to well-rounded rocks (bottom).

Rate of Erosion and Rock Type The rate of erosion sometimes depends on the type of rock. Weathering can break some types of rock, such as sandstone, into large pieces. Other rock types, such as shale or siltstone, can easily break into smaller pieces. These smaller pieces can be removed and transported faster by agents of erosion. For example, large rocks in streams usually move only short distances every few decades, but silt particles might move a kilometer or more each day.

Rounding Rock fragments bump against each other during erosion. When this happens, the shapes of the fragments can change. Rock fragments can range from poorly rounded to well-rounded. The more spherical and well-rounded a rock is, the more it has been polished during erosion. Rough edges break off as the rock fragments bump against each other. Differences in sediment rounding are shown in **Figure 3.**

Key Concept Check How can erosion affect the shape of sediment?

Sorting Erosion also affects the level of sorting of sediment. Sorting is the separating of items into groups according to one or more properties. As sediment is transported, it can become sorted by grain size, as shown in **Figure 4.** Sediment is often well-sorted when it has been moved a lot by wind or waves. Poorly sorted sediment often results from rapid transportation, perhaps by a storm, a flash flood, or a volcanic eruption. Sediment left at the edges of glaciers is also poorly sorted.

Key Concept Check How can erosion sort sediment?

Sediment Sorting by Size

Figure 4 Erosion can sort sediment according to its size.

Poorly sorted sediment has a wide range of sizes.

Moderately sorted sediment has a small range of sizes.

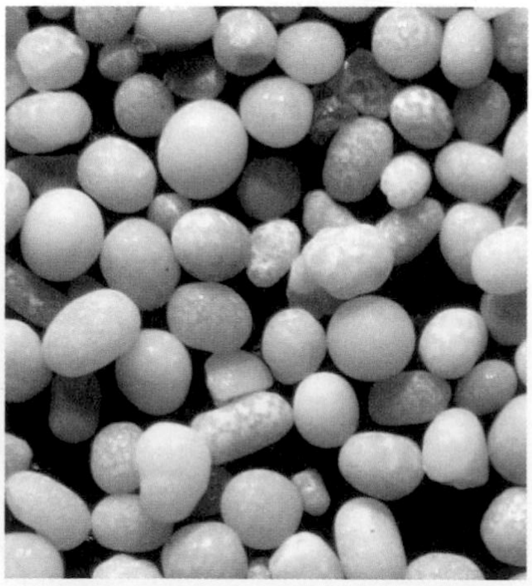

Well-sorted sediment is all about the same size.

Deposition

You have read about two destructive processes that shape Earth's surface—weathering and erosion. After material has been eroded, a constructive process takes place. **Deposition** *is the laying down or settling of eroded material.* As water or wind slows down, it has less energy and can hold less sediment. Some of the sediment can then be laid down, or deposited.

WORD ORIGIN
deposition
from French *deposer,* means "put down"

Key Concept Check How are erosion and deposition related?

Depositional Environments Sediment is deposited in locations called depositional environments. These locations are on land, along coasts, or in oceans. Examples include **swamps,** deltas, beaches, and the ocean floor.

REVIEW VOCABULARY
swamp
a wetland occasionally or partially covered with water

Reading Check What is a depositional environment?

Environments where sediment is transported and deposited quickly are high-energy environments. Examples include rushing rivers, ocean shores with large waves, and deserts with strong winds. Large grains of sediment tend to be deposited in high-energy environments.

Small grains of sediment are often deposited in low-energy environments. Deep lakes and areas of slow-moving air or water are low-energy environments. The swamp shown in **Figure 5** is an example of a low-energy environment. The material that makes up a fine-grained sedimentary rock, such as shale, was probably deposited in a low-energy environment.

Sediment Layers Sediment deposited in water typically forms layers called beds. Some examples of beds appear as "stripes" in the photo at the beginning of this lesson. Beds often form as layers of sediment at the bottom of rivers, lakes, and oceans. These layers can be preserved in sedimentary rocks.

A Low-Energy Depositional Environment

Figure 5 Silt and clay are deposited in low-energy environments such as swamps. Swamp deposits also include dark, organic material from decaying trees and other plants.

Figure 6 The tall, steep, somewhat sharp features shown in these photographs are common in landforms carved by erosion.

1

The Tepees in the Painted Desert of Arizona

2

Hoodoos at Bryce Canyon National Park

3

Glacier National Park in Montana

Visual Check How did the passage of glaciers through these mountains change the shape of the valleys?

Interpreting Landforms

What do landform characteristics, such as structure, elevation, and rock exposure, suggest about the development of landforms? Examples of landforms include mountains, valleys, plains, sea cliffs, and beaches. These landforms are always changing, although you might not observe these changes in your lifetime. Landform characteristics can be observed to determine whether destructive forces, such as erosion, or constructive forces, such as deposition, produced the landforms.

Landforms Created by Erosion

Landforms can have features that are clearly produced by erosion. These landforms are often tall, jagged structures with cuts in layers of rock, as shown in the photographs in **Figure 6.**

1 Landforms formed by erosion can expose several layers of rock. The Tepees in the Painted Desert of Arizona contain several layers of different materials. Over time, erosion wore away parts of the land, leaving behind multicolored mounds.

2 Recall that different rates of erosion can result in unusual landforms when some rocks erode and leave more erosion-resistant rocks behind. For example, tall, protruding landforms called hoodoos are shown in the middle photograph of **Figure 6.** Over time, water and ice eroded the less-resistant sedimentary rock. The remaining rocks are more resistant. If you would like to examine hoodoos more closely, look back at **Figure 2.**

3 Glacial erosion and coastal erosion also form unique landforms. Glacial erosion can produce ice-carved features in mountains. The U-shaped valleys of Glacier National Park in Montana, shown in the bottom photograph, formed by glacial erosion. Coastal erosion forms picturesque landforms, such as sea cliffs, caves, and sea arches.

Landforms Created by Deposition

Landforms created by deposition are often flat and low-lying. Wind deposition, for example, can gradually form deserts of sand. Deposition also occurs where mountain streams reach the gentle slopes of wide, flat valleys. An apron of sediment, called an alluvial fan, often forms where a stream flows from a steep, narrow canyon onto a flat plain at the foot of a mountain, as shown in **Figure 7.**

▲ **Figure 7** An alluvial fan is a gently sloping mass of sediment that forms where a stream empties onto flat land at the foot of a steep slope.

Reading Check How does an alluvial fan develop?

Water traveling in a river can slow due to friction with the edges and the bottom of the river channel. An increase in channel width or depth also can slow the current and promote deposition. Deposition along a riverbed occurs where the speed of the water slows. This deposition can form a sandbar, as shown in **Figure 8.** The endpoint for most rivers is where they reach a lake or an ocean and deposit sediment under water. Wave action along shorelines also moves and deposits sediment.

◀ **Figure 8** A sandbar is a depositional feature in rivers and near ocean shores.

As glaciers melt, they can leave behind piles of sediment and rock. For example, glaciers can create long, narrow deposits called eskers and moraines. In the United States, these features are best preserved in northern states such as Wisconsin and New York. You will read more about glacial deposition in Lesson 3.

Comparing Landforms

Look again at the landforms shown in **Figure 6, Figure 7,** and **Figure 8.** Notice how landforms produced by erosion and deposition are different. Erosion produces landforms that are often tall and jagged, but deposition usually produces landforms on flat, low land. By observing the features of a landform, you can infer whether erosion or deposition produced it.

Key Concept Check What features suggest whether erosion or deposition produced a landform?

FOLDABLES®

Make a two-tab book and label it as shown. Use your book to describe and identify some landforms created by the processes of erosion and deposition.

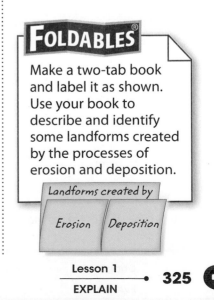

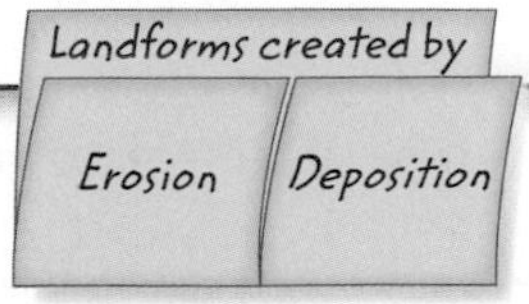

Lesson 1 Review

Assessment Online Quiz

Visual Summary

Erosion occurring at different rates can carve rock into interesting landforms.

Rock fragments with rough edges are rounded during transportation.

Landforms produced by deposition are often flat and low-lying.

FOLDABLES®

Use your lesson Foldable to review the lesson. Save your Foldable for the project at the end of the chapter.

What do you think NOW?

You first read the statements below at the beginning of the chapter.

1. Wind, water, ice, and gravity continually shape Earth's surface.
2. Different sizes of sediment tend to mix when being moved along by water.

Did you change your mind about whether you agree or disagree with the statements? Rewrite any false statements to make them true.

Use Vocabulary

1. **Define** *deposition* in your own words.
2. **Use the term** *erosion* in a complete sentence.

Understand Key Concepts

3. Which would most likely leave behind well-sorted sediment?
   - **A.** flash flood
   - **B.** melting glacier
   - **C.** ocean waves
   - **D.** volcanic eruption
4. **Describe** some features of an alluvial fan that suggest that it was formed by deposition.
5. **Explain** how erosion and deposition by a stream are related.

Interpret Graphics

6. **Examine** the illustration of sediment particle sizes shown below.

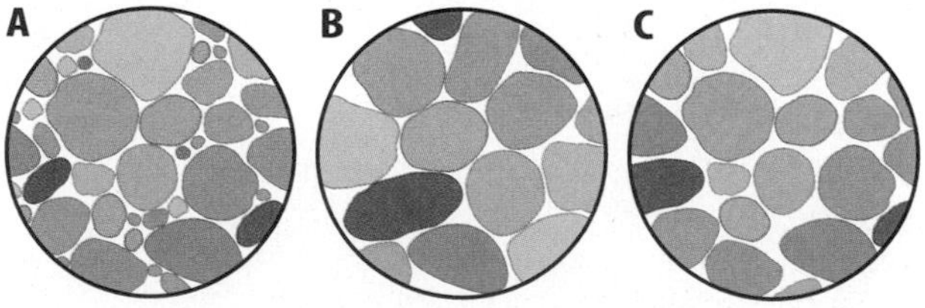

Classify each set of particles as well-sorted, moderately sorted, or poorly sorted. Explain.

7. **Sequence** Copy and fill in the graphic organizer below to describe a possible history of a grain of the mineral quartz that begins in a boulder at the top of a mountain and ends as a piece of sand on the coast.

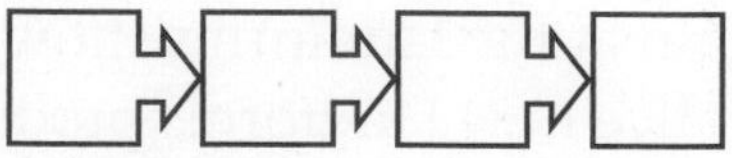

Critical Thinking

8. **Decide** Imagine a river that deposits only small particles where it flows into a sea. Is the river current most likely fast or slow? Why?

HOW NATURE WORKS

AMERICAN MUSEUM OF NATURAL HISTORY

Clues from the Canyon

Rocks of the majestic Grand Canyon tell a story about Earth's past.

Visitors to the Grand Canyon in Arizona are awestruck by its magnificent size and depth. But to many scientists, the canyon's walls are even more impressive. The soaring walls hold about 40 layers of colorful rocks in shades of red, yellow, brown, and gray. Each layer is like a page in a history book about Earth's past—and the deeper the layer, the older it is. The different layers reflect the particular types of environments in which they formed.

Weathering The canyon walls continue to weather and erode today. Rockfalls and landslides are common. Harder rock such as sandstone weathers in big chunks that break off, forming steep cliffs. The softer rocks weather and erode more easily. This forms gentle slopes.

Deposition These rock layers formed 280 to 260 million years ago. During the early part of this period, the region was covered by sand dunes and wind-deposited layers of sand. Later, shallow seas covered this area and layers of shells settled on the seafloor. Gradually, the sediments were compacted and cemented together and these multicolored layers of sedimentary rock were formed.

Erosion Several million years ago, the movement of tectonic plates pushed up the layers of rock. This formed what is called the Colorado Plateau. As the rocks rose higher, the slope of the Colorado River became steeper and its waters flowed faster and with greater force. The Colorado River cut through the weathered rock and carried away sediment. Over millions of years, this erosion formed the canyon.

It's Your Turn

DIAGRAM With a partner, find a photo of a local natural land formation. Research and write short descriptions explaining how parts of the formation were created. Attach your descriptions to the appropriate places on the photo.

Lesson 2

Reading Guide

Key Concepts
ESSENTIAL QUESTIONS

- What are the stages of stream development?
- How do water erosion and deposition change Earth's surface?
- How do wind erosion and deposition change Earth's surface?

Vocabulary
meander p. 330
longshore current p. 331
delta p. 332
abrasion p. 334
dune p. 334
loess p. 334

g Multilingual eGlossary

Academic Standards for Science
7.1.3 Recognize and explain how different ways of obtaining, transforming, and distributing energy have different environmental consequences.

7.2.6 Describe physical and chemical characteristics of soil layers and how they are influenced by the process of soil formation, including the action of bacteria, fungi, insects, and other organisms.

7.2.7 Use geological features such as karst topography and glaciation to explain how large-scale physical processes have shaped the land.

Also covers: 7.NS.1, 7.NS.2, 7.NS.7, 7.NS.9

Landforms Shaped by Water and Wind

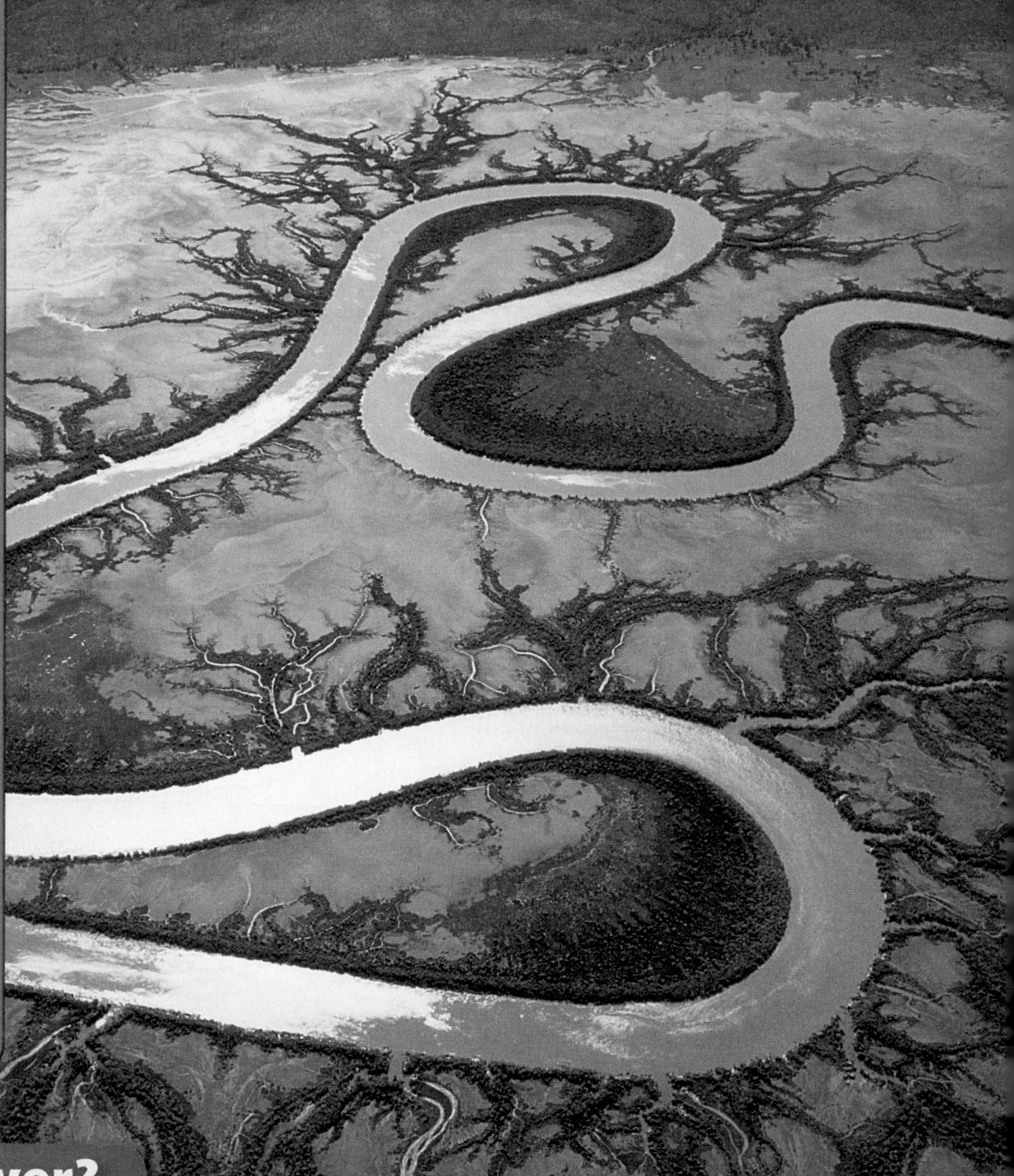

Inquiry Twisted River?

As a river flows down a mountain, it usually flows in the same general direction. What causes this river to flow side-to-side? Why doesn't it flow in a straight path?

Inquiry Launch Lab — 15 minutes

How do water and wind shape Earth?

Imagine a fast-moving river rushing over rocks or a strong wind blowing across a field. What changes on Earth do the water and the wind cause?

1. Form into groups and discuss the pictures below with others in your group.
2. Can you recognize evidence of ways water and wind have changed the land—through both erosion and deposition?

Landforms Shaped by Water and Wind

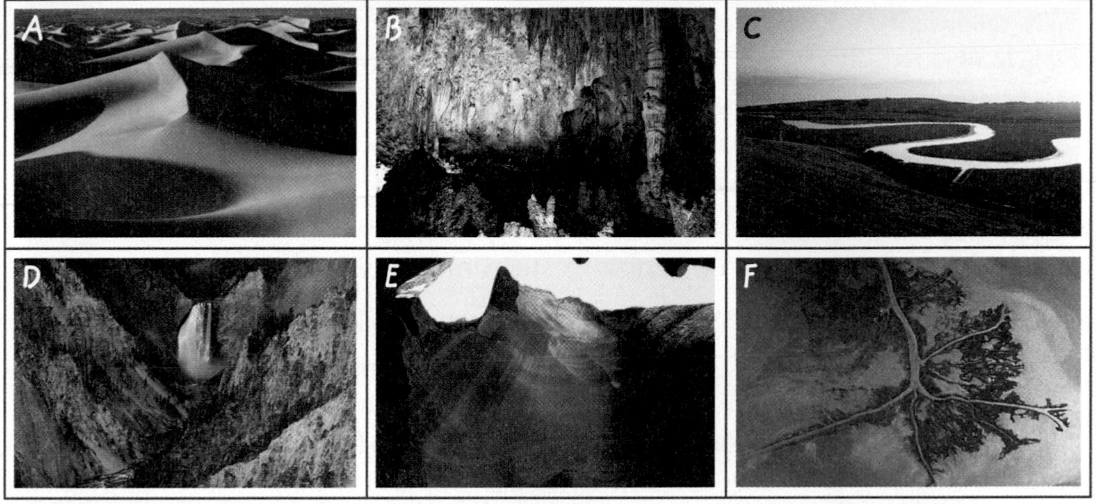

Think About This

1. What are some examples of erosion and deposition in the pictures?
2. **Key Concept** Describe ways you think water might have changed the land in the pictures. What are some ways wind might have changed the land?

Shaping the Land with Water and Wind

Recall that landforms on Earth's surface undergo continual change. Weathering and erosion are destructive processes that shape Earth's surface. These destructive processes often produce tall, jagged landforms. Deposition is a constructive process that also shapes Earth's surface. Constructive processes often produce flat, low-lying landforms.

What causes these processes that continually tear down and build up Earth's surface? In this lesson, you will read that water and wind are two important agents of weathering, erosion, and deposition. The cliffs shown in **Figure 9** are an example of how erosion by water and wind can change the shape of landforms. In the next lesson you will read about ways Earth's surface is changed by the downhill movement of rocks and soil and by the movement of glaciers.

Figure 9 Erosion by water and wind formed these cliffs along Lake Superior.

Figure 10 Water erosion carved this V-shaped valley at Lower Falls, Yellowstone National Park, in Wyoming.

Water Erosion and Deposition

Water can shape landforms on and below Earth's surface. The speed of water movement and the depositional environment often affect the shape of landforms.

Water Erosion

If you have ever had a chance to wade into an ocean and feel the waves rushing toward shore, you know that moving water can be incredibly strong. Moving water causes erosion along streams, at beaches, and underground.

Stream Erosion Streams are active systems that erode land and transport sediment. The erosion produced by a stream depends on the stream's energy. This energy is usually greatest in steep, mountainous areas where young streams flow rapidly downhill. The rushing water often carves V-shaped valleys, such as the one shown in **Figure 10.** Waterfalls and river rapids are common in steep mountain streams.

Water in a young stream slows as it reaches gentler slopes. The stream is then called a mature stream, such as the one shown in **Figure 11.** Slower moving water erodes the sides of a stream channel more than its bottom, and the stream develops curves. *A* **meander** *is a broad, C-shaped curve in a stream.*

When a stream reaches flat land, it moves even slower and is called an old stream. Over time, meanders change shape. More erosion occurs on the outside of bends where water flows faster. More deposition occurs on the inside of bends where water flows slower. Over time, the meander's size increases.

Key Concept Check Describe the stream development stages.

FOLDABLES®

Make a two-tab book and label it as shown. Use your book to organize information about landforms and features created by erosion and deposition by water and wind.

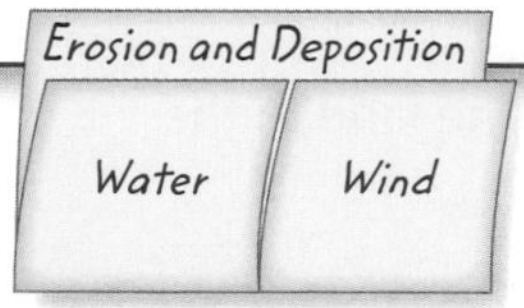

Stages of Stream Development

Concepts in Motion Animation

Figure 11 Streams change as they flow from steep slopes to gentle slopes and finally to flat plains.

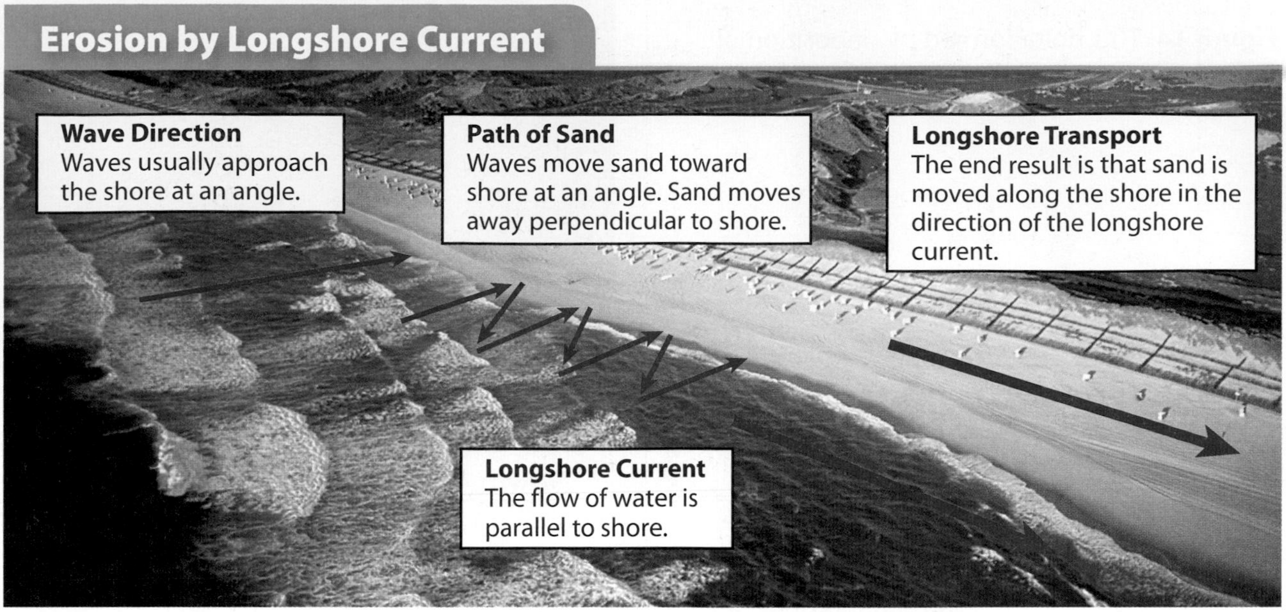

Erosion by Longshore Current
Wave Direction
Waves usually approach the shore at an angle.
Path of Sand
Waves move sand toward shore at an angle. Sand moves away perpendicular to shore.
Longshore Transport
The end result is that sand is moved along the shore in the direction of the longshore current.
Longshore Current
The flow of water is parallel to shore.

▲ **Figure 12** A longshore current erodes and deposits large amounts of sediment along a shoreline.

Visual Check What causes the sand to move away perpendicular to shore?

Coastal Erosion Like streams, coastlines continually change. Waves crashing onto shore erode loose sand, gravel, and rock along coastlines. One type of coastal erosion is shown in **Figure 12.** *A* **longshore current** *is a current that flows parallel to the shoreline.* This current moves sediment and continually changes the size and shape of beaches. Coastal erosion also occurs when the cutting action of waves along rocky shores forms sea cliffs. Erosional features such as sea caves, sea stacks (tall pillars just offshore), and sea arches (rock bridges extending into the sea) can form when waves erode less resistant rocks along the shore.

Key Concept Check How does water erosion change Earth's surface?

Groundwater Erosion Water that flows underground also can erode rock. Have you ever wondered how caves and other features of karst topography form? When carbon dioxide in the atmosphere mixes with rain, a weak acid forms. Some of this acidic rainwater becomes acidic groundwater. Acidic groundwater seeps through soil and rock layers. The water dissolves and washes away the limestone, forming a cave, as shown in **Figure 13.** Caves, sinkholes, and underground rivers and streams are characteristic of karst topography.

▲ **Figure 13** Carlsbad Caverns in New Mexico was formed by water erosion. Other karst topography regions include the Mitchell Plateau in south central Indiana.

Figure 14 This delta formed by deposition of sediment when water flowed from a river into an ocean.

Inquiry MiniLab — 20 minutes

How do stalactites form?

A stalactite forms when minerals are deposited as crystals. In this lab, you will model the formation of a stalactite.

1. Read and complete a lab safety form.
2. Use **scissors** to poke a hole in the bottom of a **small paper cup.**

3. Tie a **washer** to one end of a 25-cm length of **yarn.** Thread the other end through the hole in the cup and a hole in the top of a **box.** Place the cup on the box with the holes aligned.
4. Half-fill **another cup** with **Epsom salts.** Add **warm water** until the cup is full. Stir with a **spoon.** Pour the salt water into the cup with yarn so that it drips down the yarn into a **bowl.**
5. Record in your Science Journal observations of your model each day for one week.

Analyze and Conclude

1. **Describe** daily changes in your model.
2. **Key Concept** How did this activity model the formation of a stalactite?

Water Deposition

Flowing water deposits sediment as the water slows. A loss of speed reduces the amount of energy that the water has to carry sediment.

Deposition Along Streams Deposition by a stream can occur anywhere along its path where the water's speed decreases. As you read earlier, slower-moving water deposits sediment on the inside curves of meanders. A stream also slows and deposits sediment when it reaches flat land or a large body of water, such as a lake or an ocean. An example is the delta shown in **Figure 14.** *A* **delta** *is a large deposit of sediment that forms where a stream enters a large body of water.*

Deposition Along Coastlines Much of the sand on most ocean beaches was originally deposited by rivers. Longshore currents transport the sand along ocean coasts. Eventually, sand is deposited where currents are slower and have less energy. Sandy beaches often develop at those locations.

Key Concept Check How does water deposition change Earth's surface?

Groundwater Deposition Weathering and erosion produce caves, but deposition forms many structures within caves. Look again at **Figure 13.** The cave contains landforms that dripping groundwater formed as it deposited minerals. Over time, the deposits developed into stalactites and stalagmites. Stalactites hang from the ceiling. Stalagmites build up on the cave's floor.

Land Use Practices

Damage caused by water erosion can be affected by the ways people use land. Two areas of concern are beaches along coasts and surface areas within continental interiors.

Beach Erosion Ocean waves can erode beaches by removing sediment. To reduce this erosion, people sometimes build structures such as retaining walls, or groins, like those shown in **Figure 15.** A row of groins is constructed at right angles to the shore. They are built to trap sediment and reduce the erosive effects of longshore currents.

▲ **Figure 15** These shoreline groins prevent beach erosion by trapping sediment.

Some ways people affect beaches are unintended. For example, people build dams on rivers for purposes of flood control and other reasons. However, dams on rivers prevent river sand from reaching beaches. Beach sand that is washed out to sea by waves is not replaced.

Surface Erosion Reducing the amount of vegetation or removing it from the land increases surface erosion. Agricultural production, construction activities, and cutting trees for lumber and paper production are some reasons that people remove vegetation.

Reading Check What are some ways human activities affect water erosion?

A floodplain is a wide, flat area next to a river. It is usually dry land but can be flooded when the river overflows. Heavy rain or rapid melting of snow can cause a river to flood. Building within a floodplain is risky, as shown in **Figure 16.** However, floods supply mineral-rich soil that is ideal for farming. One way to decrease flooding on a floodplain is to build a levee. A levee is a long, low ridge of soil along a river. However, decreasing flooding also decreases the renewed supply of mineral-rich soil for farming.

◀ **Figure 16** This 2005 levee break in New Orleans caused extensive flood damage.

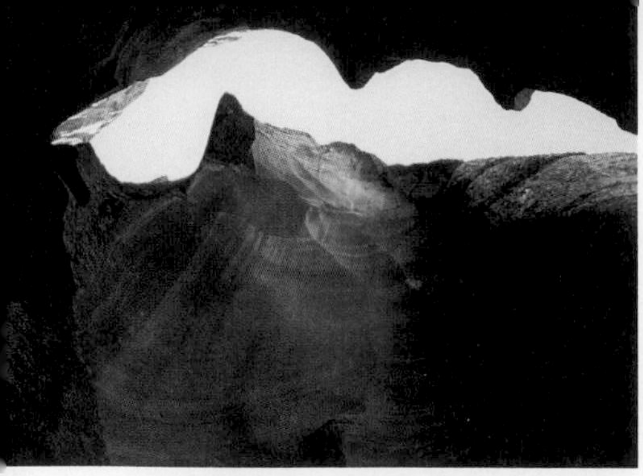

▲ **Figure 17** Wind abrasion carved this unusual landform in the red sandstone of Nevada's Valley of Fire region.

Wind Erosion and Deposition

If you think about a gentle wind that blows leaves in the autumn, it seems unlikely that the wind can cause land erosion and deposition. But strong or long-lasting winds can significantly change the land.

Wind Erosion

As wind carries sediment along, the sediment cuts and polishes exposed rock. **Abrasion** *is the grinding away of rock or other surfaces as particles carried by wind, water, or ice scrape against them.* Examples of rock surfaces carved by wind abrasion are shown in **Figure 17** and at the beginning of this chapter.

Wind Deposition

Two common types of wind-blown deposits are dunes and loess (LUHS). *A* **dune** *is a pile of windblown sand.* Over time, entire fields of dunes can travel across the land as wind continues to blow the sand. Some dunes are shown in **Figure 18.** **Loess** *is a crumbly, windblown deposit of silt and clay.* One type of loess forms from rock that was ground up and deposited by glaciers. Wind picks up this fine-grain sediment and redeposits it as thick layers of dust called loess.

Word Origin
loess
from Swiss German *Lösch,* means "loose"

Key Concept Check How do wind erosion and deposition change Earth's surface?

Land Use Practices

People contribute to wind erosion. For example, plowed fields and dry, overgrazed pastures expose soil. Strong winds can remove topsoil that is not held in place by plants. One way to slow the effects of wind erosion is to leave fields unplowed after harvesting crops. Farmers can also plant rows of trees to slow wind and protect the farmland.

Wind Erosion and Deposition

Figure 18 Dunes, such as these in Death Valley, California, formed by the deposition of wind-blown sand. ▶

Visual Check What are two effects wind has had on this landscape?

Lesson 2 Review

Assessment Online Quiz
Inquiry Virtual Lab

Visual Summary

Water erosion changes Earth's surface. An example of this is the change in features of a stream over time.

Water transports sediment and deposits it in places where the speed of the water decreases.

Wind erosion can change Earth's surface by moving sediment. A dune and loess are two types of wind deposition.

FOLDABLES®

Use your lesson Foldable to review the lesson. Save your Foldable for the project at the end of the chapter.

What do you think NOW?

You first read the statements below at the beginning of the chapter.

3. A beach is a landform that does not change over time.

4. Windblown sediment can cut and polish exposed rock surfaces.

Did you change your mind about whether you agree or disagree with the statements? Rewrite any false statements to make them true.

Use Vocabulary

1. **Distinguish** between loess and a dune.
2. **Use the term** *delta* in a complete sentence.
3. Sediment is transported parallel to the shoreline by a ________.

Understand Key Concepts

4. Which feature would a young river most likely have?
   A. meander
   B. slow movement
   C. waterfall
   D. wide channel
5. **Explain** how wind erosion might affect exposed rock.
6. **Compare and contrast** the advantages and disadvantages of farming on a floodplain.

Interpret Graphics

7. **Determine Cause and Effect** Copy and fill in the graphic organizer below to identify two ways waves cause seashore erosion.

8. **Examine** the image below.

How have erosion and deposition shaped the stream?

Critical Thinking

9. **Suppose** the amount of sand in front of a large, beachfront hotel is slowly disappearing. Explain the process that is likely causing this problem. Suggest a way to avoid further loss of sand.
10. **Recommend** What are some steps a farmer could take to avoid wind erosion and water erosion of farmland?

Inquiry **Skill Practice** **Analyze** **40 minutes**

How do water erosion and deposition occur along a stream?

Water flowing in a stream erodes the land it flows over. As stream water slows down, it deposits sediments. You can learn about this type of erosion and deposition by analyzing how water shapes land.

Materials

sand

paper cup

craft sticks

tub

stream table

small rock

Also needed: drain tube

Safety

Learn It

When you **analyze** an event, such as erosion or deposition, you observe the different things that happen. You also consider the effects of changes. In this activity, you will analyze how erosion and deposition occur along a stream.

Try It

1. Read and complete a lab safety form.
2. Half-fill a stream table with sand. Add water to dampen the sand. Tilt the table slightly, and put the drain tube in a tub.
3. Flatten the sand into a gentle slope. Slowly pour water from a paper cup onto the high end of the sand. Notice the movement of sand along the water's path. Record your observations in your Science Journal.
4. Flatten the sand again. Use a craft stick to make a straight channel for the water. Pour water into the channel slowly and then faster. Analyze the movement of sand along the channel.

Apply It

5. Test the effect of having an object, such as a rock, in the water's path. Analyze how this affects the path of the water and the movement of sand.
6. Think about how flowing water affects the shape of a meander. Test this with your damp sand and water. Describe your results.
7. **Key Concept** How did water erosion and deposition occur along the stream?

Lesson 3

Reading Guide

Key Concepts
ESSENTIAL QUESTIONS

- What are some ways gravity shapes Earth's surface?
- How do glaciers erode Earth's surface?

Vocabulary

mass wasting p. 338
landslide p. 339
talus p. 339
glacier p. 341
till p. 342
moraine p. 342
outwash p. 342

g Multilingual eGlossary

Video BrainPOP®

Academic Standards for Science

7.2.7 Use geological features such as karst topography and glaciation to explain how large-scale physical processes have shaped the land.

Also covers: 7.NS.4, 7.NS.5, 7.DP.1, 7.DP.2, 7.DP.3, 7.DP.4, 7.DP.5, 7.DP.6, 7.DP.7, 7.DP.9, 7.DP.10, 7.DP.11

Mass Wasting and Glaciers

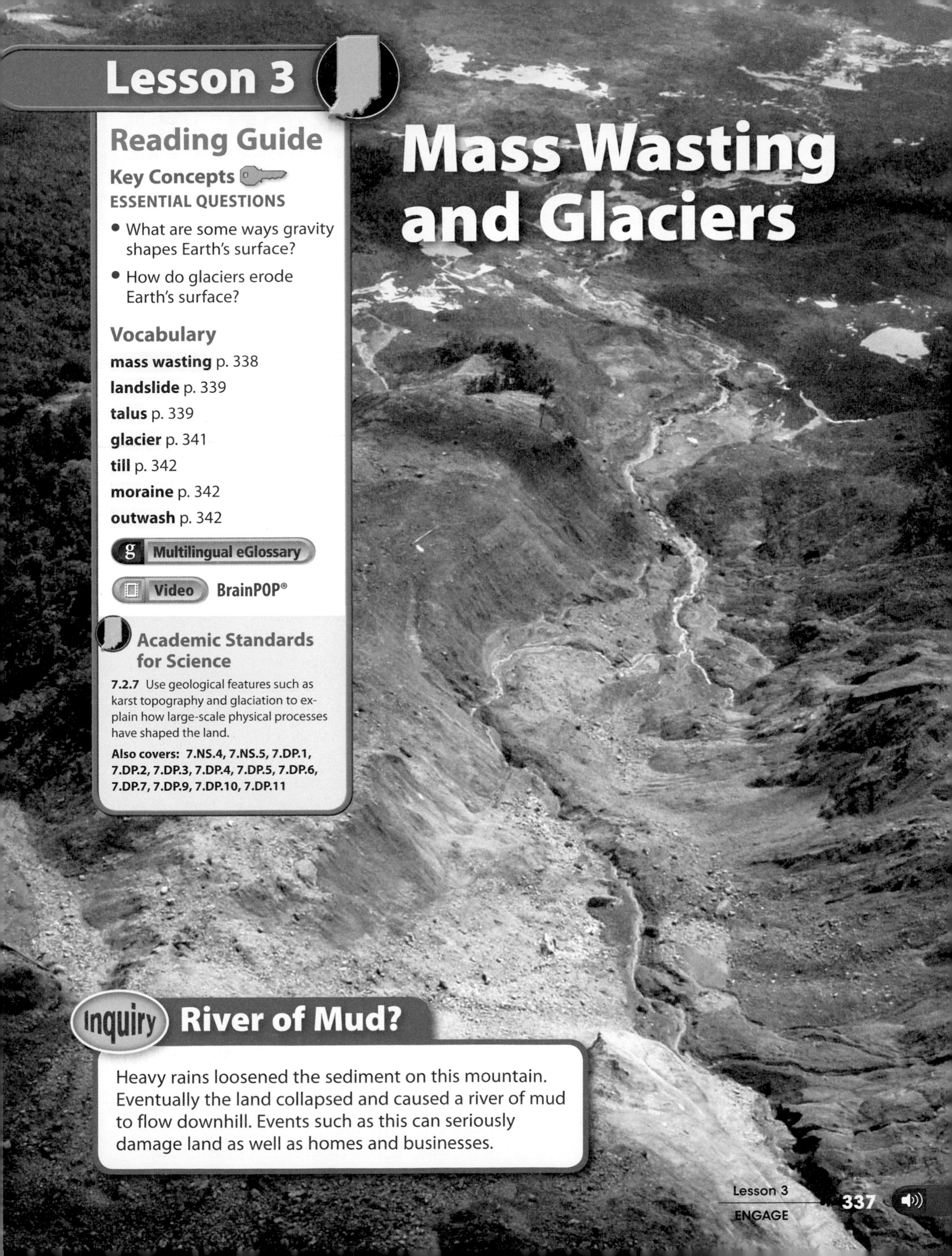

Inquiry River of Mud?

Heavy rains loosened the sediment on this mountain. Eventually the land collapsed and caused a river of mud to flow downhill. Events such as this can seriously damage land as well as homes and businesses.

Inquiry Launch Lab

15 minutes

How does a moving glacier shape Earth's surface?

A glacier is a huge mass of slow-moving ice. The weight of a glacier is so great that its movement causes significant erosion and deposition along its path. In this lab, you will use a model glacier to observe these effects.

1. Read and complete a lab safety form.
2. Half-fill an **aluminum pan** with **dirt** and **gravel.** Mix enough water so that the dirt holds together easily. Use **two books** to raise one end of the pan.
3. Sprinkle **colored sand** at the top of the dirt hill.
4. Place a **model glacier** at the top of the hill. Slowly move the glacier downhill, pressing down gently.

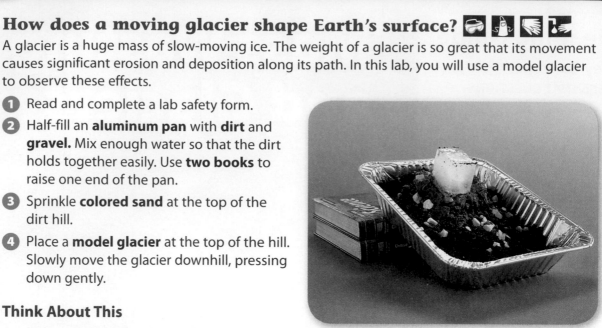

Think About This

1. What happened to the colored sand as the glacier moved downhill?
2. **Key Concept** What kinds of erosion and deposition did your model glacier cause?

Mass Wasting

Have you ever seen or heard a news report about a large pile of boulders that has fallen down a mountain onto a road? This is an example of a mass wasting event. **Mass wasting** *is the downhill movement of a large mass of rocks or soil because of the pull of gravity.* There are two important parts to this definition:

- material moves in bulk as a large mass
- gravity is the dominant cause of movement. For example, the mass moves all at once, rather than as separate pieces over a long period of time. Also, the mass is not moved by, in, on, or under a transporting agent such as water, ice, or air.

Reading Check Describe two characteristics of a mass wasting event.

Look again at the photo on the previous page. It is a photo of a mass wasting event called a mud flow. Even though water did not transport the mud, it did contribute to this mass wasting event. Mass wasting commonly occurs when soil on a hillside is soaked with rainwater. The water-soaked soil becomes so heavy that it breaks loose and slides down the hillside.

Recall that vegetation on a steep slope reduces the amount of water erosion during a heavy rainfall. The presence of thick vegetation on a slope also reduces the likelihood of a mass wasting event. Root systems of plants help hold sediment in place. Vegetation also reduces the force of falling rain. This minimizes erosion by allowing water to gently soak into the soil.

Examples of Mass Wasting

Rockfall

Slump

Creep

Figure 19 A rockfall, slump, and creep are examples of mass wasting.

Visual Check What evidence do you see in the figure that mass wasting has occurred?

Erosion by Mass Wasting

There are many types of mass wasting events. For example, *a* **landslide** *is the rapid downhill movement of soil, loose rocks, and boulders.* Two types of landslides are a rockfall, such as the one shown in **Figure 19,** and a mudslide, shown on the first page of this lesson. Slump is a type of mass wasting where the material moves slowly, in a large mass. If the material moves too slowly to be noticeable, causing trees and other objects to lean over, the event is called creep, also shown in **Figure 19.**

The amount of erosion that occurs during a mass wasting event depends on factors such as the type of rock, the amount of water in the soil, and how strongly the rock and soil are held together. Erosion also tends to be more destructive when the mass wasting occurs on steep slopes. For example, landslides on a steep hillside can cause extensive damage because they transport large amounts of material quickly.

Key Concept Check What are some ways gravity shapes Earth's surface?

Deposition by Mass Wasting

The erosion that occurs during mass wasting continues as long as gravity is greater than other forces holding the rock and soil in place. But when the material reaches a stable location, such as the base of a mountain, the material is deposited. **Talus** *is a pile of angular rocks and sediment from a rockfall,* like the pile of rock at the base of the hill in **Figure 19.**

FOLDABLES®

Make a two-tab book and label it as shown. Use your book to organize information about landforms and features created by erosion and deposition by mass wasting and by glaciers.

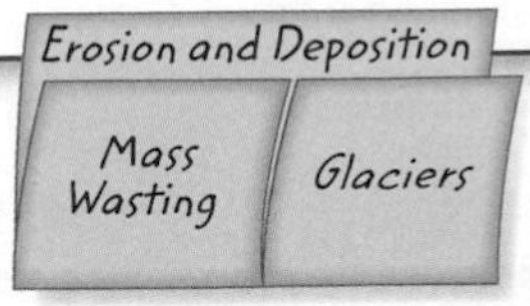

Math Skills

Use Ratios

Slope is the ratio of the change in vertical height over the change in horizontal distance. The slope of the hill in the drawing is

$$\frac{(108\text{ m} - 100\text{ m})}{40\text{ m}} = \frac{8\text{ m}}{40\text{ m}} = 0.2$$

Multiply the answer by 100 to calculate percent slope.

$$0.2 \times 100 = 20\%$$

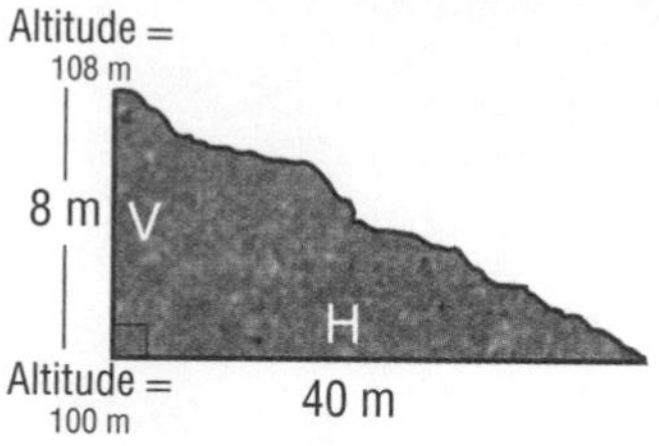

Practice

A mountain rises from 380 m to 590 m over a horizontal distance of 3,000 m. What is its percent slope?

Review

- **Math Practice**
- **Personal Tutor**

Figure 20 Building on steep slopes can increase the risk of a landslide. Construction or removal of vegetation makes the hillside even less stable.

Land Use Practices

Human activities can affect both the severity of mass wasting and the tendency for it to occur. The homes in **Figure 20** were built on steep and unstable slopes and were damaged during a landslide. Removing vegetation increases soil erosion and can promote mass wasting. The use of heavy machines or blasting can shake the ground and trigger mass wasting. In addition, landscaping can make a slope steeper. A steep slope is more likely to undergo mass wasting.

Reading Check What are some ways human activities can increase or decrease the risk of mass wasting?

Inquiry MiniLab

20 minutes

How does the slope of a hill affect erosion?

1. Read and complete a lab safety form.
2. Use **scissors** to poke holes in one end of an **aluminum pan.** Prop the other end up with a **book.** Place a **second pan** under the low end. Pile **300 mL of soil** in the high end.
3. Quickly pour **400 mL of water** over the soil. Drain the water from the second pan. Use a **balance** to measure the mass of the soil that was washed into the second pan.
4. Clean the pans. Using fresh soil, repeat steps 2 and 3 with **three books** holding up the pan.

Analyze and Conclude

1. **Predict** what your results would have been if you had sprinkled the water on slowly.
2. **Key Concept** How did the slope of the hill affect the amount of erosion?

Glacial Erosion and Deposition

You have read about erosion and deposition caused by mass wasting events. Glaciers can also cause erosion and deposition. *A* **glacier** *is a large mass of ice that formed on land and moves slowly across Earth's surface.* Glaciers form on land in areas where the amount of snowfall is greater than the amount of snowmelt. Although glaciers appear to be motionless, they can move several centimeters or more each day.

There are two main types of glaciers—alpine glaciers and ice sheets. Alpine glaciers, like the one shown in **Figure 21,** form in mountains and flow downhill. More than 100,000 alpine glaciers exist on Earth today. Ice sheets cover large areas of land and move outward from central locations. Continental ice sheets were common in past ice ages but only exist today on Antarctica and Greenland.

▲ **Figure 21** The Mendenhall Glacier in Alaska is an alpine glacier.

Glacial Erosion

Glaciers erode Earth's surface as they slide over it. They act as bulldozers, carving the land as they move. Rocks and grit frozen within the ice create grooves and scratches on underlying rocks. This is similar to the way sandpaper scratches wood. Alpine glaciers produce distinctive erosional features like the ones shown in **Figure 22.** Notice the U-shaped valleys that glaciers carved through the mountains.

Key Concept Check How do glaciers erode Earth's surface?

Figure 22 Alpine glaciers produce distinctive erosion features.

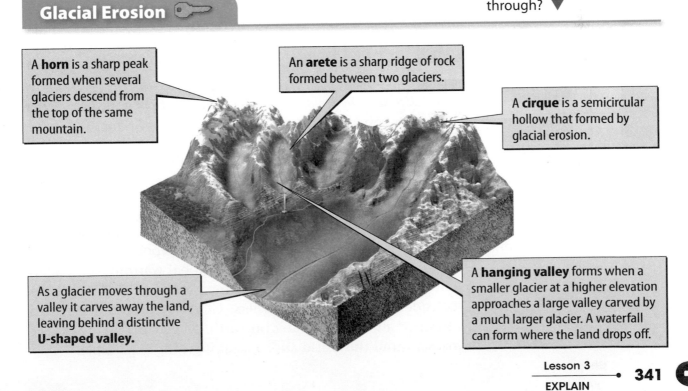

Visual Check How would the mountains and the valley be different if a glacier had not passed through? ▼

Glacial Erosion

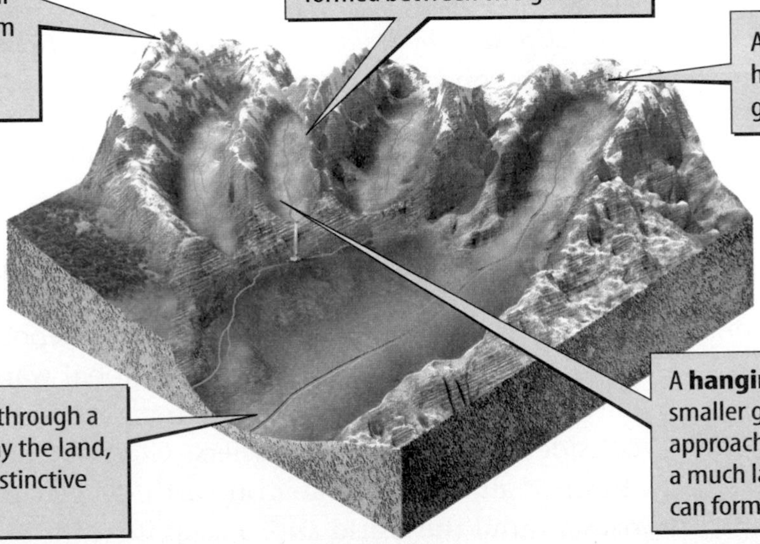

A **horn** is a sharp peak formed when several glaciers descend from the top of the same mountain.
An **arete** is a sharp ridge of rock formed between two glaciers.
A **cirque** is a semicircular hollow that formed by glacial erosion.
As a glacier moves through a valley it carves away the land, leaving behind a distinctive **U-shaped valley.**
A **hanging valley** forms when a smaller glacier at a higher elevation approaches a large valley carved by a much larger glacier. A waterfall can form where the land drops off.

Glacial Deposition

Concepts in Motion Animation

Figure 23 Melting glaciers form various land features as they deposit rock and sediment.

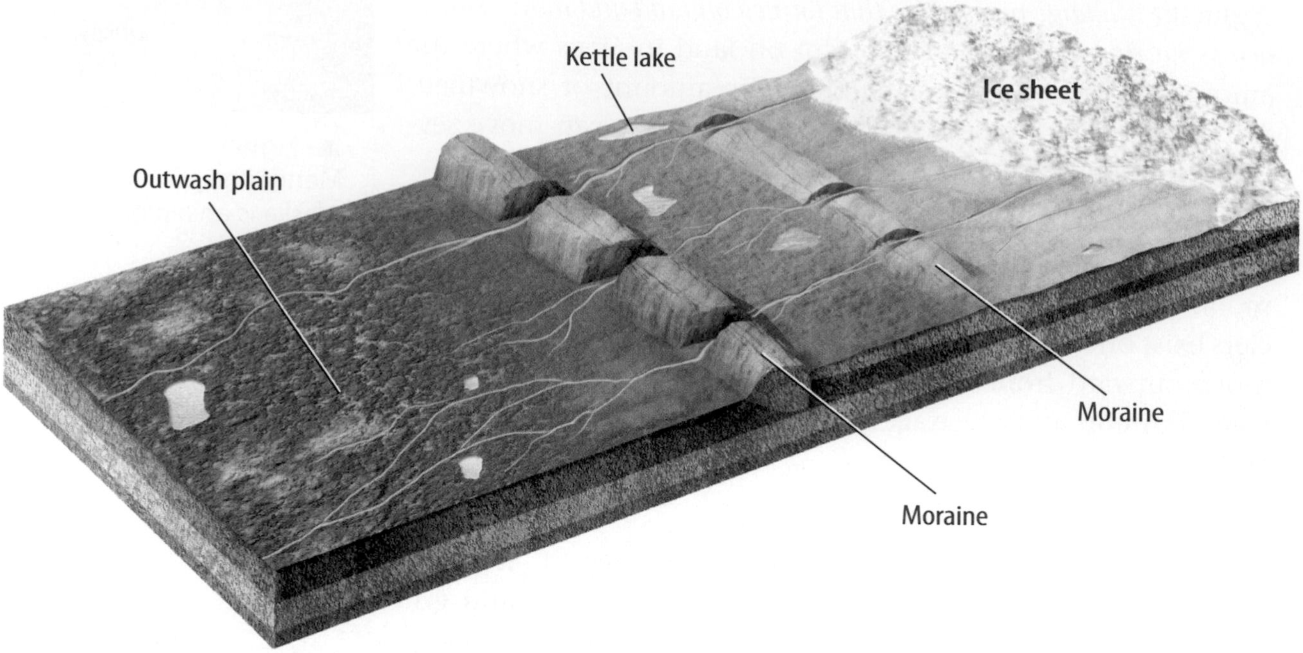

SCIENCE USE V. COMMON USE

till

Science Use rock and sediment deposited by a glacier

Common Use to work by plowing, sowing, and raising crops

WORD ORIGIN

moraine

from French *morena*, means "mound of earth"

Glacial Deposition

Glaciers slowly melt as they move down from high altitudes or when the climate in the area warms. Sediment that was once frozen in the ice eventually is deposited in various forms, as illustrated in **Figure 23.** **Till** *is a mixture of various sizes of sediment deposited by a glacier.* Deposits of till are poorly sorted. They commonly contain particles that range in size from boulders to silt. Till often piles up along the sides and fronts of glaciers. It can be shaped and streamlined into many features by the moving ice. For example, *a* **moraine** *is a mound or ridge of unsorted sediment deposited by a glacier.* **Outwash** *is layered sediment deposited by streams of water that flow from a melting glacier.* Outwash consists mostly of well sorted sand and gravel.

Reading Check How does outwash differ from a moraine?

Land Use Practices

At first, it might not seem that human activities affect glaciers. But in some ways, the effects are more significant than they are for other forms of erosion and deposition. For example, human activities contribute to global warming—the gradual increase in Earth's average temperature. This can cause considerable melting of glaciers. Glaciers contain about two-thirds of all the freshwater on Earth. As glaciers melt, sea level rises around the world and coastal flooding is possible.

Lesson 3 Review

Assessment | Online Quiz

Visual Summary

Mass wasting can occur very fast, such as when a landslide occurs, or slowly over many years.

Material moved by a mass wasting event is deposited when it reaches a relatively stable location. An example is talus deposited at the base of this hill.

A glacier erodes Earth's surface as it moves and melts. Glaciers can form U-shaped valleys when they move past mountains.

FOLDABLES®

Use your lesson Foldable to review the lesson. Save your Foldable for the project at the end of the chapter.

What do you think NOW?

You first read the statements below at the beginning of the chapter.

5. Landslides are a natural process that cannot be influenced by human activities.

6. A glacier leaves behind very smooth land as it moves through an area.

Did you change your mind about whether you agree or disagree with the statements? Rewrite any false statements to make them true.

Use Vocabulary

1. **Define** *mass wasting* in your own words.
2. **Use the term** *talus* in a complete sentence.
3. Erosion by the movement of a ________ can produce a U-shaped valley.

Understand Key Concepts

4. Which is the slowest mass wasting event?
   - **A.** creep
   - **B.** landslide
   - **C.** rockfall
   - **D.** slump
5. **Classify** each of the following as features of either erosion or deposition: (a) arete, (b) outwash, (c) cirque, and (d) till.

Interpret Graphics

6. **Examine** the drawing. What feature formed by the glacier is indicated by the arrow?

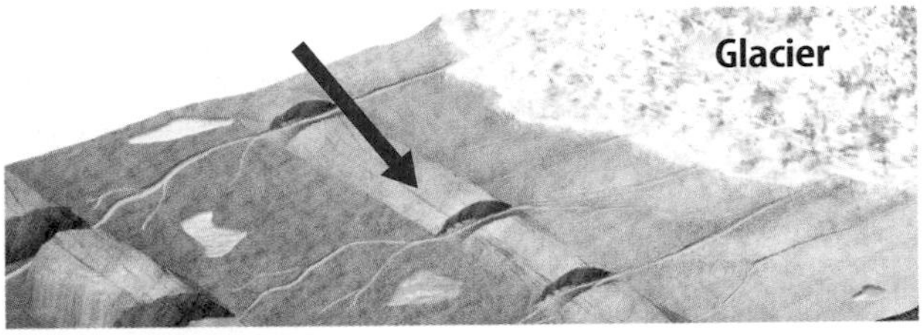

7. **Compare and Contrast** Copy and fill in the table below to compare and contrast moraine and outwash.

Similarities	Differences

Critical Thinking

8. **Compose** a list of evidence for erosion and deposition that you might find in a mountain park that would indicate that glaciers once existed in the area.

Math Skills

Review | Math Practice

9. A mountain's base is 2,500 m high. The peak is 3,500 m high. The horizontal distance covers 4,000 m. What is the percent slope?

Inquiry Lab

40 minutes

Materials

aluminum pan

sand

cup

model house

paper

collection of grass, small sticks, and pebbles

Safety

Avoiding a Landslide

The damage caused by landslides can be costly to humans. Sometimes landslides are even deadly. Landslides occur most often after a period of heavy rain in regions prone to earthquakes. In this lab, you will analyze ways to protect a house from a landslide.

Ask a Question

What are some ways to reduce the risk of a landslide?

Make Observations

1. Read and complete a lab safety form.
2. In a pan, mix two parts sand to one part water. There should be 2–3 cm of damp sand in the pan.
3. Shape the damp sand into a hill. Place a model house on top of the hill.

3

4. Using a cup, pour water over the hill, as if it were raining. Record your observations in your Science Journal.
5. Rebuild the hill and the house. This time, gently shake the pan, as if there were an earthquake. Record your observations.

Landslide Test Observations		
Setup	**Action**	**Observations**
damp sand hill, no ground cover	pour on water with no shaking	
damp sand hill, no ground cover	pour water and shake the pan	

Form a Hypothesis

6 Suppose someone built a house on the top of a hill. What are three ways to reduce the risk of a landslide? For each way, develop a hypothesis to save the house from a landslide.

Test Your Hypothesis

7 Develop a plan for testing each hypothesis. Present your plans to your teacher. When they are approved, obtain additional materials from your teacher to implement the plans.

8 Test your plans with both rain and an earthquake. Rebuild the hill and replace the house between tests, if necessary.

Analyze and Conclude

9 **Describe** the results of your tests. For each test, was your hypothesis correct? What might have worked better?

10 **Analyze** What is the relationship between the amount of water in the soil and the likelihood of a landslide? Use specific examples from the lab in your explanation.

11 **The Big Idea** What are some ways people can alter Earth's surface to reduce the risk of a landslide?

Communicate Your Results

People who live in areas prone to landslides need to take precautions to protect their homes. Write and perform a 30-second public service announcement that describes your results and how they can help people protect their homes.

Inquiry Extension

Evaluate your home for risk of a landslide. Is it on a slope? Do you get a lot of rain? Do you live in an area prone to earthquakes?

Lab Tips

- ☑ Mix the sand and water completely, but allow water to drain out to make a strong hill.
- ☑ Before testing your hypotheses, predict which method will be most effective in reducing the risk of a landslide.

Remember to use scientific methods.

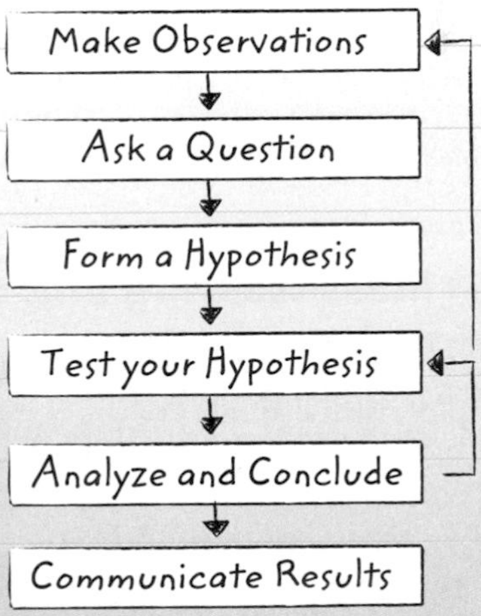

Chapter 9 Study Guide

WebQuest

THE BIG IDEA **Erosion and deposition shape Earth's surface by building up and tearing down landforms.**

Key Concepts Summary

Lesson 1: The Erosion-Deposition Process

- **Erosion** is the wearing away and transportation of weathered material. **Deposition** is the laying down of the eroded material.
- Erosion tends to make rocks more rounded. Erosion can sort sediment according to its grain size.
- Landforms produced by deposition are usually on flat, low land. Landforms produced by erosion are often tall and/or jagged.

Vocabulary

erosion p. 321
deposition p. 323

Lesson 2: Landforms Shaped by Water and Wind

- A young stream moves quickly down steep slopes. A mature stream moves more slowly and develops **meanders.** An old stream is wider and moves slowly.
- Water erosion can form V-shaped valleys. **Longshore currents** reshape beaches. Deposition of sediment from water can form **deltas.**
- Wind **abrasion** can change the shape of rock. Wind deposition can form a **dune** or **loess.**

Vocabulary

meander p. 330
longshore current p. 331
delta p. 332
abrasion p. 334
dune p. 334
loess p. 334

Lesson 3: Mass Wasting and Glaciers

- Gravity can shape Earth's surface through **mass wasting.** Creep is an example of mass wasting.
- A **glacier** erodes Earth's surface as it moves by carving grooves and scratches into rock.

Vocabulary

mass wasting p. 338
landslide p. 339
talus p. 339
glacier p. 341
till p. 342
moraine p. 342
outwash p. 342

Review
- Personal Tutor
- Vocabulary eGames
- Vocabulary eFlashcards

FOLDABLES® Chapter Project

Assemble your lesson Foldables as shown to make a Chapter Project. Use the project to review what you have learned in this chapter.

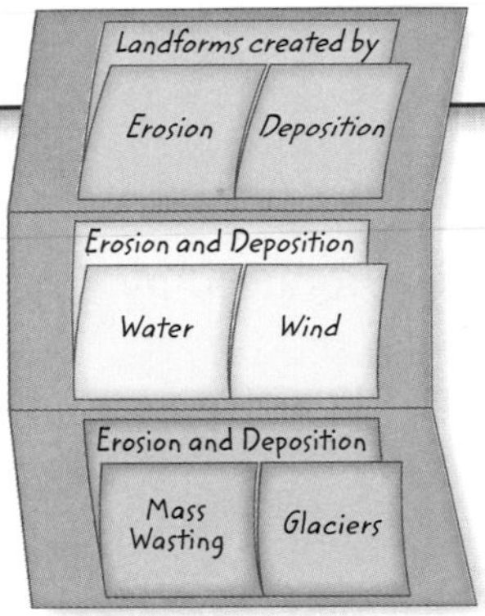

Use Vocabulary

1. Water moving sediment down slopes and a glacier forming a U-shaped valley as it moves past mountains are examples of ________.
2. Wind has less energy as it slows, and ________ of sediment occurs.
3. The grinding of rock as water, wind, or glaciers move sediment is ________.
4. An apron of sediment known as a(n) ________ forms where a stream enters a lake or an ocean.
5. A landslide and creep are types of ________.
6. A large pile of rocks formed from a rockfall is ________.

Link Vocabulary and Key Concepts

Concepts in Motion Interactive Concept Map

Copy this concept map, and then use vocabulary terms from the previous page to complete the concept map.

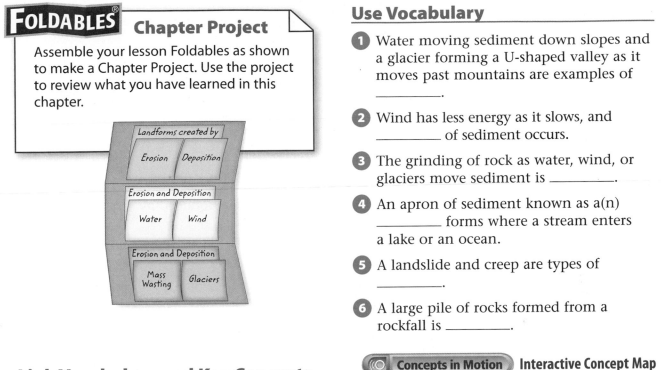

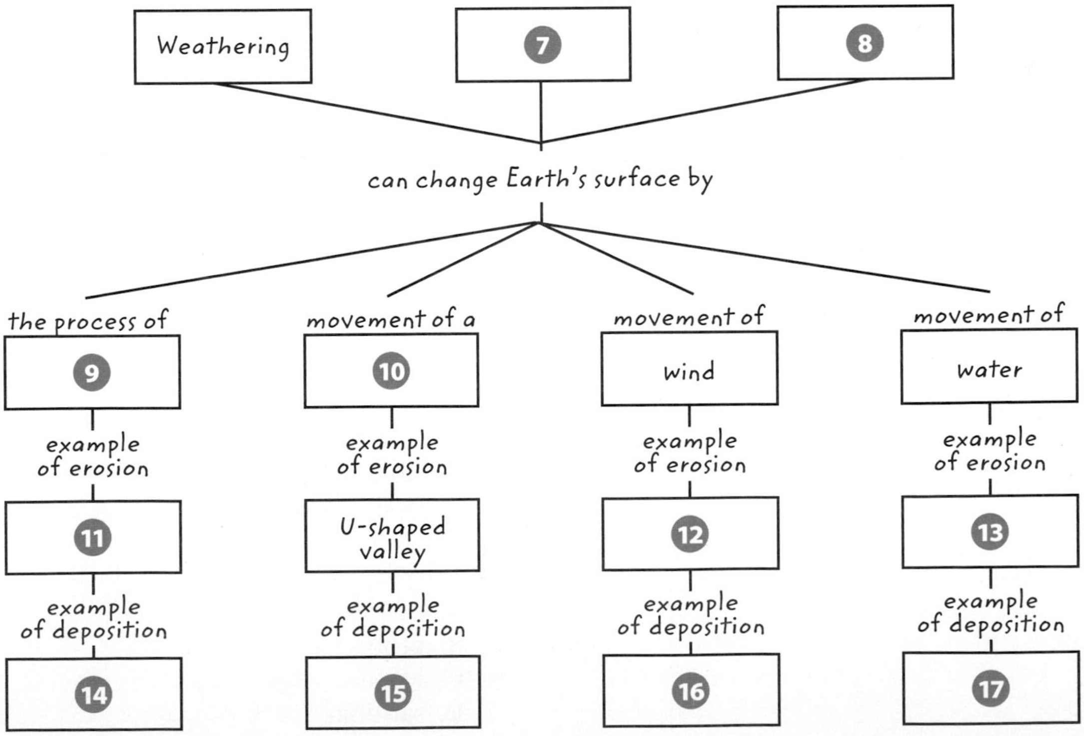

Chapter 9 Review

Understand Key Concepts

1 Which is a structure created mostly by deposition?

A. cirque
B. hoodoo
C. sandbar
D. slump

2 Which shows an example of sediment that is both poorly rounded and well-sorted?

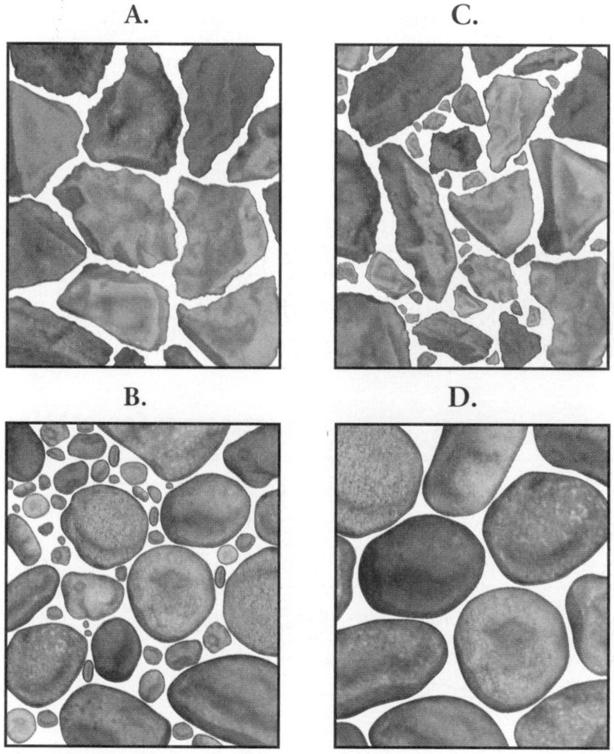

3 Which is typically a low-energy depositional environment?

A. a fast-moving river
B. an ocean shore with waves
C. a stream with meanders
D. a swamp with decaying trees

4 Which would most likely produce a moraine?

A. a glacier
B. an ocean
C. a river
D. the wind

5 The illustration below shows a type of mass wasting.

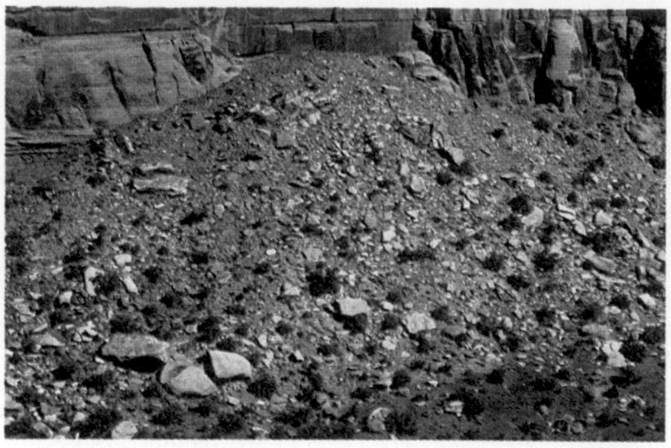

Which was produced by this event?

A. cirque
B. moraine
C. talus
D. till

6 What is the main difference between slump and creep?

A. the type of land that is affected
B. the place where they occur
C. the speed at which they occur
D. the amount of rain that causes them

7 Which best describes the difference between a dune and loess?

A. They are produced in different places.
B. One is erosion, and the other is deposition.
C. They are deposits of different-sized particles.
D. One is caused by wind, and the other is caused by water.

8 Where would you most likely find a meander?

A. in a cave
B. in a mature stream
C. under a glacier
D. beside a waterfall

9 Which is built to prevent beach erosion?

A. delta
B. groin
C. levee
D. sandbar

Assessment

Online Test Practice

Critical Thinking

10 **Describe** one erosion feature and one deposition feature you might expect to find (a) in a valley, (b) in a desert, and (c) high in the mountains.

11 **Classify** these landforms as formed mostly by erosion or deposition: (a) cirque, (b) sand dune, (c) alluvial fan, (d) hoodoo.

12 **Construct** a chart that lists three careless land uses that result in mass wasting that could be dangerous to humans. Include in your chart details about how each land use could be changed to be safer.

13 **Produce** a list of at least three hazardous erosion or deposition conditions that would be worse during a particularly stormy, rainy season.

14 **Predict** several ways the mountains and the valleys shown below might change as the glaciers slide down slopes.

15 **Contrast** the rounding and sorting of sediment caused by a young stream to that caused by an old stream.

Writing in Science

16 **Write** Imagine you are planning to build a home on a high cliff overlooking the sea. Write a paragraph that assesses the potential for mass wasting along the cliff. Describe at least four features that would concern you.

REVIEW THE BIG IDEA

17 How do erosion and deposition shape Earth's surface?

18 The photo below shows a landform known as The Wave in Arizona. Explain how erosion and deposition might have produced this landform.

Math Skills

Review

Math Practice

Use Ratios

19 Calculate the average percent slope of the mountains in parts a and b.

a. Mountain A rises from 3,200 m to 6,700 m over a horizontal distance of 10,000 m.

b. Mountain B rises from 1,400 m to 9,400 m over a horizontal distance of 2.5 km.

c. If mountains A and B are composed of the same materials, which mountain is more likely to experience mass wasting?

20 If the slope of a hill is 10 percent, how many meters does the hill rise for every 10 m of horizontal distance?

Standardized Test Practice

Record your answers on the answer sheet provided by your teacher or on a sheet of paper.

Multiple Choice

1 Which landform is created by deposition?

A alluvial fan

B glacial valley

C mountain range

D river channel

Use the diagram below to answer question 2.

2 Which process formed the features shown in the diagram above?

A A stream eroded and deposited sediment.

B Groundwater deposited minerals in a cave.

C Groundwater dissolved several layers of rock.

D Wind and ice wore away soft sedimentary rock.

3 Which causes movement in mass wasting?

A gravity

B ice

C magnetism

D wind

4 Which typically is NOT a depositional environment?

A delta

B mountain peak

C ocean floor

D swamp

Use the diagram below to answer questions 5 and 6.

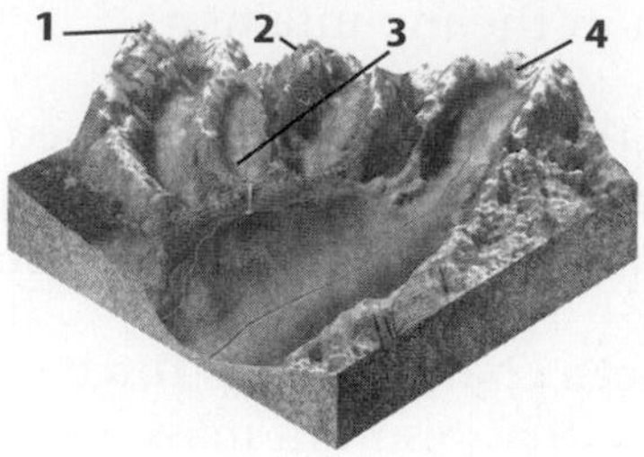

5 Which landform on the diagram above is a cirque?

A 1

B 2

C 3

D 4

6 How did structure *1* form in the diagram above?

A A glacier deposited a large amount of land as it moved.

B A small glacier approached a valley carved by a large glacier.

C Several glaciers descended from the top of the same mountain.

D Two glaciers formed on either side of a ridge.

7 Which agent of erosion can create a limestone cave?

A acidic water

B freezing and melting ice

C growing plant roots

D gusty wind

8 Which deposit does mass wasting create?

A loess

B outwash

C talus

D till

Assessment
Online Standardized Test Practice

Use the diagram below to answer question 9.

9 Which river feature does the arrow point to in the diagram above?

A a current

B a meander

C a valley

D an alluvial fan

10 Which is true of a longshore current?

A It ALWAYS flows perpendicular to the shoreline.

B It can form large underground caves.

C It continually changes the size and shape of beaches.

D It creates stretches of sand dunes along the beach.

11 Which geological process is often caused by the growth of plant roots?

A deposition

B erosion

C sorting

D weathering

Constructed Response

Use the diagram below to answer questions 12 and 13.

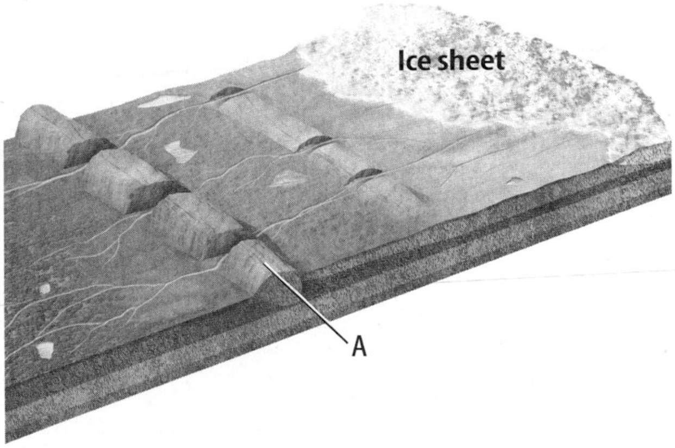

12 Describe the characteristics of deposits found in the feature labeled *A*.

13 How did feature *A* form?

14 A sedimentary rock formation contains alternating layers of fine-grained rock and conglomerate rock, which contains smooth pebble-sized sediments. What is the process that most likely deposited the sediments that make up this rock formation?

15 What factors determine the amount of erosion that occurs during a mass wasting event? How does slope affect the destructive power of this event?

16 What is the typical appearance of a landform formed by erosion?

NEED EXTRA HELP?																
If You Missed Question...	1	2	3	4	5	6	7	8	9	10	11	12	13	14	15	16
Go to Lesson...	1	2	3	1	3	3	2	3	2	2	1	3	3	1, 2	3	1

Chapter 10

Weathering and Soil

THE BIG IDEA What natural processes break down rocks and begin soil formation?

Inquiry What is dust?

Dust is weathered rock or rock broken into tiny pieces. These tiny pieces of rock make up a large part of soil. Sometimes they are so small that they are easily blown by the wind.

- How does rock break into tiny pieces of dust?
- What natural processes break down rocks and begin soil formation?

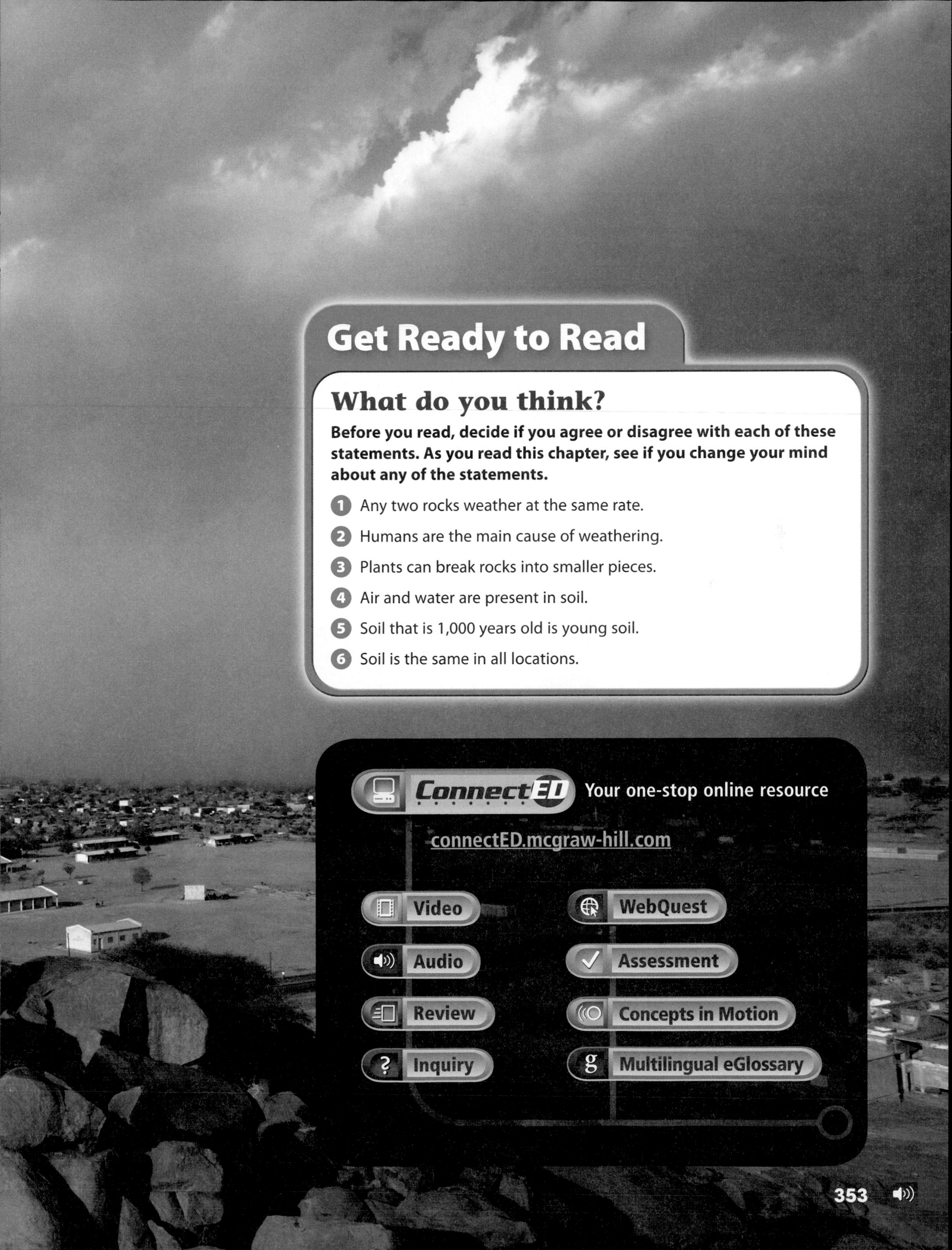

Get Ready to Read

What do you think?

Before you read, decide if you agree or disagree with each of these statements. As you read this chapter, see if you change your mind about any of the statements.

1. Any two rocks weather at the same rate.
2. Humans are the main cause of weathering.
3. Plants can break rocks into smaller pieces.
4. Air and water are present in soil.
5. Soil that is 1,000 years old is young soil.
6. Soil is the same in all locations.

ConnectED Your one-stop online resource

connectED.mcgraw-hill.com

- Video
- Audio
- Review
- Inquiry
- WebQuest
- Assessment
- Concepts in Motion
- Multilingual eGlossary

Lesson 1

Weathering

Reading Guide

Key Concepts
ESSENTIAL QUESTIONS

- How does weathering break down or change rock?
- How do mechanical processes break rocks into smaller pieces?
- How do chemical processes change rocks?

Vocabulary

weathering p. 355

mechanical weathering p. 356

chemical weathering p. 358

oxidation p. 359

g Multilingual eGlossary

Video BrainPOP®

Academic Standards for Science

7.2.6 Describe physical and chemical characteristics of soil layers and how they are influenced by the process of soil formation, including the action of bacteria, fungi, insects, and other organisms.

Also covers: 7.NS.3, 7.NS.7

Inquiry What carved this rock?

Rocks carved like this can be along ocean shores and rivers, in deserts, and even underground. What carved them? What do they have in common?

Inquiry Launch Lab

10 minutes

How can rocks be broken down?

Have you ever looked at the rocks in a stream? What makes some rocks look different from other rocks?

1. Read and complete a lab safety form.
2. Obtain 12 pieces of **candy-coated chocolate candies.** Put four of them in a **plastic cup.** Place the rest into a **container with a lid.**
3. Fasten the lid tightly. Shake the container vigorously 300 times.
4. Remove about half of the pieces. Place them in another plastic cup.
5. Replace the lid, and shake the container 300 more times. Remove the remaining "rocks" and place them in another cup.

Think About This

1. Compare and contrast the "rocks" from each cup.
2. **Key Concept** What do you think caused your "rocks" to change?

Weathering and Its Effects

Everything around you changes over time. Brightly painted walls and signs slowly fade. Shiny cars become rusty. Things made of wood dry out and change color. These changes are some examples of weathering. *The mechanical and chemical processes that change objects on Earth's surface over time are called* **weathering.**

Weathering also changes Earth's surface. Earth's surface today is different from what it was in the past and what it will be in the future. Weathering processes break, wear, abrade, and chemically alter rocks and rock surfaces. Weathering can produce strangely shaped rocks like those on the previous page as well.

Over thousands of years, weathering can break rock into smaller and smaller pieces. These pieces, also known as sediment, are called sand, silt, and clay. The largest soil pieces are sand grains and the smallest ones are clay. Weathering also can change the chemical makeup of a rock. Often, chemical changes can make a rock easier to break down.

Key Concept Check How does weathering break down or change rock?

SCIENCE USE V. COMMON USE

weather

Science Use to change from the action of the environment

Common Use the state of the atmosphere

FOLDABLES®

Make a two-tab book and label it as shown. Use it to organize your notes about how mechanical and chemical weathering affect rocks.

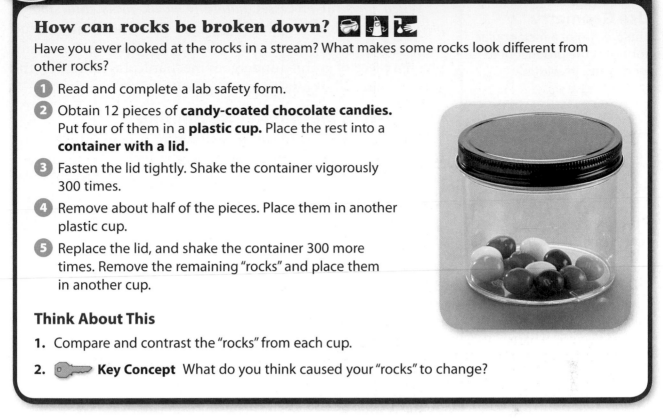

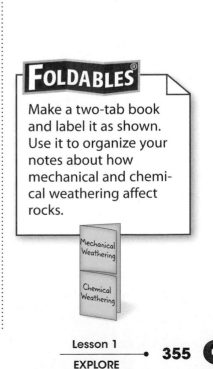

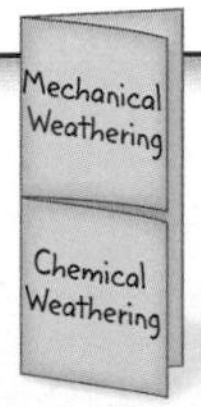

Math Skills

Use Geometry

The area (A) of a rectangular surface is the product of its length and its width.

$$A = \ell \times w$$

Area has square units, such as square centimeters (cm^2).

The surface area (SA) of a regular solid is the sum of the areas of all of its sides.

Practice

A rock sample is a cube and measures 3 cm on each side.

1. What is the surface area of the rock?
2. If you break the sample into two equal parts, what is the total surface area now?

Review

- **Math Practice**
- **Personal Tutor**

Mechanical Weathering

When physical processes naturally break rocks into smaller pieces, **mechanical weathering** occurs. The chemical makeup of a rock is not changed by mechanical weathering. For example, if a piece of granite undergoes mechanical weathering, the smaller pieces that result are still granite.

Examples of Mechanical Weathering

An example of mechanical weathering is when the intense temperature of a forest fire causes nearby rocks to expand and crack. Other causes of mechanical weathering are described in **Table 1** on the next page.

Key Concept Check What is the result of a rock undergoing mechanical weathering?

Surface Area

As shown in **Figure 1,** when something is broken into smaller pieces, the total surface area increases. Surface area is the amount of space on the outside of an object. The rate of weathering depends on a rock's surface area that is exposed to the environment.

Sand and clay are both the result of mechanical weathering. If you pour water on sand, some of the water sticks to the surface. Suppose you pour the same amount of water on an equal volume of clay. Clay particles are only about one-hundredth the size of sand. The greater total surface area of clay particles means more water sticks to its surfaces, along with any substances the water contains. The increased surface area means that weathering has a greater effect on soil with smaller particles. It also increases the rate of chemical weathering.

Reading Check Why is the surface area of a rock important?

Surface Area

Figure 1 The surface area of an object is all of the area on its exposed surfaces.

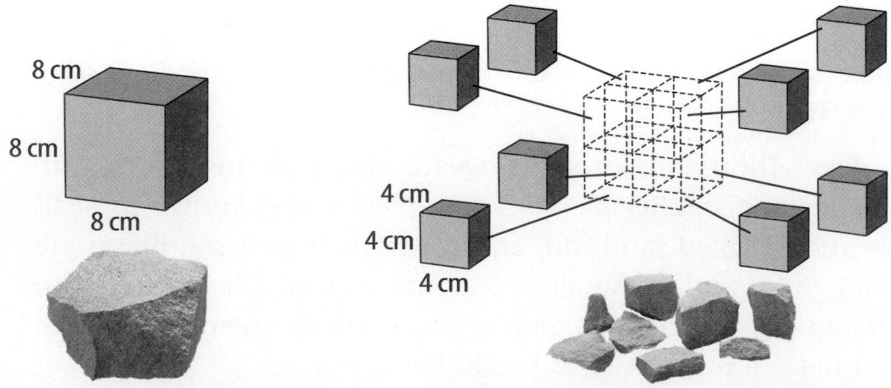

Surface area of cube = 6 equal squares
Surface area = 6 squares × 64 cm^2/square
Surface area = 384 cm^2

Surface area of 8 cubes = 48 equal squares
Surface area = 48 squares × 16 cm^2/square
Surface area = 768 cm^2

Table 1 Causes of Mechanical Weathering

Ice Wedging One of the most effective weathering processes is ice wedging—also called frost wedging. Water enters cracks in rocks. When the temperature reaches 0°C, the water freezes. Water expands as it freezes and the expansion widens the crack. As shown in the photo, repeated freezing and thawing can break rocks apart.	
Abrasion Another effective mechanical weathering process is abrasion—the grinding away of rock by friction or impact. For example, a strong current in a stream can carry loose fragments of rock downstream. The rock fragments tumble and grind against one another. Eventually, the fragments grind themselves into smaller and smaller pieces. Glaciers, wind, and waves along ocean or lake shores can also cause abrasion.	
Plants Plants can cause weathering by crumbling rocks. Imagine a plant growing into a crack in a rock. Roots absorb minerals from the rock, making it weaker. As the plant grows, its stem and roots not only get longer, they also get wider. The growing plant pushes on the sides of the crack. Over time, the rock breaks.	
Animals Animals that live in soil create holes in the soil where water enters and causes weathering. Animals burrowing through loose rock can also help to break down rocks as they dig.	

Figure 2 These granite obelisks were carved in a dry climate, then one was moved to a different, wetter climate.

Visual Check What is the evidence that chemical weathering occurred?

Review
Personal Tutor

Chemical Weathering

Figure 2 shows how chemical weathering can affect some rock. Both obelisks were carved in Egypt about 3,500 years ago. One was moved to New York City in the 1800s. There it has been exposed to more agents of chemical weathering. **Chemical weathering** *changes the materials that are part of a rock into new materials.* If a piece of granite weathers chemically, the composition and size of the granite changes.

Reading Check How does chemical weathering differ from mechanical weathering?

Water and Chemical Weathering

Water is important in chemical weathering because most substances dissolve in water. The minerals that make up most rocks dissolve very slowly in water. Sometimes the amount that dissolves over several years is so small that it seems as though the mineral does not dissolve at all.

For a rock, the process of dissolving happens when minerals in the rock break into smaller parts in solution. For example, table salt is the mineral sodium chloride. When table salt dissolves in water, it breaks into smaller sodium ions and chlorine ions. Ions are atoms that have electrical charges.

Dissolving by Acids

Acids increase the rate of chemical weathering more than rain or water does. The action of acids attracts atoms away from rock minerals and dissolves them in the acid.

Scientists use pH, which is a property of solutions, to learn if a solution is acidic, basic, or neutral. They rate the pH of a solution on a scale from 0 to 14. The pH of an acid is between 0 and 7. Vinegar has a pH of 2 to 3, so it is an acid.

Normal rain is slightly acidic, around 5.6, because carbon dioxide in the air forms a weak acid when it reacts with rain. This means rain can dissolve rocks, as it did to the obelisk in **Figure 2.**

Acid-forming chemicals enter the air from natural sources such as volcanoes. Pollutants in the air also react with rain and make it more acidic. For example, when coal burns, sulfur oxides form and enter the atmosphere. When these oxides dissolve in rain, they ionize the water to produce acid rain. Acid rain has a pH of 4.5 or less. It can cause more chemical weathering than normal rain causes.

Reading Check How can pollutants create acid rain?

Oxidation

Another process that causes chemical weathering is called oxidation. **Oxidation** *combines the element oxygen with other elements or molecules.* Most of the oxygen needed for oxidation comes from the air.

The addition of oxygen to a substance produces an oxide. Iron oxide is a common oxide of Earth materials. Useful ores, such as bauxite and hematite, are oxides of aluminum and iron, respectively.

Do all parts of an iron-containing rock oxidize at the same rate? The outside of the rock has the most contact with oxygen in the air. Therefore, this outer part oxidizes the most. When rocks that contain iron oxidize, a layer of red iron oxide forms on the gray, outside surface, as shown in **Figure 3.**

Key Concept Check How does chemical weathering change rock?

Figure 3 The red outer layer of this rock is created by oxidation. The oxidized minerals in the outer layer are different from the minerals in the center of the rock.

Inquiry MiniLab — 20 minutes

How are rocks weathered?

Chemical weathering can be caused by weak acids. These acids react with minerals in the rock and produce new substances.

1. Read and complete a lab safety form.
2. Use a **magnifying lens** to carefully examine the **rocks** provided by your teacher. Note details such as color, texture, and size of grains.
3. Use a **thin-stem pipette** to place several drops of **water** on each rock.
4. Observe what happens to each rock. Record your observations in your Science Journal.
5. Use the pipette to place several drops of dilute **hydrochloric acid** on each rock. Again, record your observations.

Analyze and Conclude

1. **Recognize Cause and Effect** Which substance reacted with the rock? How do you know a reaction occurred?
2. **Key Concept** What might happen to rocks exposed to such a substance in the environment?

Figure 4 The NIST wall was constructed of rock from every state and several foreign countries. It has been exposed to continuous weathering since 1948.

Visual Check Point out which rocks have been weathered most.

What affects weathering rates?

You saw in **Figure 2** that similar rocks can weather at different rates. What causes this difference?

The **environment** in which weathering occurs helps determine the rate of weathering. Both types of weathering depend on water and temperature. Mechanical weathering occurs fastest in locations that have frequent temperature changes. This type of weathering requires cycles of either wetting and drying or freezing and thawing. Chemical weathering is fastest in warm, wet places. As a result, weathering often occurs fastest in the regions near the equator.

ACADEMIC VOCABULARY
environment
the physical, chemical, and biotic factors acting in a community

Reading Check Why is weathering slow in cold, dry places?

The type of rock being weathered also affects the rate of weathering and the kinds of products that result. Examine **Figure 4** to see how different rocks weather under the same conditions.

Rocks can be made of one mineral or many minerals. The most easily weathered mineral determines the rate that the entire rock weathers. For example, rocks containing minerals with low hardness undergo mechanical weathering more easily. This increases the surface area of the rock. Because more surface area is exposed, these rocks more easily undergo chemical weathering. The size and number of holes in a rock also affect the rate at which a rock weathers.

Lesson 1 Review

Assessment Online Quiz
Inquiry Virtual Lab

Visual Summary

Weathering is the mechanical and chemical processes that change things over time.

Mechanical weathering does not change the identity of the materials that make up rocks. It breaks up rocks into smaller pieces.

Chemical weathering is the process that changes the minerals in rock into different materials. Oxidation is a type of chemical weathering, as is reaction with an acid.

FOLDABLES®

Use your lesson Foldable to review the lesson. Save your Foldable for the project at the end of the chapter.

What do you think NOW?

You first read the statements below at the beginning of the chapter.

1. Any two rocks weather at the same rate.
2. Humans are the main cause of weathering.
3. Plants can break rocks into smaller pieces.

Did you change your mind about whether you agree or disagree with the statements? Rewrite any false statements to make them true.

Use Vocabulary

1. The chemical and physical processes that change things over time are called ______.
2. **Define** *mechanical weathering* in your own words.
3. **Use the term** *oxidation* correctly in a sentence.

Understand Key Concepts

4. **Identify** What kinds of rocks weather most rapidly?
5. What conditions produce the fastest weathering?
   A. cold and dry
   B. hot and dry
   C. hot and wet
   D. cold and wet
6. **Summarize** How does weathering change rocks and minerals?

Interpret Graphics

7. **Explain** How might chemical weathering change the appearance of this obelisk?

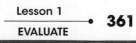

8. **Compare and contrast** types of weathering by copying and completing this table.

Weathering	Alike	Different
Chemical and Physical		

Critical Thinking

9. **Explain** how rates of chemical weathering change as temperature increases.

Math Skills

Review
Math Practice

10. A block of stone measures 15 cm × 15 cm × 20 cm. What is the total surface area of the stone? Hint: A block has six sides.

Inquiry **Skill Practice** **Model** **30 minutes**

What causes weathering?

Over time, rocks that are exposed at Earth's surface undergo mechanical and chemical weathering. You have already seen how mechanical processes break down a rock into small particles called sediment. Now you will model the mechanical weathering of rock and determine how much rock is weathered.

Materials

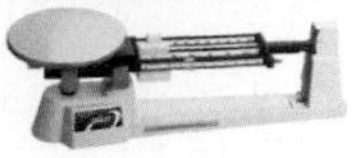
balance

rock chips

wide-mouthed plastic bottle with lid

water

timer

paper towels

Safety

Learn It

Scientists use **models** in a lab for many reasons. One use of a model is to study processes that happen too slowly to study them efficiently outside of the lab. Weathering is such a process.

Try It

1. Read and complete a lab safety form.
2. Copy the data table into your Science Journal.
3. Soak some rock chips in water. Then drain off the water and pat dry. Use a balance to measure 10.0 g of the soaked rock chips.
4. Place the rock chips in a bottle. Add enough water to cover the chips. Put the lid on the bottle. Shake the bottle vigorously for 3 minutes.
5. Drain the water and carefully remove the rock chips. Pat off the water with a paper towel. Measure the mass of the damp rock chips to the nearest tenth of a gram. Record the results in the data table.
6. Repeat steps 4 and 5 four additional times.
7. Calculate the percent of mass lost in each trial. Use the following steps. Record each answer in your data table.
   a. **Find the amount of mass lost.** Subtract the mass at the end of the trial from the mass at the start of the trial.
   b. **Find the percent of mass lost.** Divide the amount of mass lost (step a) by the mass at the start of the trial. Your answer should be to three decimal places. Then multiply by 100 to change the answer to a percent.

Apply It

8. How did this percentage change during the experiment?
9. **Key Concept** What type of weathering did you model in this experiment? How is this model similar to the natural process that it represents? How does it differ?

Data Table

Trial	Mass of Rocks at End of Trial (g)	Amount of Mass Lost (g)	Percent of Mass Lost
Start	10.0	None	None
1			
2			
3			
4			
5			

Lesson 2

Soil

Reading Guide

Key Concepts
ESSENTIAL QUESTIONS
- How is soil created?
- What are soil horizons?
- Which soil properties can be observed and measured?
- How are soils and soil conditions related to life?

Vocabulary
soil p. 364
organic matter p. 364
pore p. 364
decomposition p. 365
parent material p. 366
climate p. 366
topography p. 367
biota p. 367
horizon p. 368

g Multilingual eGlossary

Academic Standards for Science
7.2.6 Describe physical and chemical characteristics of soil layers and how they are influenced by the process of soil formation, including the action of bacteria, fungi, insects, and other organisms.
Also covers: 7.NS.7, 7.DP.1, 7.DP.2, 7.DP.3, 7.DP.4, 7.DP.6, 7.DP.9, 7.DP.10, 7.DP.11

Inquiry Why is the soil so red?

Soils have different colors because of what they contain. This soil contains iron, which makes it red. Why do iron-rich soils turn red? Is it red underground, too? What color is your soil?

Inquiry Launch Lab

10 minutes

What is in your soil?

Soils are different in different places. Suppose you look at the soil along a river bank. Is this soil like the soil in a field? Are either of these soils like the soil near your home? What is in the soil where you live?

1. Read and complete a lab safety form.
2. Place about a cup of **local soil** in a **jar** that has a **lid.** Add a few drops of **liquid detergent.**
3. Add **water** to the jar until it is almost full. Firmly attach the lid.
4. Shake for 1 minute and place it on your desk.
5. Observe the contents of the jar after 2 minutes and again after 5 minutes.

Think About This

1. How many different layers did your sample form?
2. **Key Concept** From your observations, what do you think makes up each layer?

What is soil?

A soil scientist might think of soil as the "active skin of Earth." Soil is full of life, and life on Earth depends on soil.

If you were to dig into soil, what would you find? About half the volume of soil is solid materials. The other half is liquids and gases. **Soil** *is a mixture of weathered rock, rock fragments, decayed organic matter, water, and air.*

As you read in Lesson 1, weathering gradually breaks rocks into smaller and smaller fragments. These fragments, however, do not become good soil until plants and animals live in them. Plants and animals add organic matter to the rock fragments. **Organic matter** *is the remains of something that was once alive.*

Water and air are in varying amounts in the small holes and spaces in soil. *These small holes and spaces in soil are called* **pores.** Soil pores are important because water flows in and through them. The movement of water through the pore spaces is known as porosity. Pores can vary greatly in size depending on the particles that make up the soil. **Figure 5** indicates how the sizes of pores change with differences in particle sizes or differences in soil types. Larger particles have larger spaces.

Word Origin
pore
from Greek *poros,* means "passage"

Reading Check What is in a pore?

The Organic Part of Soil

Recall that the solid part of soil that was once part of an organism is called organic matter. Pieces of leaves, dead insects, and waste products of animals that are in the soil are examples of organic matter.

How does organic matter form? Soil is home to many organisms, from roots of plants to tiny bacteria. Over time, roots die, and leaves and twigs fall to the ground. Organisms living in the soil decompose these materials for food. **Decomposition** *is the process of changing once-living material into dark-colored organic matter.* In the end, something that was once recognizable as a pine needle becomes organic matter.

Reading Check How is decomposition related to organic matter?

Organic matter gives soil important properties. Dark soil absorbs sunlight while organic matter holds water and provides plant nutrients. Organic material holds minerals together in clusters. This helps keep soil pores open for the movement of water and air in soil.

The Inorganic Part of Soil

The term *inorganic* describes materials that have never been alive. Mechanical and chemical weathering of rocks into fragments forms inorganic matter in soil. Soil scientists classify the soil fragments according to their sizes. Rock fragments can be boulders, cobbles, gravel, sand, silt, or clay. **Figure 5** shows a magnified image of the three smallest sizes of soil particles. Between large particles are large pores, which affect soil properties such as drainage and water storage.

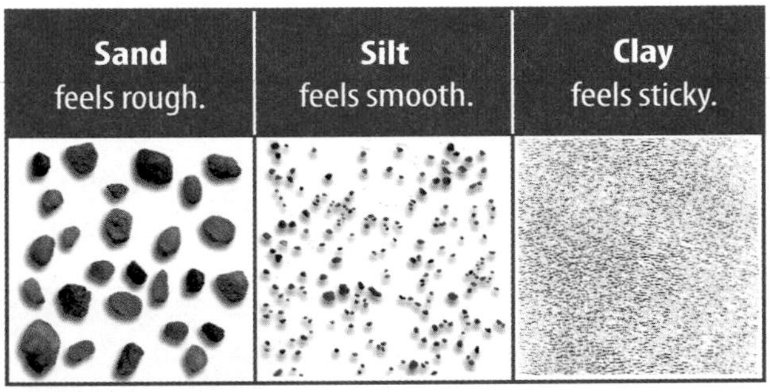

Sand
feels rough.
Silt
feels smooth.
Clay
feels sticky.

Figure 5 Inorganic matter contributes different properties to soil. Large pores occur between large particles, which drain rapidly; small particle pores retain more water in the soil.

Inquiry MiniLab

20 minutes

How can you determine soil composition?

Scientists can sometimes feel soil to help identify the soil's composition. Can you identify soil composition by how it feels?

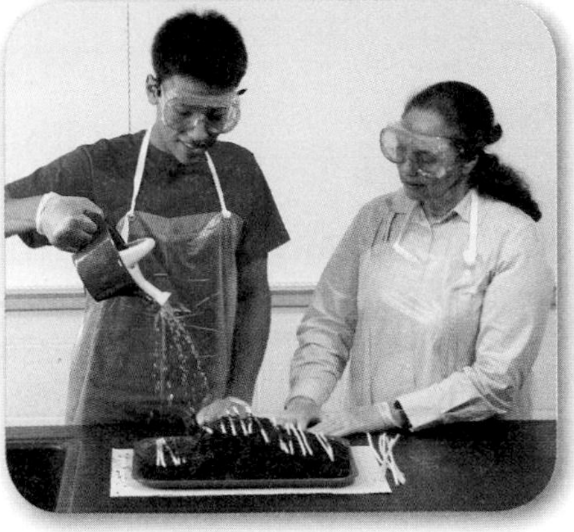

1. Read and complete a lab safety form.
2. Carefully observe your **soil** sample with a **magnifying lens.** In your Science Journal, record the sizes of the particles you observe.
3. Fill a **spray bottle** or a **sprinkling can** with **water.** Use the water to moisten the soil.
4. Rub some moist soil between your fingers.
5. Use **Figure 5** and your observations to classify your soil as mostly sand, mostly silt, or mostly clay.

Analyze and Conclude

1. **Classify** What texture does the soil have?
2. **Key Concept** What other properties of your soil sample did you observe?

FOLDABLES®

Divide a circle into five parts and label it as shown. Use the circle organizer to record information about the factors of soil formation.

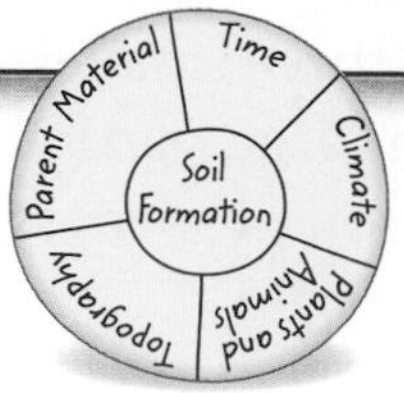

Formation of Soil

Why is the soil near your school different from the soil along a river bank or soil in a desert? The many kinds of soils that form depend on five factors, called the factors of soil formation. The five factors are parent material, climate, topography, biota, and time.

Parent Material

The starting material of soil is **parent material.** It is made of the rock or **sediment** that weathers and forms the soil, as shown in **Figure 6.** Soil can develop from rock that weathered in the same place where the rock first formed. This rock is known as bedrock. Soil also can develop from weathered pieces of rock that were carried by wind or water from another location. The particle size and the type of the parent material can determine the properties of the soil that develops.

Key Concept Check What is the role of parent material in creating soil?

Parent Material

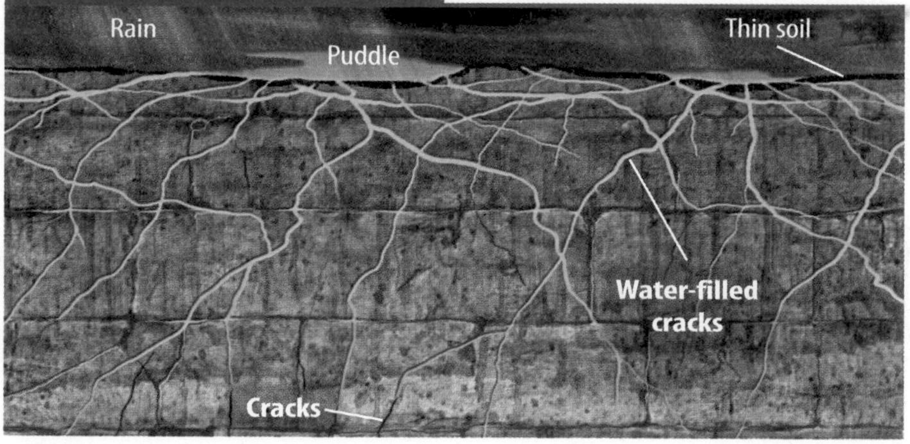

Figure 6 Parent material is broken down by mechanical and chemical weathering.

Concepts in Motion

Animation

Climate

The average weather of an area is its **climate.** How can you describe the climate where you live? The amount of precipitation and the daily and average annual temperatures are some measures of climate. If the parent material is in a warm, wet climate, soil formation can be rapid. Large amounts of rain can speed up weathering as it contacts the surface of the rock. Warm temperatures also speed up weathering by increasing the rate of chemical changes. Weathering rates also increase in locations where freezing and thawing occur.

Reading Check Why do soils form rapidly in warm, moist climates?

REVIEW VOCABULARY

sediment
rock material that has been broken down or dissolved in water

Topography

Is the land where you live flat or hilly? If it is hilly, are the hills steep or gentle? **Topography** *is the shape and steepness of the landscape.* The topography of an area determines what happens to water that reaches the soil surface. For example, in flat landscapes, most of the water enters the soil. Water speeds weathering. In steep landscapes, much of the water runs downhill. Water running downhill can carry soil with it, leaving some slopes bare of soil. **Figure 7** shows that broken rock and sediments collect at the bottom of a steep slope. There, they undergo further weathering.

Figure 7 Broken rock and sediment collects at the bottom of steep slopes. Sediment is redistributed by streams and moving water as sandbars and shoreline deposition.

Reading Check What is topography?

Biota

Soil is home to a large number and variety of organisms that speed up the process of soil formation. They range from the smallest bacteria to small rodents. **Biota** (bi OH tuh) *is all of the organisms that live in a region.* Biota in the soil help speed up the process of soil formation. Insects and rodents form passages for water to move through. Organisms such as insects and fungi are involved in the decomposition of materials that form organic matter. As **Figure 8** shows, rock and soil are affected by organism activity.

Key Concept Check How does biota aid in soil formation?

Time

As time passes, weathering is constantly acting on rock and sediment. Therefore, soil formation is a constant, but slow, process. A 90 year-old person is considered old, but soil is still young after a thousand years. It is difficult to see all the soil-producing changes in one human lifetime.

As **Figure 8** shows, mature soils develop layers as new soil forms on top of older soil. Each layer has different characteristics as organic matter is added or as water carries elements and nutrients downward.

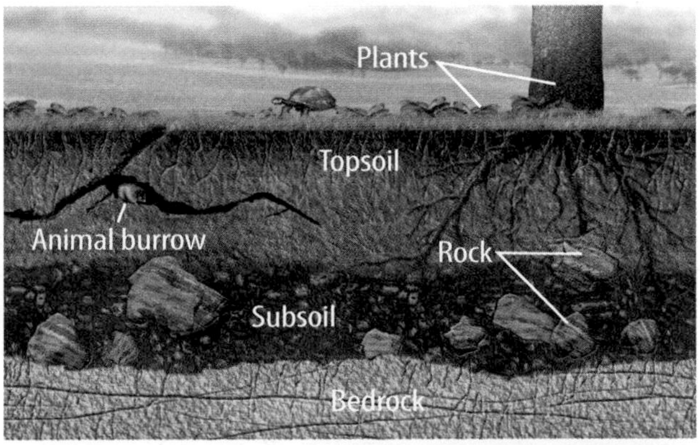

Figure 8 Mature soils form over thousands of years as plants, animals, and other processes break down the bedrock and subsoil.

Horizons

You know that soil is more than what you see when you look at the ground. If you dig into the soil, you see that it is different as you dig deeper. You might see dark soil on or near the surface. The soil you see deeper down is lighter in color and probably contains larger pieces of rock. Soil might be loosely packed on the surface, but deeper soil is more tightly packed.

Word Origin
horizon
from Latin *horizontem*, means "bounding circle"

Soil has layers, called horizons. **Horizons** *are layers of soil formed from the movement of the products of weathering.* Each horizon has characteristics based on the type of materials it contains. The three horizons common to most soils are identified as A-horizon, B-horizon, and C-horizon, as shown in **Figure 9**. Each horizon can appear quite different depending on where the soil forms. The top, organic layer is called the O-horizon and the unweathered, bedrock layer is the R-horizon.

Key Concept Check What are soil horizons?

Common Soil Horizons

Figure 9 A-, B-, and C-horizons are commonly found in soil. Some soils contain other kinds of horizons. Not every kind of horizon is found in every soil.

Visual Check One horizon contains a lot of clay, and another horizon is dark. Of these two horizons, which is on top? Explain your answer.

A-horizon
The A-horizon is the part of the soil that you are the most likely to see when you dig a shallow hole in the soil with your fingers. Organic matter from the decay of roots and the action of soil organisms often makes this horizon excellent for plant growth. Because the A-horizon contains most of the organic matter in the soil, it is usually darker than other horizons.

B-horizon
When water from rain or snow seeps through pores in the A-horizon, it carries clay particles. The clay is then deposited below the upper layer, forming a B-horizon. Other materials also accumulate in B-horizons.

C-horizon
The layer of weathered parent material is called the C-horizon. Parent material can be rock or sediments.

Soil Properties and Uses

Soil horizons in different locations have different properties. Recall that properties are characteristics used to describe something. Several soil properties are listed and described in **Table 2.** The properties of a soil determine the best use of that soil. For example, soil that is young, deep, and has few horizons is good for plant growth.

Observing and Measuring Soil Properties

Some properties of soil can be determined just by observation. The amount of sand, silt, and clay in a soil can be estimated by feeling the soil. The types of horizons also provide information about the soil. The color of a soil is easily observed and shows how much organic matter it contains.

Many soil properties can be measured more accurately in a laboratory. Laboratory measurements can determine exactly what is in each sample of soil. Measuring nutrient content and soil pH to determine the suitability for farming or gardening requires careful laboratory analysis.

Key Concept Check List soil properties that can be observed and measured.

Soil Properties That Support Life

Plants depend on the nutrients that come from organic matter and the weathering of rocks. Plant growers can observe how well plants grow in the soil to get information about soil nutrients. Crop plants depend less on weathering for nutrients because farmers usually use fertilizers that add nutrients to the soil.

It takes thousands of years to form soil from parent material. Soil that is damaged or misused is slow to replenish its nutrients. The restoration can take many human lifetimes.

Key Concept Check How are soil nutrients related to life?

Table 2 Soil Properties

Color	Soil can be described based on the color, such as how yellow, brown, or red it is; how light or dark it is; and how intense the color is.
Texture	The texture of soil ranges from boulder-sized pieces to very fine clay.
Structure	Soil structure describes the shape of soil clumps and how the particles are held together. Structure can look grainy, blocky, or prism shaped.
Consistency	The hardness or softness of a soil is the measure of its consistency. Consistency varies with moisture. For example, some soils have a soft, slippery consistency when they are moist.
Infiltration	Infiltration describes how fast water enters a soil.
Soil moisture	The amount of water in soil pores is its moisture content. Soil scientists determine weight loss by drying samples in an oven at 100°C. The weight difference is the amount of moisture in the soil.
pH	Most soils have a pH between 5.5 and 8.2. Soils can be more acidic in humid environments.
Fertility	Soil fertility is the measure of the ability of a soil to support plant growth. Soil fertility includes the amount of certain elements that are essential for good plant growth.
Temperature	On the ground surface, soil temperature changes with daily cycles and the weather. Soil temperature in lower layers changes less.

Table 2 Many soil properties are observed. Others are more likely to be measured. These properties can predict soil quality.

Soil Types of North America

Figure 10 There are 12 major soil types in the world. The colors in the key match the colors on the map.

Visual Check What soil property might be typical of a desert in the Southwest?

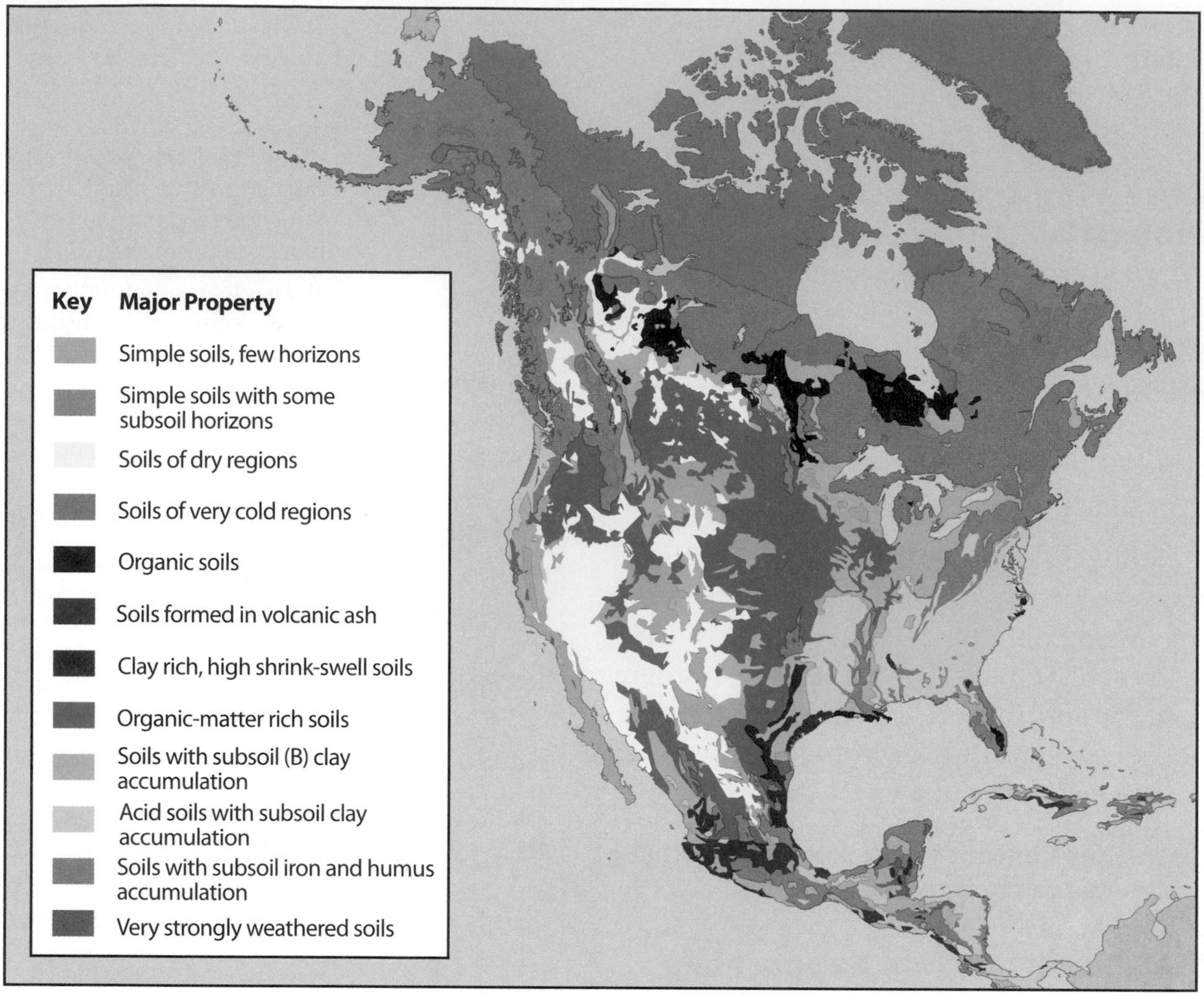

Soil Types and Locations

Recall that the type of soil formed depends partly on climate. Can you see how the soil types shown in **Figure 10** depend on the climate where they form? For example, in northern parts of Canada and Alaska, and along mountain ranges, some soils stay frozen throughout the year. These soils are very simple and have few horizons. In the mid-latitudes, you can see a wide variety of soil types and depths. Farther toward the warm and wet climate of the tropics, soils are deeply weathered. Soils formed near volcanoes, such as those in Alaska and California, are acidic and have fine ash particles from volcanic activity.

Key Concept Check Are soils the same everywhere?

Lesson 2 Review

Assessment Online Quiz

Visual Summary

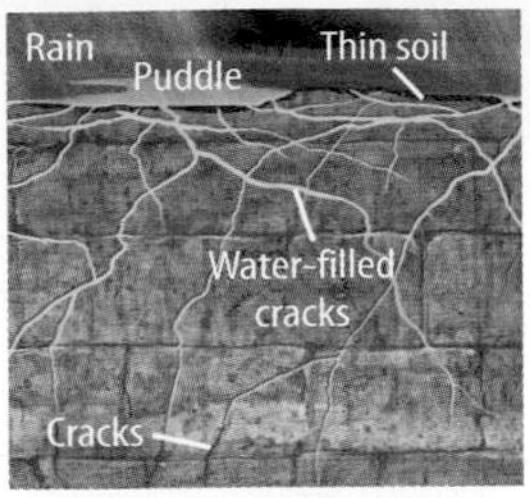

The inorganic matter in soil is made up of weathered parent material. The organic matter in soil is made by the decomposition of things that once lived.

The five factors that contribute to soil formation are parent material, topography, climate, biota, and time.

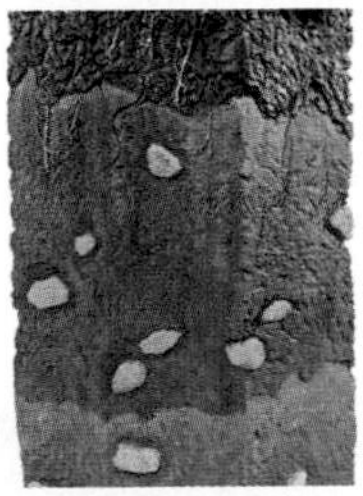

Soil contains horizons, which are layers formed from the movement of the products of weathering. Most soil contains A-, B-, and C-horizons.

FOLDABLES®

Use your lesson Foldable to review the lesson. Save your Foldable for the project at the end of the chapter.

What do you think NOW?

You first read the statements below at the beginning of the chapter.

4. Air and water are present in soil.

5. Soil that is 1,000 years old is a young soil.

6. Soil is the same in all locations.

Did you change your mind about whether you agree or disagree with the statements? Rewrite any false statements to make them true.

Use Vocabulary

1. **Use the term** *decomposition* correctly in a sentence.
2. **Explain** how a leaf is organic matter.
3. **Define** *biota* in your own words.

Understand Key Concepts

4. What is in the C-horizon?
   - **A.** bedrock
   - **B.** clay
   - **C.** weathered stone
   - **D.** organic material
5. **Contrast** rocks and soil. List three differences.
6. **Describe** what fills soil pores.

Interpret Graphics

7. **Identify** Use the diagram to identify the soil horizon that contains the most organic matter.

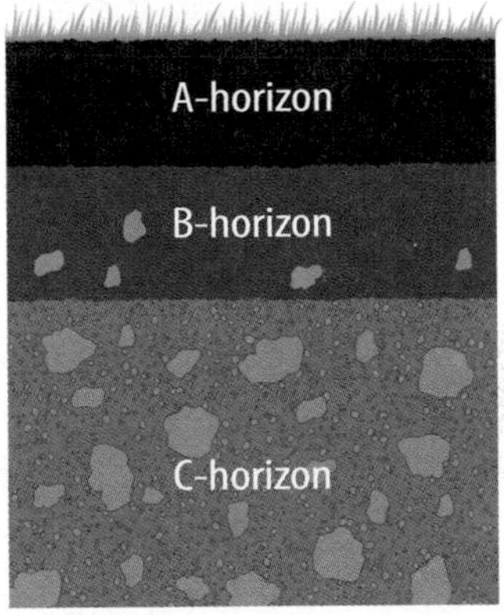

8. **Sequence** Copy the graphic organizer below. Starting with parent material, list steps that lead to the formation of an A-horizon.

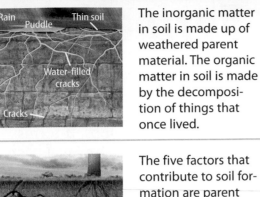

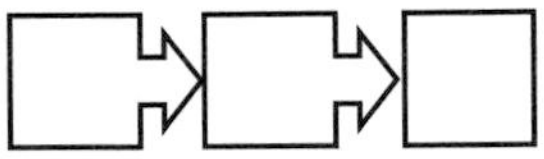

Critical Thinking

9. **Explain** What three things does soil provide for plants?
10. **Apply** Describe the soil-forming factors around your school.

Inquiry **Lab**

40 minutes

Materials

index cards

glue

colored pencils

silt

clay

sand

topsoil

Safety

Soil Horizons and Soil Formation

Soil, the complex mixture of weathered rock and partially decayed organic matter, covers most of Earth's land surfaces. Soil is different in different locations because it forms from different rocks and in different climates and topography. As soil develops, it forms horizontal layers that have different properties. These layers vary in color and thickness. Together, they form a soil profile. How can you model a soil profile and relate it to how soil formed at that location?

Question

How is a soil profile in a certain location determined by the soil-forming factors there?

Procedure

1. Discuss the types of rocks, the climate, and the topography of Minnesota, Colorado, and Florida. You can use reference materials to obtain this information. Record some similarities and differences in your Science Journal.
2. Examine the soil profile from each of the samples shown on these pages. Record some similarities and differences.
3. Draw the sample profiles and mark the A-, B-, and C-horizons that are present on each drawing.
4. Use what you know about soil formation and the sample profiles to state how each soil horizon relates to factors of soil formation.

Florida

5. Choose one of the three soil profiles shown in this activity. Use the provided materials to model this profile. Label the model with the state name and the horizons you see.
6. Examine the information about parent material, climate, and topography for the state you chose. Make generalizations about how soil profiles are affected by soil-forming factors.

Analyze and Conclude

7. Were any of the profiles missing an A-, B-, or C-horizon? Explain why a horizon might not be present in a profile.
8. Was one of the horizons thicker in any of the profiles? What could explain this?
9. **The Big Idea** What did your conclusions show about how a soil profile relates to soil-forming factors?

Minnesota

Colorado

Communicate Your Results

As a class, place a soil-profile model for each listed state on a map of the United States. For each profile, discuss what other states might have a similar soil profile.

Inquiry Extension

Choose a location on another continent. Find out whether the soil profile and soil-forming factors there support your hypothesis.

Lab Tips

☑ Review where silt, clay, sand, and topsoil appear in soil horizons before modeling a soil profile.

Remember to use scientific methods.

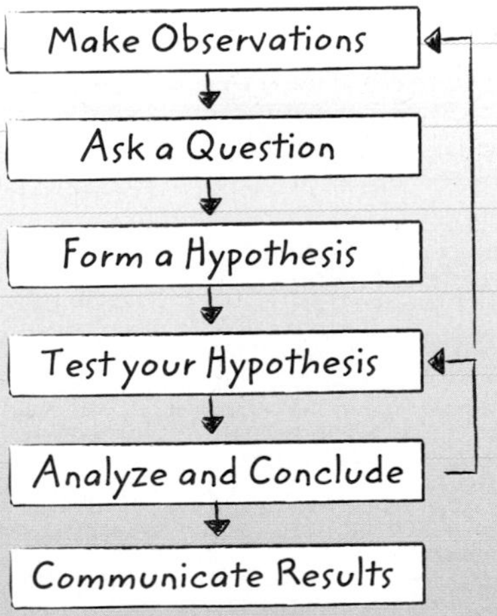

Chapter 10 Study Guide

WebQuest

THE BIG IDEA **Mechanical and chemical weathering break down rocks, which begins the formation of soil.**

Key Concepts Summary

Lesson 1: Weathering

- **Weathering** acts mechanically and chemically and breaks down rocks.
- Through the action of Earth processes such as freezing and thawing, **mechanical weathering** breaks rocks into smaller pieces.
- **Chemical weathering** by water and acids change the materials in rocks into new materials.

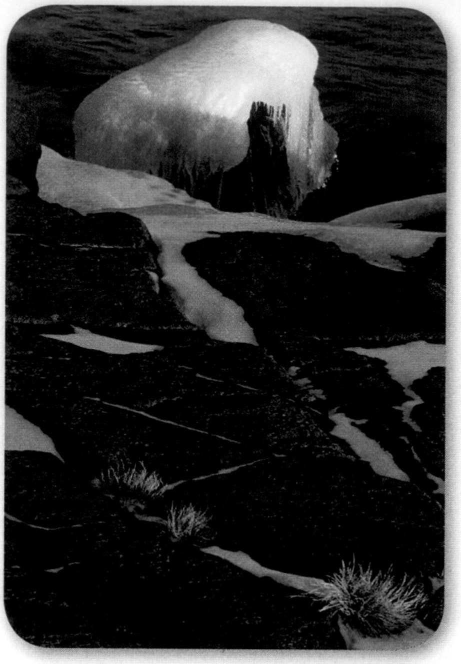

Vocabulary

weathering p. 355
mechanical weathering p. 356
chemical weathering p. 358
oxidation p. 359

Lesson 2: Soil

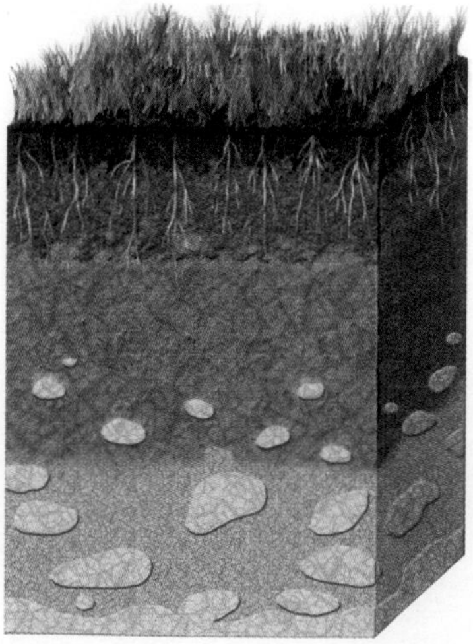

- Five factors—**parent material, climate, topography, biota,** and time—affect the formation of soil.
- **Horizons** are soil layers formed from the movement of the various products of weathering.
- Soil can be characterized by properties such as the amount of **organic matter** and inorganic matter.
- Plants depend on certain characteristics of soil, such as organic matter and amount of weathering.

Vocabulary

soil p. 364
organic matter p. 364
pore p. 364
decomposition p. 365
parent material p. 366
climate p. 366
topography p. 367
biota p. 367
horizon p. 368

Review
- Personal Tutor
- Vocabulary eGames
- Vocabulary eFlashcards

FOLDABLES® Chapter Project

Assemble your lesson Foldables as shown to make a Chapter Project. Use the project to review what you have learned in this chapter.

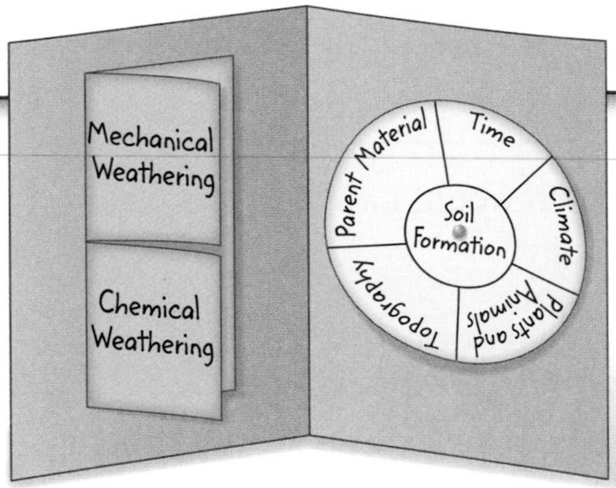

Use Vocabulary

1. When rock undergoes ________, the product is smaller pieces of the same kind of rock.
2. Rock fragments and other materials combine to form ________.
3. The part of soil that comes from plants and animals is ________.
4. An important soil-forming factor that includes trees and microorganisms is ________.
5. Oxygen combines with other elements or compounds during the process of ________.
6. The shape of the land is its ________.

Concepts in Motion Interactive Concept Map

Link Vocabulary and Key Concepts

Copy this concept map, and then use vocabulary terms from the previous page to complete the concept map.

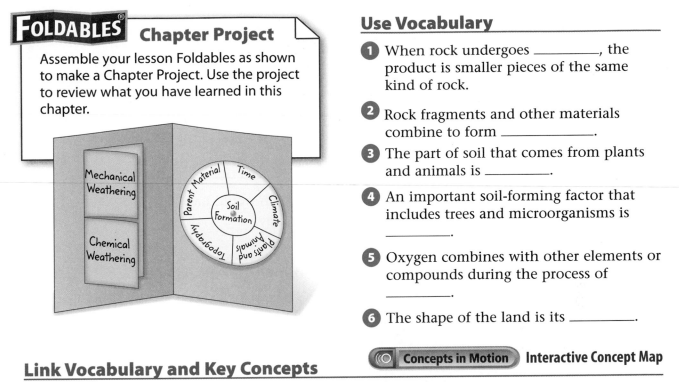

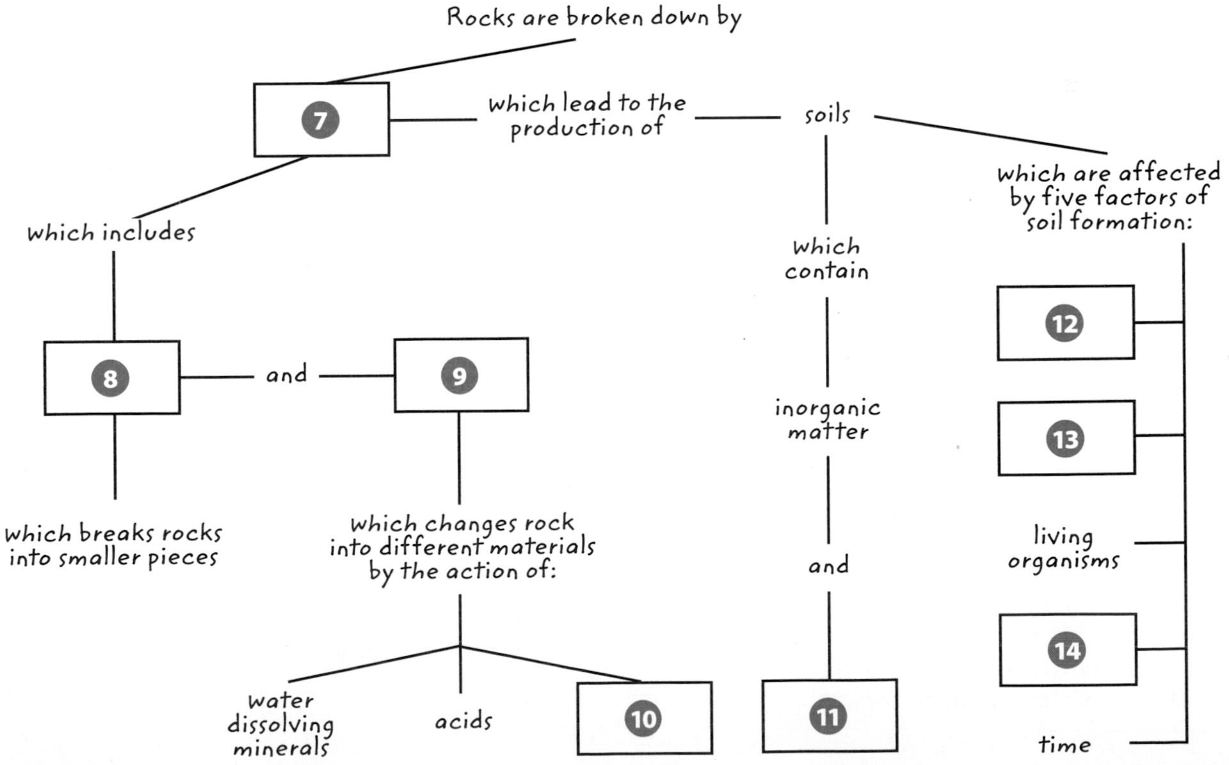

Chapter 10 Review

Understand Key Concepts

1 Which is an example of chemical weathering?

A. abrasion
B. ice wedging
C. organisms
D. oxidation

2 A statue made of limestone is damaged by its environment. What most likely caused this damage?

A. acid
B. a root
C. topography
D. wind

3 The picture below shows how mechanical and chemical weathering changes a rock.

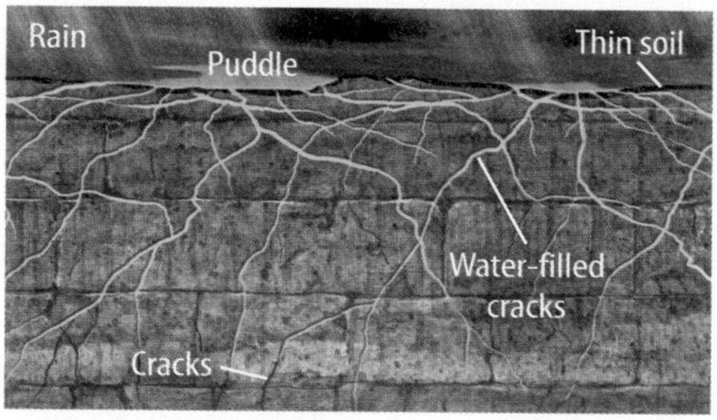

What kind of chemical weathering is most likely illustrated above?

A. acid rain reactions
B. ice wedging
C. mineral absorption
D. root pressure

4 What kind of climate has the fastest weathering?

A. cold and dry
B. cold and wet
C. hot and dry
D. hot and wet

5 How does organic matter help soil?

A. It decomposes bacteria in the soil.
B. It holds water.
C. It weathers and forms clay.
D. It weathers nearby rocks.

6 The table below shows different sizes of soil particles.

Sand feels rough.	**Silt** feels smooth.	**Clay** feels sticky.
	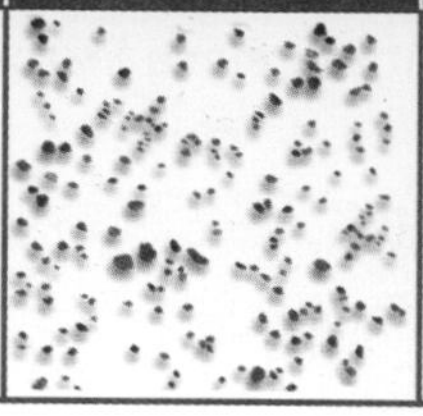	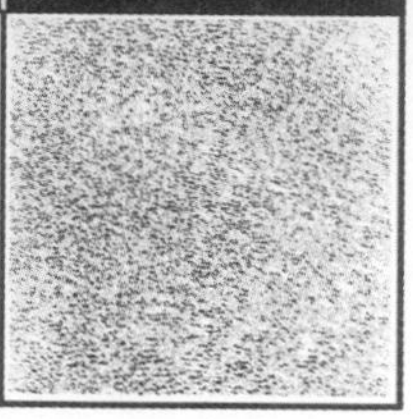

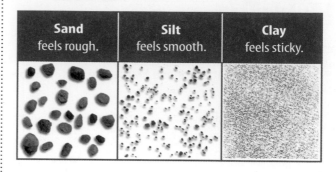

Which would have the largest pores?

A. clay
B. sand
C. a mixture of clay and silt
D. a mixture of sand and silt

7 What is the main material in a B-horizon?

A. clay
B. iron
C. organic matter
D. parent material

8 Which statement is true about soils worldwide?

A. They are the same color.
B. They are the same age.
C. They are different in many ways.
D. They differ only in thickness.

9 Which process causes river gravel to have rounded edges?

A. abrasion
B. acid rain
C. ice wedging
D. oxidation

10 Which is NOT a soil property?

A. color
B. pH
C. texture
D. topography

Assessment
Online Test Practice

Critical Thinking

11 **Infer** A student notices that when it rains, most of the water that falls on her yard runs off instead of soaking in. Is it more likely that the soil in her yard contains mostly clay or mostly sand? Explain.

12 **Explain** The diagram below shows an example of soil biota.

How does this biota help form soil?

13 **Explain** how climate helps to create soil.

14 **Describe** how soil horizons are produced and identified.

15 **Compare** Stone buildings near cities usually undergo more chemical weathering than buildings away from cities. Explain why this is true.

16 **Summarize** how soil is important to life.

17 **Identify** how chemical weathering and mechanical weathering make soil.

18 **Describe** how ice wedging and plant roots are similar in breaking rocks down.

Writing in Science

19 **Write** a short story that explains how a large boulder becomes sand through weathering. In your story, include both mechanical and chemical weathering. Include main ideas and supporting details.

REVIEW THE BIG IDEA

20 What processes might have created the dust in the chapter opener photo?

21 How might dust become an agent of soil formation?

Math Skills

Review
Math Practice

Use the following data to answer the questions.

Rock Sample	Length	Width	Height
X	8 cm	8 cm	8 cm
Y	2 cm	16 cm	16 cm

22 How do the surface areas of rock sample X and rock sample Y compare?

23 What is the surface area of each face of rock X? Rock Y?

24 Rock sample X breaks into 8 equal cubes.

a. What is the surface area of each cube?

b. What is the total surface area of the broken rock?

c. How does this area compare with the original surface area?

Standardized Test Practice

Record your answers on the answer sheet provided by your teacher or on a sheet of paper.

Multiple Choice

1 Which is true of oxidation?

A It is a mechanical process.

B No change occurs in the makeup of rock.

C Rock parts weather at different rates.

D Water enters cracks in rock.

2 What does the term *biota* describe?

A ALL of the organisms living in a region

B how burrowing animals change soil and rock

C the ability of a certain type of soil to support plant life

D the remains of once-living things in soil

Use the table below to answer question 3.

Rain sample	pH
1	5.3
2	4.7
3	5.5
4	4.3

3 Students collected and recorded the pH of four samples of rainwater in the table above. Which sample is the most acidic?

A 1

B 2

C 3

D 4

4 Which soil property is a measure of the consistency of soil?

A the moisture content

B its ability to support plant growth

C its hardness or softness

D the size of its particles

Use the diagram below to answer question 5.

5 At which spot in the landscape above would you most likely find a pile of broken, weathering rocks?

A 1

B 2

C 3

D 4

6 What is the pH range of most soils?

A 2.0–3.0

B 4.4–7.0

C 5.5–8.2

D 7.5–10.5

7 The grinding of rock by friction or impact is called

A abrasion.

B decomposition.

C erosion.

D infiltration.

8 Which is NOT organic matter?

A animal wastes

B dead insects

C decayed leaves

D mineral fragments

Use the diagram below to answer question 9.

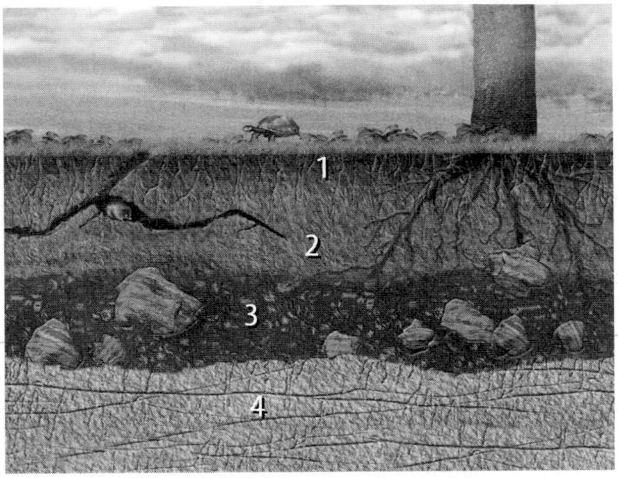

9 Which area pictured in the diagram above contains the most organic matter?

A 1

B 2

C 3

D 4

10 Which is LEAST likely to weather bedrock buried beneath layers of soil?

A abrasion

B acidic water

C ice

D plant roots

11 If volume were the same, which would have the greatest surface area?

A clay

B gravel

C sand

D silt

Constructed Response

Use the table below to answer questions 12 and 13.

Soil Horizon	Description
O	
A	
B	the clay-rich layer beneath the A-horizon.
C	
R	unweathered bedrock that makes up the parent material for the soil.

12 Describe the O-, A-, and C- horizons to complete the table above.

13 Why is the B-horizon rich in clay?

14 What are the five factors of soil formation? Describe each.

15 What are pores in soil? Why are they important?

NEED EXTRA HELP?															
If You Missed Question...	1	2	3	4	5	6	7	8	9	10	11	12	13	14	15
Go to Lesson...	1	2	1	2	2	2	1	2	2	1	1	2	2	2	2

Unit 4

LIFE: Structure & Function

1600 — 1650 — 1800

1665
Robert Hooke discovers cells while examining thin slices of cork under a microscope.

1674
Anton van Leeuwenhoek observes living cells under a microscope and names the moving organisms *animalcules*.

1831
The nucleus is given its name by Robert Brown.

1839
Theodor Schwann publishes a book suggesting that the cell is the basic unit of life.

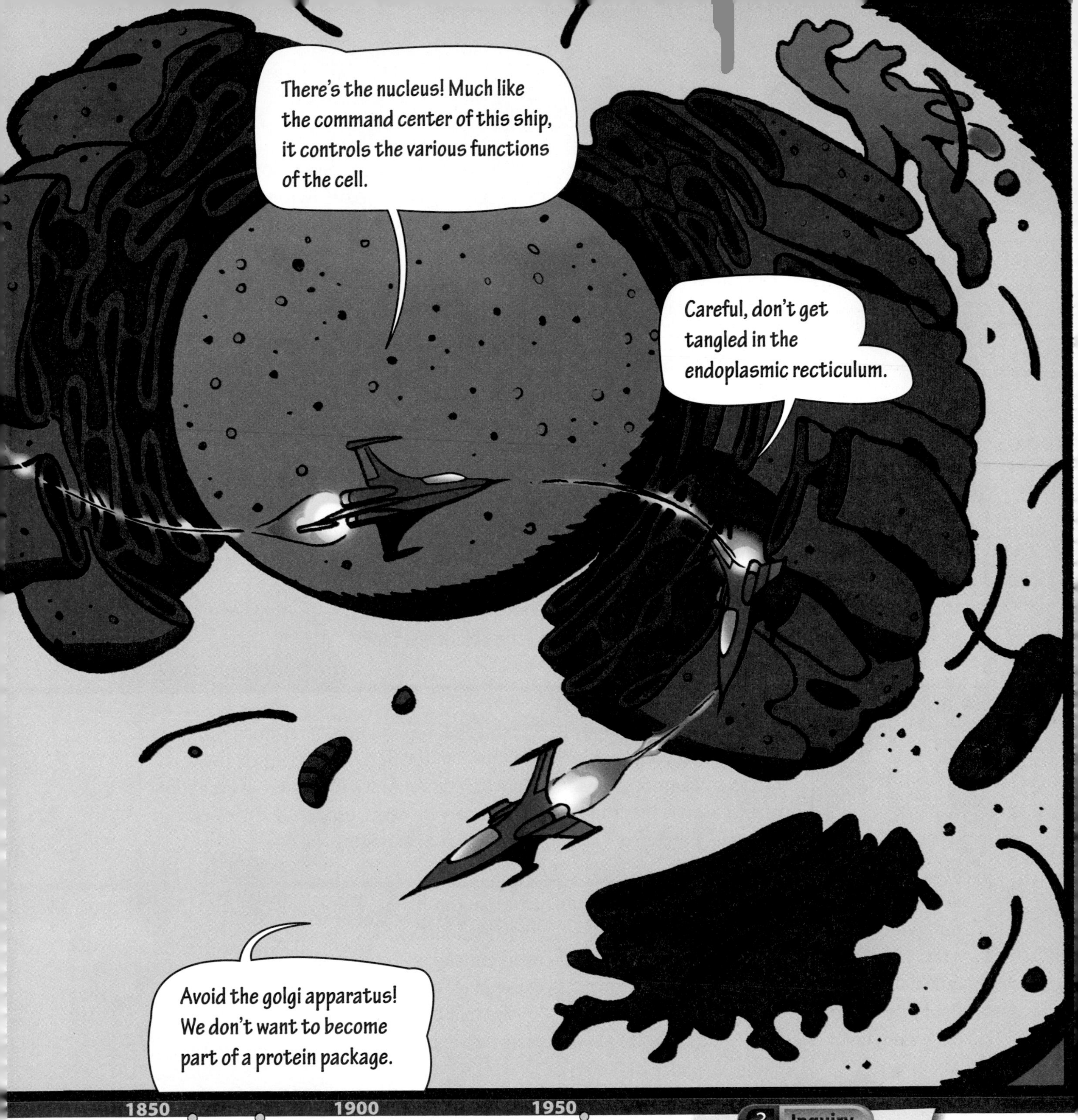

1850 · 1900 · 1950

1858
Rudolf Virchow concludes that all cells come from preexisting cells.

1875
Walther Flemming introduces the term *mitosis* and notes that chromosomes split longitudinally during this process.

1953
James Watson and Francis Crick develop the double-helix model of DNA.

? Inquiry
Visit ConnectED for this unit's **STEM** activity.

Models

What would you do without your heart—one of the most important muscles in your body? Worldwide, people are on donor lists, patiently waiting for heart transplants because their hearts are not working properly. Today, doctors can diagnose and treat heart problems with the help of models.

A **model** is a representation of an object, a process, an event, or a system that is similar to the physical object or idea being studied. Models can be used to study things that are too big or too small, happen too quickly or too slowly, or are too dangerous or too expensive to study directly. However, some models can replace organs or bones in the body that are not functioning properly.

A magnetic resonance image (MRI) is a type of model created by using a strong magnetic field and radio waves. MRI machines produce high-resolution images of the body from a series of images of different layers of the heart. For example, an MRI model of the heart allows cardiologists to diagnose heart disease or damage. To obtain a clear MRI, the patient must be still. Even the beating of the heart can limit the ability of an MRI to capture clear images.

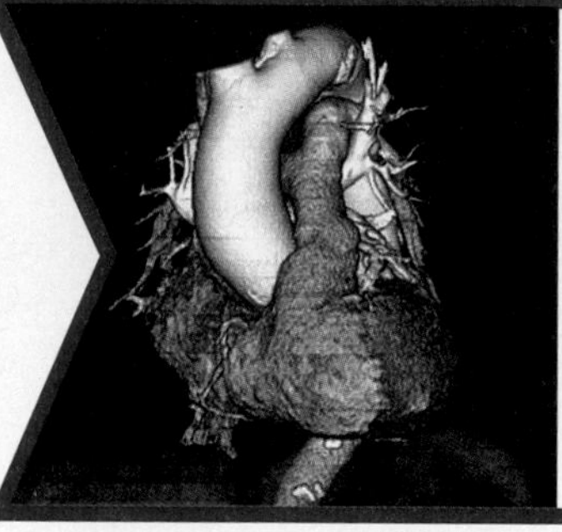

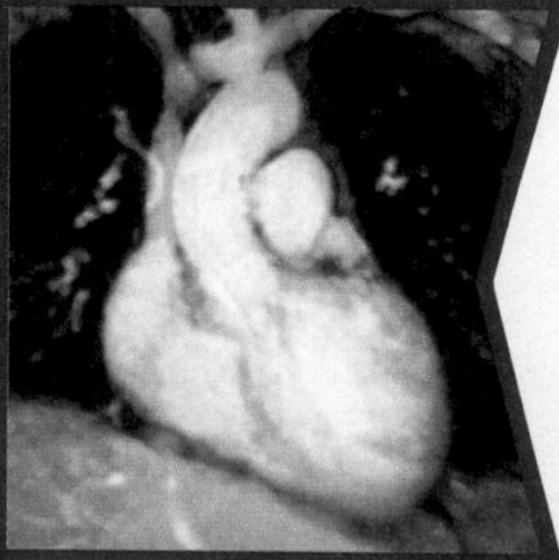

A computer tomography (CT) scan combines multiple X-ray images into a detailed 3-D visual model of structures in the body. Cardiologists use this model to diagnose a malfunctioning heart or blocked arteries. A limitation of a CT scan is that some coronary artery diseases, especially if they do not involve a buildup of calcium, may not be detected by the scan.

An artificial heart is a physical model of a human heart that can pump blood throughout the body. For a patient with heart failure, a doctor might suggest temporarily replacing the heart with an artificial model while they wait for a transplant. Because of its size, the replacement heart is suitable for about only 50 percent of the male population. And, it is stable only for about 2 years before it wears out.

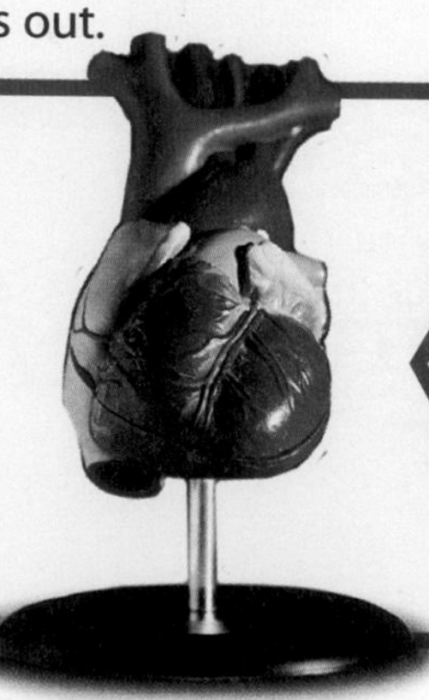

A cardiologist might use a physical model of a heart to explain a diagnosis to a patient. The parts of the heart can be touched and manipulated to explain how a heart works and the location of any complications. However, this physical model does not function like a real heart, and it cannot be used to diagnose disease.

Maps as Models

One way to think of a computer model, such as an MRI or a CT scan, is as a map. A map is a model that shows how locations are arranged in space. A map can be a model of a small area, such as your street. Or, maps can be models of very large areas, such as a state, a country, or the world.

Biologists study maps to understand where different animal species live, how they interact, and how they migrate. Most animals travel in search of food, water, specific weather, or a place to mate. By placing small electronic tracking devices on migrating animals biologists can create maps of their movements, such as the map of elephant movement in **Figure 1.** These maps are models that help determine how animals survive, repeat the patterns of their life cycle, and respond to environmental changes.

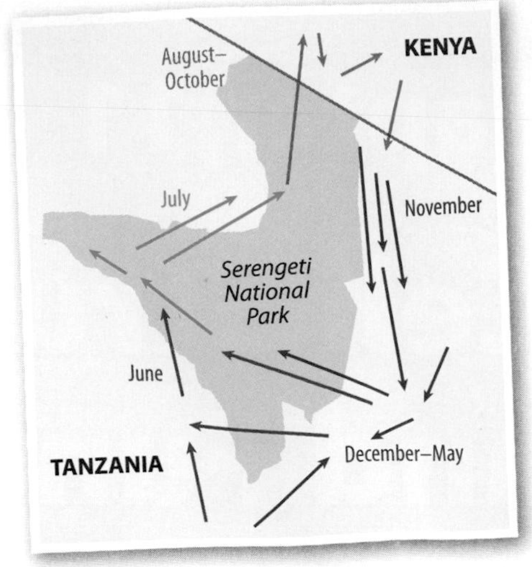

Figure 1 This map is a model of elephants' movements. The colored lines show the paths of three elephants that were equipped with tracking devices for a year.

Limitations of Models

It is impossible to include all the details about an object or an idea in one model. A map of elephant migration does not tell you whether the elephant is eating, sleeping, or playing with other elephants. Scientists must consider the limitations of the models they use when drawing conclusions about animal behavior.

All models have limitations. When making decisions about a patient's diagnosis and treatment, a cardiologist must be aware of the information each type of model does and does not provide. CT scans and MRIs each provide different diagnostic information. A doctor needs to know what information is needed before choosing which model to use. Scientists and doctors consider the purpose and limitations of the models they use to ensure that they draw the most accurate conclusions possible.

Inquiry MiniLab — 40 minutes

How can you model an elephant enclosure?

You are part of a zoo design firm hired to design a model of a new elephant enclosure that mimics a natural habitat.

1. Read and complete a lab safety form.
2. Research elephants and study the map above to understand the needs of elephants.
3. Create a detailed map of your enclosure using **colored pencils** and a **ruler.** Be sure to include the scale, labels, and a legend.
4. Trade maps with a classmate.
5. Using **salt dough** and **craft supplies,** build a physical 3-D model of the elephant enclosure.

Analyze and Conclude

1. **Describe** How did you decide on the scale for your map?
2. **Compare** What are some similarities between your map and your physical model?
3. **Contrast** What are the benefits and the limitations of your physical model?

Chapter 11

Cell Structure and Function

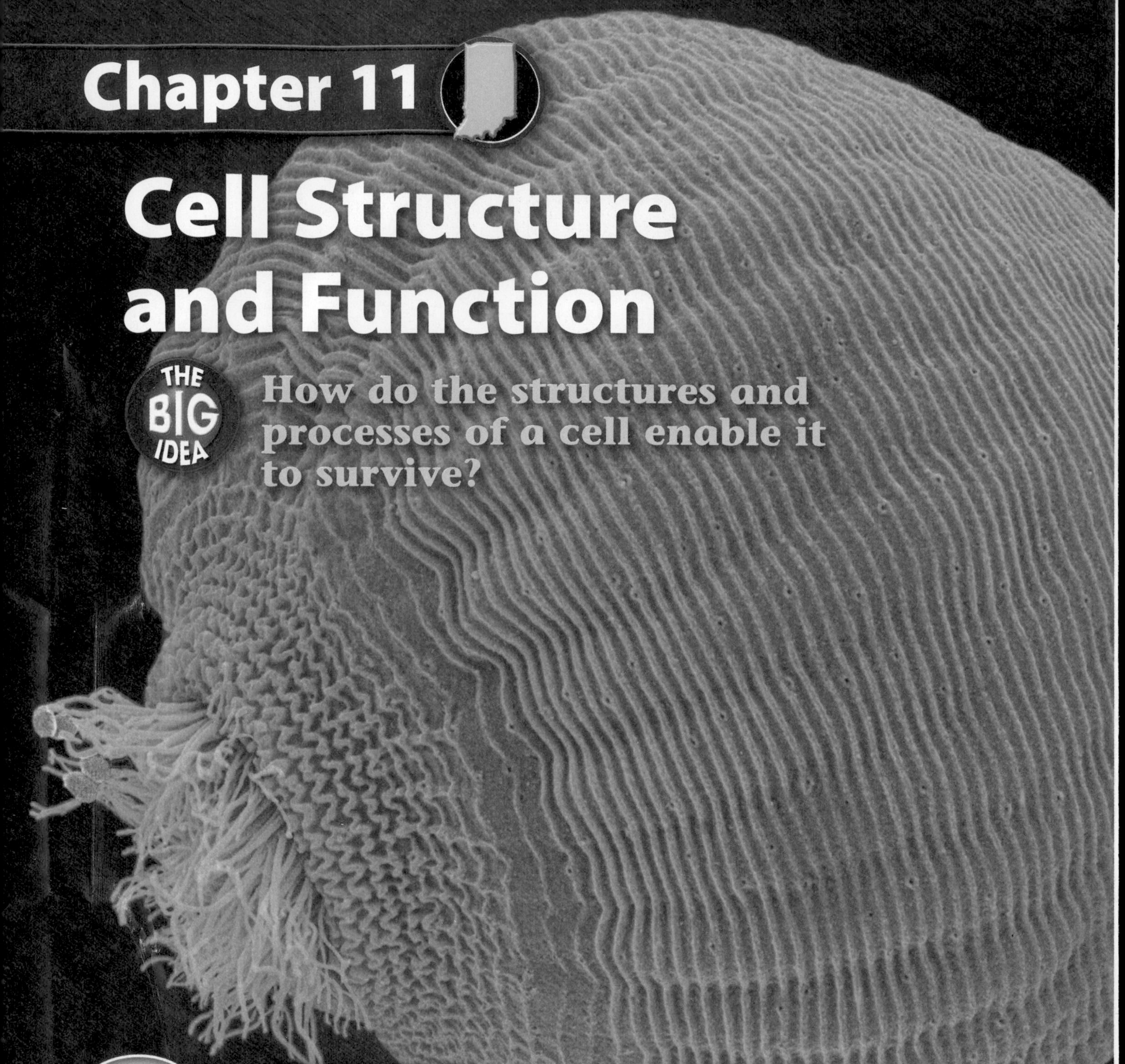

THE BIG IDEA

How do the structures and processes of a cell enable it to survive?

Inquiry Alien Life?

You might think this unicellular organism looks like something out of a science-fiction movie. Although it looks scary, the hairlike structures in its mouth enable the organism to survive.

- What do you think the hairlike structures do?
- How might the shape of the hairlike structures relate to their function?
- How do you think the structures and processes of a cell enable it to survive?

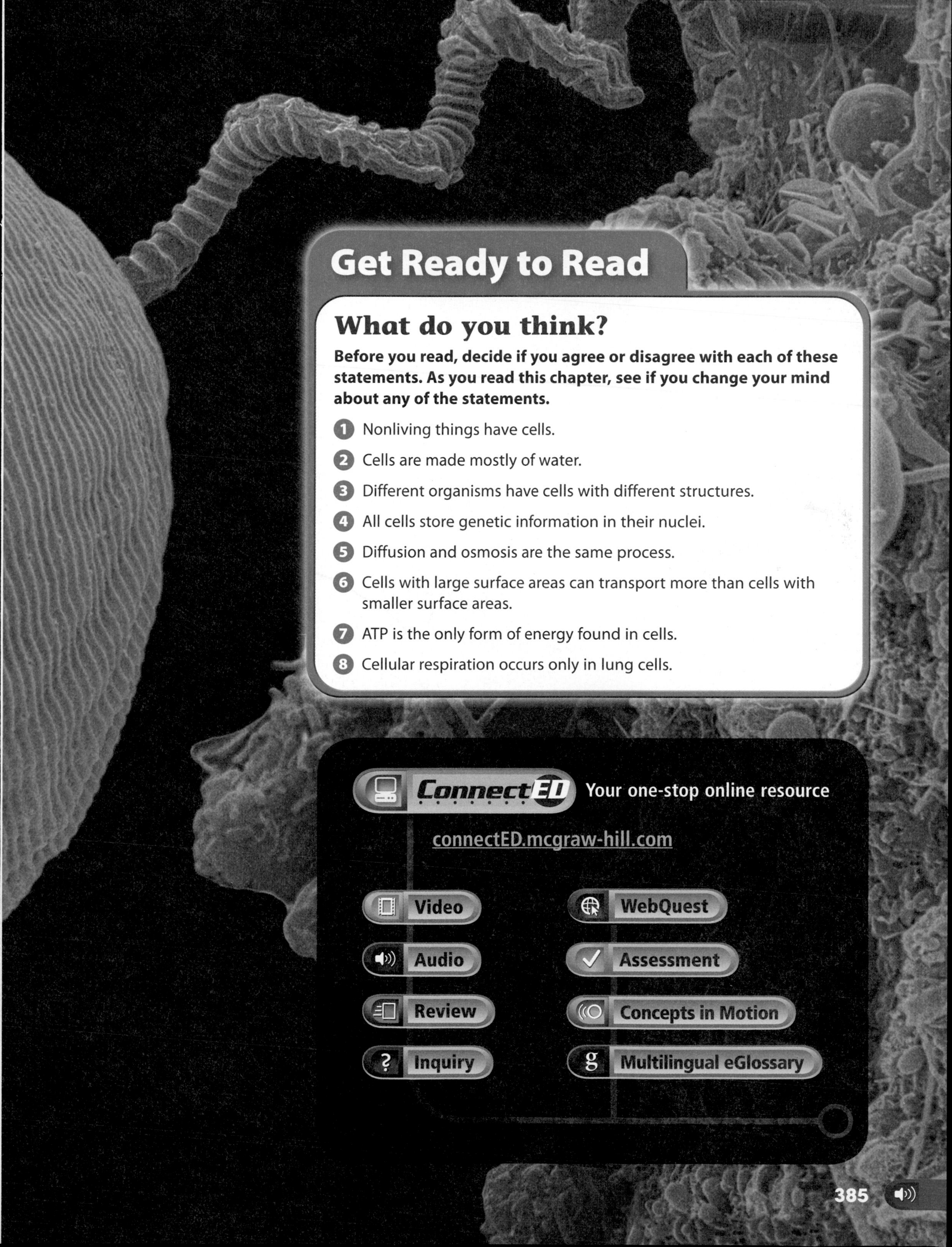

Get Ready to Read

What do you think?

Before you read, decide if you agree or disagree with each of these statements. As you read this chapter, see if you change your mind about any of the statements.

1. Nonliving things have cells.
2. Cells are made mostly of water.
3. Different organisms have cells with different structures.
4. All cells store genetic information in their nuclei.
5. Diffusion and osmosis are the same process.
6. Cells with large surface areas can transport more than cells with smaller surface areas.
7. ATP is the only form of energy found in cells.
8. Cellular respiration occurs only in lung cells.

ConnectED Your one-stop online resource

connectED.mcgraw-hill.com

- Video
- Audio
- Review
- Inquiry
- WebQuest
- Assessment
- Concepts in Motion
- Multilingual eGlossary

Lesson 1

Cells and Life

Reading Guide

Key Concepts
ESSENTIAL QUESTIONS

- How did scientists' understanding of cells develop?
- What basic substances make up a cell?

Vocabulary

cell theory p. 388

macromolecule p. 389

nucleic acid p. 390

protein p. 391

lipid p. 391

carbohydrate p. 391

g Multilingual eGlossary

Academic Standards for Science

7.3.1 Explain that all living organisms are composed of one or more cells and that the many functions needed to sustain life are carried out within such cells.

7.3.2 Understand that water is a major component within all cells and is required to carry out many cellular functions.

7.3.4 Compare and contrast similarities and differences between specialized subcellular components within plant and animal cells, including organelles and cell walls that perform essential functions and give a cell its shape and structure.

Also covers: 7.NS.2, 7.NS.3, 7.NS.7, 7.NS.8

Inquiry Two of a Kind?

At first glance, the plant and animal in the photo might seem like they have nothing in common. The plant is rooted in the ground, and the iguana can move quickly. Are they more alike than they appear? How can you find out?

Inquiry Launch Lab — 10 minutes

What's in a cell?

Most plants grow from seeds. A seed began as one cell, but a mature plant can be made up of millions of cells. How does a seed change and grow into a mature plant?

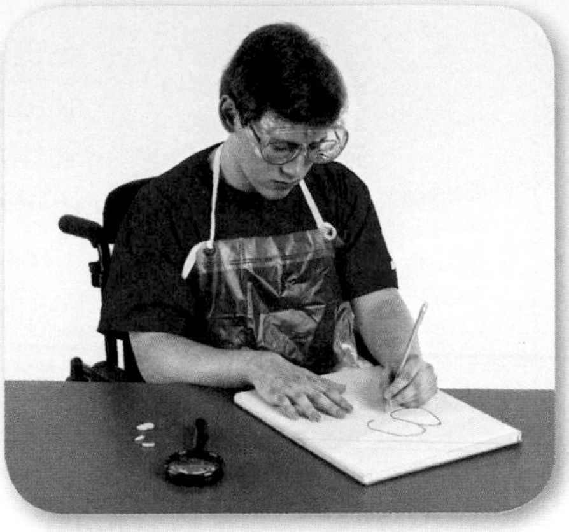

1. Read and complete a lab safety form.
2. Use a **toothpick** to gently remove the thin outer covering of a **bean seed** that has soaked overnight.
3. Open the seed with a **plastic knife,** and observe its inside with a **magnifying lens.** Draw the inside of the seed in your Science Journal.
4. Gently remove the small, plantlike embryo, and weigh it on a **balance.** Record its mass in your Science Journal.
5. Gently pull a **bean seedling** from the soil. Rinse the soil from the roots. Weigh the seedling, and record the mass.

Think About This

1. How did the mass of the embryo and the bean seedling differ?
2. **Key Concept** If a plant begins as one cell, where do all the cells come from?

Understanding Cells

Have you ever looked up at the night sky and tried to find other planets in our solar system? It is hard to see them without using a telescope. This is because the other planets are millions of kilometers away. Just like we can use telescopes to see other planets, we can use microscopes to see the basic units of all living things—cells. But people didn't always know about cells. Because cells are so small, early scientists had no tools to study them. It took hundreds of years for scientists to learn about cells.

More than 300 years ago, an English scientist named Robert Hooke built a microscope. He used the microscope to look at cork, which is part of a cork oak tree's bark. What he saw looked like the openings in a honeycomb, as shown in **Figure 1.** The openings reminded him of the small rooms, called cells, where monks lived. He called the structures cells, from the Latin word *cellula* (SEL yuh luh), which means "small rooms."

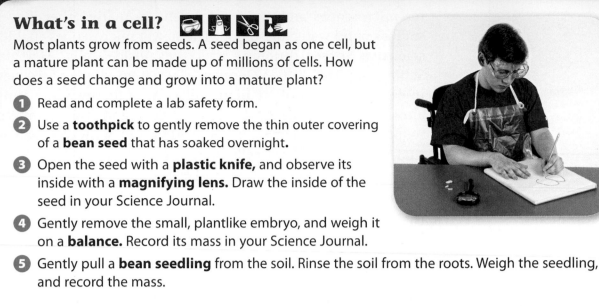

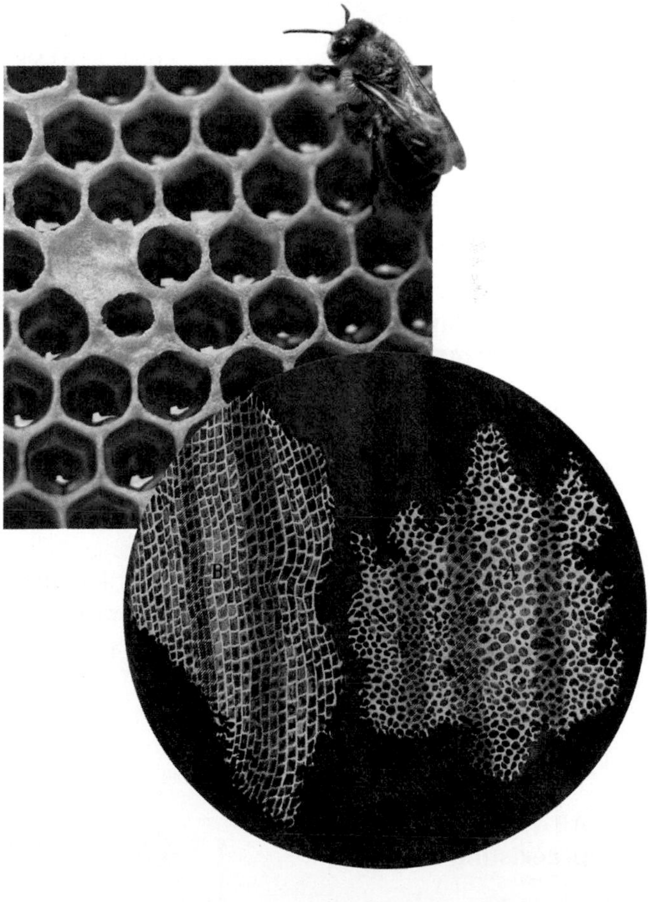

Figure 1 To Robert Hooke, the cells of cork looked like the openings in a honeycomb.

The Cell Theory

After Hooke's discovery, other scientists began making better microscopes and looking for cells in many other places, such as pond water and blood. The newer microscopes enabled scientists to see different structures inside cells. Matthias Schleiden (SHLI dun), a German scientist, used one of the new microscopes to look at plant cells. Around the same time, another German scientist, Theodor Schwann, used a microscope to study animal cells. Schleiden and Schwann realized that plant and animal cells have similar features. You'll read about many of these features in Lesson 2.

Almost two decades later, Rudolf Virchow (VUR koh), a German doctor, proposed that all cells come from preexisting cells, or cells that already exist. The observations made by Schleiden, Schwann, and Virchow were combined into one **theory.** As illustrated in **Table 1,** *the* **cell theory** *states that all living things are made of one or more cells, the cell is the smallest unit of life, and all new cells come from preexisting cells.* After the development of the cell theory, scientists raised more questions about cells. If all living things are made of cells, what are cells made of?

Key Concept Check How did scientists' understanding of cells develop?

REVIEW VOCABULARY

theory
explanation of things or events based on scientific knowledge resulting from many observations and experiments

Table 1 Scientists developed the cell theory after studying cells with microscopes.

Table 1 The Cell Theory

Principle	Example
All living things are made of one or more cells.	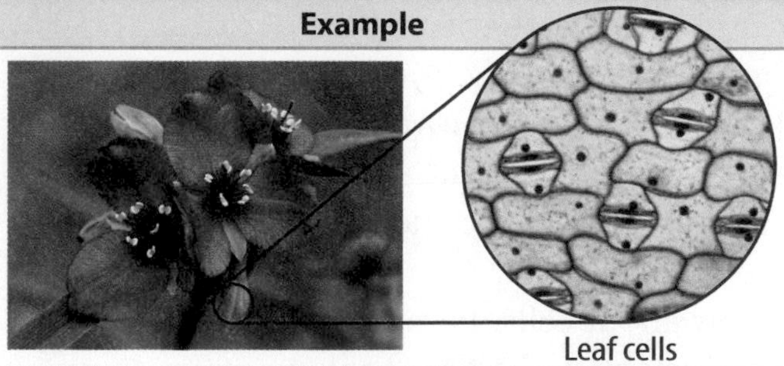 Leaf cells
The cell is the smallest unit of life.	This unicellular amoeba is surrounding an algal cell to get food and energy. 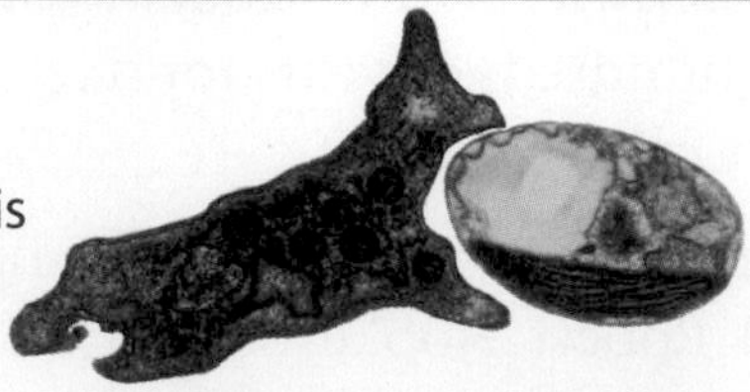 Amoeba; Algal cell
All new cells come from preexisting cells.	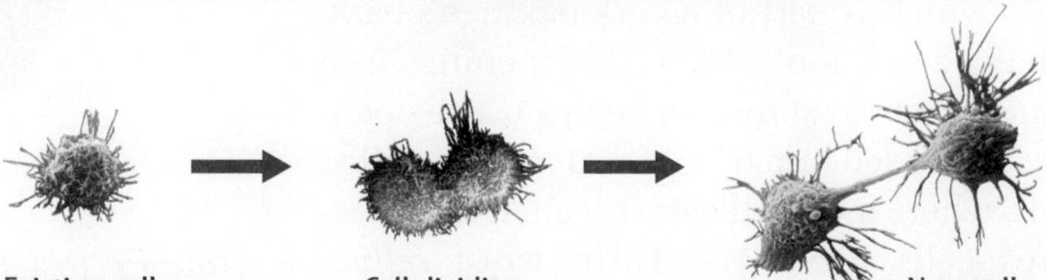 Existing cell → Cell dividing → New cells

Basic Cell Substances

Have you ever watched a train travel down a railroad track? The locomotive pulls train cars that are hooked together. Like a train, many of the substances in cells are made of smaller parts that are joined together. *These substances, called* **macromolecules,** *form by joining many small molecules together.* As you will read later in this lesson, macromolecules have many important roles in cells. But macromolecules cannot function without one of the most important substances in cells—water.

WORD ORIGIN
macromolecule
from Greek *makro–*, means "long"; and Latin *molecula*, means "mass"

The Main Ingredient—Water

The main ingredient in any cell is water. It makes up more than 70 percent of a cell's volume and is essential for life. Why is water such an important molecule? In addition to making up a large part of the inside of cells, water also surrounds cells. The water surrounding your cells helps to insulate your body, which maintains homeostasis, or a stable internal environment.

The structure of a water molecule makes it ideal for dissolving many other substances. Substances must be in a liquid to move into and out of cells. A water molecule has two areas:

- An area that is more negative (–), called the negative end; this end can attract the positive part of another substance.
- An area that is more positive (+), called the positive end; this end can attract the negative part of another substance.

Examine **Figure 2** to see how the positive and negative ends of water molecules dissolve salt crystals.

Figure 2 The positive and negative ends of a water molecule attract the positive and negative parts of another substance, similar to the way magnets are attracted to each other.

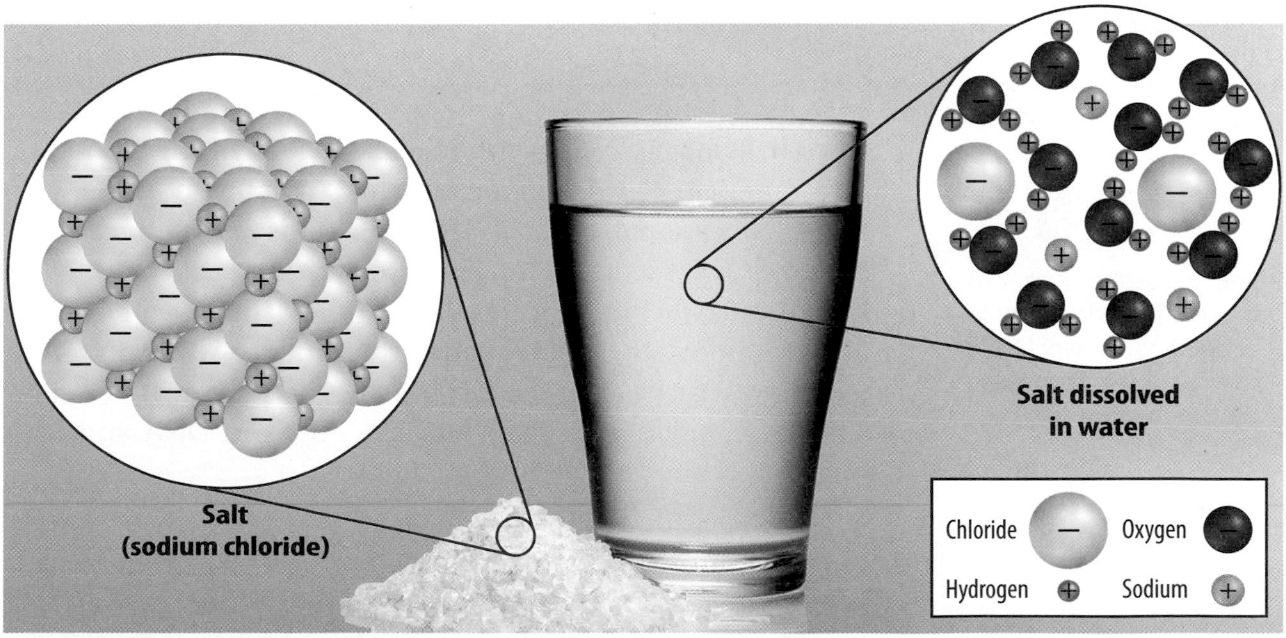

Visual Check Which part of the salt crystal is attracted to the oxygen in the water molecule?

Macromolecules

Although water is essential for life, all cells contain other substances that enable them to function. Recall that macromolecules are large molecules that form when smaller molecules join together. As shown in **Figure 3,** there are four types of macromolecules in cells: nucleic acids, proteins, lipids, and carbohydrates. Each type of macromolecule has unique functions in a cell. These functions range from growth and communication to movement and storage.

Cell Macromolecules

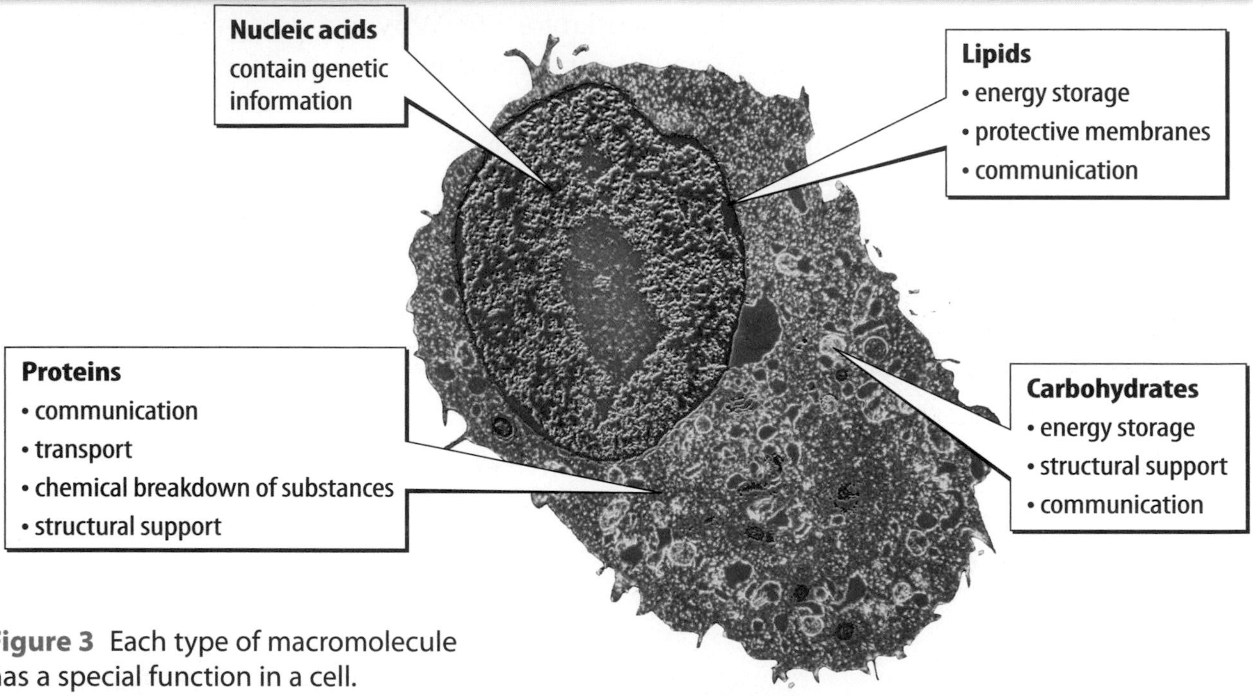

Figure 3 Each type of macromolecule has a special function in a cell.

Color-Enhanced TEM Magnification: 300×

Nucleic Acids Both deoxyribonucleic (dee AHK sih ri boh noo klee ihk) acid (DNA) and ribonucleic (ri boh noo KLEE ihk) acid (RNA) are nucleic acids. **Nucleic acids** *are macromolecules that form when long chains of molecules called nucleotides* (NEW klee uh tidz) *join together.* The order of nucleotides in DNA and RNA is important. If you change the order of words in a sentence, you can change the meaning of the sentence. In a similar way, changing the order of nucleotides in DNA and RNA can change the genetic information in a cell.

Nucleic acids are important in cells because they contain genetic information. This information can pass from parents to offspring. DNA includes instructions for cell growth, cell reproduction, and cell processes that enable a cell to respond to its environment. DNA is used to make RNA. RNA is used to make proteins.

FOLDABLES®

Fold a sheet of paper to make a four-door book. Label it as shown. Use it to organize your notes on the macromolecules and their uses in a cell.

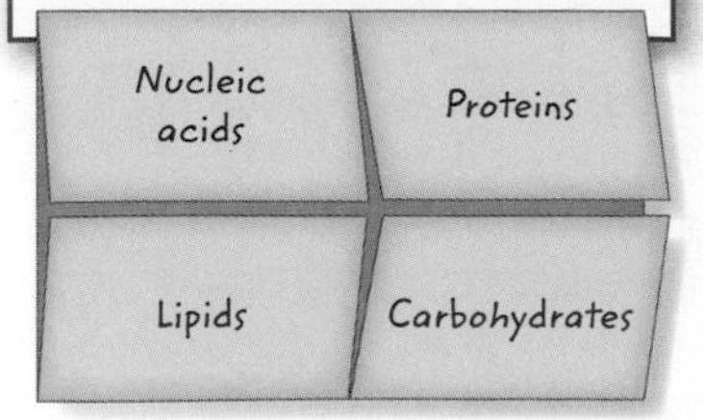

Proteins The macromolecules necessary for nearly everything cells do are proteins. **Proteins** *are long chains of amino acid molecules*. You just read that RNA is used to make proteins. RNA contains instructions for joining amino acids together.

Cells contain hundreds of proteins. Each protein has a unique function. Some proteins help cells communicate with each other. Other proteins transport substances around inside cells. Some proteins, such as amylase (AM uh lays) in saliva, help break down nutrients in food. Other proteins, such as keratin (KER uh tun)—a protein found in hair, horns, and feathers—provide structural support.

Lipids Another group of macromolecules found in cells is lipids. *A* **lipid** *is a large macromolecule that does not dissolve in water.* Because lipids do not mix with water, they play an important role as protective barriers in cells. They are also the major part of cell membranes. Lipids play roles in energy storage and in cell communication. Examples of lipids are cholesterol (kuh LES tuh rawl), phospholipids (fahs foh LIH pids), and vitamin A.

Reading Check Why are lipids important to cells?

Carbohydrates *One sugar molecule, two sugar molecules, or a long chain of sugar molecules make up* **carbohydrates** (kar boh HI drayts). Carbohydrates store energy, provide structural support, and are needed for communication between cells. Sugars and starches are carbohydrates that store energy. Fruits contain sugars. Breads and pastas are mostly starch. The energy in sugars and starches can be released quickly through chemical reactions in cells. Cellulose is a carbohydrate in the cell walls in plants that provides structural support.

Key Concept Check What basic substances make up a cell?

Inquiry MiniLab — 25 minutes

How can you observe DNA?

Nucleic acids are macromolecules that are important in cells because they contain an organism's genetic information. In this lab, you will observe one type of nucleic acid, DNA, in onion root-tip cells using a compound light microscope.

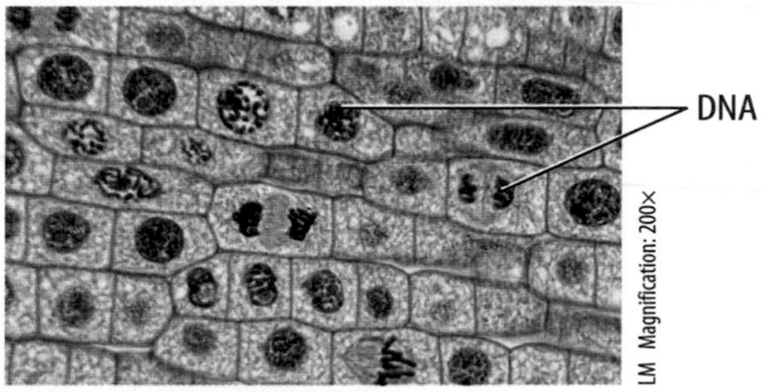

1. Read and complete a lab safety form.
2. Obtain a **microscope** and a **slide** from your teacher. Use care and properly handle your microscope.
3. Observe the **onion root-tip cells** at the magnifications assigned by your teacher.
4. Determine the approximate number of cells in your field of view and the number of cells with visible DNA. Record these numbers in your Science Journal.

Analyze and Conclude

1. **Calculate** Using your data, find the percentage of cells with visible DNA that you saw in your microscope's field of view.
2. **Compare** your results with the results of other students. Are all the results the same? Explain.
3. **Create** a data table for the entire class that lists individual results.
4. **Calculate** the total percentage of cells with visible DNA at each magnification.
5. **Key Concept** Did looking at the cells at different magnifications change the percentage of cells with visible DNA? Explain.

Lesson 1 Review

Assessment Online Quiz

Visual Summary

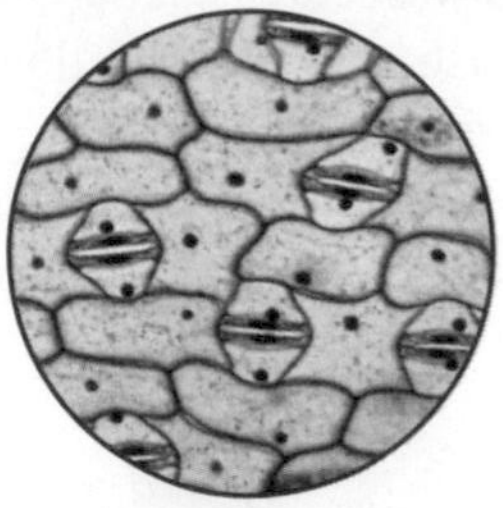

The cell theory summarizes the main principles for understanding that the cell is the basic unit of life.

Water is the main ingredient in every cell.

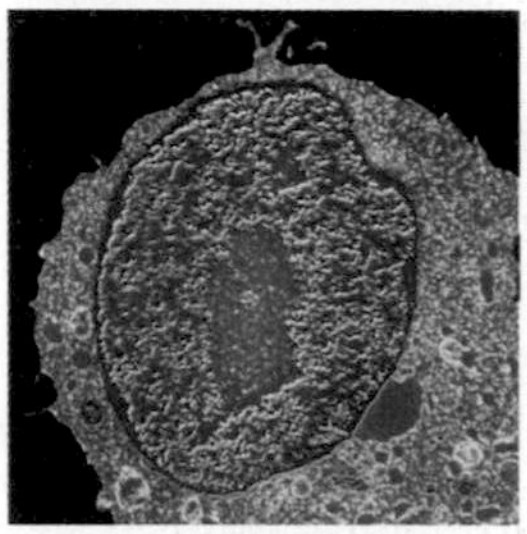

A nucleic acid, such as DNA, contains the genetic information for a cell.

FOLDABLES®

Use your lesson Foldable to review the lesson. Save your Foldable for the project at the end of the chapter.

What do you think NOW?

You first read the statements below at the beginning of the chapter.

1. Nonliving things have cells.

2. Cells are made mostly of water.

Did you change your mind about whether you agree or disagree with the statements? Rewrite any false statements to make them true.

Use Vocabulary

1. The ________ ________ states that the cell is the basic unit of all living things.
2. **Distinguish** between a carbohydrate and a lipid.
3. **Use the term** *nucleic acid* in a sentence.

Understand Key Concepts

4. Which macromolecule is made from amino acids?
   - **A.** lipid
   - **B.** protein
   - **C.** carbohydrate
   - **D.** nucleic acid
5. **Describe** how the invention of the microscope helped scientists understand cells.
6. **Compare** the functions of DNA and proteins in a cell.

Interpret Graphics

7. **Summarize** Copy and fill in the graphic organizer below to summarize the main principles of the cell theory.

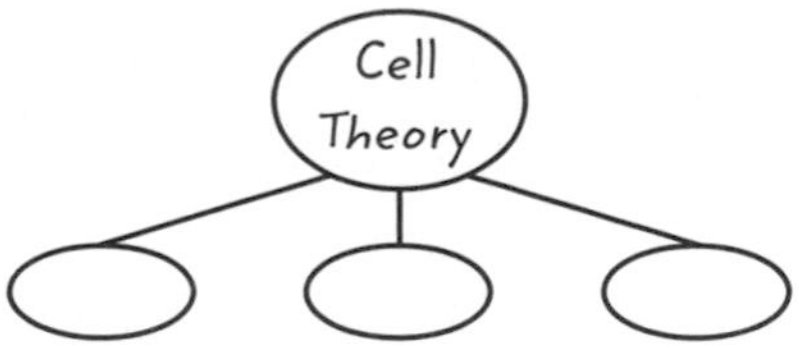

8. **Analyze** How does the structure of the water molecule shown below enable it to interact with other water molecules?

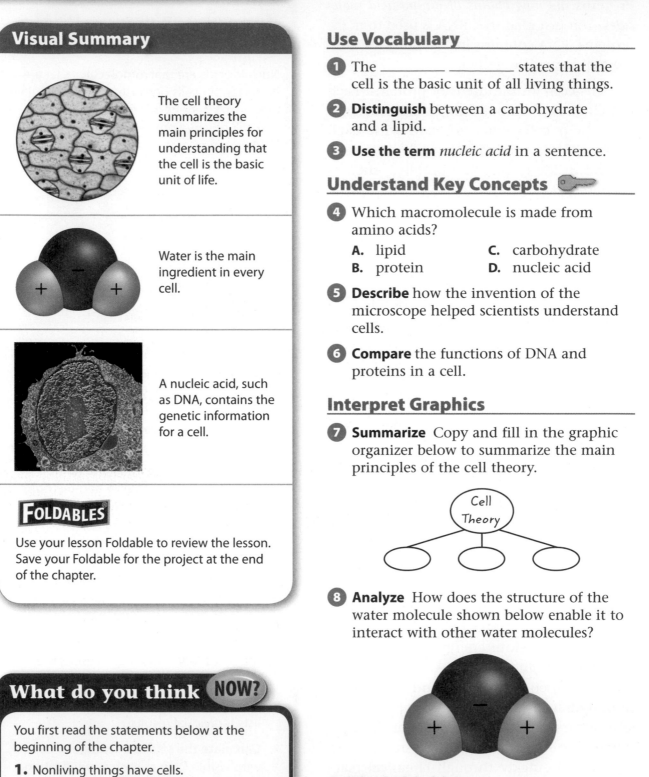

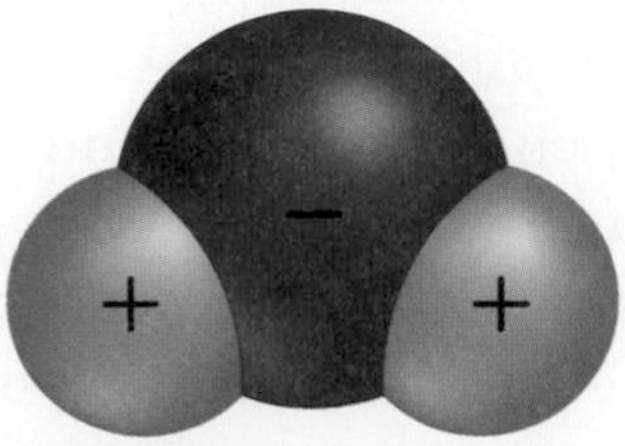

Critical Thinking

9. **Summarize** the functions of lipids in cells.
10. **Hypothesize** why carbohydrates are found in plant cell walls.

A Very Powerful Microscope

Using technology to look inside cells

If Robert Hooke had used an atomic force microscope (AFM), he would have observed more than just cells. He would have seen the macromolecules inside them! An AFM can scan objects that are only nanometers in size. A nanometer is one one-billionth of a meter. That's 100,000 times smaller than the width of a human hair. AFM technology has enabled scientists to better understand how cells function. It also has given them a three-dimensional look at the macromolecules that make life possible. This is how it works.

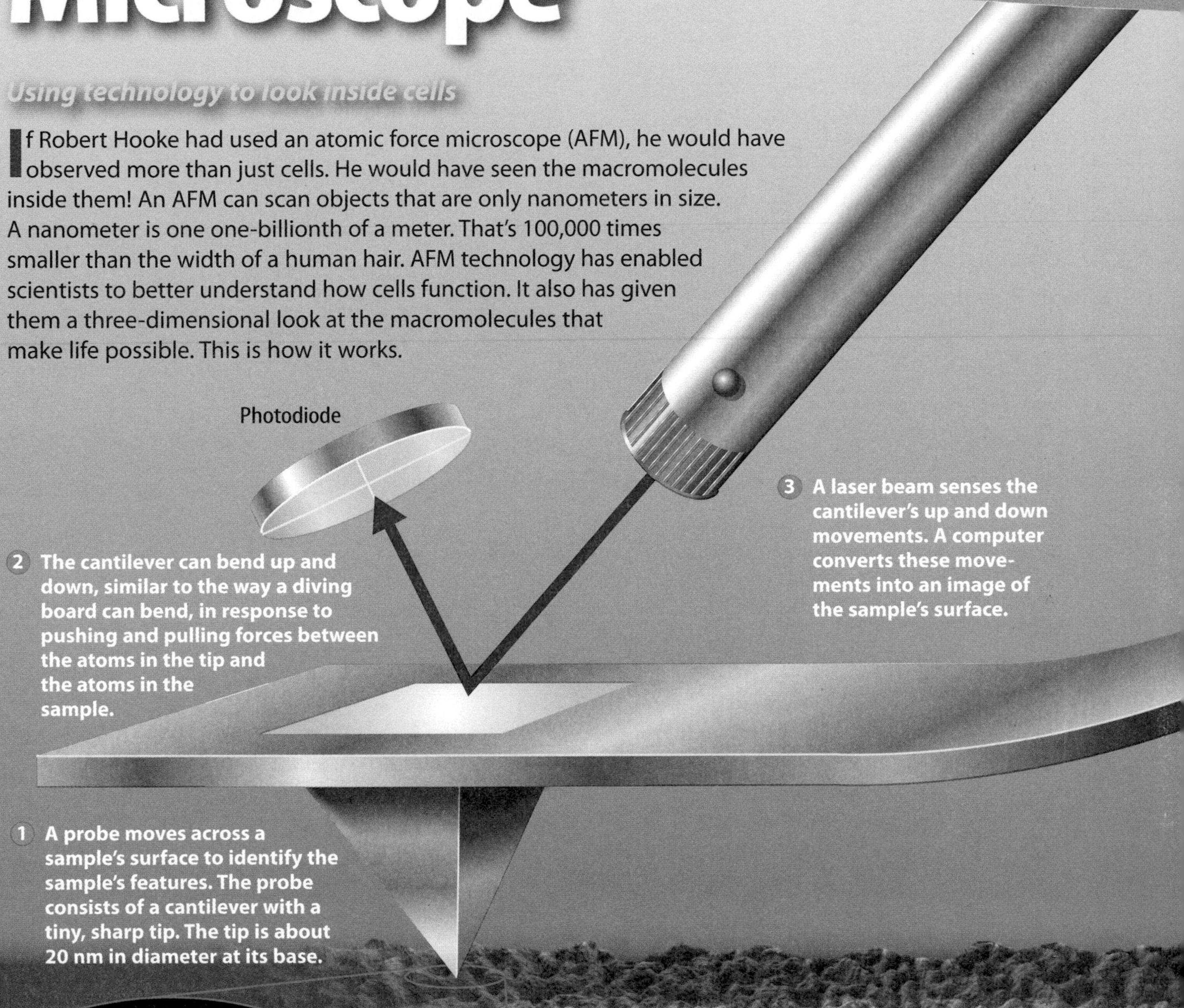

Photodiode
1 A probe moves across a sample's surface to identify the sample's features. The probe consists of a cantilever with a tiny, sharp tip. The tip is about 20 nm in diameter at its base.
2 The cantilever can bend up and down, similar to the way a diving board can bend, in response to pushing and pulling forces between the atoms in the tip and the atoms in the sample.
3 A laser beam senses the cantilever's up and down movements. A computer converts these movements into an image of the sample's surface.

It's Your Turn

RESEARCH NASA's Phoenix Mars Lander included an atomic force microscope. Find out what scientists discovered on Mars with this instrument.

Lesson 2

The Cell

Reading Guide

Key Concepts
ESSENTIAL QUESTIONS

- How are prokaryotic cells and eukaryotic cells similar, and how are they different?
- What do the structures in a cell do?

Vocabulary

cell membrane p. 396
cell wall p. 396
cytoplasm p. 397
cytoskeleton p. 397
organelle p. 398
nucleus p. 399
chloroplast p. 401

g Multilingual eGlossary

Video BrainPOP®

Academic Standards for Science

7.3.1 Explain that all living organisms are composed of one or more cells and that the many functions needed to sustain life are carried out within such cells.

7.3.4 Compare and contrast similarities and differences between specialized subcellular components within plant and animal cells, including organelles and cell walls that perform essential functions and give a cell its shape and structure.

Also covers: 7.NS.7, 7.DP.1, 7.DP.3, 7.DP.4, 7.DP.5, 7.DP.6, 7.DP.7, 7.DP.10, 7.DP.11

Inquiry Hooked Together?

What do you think happens when one of the hooks in the photo above goes through one of the loops? The two sides fasten together. The shapes of the hooks and loops in the hook-and-loop tape are suited to their function—to hold the two pieces together.

Inquiry Launch Lab

10 minutes

Why do eggs have shells?

Bird eggs have different structures, such as a shell, a membrane, and a yolk. Each structure has a different function that helps keep the egg safe and assists in development of the baby bird inside of it.

1. Read and complete a lab safety form.
2. Place an **uncooked egg** in a bowl.
3. Feel the shell, and record your observations in your Science Journal.
4. Crack open the egg. Pour the contents into the bowl.
5. Observe the inside of the shell and the contents of the bowl. Record your observations in your Science Journal.

Think About This

1. What do you think is the role of the eggshell?
2. Are there any structures in the bowl that have the same function as the eggshell? Explain.
3. **Key Concept** What does the structure of the eggshell tell you about its function?

Cell Shape and Movement

You might recall from Lesson 1 that all living things are made up of one or more cells. As illustrated in **Figure 4,** cells come in many shapes and sizes. The size and shape of a cell relates to its job or function. For example, a human red blood cell cannot be seen without a microscope. Its small size and disk shape enable it to pass easily through the smallest blood vessels. The shape of a nerve cell enables it to send signals over long distances. Some plant cells are hollow and make up tubelike structures that carry materials throughout a plant.

The structures that make up a cell also have unique functions. Think about how the players on a football team perform different tasks to move the ball down the field. In a similar way, a cell is made of different structures that perform different functions that keep a cell alive. You will read about some of these structures in this lesson.

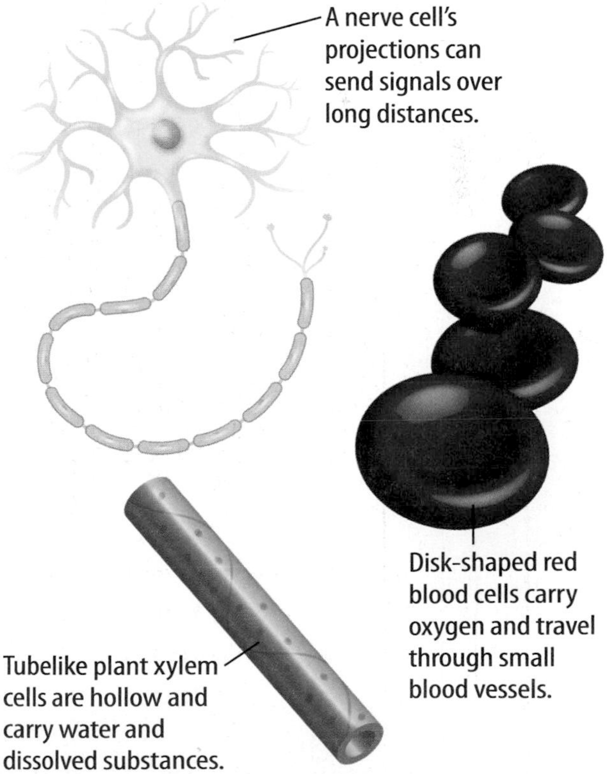

A nerve cell's projections can send signals over long distances.
Disk-shaped red blood cells carry oxygen and travel through small blood vessels.
Tubelike plant xylem cells are hollow and carry water and dissolved substances.

Figure 4 The shape of a cell relates to the function it performs.

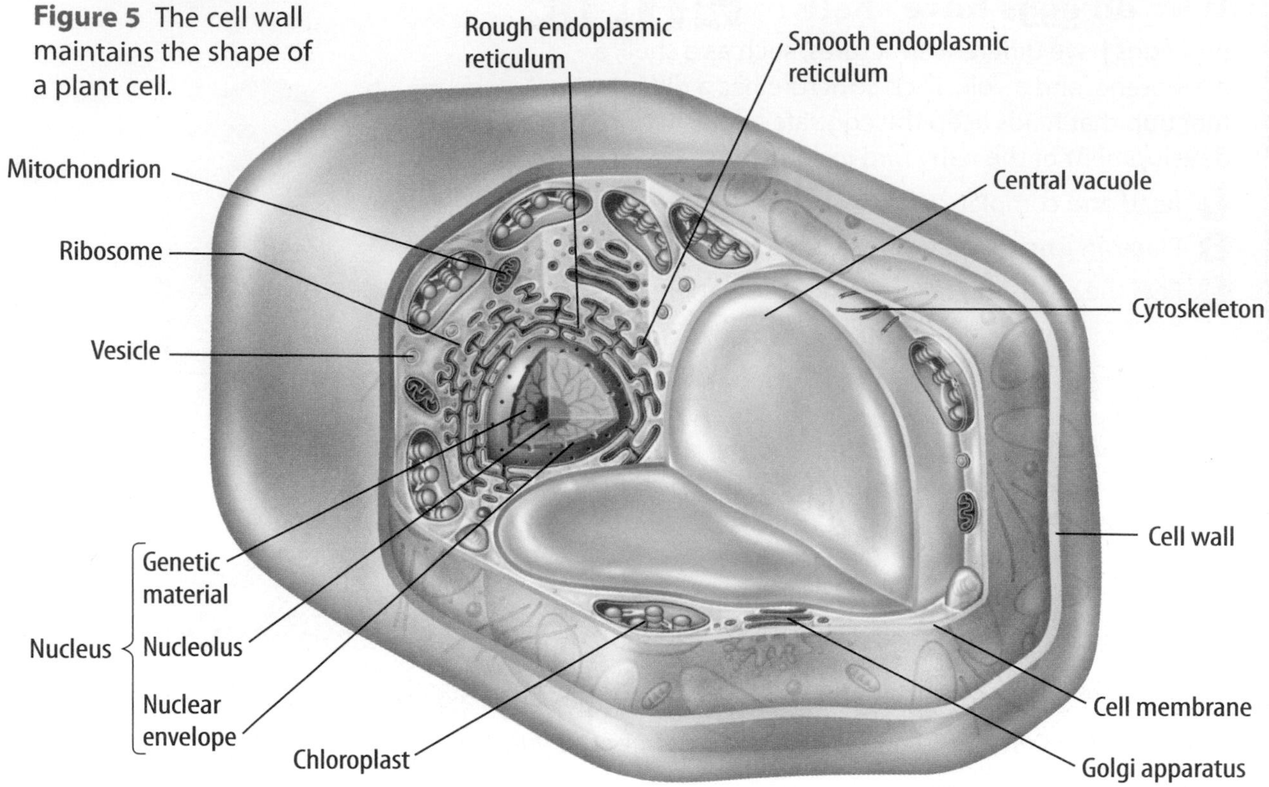

Figure 5 The cell wall maintains the shape of a plant cell.

Cell Membrane

Although different types of cells perform different **functions,** all cells have some structures in common. As shown in **Figure 5** and **Figure 6,** every cell is surrounded by a protective covering called a membrane. *The* **cell membrane** *is a flexible covering that protects the inside of a cell from the environment outside a cell.* Cell membranes are mostly made of two different macromolecules—proteins and a type of lipid called phospholipids. Think again about a football team. The defensive line tries to stop the other team from moving forward with the football. In a similar way, a cell membrane protects the cell from the outside environment.

Academic Vocabulary
function
(noun) the purpose for which something is used

Reading Check What are cell membranes made of?

Cell Wall

Every cell has a cell membrane, but some cells are also surrounded by a structure called the cell wall. Plant cells such as the one in **Figure 5,** fungal cells, bacteria, and some types of protists have cell walls. *A* **cell wall** *is a stiff structure outside the cell membrane.* A cell wall protects a cell from attack by viruses and other harmful organisms. In some plant cells and fungal cells, a cell wall helps maintain the cell's shape and gives structural support.

Figure 6 The cytoskeleton maintains the shape of an animal cell.

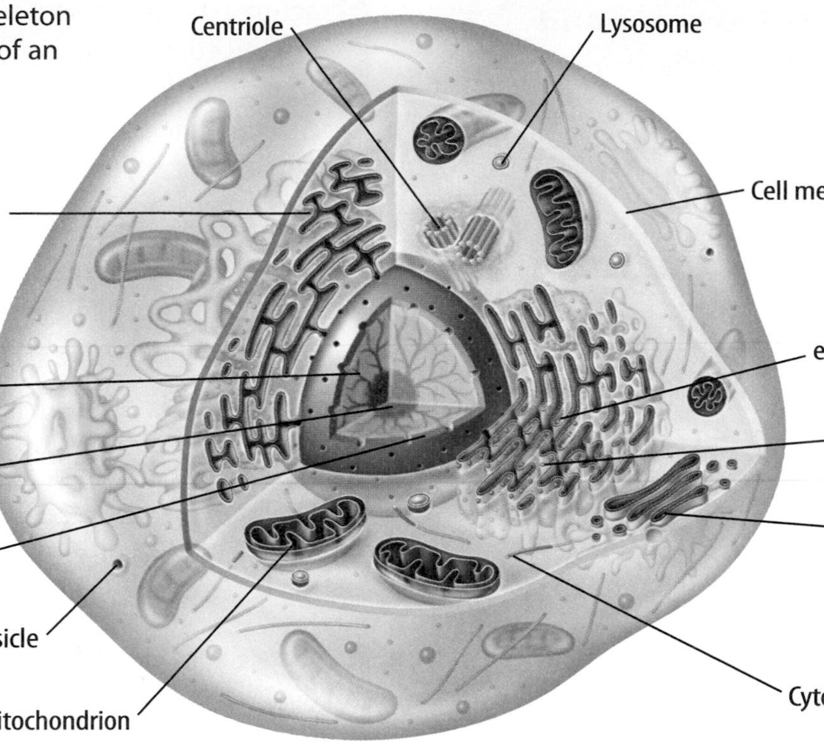

Visual Check Compare this animal cell to the plant cell in **Figure 5.**

Cell Appendages

Arms, legs, claws, and antennae are all types of appendages. Cells can have appendages too. Cell appendages are often used for movement. Flagella (fluh JEH luh; singular, flagellum) are long, tail-like appendages that whip back and forth and move a cell. A cell can also have cilia (SIH lee uh; singular, cilium) like the ones shown in **Figure 7.** Cilia are short, hairlike structures. They can move a cell or move molecules away from a cell. A microscopic organism called a paramecium (pa ruh MEE shee um) moves around its watery environment using its cilia. The cilia in your windpipe move harmful substances away from your lungs.

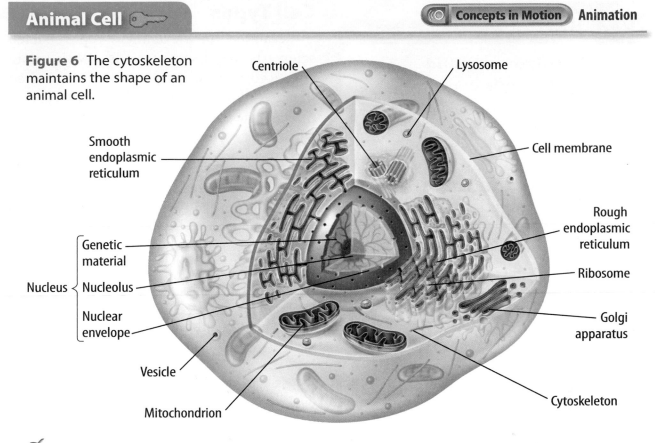

Figure 7 Lung cells have cilia that help move fluids and foreign materials.

Cytoplasm and the Cytoskeleton

In Lesson 1, you read that water is the main ingredient in a cell. Most of this water is in the **cytoplasm,** *a fluid inside a cell that contains salts and other molecules.* The cytoplasm also contains a cell's cytoskeleton. *The* **cytoskeleton** *is a network of threadlike proteins that are joined together.* The proteins form a framework inside a cell. This framework gives a cell its shape and helps it move. Cilia and flagella are made from the same proteins that make up the cytoskeleton.

WORD ORIGIN
cytoplasm
from Greek *kytos,* means "hollow vessel"; and *plasma,* means "something molded"

Inquiry MiniLab 25 minutes

How do eukaryotic and prokaryotic cells compare?

With the use of better microscopes, scientists discovered that cells can be classified as one of two types—prokaryotic or eukaryotic.

1. Read and complete a lab safety form.

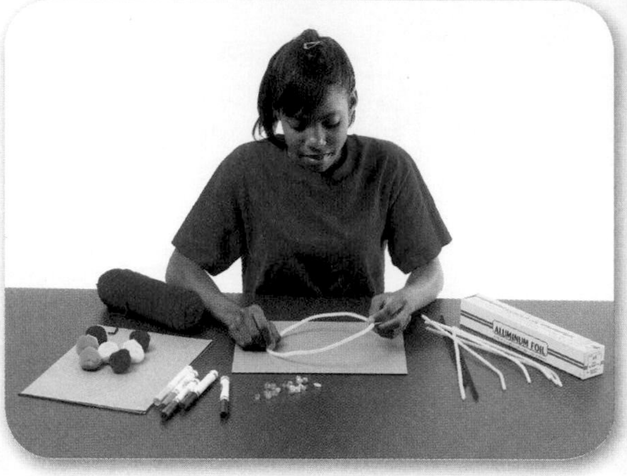

2. Using different **craft items,** make a two-dimensional model of a eukaryotic cell.
3. In your cell model, include the number of cell structures assigned by your teacher.
4. Make each cell structure the correct shape, as shown in this lesson.
5. Make a label for each cell structure of your model.

Analyze and Conclude

1. **Describe** the nucleus of your cell.
2. **Classify** your cell as either a plant cell or an animal cell, and support your classification with evidence.
3. **Key Concept** Compare and contrast a prokaryotic cell, as shown in **Figure 8,** with your eukaryotic cell model.

Cell Types

Recall that the use of microscopes enabled scientists to discover cells. With more advanced microscopes, scientists discovered that all cells can be grouped into two types—prokaryotic (proh ka ree AH tihk) cells and eukaryotic (yew ker ee AH tihk) cells.

Prokaryotic Cells

The genetic material in a prokaryotic cell is not surrounded by a membrane, as shown in **Figure 8.** This is the most important feature of a prokaryotic cell. Prokaryotic cells also do not have many of the other cell parts that you will read about later in this lesson. Most prokaryotic cells are unicellular organisms and are called prokaryotes.

Figure 8 In prokaryotic cells, the genetic material floats freely in the cytoplasm.

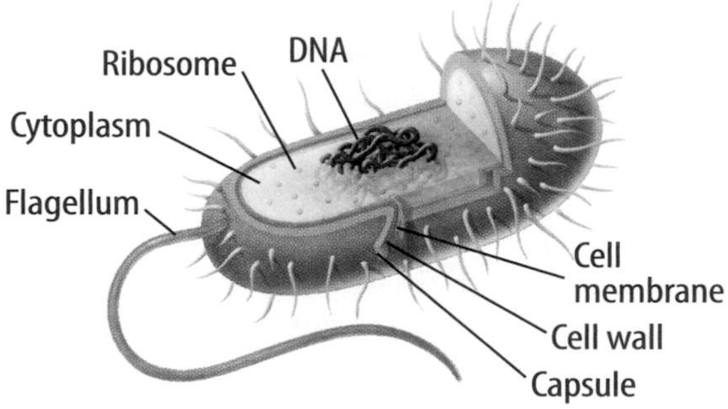

Eukaryotic Cells

Plants, animals, fungi, and protists are all made of eukaryotic cells, such as the ones shown in **Figure 5** and **Figure 6,** and are called eukaryotes. With few exceptions, each eukaryotic cell has genetic material that is surrounded by a membrane. Every eukaryotic cell also has *other structures, called* **organelles**, *which have specialized functions. Most organelles are surrounded by membranes.* Eukaryotic cells are usually larger than prokaryotic cells. About ten prokaryotic cells would fit inside one eukaryotic cell.

Key Concept Check How are prokaryotic cells and eukaryotic cells similar, and how are they different?

Cell Organelles

As you have just read, organelles are eukaryotic cell structures with specific functions. Organelles enable cells to carry out different functions at the same time. For example, cells can obtain energy from food, store information, make macromolecules, and get rid of waste materials all at the same time because different organelles perform the different tasks.

The Nucleus

The largest organelle inside most eukaryotic cells is the nucleus, shown in **Figure 9.** *The* **nucleus** *is the part of a eukaryotic cell that directs cell activities and contains genetic information stored in DNA.* DNA is organized into structures called chromosomes. The number of chromosomes in a nucleus is different for different species of organisms. For example, kangaroo cells contain six pairs of chromosomes. Most human cells contain 23 pairs of chromosomes.

FOLDABLES®

Fold a sheet of paper into a vertical half book. Use it to record information about cell organelles and their functions.

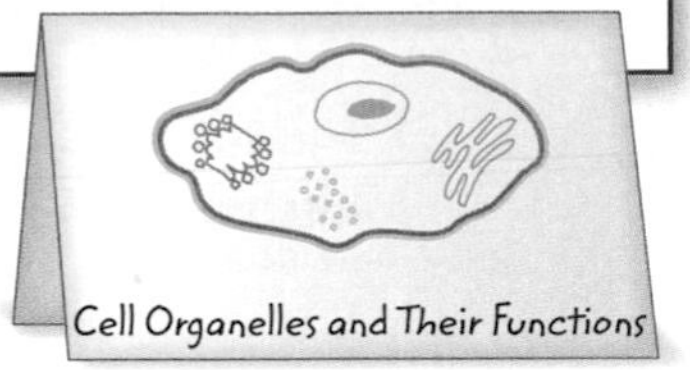

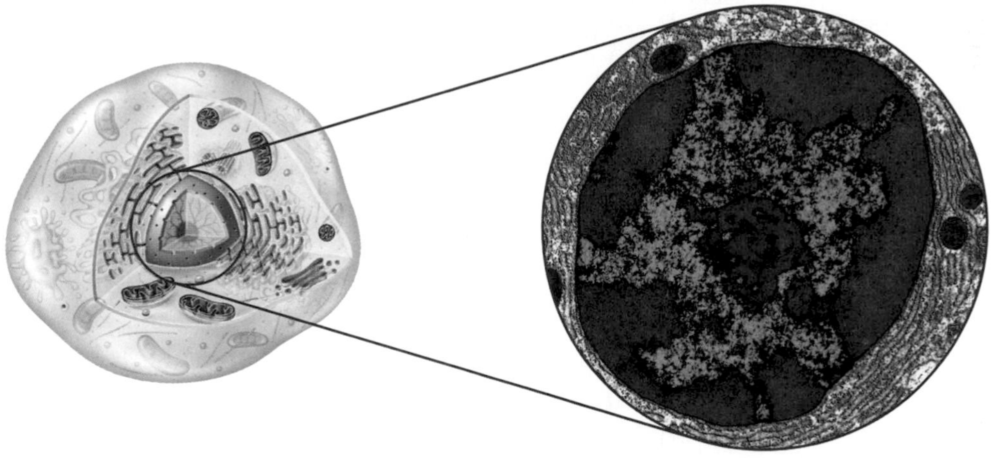

Nucleus
Color-Enhanced TEM Magnification: 15,500×

Figure 9 The nucleus directs cell activity and is surrounded by a membrane.

In addition to chromosomes, the nucleus contains proteins and an organelle called the nucleolus (new KLEE uh lus). The nucleolus is often seen as a large dark spot in the nucleus of a cell. The nucleolus makes ribosomes, organelles that are involved in the production of proteins. You will read about ribosomes later in this lesson.

Surrounding the nucleus are two membranes that form a structure called the nuclear **envelope.** The nuclear envelope contains many pores. Certain molecules, such as ribosomes and RNA, move into and out of the nucleus through these pores.

Science Use v. Common Use

envelope

Science Use an outer covering

Common Use a flat paper container for a letter

Reading Check What is the nuclear envelope?

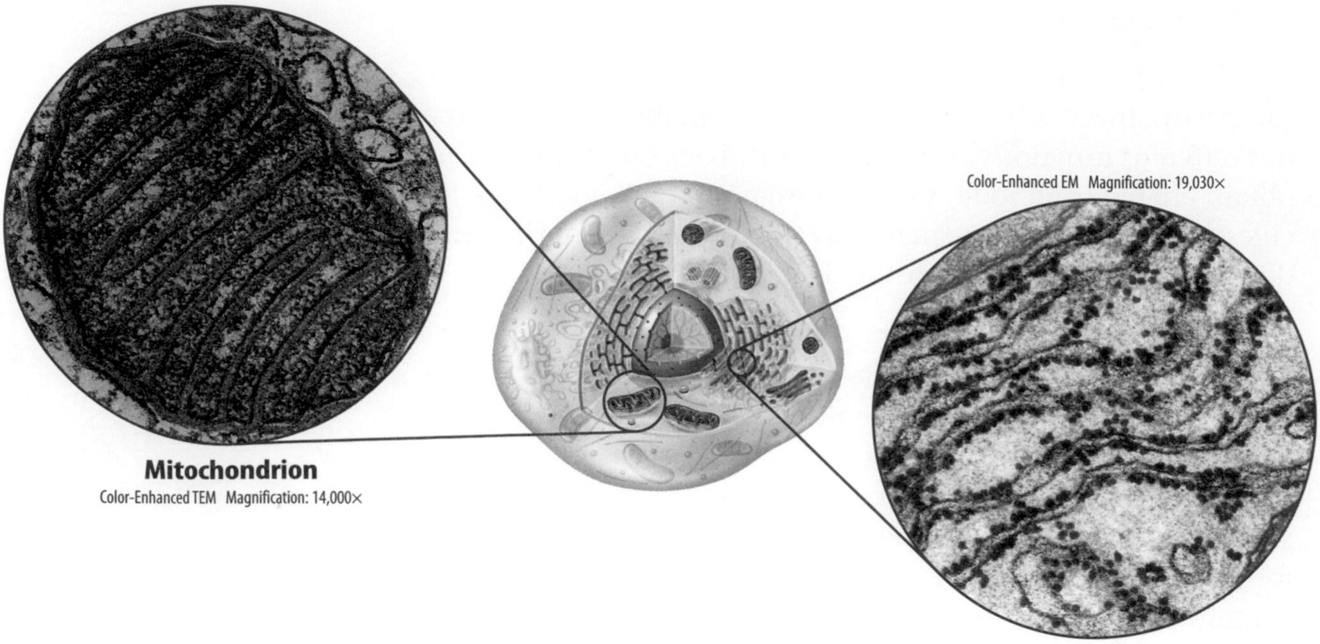

Figure 10 The endoplasmic reticulum is made of many folded membranes. Mitochondria provide a cell with usable energy.

Manufacturing Molecules

You might recall from Lesson 1 that proteins are important molecules in cells. Proteins are made on small structures called ribosomes. Unlike other cell organelles, a ribosome is not surrounded by a membrane. Ribosomes are in a cell's cytoplasm. They also can be attached to a weblike organelle called the endoplasmic reticulum (en duh PLAZ mihk • rih TIHK yuh lum), or ER. As shown in **Figure 10,** the ER spreads from the nucleus throughout most of the cytoplasm. ER with ribosomes on its surface is called rough ER. Rough ER is the site of protein production. ER without ribosomes is called smooth ER. It makes lipids such as cholesterol. Smooth ER is important because it helps remove harmful substances from a cell.

Reading Check Contrast smooth ER and rough ER.

Processing Energy

All living things require energy in order to survive. Cells process some energy in specialized organelles. Most eukaryotic cells contain hundreds of organelles called mitochondria (mi tuh KAHN dree uh; singular, mitochondrion), shown in **Figure 10.** Some cells in a human heart can contain a thousand mitochondria.

Like the nucleus, a mitochondrion is surrounded by two membranes. Energy is released during chemical reactions that occur in the mitochondria. This energy is stored in high-energy molecules called ATP—adenosine triphosphate (uh DEH nuh seen • tri FAHS fayt). ATP is the fuel for cellular processes such as growth, cell division, and material transport.

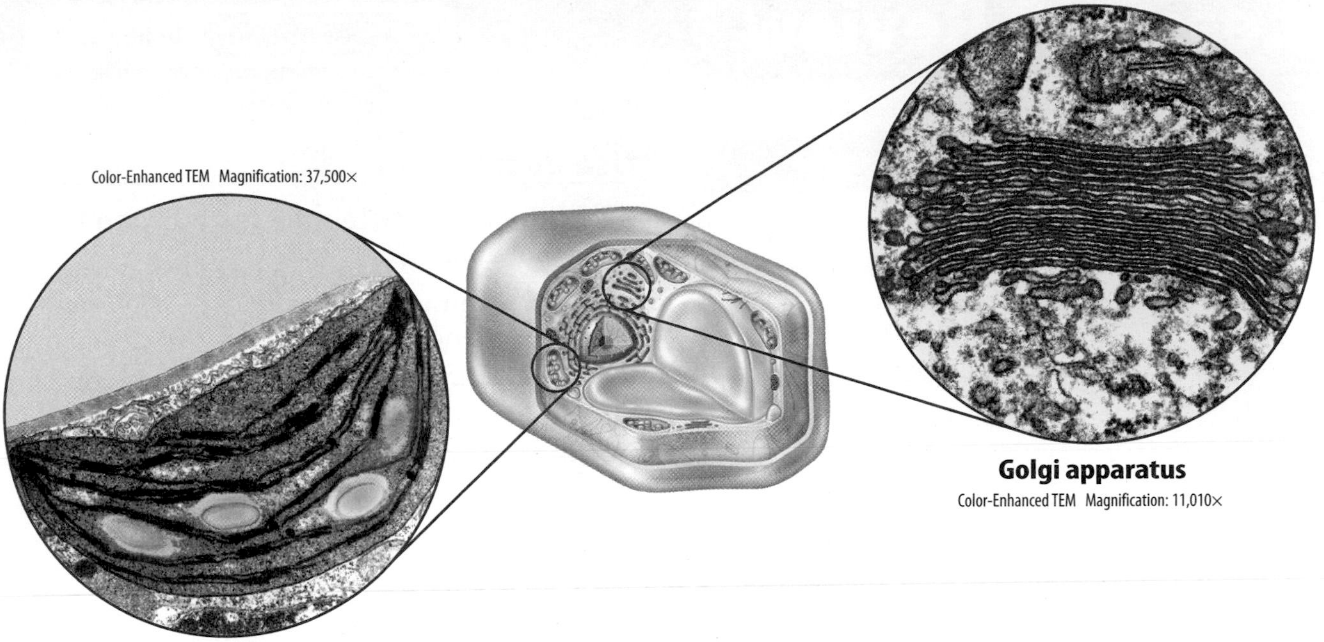

Figure 11 Plant cells have chloroplasts that use light energy and make food. The Golgi apparatus packages materials into vesicles.

Plant cells and some protists, such as algae, also contain organelles called chloroplasts (KLOR uh plasts), shown in **Figure 11.** **Chloroplasts** *are membrane-bound organelles that use light energy and make food—a sugar called glucose—from water and carbon dioxide in a process known as photosynthesis* (foh toh SIHN thuh sus). The sugar contains stored chemical energy that can be released when a cell needs it. You will read more about photosynthesis in Lesson 4.

Reading Check Which types of cells contain chloroplasts?

Processing, Transporting, and Storing Molecules

Near the ER is an organelle that looks like a stack of pancakes. This is the Golgi (GAWL jee) apparatus, shown in **Figure 11.** It prepares proteins for their specific jobs or functions. Then it packages the proteins into tiny, membrane-bound, ball-like structures called vesicles. Vesicles are organelles that transport substances from one area of a cell to another area of a cell. Some vesicles in an animal cell are called lysosomes. Lysosomes contain substances that help break down and recycle cellular components.

Some cells also have saclike structures called vacuoles (VA kyuh wohlz). Vacuoles are organelles that store food, water, and waste material. A typical plant cell usually has one large vacuole that stores water and other substances. Some animal cells have many small vacuoles.

Key Concept Check What is the function of the Golgi apparatus?

Lesson 2 Review

Assessment Online Quiz

Visual Summary

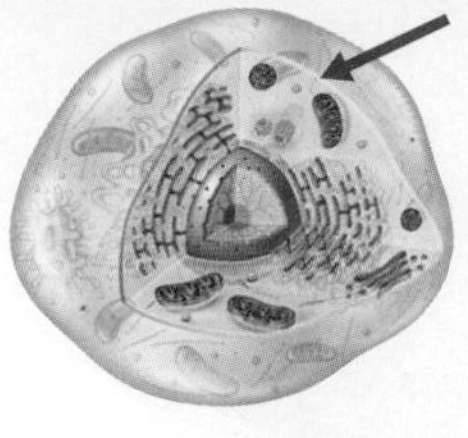

A cell is protected by a flexible covering called the cell membrane.

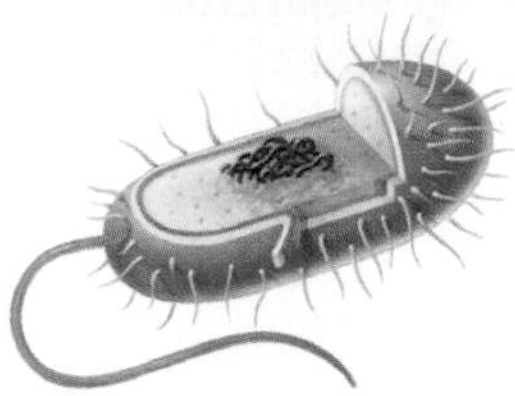

Cells can be grouped into two types—prokaryotic cells and eukaryotic cells.

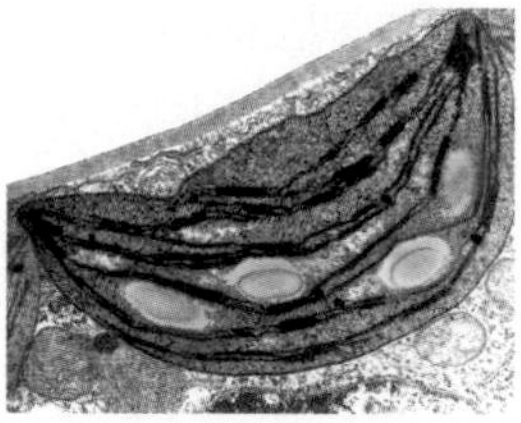

In a chloroplast, light energy is used for making sugars in a process called photosynthesis.

FOLDABLES®

Use your lesson Foldable to review the lesson. Save your Foldable for the project at the end of the chapter.

What do you think NOW?

You first read the statements below at the beginning of the chapter.

3. Different organisms have cells with different structures.

4. All cells store genetic information in their nuclei.

Did you change your mind about whether you agree or disagree with the statements? Rewrite any false statements to make them true.

Use Vocabulary

1. **Distinguish** between the cell wall and the cell membrane.
2. **Use the terms** *mitochondria* and *chloroplasts* in a sentence.
3. **Define** *organelle* in your own words.

Understand Key Concepts

4. Which organelle is used to store water?
   - **A.** chloroplast
   - **B.** lysosome
   - **C.** nucleus
   - **D.** vacuole
5. **Explain** the role of the cytoskeleton.
6. **Draw** a prokaryotic cell and label its parts.
7. **Compare** the roles of the endoplasmic reticulum and the Golgi apparatus.

Interpret Graphics

8. **Explain** how the structure of the cells below relates to their function.

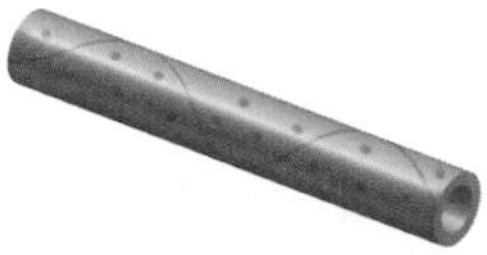

9. **Compare** Copy the table below and fill it in to compare the structures of a plant cell to the structures of an animal cell.

Structure	Plant Cell	Animal Cell
Cell membrane	yes	yes
Cell wall		
Mitochondrion		
Chloroplast		
Nucleus		
Vacuole		
Lysosome		

Critical Thinking

10. **Analyze** Why are most organelles surrounded by membranes?
11. **Compare** the features of eukaryotic and prokaryotic cells.

Inquiry **Skill Practice** **Compare and Contrast** **45 minutes**

How are plant cells and animal cells similar and how are they different?

A light microscope enables you to observe many of the structures in cells. Increasing the magnification means you see a smaller portion of the object, but lets you see more detail. As you see more details, you can **compare and contrast** different cell types. How are they alike? How are they different?

Materials

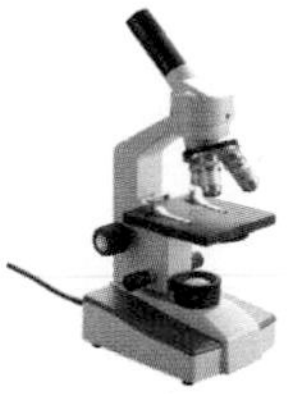

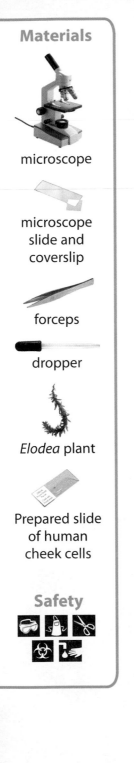

microscope

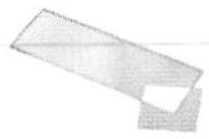

microscope slide and coverslip

forceps

dropper

Elodea plant

Prepared slide of human cheek cells

Safety

Learn It

Observations can be analyzed by noting the similarities and differences between two or more objects that you observe. You **compare** objects by noting similarities. You **contrast** objects by looking for differences.

Try It

1. Read and complete a lab safety form.
2. Using forceps, make a wet-mount slide of a young leaf from the tip of an *Elodea* plant.
3. Use a microscope to observe the leaf on low power. Focus on the top layer of cells.
4. Switch to high power and focus on one cell. The large organelle in the center of the cell is the central vacuole. Moving around the central vacuole are green, disklike objects called chloroplasts. Try to find the nucleus. It looks like a clear ball.
5. Draw a diagram of an *Elodea* cell in your Science Journal. Label the cell wall, central vacuole, chloroplasts, cytoplasm, and nucleus. Return to low power and remove the slide. Properly dispose of the slide.
6. Observe the prepared slide of cheek cells under low power.
7. Switch to high power and focus on one cell. Draw a diagram of one cheek cell. Label the cell membrane, cytoplasm, and nucleus. Return to low power and remove the slide.

Apply It

8. Based on your diagrams, how do the shapes of the *Elodea* cell and cheek cell compare?
9. **Key Concept** Compare and contrast the cell structures in your two diagrams. Which structures did you observe in both cells? Which structures did you observe in only one of the cells?

Lesson 3

Moving Cellular Material

Reading Guide

Key Concepts
ESSENTIAL QUESTIONS

- How do materials enter and leave cells?
- How does cell size affect the transport of materials?

Vocabulary

passive transport p. 405
diffusion p. 406
osmosis p. 406
facilitated diffusion p. 407
active transport p. 408
endocytosis p. 408
exocytosis p. 408

g Multilingual eGlossary

Academic Standards for Science

7.3.1 Explain that all living organisms are composed of one or more cells and that the many functions needed to sustain life are carried out within such cells.

7.3.2 Understand that water is a major component within all cells and is required to carry out many cellular functions.

Also covers: 7.NS.3, 7.NS.5, 7.NS.7

Inquiry Why the Veil?

A beekeeper often wears a helmet with a face-covering veil made of mesh. The openings in the mesh are large enough to let air through, yet small enough to keep bees out. In a similar way, some things must be allowed in or out of a cell, while other things must be kept in or out. How do the right things enter or leave a cell?

Inquiry Launch Lab

5 minutes

What does the cell membrane do?

All cells have a membrane around the outside of the cell. The cell membrane separates the inside of a cell from the environment outside a cell. What else might a cell membrane do?

1. Read and complete a lab safety form.
2. Place a square of **wire mesh** on top of a **beaker.**
3. Pour a small amount of **birdseed** on top of the wire mesh. Record your observations in your Science Journal.

Think About This

1. What part of a cell does the wire mesh represent?
2. What happened when you poured birdseed on the wire mesh?
3. **Key Concept** How do you think the cell membrane affects materials that enter and leave a cell?

Passive Transport

Recall from Lesson 2 that membranes are the boundaries between cells and between organelles. Another important role of membranes is to control the movement of substances into and out of cells. A cell membrane is semipermeable. This means it allows only certain substances to enter or leave a cell. Substances can pass through a cell membrane by one of several different processes. The type of process depends on the physical and chemical properties of the substance passing through the membrane.

Small molecules, such as oxygen and carbon dioxide, pass through membranes by a process called passive transport. **Passive transport** *is the movement of substances through a cell membrane without using the cell's energy.* Passive transport depends on the amount of a substance on each side of a membrane. For example, suppose there are more molecules of oxygen outside a cell than inside it. Oxygen will move into that cell until the amount of oxygen is equal on both sides of the cell's membrane. Since oxygen is a small molecule, it passes through a cell membrane without using the cell's energy. The different types of passive transport are explained on the following pages.

Reading Check Describe a semipermeable membrane.

FOLDABLES®

Fold a sheet of paper into a two-tab book. Label the tabs as shown. Use it to organize information about the different types of passive and active transport.

Diffusion

What happens when the concentration, or amount per unit of volume, of a substance is unequal on each side of a membrane? The molecules will move from the side with a higher concentration of that substance to the side with a lower concentration. **Diffusion** *is the movement of substances from an area of higher concentration to an area of lower concentration.*

Word Origin
diffusion
from Latin *diffusionem*, means "scatter, pour out"

Usually, diffusion continues through a membrane until the concentration of a substance is the same on both sides of the membrane. When this happens, a substance is in equilibrium. Compare the two diagrams in **Figure 12.** What happened to the red dye that was added to the water on one side of the membrane? Water and dye passed through the membrane in both directions until there were equal concentrations of water and dye on both sides of the membrane.

Diffusion

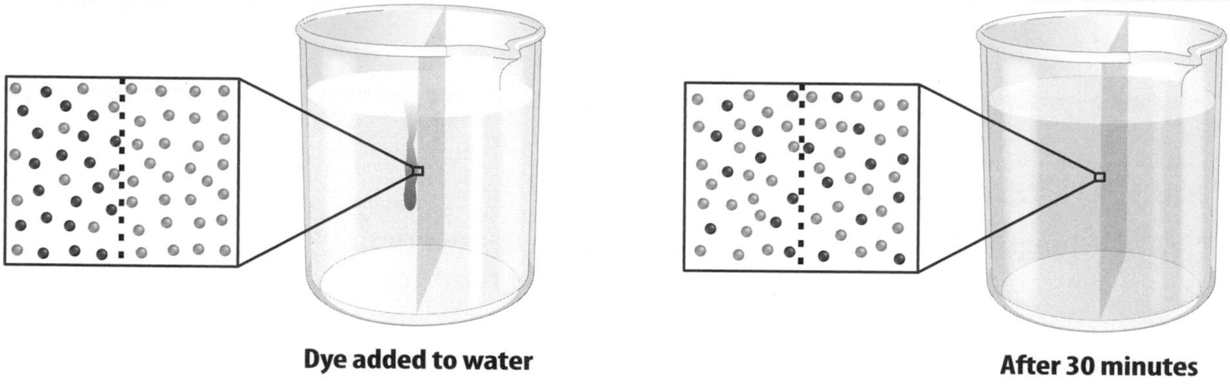

Visual Check What would the water in the beaker on the right look like if the membrane did not let anything through?

Figure 12 Over time, the concentration of dye on either side of the membrane becomes the same.

Osmosis—The Diffusion of Water

Diffusion refers to the movement of any small molecules from higher to lower concentrations. However, **osmosis** *is the diffusion of water molecules only through a membrane.* Semipermeable cell membranes also allow water to pass through them until equilibrium occurs. For example, the amount of water stored in the vacuoles of plant cells can decrease because of osmosis. That is because the concentration of water in the air surrounding the plant is less than the concentration of water inside the vacuoles of plant cells. Water will continue to diffuse into the air until the concentrations of water inside the plant's cells and in the air are equal. If the plant is not watered to replace the lost water, it will wilt and eventually die.

Facilitated Diffusion

Some molecules are too large or are chemically unable to travel through a membrane by diffusion. *When molecules pass through a cell membrane using special proteins called transport proteins, this is* **facilitated diffusion.** Like diffusion and osmosis, facilitated diffusion does not require a cell to use energy. As shown in **Figure 13,** a cell membrane has transport proteins. The two types of transport proteins are carrier proteins and channel proteins. Carrier proteins carry large molecules, such as the sugar molecule glucose, through the cell membrane. Channel proteins form pores through the membrane. Atomic particles, such as sodium ions and potassium ions, pass through the cell membrane by channel proteins.

Reading Check How do materials move through the cell membrane in facilitated diffusion?

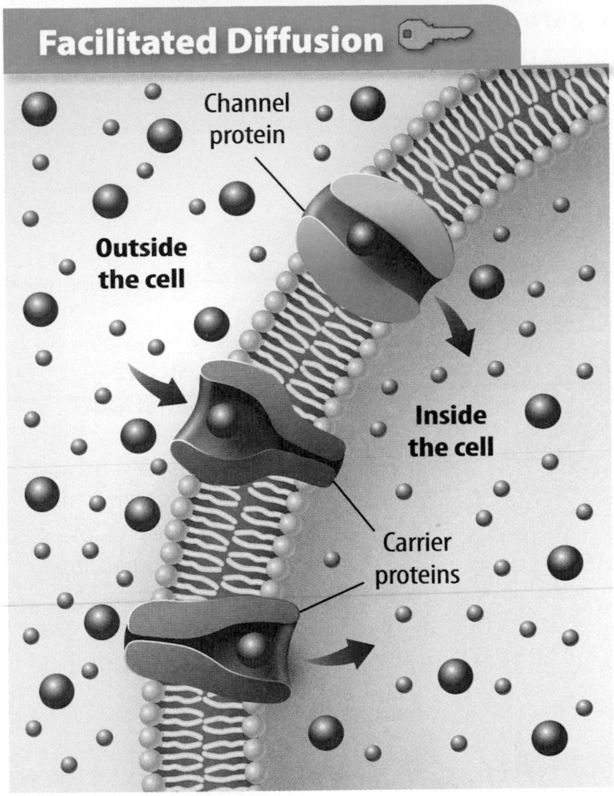

Figure 13 Transport proteins are used to move large molecules into and out of a cell.

Inquiry MiniLab

20 minutes

How is a balloon like a cell membrane?

Substances within a cell are constantly in motion. How can a balloon act like a cell membrane?

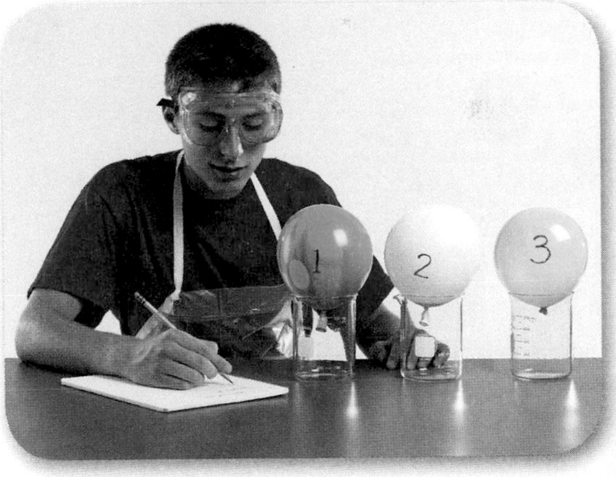

1. Read and complete a lab safety form.
2. Make a three-column table in your Science Journal to record your data. Label the first column *Balloon Number*, the second column *Substance*, and the third column *Supporting Evidence*.
3. Use your senses to identify what substance is in each of the **numbered balloons.**
4. Record what you think each substance is.
5. Record the evidence supporting your choice.

Analyze and Conclude

1. **List** the senses that were most useful in identifying the substances.
2. **Infer** if you could identify the substances if you were blindfolded. If so, how?
3. **Describe** how the substances moved, and explain why they moved this way.
4. **Key Concept** Explain how a balloon is like a cell membrane in terms of the movement of substances.

Figure 14 Active transport is most often used to bring needed nutrients into a cell. Endocytosis and exocytosis move materials that are too large to pass through the cell membrane by other methods.

Active Transport

Concepts in Motion Animation

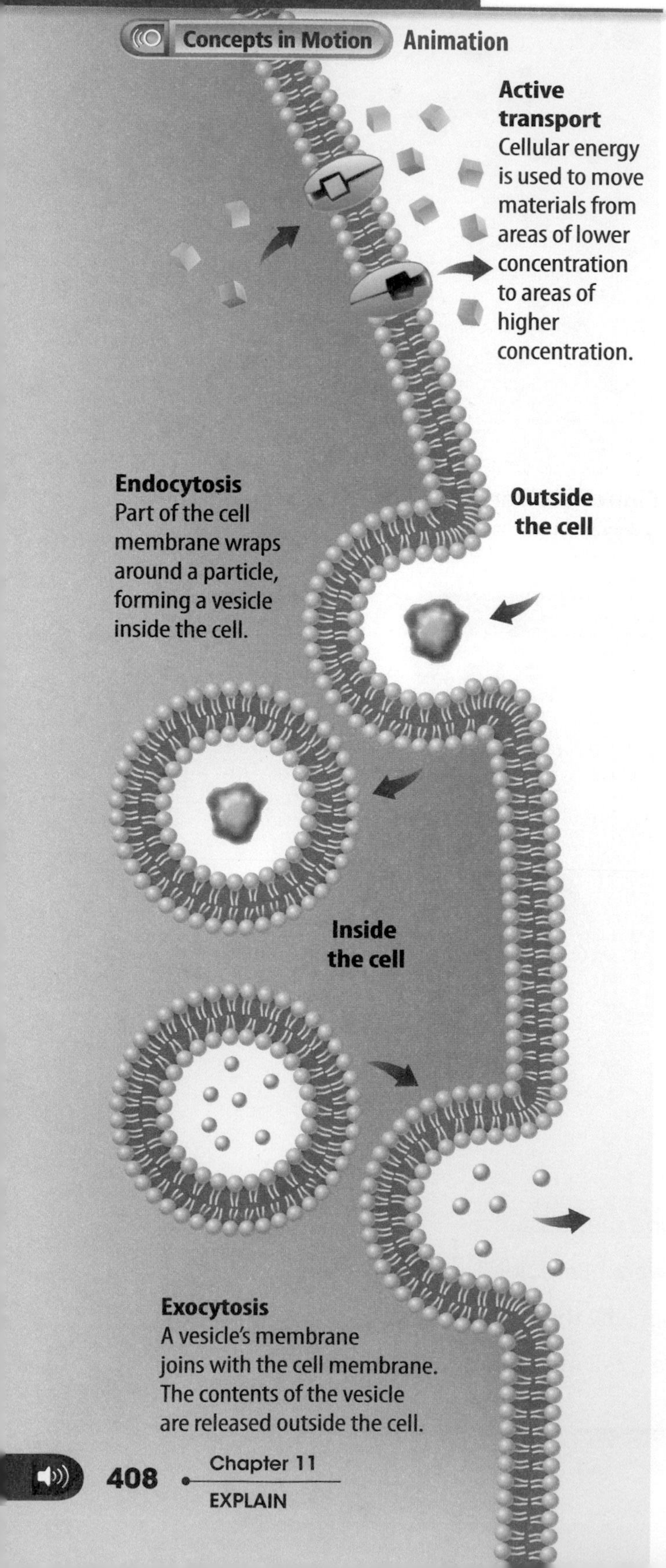

Active transport
Cellular energy is used to move materials from areas of lower concentration to areas of higher concentration.
Endocytosis
Part of the cell membrane wraps around a particle, forming a vesicle inside the cell.
Outside the cell
Inside the cell
Exocytosis
A vesicle's membrane joins with the cell membrane. The contents of the vesicle are released outside the cell.

Active Transport

Sometimes when cellular materials pass through membranes it requires a cell to use energy. **Active transport** *is the movement of substances through a cell membrane only by using the cell's energy.*

Recall that passive transport is the movement of substances from areas of higher concentration to areas of lower concentration. However, substances moving by active transport move from areas of lower concentration to areas of higher concentration, as shown in **Figure 14.**

Active transport is important for cells and organelles. Cells can take in needed nutrients from the environment through carrier proteins by using active transport. This occurs even when concentrations of these nutrients are lower in the environment than inside the cell. Some other molecules and waste materials also leave cells by active transport.

Endocytosis and Exocytosis

Some substances are too large to enter a cell membrane by diffusion or by using a transport protein. These substances can enter a cell by another process. **Endocytosis** (en duh si TOH sus), shown in **Figure 14,** *is the process during which a cell takes in a substance by surrounding it with the cell membrane.* Many different types of cells use endocytosis. For example, some cells take in bacteria and viruses using endocytosis.

Some substances are too large to leave a cell by diffusion or by using a transport protein. These substances can leave a cell another way. **Exocytosis** (ek soh si TOH sus), shown in **Figure 14,** *is the process during which a cell's vesicles release their contents outside the cell.* Proteins and other substances are removed from a cell through this process.

Key Concept Check How do materials enter and leave cells?

Cell Size and Transport

Recall that the movement of nutrients, waste material, and other substances into and out of a cell is important for survival. For this movement to happen, the area of the cell membrane must be large compared to its volume. The area of the cell membrane is the cell's surface area. The volume is the amount of space inside the cell. As a cell grows, both its volume and its surface area increase. The volume of a cell increases faster than its surface area. If a cell were to keep growing, it would need large amounts of nutrients and would produce large amounts of waste material. However, the surface area of the cell's membrane would be too small to move enough nutrients and wastes through it for the cell to survive.

Key Concept Check How does cell size affect the transport of materials?

Review
- **Math Practice**
- **Personal Tutor**

Math Skills — Use Ratios

A ratio is a comparison of two numbers, such as surface area and volume. If a cell were cube-shaped, you would calculate surface area by multiplying its length (ℓ) by its width (w) by the number of sides (6).

Surface area $= \ell \times w \times 6$

You would calculate the volume of the cell by multiplying its length (ℓ) by its width (w) by its height (h).

Volume $= \ell \times w \times h$

To find the surface-area-to-volume ratio of the cell, divide its surface area by its volume.

$\frac{\text{Surface area}}{\text{Volume}}$

In the table below, surface-area-to-volume ratios are calculated for cells that are 1 mm, 2 mm, and 4 mm per side. Notice how the ratios change as the cell's size increases.

		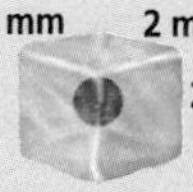	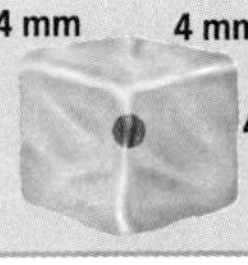
Length	1 mm	2 mm	4 mm
Width	1 mm	2 mm	4 mm
Height	1 mm	2 mm	4 mm
Number of sides	6	6	6
Surface area ($\ell \times w \times$ no. of sides)	1 mm $\times$ 1 mm $\times$ 6 $= 6\ mm^2$	2 mm $\times$ 2 mm $\times$ 6 $= 24\ mm^2$	4 mm $\times$ 4 mm $\times$ 6 $= 96\ mm^2$
Volume ($\ell \times w \times h$)	1 mm $\times$ 1 mm $\times$ 1 mm $= 1\ mm^3$	2 mm $\times$ 2 mm $\times$ 2 mm $= 8\ mm^3$	4 mm $\times$ 4 mm $\times$ 4 mm $= 64\ mm^3$
Surface-area-to-volume ratio	$\frac{6\ mm^2}{1\ mm^3} = \frac{6}{1}$ or 6:1	$\frac{24\ mm^2}{8\ mm^3} = \frac{3}{1}$ or 3:1	$\frac{96\ mm^2}{64\ mm^3} = \frac{1.5}{1}$ or 1.5:1

Practice

What is the surface-area-to-volume ratio of a cell whose six sides are 3 mm long?

Lesson 3 Review

Assessment Online Quiz
Inquiry Virtual Lab

Visual Summary

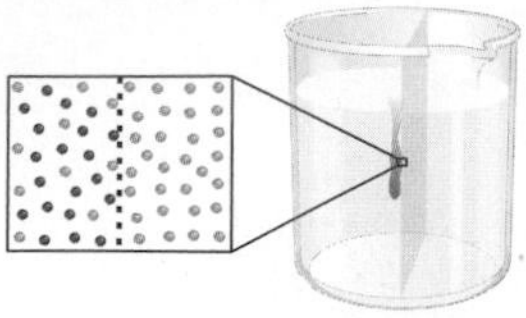

Small molecules can move from an area of higher concentration to an area of lower concentration by diffusion.

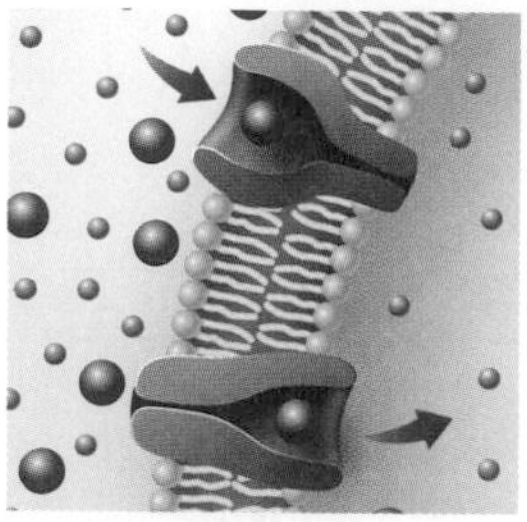

In facilitated diffusion, proteins transport larger molecules through a cell membrane.

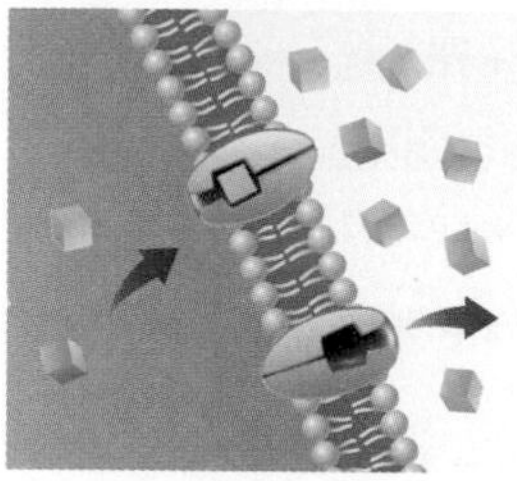

Some molecules move from areas of lower concentration to areas of higher concentration through active transport.

FOLDABLES®

Use your lesson Foldable to review the lesson. Save your Foldable for the project at the end of the chapter.

What do you think NOW?

You first read the statements below at the beginning of the chapter.

5. Diffusion and osmosis are the same process.

6. Cells with large surface areas can transport more than cells with smaller surface areas.

Did you change your mind about whether you agree or disagree with the statements? Rewrite any false statements to make them true.

Use Vocabulary

1. **Use the term** *osmosis* in a sentence.
2. **Distinguish** between active transport and passive transport.
3. The process by which vesicles move substances out of a cell is ________.

Understand Key Concepts

4. **Explain** why energy is needed in active transport.
5. **Summarize** the function of endocytosis.
6. **Contrast** osmosis and diffusion.
7. What is limited by a cell's surface-area-to-volume ratio?
   A. cell shape
   B. cell size
   C. cell surface area
   D. cell volume

Interpret Graphics

8. **Identify** the process shown below, and explain how it works.

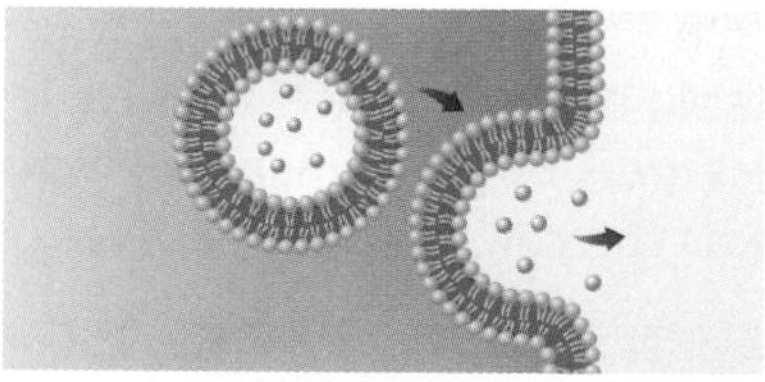

9. **Copy** and fill in the graphic organizer below to describe ways that cells transport substances.

Critical Thinking

10. **Relate** the surface area of a cell to the transport of materials.

Math Skills

Review
Math Practice

11. **Calculate** the surface-area-to-volume ratio of a cube whose sides are 6 cm long.

Inquiry **Skill Practice** **Analyze and Conclude** **30 minutes**

How does an object's size affect the transport of materials?

Materials

hard-cooked eggs

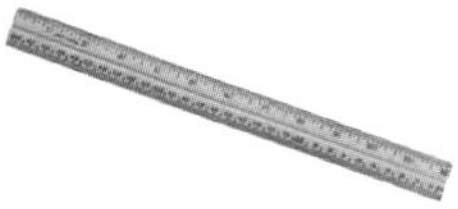

metric ruler

blue food coloring

250-mL beaker

plastic spoon

plastic knife

paper towels

Safety

Nutrients, oxygen, and other materials enter and leave a cell through the cell membrane. Does the size of a cell affect the transport of these materials throughout the cell? In this lab, you will **analyze and conclude** how the size of a cube of egg white affects material transport.

Learn It

To **analyze** how an object's size affects material transport, you will need to calculate each object's surface-area-to-volume ratio. The following formulas are used to calculate surface area and volume of a cube.

surface area (mm^2) = (length of 1 side)$^2 \times 6$

volume (mm^3) = (length of 1 side)^3

To calculate the ratio of surface area to volume, divide surface area by volume.

Try It

1. Read and complete a lab safety form.
2. Measure and cut one large cube of egg white that is 20 mm on each side. Then, measure and cut one small cube of egg white that is 10 mm on each side.
3. Place 100 mL of water in a plastic cup. Add 10 drops of food coloring. Gently add the egg-white cubes, and soak overnight.
4. Remove the cubes from the cup with a plastic spoon and place them on a paper towel. Cut each cube in half.
5. Examine the inside surface of each cube. Measure and record in millimeters how deep the blue food coloring penetrated into each cube.

Apply It

6. How does the depth of the color compare on the two cubes?
7. Calculate the surface area, the volume, and the surface-area-to-volume ratio of each cube. How do the surface-area-to-volume ratios of the two cubes compare?
8. **Key Concept** Would a cell with a small surface-area-to-volume ratio be able to transport nutrients and waste through the cell as efficiently as a cell with a large surface-area-to-volume ratio?

4

Lesson 4

Reading Guide

Key Concepts
ESSENTIAL QUESTIONS

- How does a cell obtain energy?
- How do some cells make food molecules?

Vocabulary

cellular respiration p. 413
glycolysis p. 413
fermentation p. 414
photosynthesis p. 415

g Multilingual eGlossary

Academic Standards for Science

7.3.1 Explain that all living organisms are composed of one or more cells and that the many functions needed to sustain life are carried out within such cells.

Also covers: 7.NS.1, 7.NS.3, 7.NS.4, 7.NS.5, 7.NS.7, 7.NS.9, 7.NS.11

Cells and Energy

Inquiry Why are there bubbles?

Have you ever seen bubbles on a green plant in an aquarium? Where did the bubbles come from? Green plants use light energy and make sugars and oxygen.

Inquiry Launch Lab

5 minutes

What do you exhale?

Does the air you breathe in differ from the air you breathe out?

1. Read and complete a lab safety form.
2. Unwrap a **straw.** Use the straw to slowly blow into a small **cup** of **bromthymol blue.** Do not splash the liquid out of the cup.
3. In your Science Journal, record any changes in the solution.

Think About This

1. What changes did you observe in the solution?
2. What do you think caused the changes in the solution?
3. **Key Concept** Why do you think the air you inhale differs from the air you exhale?

Cellular Respiration

When you are tired, you might eat something to give you energy. All living things, from one-celled organisms to humans, need energy to survive. Recall that cells process energy from food into the energy-storage compound ATP. **Cellular respiration** *is a series of chemical reactions that convert the energy in food molecules into a usable form of energy called ATP.* Cellular respiration is a complex process that occurs in two parts of a cell—the cytoplasm and the mitochondria.

Reactions in the Cytoplasm

The first step of cellular respiration, called glycolysis, occurs in the cytoplasm of all cells. **Glycolysis** *is a process by which glucose, a sugar, is broken down into smaller molecules.* As shown in **Figure 15,** glycolysis produces some ATP molecules. It also uses energy from other ATP molecules. You will read on the following page that more ATP is made during the second step of cellular respiration than during glycolysis.

Reading Check What is produced during glycolysis?

Glycolysis

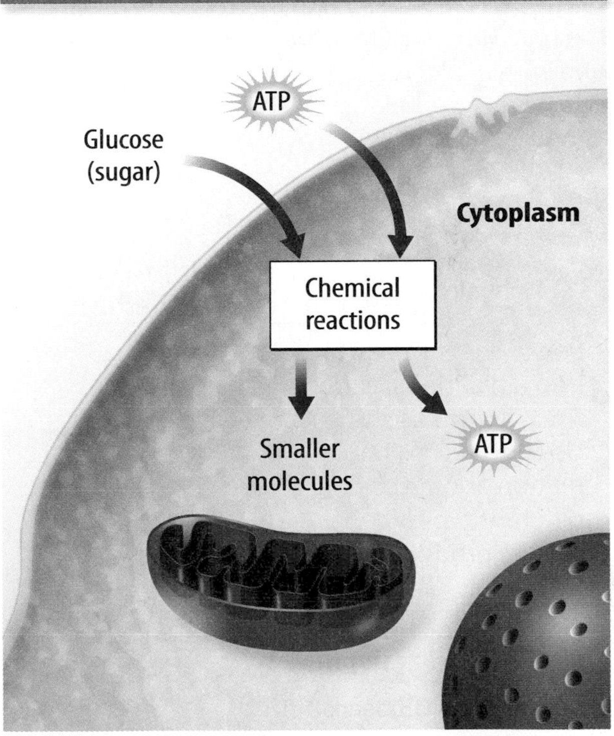

Figure 15 Glycolysis is the first step of cellular respiration.

Reactions in the Mitochondria

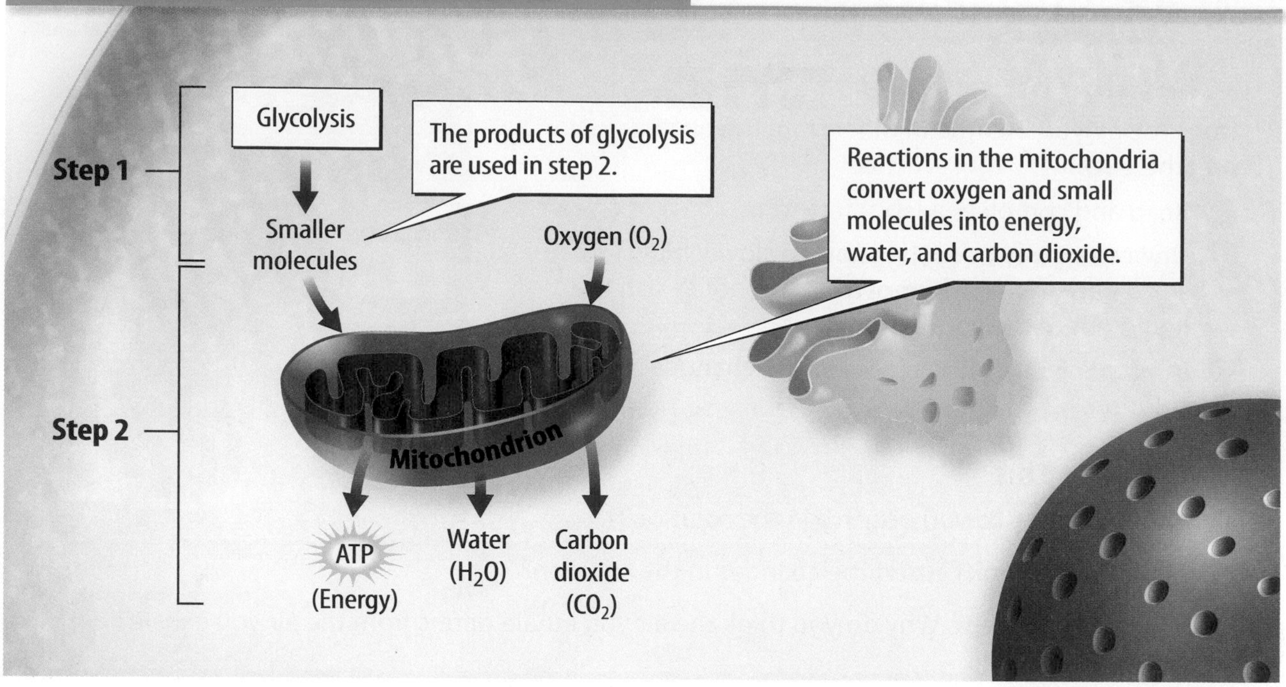

Figure 16 After glycolysis, cellular respiration continues in the mitochondria.

Visual Check Compare the reactions in mitochondria with glycolysis.

Reactions in the Mitochondria

The second step of cellular respiration occurs in the mitochondria of eukaryotic cells, as shown in **Figure 16.** This step of cellular respiration requires oxygen. The smaller molecules made from glucose during glycolysis are broken down. Large amounts of ATP—usable energy—are produced. Cells use ATP to power all cellular processes. Two waste products—water and carbon dioxide (CO_2)—are given off during this step.

The CO_2 released by cells as a waste product is used by plants and some unicellular organisms in another process called photosynthesis. You will read more about the chemical reactions that take place during photosynthesis in this lesson.

FOLDABLES®

Fold a sheet of paper into a half book. Label the columns as shown. Use it to record information about the different types of energy production.

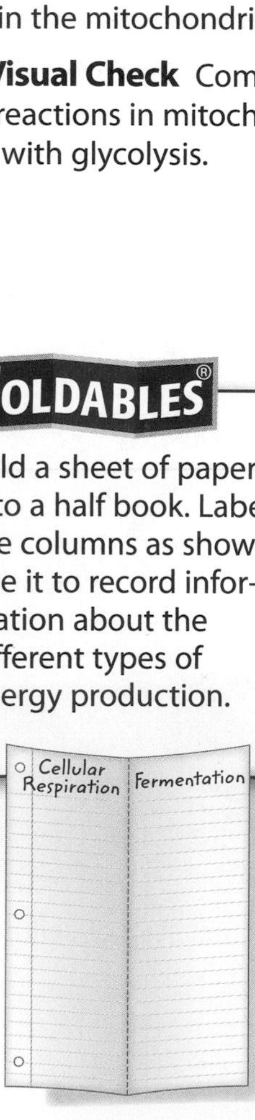

Fermentation

Have you ever felt out of breath after exercising? Sometimes when you exercise, your cells don't have enough oxygen to make ATP through cellular respiration. Then, chemical energy is obtained through a different process called fermentation. This process does not use oxygen.

Fermentation *is a reaction that eukaryotic and prokaryotic cells can use to obtain energy from food when oxygen levels are low.* Because no oxygen is used, fermentation makes less ATP than cellular respiration does. Fermentation occurs in a cell's cytoplasm, not in mitochondria.

Key Concept Check How does a cell obtain energy?

Types of Fermentation

One type of fermentation occurs when glucose is converted into ATP and a waste product called lactic acid, as illustrated in **Figure 17.** Some bacteria and fungi help produce cheese, yogurt, and sour cream using lactic-acid fermentation. Muscle cells in humans and other animals can use lactic-acid fermentation and obtain energy during exercise.

Some types of bacteria and yeast make ATP through a process called alcohol fermentation. However, instead of producing lactic acid, alcohol fermentation produces an alcohol called ethanol and CO_2, also illustrated in **Figure 17.** Some types of breads are made using yeast. The CO_2 produced by yeast during alcohol fermentation makes the dough rise.

Reading Check Compare lactic-acid fermentation and alcohol fermentation.

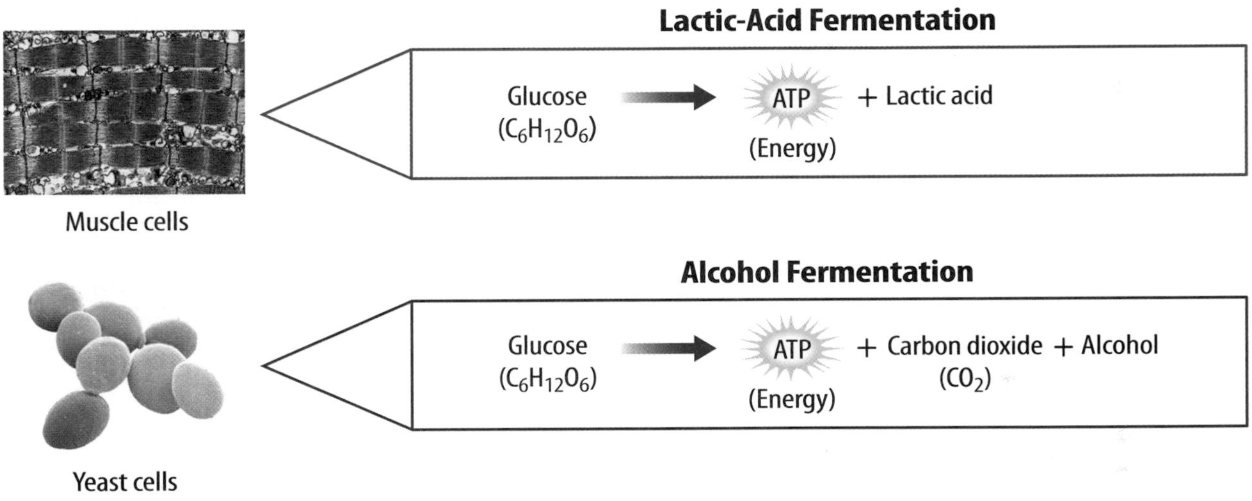

Figure 17 Your muscle cells produce lactic acid as a waste during fermentation. Yeast cells produce carbon dioxide and alcohol as wastes during fermentation.

Photosynthesis

Humans and other animals convert food energy into ATP through cellular respiration. However, plants and some unicellular organisms obtain energy from light. **Photosynthesis** *is a series of chemical reactions that convert light energy, water, and* CO_2 *into the food-energy molecule glucose and give off oxygen.*

WORD ORIGIN

photosynthesis
from Greek *photo,* means "light"; and *synthesis,* means "composition"

Lights and Pigments

Photosynthesis requires light energy. In plants, pigments such as chlorophyll absorb light energy. When chlorophyll absorbs light, it absorbs all colors except green. Green light is reflected as the green color seen in leaves. However, plants contain many pigments that reflect other colors, such as yellow and red.

Reactions in Chloroplasts

The light energy absorbed by chlorophyll and other pigments powers the chemical reactions of photosynthesis. These reactions occur in chloroplasts, the organelles in plant cells that convert light energy to chemical energy in food. During photosynthesis, light energy, water, and carbon dioxide combine and make sugars. Photosynthesis also produces oxygen that is released into the atmosphere, as shown in **Figure 18.**

Key Concept Check How do some cells make food molecules?

Importance of Photosynthesis

Recall that photosynthesis uses light energy and CO_2 and makes food energy and releases oxygen. This food energy is stored in the form of glucose. When an organism, such as the bird in **Figure 18,** eats plant material, such as fruit, it takes in food energy. An organism's cells use the oxygen released during photosynthesis and convert the food energy into usable energy through cellular respiration. **Figure 18** illustrates the important relationship between cellular respiration and photosynthesis.

Figure 18 The relationship between cellular respiration and photosynthesis is important for life.

Cellular Respiration and Photosynthesis

Review Personal Tutor

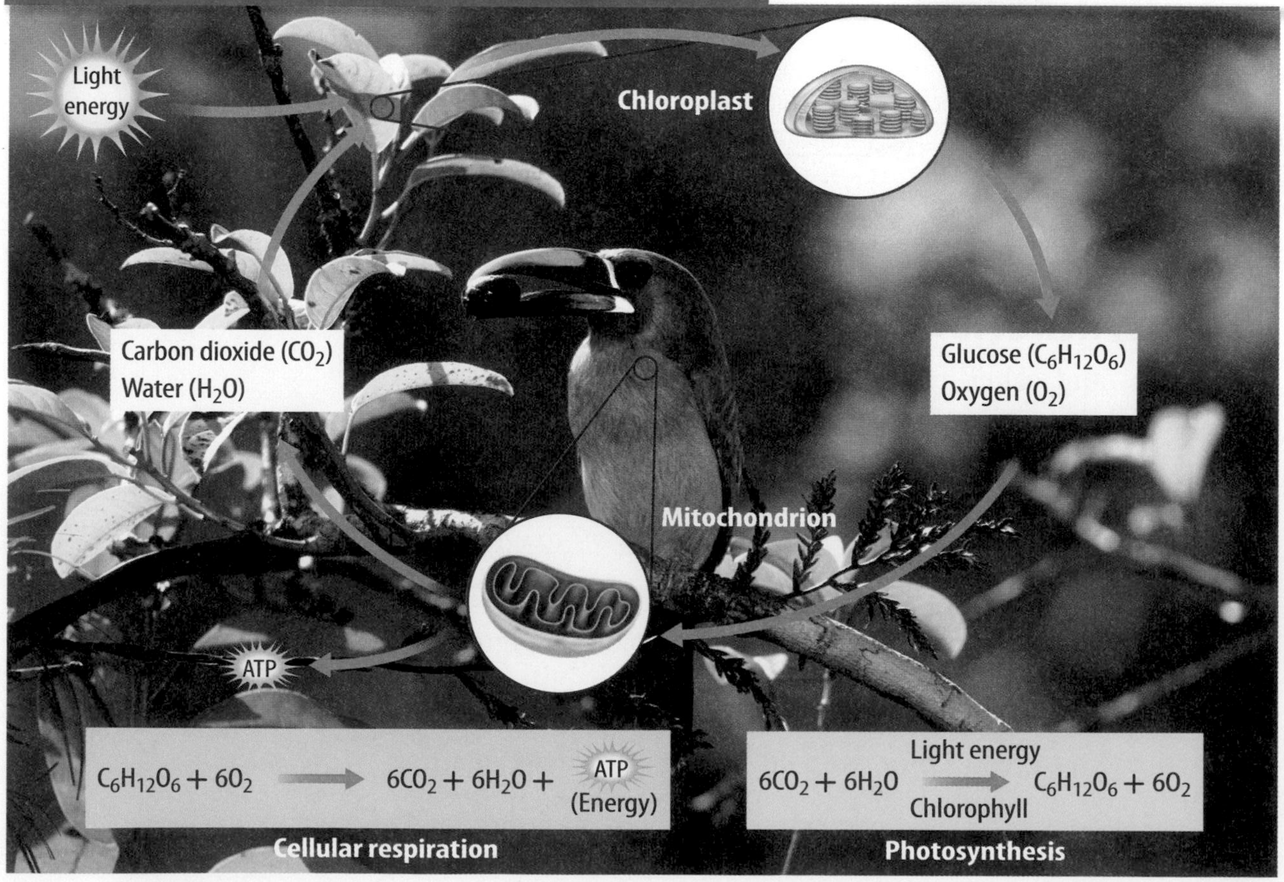

Lesson 4 Review

Assessment | Online Quiz

Visual Summary

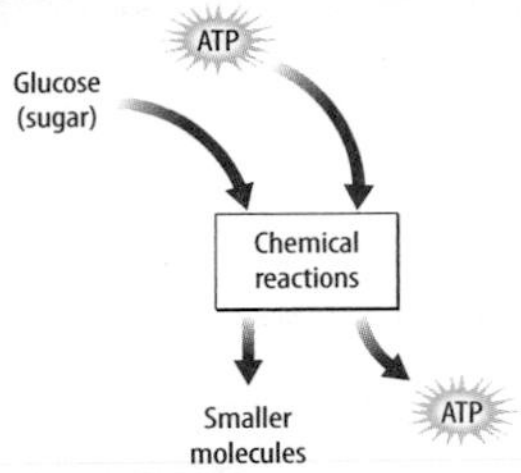

Glycolysis is the first step in cellular respiration.

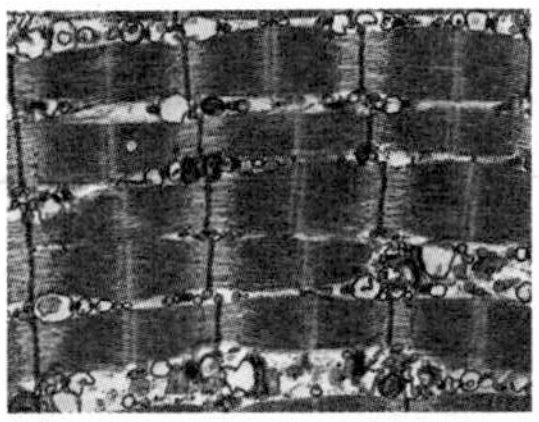

Fermentation provides cells, such as muscle cells, with energy when oxygen levels are low.

Light energy powers the chemical reactions of photosynthesis.

FOLDABLES®

Use your lesson Foldable to review the lesson. Save your Foldable for the project at the end of the chapter.

What do you think NOW?

You first read the statements below at the beginning of the chapter.

7. ATP is the only form of energy found in cells.

8. Cellular respiration occurs only in lung cells.

Did you change your mind about whether you agree or disagree with the statements? Rewrite any false statements to make them true.

Use Vocabulary

1. **Define** *glycolysis* using your own words.
2. **Distinguish** between cellular respiration and fermentation.
3. A process used by plants to convert light energy into food energy is ________.

Understand Key Concepts

4. Which contains pigments that absorb light energy?
   A. chloroplast
   B. mitochondrion
   C. nucleus
   D. vacuole
5. **Relate** mitochondria to cellular respiration.
6. **Describe** the role of chlorophyll in photosynthesis.
7. **Give an example** of how fermentation is used in the food industry.

Interpret Graphics

8. **Draw** a graphic organizer like the one below. Fill in the boxes with the substances used and produced during photosynthesis.

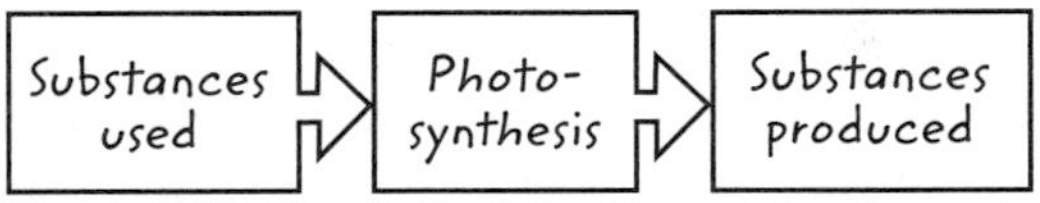

9. **Summarize** the steps of cellular respiration using the figure below.

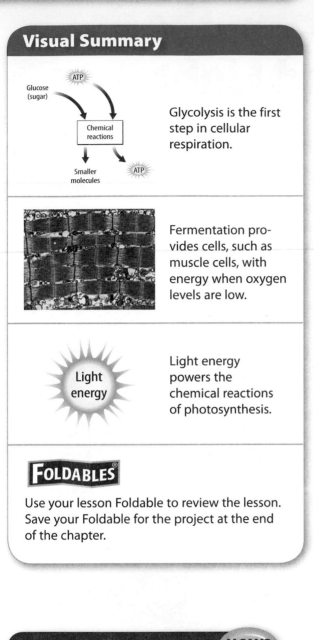

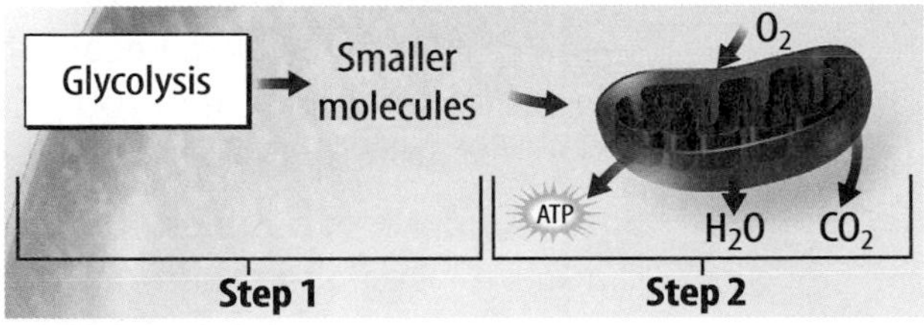

Critical Thinking

10. **Design** a concept map to show the relationship between cellular respiration in animals and photosynthesis in plants.
11. **Summarize** the roles of glucose and ATP in energy processing.

Inquiry **Lab** — 50 minutes

Photosynthesis and Light

Materials

test tube

Elodea

scissors

beaker

lamp

watch or clock

thermometer

Safety

You might think of photosynthesis as a process of give and take. Plant cells take in water and carbon dioxide, and, powered by light energy, make their own food. Plants give off oxygen as a waste product during photosynthesis. Can you determine how the intensity of light affects the rate of photosynthesis?

Ask a Question

How does the intensity of light affect photosynthesis?

Make Observations

1. Read and complete a lab safety form.
2. Cut the bottom end of an *Elodea* stem at an angle, and lightly crush the cut end. Place the *Elodea* in a test tube with the cut side at the top. Fill the test tube with water. Stand the test tube and a thermometer in a beaker filled with water. (The water in the beaker keeps the water in the test tube from getting too warm under the lamp.)
3. Place the beaker containing your test tube on a sheet of paper under a lamp. Measure the temperature of the water in the beaker. Record the temperature in your Science Journal.
4. When bubbles of oxygen begin to rise from the plant, start counting the number of bubbles per minute. Continue to record this data for 10 minutes.
5. Record the temperature of the water in the beaker at the end of the test.
6. Calculate the average number of bubbles produced per minute by your plant.
7. Compare your data with your classmates' data.

Form a Hypothesis

8. Use your data to form a hypothesis relating the amount of light to the rate of photosynthesis.

Test Your Hypothesis

9. Repeat the experiment, changing the light variable so that you are observing your plant's reaction to getting either more or less light. An increase or decrease in water temperature will indicate a change in the amount of light. Keep all other conditions the same.
10. Record your data in a table similar to the one shown at right, and calculate the average number of bubbles per minute.

Analyze and Conclude

11. **Use Variables** How does the amount of light affect photosynthesis? What is your evidence?
12. **The Big Idea** How do plant cells make food? What do they take in and what do they give off? What source of energy do they use?

Communicate Your Results

Compile all the class data on one graph to show the effects of varying amounts of light on the rate of photosynthesis.

Number of Bubbles per Minute

Time	Control	Less Light
1		
2		
3		
4		
5		
6		
7		
8		
9		
10		

Remember to use scientific methods.

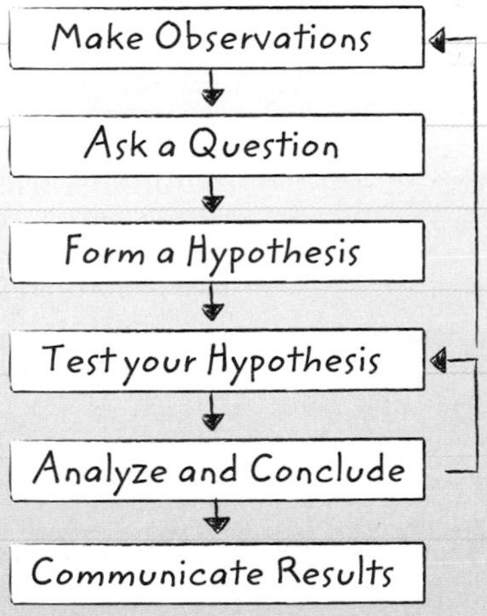

Inquiry Extension

What other variables might affect the rate of photosynthesis? For example, how does different-colored light or a change in temperature affect the rate of photosynthesis? To investigate your question, design a controlled experiment.

Lab Tips

☑ To calculate the average number of bubbles per minute, add the total number of bubbles observed in 10 minutes, and then divide by 10.

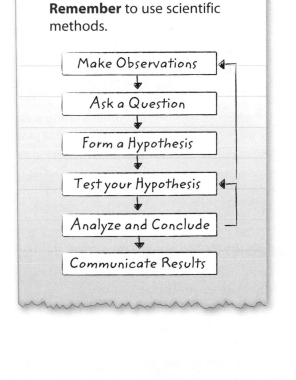

Chapter 11 Study Guide

WebQuest

THE BIG IDEA **A cell is made up of structures that provide support and movement; process energy; and transport materials into, within, and out of a cell.**

Key Concepts Summary

Lesson 1: Cells and Life

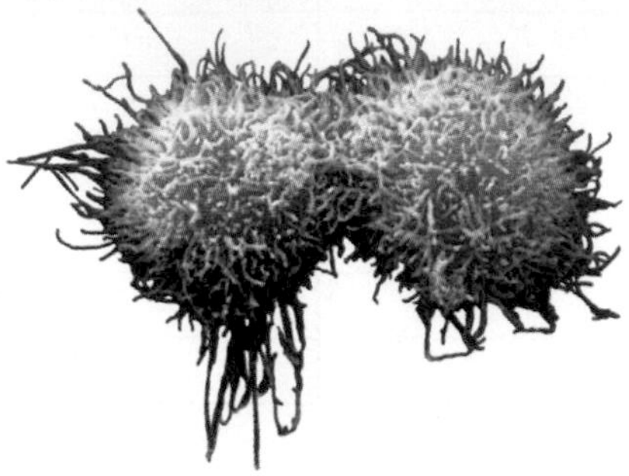

- The invention of the microscope led to discoveries about cells. In time, scientists used these discoveries to develop the **cell theory,** which explains how cells and living things are related.
- Cells are composed mainly of water, **proteins, nucleic acids, lipids,** and **carbohydrates.**

Vocabulary

cell theory p. 388
macromolecule p. 389
nucleic acid p. 390
protein p. 391
lipid p. 391
carbohydrate p. 391

Lesson 2: The Cell

- Cell structures have specific functions, such as supporting a cell, moving a cell, controlling cell activities, processing energy, and transporting molecules.
- A prokaryotic cell lacks a nucleus and other **organelles,** while a eukaryotic cell has a nucleus and other organelles.

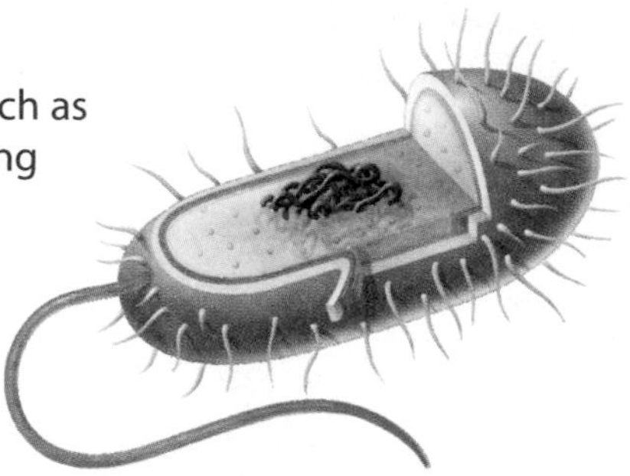

Vocabulary

cell membrane p. 396
cell wall p. 396
cytoplasm p. 397
cytoskeleton p. 397
organelle p. 398
nucleus p. 399
chloroplast p. 401

Lesson 3: Moving Cellular Material

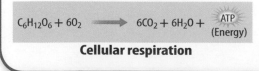

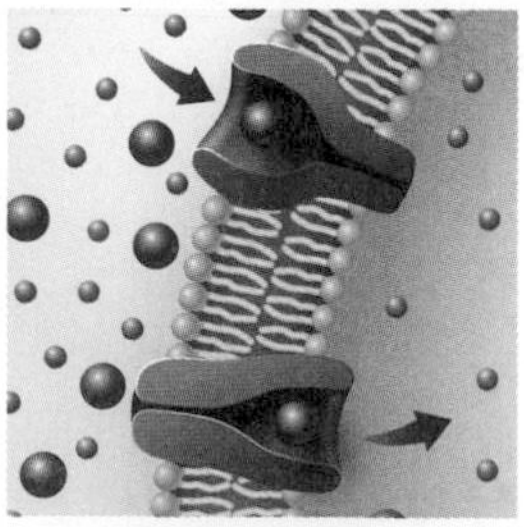

- Materials enter and leave a cell through the cell membrane using **passive transport** or **active transport, endocytosis,** and **exocytosis.**
- The ratio of surface area to volume limits the size of a cell. In a smaller cell, the high surface-area-to-volume ratio allows materials to move easily to all parts of a cell.

Vocabulary

passive transport p. 405
diffusion p. 406
osmosis p. 406
facilitated diffusion p. 407
active transport p. 408
endocytosis p. 408
exocytosis p. 408

Lesson 4: Cells and Energy

- All living cells release energy from food molecules through **cellular respiration** and/or **fermentation.**
- Some cells make food molecules using light energy through the process of **photosynthesis.**

$$C_6H_{12}O_6 + 6O_2 \longrightarrow 6CO_2 + 6H_2O + \text{ATP (Energy)}$$

Cellular respiration

$$6CO_2 + 6H_2O \xrightarrow[\text{Chlorophyll}]{\text{Light energy}} C_6H_{12}O_6 + 6O_2$$

Photosynthesis

Vocabulary

cellular respiration p. 413
glycolysis p. 413
fermentation p. 414
photosynthesis p. 415

Review
- Vocabulary eFlashcards
- Vocabulary eGames
- Personal Tutor

FOLDABLES® Chapter Project

Assemble your lesson Foldables as shown to make a Chapter Project. Use the project to review what you have learned in this chapter.

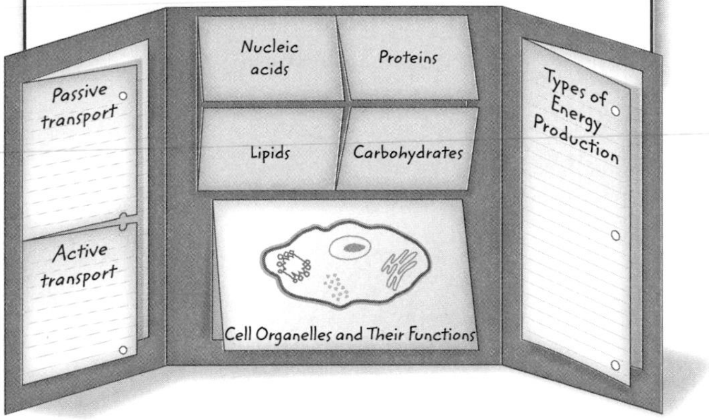

Use Vocabulary

1. Substances formed by joining smaller molecules together are called ________.
2. The ________ consists of proteins joined together to create fiberlike structures inside cells.
3. The movement of substances from an area of high concentration to an area of low concentration is called ________.
4. A process that uses oxygen to convert energy from food into ATP is ________ ________.

Link Vocabulary and Key Concepts

Concepts in Motion **Interactive Concept Map**

Copy this concept map, and then use vocabulary terms from the previous page to complete the concept map.

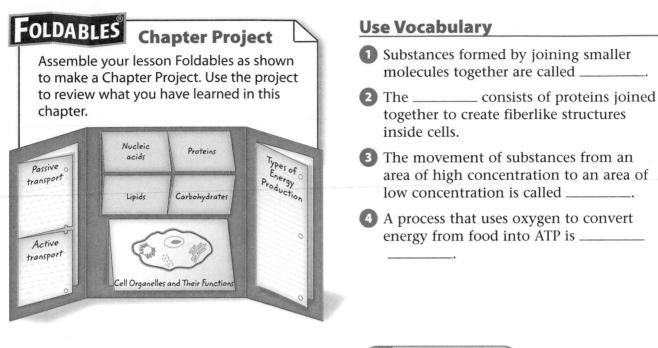

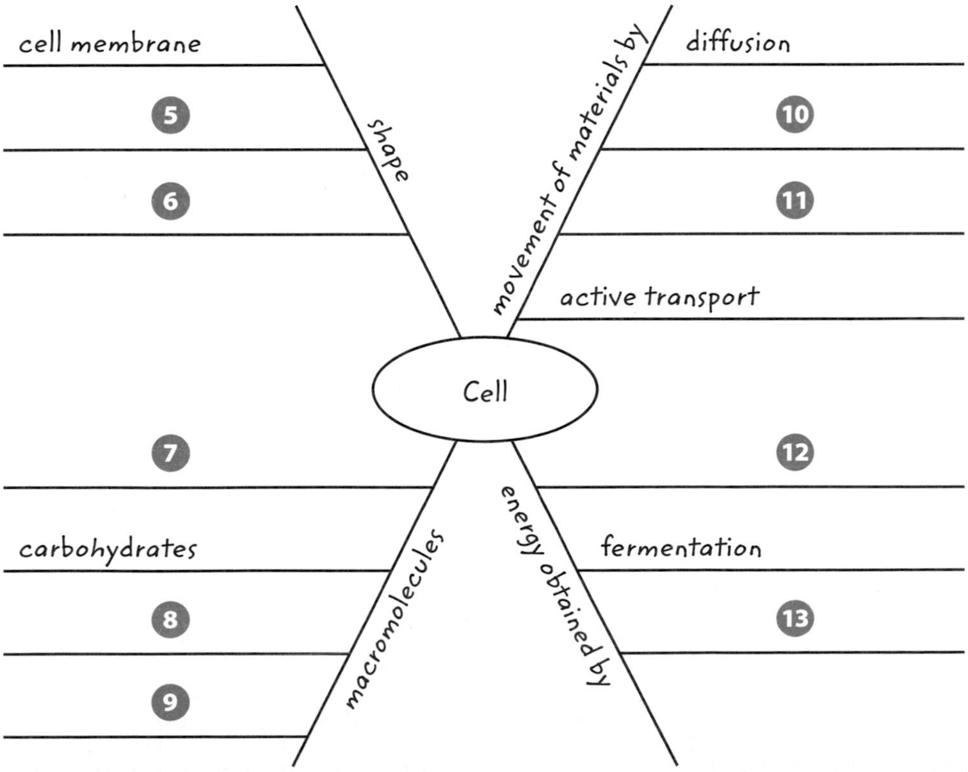

Chapter 11 Review

Understand Key Concepts

1 Cholesterol is which type of macromolecule?
- A. carbohydrate
- B. lipid
- C. nucleic acid
- D. protein

2 Genetic information is stored in which macromolecule?
- A. DNA
- B. glucose
- C. lipid
- D. starch

3 The arrow below is pointing to which cell part?

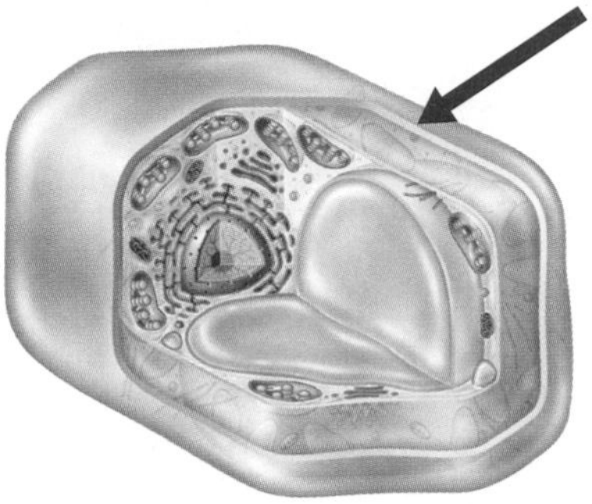

- A. chloroplast
- B. mitochondrion
- C. cell membrane
- D. cell wall

4 Which best describes vacuoles?
- A. lipids
- B. proteins
- C. contained in mitochondria
- D. storage compartments

5 Which is true of fermentation?
- A. does not generate energy
- B. does not require oxygen
- C. occurs in mitochondria
- D. produces lots of ATP

6 Which process eliminates substances from cells in vesicles?
- A. endocytosis
- B. exocytosis
- C. osmosis
- D. photosynthesis

7 Which cell shown below can send signals over long distances?

A. 

B. 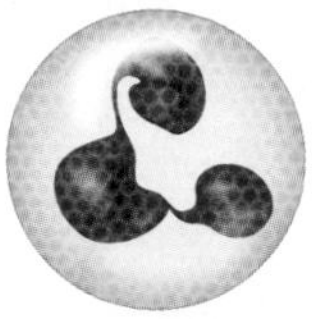

C. 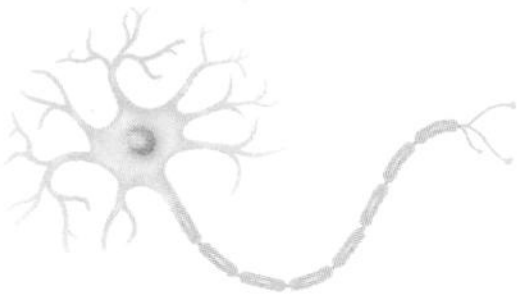

D. 

8 The figure below shows a cell. What is the arrow pointing to?

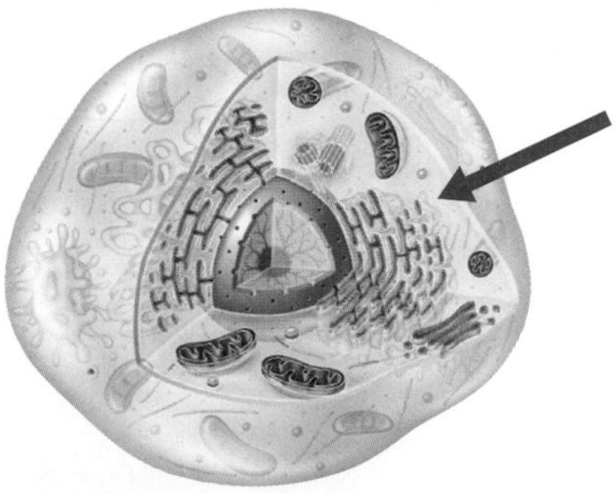

- A. chloroplast
- B. cytoplasm
- C. mitochondrion
- D. nucleus

Assessment
- Chapter Test
- Math Practice

Critical Thinking

9 **Evaluate** the importance of the microscope to biology.

10 **Summarize** the role of water in cells.

11 **Hypothesize** how new cells form from existing cells.

12 **Distinguish** between channel proteins and carrier proteins.

13 **Explain** osmosis.

14 **Infer** Why do cells need carrier proteins that transport glucose?

15 **Compare** the amounts of ATP generated in cellular respiration and fermentation.

16 **Assess** the role of fermentation in baking bread.

17 **Hypothesize** how air pollution like smog affects photosynthesis.

18 **Compare** prokaryotes and eukaryotes by copying and filling in the table below.

Structure	Prokaryote (yes or no)	Eukaryote (yes or no)
Cell membrane		
DNA		
Nucleus		
Endoplasmic reticulum		
Golgi apparatus		
Cell wall		

Writing in Science

19 **Write** a five-sentence paragraph relating the cytoskeleton to the walls of a building. Be sure to include a topic sentence and a concluding sentence in your paragraph.

REVIEW THE BIG IDEA

20 How do the structures and processes of a cell enable it to survive? As an example, explain how chloroplasts help plant cells.

21 The photo below shows a protozoan. What structures enable it to get food into its mouth?

Math Skills

Review
Math Practice

Use Ratios

22 A rectangular solid measures 4 cm long by 2 cm wide by 2 cm high. What is the surface-area-to-volume ratio of the solid?

23 At different times during its growth, a cell has the following surface areas and volumes:

Time	Surface area (μm)	Volume (μm)
1	6	1
2	24	8
3	54	27

What happens to the surface-area-to-volume ratio as the cell grows?

Standardized Test Practice

Record your answers on the answer sheet provided by your teacher or on a sheet of paper.

Multiple Choice

1 Which process do plant cells use to capture and store energy from sunlight?

 A endocytosis

 B fermentation

 C glycolysis

 D photosynthesis

Use the diagram below to answer question 2.

Chloride	—	Oxygen	●
Hydrogen	+	Sodium	+

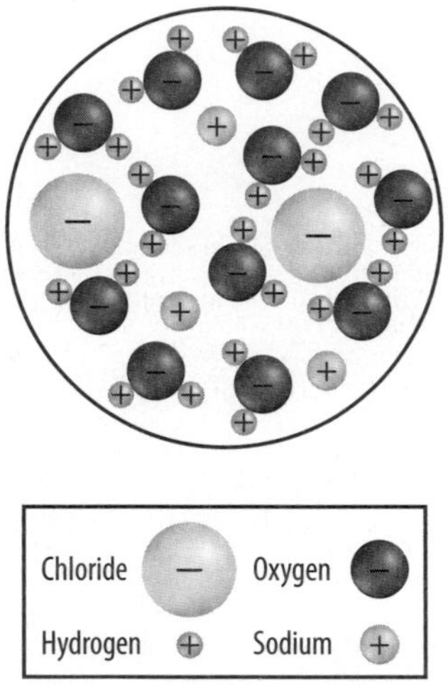

2 The diagram shows salt dissolved in water. What does it show about water molecules and chloride ions?

 A A water molecule consists of oxygen and chloride ions.

 B A water molecule is surrounded by several chloride ions.

 C A water molecule moves away from a chloride ion.

 D A water molecule points its positive end toward a chloride ion.

3 Which transport process requires the use of a cell's energy?

 A diffusion

 B osmosis

 C active transport

 D facilitated diffusion

4 Diffusion differs from active cell transport processes because it

 A forces large molecules from a cell.

 B keeps a cell's boundary intact.

 C moves substances into a cell.

 D needs none of a cell's energy.

Use the diagram below to answer questions 5 and 6.

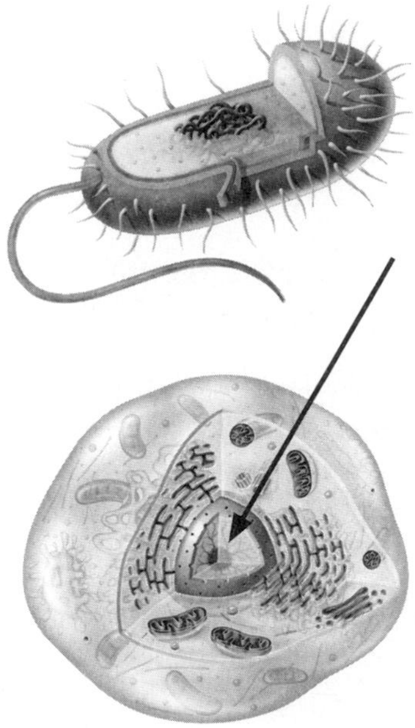

5 Which structure does the arrow point to in the eukaryotic cell?

 A cytoplasm

 B lysosome

 C nucleus

 D ribosome

6 Which feature does a typical prokaryotic cell have that is missing from some eukaryotic cells, like the one above?

 A cytoplasm

 B DNA

 C cell membrane

 D cell wall

7 Which explains why the ratio of cell surface area to volume affects the cell size? Cells with a high surface-to-volume ratio

A consume energy efficiently.

B produce waste products slowly.

C suffer from diseases frequently.

D transport substances effectively.

Use the diagram below to answer question 8.

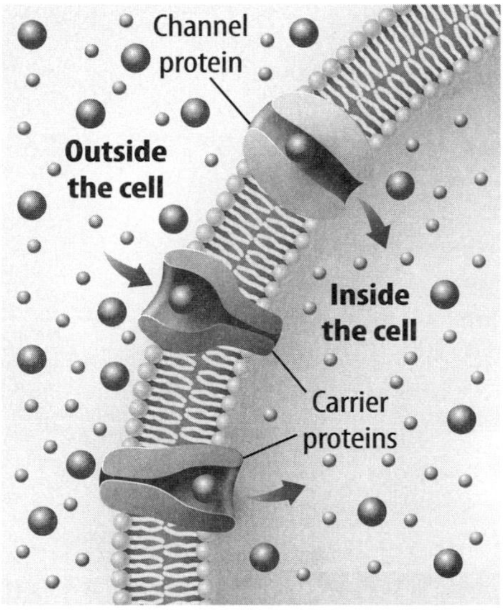

8 Which statement is NOT true of carrier proteins and channel proteins?

A Carrier proteins change shape as they function but channel proteins do not.

B Carrier proteins and channel proteins extend through the cell membrane.

C Channel proteins move items inside a cell but carrier proteins do not.

D Channel proteins and carrier proteins perform facilitated diffusion.

Constructed Response

9 Copy the table below and complete it using these terms: *cell membrane, cell wall, chloroplast, cytoplasm, cytoskeleton, nucleus.*

Cell Structure	Function
	Maintains the shape of an animal cell
	Controls the activities of a cell
	Traps energy from the Sun
	Controls the materials going in and out of a cell
	Holds the structures of a cell in a watery mix
	Maintains the shape of some plant cells

10 Name the kinds of organisms that have cells with cell walls. Name the kinds of organisms that have cells without cell walls. Briefly describe the benefits of cell walls for organisms.

11 Draw simple diagrams of an animal cell and a plant cell. Label the nucleus, the cytoplasm, the mitochondria, the cell membrane, the chloroplasts, the cell wall, and the central vacuole in the appropriate cells. Briefly describe the main differences between the two cells.

NEED EXTRA HELP?											
If You Missed Question...	1	2	3	4	5	6	7	8	9	10	11
Go to Lesson...	4	1	3	3	2	2	3	3	2	2	2

Chapter 12

From a Cell to an Organism

THE BIG IDEA **How can one cell become a multicellular organism?**

Inquiry What's happening inside?

From the outside, a chicken egg looks like a simple oval object. But big changes are taking place inside the egg. Over several weeks, the one cell in the egg will grow and divide and become a chick.

- How did the original cell change over time?
- What might have happened to the chick's cells as the chick grew?
- How can one cell become a multicellular chick?

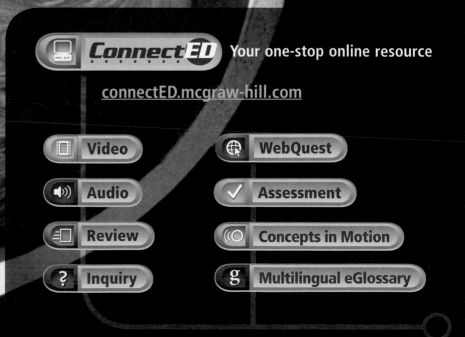

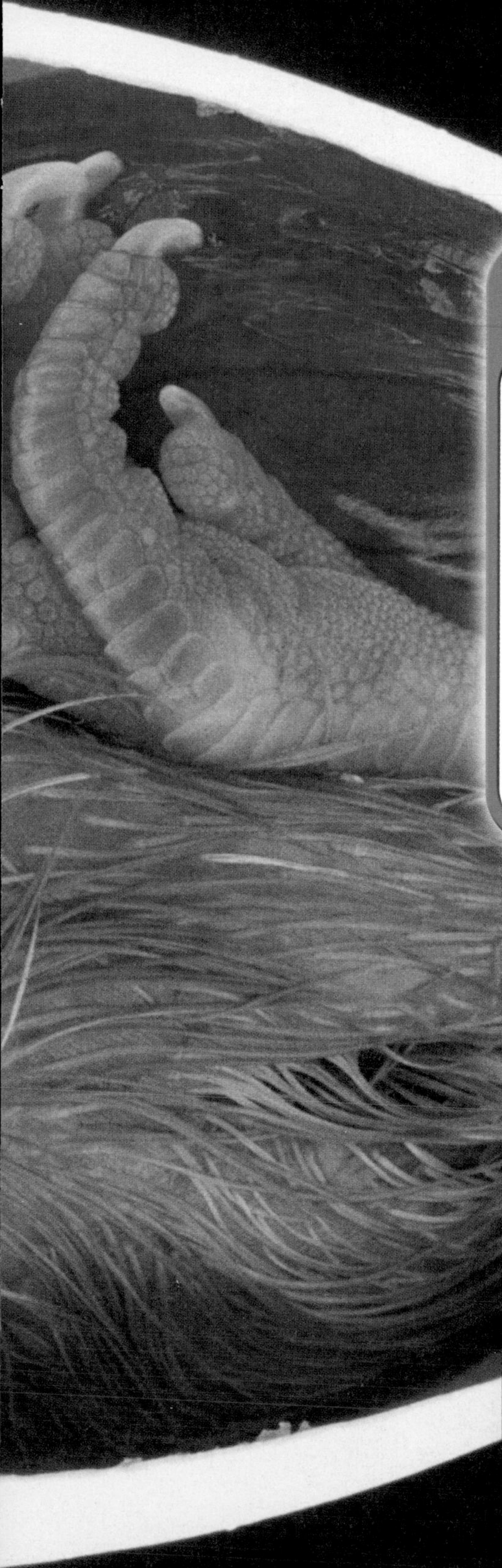

Get Ready to Read

What do you think?

Before you read, decide if you agree or disagree with each of these statements. As you read this chapter, see if you change your mind about any of the statements.

1. Cell division produces two identical cells.
2. Cell division is important for growth.
3. At the end of the cell cycle, the original cell no longer exists.
4. Unicellular organisms do not have all the characteristics of life.
5. All the cells in a multicellular organism are the same.
6. Some organs work together as part of an organ system.

ConnectED Your one-stop online resource

connectED.mcgraw-hill.com

Video

WebQuest

Audio

Assessment

Review

Concepts in Motion

Inquiry

Multilingual eGlossary

Lesson 1

Reading Guide

Key Concepts
ESSENTIAL QUESTIONS

- What are the phases of the cell cycle?
- Why is the result of the cell cycle important?

Vocabulary

cell cycle p. 429
interphase p. 430
sister chromatid p. 432
centromere p. 432
mitosis p. 433
cytokinesis p. 433
daughter cell p. 433

g Multilingual eGlossary

Video BrainPOP®

Academic Standards for Science

7.3.5 Explain that cells in multicellular organisms repeatedly divide to make more cells for growth and repair.

Also covers: 7.NS.9, 7.NS.11

The Cell Cycle and Cell Division

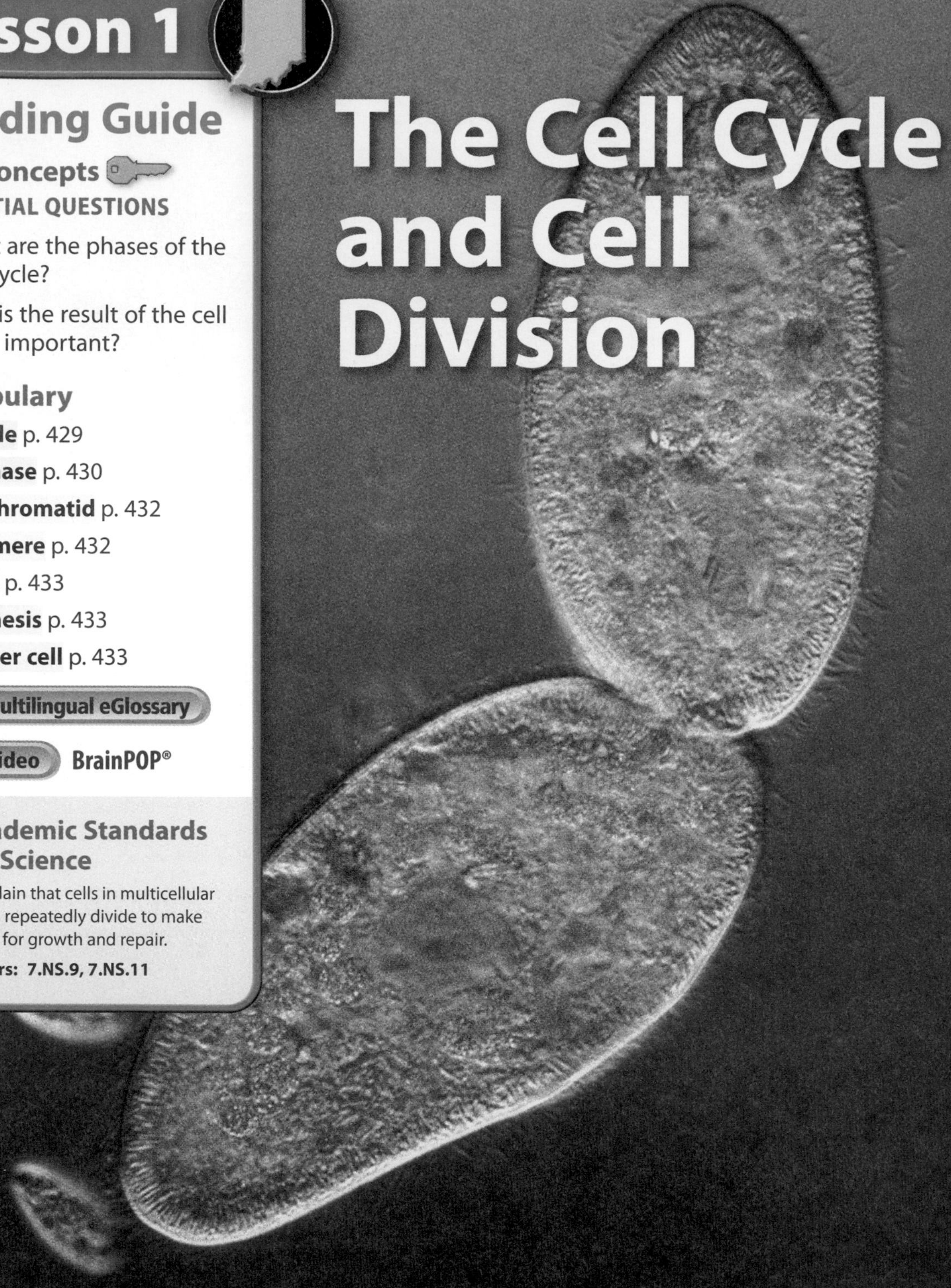

Inquiry Time to Split?

Unicellular organisms such as these reproduce when one cell divides into two new cells. The two cells are identical to each other. What do you think happened to the contents of the original cell before it divided?

Inquiry Launch Lab

15 minutes

Why isn't your cell like mine?

All living things are made of cells. Some are made of only one cell, while others are made of trillions of cells. Where do all those cells come from?

1. Read and complete a lab safety form.
2. Ask your team members to face away from you. Draw an animal cell on a sheet of **paper.** Include as many organelles as you can.
3. Use **scissors** to cut the cell drawing into equal halves. Fold each sheet of paper in half so the drawing cannot be seen.
4. Ask your team members to face you. Give each team member half of the cell drawing.
5. Have team members sit facing away from each other. Each person should use a **glue stick** to attach the cell half to one side of a sheet of paper. Then, each person should draw the missing cell half.
6. Compare the two new cells to your original cell.

Think About This

1. How did the new cells compare to the original cell?
2. **Key Concept** What are some things that might be done in the early steps to produce two new cells that are more like the original cell?

The Cell Cycle

No matter where you live, you have probably noticed that the weather changes in a regular pattern each year. Some areas experience four seasons—winter, spring, summer, and fall. In other parts of the world, there are only two seasons—rainy and dry. As seasons change, temperature, precipitation, and the number of hours of sunlight vary in a regular cycle.

These changes can affect the life cycles of organisms such as trees. Notice how the tree in **Figure 1** changes with the seasons. Like changing seasons or the growth of trees, cells go through cycles. *Most cells in an organism go through a cycle of growth, development, and division called the* **cell cycle.** Through the cell cycle, organisms grow, develop, replace old or damaged cells, and produce new cells.

Figure 1 This maple tree changes in response to a seasonal cycle.

Visual Check List the seasonal changes of this maple tree.

FOLDABLES®

Make a folded book from a sheet of paper. Label the front *The Cell Cycle,* and label the inside of the book as shown. Open the book completely and use the full sheet to illustrate the cell cycle.

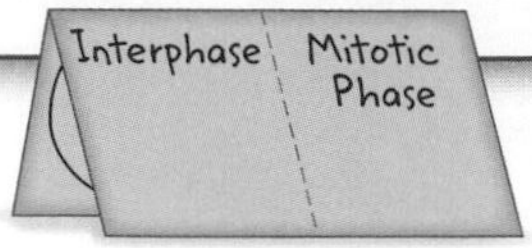

Phases of the Cell Cycle

There are two main phases in the cell cycle—interphase and the mitotic (mi TAH tihk) phase. **Interphase** *is the period during the cell cycle of a cell's growth and development.* A cell spends most of its life in interphase, as shown in **Figure 2.** During interphase, most cells go through three stages:

- rapid growth and replication, or copying, of the membrane-bound structures called organelles;
- copying of DNA, the genetic information in a cell; and
- preparation for cell division.

Interphase is followed by a shorter period of the cell cycle known as the mitotic phase. A cell reproduces during this phase. The mitotic phase has two stages, as illustrated in **Figure 2.** The nucleus divides in the first stage, and the cell's fluid, called the cytoplasm, divides in the second stage. The mitotic phase creates two new identical cells. At the end of this phase, the original cell no longer exists.

Key Concept Check What are the two main phases of the cell cycle?

The Cell Cycle

Figure 2 A cell spends most of its life growing and developing during interphase.

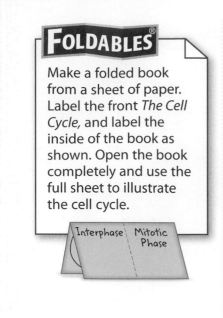

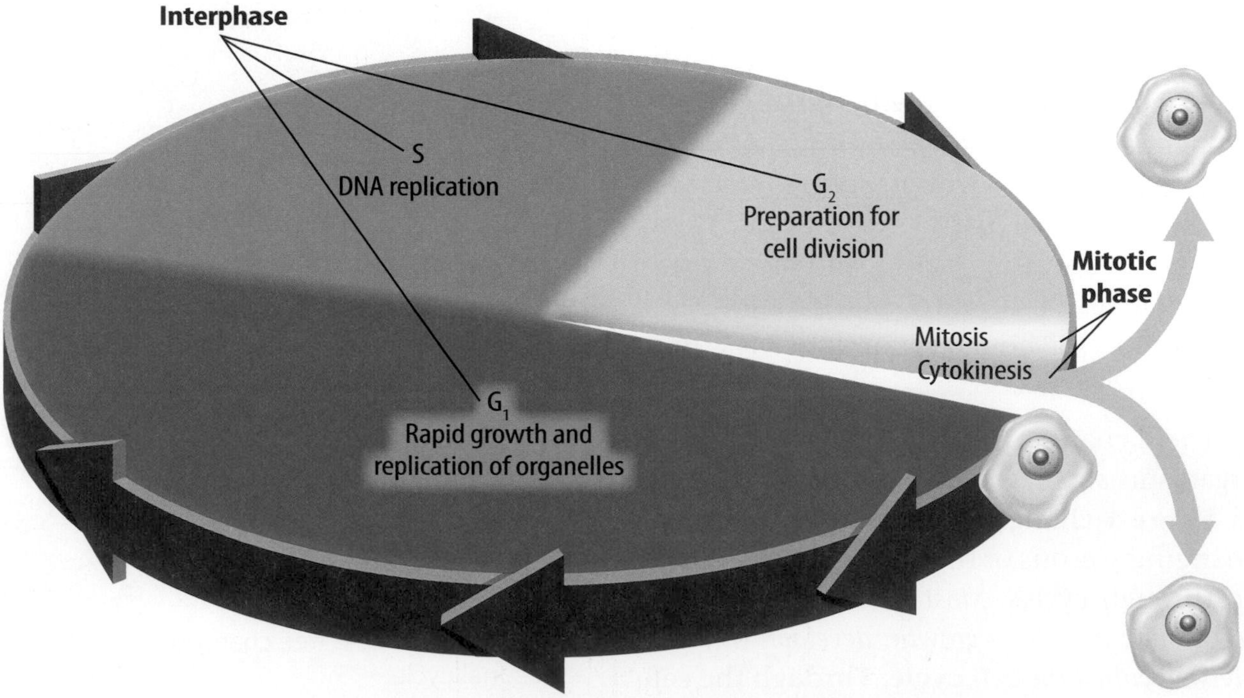

Visual Check Which stage of interphase is the longest?

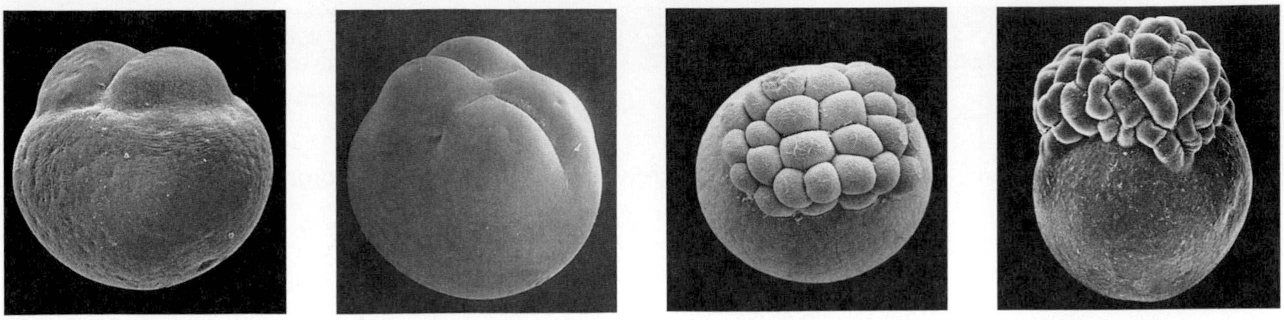

▲ **Figure 3** The fertilized egg of a zebra fish divides into 256 cells in 2.5 hours.

Length of a Cell Cycle

The time it takes a cell to complete the cell cycle depends on the type of cell that is dividing. Recall that a **eukaryotic** cell has membrane-bound organelles, including a nucleus. For some eukaryotic cells, the cell cycle might last only eight minutes. For other cells, the cycle might take as long as one year. Most dividing human cells normally complete the cell cycle in about 24 hours. As illustrated in **Figure 3,** the cells of some organisms divide very quickly.

REVIEW VOCABULARY

eukaryotic
a cell with membrane-bound structures

Interphase

As you have read, interphase makes up most of the cell cycle. Newly produced cells begin interphase with a period of rapid growth—the cell gets bigger. This is followed by cellular activities such as making proteins. Next, actively dividing cells make copies of their DNA and prepare for cell division. During interphase, the DNA is called chromatin (KROH muh tun). Chromatin is long, thin strands of DNA, as shown in **Figure 4.** When scientists dye a cell in interphase, the nucleus looks like a plate of spaghetti. This is because the nucleus contains many strands of chromatin tangled together.

Figure 4 During interphase, the nuclei of an animal cell and a plant cell contain long, thin strands of DNA called chromatin. ▼

Interphase

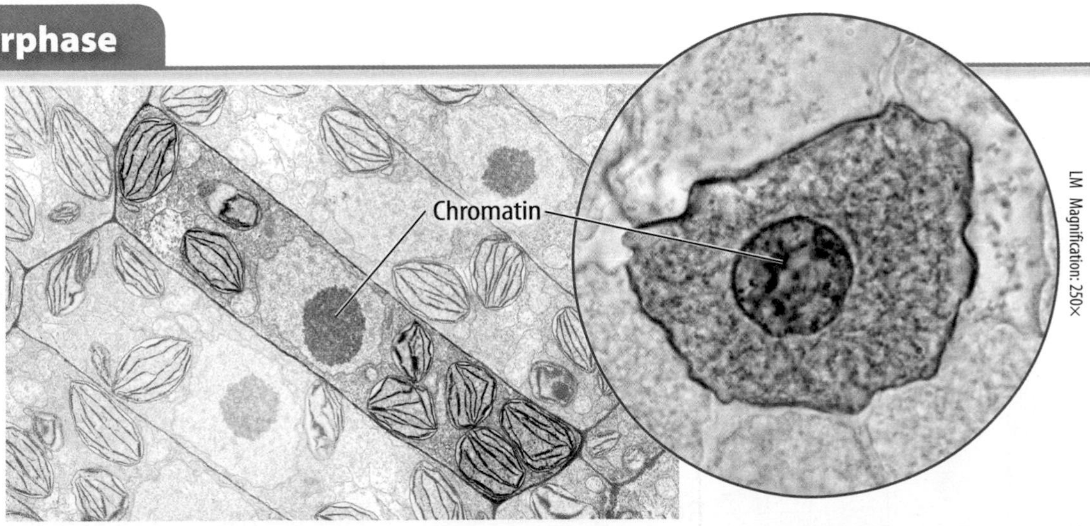

Plant Cell

Animal Cell

Table 1 Phases of the Cell Cycle	Concepts in Motion Interactive Table	
Phase	**Stage**	**Description**
Interphase	G_1	growth and cellular functions; organelle replication
	S	growth and chromosome replication; organelle replication
	G_2	growth and cellular functions; organelle replication
Mitotic phase	mitosis	division of nucleus
	cytokinesis	division of cytoplasm

▲ **Table 1** The two phases of the cell cycle can each be divided into different stages.

Phases of Interphase

Scientists divide interphase into three stages, as shown in **Table 1.** Interphase begins with a period of rapid growth—the G_1 stage. This stage lasts longer than other stages of the cell cycle. During G_1, a cell grows and carries out its normal cell functions. For example, during G_1, cells that line your stomach make enzymes that help digest your food. Although most cells continue the cell cycle, some cells stop the cell cycle at this point. For example, mature nerve cells in your brain remain in G_1 and do not divide again.

During the second stage of interphase—the S stage—a cell continues to grow and copies its DNA. There are now identical strands of DNA. These identical strands of DNA ensure that each new cell gets a copy of the original cell's genetic information. Each strand of DNA coils up and forms a chromosome. Identical chromosomes join together. The cell's DNA is now arranged as pairs of identical chromosomes. Each pair is called a duplicated chromosome. *Two identical chromosomes, called* **sister chromatids,** *make up a duplicated chromosome,* as shown in **Figure 5.** Notice that the *sister chromatids are held together by a structure called the* **centromere.**

The final stage of interphase—the G_2 stage—is another period of growth and the final preparation for mitosis. A cell uses energy copying DNA during the S stage. During G_2, the cell stores energy that will be used during the mitotic phase of the cell cycle.

Reading Check Describe what happens in the G_2 phase.

Figure 5 The coiled DNA forms a duplicated chromosome made of two sister chromatids connected at the centromere. ▼

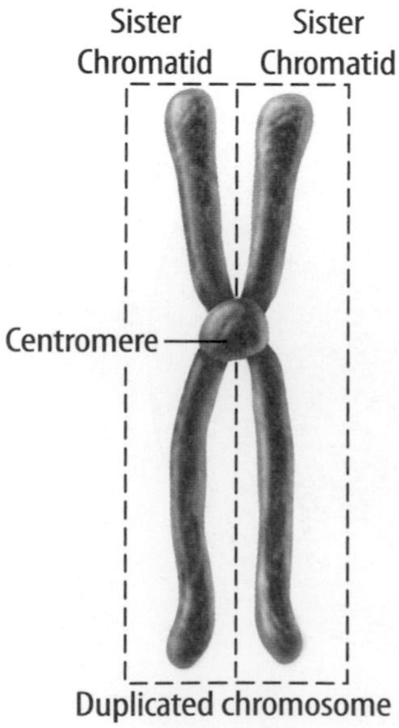

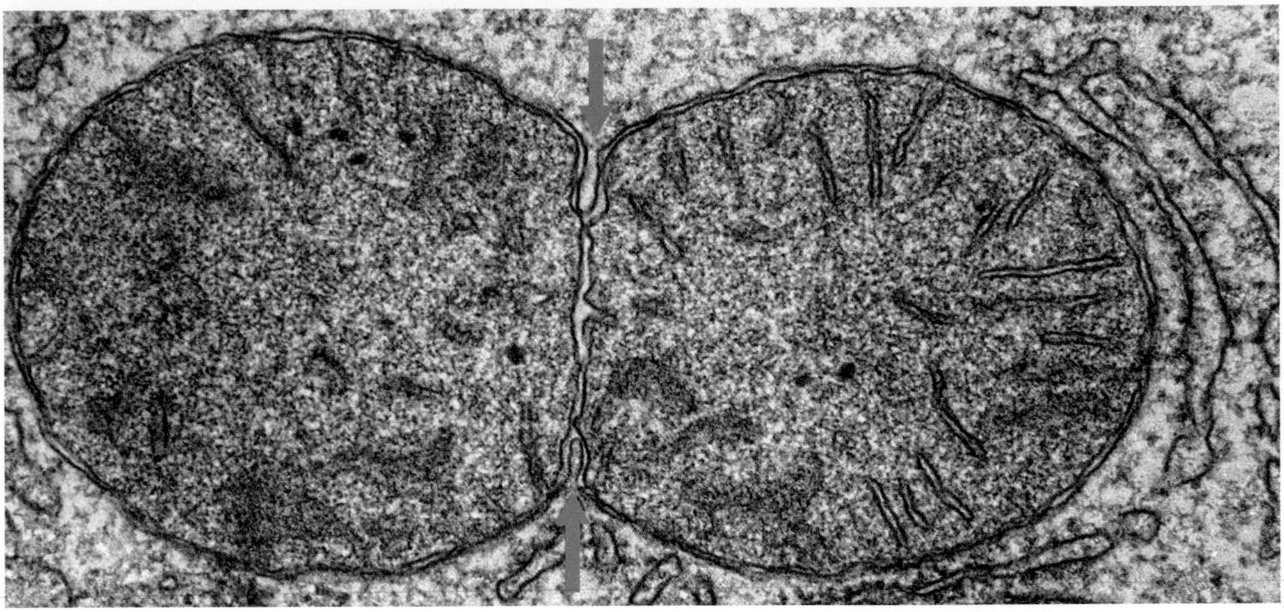

TEM Magnification: Unavailable

Figure 6 This mitochondrion is in the final stage of dividing.

Organelle Replication

During cell division, the organelles in a cell are distributed between the two new cells. Before a cell divides, it makes a copy of each organelle. This enables the two new cells to function properly. Some organelles, such as the energy-processing mitochondria and chloroplasts, have their own DNA. These organelles can make copies of themselves on their own, as shown in **Figure 6.** A cell produces other organelles from materials such as proteins and lipids. A cell makes these materials using the information contained in the DNA inside the nucleus. Organelles are copied during all stages of interphase.

The Mitotic Phase

The mitotic phase of the cell cycle follows interphase. It consists of two stages: mitosis (mi TOH sus) and cytokinesis (si toh kuh NEE sus). *In* **mitosis,** *the nucleus and its contents divide. In* **cytokinesis,** *the cytoplasm and its contents divide.* **Daughter cells** *are the two new cells that result from mitosis and cytokinesis.*

WORD ORIGIN

mitosis
from Greek *mitos,* means "warp thread"; and Latin *-osis,* means "process"

During mitosis, the contents of the nucleus divide, forming two identical nuclei. The sister chromatids of the duplicated chromosomes separate from each other. This gives each daughter cell the same genetic information. For example, a cell that has ten duplicated chromosomes actually has 20 chromatids. When the cell divides, each daughter cell will have ten different chromatids. Chromatids are now called chromosomes.

In cytokinesis, the cytoplasm divides and forms the two new daughter cells. Organelles that were made during interphase are divided between the daughter cells.

Phases of Mitosis

Like interphase, mitosis is a continuous process that scientists divide into different phases, as shown in **Figure 7.**

Prophase During the first phase of mitosis, called prophase, the copied chromatin coils together tightly. The coils form visible duplicated chromosomes. The nucleolus disappears, and the nuclear membrane breaks down. Structures called spindle fibers form in the cytoplasm.

Metaphase During metaphase, the spindle fibers pull and push the duplicated chromosomes to the middle of the cell. Notice in **Figure 7** that the chromosomes line up along the middle of the cell. This arrangement ensures that each new cell will receive one copy of each chromosome. Metaphase is the shortest phase in mitosis, but it must be completed successfully for the new cells to be identical.

Concepts in Motion **Animation**

Phases of Mitosis

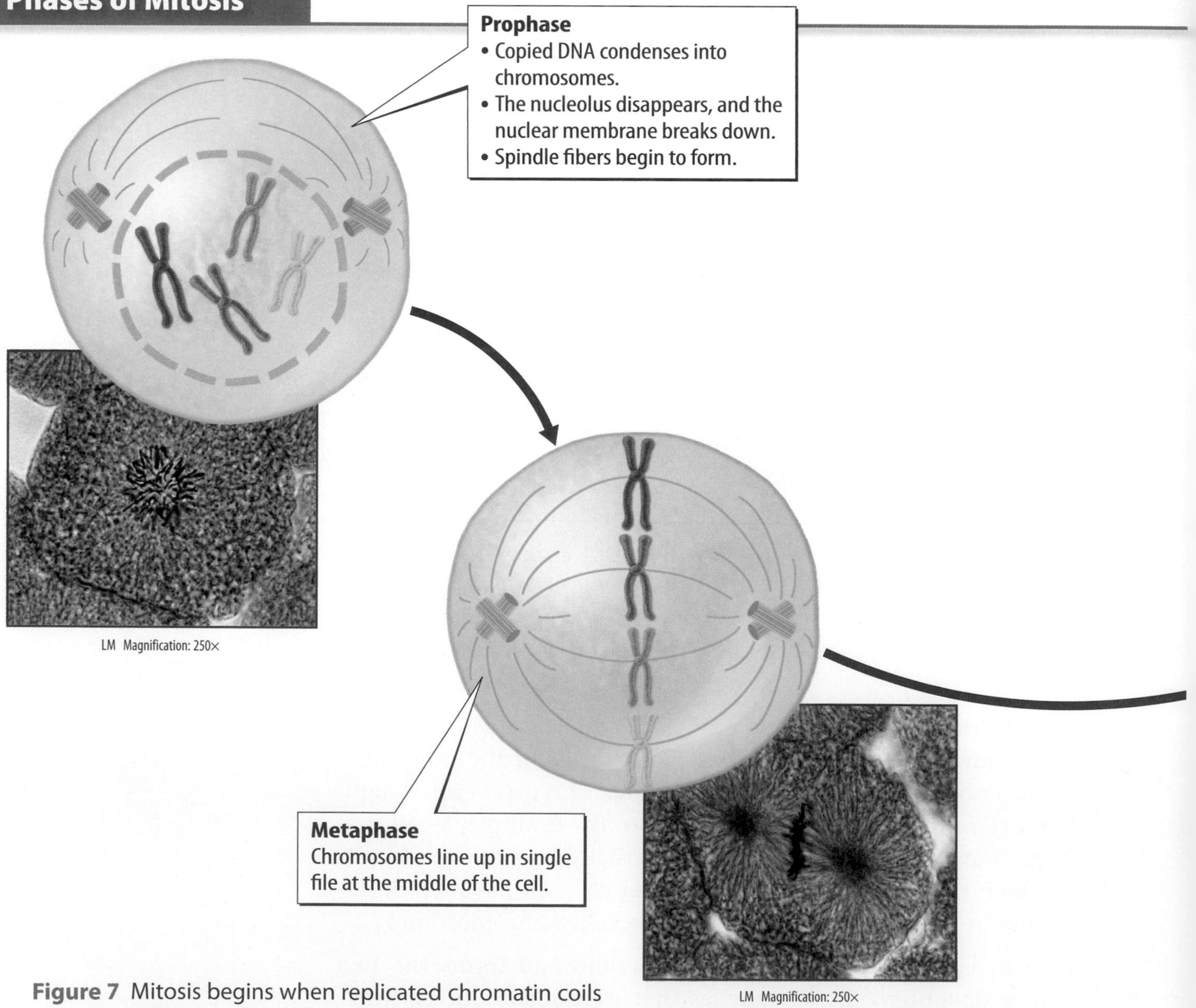
Prophase
• Copied DNA condenses into chromosomes.
• The nucleolus disappears, and the nuclear membrane breaks down.
• Spindle fibers begin to form.
LM Magnification: 250×
Metaphase
Chromosomes line up in single file at the middle of the cell.
LM Magnification: 250×

Figure 7 Mitosis begins when replicated chromatin coils together and ends when two identical nuclei are formed.

Anaphase In anaphase, the third stage of mitosis, the two sister chromatids in each chromosome separate from each other. The spindle fibers pull them in opposite directions. Once separated, the chromatids are now two identical single-stranded chromosomes. As they move to opposite sides of a cell, the cell begins to get longer. Anaphase is complete when the two identical sets of chromosomes are at opposite ends of a cell.

Telophase During telophase, the spindle fibers begin to disappear. Also, the chromosomes begin to uncoil. A nuclear membrane forms around each set of chromosomes at either end of the cell. This forms two new identical nuclei. Telophase is the final stage of mitosis. It is often described as the reverse of prophase because many of the processes that occur during prophase are reversed during telophase.

Reading Check What are the phases of mitosis?

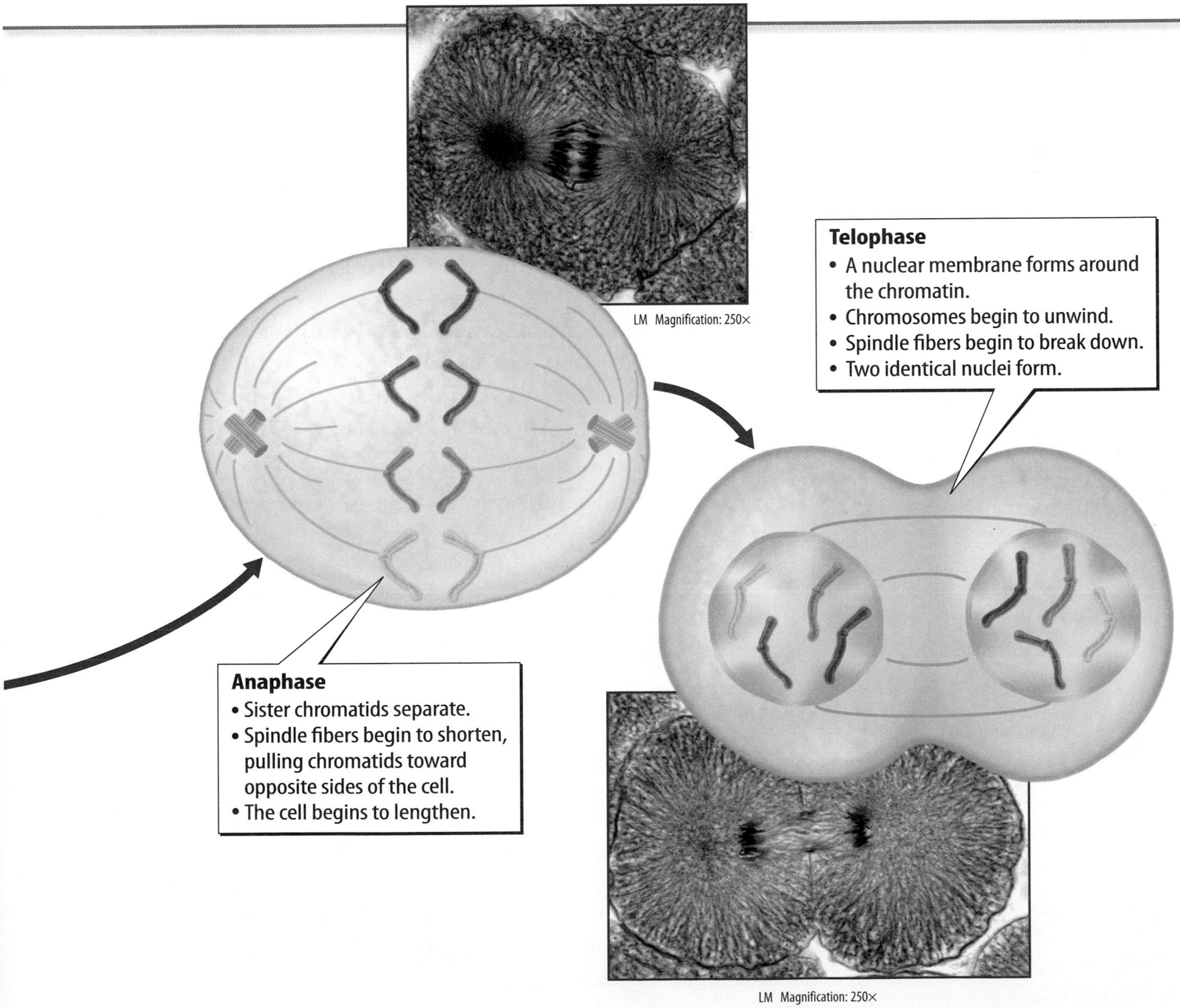

LM Magnification: 250×
Telophase
• A nuclear membrane forms around the chromatin.
• Chromosomes begin to unwind.
• Spindle fibers begin to break down.
• Two identical nuclei form.
Anaphase
• Sister chromatids separate.
• Spindle fibers begin to shorten, pulling chromatids toward opposite sides of the cell.
• The cell begins to lengthen.
LM Magnification: 250×

Furrow

Animal Cell
Color-Enhanced SEM Magnification: 1500×

Cell plate

Plant Cell
LM Magnification: 400×

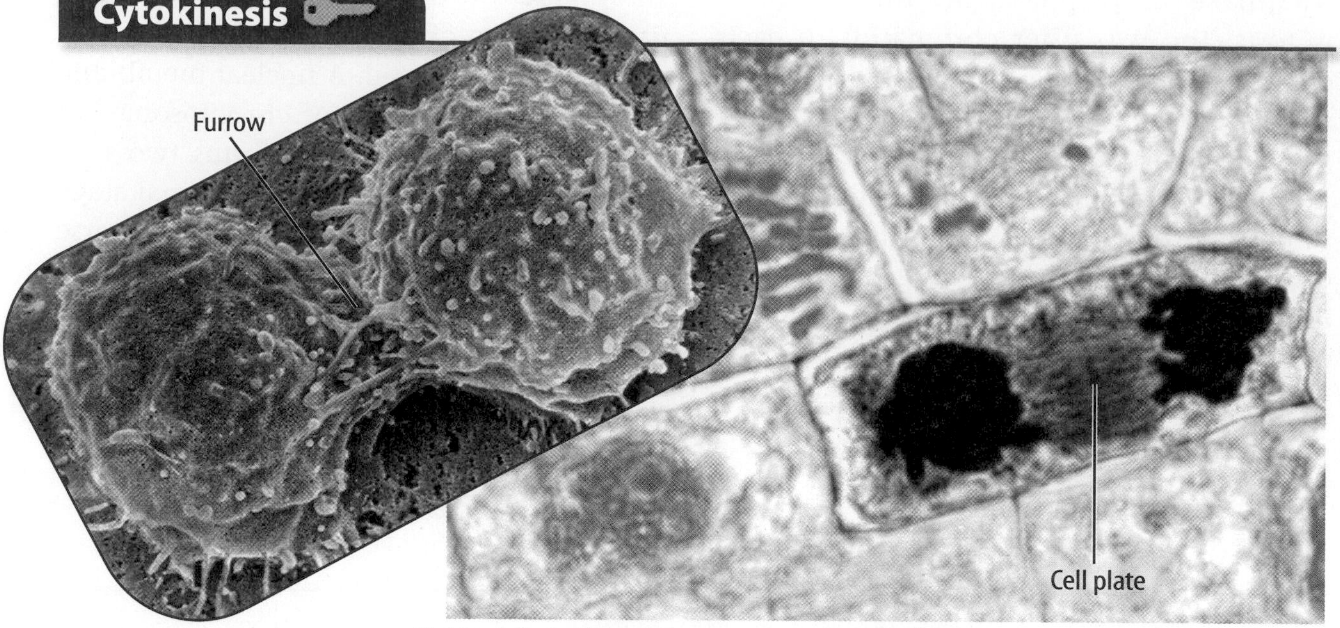

Figure 8 Cytokinesis differs in animal cells and plant cells.

Math Skills ✕÷

Use Percentages
A percentage is a ratio that compares a number to 100. If the length of the entire cell cycle is 24 hours, 24 hours equals 100%. If part of the cycle takes 6.0 hours, it can be expressed as 6.0 hours/ 24 hours. To calculate percentage, divide and multiply by 100. Add a percent sign.

$$\frac{6.0}{24} = 0.25 \times 100 = 25\%$$

Practice
Interphase in human cells takes about 23 hours. If the cell cycle is 24 hours, what percentage is interphase?

 Review

- **Math Practice**
- **Personal Tutor**

Dividing the Cell's Components

Following the last phase of mitosis, a cell's cytoplasm divides in a process called cytokinesis. The specific steps of cytokinesis differ depending on the type of cell that is dividing. In animal cells, the cell membrane contracts, or squeezes together, around the middle of the cell. Fibers around the center of the cell pull together. This forms a crease, called a furrow, in the middle of the cell. The furrow gets deeper and deeper until the cell membrane comes together and divides the cell. An animal cell undergoing cytokinesis is shown in **Figure 8.**

Cytokinesis in plants happens in a different way. As shown in **Figure 8,** a new cell wall forms in the middle of a plant cell. First, organelles called vesicles join together to form a membrane-bound disk called a cell plate. Then the cell plate grows outward toward the cell wall until two new cells form.

✓ **Reading Check** Compare cytokinesis in plant and animal cells.

Results of Cell Division

Recall that the cell cycle results in two new cells. These daughter cells are genetically identical to each other and to the original cell that no longer exists. For example, a human cell has 46 chromosomes. When that cell divides, it will produce two new cells with 46 chromosomes each. The cell cycle is important for reproduction in some organisms, growth in multicellular organisms, replacement of worn out or damaged cells, and repair of damaged tissues.

Reproduction

In some unicellular organisms, cell division is a form of reproduction. For example, an organism called a paramecium often reproduces by dividing into two new daughter cells or two new paramecia. Cell division is also important in other methods of reproduction in which the offspring are identical to the parent organism.

Growth

Cell division allows multicellular organisms, such as humans, to grow and develop from one cell (a fertilized egg). In humans, cell division begins about 24 hours after fertilization and continues rapidly during the first few years of life. It is likely that during the next few years you will go through another period of rapid growth and development. This happens because cells divide and increase in number as you grow and develop.

Replacement

Even after an organism is fully grown, cell division continues. It replaces cells that wear out or are damaged. The outermost layer of your skin is always rubbing or flaking off. A layer of cells below the skin's surface is constantly dividing. This produces millions of new cells daily to replace the ones that are rubbed off.

Repair

Cell division is also critical for repairing damage. When a bone breaks, cell division produces new bone cells that patch the broken pieces back together.

Not all damage can be repaired, however, because not all cells continue to divide. Recall that mature nerve cells stop the cell cycle in interphase. For this reason, injuries to nerve cells often cause permanent damage.

Key Concept Check Why is the result of the cell cycle important?

Inquiry MiniLab — 20 minutes

How does mitosis work?

The dolix is a mythical animal whose cells contain just two chromosomes. What happens to a dolix cell nucleus during mitosis?

1. Read and complete a lab safety form.
2. Form four 60-cm lengths of **yarn** into large circles on four separate sheets of **paper.** Each piece of paper represents one phase of mitosis, and the yarn represents the cell membrane.
3. On each sheet of paper, model one phase of mitosis using different colors of yarn to represent the nuclear membrane, the spindles, and the chromosomes. Use **twist ties** to represent centromeres. **Tape** the yarn in place.
4. Label your models, or develop a key to indicate which color is used for which part.

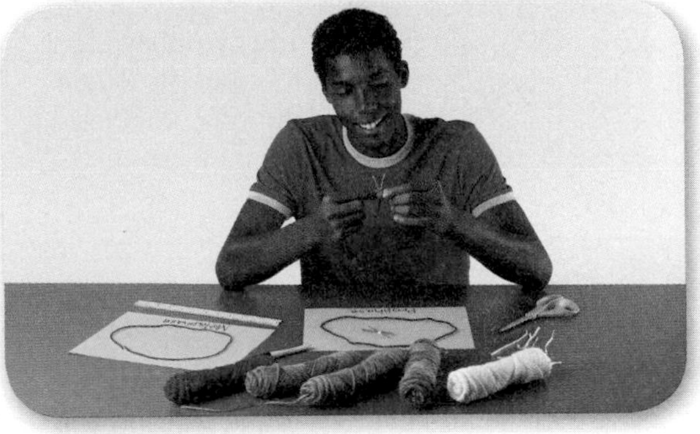

Analyze and Conclude

1. **Identify** If you were to model a dolix cell's nucleus before mitosis began, what would your model look like? Would you be able to see the individual chromosomes?
2. **Integrate** What would a model of your cell look like during the stage immediately following mitosis? What is this stage?
3. **Key Concept** During mitosis, a cell forms two new, identical nuclei. Use your models to explain why, in order to do this, mitosis must occur after events in interphase.

Lesson 1 Review

Assessment Online Quiz

Visual Summary

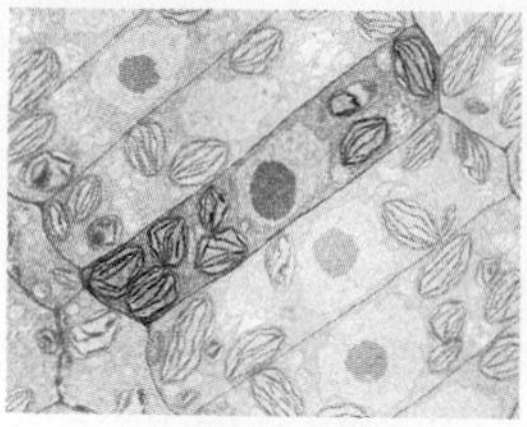

During interphase, most cells go through periods of rapid growth and replication of organelles, copying DNA, and preparation for cell division.

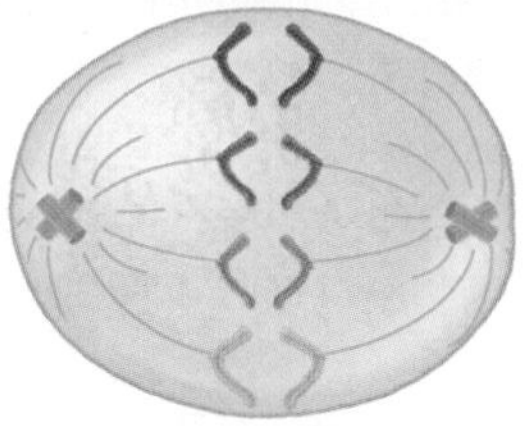

The nucleus and its contents divide during mitosis.

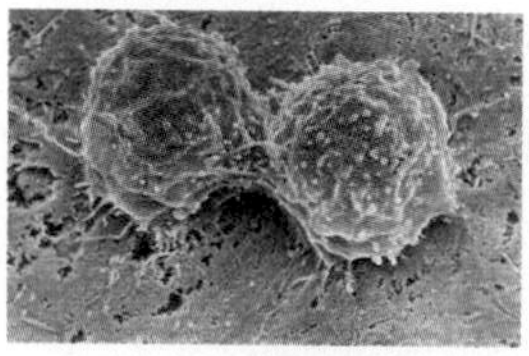

The cytoplasm and its contents divide during cytokinesis.

FOLDABLES®

Use your lesson Foldable to review the lesson. Save your Foldable for the project at the end of the chapter.

What do you think NOW?

You first read the statements below at the beginning of the chapter.

1. Cell division produces two identical cells.

2. Cell division is important for growth.

3. At the end of the cell cycle, the original cell no longer exists.

Did you change your mind about whether you agree or disagree with the statements? Rewrite any false statements to make them true.

Use Vocabulary

1 **Distinguish** between mitosis and cytokinesis.

2 A duplicated chromosome is made of two ________.

3 **Use the term** *interphase* in a sentence.

Understand Key Concepts

4 Which is NOT part of mitosis?

A. anaphase **C.** prophase
B. interphase **D.** telophase

5 **Construct** a table to show the different phases of mitosis and what happens during each.

6 **Give three examples** of why the result of the cell cycle is important.

Interpret Graphics

7 **Identify** The animal cell on the right is in what phase of mitosis? Explain your answer.

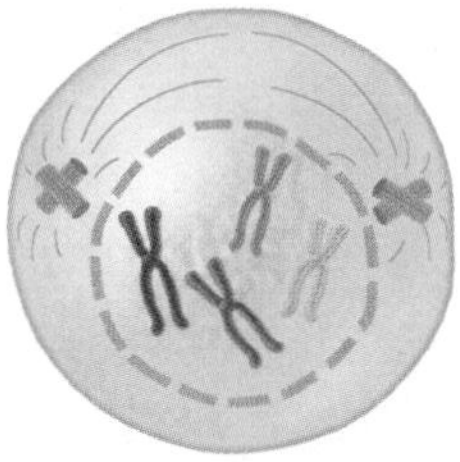

8 **Organize** Copy and fill in the graphic organizer below to show the results of cell division.

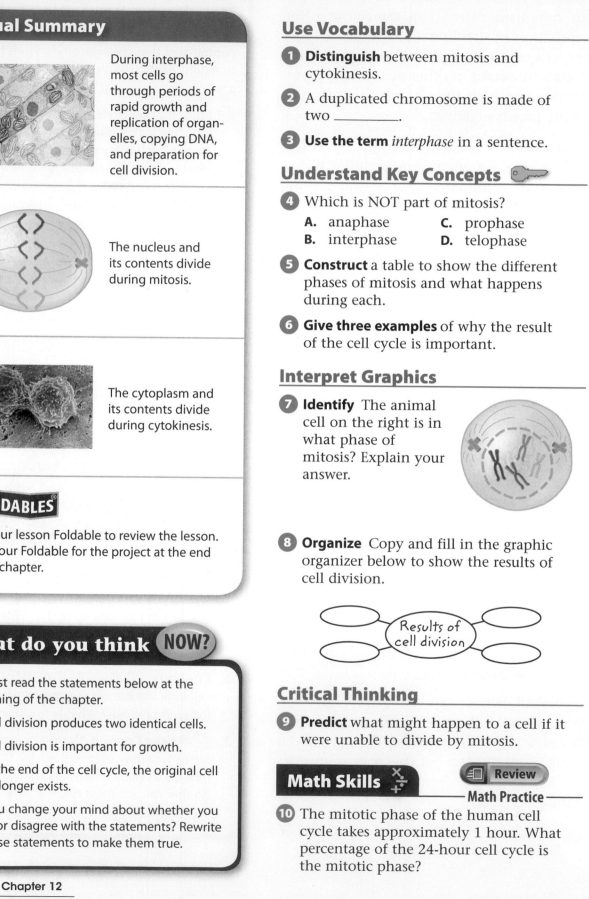

Critical Thinking

9 **Predict** what might happen to a cell if it were unable to divide by mitosis.

Math Skills

Review Math Practice

10 The mitotic phase of the human cell cycle takes approximately 1 hour. What percentage of the 24-hour cell cycle is the mitotic phase?

DNA Fingerprinting

SCIENCE & SOCIETY

Solving Crimes One Strand at a Time

Every cell in your body has the same DNA in its nucleus. Unless you are an identical twin, your DNA is entirely unique. Identical twins have identical DNA because they begin as one cell that divides and separates. When your cells begin mitosis, they copy their DNA. Every new cell has the same DNA as the original cells. That is why DNA can be used to identify people. Just as no two people have the same fingerprints, your DNA belongs to you alone.

Using scientific methods to solve crimes is called forensics. DNA fingerprinting is now a basic tool in forensics. Samples collected from a crime scene can be compared to millions of samples previously collected and indexed in a computer.

Every day, everywhere you go, you leave a trail of DNA. It might be in skin cells. It might be in hair or in the saliva you used to lick an envelope. If you commit a crime, you will most likely leave DNA behind. An expert crime scene investigator will know how to collect that DNA.

DNA evidence can prove innocence as well. Investigators have reexamined DNA found at old crime scenes. Imprisoned persons have been proven not guilty through DNA fingerprinting methods that were not yet available when a crime was committed.

DNA fingerprinting can also be used to identify bodies that had previously been known only as a John or Jane Doe.

▼ DNA

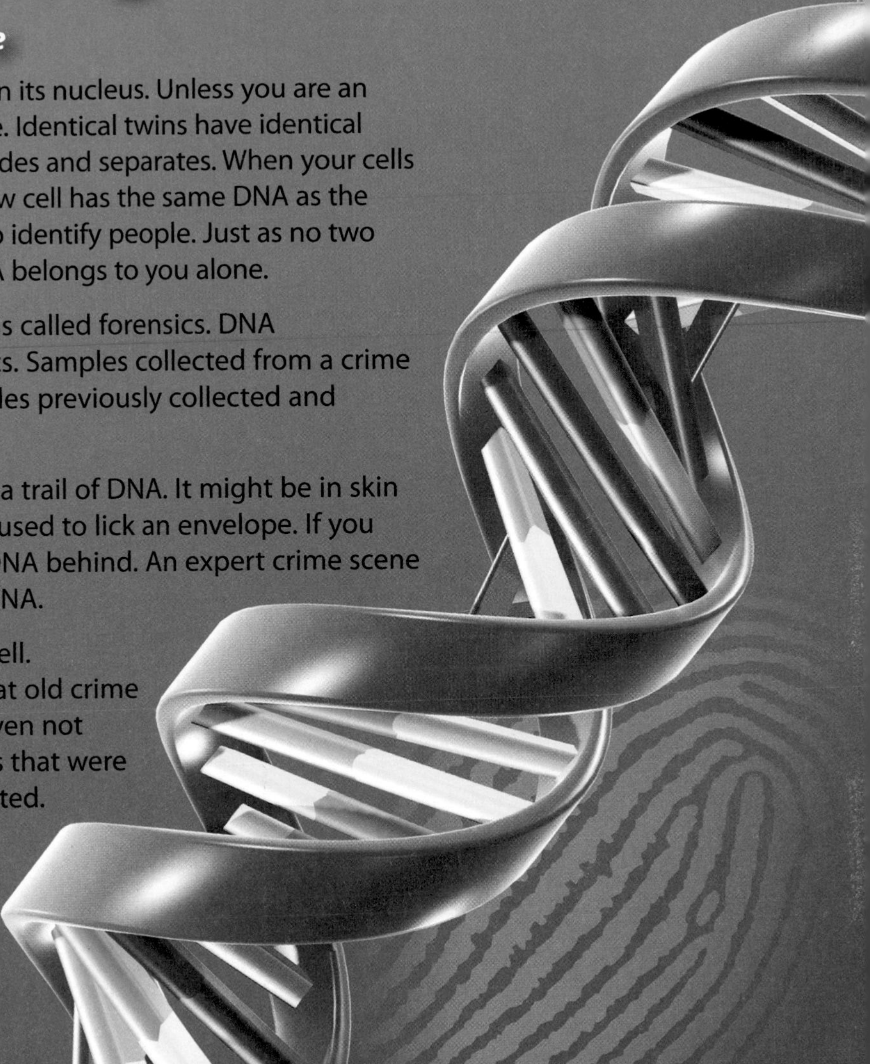

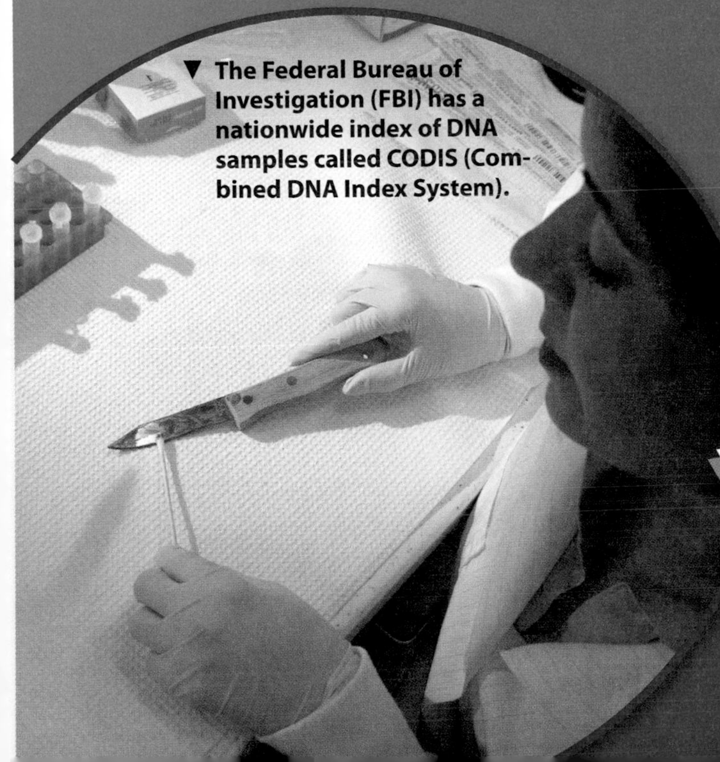

▼ **The Federal Bureau of Investigation (FBI) has a nationwide index of DNA samples called CODIS (Combined DNA Index System).**

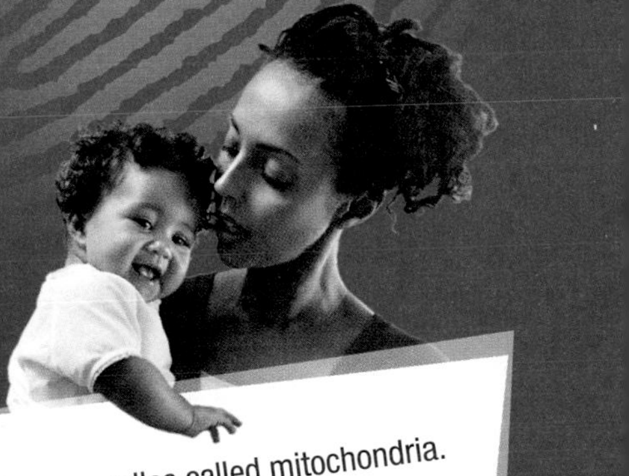

It's Your Turn

DISCOVER Your cells contain organelles called mitochondria. They have their own DNA, called mitochondrial DNA. Your mitochondrial DNA is identical to your mother's mitochondrial DNA. Find out how this information is used.

Lesson 2

Levels of Organization

Reading Guide

Key Concepts
ESSENTIAL QUESTIONS

- How do unicellular and multicellular organisms differ?
- How does cell differentiation lead to the organization within a multicellular organism?

Vocabulary

cell differentiation p. 443
stem cell p. 444
tissue p. 445
organ p. 446
organ system p. 447

g Multilingual eGlossary

Video BrainPOP®

Academic Standards for Science

7.3.3 Explain that although the way cells function is similar in all living organisms, multicellular organisms also have specialized cells whose specialized functions are directly related to their structure.

7.3.6 Explain that after fertilization, a small cluster of cells divides to form the basic tissues of an embryo which further develops into all the specialized tissues and organs within a multicellular organism.

7.3.8 Describe how various organs and tissues serve the needs of cells for nutrient and oxygen delivery and waste removal.

Also covers: 7.NS.2, 7.NS.5, 7.NS.7, 7.NS.11

Inquiry Scales on Wings?

This butterfly has a distinctive pattern of colors on its wings. The pattern is formed by clusters of tiny scales. In a similar way, multicellular organisms are made of many small parts working together.

Inquiry Launch Lab

15 minutes

How is a system organized?

The places people live are organized in a system. Do you live in or near a city? Cities contain things such as schools and stores that enable them to function on their own. Many cities together make up another level of organization.

1. Read and complete a lab safety form.
2. Using a **metric ruler** and **scissors,** measure and cut squares of **construction paper** that are 4 cm, 8 cm, 12 cm, 16 cm, and 20 cm on each side. Use a different color for each square.
3. Stack the squares from largest to smallest, and glue them together.
4. Cut apart the *City, Continent, Country, County,* and *State* labels your teacher gives you.
5. Use a **glue stick** to attach the *City* label to the smallest square. Sort the remaining labels from smallest to largest, and glue to the corresponding square.

Think About This

1. What is the largest level of organization a city belongs to?
2. Can any part of the system function without the others? Explain.
3. **Key Concept** How do you think the system used to organize where people live is similar to how your body is organized?

Life's Organization

You might recall that all matter is made of atoms and that atoms combine and form molecules. Molecules make up cells. A large animal, such as a Komodo dragon, is not made of one cell. Instead, it is composed of trillions of cells working together. Its skin, shown in **Figure 9,** is made of many cells that are specialized for protection. The Komodo dragon has other types of cells, such as blood cells and nerve cells, that perform other functions. Cells work together in the Komodo dragon and enable it to function. In the same way, cells work together in you and in other multicellular organisms.

Recall that some organisms are made of only one cell. These unicellular organisms carry out all the activities necessary to survive, such as absorbing nutrients and getting rid of wastes. But no matter their sizes, all organisms are made of cells.

Figure 9 Skin cells are only one of the many kinds of cells that make up a Komodo dragon.

Unicellular Organisms

Figure 10 Unicellular organisms carry out life processes within one cell.

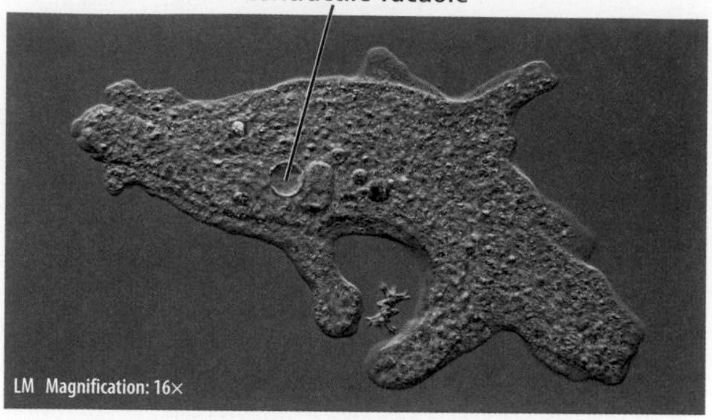

This unicellular amoeba captures a desmid for food.

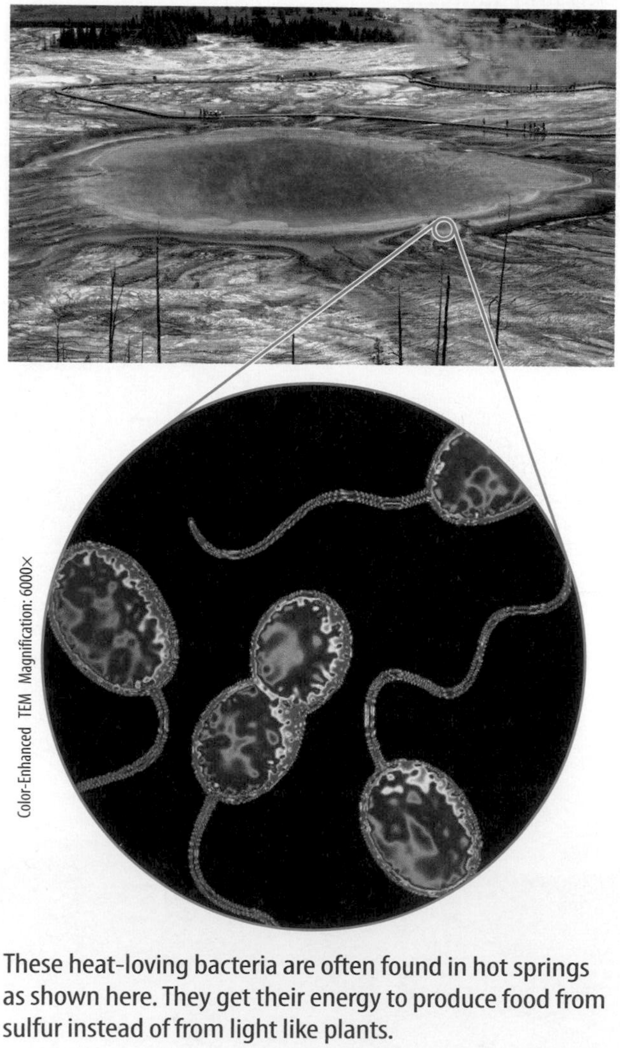

These heat-loving bacteria are often found in hot springs as shown here. They get their energy to produce food from sulfur instead of from light like plants.

Unicellular Organisms

As you read on the previous page, some organisms have only one cell. Unicellular organisms do all the things needed for their survival within that one cell. For example, the amoeba in **Figure 10** is ingesting another unicellular organism, a type of green algae called a desmid, for food. Unicellular organisms also respond to their environment, get rid of waste, grow, and even reproduce on their own. Unicellular organisms include both prokaryotes and some eukaryotes.

Prokaryotes

Recall that a cell without a membrane-bound nucleus is a prokaryotic cell. In general, prokaryotic cells are smaller than eukaryotic cells and have fewer cell structures. A unicellular organism made of one prokaryotic cell is called a prokaryote. Some prokaryotes live in groups called colonies. Some can also live in extreme environments, as shown in **Figure 10.**

Eukaryotes

You might recall that a eukaryotic cell has a nucleus surrounded by a membrane and many other specialized organelles. For example, the amoeba shown in **Figure 10** has an organelle called a contractile vacuole. It functions like a bucket that is used to bail water out of a boat. A contractile vacuole collects excess water from the amoeba's cytoplasm. Then it pumps the water out of the amoeba. This prevents the amoeba from swelling and bursting.

A unicellular organism that is made of one eukaryotic cell is called a eukaryote. There are thousands of different unicellular eukaryotes, such as algae that grow on the inside of an aquarium and the fungus that causes athlete's foot.

Reading Check Give an example of a unicellular eukaryotic organism.

Multicellular Organisms

Multicellular organisms are made of many eukaryotic cells working together, like the crew on an airplane. Each member of the crew, from the pilot to the mechanic, has a specific job that is important for the plane's operation. Similarly, each type of cell in a multicellular organism has a specific job that is important to the survival of the organism.

Key Concept Check How do unicellular and multicellular organisms differ?

Cell Differentiation

As you read in the last lesson, all cells in a multicellular organism come from one cell—a fertilized egg. Cell division starts quickly after fertilization. The first cells made can become any type of cell, such as a muscle cell, a nerve cell, or a blood cell. *The process by which cells become different types of cells is called* **cell differentiation** (dihf uh ren shee AY shun).

You might recall that a cell's instructions are contained in its chromosomes. Also, nearly all the cells of an organism have identical sets of chromosomes. If an organism's cells have identical sets of instructions, how can cells be different? Different cell types use different parts of the instructions on the chromosomes. A few of the many different types of cells that can result from human cell differentiation are shown in **Figure 11.**

FOLDABLES®

Make a layered book from three sheets of notebook paper. Label it as shown. Use your book to describe the levels of organization that make up organisms.

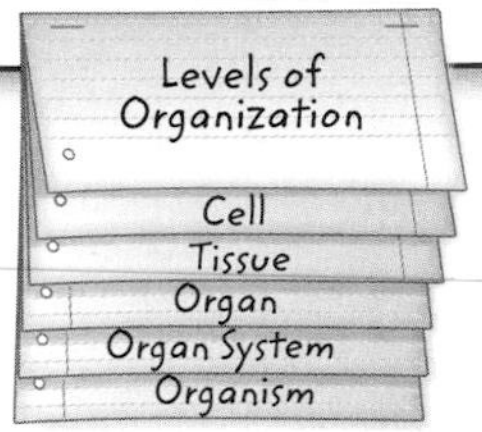

Figure 11 A fertilized egg produces cells that can differentiate into a variety of cell types.

Cell Differentiation in Eukaryotes

Review **Personal Tutor**

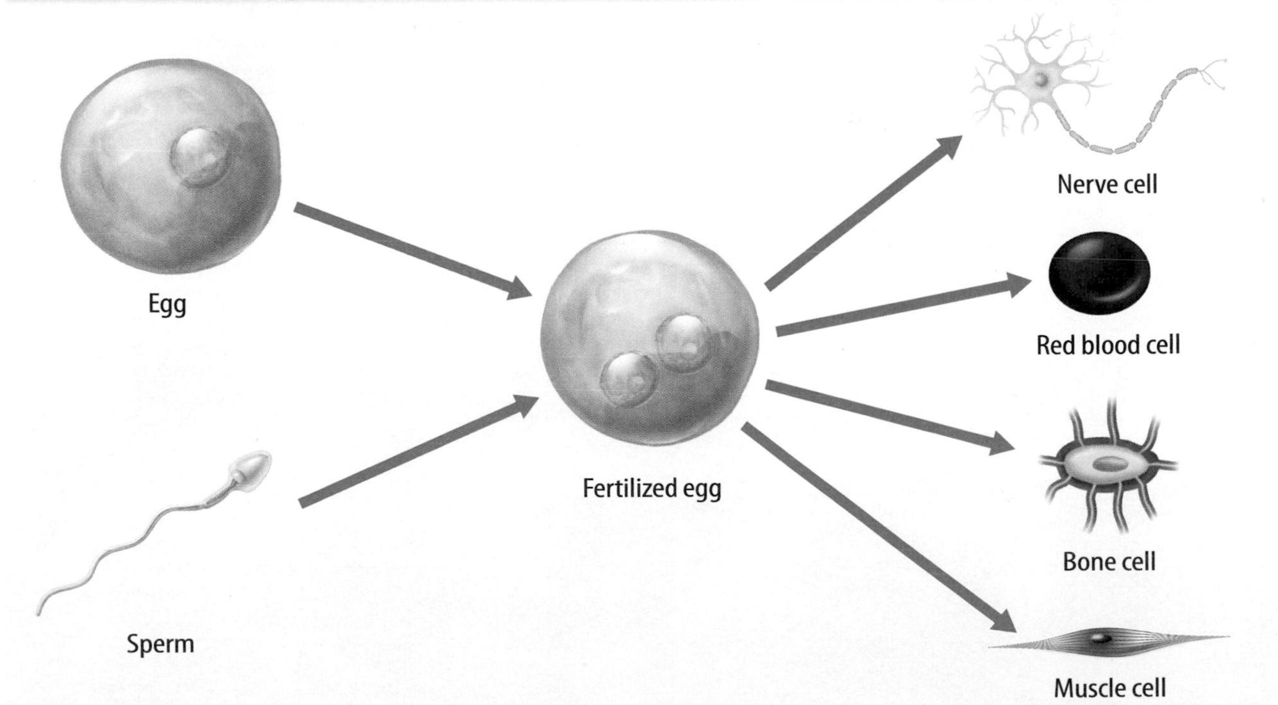

Animal Stem Cells Not all cells in a developing animal differentiate. **Stem cells** *are unspecialized cells that are able to develop into many different cell types*. There are many stem cells in embryos but fewer in adult organisms. Adult stem cells are important for the cell repair and replacement you read about in Lesson 1. For example, stem cells in your bone marrow can produce more than a dozen different types of blood cells. These replace ones that are damaged or worn out. Stem cells have also been discovered in skeletal muscles. These stem cells can produce new muscle cells when the **fibers** that make up the muscle are torn.

SCIENCE USE V. COMMON USE
fiber
Science Use a long muscle cell
Common Use a thread

Plant Cells Plants also have unspecialized cells similar to animal stem cells. These cells are grouped in areas of a plant called meristems (MER uh stemz). Meristems are in different areas of a plant, including the tips of roots and stems, as shown in **Figure 12.** Cell division in meristems produces different types of plant cells with specialized structures and functions, such as transporting materials, making food, storing food, or protecting the plant. These cells might become parts of stems, leaves, flowers, or roots.

Figure 12 Plant meristems produce cells that can become part of stems, leaves, flowers, or roots.

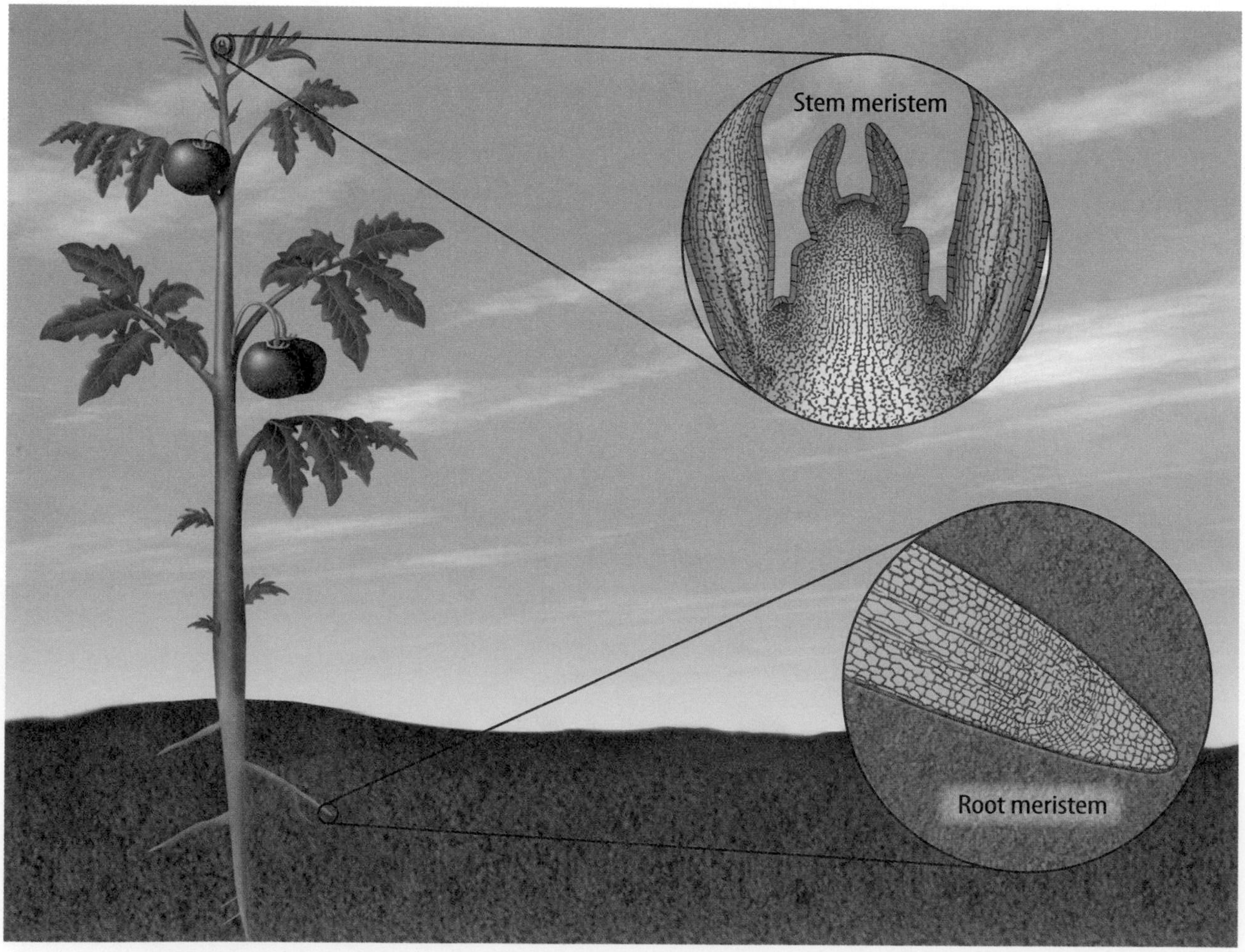

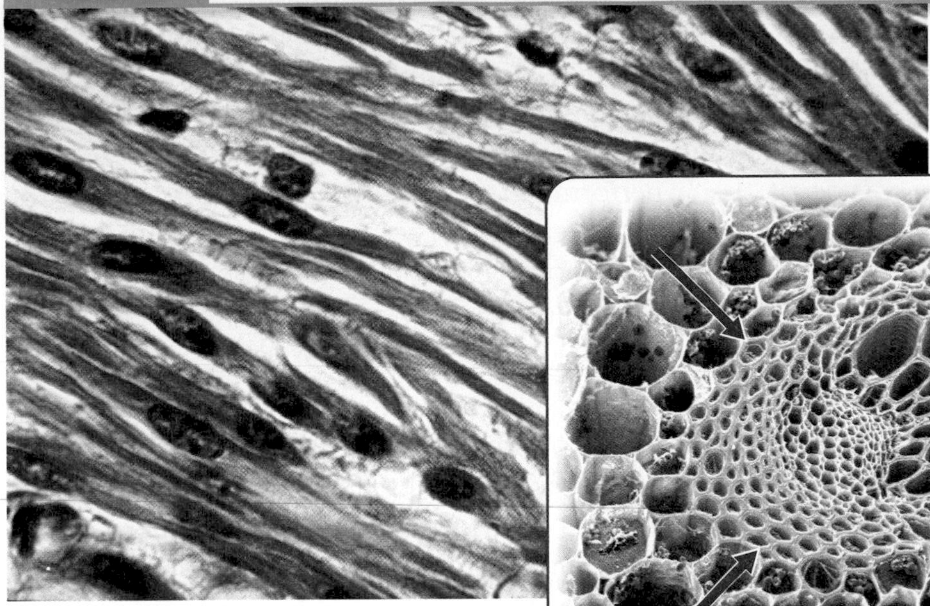

Animal muscle tissue

LM Magnification: 100×

Color-Enhanced SEM Magnification: 113×

Plant vascular tissue

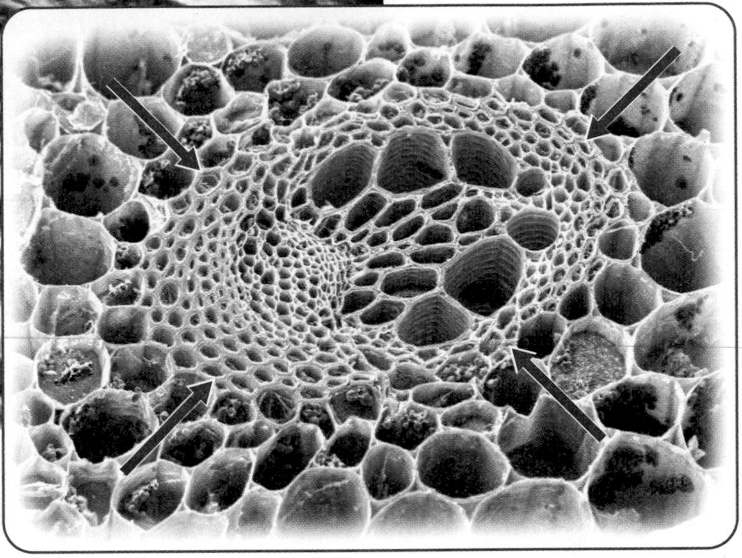

Figure 13 Similar cells work together and form tissues such as this animal muscle tissue that contracts the stomach to help digestion. Plant vascular tissue, indicated by red arrows, moves water and nutrients throughout a plant.

Tissues

In multicellular organisms, similar types of cells are organized into groups. **Tissues** *are groups of similar types of cells that work together to carry out specific tasks.* Humans, like most other animals, have four main types of tissue—muscle, connective, nervous, and epithelial (eh puh THEE lee ul). For example, the animal tissue shown in **Figure 13** is smooth muscle tissue that is part of the stomach. Muscle tissue causes movement. Connective tissue provides structure and support and often connects other types of tissue together. Nervous tissue carries messages to and from the brain. Epithelial tissue forms the protective outer layer of the skin and the lining of major organs and internal body cavities.

Plants also have different types of tissues. The three main types of plant tissue are dermal, vascular (VAS kyuh lur), and ground tissue. Dermal tissue provides protection and helps reduce water loss. Vascular tissue, shown in **Figure 13,** transports water and nutrients from one part of a plant to another. Ground tissue provides storage and support and is where photosynthesis takes place.

Reading Check Compare animal and plant tissues.

WORD ORIGIN

tissue
from Latin *texere,* means "weave"

Organs

ACADEMIC VOCABULARY

complex
(adjective) made of two or more parts

Complex jobs in organisms require more than one type of tissue. **Organs** *are groups of different tissues working together to perform a particular job.* For example, your stomach is an organ specialized for breaking down food. It is made of all four types of tissue: muscle, epithelial, nervous, and connective. Each type of tissue performs a specific function necessary for the stomach to work properly. Layers of muscle tissue contract and break up pieces of food, epithelial tissue lines the stomach, nervous tissue sends signals to indicate the stomach is full, and connective tissue supports the stomach wall.

Plants also have organs. The leaves shown in **Figure 14** are organs specialized for photosynthesis. Each leaf is made of dermal, ground, and vascular tissues. Dermal tissue covers the outer surface of a leaf. The leaf is a vital organ because it contains ground tissue that produces food for the rest of the plant. Ground tissue is where photosynthesis takes place. The ground tissue is tightly packed on the top half of a leaf. The vascular tissue moves both the food produced by photosynthesis and water throughout the leaf and the rest of the plant.

Reading Check List the tissues in a leaf organ.

Figure 14 A plant leaf is an organ made of several different tissues.

Visual Check Which plant tissue makes up the thinnest layer?

Organ Systems

Usually organs do not function alone. Instead, **organ systems** *are groups of different organs that work together to complete a series of tasks*. Human organ systems can be made of many different organs working together. For example, the human digestive system is made of many organs, including the stomach, the small intestine, the liver, and the large intestine. These organs and others all work together to break down food and take it into the body. Blood absorbs and transports nutrients from broken down food to cells throughout the body.

Plants have two major organ systems—the shoot system and the root system. The shoot system includes leaves, stems, and flowers. Food and water are transported throughout the plant by the shoot system. The root system anchors the plant and takes in water and nutrients.

Reading Check What are the major organ systems in plants?

Inquiry MiniLab

25 minutes

How do cells work together to make an organism?

In a multicellular organism, similar cells work together and make a tissue. A tissue can perform functions that individual cells cannot. Tissues are organized into organs, then organ systems, then organisms. How can you model the levels of organization in an organism?

1. Read and complete a lab safety form.
2. Your teacher will give you a **cardboard shape, macaroni,** and a **permanent marker.**
3. The macaroni represent cells. Use the marker to draw a small circle on each piece of macaroni. This represents the nucleus.
4. Arrange and **glue** enough macaroni on the blank side of the cardboard shape to cover it. Your group of similar cells represents a tissue.
5. One of the squares on the back of your shape is labeled *A, B, C,* or *D*. Find the group with a matching letter. Line up these squares, and use **tape** to connect the two tissues. This represents an organ.
6. Repeat step 4 with the squares labeled *E* or *F*. This represents an organ system.
7. Connect the organ systems by aligning the squares labeled *G* to represent an organism.

Analyze and Conclude

1. Each group had to work with other groups to make a model of an organism. Do cells, tissues, and organs need to work together in organisms? Explain.
2. **Key Concept** How does your model show the levels of organization in living things?

Organisms

Multicellular organisms usually have many organ systems. These systems work together to carry out all the jobs needed for the survival of the organisms. For example, the cells in the leaves and the stems of a plant need water to live. They cannot absorb water directly. Water diffuses into the roots and is transported through the stem to the leaves by the transport system.

In the human body, there are many major organ systems. Each organ system depends on the others and cannot work alone. For example, the cells in the muscle tissue of the stomach cannot survive without oxygen. The stomach cannot get oxygen without working together with the respiratory and circulatory systems. **Figure 15** will help you review how organisms are organized.

Key Concept Check How does cell differentiation lead to the organization within a multicellular organism?

Concepts in Motion **Animation**

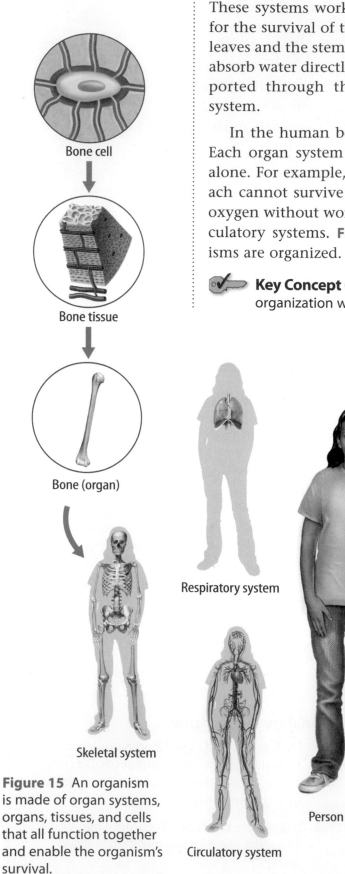

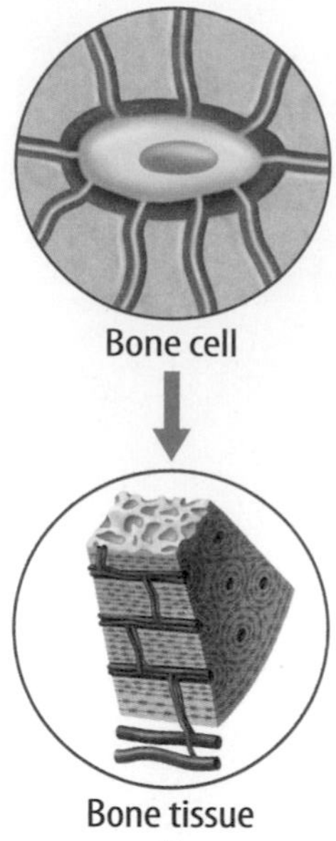

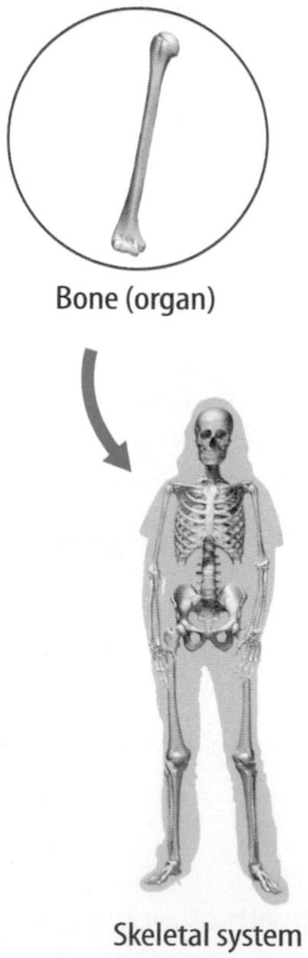

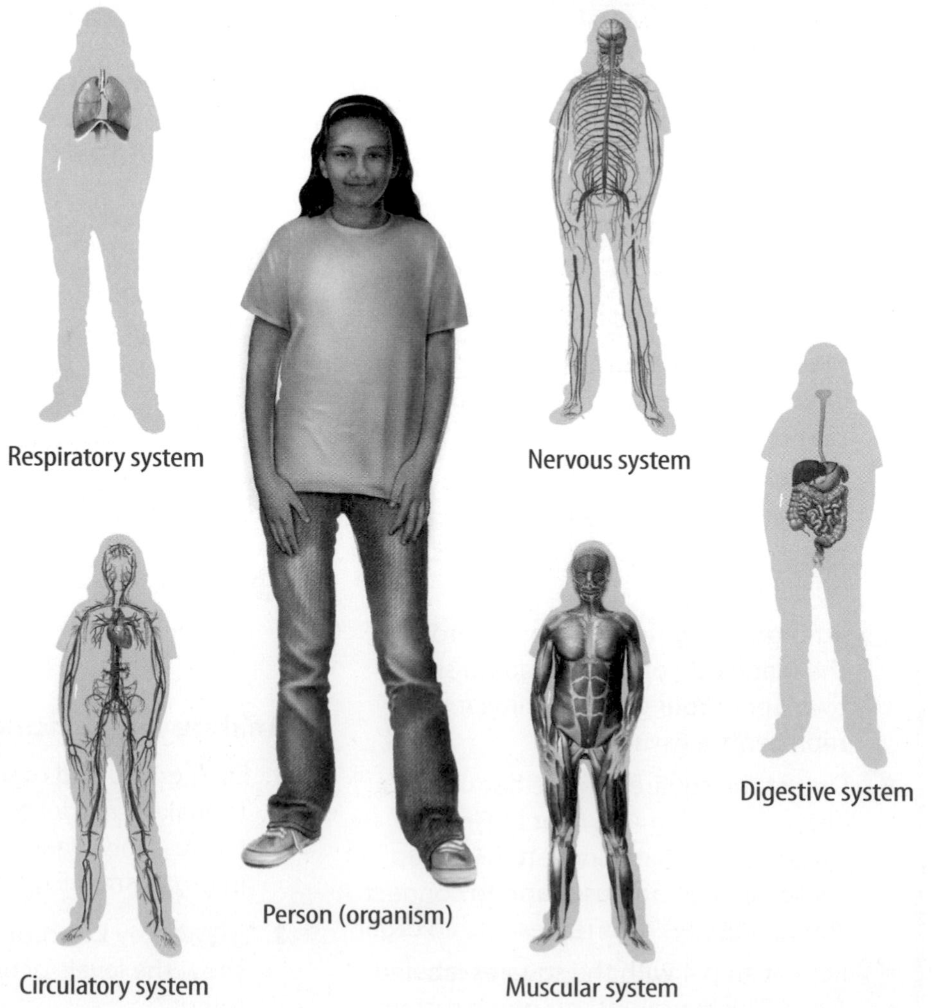

Figure 15 An organism is made of organ systems, organs, tissues, and cells that all function together and enable the organism's survival.

Lesson 2 Review

Assessment Online Quiz
Inquiry Virtual Lab

Visual Summary

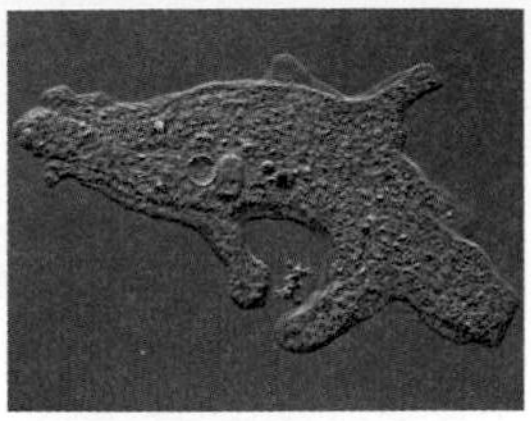

A unicellular organism carries out all the activities necessary for survival within one cell.

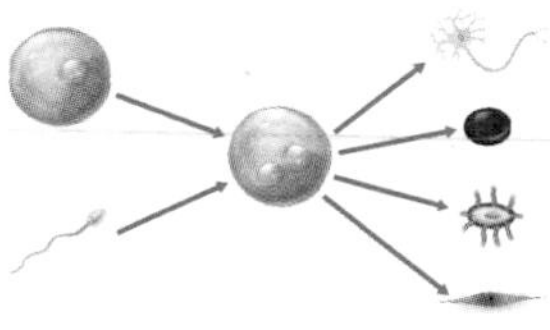

Cells become specialized in structure and function during cell differentiation.

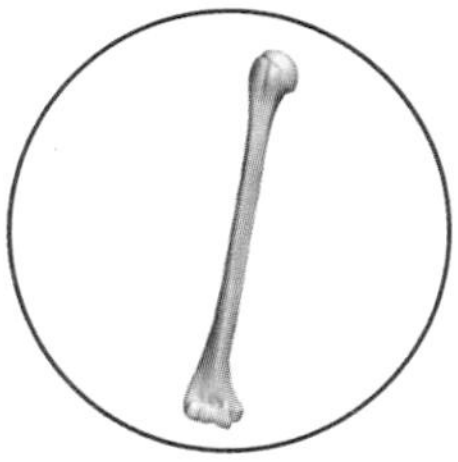

Organs are groups of different tissues that work together to perform a job.

FOLDABLES®

Use your lesson Foldable to review the lesson. Save your Foldable for the project at the end of the chapter.

What do you think NOW?

You first read the statements below at the beginning of the chapter.

4. Unicellular organisms do not have all the characteristics of life.

5. All the cells in a multicellular organism are the same.

6. Some organs work together as part of an organ system.

Did you change your mind about whether you agree or disagree with the statements? Rewrite any false statements to make them true.

Use Vocabulary

1. **Define** *cell differentiation* in your own words.
2. **Distinguish** between an organ and an organ system.

Understand Key Concepts

3. **Explain** the difference between a unicellular organism and a multicellular organism.
4. **Describe** how cell differentiation produces different types of cells in animals.
5. Which is the correct sequence of the levels of organization?
   A. cell, organ, tissue, organ system, organism
   B. organism, organ, organ system, tissue, cell
   C. cell, tissue, organ, organ system, organism
   D. tissue, organ, organism, organ system, cell

Interpret Graphics

6. **Organize** Copy and fill in the table below to summarize the characteristics of unicellular and multicellular organisms.

Organism Characteristics	
Unicellular	Multicellular

Critical Thinking

7. **Predict** A mistake occurs during mitosis of a muscle stem cell. How might this affect muscle tissue?
8. **Compare** the functions of a cell to the functions of an organism, such as getting rid of wastes.

Inquiry Lab

90 minutes

Cell Differentiation

Materials

cooked eggs

boiled chicken leg

forceps

dissecting scissors

plastic knife

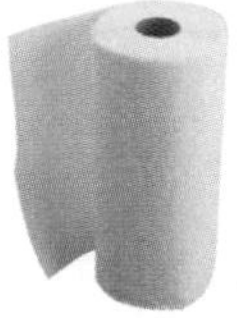

paper towels

Safety

It's pretty amazing that a whole chicken with wings, feet, beak, feathers, and internal organs can come from one cell, a fertilized egg. Shortly after fertilization, the cell begins to divide. The new cells in the developing embryo become specialized both in structure and function. The process by which cells become specialized is called cellular differentiation.

Question

How does a single cell become a multicellular organism?

Procedure

1. Read and complete a lab safety form.
2. Carefully examine the outside of your egg. Remove the shell.
3. Dissect the egg on a paper towel, cutting it in half from tip to rounded end. Examine the inside.
4. Record your observations in your Science Journal. Include a labeled drawing. Infer the function of each part.
5. Discard all your trash in the container provided.
6. Examine the outside of the chicken leg. Describe the skin and its functions.

3

7 Carefully remove the skin using forceps and dissecting scissors. Put the skin in your discard container. Now you should see evidence of fat and muscles. You may also be able to see some blood vessels and tendons, but these are not always visible after cooking. Describe each part that you see and explain its function.

8 Peel back the muscles to reveal the bones. Tendons, ligaments, and cartilage holding the bones in place may also be evident.

9 Put all your trash in the discard container. Your teacher will give you instructions about cleaning up.

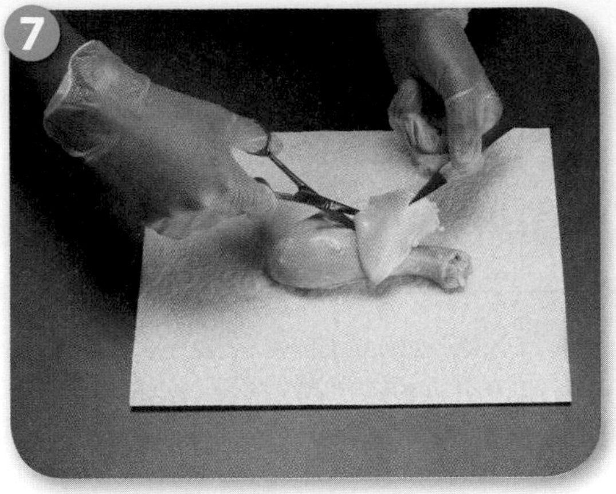

Analyze and Conclude

10 **The Big Idea** A single cell can become a multicellular organism through the process of cell differentiation. How do the organization of the egg and the chicken leg compare?

11 **Summarize** How many different types of cell differentiation did you observe in the chicken leg?

Lab TIPS

☑ Work slowly and carefully on your dissections so as not to destroy any structures. Report any accidents to your teacher immediately. Cleaning up is important!

Communicate Your Results

Make a poster about how an egg transforms into a chicken through the process of cell differentiation.

Inquiry Extension

Examine a whole raw chicken or a raw chicken leg that is still attached to a thigh. You might be able to move the muscles in the legs or wings and see parts that were not visible in this lab. Be sure to wear gloves and to wash well with soap and water after touching the raw chicken.

Remember to use scientific methods.

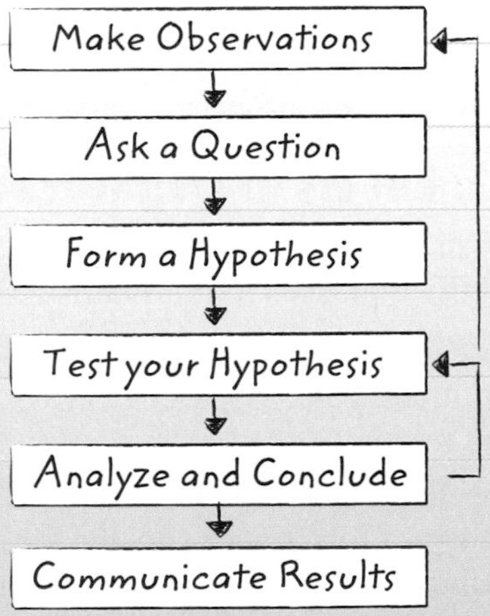

Chapter 12 Study Guide

WebQuest

THE BIG IDEA **Through cell division, one cell can produce new cells to grow and develop into a multicellular organism.**

Key Concepts Summary

Lesson 1: The Cell Cycle and Cell Division

- The **cell cycle** consists of two phases. During **interphase,** a cell grows and its chromosomes and organelles replicate. During the mitotic phase of the cell cycle, the nucleus divides during **mitosis,** and the cytoplasm divides during **cytokinesis.**
- The cell cycle results in two genetically identical **daughter cells.** The original parent cell no longer exists.
- The cell cycle is important for growth in multicellular organisms, reproduction in some organisms, replacement of worn-out cells, and repair of damaged cells.

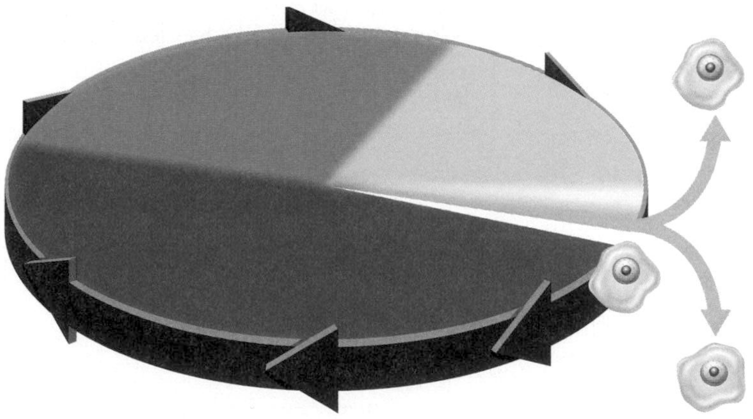

Vocabulary

cell cycle p. 429
interphase p. 430
sister chromatid p. 432
centromere p. 432
mitosis p. 433
cytokinesis p. 433
daughter cell p. 433

Lesson 2: Levels of Organization

- The one cell of a unicellular organism is able to obtain all the materials that it needs to survive.
- In a multicellular organism, cells cannot survive alone and must work together to provide the organism's needs.
- Through **cell differentiation,** cells become different types of cells with specific functions. Cell differentiation leads to the formation of **tissues, organs,** and **organ systems.**

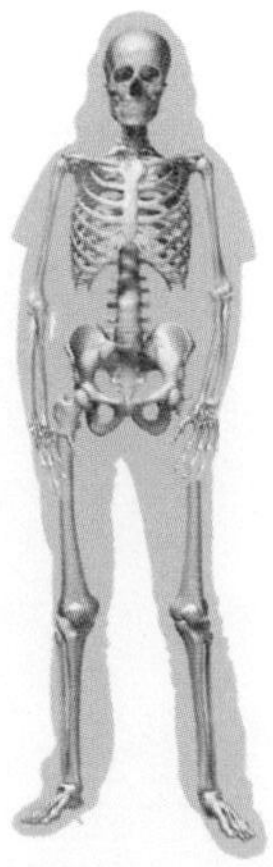

Vocabulary

cell differentiation p. 443
stem cell p. 444
tissue p. 445
organ p. 446
organ system p. 447

Review
- Personal Tutor
- Vocabulary eGames
- Vocabulary eFlashcards

FOLDABLES® Chapter Project

Assemble your lesson Foldables as shown to make a Chapter Project. Use the project to review what you have learned in this chapter.

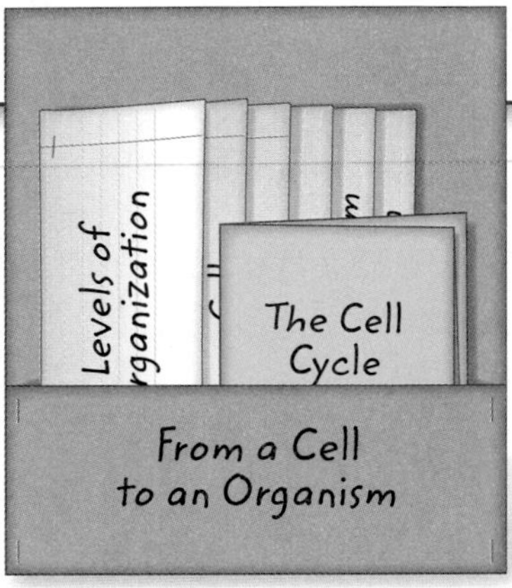

Use Vocabulary

1. Use the term *sister chromatids* in a sentence.
2. Define the term *centromere* in your own words.
3. The new cells formed by mitosis are called ________.
4. Use the term *cell differentiation* in a sentence.
5. Define the term *stem cell* in your own words.
6. Organs are groups of ________ working together to perform a specific task.

Link Vocabulary and Key Concepts

Concepts in Motion Interactive Concept Map

Copy this concept map, and then use vocabulary terms from the previous page and from the chapter to complete the concept map.

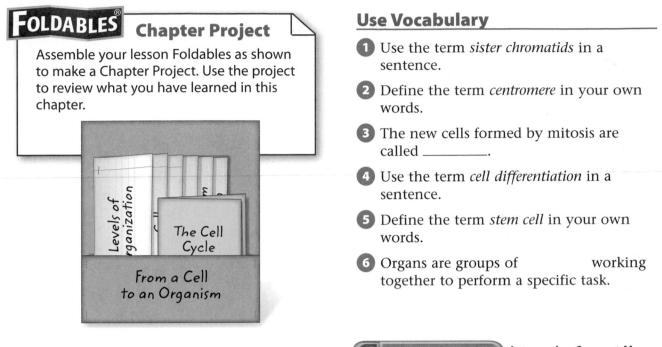

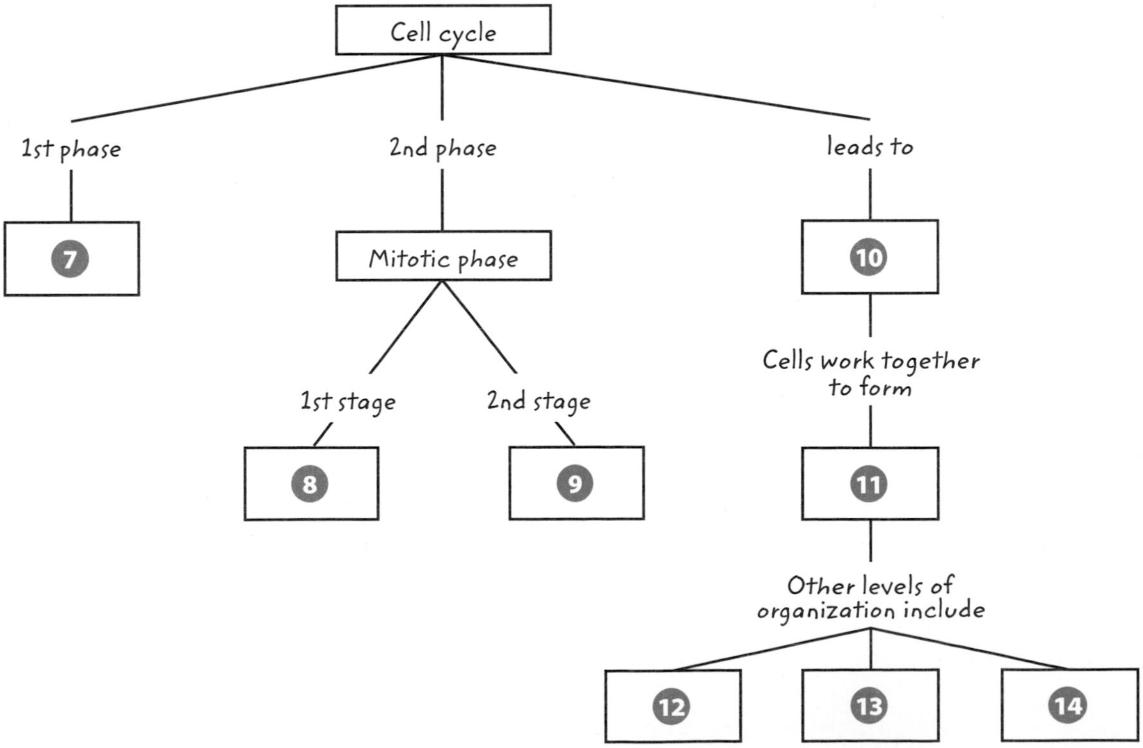

Chapter 12 Review

Understand Key Concepts

1. Chromosomes line up in the center of the cell during which phase?
   A. anaphase
   B. metaphase
   C. prophase
   D. telophase

2. Which stage of the cell cycle precedes cytokinesis?
   A. G_1
   B. G_2
   C. interphase
   D. mitosis

Use the figure below to answer questions 3 and 4.

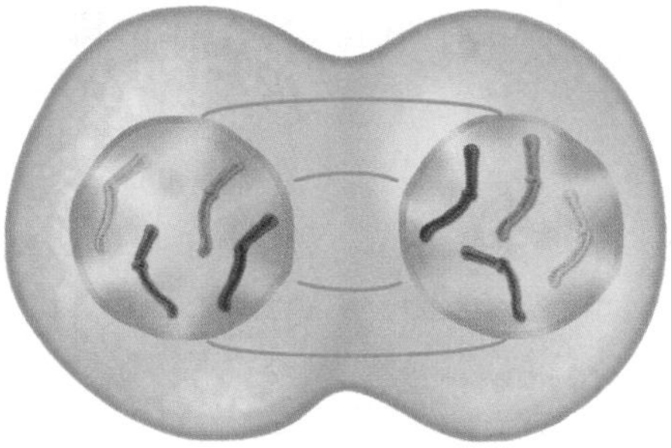

3. The figure represents which stage of mitosis?
   A. anaphase
   B. metaphase
   C. prophase
   D. telophase

4. What forms during this phase?
   A. centromere
   B. furrow
   C. sister chromatid
   D. two nuclei

5. What is the longest part of the cell cycle?
   A. anaphase
   B. cytokinesis
   C. interphase
   D. mitosis

6. A plant's root system is which level of organization?
   A. cell
   B. organ
   C. organ system
   D. tissue

7. Where is a meristem often found?
   A. liver cells
   B. muscle tissue
   C. tip of plant root
   D. unicellular organism

8. Which is NOT a type of human tissue?
   A. connective
   B. meristem
   C. muscle
   D. nervous

9. Which are unspecialized cells?
   A. blood cells
   B. muscle cells
   C. nerve cells
   D. stem cells

10. Which level of organization is shown in the figure below?
    A. cell
    B. organ
    C. organ system
    D. tissue

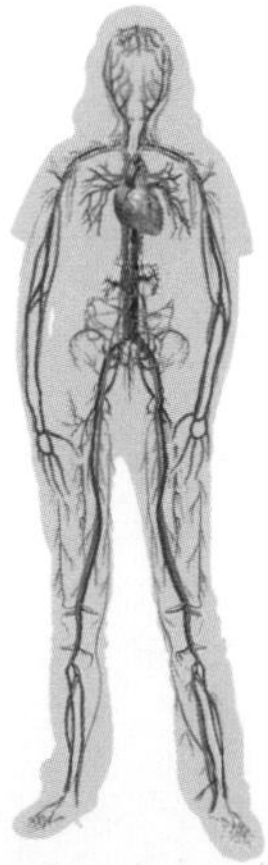

11. Which level of organization completes a series of tasks?
    A. cell
    B. organ
    C. organ system
    D. tissue

Assessment
Online Test Practice

Critical Thinking

12 **Sequence** the events that occur during the phases of mitosis.

13 **Infer** why the chromatin condenses into chromosomes before mitosis begins.

14 **Create** Use the figure below to create a cartoon that shows a duplicated chromosome separating into two sister chromatids.

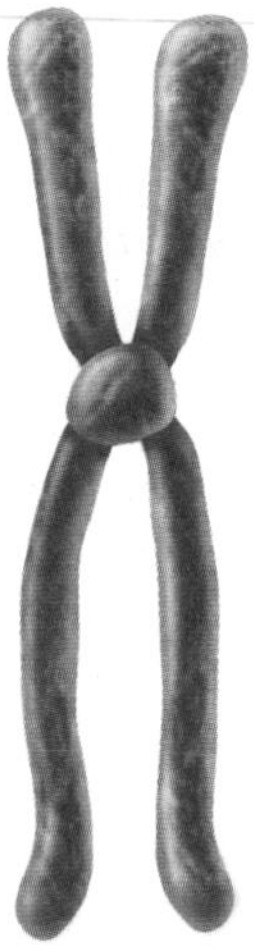

15 **Classify** a leaf as a tissue or an organ. Explain your choice.

16 **Distinguish** between a tissue and an organ.

17 **Construct** a table that lists and defines the different levels of organization.

18 **Summarize** the differences between unicellular organisms and multicellular organisms.

Writing in Science

19 **Write** a five-sentence paragraph describing a human organ system. Include a main idea, supporting details, and a concluding statement.

REVIEW THE BIG IDEA

20 Why is cell division important for multicellular organisms?

21 The photo below shows a chick growing inside an egg. An egg begins as one cell. How can one cell become a chick?

Math Skills

Review
Math Practice

Use Percentages

22 During an interphase lasting 23 hours, the S stage takes an average of 8.0 hours. What percentage of interphase is taken up by the S stage?

Use the following information to answer questions 23 through 25.

During a 23-hour interphase, the G_1 stage takes 11 hours and the S stage takes 8.0 hours.

23 What percentage of interphase is taken up by the G_1 and S stages?

24 What percentage of interphase is taken up by the G_2 phase?

25 How many hours does the G_2 phase last?

Standardized Test Practice

Record your answers on the answer sheet provided by your teacher or on a sheet of paper.

Multiple Choice

1 Which tissue carries messages to and from the brain?

A connective

B epithelial

C muscle

D nervous

Use the diagram below to answer question 2.

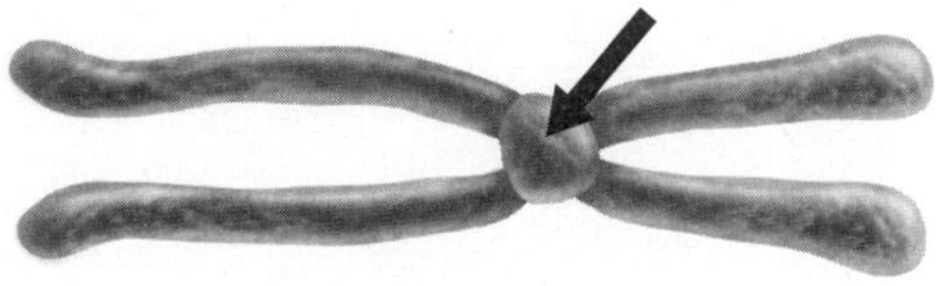

2 What is indicated by the arrow?

A centromere

B chromatid

C chromosome

D nucleus

3 In which stage of mitosis do spindle fibers form?

A anaphase

B metaphase

C prophase

D telophase

4 What structures separate during anaphase?

A centromeres

B chromatids

C nuclei

D organelles

Use the diagram below to answer question 5.

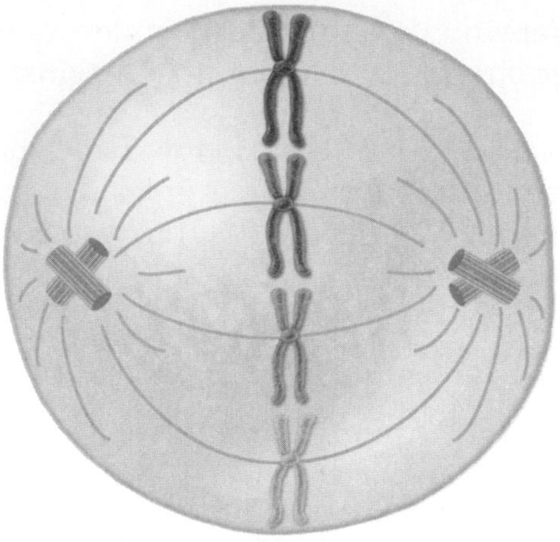

5 What stage of mitosis does the image above represent?

A anaphase

B metaphase

C prophase

D telophase

6 A plant's dermal tissue

A produces food for the rest of the plant.

B provides protection and helps reduce water loss.

C takes in water and nutrients for use throughout the plant.

D transports water and nutrients throughout the plant.

7 Which is the most accurate description of a leaf or your stomach?

A a cell

B an organ

C an organ system

D a tissue

Use the figure below to answer question 8.

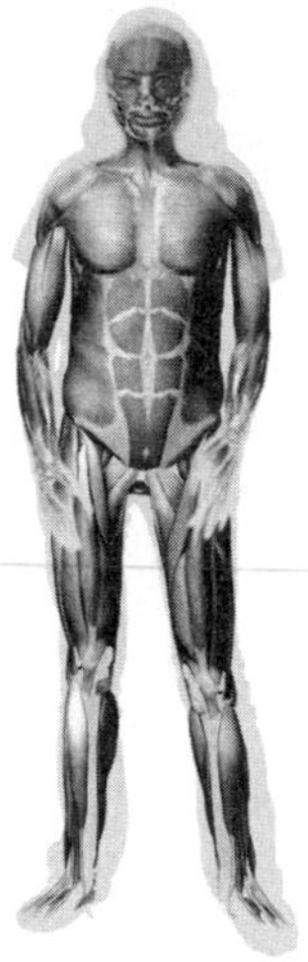

8 Which does this figure illustrate?

A an organ

B an organism

C an organ system

D a tissue

9 If a cell has 30 chromosomes at the start of mitosis, how many chromosomes will be in each new daughter cell?

A 10

B 15

C 30

D 60

10 What areas of plants have unspecialized cells?

A flowers

B fruits

C leaves

D meristems

Constructed Response

Use the figure below to answer questions 11 and 12.

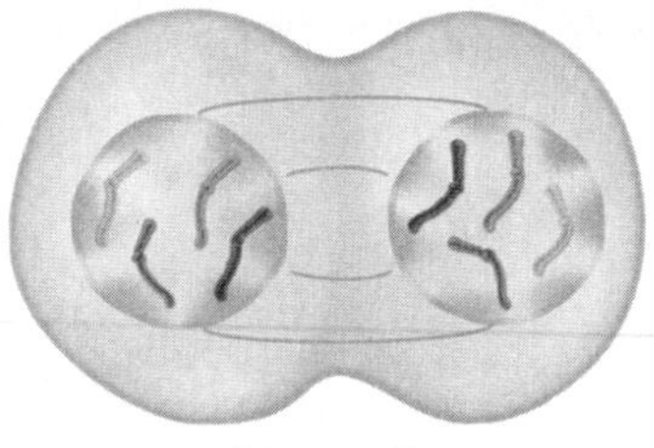

Figure A

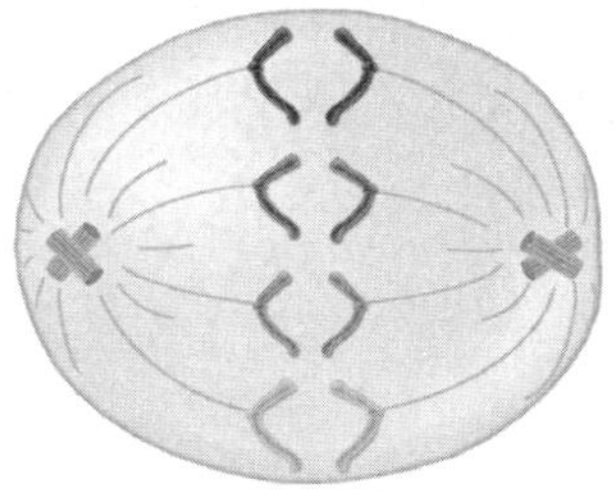

Figure B

11 The figures illustrate two phases of mitosis. Which occurs first: A or B? Explain your reasoning.

12 What stage of the mitotic phase follows those illustrated above? Explain how this stage differs between plant and animal cells.

13 What are some similarities and differences between the G_1 and S stages of interphase?

14 Are all human cells capable of mitosis and cell division? How does this affect the body's ability to repair itself? Support your answer with specific examples.

NEED EXTRA HELP?														
If You Missed Question...	1	2	3	4	5	6	7	8	9	10	11	12	13	14
Go to Lesson...	2	1	1	1	1	2	2	2	1	2	1	1	1	1

Student Resources

For Students and Parents/Guardians

These resources are designed to help you achieve success in science. You will find useful information on laboratory safety, math skills, and science skills. In addition, science reference materials are found in the Reference Handbook. You'll find the information you need to learn and sharpen your skills in these resources.

Table of Contents

Scientific Methods

Scientists use an orderly approach called the scientific method to solve problems. This includes organizing and recording data so others can understand them. Scientists use many variations in this method when they solve problems.

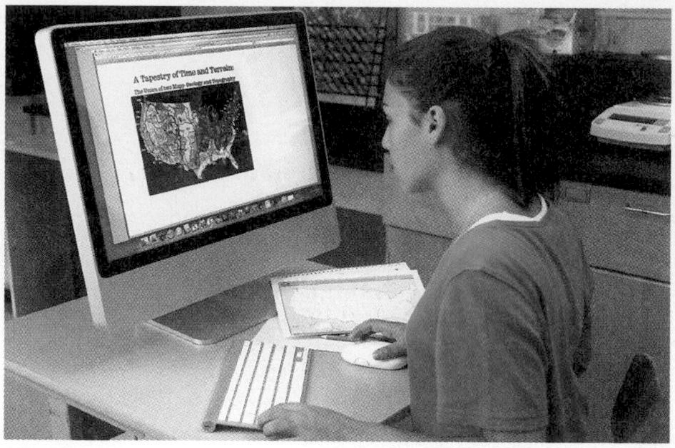

Figure 1 The Internet can be a valuable research tool.

Identify a Question

The first step in a scientific investigation or experiment is to identify a question to be answered or a problem to be solved. For example, you might ask which gasoline is the most efficient.

Gather and Organize Information

After you have identified your question, begin gathering and organizing information. There are many ways to gather information, such as researching in a library, interviewing those knowledgeable about the subject, testing and working in the laboratory and field. Fieldwork is investigations and observations done outside of a laboratory.

Researching Information Before moving in a new direction, it is important to gather the information that already is known about the subject. Start by asking yourself questions to determine exactly what you need to know. Then you will look for the information in various reference sources, like the student is doing in **Figure 1.** Some sources may include textbooks, encyclopedias, government documents, professional journals, science magazines, and the Internet. Always list the sources of your information.

Evaluate Sources of Information Not all sources of information are reliable. You should evaluate all of your sources of information, and use only those you know to be dependable. For example, if you are researching ways to make homes more energy efficient, a site written by the U.S. Department of Energy would be more reliable than a site written by a company that is trying to sell a new type of weatherproofing material. Also, remember that research always is changing. Consult the most current resources available to you. For example, a 1985 resource about saving energy would not reflect the most recent findings.

Sometimes scientists use data that they did not collect themselves, or conclusions drawn by other researchers. This data must be evaluated carefully. Ask questions about how the data were obtained, if the investigation was carried out properly, and if it has been duplicated exactly with the same results. Would you reach the same conclusion from the data? Only when you have confidence in the data can you believe it is true and feel comfortable using it.

Interpret Scientific Illustrations As you research a topic in science, you will see drawings, diagrams, and photographs to help you understand what you read. Some illustrations are included to help you understand an idea that you can't see easily by yourself, like the tiny particles in an atom in **Figure 2.** A drawing helps many people to remember details more easily and provides examples that clarify difficult concepts or give additional information about the topic you are studying. Most illustrations have labels or a caption to identify or to provide more information.

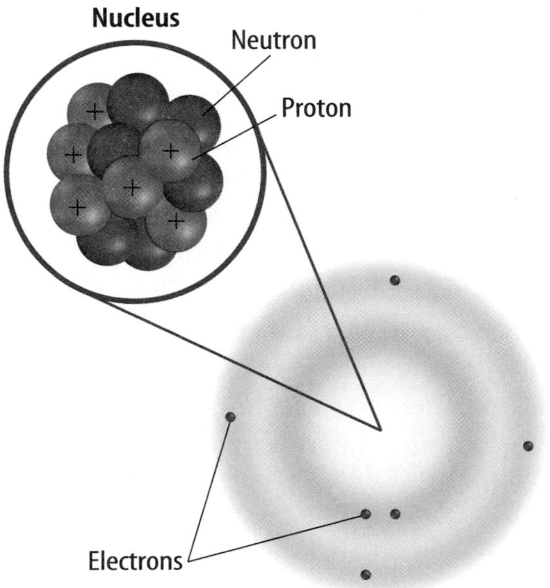

Figure 2 This drawing shows an atom of carbon with its six protons, six neutrons, and six electrons.

Concept Maps One way to organize data is to draw a diagram that shows relationships among ideas (or concepts). A concept map can help make the meanings of ideas and terms more clear, and help you understand and remember what you are studying. Concept maps are useful for breaking large concepts down into smaller parts, making learning easier.

Network Tree A type of concept map that not only shows a relationship, but how the concepts are related is a network tree, shown in **Figure 3.** In a network tree, the words are written in the ovals, while the description of the type of relationship is written across the connecting lines.

When constructing a network tree, write down the topic and all major topics on separate pieces of paper or notecards. Then arrange them in order from general to specific. Branch the related concepts from the major concept and describe the relationship on the connecting line. Continue to more specific concepts until finished.

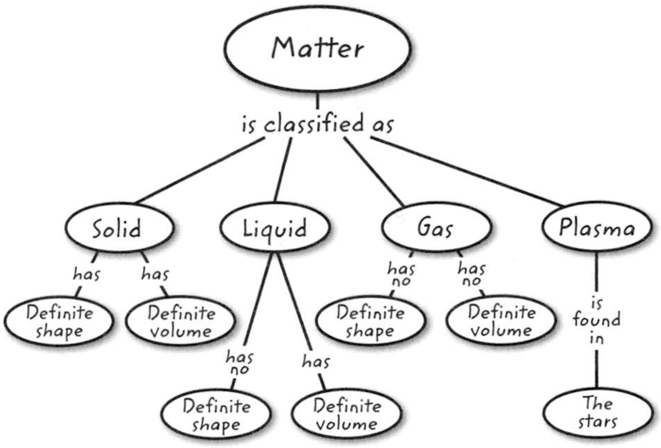

Figure 3 A network tree shows how concepts or objects are related.

Events Chain Another type of concept map is an events chain. Sometimes called a flow chart, it models the order or sequence of items. An events chain can be used to describe a sequence of events, the steps in a procedure, or the stages of a process.

When making an events chain, first find the one event that starts the chain. This event is called the initiating event. Then, find the next event and continue until the outcome is reached, as shown in **Figure 4.**

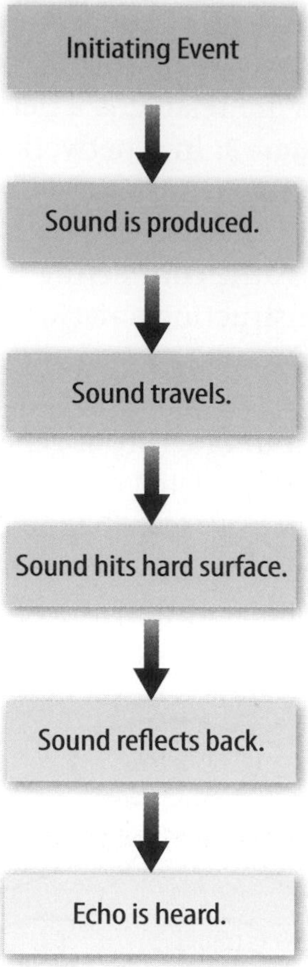

Figure 4 Events-chain concept maps show the order of steps in a process or event. This concept map shows how a sound makes an echo.

Cycle Map A specific type of events chain is a cycle map. It is used when the series of events do not produce a final outcome, but instead relate back to the beginning event, such as in **Figure 5.** Therefore, the cycle repeats itself.

To make a cycle map, first decide what event is the beginning event. This is also called the initiating event. Then list the next events in the order that they occur, with the last event relating back to the initiating event. Words can be written between the events that describe what happens from one event to the next. The number of events in a cycle map can vary, but usually contain three or more events.

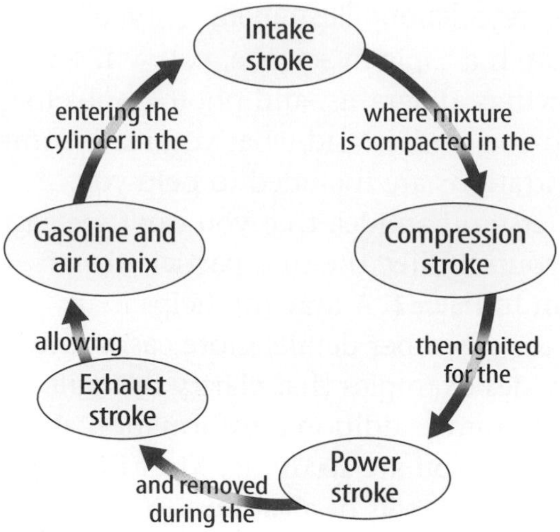

Figure 5 A cycle map shows events that occur in a cycle.

Spider Map A type of concept map that you can use for brainstorming is the spider map. When you have a central idea, you might find that you have a jumble of ideas that relate to it but are not necessarily clearly related to each other. The spider map on sound in **Figure 6** shows that if you write these ideas outside the main concept, then you can begin to separate and group unrelated terms so they become more useful.

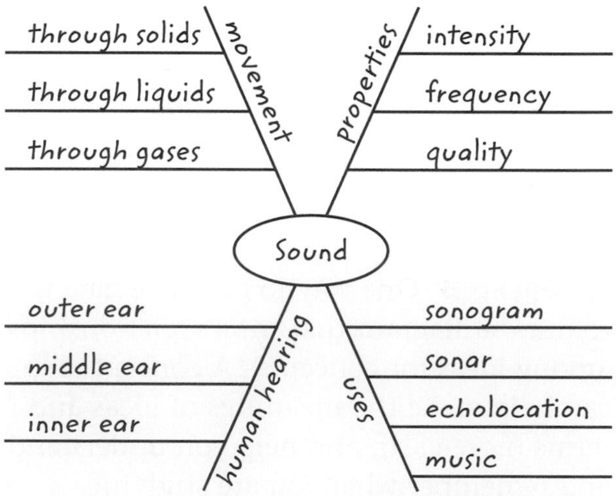

Figure 6 A spider map allows you to list ideas that relate to a central topic but not necessarily to one another.

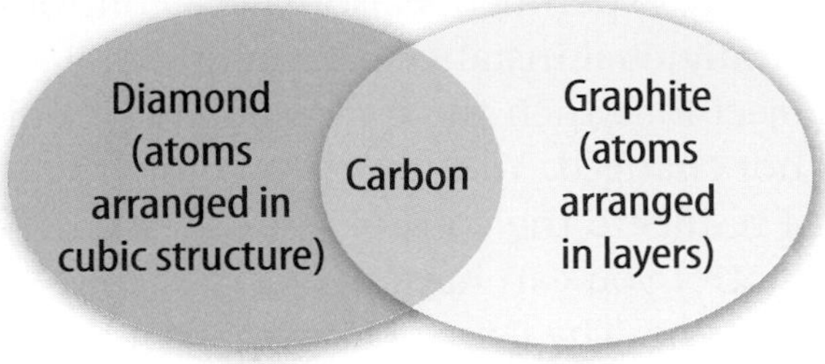

Figure 7 This Venn diagram compares and contrasts two substances made from carbon.

Venn Diagram To illustrate how two subjects compare and contrast you can use a Venn diagram. You can see the characteristics that the subjects have in common and those that they do not, shown in **Figure 7.**

To create a Venn diagram, draw two overlapping ovals that that are big enough to write in. List the characteristics unique to one subject in one oval, and the characteristics of the other subject in the other oval. The characteristics in common are listed in the overlapping section.

Make and Use Tables One way to organize information so it is easier to understand is to use a table. Tables can contain numbers, words, or both.

To make a table, list the items to be compared in the first column and the characteristics to be compared in the first row. The title should clearly indicate the content of the table, and the column or row heads should be clear. Notice that in **Table 1** the units are included.

Table 1 Recyclables Collected During Week

Day of Week	Paper (kg)	Aluminum (kg)	Glass (kg)
Monday	5.0	4.0	12.0
Wednesday	4.0	1.0	10.0
Friday	2.5	2.0	10.0

Make a Model One way to help you better understand the parts of a structure, the way a process works, or to show things too large or small for viewing is to make a model. For example, an atomic model made of a plastic-ball nucleus and pipe-cleaner electron shells can help you visualize how the parts of an atom relate to each other. Other types of models can be devised on a computer or represented by equations.

Form a Hypothesis

A possible explanation based on previous knowledge and observations is called a hypothesis. After researching gasoline types and recalling previous experiences in your family's car you form a hypothesis—our car runs more efficiently because we use premium gasoline. To be valid, a hypothesis has to be something you can test by using an investigation.

Predict When you apply a hypothesis to a specific situation, you predict something about that situation. A prediction makes a statement in advance, based on prior observation, experience, or scientific reasoning. People use predictions to make everyday decisions. Scientists test predictions by performing investigations. Based on previous observations and experiences, you might form a prediction that cars are more efficient with premium gasoline. The prediction can be tested in an investigation.

Design an Experiment A scientist needs to make many decisions before beginning an investigation. Some of these include: how to carry out the investigation, what steps to follow, how to record the data, and how the investigation will answer the question. It also is important to address any safety concerns.

Test the Hypothesis

Now that you have formed your hypothesis, you need to test it. Using an investigation, you will make observations and collect data, or information. This data might either support or not support your hypothesis. Scientists collect and organize data as numbers and descriptions.

Follow a Procedure In order to know what materials to use, as well as how and in what order to use them, you must follow a procedure. **Figure 8** shows a procedure you might follow to test your hypothesis.

Procedure

Step 1	Use regular gasoline for two weeks.
Step 2	Record the number of kilometers between fill-ups and the amount of gasoline used.
Step 3	Switch to premium gasoline for two weeks.
Step 4	Record the number of kilometers between fill-ups and the amount of gasoline used.

Figure 8 A procedure tells you what to do step by step.

Identify and Manipulate Variables and Controls In any experiment, it is important to keep everything the same except for the item you are testing. The one factor you change is called the independent variable. The change that results is the dependent variable. Make sure you have only one independent variable, to assure yourself of the cause of the changes you observe in the dependent variable. For example, in your gasoline experiment the type of fuel is the independent variable. The dependent variable is the efficiency.

Many experiments also have a control—an individual instance or experimental subject for which the independent variable is not changed. You can then compare the test results to the control results. To design a control you can have two cars of the same type. The control car uses regular gasoline for four weeks. After you are done with the test, you can compare the experimental results to the control results.

Collect Data

Whether you are carrying out an investigation or a short observational experiment, you will collect data, as shown in **Figure 9.** Scientists collect data as numbers and descriptions and organize it in specific ways.

Observe Scientists observe items and events, then record what they see. When they use only words to describe an observation, it is called qualitative data. Scientists' observations also can describe how much there is of something. These observations use numbers, as well as words, in the description and are called quantitative data. For example, if a sample of the element gold is described as being "shiny and very dense" the data are qualitative. Quantitative data on this sample of gold might include "a mass of 30 g and a density of 19.3 g/cm^3."

Figure 9 Collecting data is one way to gather information directly.

Figure 10 Record data neatly and clearly so it is easy to understand.

When you make observations you should examine the entire object or situation first, and then look carefully for details. It is important to record observations accurately and completely. Always record your notes immediately as you make them, so you do not miss details or make a mistake when recording results from memory. Never put unidentified observations on scraps of paper. Instead they should be recorded in a notebook, like the one in **Figure 10.** Write your data neatly so you can easily read it later. At each point in the experiment, record your observations and label them. That way, you will not have to determine what the figures mean when you look at your notes later. Set up any tables that you will need to use ahead of time, so you can record any observations right away. Remember to avoid bias when collecting data by not including personal thoughts when you record observations. Record only what you observe.

Estimate Scientific work also involves estimating. To estimate is to make a judgment about the size or the number of something without measuring or counting. This is important when the number or size of an object or population is too large or too difficult to accurately count or measure.

Sample Scientists may use a sample or a portion of the total number as a type of estimation. To sample is to take a small, representative portion of the objects or organisms of a population for research. By making careful observations or manipulating variables within that portion of the group, information is discovered and conclusions are drawn that might apply to the whole population. A poorly chosen sample can be unrepresentative of the whole. If you were trying to determine the rainfall in an area, it would not be best to take a rainfall sample from under a tree.

Measure You use measurements every day. Scientists also take measurements when collecting data. When taking measurements, it is important to know how to use measuring tools properly. Accuracy also is important.

Length To measure length, the distance between two points, scientists use meters. Smaller measurements might be measured in centimeters or millimeters.

Length is measured using a metric ruler or meter stick. When using a metric ruler, line up the 0-cm mark with the end of the object being measured and read the number of the unit where the object ends. Look at the metric ruler shown in **Figure 11.** The centimeter lines are the long, numbered lines, and the shorter lines are millimeter lines. In this instance, the length would be 4.50 cm.

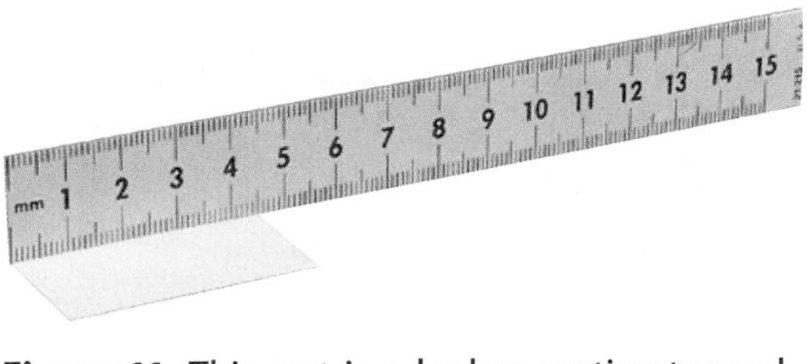

Figure 11 This metric ruler has centimeter and millimeter divisions.

Science Skill Handbook
Math Skill Handbook
Foldables Handbook
Reference Handbook
Glossary/Glosario
Index

Mass The SI unit for mass is the kilogram (kg). Scientists can measure mass using units formed by adding metric prefixes to the unit gram (g), such as milligram (mg). To measure mass, you might use a triple-beam balance similar to the one shown in **Figure 12.** The balance has a pan on one side and a set of beams on the other side. Each beam has a rider that slides on the beam.

When using a triple-beam balance, place an object on the pan. Slide the largest rider along its beam until the pointer drops below zero. Then move it back one notch. Repeat the process for each rider proceeding from the larger to smaller until the pointer swings an equal distance above and below the zero point. Sum the masses on each beam to find the mass of the object. Move all riders back to zero when finished.

Instead of putting materials directly on the balance, scientists often take a tare of a container. A tare is the mass of a container into which objects or substances are placed for measuring their masses. To mass objects or substances, find the mass of a clean container. Remove the container from the pan, and place the object or substances in the container. Find the mass of the container with the materials in it. Subtract the mass of the empty container from the mass of the filled container to find the mass of the materials you are using.

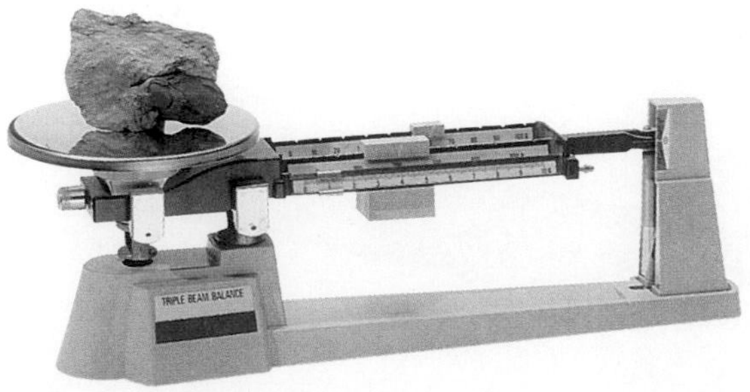

Figure 12 A triple-beam balance is used to determine the mass of an object.

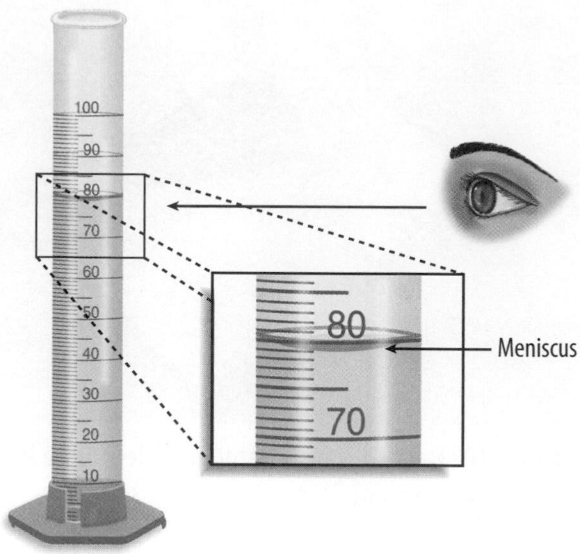

Figure 13 Graduated cylinders measure liquid volume.

Liquid Volume To measure liquids, the unit used is the liter. When a smaller unit is needed, scientists might use a milliliter. Because a milliliter takes up the volume of a cube measuring 1 cm on each side it also can be called a cubic centimeter ($cm^3 = cm \times cm \times cm$).

You can use beakers and graduated cylinders to measure liquid volume. A graduated cylinder, shown in **Figure 13,** is marked from bottom to top in milliliters. In lab, you might use a 10-mL graduated cylinder or a 100-mL graduated cylinder. When measuring liquids, notice that the liquid has a curved surface. Look at the surface at eye level, and measure the bottom of the curve. This is called the meniscus. The graduated cylinder in **Figure 13** contains 79.0 mL, or 79.0 cm^3, of a liquid.

Temperature Scientists often measure temperature using the Celsius scale. Pure water has a freezing point of 0°C and boiling point of 100°C. The unit of measurement is degrees Celsius. Two other scales often used are the Fahrenheit and Kelvin scales.

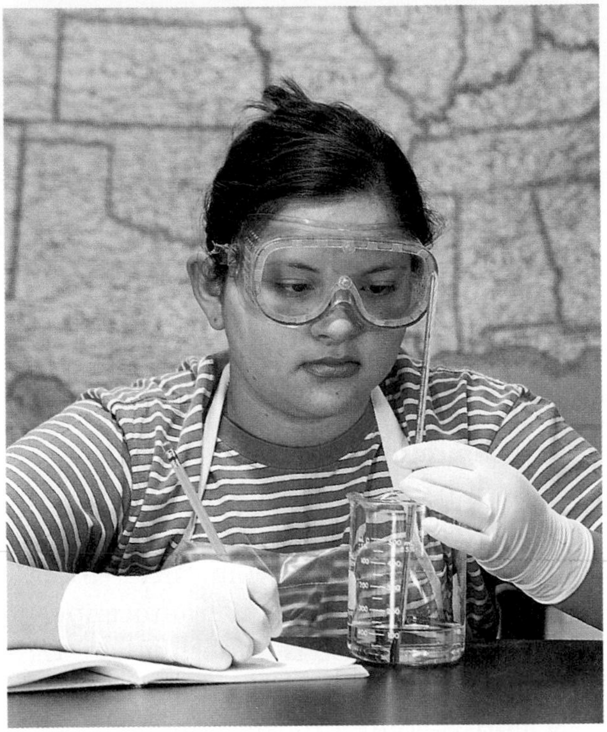

Figure 14 A thermometer measures the temperature of an object.

Scientists use a thermometer to measure temperature. Most thermometers in a laboratory are glass tubes with a bulb at the bottom end containing a liquid such as colored alcohol. The liquid rises or falls with a change in temperature. To read a glass thermometer like the thermometer in **Figure 14,** rotate it slowly until a red line appears. Read the temperature where the red line ends.

Form Operational Definitions An operational definition defines an object by how it functions, works, or behaves. For example, when you are playing hide and seek and a tree is home base, you have created an operational definition for a tree.

Objects can have more than one operational definition. For example, a ruler can be defined as a tool that measures the length of an object (how it is used). It can also be a tool with a series of marks used as a standard when measuring (how it works).

Analyze the Data

To determine the meaning of your observations and investigation results, you will need to look for patterns in the data. Then you must think critically to determine what the data mean. Scientists use several approaches when they analyze the data they have collected and recorded. Each approach is useful for identifying specific patterns.

Interpret Data The word *interpret* means "to explain the meaning of something." When analyzing data from an experiment, try to find out what the data show. Identify the control group and the test group to see whether or not changes in the independent variable have had an effect. Look for differences in the dependent variable between the control and test groups.

Classify Sorting objects or events into groups based on common features is called classifying. When classifying, first observe the objects or events to be classified. Then select one feature that is shared by some members in the group, but not by all. Place those members that share that feature in a subgroup. You can classify members into smaller and smaller subgroups based on characteristics. Remember that when you classify, you are grouping objects or events for a purpose. Keep your purpose in mind as you select the features to form groups and subgroups.

Compare and Contrast Observations can be analyzed by noting the similarities and differences between two or more objects or events that you observe. When you look at objects or events to see how they are similar, you are comparing them. Contrasting is looking for differences in objects or events.

Recognize Cause and Effect A cause is a reason for an action or condition. The effect is that action or condition. When two events happen together, it is not necessarily true that one event caused the other. Scientists must design a controlled investigation to recognize the exact cause and effect.

Draw Conclusions

When scientists have analyzed the data they collected, they proceed to draw conclusions about the data. These conclusions are sometimes stated in words similar to the hypothesis that you formed earlier. They may confirm a hypothesis, or lead you to a new hypothesis.

Infer Scientists often make inferences based on their observations. An inference is an attempt to explain observations or to indicate a cause. An inference is not a fact, but a logical conclusion that needs further investigation. For example, you may infer that a fire has caused smoke. Until you investigate, however, you do not know for sure.

Apply When you draw a conclusion, you must apply those conclusions to determine whether the data supports the hypothesis. If your data do not support your hypothesis, it does not mean that the hypothesis is wrong. It means only that the result of the investigation did not support the hypothesis. Maybe the experiment needs to be redesigned, or some of the initial observations on which the hypothesis was based were incomplete or biased. Perhaps more observation or research is needed to refine your hypothesis. A successful investigation does not always come out the way you originally predicted.

Avoid Bias Sometimes a scientific investigation involves making judgments. When you make a judgment, you form an opinion. It is important to be honest and not to allow any expectations of results to bias your judgments. This is important throughout the entire investigation, from researching to collecting data to drawing conclusions.

Communicate

The communication of ideas is an important part of the work of scientists. A discovery that is not reported will not advance the scientific community's understanding or knowledge. Communication among scientists also is important as a way of improving their investigations.

Scientists communicate in many ways, from writing articles in journals and magazines that explain their investigations and experiments, to announcing important discoveries on television and radio. Scientists also share ideas with colleagues on the Internet or present them as lectures, like the student is doing in **Figure 15.**

Figure 15 A student communicates to his peers about his investigation.

These safety symbols are used in laboratory and field investigations in this book to indicate possible hazards. Learn the meaning of each symbol and refer to this page often. *Remember to wash your hands thoroughly after completing lab procedures.*

PROTECTIVE EQUIPMENT

Do not begin any lab without the proper protection equipment.

GOGGLES	Proper eye protection must be worn when performing or observing science activities which involve items or conditions as listed below.	**APRON**	Wear an approved apron when using substances that could stain, wet, or destroy cloth.	**SOAP**	Wash hands with soap and water before removing goggles and after all lab activities.	**GLOVES**	Wear gloves when working with biological materials, chemicals, animals, or materials that can stain or irritate hands.

LABORATORY HAZARDS

Symbols	Potential Hazards	Precaution	Response
DISPOSAL	contamination of classroom or environment due to improper disposal of materials such as chemicals and live specimens	• DO NOT dispose of hazardous materials in the sink or trash can. • Dispose of wastes as directed by your teacher.	• If hazardous materials are disposed of improperly, notify your teacher immediately.
EXTREME TEMPERATURE	skin burns due to extremely hot or cold materials such as hot glass, liquids, or metals; liquid nitrogen; dry ice	• Use proper protective equipment, such as hot mitts and/or tongs, when handling objects with extreme temperatures.	• If injury occurs, notify your teacher immediately.
SHARP OBJECTS	punctures or cuts from sharp objects such as razor blades, pins, scalpels, and broken glass	• Handle glassware carefully to avoid breakage. • Walk with sharp objects pointed downward, away from you and others.	• If broken glass or injury occurs, notify your teacher immediately.
ELECTRICAL	electric shock or skin burn due to improper grounding, short circuits, liquid spills, or exposed wires	• Check condition of wires and apparatus for fraying or uninsulated wires, and broken or cracked equipment. • Use only GFCI-protected outlets	• DO NOT attempt to fix electrical problems. Notify your teacher immediately.
CHEMICAL	skin irritation or burns, breathing difficulty, and/or poisoning due to touching, swallowing, or inhalation of chemicals such as acids, bases, bleach, metal compounds, iodine, poinsettias, pollen, ammonia, acetone, nail polish remover, heated chemicals, mothballs, and any other chemicals labeled or known to be dangerous	• Wear proper protective equipment such as goggles, apron, and gloves when using chemicals. • Ensure proper room ventilation or use a fume hood when using materials that produce fumes. • NEVER smell fumes directly. • NEVER taste or eat any material in the laboratory.	• If contact occurs, immediately flush affected area with water and notify your teacher. • If a spill occurs, leave the area immediately and notify your teacher.
FLAMMABLE	unexpected fire due to liquids or gases that ignite easily such as rubbing alcohol	• Avoid open flames, sparks, or heat when flammable liquids are present.	• If a fire occurs, leave the area immediately and notify your teacher.
OPEN FLAME	burns or fire due to open flame from matches, Bunsen burners, or burning materials	• Tie back loose hair and clothing. • Keep flame away from all materials. • Follow teacher instructions when lighting and extinguishing flames. • Use proper protection, such as hot mitts or tongs, when handling hot objects.	• If a fire occurs, leave the area immediately and notify your teacher.
ANIMAL SAFETY	injury to or from laboratory animals	• Wear proper protective equipment such as gloves, apron, and goggles when working with animals. • Wash hands after handling animals.	• If injury occurs, notify your teacher immediately.
BIOLOGICAL	infection or adverse reaction due to contact with organisms such as bacteria, fungi, and biological materials such as blood, animal or plant materials	• Wear proper protective equipment such as gloves, goggles, and apron when working with biological materials. • Avoid skin contact with an organism or any part of the organism. • Wash hands after handling organisms.	• If contact occurs, wash the affected area and notify your teacher immediately.
FUME	breathing difficulties from inhalation of fumes from substances such as ammonia, acetone, nail polish remover, heated chemicals, and mothballs	• Wear goggles, apron, and gloves. • Ensure proper room ventilation or use a fume hood when using substances that produce fumes. • NEVER smell fumes directly.	• If a spill occurs, leave area and notify your teacher immediately.
IRRITANT	irritation of skin, mucous membranes, or respiratory tract due to materials such as acids, bases, bleach, pollen, mothballs, steel wool, and potassium permanganate	• Wear goggles, apron, and gloves. • Wear a dust mask to protect against fine particles.	• If skin contact occurs, immediately flush the affected area with water and notify your teacher.
RADIOACTIVE	excessive exposure from alpha, beta, and gamma particles	• Remove gloves and wash hands with soap and water before removing remainder of protective equipment.	• If cracks or holes are found in the container, notify your teacher immediately.

Safety in the Science Laboratory

Introduction to Science Safety

The science laboratory is a safe place to work if you follow standard safety procedures. Being responsible for your own safety helps to make the entire laboratory a safer place for everyone. When performing any lab, read and apply the caution statements and safety symbol listed at the beginning of the lab.

General Safety Rules

1. Complete the *Lab Safety Form* or other safety contract BEFORE starting any science lab.
2. Study the procedure. Ask your teacher any questions. Be sure you understand safety symbols shown on the page.
3. Notify your teacher about allergies or other health conditions which can affect your participation in a lab.
4. Learn and follow use and safety procedures for your equipment. If unsure, ask your teacher.

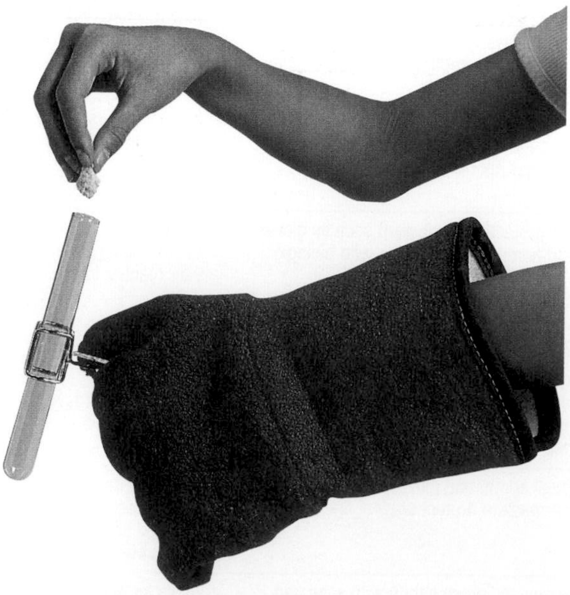

5. Never eat, drink, chew gum, apply cosmetics, or do any personal grooming in the lab. Never use lab glassware as food or drink containers. Keep your hands away from your face and mouth.
6. Know the location and proper use of the safety shower, eye wash, fire blanket, and fire alarm.

Prevent Accidents

1. Use the safety equipment provided to you. Goggles and a safety apron should be worn during investigations.
2. Do NOT use hair spray, mousse, or other flammable hair products. Tie back long hair and tie down loose clothing.
3. Do NOT wear sandals or other open-toed shoes in the lab.
4. Remove jewelry on hands and wrists. Loose jewelry, such as chains and long necklaces, should be removed to prevent them from getting caught in equipment.
5. Do not taste any substances or draw any material into a tube with your mouth.
6. Proper behavior is expected in the lab. Practical jokes and fooling around can lead to accidents and injury.
7. Keep your work area uncluttered.

Laboratory Work

1. Collect and carry all equipment and materials to your work area before beginning a lab.
2. Remain in your own work area unless given permission by your teacher to leave it.

3. Always slant test tubes away from yourself and others when heating them, adding substances to them, or rinsing them.
4. If instructed to smell a substance in a container, hold the container a short distance away and fan vapors towards your nose.
5. Do NOT substitute other chemicals/substances for those in the materials list unless instructed to do so by your teacher.
6. Do NOT take any materials or chemicals outside of the laboratory.
7. Stay out of storage areas unless instructed to be there and supervised by your teacher.

Laboratory Cleanup

1. Turn off all burners, water, and gas, and disconnect all electrical devices.
2. Clean all pieces of equipment and return all materials to their proper places.
3. Dispose of chemicals and other materials as directed by your teacher. Place broken glass and solid substances in the proper containers. Never discard materials in the sink.
4. Clean your work area.
5. Wash your hands with soap and water thoroughly BEFORE removing your goggles.

Emergencies

1. Report any fire, electrical shock, glassware breakage, spill, or injury, no matter how small, to your teacher immediately. Follow his or her instructions.
2. If your clothing should catch fire, STOP, DROP, and ROLL. If possible, smother it with the fire blanket or get under a safety shower. NEVER RUN.
3. If a fire should occur, turn off all gas and leave the room according to established procedures.
4. In most instances, your teacher will clean up spills. Do NOT attempt to clean up spills unless you are given permission and instructions to do so.
5. If chemicals come into contact with your eyes or skin, notify your teacher immediately. Use the eyewash, or flush your skin or eyes with large quantities of water.
6. The fire extinguisher and first-aid kit should only be used by your teacher unless it is an extreme emergency and you have been given permission.
7. If someone is injured or becomes ill, only a professional medical provider or someone certified in first aid should perform first-aid procedures.

Math Review

Use Fractions

A fraction compares a part to a whole. In the fraction $\frac{2}{3}$, the 2 represents the part and is the numerator. The 3 represents the whole and is the denominator.

Reduce Fractions To reduce a fraction, you must find the largest factor that is common to both the numerator and the denominator, the greatest common factor (GCF). Divide both numbers by the GCF. The fraction has then been reduced, or it is in its simplest form.

Example

Twelve of the 20 chemicals in the science lab are in powder form. What fraction of the chemicals used in the lab are in powder form?

Step 1 Write the fraction.

$\frac{\text{part}}{\text{whole}} = \frac{12}{20}$

Step 2 To find the GCF of the numerator and denominator, list all of the factors of each number.

Factors of 12: 1, 2, 3, 4, 6, 12
(the numbers that divide evenly into 12)

Factors of 20: 1, 2, 4, 5, 10, 20
(the numbers that divide evenly into 20)

Step 3 List the common factors.

1, 2, 4

Step 4 Choose the greatest factor in the list. The GCF of 12 and 20 is 4.

Step 5 Divide the numerator and denominator by the GCF.

$\frac{12 \div 4}{20 \div 4} = \frac{3}{5}$

In the lab, $\frac{3}{5}$ of the chemicals are in powder form.

Practice Problem At an amusement park, 66 of 90 rides have a height restriction. What fraction of the rides, in its simplest form, has a height restriction?

Add and Subtract Fractions with Like Denominators To add or subtract fractions with the same denominator, add or subtract the numerators and write the sum or difference over the denominator. After finding the sum or difference, find the simplest form for your fraction.

Example 1

In the forest outside your house, $\frac{1}{8}$ of the animals are rabbits, $\frac{3}{8}$ are squirrels, and the remainder are birds and insects. How many are mammals?

Step 1 Add the numerators.

$\frac{1}{8} + \frac{3}{8} = \frac{(1 + 3)}{8} = \frac{4}{8}$

Step 2 Find the GCF.

$\frac{4}{8}$ (GCF, 4)

Step 3 Divide the numerator and denominator by the GCF.

$\frac{4 \div 4}{8 \div 4} = \frac{1}{2}$

$\frac{1}{2}$ of the animals are mammals.

Example 2

If $\frac{7}{16}$ of the Earth is covered by freshwater, and $\frac{1}{16}$ of that is in glaciers, how much freshwater is not frozen?

Step 1 Subtract the numerators.

$\frac{7}{16} - \frac{1}{16} = \frac{(7 - 1)}{16} = \frac{6}{16}$

Step 2 Find the GCF.

$\frac{6}{16}$ (GCF, 2)

Step 3 Divide the numerator and denominator by the GCF.

$\frac{6 \div 2}{16 \div 2} = \frac{3}{8}$

$\frac{3}{8}$ of the freshwater is not frozen.

Practice Problem A bicycle rider is riding at a rate of 15 km/h for $\frac{4}{9}$ of his ride, 10 km/h for $\frac{2}{9}$ of his ride, and 8 km/h for the remainder of the ride. How much of his ride is he riding at a rate greater than 8 km/h?

Add and Subtract Fractions with Unlike Denominators To add or subtract fractions with unlike denominators, first find the least common denominator (LCD). This is the smallest number that is a common multiple of both denominators. Rename each fraction with the LCD, and then add or subtract. Find the simplest form if necessary.

Example 1

A chemist makes a paste that is $\frac{1}{2}$ table salt (NaCl), $\frac{1}{3}$ sugar ($C_6H_{12}O_6$), and the remainder is water (H_2O). How much of the paste is a solid?

Step 1 Find the LCD of the fractions.

$\frac{1}{2} + \frac{1}{3}$ (LCD, 6)

Step 2 Rename each numerator and each denominator with the LCD.

Step 3 Add the numerators.

$\frac{3}{6} + \frac{2}{6} = \frac{(3 + 2)}{6} = \frac{5}{6}$

$\frac{5}{6}$ of the paste is a solid.

Example 2

The average precipitation in Grand Junction, CO, is $\frac{7}{10}$ inch in November, and $\frac{3}{5}$ inch in December. What is the total average precipitation?

Step 1 Find the LCD of the fractions.

$\frac{7}{10} + \frac{3}{5}$ (LCD, 10)

Step 2 Rename each numerator and each denominator with the LCD.

Step 3 Add the numerators.

$\frac{7}{10} + \frac{6}{10} = \frac{(7 + 6)}{10} = \frac{13}{10}$

$\frac{13}{10}$ inches total precipitation, or $1\frac{3}{10}$ inches.

Practice Problem On an electric bill, about $\frac{1}{8}$ of the energy is from solar energy and about $\frac{1}{10}$ is from wind power. How much of the total bill is from solar energy and wind power combined?

Example 3

In your body, $\frac{7}{10}$ of your muscle contractions are involuntary (cardiac and smooth muscle tissue). Smooth muscle makes $\frac{3}{15}$ of your muscle contractions. How many of your muscle contractions are made by cardiac muscle?

Step 1 Find the LCD of the fractions.

$\frac{7}{10} - \frac{3}{15}$ (LCD, 30)

Step 2 Rename each numerator and each denominator with the LCD.

$\frac{7 \times 3}{10 \times 3} = \frac{21}{30}$

$\frac{3 \times 2}{15 \times 2} = \frac{6}{30}$

Step 3 Subtract the numerators.

$\frac{21}{30} - \frac{6}{30} = \frac{(21 - 6)}{30} = \frac{15}{30}$

Step 4 Find the GCF.

$\frac{15}{30}$ (GCF, 15)

$\frac{1}{2}$

$\frac{1}{2}$ of all muscle contractions are cardiac muscle.

Example 4

Tony wants to make cookies that call for $\frac{3}{4}$ of a cup of flour, but he only has $\frac{1}{3}$ of a cup. How much more flour does he need?

Step 1 Find the LCD of the fractions.

$\frac{3}{4} - \frac{1}{3}$ (LCD, 12)

Step 2 Rename each numerator and each denominator with the LCD.

$\frac{3 \times 3}{4 \times 3} = \frac{9}{12}$

$\frac{1 \times 4}{3 \times 4} = \frac{4}{12}$

Step 3 Subtract the numerators.

$\frac{9}{12} - \frac{4}{12} = \frac{(9 - 4)}{12} = \frac{5}{12}$

$\frac{5}{12}$ of a cup of flour

Practice Problem Using the information provided to you in Example 3 above, determine how many muscle contractions are voluntary (skeletal muscle).

Multiply Fractions To multiply with fractions, multiply the numerators and multiply the denominators. Find the simplest form if necessary.

Example

Multiply $\frac{3}{5}$ by $\frac{1}{3}$.

Step 1 Multiply the numerators and denominators.

$$\frac{3}{5} \times \frac{1}{3} = \frac{(3 \times 1)}{(5 \times 3)} \; \frac{3}{15}$$

Step 2 Find the GCF.

$\frac{3}{15}$ (GCF, 3)

Step 3 Divide the numerator and denominator by the GCF.

$$\frac{3 \div 3}{15 \div 3} = \frac{1}{5}$$

$\frac{3}{5}$ multiplied by $\frac{1}{3}$ is $\frac{1}{5}$.

Practice Problem Multiply $\frac{3}{14}$ by $\frac{5}{16}$.

Find a Reciprocal Two numbers whose product is 1 are called multiplicative inverses, or reciprocals.

Example

Find the reciprocal of $\frac{3}{8}$.

Step 1 Inverse the fraction by putting the denominator on top and the numerator on the bottom.

$\frac{8}{3}$

The reciprocal of $\frac{3}{8}$ is $\frac{8}{3}$.

Practice Problem Find the reciprocal of $\frac{4}{9}$.

Divide Fractions To divide one fraction by another fraction, multiply the dividend by the reciprocal of the divisor. Find the simplest form if necessary.

Example 1

Divide $\frac{1}{9}$ by $\frac{1}{3}$.

Step 1 Find the reciprocal of the divisor.

The reciprocal of $\frac{1}{3}$ is $\frac{3}{1}$.

Step 2 Multiply the dividend by the reciprocal of the divisor.

$$\frac{\frac{1}{9}}{\frac{1}{3}} = \frac{1}{9} \times \frac{3}{1} = \frac{(1 \times 3)}{(9 \times 1)} = \frac{3}{9}$$

Step 3 Find the GCF.

$\frac{3}{9}$ (GCF, 3)

Step 4 Divide the numerator and denominator by the GCF.

$$\frac{3 \div 3}{9 \div 3} = \frac{1}{3}$$

$\frac{1}{9}$ divided by $\frac{1}{3}$ is $\frac{1}{3}$.

Example 2

Divide $\frac{3}{5}$ by $\frac{1}{4}$.

Step 1 Find the reciprocal of the divisor.

The reciprocal of $\frac{1}{4}$ is $\frac{4}{1}$.

Step 2 Multiply the dividend by the reciprocal of the divisor.

$$\frac{\frac{3}{5}}{\frac{1}{4}} = \frac{3}{5} \times \frac{4}{1} = \frac{(3 \times 4)}{(5 \times 1)} = \frac{12}{5}$$

$\frac{3}{5}$ divided by $\frac{1}{4}$ is $\frac{12}{5}$ or $2\frac{2}{5}$.

Practice Problem Divide $\frac{3}{11}$ by $\frac{7}{10}$.

Use Ratios

When you compare two numbers by division, you are using a ratio. Ratios can be written 3 to 5, 3:5, or $\frac{3}{5}$. Ratios, like fractions, also can be written in simplest form.

Ratios can represent one type of probability, called odds. This is a ratio that compares the number of ways a certain outcome occurs to the number of possible outcomes. For example, if you flip a coin 100 times, what are the odds that it will come up heads? There are two possible outcomes, heads or tails, so the odds of coming up heads are 50:100. Another way to say this is that 50 out of 100 times the coin will come up heads. In its simplest form, the ratio is 1:2.

Example 1

A chemical solution contains 40 g of salt and 64 g of baking soda. What is the ratio of salt to baking soda as a fraction in simplest form?

Step 1 Write the ratio as a fraction.

$$\frac{\text{salt}}{\text{baking soda}} = \frac{40}{64}$$

Step 2 Express the fraction in simplest form. The GCF of 40 and 64 is 8.

$$\frac{40}{64} = \frac{40 \div 8}{64 \div 8} = \frac{5}{8}$$

The ratio of salt to baking soda in the sample is 5:8.

Example 2

Sean rolls a 6-sided die 6 times. What are the odds that the side with a 3 will show?

Step 1 Write the ratio as a fraction.

$$\frac{\text{number of sides with a 3}}{\text{number of possible sides}} = \frac{1}{6}$$

Step 2 Multiply by the number of attempts.

$\frac{1}{6} \times 6$ attempts $= \frac{6}{6}$ attempts $= 1$ attempt

1 attempt out of 6 will show a 3.

Practice Problem Two metal rods measure 100 cm and 144 cm in length. What is the ratio of their lengths in simplest form?

Use Decimals

A fraction with a denominator that is a power of ten can be written as a decimal. For example, 0.27 means $\frac{27}{100}$. The decimal point separates the ones place from the tenths place.

Any fraction can be written as a decimal using division. For example, the fraction $\frac{5}{8}$ can be written as a decimal by dividing 5 by 8. Written as a decimal, it is 0.625.

Add or Subtract Decimals When adding and subtracting decimals, line up the decimal points before carrying out the operation.

Example 1

Find the sum of 47.68 and 7.80.

Step 1 Line up the decimal places when you write the numbers.

$$\begin{array}{r} 47.68 \\ +\ 7.80 \\ \hline \end{array}$$

Step 2 Add the decimals.

$$\begin{array}{r} \scriptstyle 1\ 1 \\ 47.68 \\ +\ 7.80 \\ \hline 55.48 \end{array}$$

The sum of 47.68 and 7.80 is 55.48.

Example 2

Find the difference of 42.17 and 15.85.

Step 1 Line up the decimal places when you write the number.

$$\begin{array}{r} 42.17 \\ -15.85 \\ \hline \end{array}$$

Step 2 Subtract the decimals.

$$\begin{array}{r} \scriptstyle 3\ 11\ 1 \\ 42.17 \\ -15.85 \\ \hline 26.32 \end{array}$$

The difference of 42.17 and 15.85 is 26.32.

Practice Problem Find the sum of 1.245 and 3.842.

Multiply Decimals To multiply decimals, multiply the numbers like numbers without decimal points. Count the decimal places in each factor. The product will have the same number of decimal places as the sum of the decimal places in the factors.

Example

Multiply 2.4 by 5.9.

Step 1 Multiply the factors like two whole numbers.

$24 \times 59 = 1416$

Step 2 Find the sum of the number of decimal places in the factors. Each factor has one decimal place, for a sum of two decimal places.

Step 3 The product will have two decimal places.

14.16

The product of 2.4 and 5.9 is 14.16.

Practice Problem Multiply 4.6 by 2.2.

Divide Decimals When dividing decimals, change the divisor to a whole number. To do this, multiply both the divisor and the dividend by the same power of ten. Then place the decimal point in the quotient directly above the decimal point in the dividend. Then divide as you do with whole numbers.

Example

Divide 8.84 by 3.4.

Step 1 Multiply both factors by 10.

$3.4 \times 10 = 34, 8.84 \times 10 = 88.4$

Step 2 Divide 88.4 by 34.

$$\begin{array}{r} 2.6 \\ 34\overline{)88.4} \\ -68 \\ \hline 204 \\ -204 \\ \hline 0 \end{array}$$

8.84 divided by 3.4 is 2.6.

Practice Problem Divide 75.6 by 3.6.

Use Proportions

An equation that shows that two ratios are equivalent is a proportion. The ratios $\frac{2}{4}$ and $\frac{5}{10}$ are equivalent, so they can be written as $\frac{2}{4} = \frac{5}{10}$. This equation is a proportion.

When two ratios form a proportion, the cross products are equal. To find the cross products in the proportion $\frac{2}{4} = \frac{5}{10}$, multiply the 2 and the 10, and the 4 and the 5. Therefore $2 \times 10 = 4 \times 5$, or $20 = 20$.

Because you know that both ratios are equal, you can use cross products to find a missing term in a proportion. This is known as solving the proportion.

Example

The heights of a tree and a pole are proportional to the lengths of their shadows. The tree casts a shadow of 24 m when a 6-m pole casts a shadow of 4 m. What is the height of the tree?

Step 1 Write a proportion.

$$\frac{\text{height of tree}}{\text{height of pole}} = \frac{\text{length of tree's shadow}}{\text{length of pole's shadow}}$$

Step 2 Substitute the known values into the proportion. Let *h* represent the unknown value, the height of the tree.

$\frac{h}{6} \times \frac{24}{4}$

Step 3 Find the cross products.

$h \times 4 = 6 \times 24$

Step 4 Simplify the equation.

$4h \times 144$

Step 5 Divide each side by 4.

$\frac{4h}{4} \times \frac{144}{4}$

$h = 36$

The height of the tree is 36 m.

Practice Problem The ratios of the weights of two objects on the Moon and on Earth are in proportion. A rock weighing 3 N on the Moon weighs 18 N on Earth. How much would a rock that weighs 5 N on the Moon weigh on Earth?

Use Percentages

The word *percent* means "out of one hundred." It is a ratio that compares a number to 100. Suppose you read that 77 percent of Earth's surface is covered by water. That is the same as reading that the fraction of Earth's surface covered by water is $\frac{77}{100}$. To express a fraction as a percent, first find the equivalent decimal for the fraction. Then, multiply the decimal by 100 and add the percent symbol.

Example 1

Express $\frac{13}{20}$ as a percent.

Step 1 Find the equivalent decimal for the fraction.

$$\begin{array}{r} 0.65 \\ 20\overline{)13.00} \\ \underline{12\ 0} \\ 1\ 00 \\ \underline{1\ 00} \\ 0 \end{array}$$

Step 2 Rewrite the fraction $\frac{13}{20}$ as 0.65.

Step 3 Multiply 0.65 by 100 and add the % symbol.

$$0.65 \times 100 = 65 = 65\%$$

So, $\frac{13}{20} = 65\%$.

This also can be solved as a proportion.

Example 2

Express $\frac{13}{20}$ as a percent.

Step 1 Write a proportion.

$$\frac{13}{20} = \frac{x}{100}$$

Step 2 Find the cross products.

$$1300 = 20x$$

Step 3 Divide each side by 20.

$$\frac{1300}{20} = \frac{20x}{20}$$

$$65\% = x$$

Practice Problem In one year, 73 of 365 days were rainy in one city. What percent of the days in that city were rainy?

Solve One-Step Equations

A statement that two expressions are equal is an equation. For example, $A = B$ is an equation that states that A is equal to B.

An equation is solved when a variable is replaced with a value that makes both sides of the equation equal. To make both sides equal the inverse operation is used. Addition and subtraction are inverses, and multiplication and division are inverses.

Example 1

Solve the equation $x - 10 = 35$.

Step 1 Find the solution by adding 10 to each side of the equation.

$$x - 10 = 35$$
$$x - 10 + 10 = 35 - 10$$
$$x = 45$$

Step 2 Check the solution.

$$x - 10 = 35$$
$$45 - 10 = 35$$
$$35 = 35$$

Both sides of the equation are equal, so $x = 45$.

Example 2

In the formula $a = bc$, find the value of c if $a = 20$ and $b = 2$.

Step 1 Rearrange the formula so the unknown value is by itself on one side of the equation by dividing both sides by b.

$$a = bc$$
$$\frac{a}{b} = \frac{bc}{b}$$
$$\frac{a}{b} = c$$

Step 2 Replace the variables a and b with the values that are given.

$$\frac{a}{b} = c$$
$$\frac{20}{2} = c$$
$$10 = c$$

Step 3 Check the solution.

$$a = bc$$
$$20 = 2 \times 10$$
$$20 = 20$$

Both sides of the equation are equal, so $c = 10$ is the solution when $a = 20$ and $b = 2$.

Practice Problem In the formula $h = gd$, find the value of d if $g = 12.3$ and $h = 17.4$.

Use Statistics

The branch of mathematics that deals with collecting, analyzing, and presenting data is statistics. In statistics, there are three common ways to summarize data with a single number—the mean, the median, and the mode.

The **mean** of a set of data is the arithmetic average. It is found by adding the numbers in the data set and dividing by the number of items in the set.

The **median** is the middle number in a set of data when the data are arranged in numerical order. If there were an even number of data points, the median would be the mean of the two middle numbers.

The **mode** of a set of data is the number or item that appears most often.

Another number that often is used to describe a set of data is the range**.** The **range** is the difference between the largest number and the smallest number in a set of data.

Example

The speeds (in m/s) for a race car during five different time trials are 39, 37, 44, 36, and 44.

To find the mean:

Step 1 Find the sum of the numbers.

$39 + 37 + 44 + 36 + 44 = 200$

Step 2 Divide the sum by the number of items, which is 5.

$200 \div 5 = 40$

The mean is 40 m/s.

To find the median:

Step 1 Arrange the measures from least to greatest.

36, 37, 39, 44, 44

Step 2 Determine the middle measure.

36, 37, 39, 44, 44

The median is 39 m/s.

To find the mode:

Step 1 Group the numbers that are the same together.

44, 44, 36, 37, 39

Step 2 Determine the number that occurs most in the set.

44, 44, 36, 37, 39

The mode is 44 m/s.

To find the range:

Step 1 Arrange the measures from greatest to least.

44, 44, 39, 37, 36

Step 2 Determine the greatest and least measures in the set.

44, 44, 39, 37, 36

Step 3 Find the difference between the greatest and least measures.

$44 - 36 = 8$

The range is 8 m/s.

Practice Problem Find the mean, median, mode, and range for the data set 8, 4, 12, 8, 11, 14, 16.

A **frequency table** shows how many times each piece of data occurs, usually in a survey. **Table 1** below shows the results of a student survey on favorite color.

Table 1 Student Color Choice

Color	Tally	Frequency
red	IIII	4
blue	卌	5
black	II	2
green	III	3
purple	卌 II	7
yellow	卌 I	6

Based on the frequency table data, which color is the favorite?

Use Geometry

The branch of mathematics that deals with the measurement, properties, and relationships of points, lines, angles, surfaces, and solids is called geometry.

Perimeter The **perimeter** (P) is the distance around a geometric figure. To find the perimeter of a rectangle, add the length and width and multiply that sum by two, or $2(l + w)$. To find perimeters of irregular figures, add the length of the sides.

Example 1

Find the perimeter of a rectangle that is 3 m long and 5 m wide.

Step 1 You know that the perimeter is 2 times the sum of the width and length.

$P = 2(3 \text{ m} + 5 \text{ m})$

Step 2 Find the sum of the width and length.

$P = 2(8 \text{ m})$

Step 3 Multiply by 2.

$P = 16 \text{ m}$

The perimeter is 16 m.

Example 2

Find the perimeter of a shape with sides measuring 2 cm, 5 cm, 6 cm, 3 cm.

Step 1 You know that the perimeter is the sum of all the sides.

$P = 2 + 5 + 6 + 3$

Step 2 Find the sum of the sides.

$P = 2 + 5 + 6 + 3$

$P = 16$

The perimeter is 16 cm.

Practice Problem Find the perimeter of a rectangle with a length of 18 m and a width of 7 m.

Practice Problem Find the perimeter of a triangle measuring 1.6 cm by 2.4 cm by 2.4 cm.

Area of a Rectangle The **area** (A) is the number of square units needed to cover a surface. To find the area of a rectangle, multiply the length times the width, or $l \times w$. When finding area, the units also are multiplied. Area is given in square units.

Example

Find the area of a rectangle with a length of 1 cm and a width of 10 cm.

Step 1 You know that the area is the length multiplied by the width.

$A = (1 \text{ cm} \times 10 \text{ cm})$

Step 2 Multiply the length by the width. Also multiply the units.

$A = 10 \text{ cm}^2$

The area is 10 cm^2.

Practice Problem Find the area of a square whose sides measure 4 m.

Area of a Triangle To find the area of a triangle, use the formula:

$A = \frac{1}{2}(\text{base} \times \text{height})$

The base of a triangle can be any of its sides. The height is the perpendicular distance from a base to the opposite endpoint, or vertex.

Example

Find the area of a triangle with a base of 18 m and a height of 7 m.

Step 1 You know that the area is $\frac{1}{2}$ the base times the height.

$A = \frac{1}{2}(18 \text{ m} \times 7 \text{ m})$

Step 2 Multiply $\frac{1}{2}$ by the product of 18×7. Multiply the units.

$A = \frac{1}{2}(126 \text{ m}^2)$

$A = 63 \text{ m}^2$

The area is 63 m^2.

Practice Problem Find the area of a triangle with a base of 27 cm and a height of 17 cm.

Circumference of a Circle The **diameter** (d) of a circle is the distance across the circle through its center, and the **radius** (r) is the distance from the center to any point on the circle. The radius is half of the diameter. The distance around the circle is called the **circumference** (C). The formula for finding the circumference is:

$C = 2\pi r$ or $C = \pi d$

The circumference divided by the diameter is always equal to 3.1415926... This nonterminating and nonrepeating number is represented by the Greek letter π (pi). An approximation often used for π is 3.14.

Example 1

Find the circumference of a circle with a radius of 3 m.

Step 1 You know the formula for the circumference is 2 times the radius times π.

$C = 2\pi(3)$

Step 2 Multiply 2 times the radius.

$C = 6\pi$

Step 3 Multiply by π.

$C \approx 19$ m

The circumference is about 19 m.

Example 2

Find the circumference of a circle with a diameter of 24.0 cm.

Step 1 You know the formula for the circumference is the diameter times π.

$C = \pi(24.0)$

Step 2 Multiply the diameter by π.

$C \approx 75.4$ cm

The circumference is about 75.4 cm.

Practice Problem Find the circumference of a circle with a radius of 19 cm.

Area of a Circle The formula for the area of a circle is: $A = \pi r^2$

Example 1

Find the area of a circle with a radius of 4.0 cm.

Step 1 $A = \pi(4.0)^2$

Step 2 Find the square of the radius.

$A = 16\pi$

Step 3 Multiply the square of the radius by π.

$A \approx 50\ cm^2$

The area of the circle is about 50 cm^2.

Example 2

Find the area of a circle with a radius of 225 m.

Step 1 $A = \pi(225)^2$

Step 2 Find the square of the radius.

$A = 50625\pi$

Step 3 Multiply the square of the radius by π.

$A \approx 159043.1$

The area of the circle is about 159043.1 m^2.

Example 3

Find the area of a circle whose diameter is 20.0 mm.

Step 1 Remember that the radius is half of the diameter.

$A = \pi\left(\frac{20.0}{2}\right)^2$

Step 2 Find the radius.

$A = \pi(10.0)^2$

Step 3 Find the square of the radius.

$A = 100\pi$

Step 4 Multiply the square of the radius by π.

$A \approx 314\ mm^2$

The area of the circle is about 314 mm^2.

Practice Problem Find the area of a circle with a radius of 16 m.

Volume The measure of space occupied by a solid is the **volume** (V). To find the volume of a rectangular solid multiply the length times width times height, or $V = l \times w \times h$. It is measured in cubic units, such as cubic centimeters (cm^3).

Example

Find the volume of a rectangular solid with a length of 2.0 m, a width of 4.0 m, and a height of 3.0 m.

Step 1 You know the formula for volume is the length times the width times the height.

$V = 2.0\text{ m} \times 4.0\text{ m} \times 3.0\text{ m}$

Step 2 Multiply the length times the width times the height.

$V = 24\text{ m}^3$

The volume is 24 m^3.

Practice Problem Find the volume of a rectangular solid that is 8 m long, 4 m wide, and 4 m high.

To find the volume of other solids, multiply the area of the base times the height.

Example 1

Find the volume of a solid that has a triangular base with a length of 8.0 m and a height of 7.0 m. The height of the entire solid is 15.0 m.

Step 1 You know that the base is a triangle, and the area of a triangle is $\frac{1}{2}$ the base times the height, and the volume is the area of the base times the height.

$V = \left[\frac{1}{2}(b \times h)\right] \times 15$

Step 2 Find the area of the base.

$V = \left[\frac{1}{2}(8 \times 7)\right] \times 15$

$V = \left(\frac{1}{2} \times 56\right) \times 15$

Step 3 Multiply the area of the base by the height of the solid.

$V = 28 \times 15$

$V = 420\text{ m}^3$

The volume is 420 m^3.

Example 2

Find the volume of a cylinder that has a base with a radius of 12.0 cm, and a height of 21.0 cm.

Step 1 You know that the base is a circle, and the area of a circle is the square of the radius times π, and the volume is the area of the base times the height.

$V = (\pi r^2) \times 21$

$V = (\pi 12^2) \times 21$

Step 2 Find the area of the base.

$V = 144\pi \times 21$

$V = 452 \times 21$

Step 3 Multiply the area of the base by the height of the solid.

$V \approx 9{,}500\text{ cm}^3$

The volume is about 9,500 cm^3.

Example 3

Find the volume of a cylinder that has a diameter of 15 mm and a height of 4.8 mm.

Step 1 You know that the base is a circle with an area equal to the square of the radius times π. The radius is one-half the diameter. The volume is the area of the base times the height.

$V = (\pi r^2) \times 4.8$

$V = \left[\pi\left(\frac{1}{2} \times 15\right)^2\right] \times 4.8$

$V = (\pi 7.5^2) \times 4.8$

Step 2 Find the area of the base.

$V = 56.25\pi \times 4.8$

$V \approx 176.71 \times 4.8$

Step 3 Multiply the area of the base by the height of the solid.

$V \approx 848.2$

The volume is about 848.2 mm^3.

Practice Problem Find the volume of a cylinder with a diameter of 7 cm in the base and a height of 16 cm.

Science Applications

Measure in SI

The metric system of measurement was developed in 1795. A modern form of the metric system, called the International System (SI), was adopted in 1960 and provides the standard measurements that all scientists around the world can understand.

The SI system is convenient because unit sizes vary by powers of 10. Prefixes are used to name units. Look at **Table 2** for some common SI prefixes and their meanings.

Table 2 Common SI Prefixes

Prefix	Symbol	Meaning	
kilo-	k	1,000	thousandth
hecto-	h	100	hundred
deka-	da	10	ten
deci-	d	0.1	tenth
centi-	c	0.01	hundreth
milli-	m	0.001	thousandth

Example

How many grams equal one kilogram?

Step 1 Find the prefix *kilo-* in **Table 2.**

Step 2 Using **Table 2,** determine the meaning of *kilo-*. According to the table, it means 1,000. When the prefix *kilo-* is added to a unit, it means that there are 1,000 of the units in a "kilounit."

Step 3 Apply the prefix to the units in the question. The units in the question are grams. There are 1,000 grams in a kilogram.

Practice Problem Is a milligram larger or smaller than a gram? How many of the smaller units equal one larger unit? What fraction of the larger unit does one smaller unit represent?

Dimensional Analysis

Convert SI Units In science, quantities such as length, mass, and time sometimes are measured using different units. A process called dimensional analysis can be used to change one unit of measure to another. This process involves multiplying your starting quantity and units by one or more conversion factors. A conversion factor is a ratio equal to one and can be made from any two equal quantities with different units. If 1,000 mL equal 1 L then two ratios can be made.

$$\frac{1{,}000\text{ mL}}{1\text{ L}} = \frac{1\text{ L}}{1{,}000\text{ mL}} = 1$$

One can convert between units in the SI system by using the equivalents in **Table 2** to make conversion factors.

Example

How many cm are in 4 m?

Step 1 Write conversion factors for the units given. From **Table 2,** you know that 100 cm = 1 m. The conversion factors are

$$\frac{100\text{ cm}}{1\text{ m}} \text{ and } \frac{1\text{ m}}{100\text{ cm}}$$

Step 2 Decide which conversion factor to use. Select the factor that has the units you are converting from (m) in the denominator and the units you are converting to (cm) in the numerator.

$$\frac{100\text{ cm}}{1\text{ m}}$$

Step 3 Multiply the starting quantity and units by the conversion factor. Cancel the starting units with the units in the denominator. There are 400 cm in 4 m.

$$4\ \cancel{\text{m}} = \frac{100\text{ cm}}{1\ \cancel{\text{m}}} = 400\text{ cm}$$

Practice Problem How many milligrams are in one kilogram? (Hint: You will need to use two conversion factors from **Table 2.**)

Table 3 Unit System Equivalents

Type of Measurement	Equivalent
Length	1 in = 2.54 cm 1 yd = 0.91 m 1 mi = 1.61 km
Mass and weight*	1 oz = 28.35 g 1 lb = 0.45 kg 1 ton (short) = 0.91 tonnes (metric tons) 1 lb = 4.45 N
Volume	1 in^3 = 16.39 cm^3 1 qt = 0.95 L 1 gal = 3.78 L
Area	1 in^2 = 6.45 cm^2 1 yd^2 = 0.83 m^2 1 mi^2 = 2.59 km^2 1 acre = 0.40 hectares
Temperature	$°C = \frac{(°F - 32)}{1.8}$ K = °C + 273

*Weight is measured in standard Earth gravity.

Convert Between Unit Systems **Table 3** gives a list of equivalents that can be used to convert between English and SI units.

Example

If a meterstick has a length of 100 cm, how long is the meterstick in inches?

Step 1 Write the conversion factors for the units given. From **Table 3,** 1 in = 2.54 cm.

$$\frac{1 \text{ in}}{2.54 \text{ cm}} \textit{ and } \frac{2.54 \text{ cm}}{1 \text{ in}}$$

Step 2 Determine which conversion factor to use. You are converting from cm to in. Use the conversion factor with cm on the bottom.

$$\frac{1 \text{ in}}{2.54 \text{ cm}}$$

Step 3 Multiply the starting quantity and units by the conversion factor. Cancel the starting units with the units in the denominator. Round your answer to the nearest tenth.

$$100 \cancel{\text{cm}} \times \frac{1 \text{ in}}{2.54 \cancel{\text{cm}}} = 39.37 \text{ in}$$

The meterstick is about 39.4 in long.

Practice Problem 1 A book has a mass of 5 lb. What is the mass of the book in kg?

Practice Problem 2 Use the equivalent for in and cm (1 in = 2.54 cm) to show how 1 $in^3 \approx$ 16.39 cm^3.

Precision and Significant Digits

When you make a measurement, the value you record depends on the precision of the measuring instrument. This precision is represented by the number of significant digits recorded in the measurement. When counting the number of significant digits, all digits are counted except zeros at the end of a number with no decimal point such as 2,050, and zeros at the beginning of a decimal such as 0.03020. When adding or subtracting numbers with different precision, round the answer to the smallest number of decimal places of any number in the sum or difference. When multiplying or dividing, the answer is rounded to the smallest number of significant digits of any number being multiplied or divided.

Example

The lengths 5.28 and 5.2 are measured in meters. Find the sum of these lengths and record your answer using the correct number of significant digits.

Step 1 Find the sum.

5.28 m	2 digits after the decimal
+ 5.2 m	1 digit after the decimal
10.48 m	

Step 2 Round to one digit after the decimal because the least number of digits after the decimal of the numbers being added is 1.

The sum is 10.5 m.

Practice Problem 1 How many significant digits are in the measurement 7,071,301 m? How many significant digits are in the measurement 0.003010 g?

Practice Problem 2 Multiply 5.28 and 5.2 using the rule for multiplying and dividing. Record the answer using the correct number of significant digits.

Scientific Notation

Many times numbers used in science are very small or very large. Because these numbers are difficult to work with scientists use scientific notation. To write numbers in scientific notation, move the decimal point until only one non-zero digit remains on the left. Then count the number of places you moved the decimal point and use that number as a power of ten. For example, the average distance from the Sun to Mars is 227,800,000,000 m. In scientific notation, this distance is 2.278×10^{11} m. Because you moved the decimal point to the left, the number is a positive power of ten.

The mass of an electron is about 0.000 000 000 000 000 000 000 000 000 000 911 kg. Expressed in scientific notation, this mass is 9.11×10^{-31} kg. Because the decimal point was moved to the right, the number is a negative power of ten.

Example

Earth is 149,600,000 km from the Sun. Express this in scientific notation.

Step 1 Move the decimal point until one non-zero digit remains on the left.

1.496 000 00

Step 2 Count the number of decimal places you have moved. In this case, eight.

Step 2 Show that number as a power of ten, 10^8.

Earth is 1.496×10^8 km from the Sun.

Practice Problem 1 How many significant digits are in 149,600,000 km? How many significant digits are in 1.496×10^8 km?

Practice Problem 2 Parts used in a high performance car must be measured to 7×10^{-6} m. Express this number as a decimal.

Practice Problem 3 A CD is spinning at 539 revolutions per minute. Express this number in scientific notation.

Make and Use Graphs

Data in tables can be displayed in a graph—a visual representation of data. Common graph types include line graphs, bar graphs, and circle graphs.

Line Graph A line graph shows a relationship between two variables that change continuously. The independent variable is changed and is plotted on the x-axis. The dependent variable is observed, and is plotted on the *y*-axis.

Example

Draw a line graph of the data below from a cyclist in a long-distance race.

Table 4 Bicycle Race Data

Time (h)	Distance (km)
0	0
1	8
2	16
3	24
4	32
5	40

Step 1 Determine the *x*-axis and *y*-axis variables. Time varies independently of distance and is plotted on the *x*-axis. Distance is dependent on time and is plotted on the *y*-axis.

Step 2 Determine the scale of each axis. The *x*-axis data ranges from 0 to 5. The *y*-axis data ranges from 0 to 50.

Step 3 Using graph paper, draw and label the axes. Include units in the labels.

Step 4 Draw a point at the intersection of the time value on the *x*-axis and corresponding distance value on the *y*-axis. Connect the points and label the graph with a title, as shown in **Figure 8.**

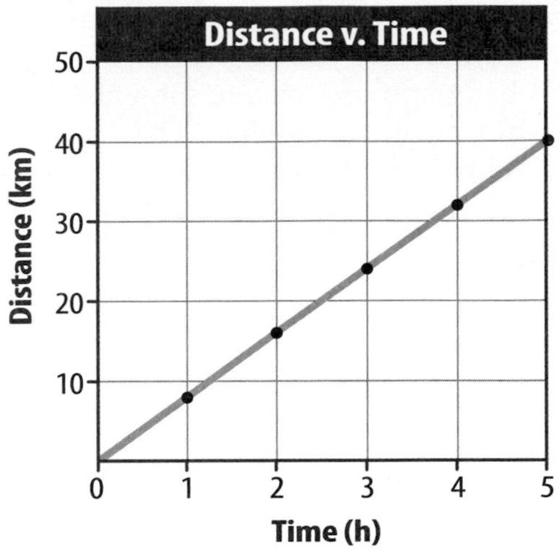

Figure 8 This line graph shows the relationship between distance and time during a bicycle ride.

Practice Problem A puppy's shoulder height is measured during the first year of her life. The following measurements were collected: (3 mo, 52 cm), (6 mo, 72 cm), (9 mo, 83 cm), (12 mo, 86 cm). Graph this data.

Find a Slope The slope of a straight line is the ratio of the vertical change, rise, to the horizontal change, run.

$$\text{Slope} = \frac{\text{vertical change (rise)}}{\text{horizontal change (run)}} = \frac{\text{change in } y}{\text{change in } x}$$

Example

Find the slope of the graph in **Figure 8**.

Step 1 You know that the slope is the change in *y* divided by the change in *x*.

$$\text{Slope} = \frac{\text{change in } y}{\text{change in } x}$$

Step 2 Determine the data points you will be using. For a straight line, choose the two sets of points that are the farthest apart.

$$\text{Slope} = \frac{(40 - 0)\text{ km}}{(5 - 0)\text{ h}}$$

Step 3 Find the change in *y* and *x*.

$$\text{Slope} = \frac{40\text{ km}}{5\text{ h}}$$

Step 4 Divide the change in *y* by the change in *x*.

$$\text{Slope} = \frac{8\text{ km}}{\text{h}}$$

The slope of the graph is 8 km/h.

Bar Graph To compare data that does not change continuously you might choose a bar graph. A bar graph uses bars to show the relationships between variables. The *x*-axis variable is divided into parts. The parts can be numbers such as years, or a category such as a type of animal. The *y*-axis is a number and increases continuously along the axis.

Example

A recycling center collects 4.0 kg of aluminum on Monday, 1.0 kg on Wednesday, and 2.0 kg on Friday. Create a bar graph of this data.

Step 1 Select the *x*-axis and *y*-axis variables. The measured numbers (the masses of aluminum) should be placed on the *y*-axis. The variable divided into parts (collection days) is placed on the *x*-axis.

Step 2 Create a graph grid like you would for a line graph. Include labels and units.

Step 3 For each measured number, draw a vertical bar above the *x*-axis value up to the *y*-axis value. For the first data point, draw a vertical bar above Monday up to 4.0 kg.

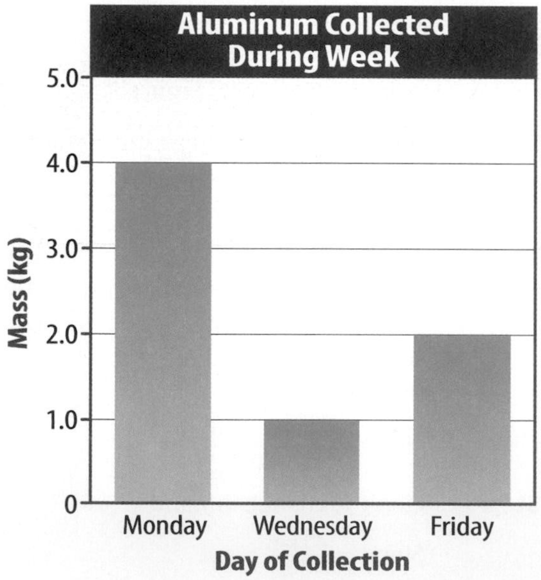

Practice Problem Draw a bar graph of the gases in air: 78% nitrogen, 21% oxygen, 1% other gases.

Circle Graph To display data as parts of a whole, you might use a circle graph. A circle graph is a circle divided into sections that represent the relative size of each piece of data. The entire circle represents 100%, half represents 50%, and so on.

Example

Air is made up of 78% nitrogen, 21% oxygen, and 1% other gases. Display the composition of air in a circle graph.

Step 1 Multiply each percent by 360° and divide by 100 to find the angle of each section in the circle.

$$78\% \times \frac{360°}{100} = 280.8°$$

$$21\% \times \frac{360°}{100} = 75.6°$$

$$1\% \times \frac{360°}{100} = 3.6°$$

Step 2 Use a compass to draw a circle and to mark the center of the circle. Draw a straight line from the center to the edge of the circle.

Step 3 Use a protractor and the angles you calculated to divide the circle into parts. Place the center of the protractor over the center of the circle and line the base of the protractor over the straight line.

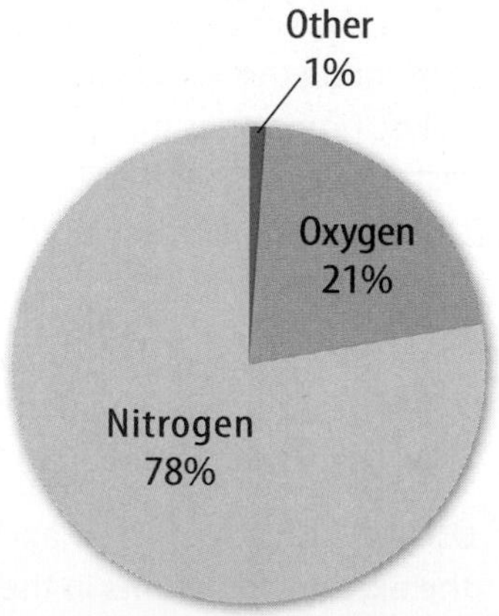

Practice Problem Draw a circle graph to represent the amount of aluminum collected during the week shown in the bar graph to the left.

Student Study Guides & Instructions
By Dinah Zike

1. You will find suggestions for Study Guides, also known as Foldables or books, in each chapter lesson and as a final project. Look at the end of the chapter to determine the project format and glue the Foldables in place as you progress through the chapter lessons.

2. Creating the Foldables or books is simple and easy to do by using copy paper, art paper, and Internet printouts. Photocopies of maps, diagrams, or your own illustrations may also be used for some of the Foldables. Notebook paper is the most common source of material for study guides and 83% of all Foldables are created from it. When folded to make books, notebook paper Foldables easily fit into 11″ × 17″ or 12″ × 18″ chapter projects with space left over. Foldables made using photocopy paper are slightly larger and they fit into Projects, but snugly. Use the least amount of glue, tape, and staples needed to assemble the Foldables.

3. Seven of the Foldables can be made using either small or large paper. When 11″ × 17″ or 12″ × 18″ paper are used, these become projects for housing smaller Foldables. Project format boxes are located within the instructions to remind you of this option.

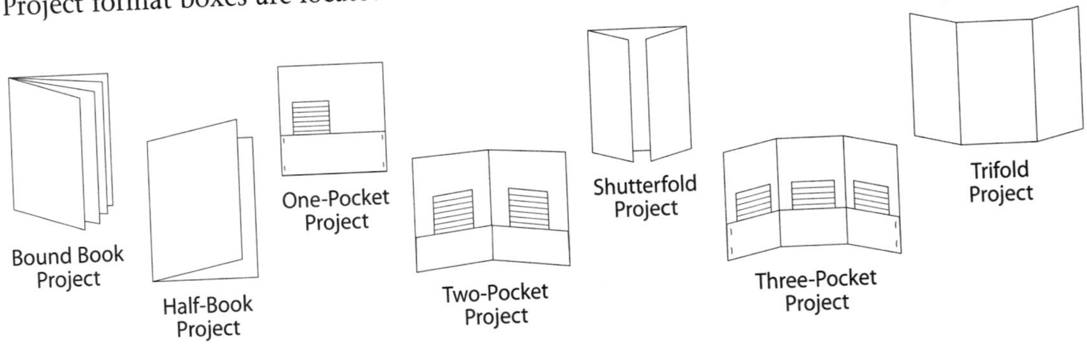

4. Use one-gallon self-locking plastic bags to store your projects. Place strips of two-inch clear tape along the left, long side of the bag and punch holes through the taped edge. Cut the bottom corners off the bag so it will not hold air. Store this Project Portfolio inside a three-hole binder. To store a large collection of project bags, use a giant laundry-soap box. Holes can be punched in some of the Foldable Projects so they can be stored in a three-hole binder without using a plastic bag. Punch holes in the pocket books before gluing or stapling the pocket.

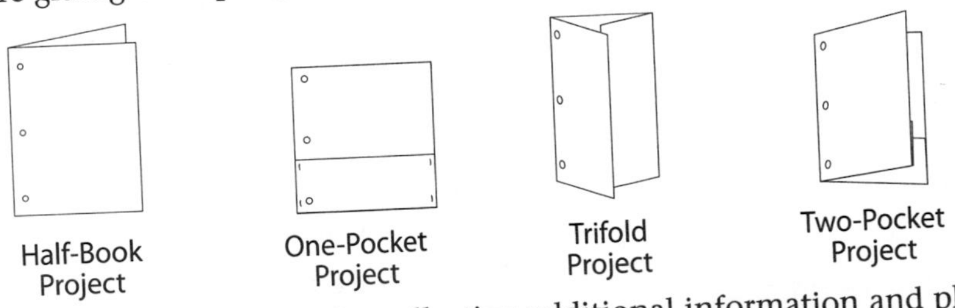

5. Maximize the use of the projects by collecting additional information and placing it on the back of the project and other unused spaces of the large Foldables.

Half-Book Foldable® By Dinah Zike

Step 1 Fold a sheet of notebook or copy paper in half.

Label the exterior tab and use the inside space to write information.

PROJECT FORMAT
Use 11″ × 17″ or 12″ × 18″ paper on the horizontal axis to make a large project book.

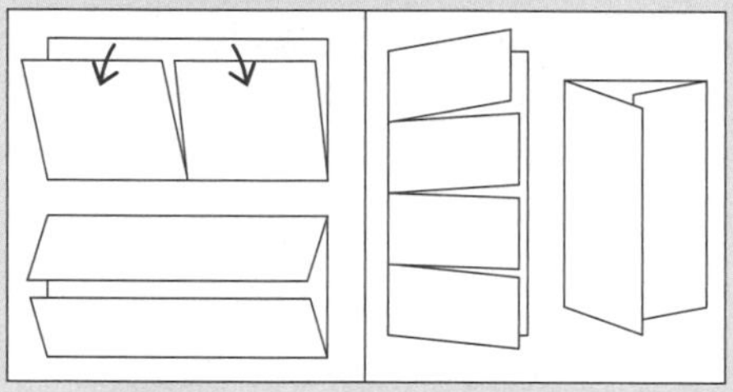

Variations

Paper can be folded vertically, like a *hamburger* or horizontally, like a *hotdog*.

A

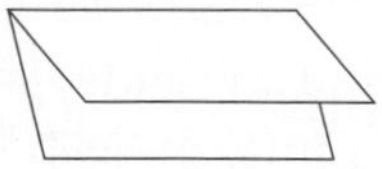

B

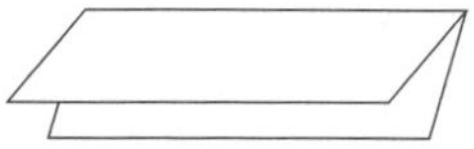

C Half-books can be folded so that one side is ½ inch longer than the other side. A title or question can be written on the extended tab.

Worksheet Foldable or Folded Book® By Dinah Zike

Step 1 Make a half-book (see above) using work sheets, Internet print-outs, diagrams, or maps.

Step 2 Fold it in half again.

Variations

A This folded sheet as a small book with two pages can be used for comparing and contrasting, cause and effect, or other skills.

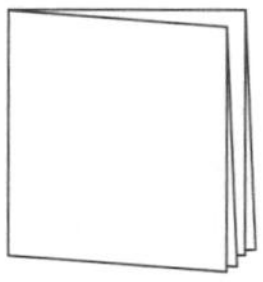

B When the sheet of paper is open, the four sections can be used separately or used collectively to show sequences or steps.

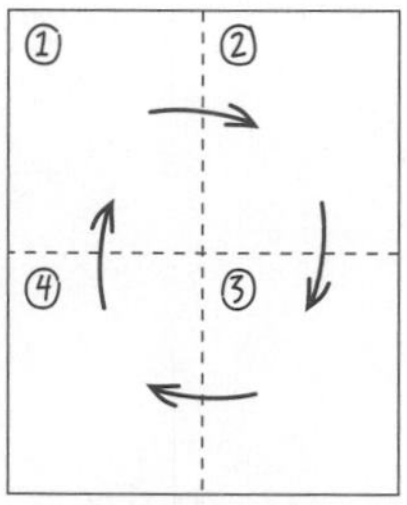

Two-Tab and Concept-Map Foldable® By Dinah Zike

Step 1 Fold a sheet of notebook or copy paper in half vertically or horizontally.

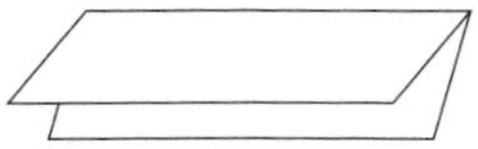

Step 2 Fold it in half again, as shown.

Step 3 Unfold once and cut along the fold line or valley of the top flap to make two flaps.

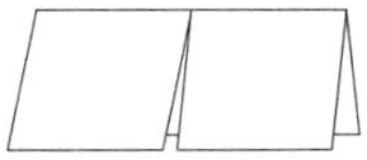

Variations

A Concept maps can be made by leaving a ½ inch tab at the top when folding the paper in half. Use arrows and labels to relate topics to the primary concept.

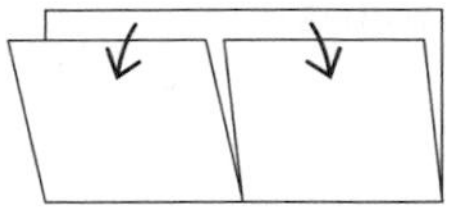

B Use two sheets of paper to make multiple page tab books. Glue or staple books together at the top fold.

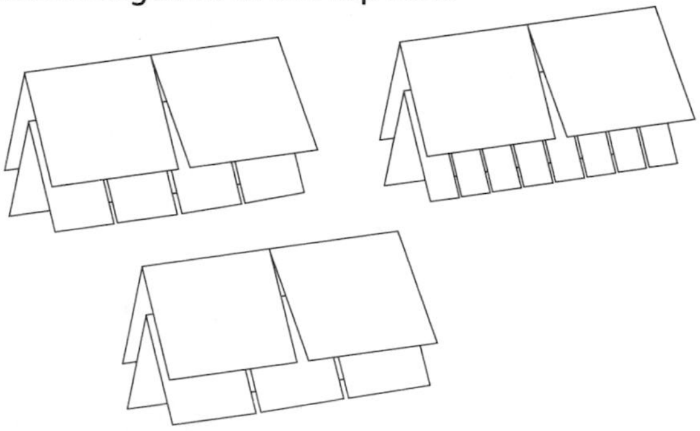

Three-Quarter Foldable® By Dinah Zike

Step 1 Make a two-tab book (see above) and cut the left tab off at the top of the fold line.

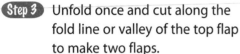

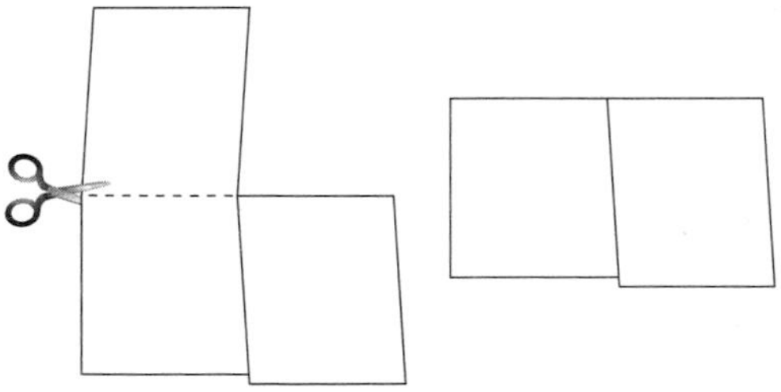

Variations

A Use this book to draw a diagram or a map on the exposed left tab. Write questions about the illustration on the top right tab and provide complete answers on the space under the tab.

B Compose a self-test using multiple choice answers for your questions. Include the correct answer with three wrong responses. The correct answers can be written on the back of the book or upside down on the bottom of the inside page.

Three-Tab Foldable® By Dinah Zike

Step 1 Fold a sheet of paper in half horizontally.

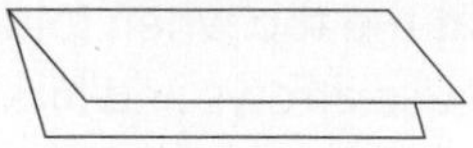

Step 2 Fold into thirds.

Step 3 Unfold and cut along the folds of the top flap to make three sections.

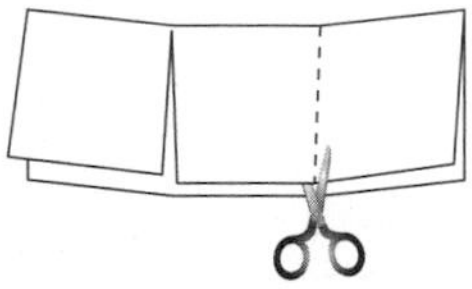

Variations

A Before cutting the three tabs draw a Venn diagram across the front of the book.

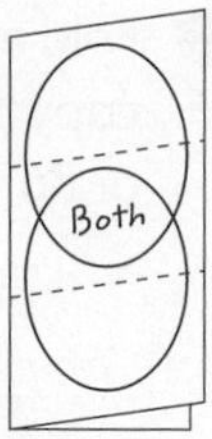

B Make a space to use for titles or concept maps by leaving a ½ inch tab at the top when folding the paper in half.

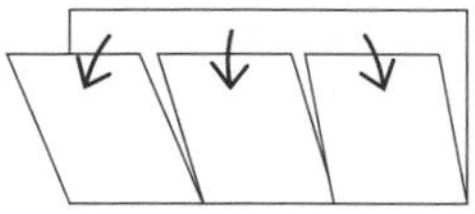

Four-Tab Foldable® By Dinah Zike

Step 1 Fold a sheet of paper in half horizontally.

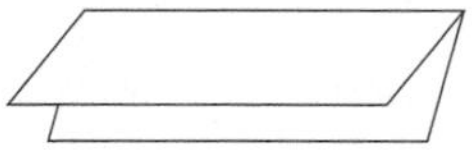

Step 2 Fold in half and then fold each half as shown below.

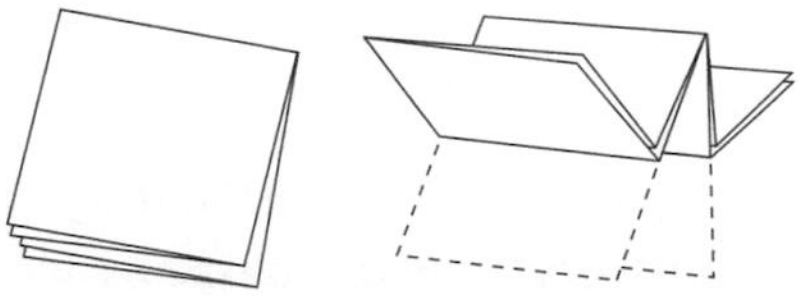

Step 3 Unfold and cut along the fold lines of the top flap to make four tabs.

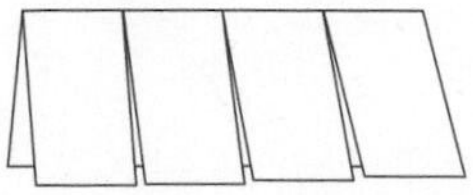

Variations

A Make a space to use for titles or concept maps by leaving a ½ inch tab at the top when folding the paper in half.

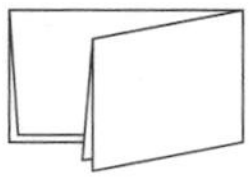

B Use the book on the vertical axis, with or without an extended tab.

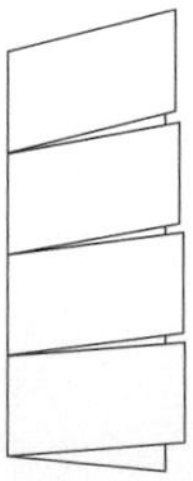

Folding Fifths for a Foldable® By Dinah Zike

Step 1 Fold a sheet of paper in half horizontally.

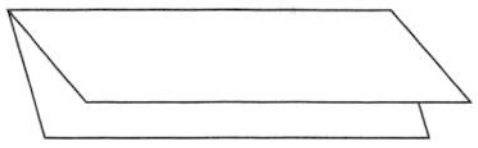

Step 2 Fold again so one-third of the paper is exposed and two-thirds are covered.

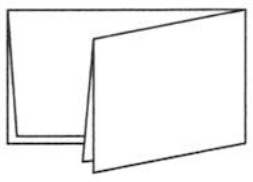

Step 3 Fold the two-thirds section in half.

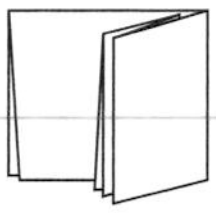

Step 4 Fold the one-third section, a single thickness, backward to make a fold line.

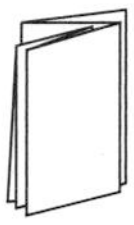

Variations

A Unfold and cut along the fold lines to make five tabs.

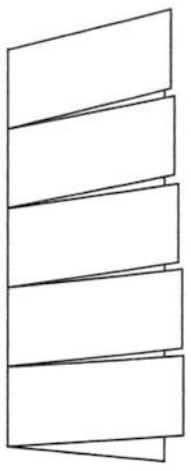

B Make a five-tab book with a ½ inch tab at the top (see two-tab instructions).

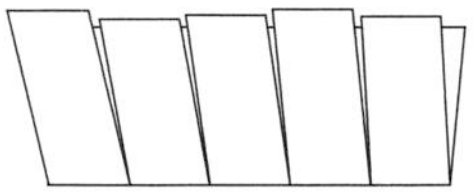

C Use 11″ × 17″ or 12″ × 18″ paper and fold into fifths for a five-column and/or row table or chart.

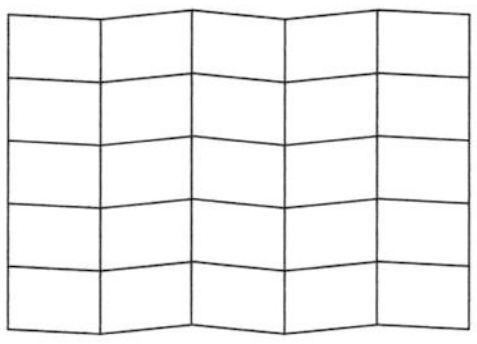

Folded Table or Chart, and Trifold Foldable® By Dinah Zike

Step 1 Fold a sheet of paper in the required number of vertical columns for the table or chart.

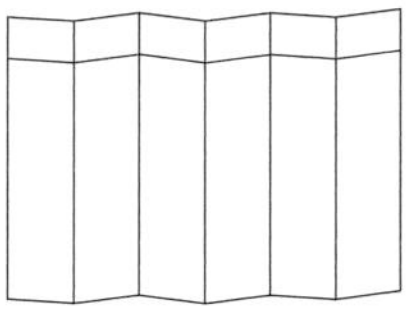

Step 2 Fold the horizontal rows needed for the table or chart.

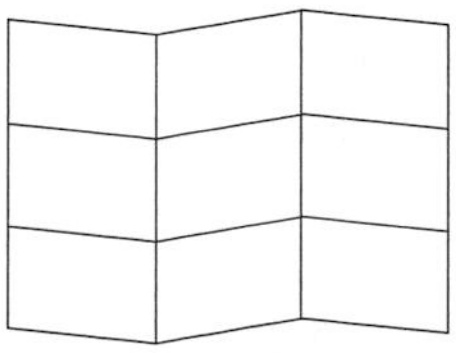

PROJECT FORMAT
Use 11″ × 17″ or 12″ × 18″ paper and fold it to make a large trifold project book or larger tables and charts.

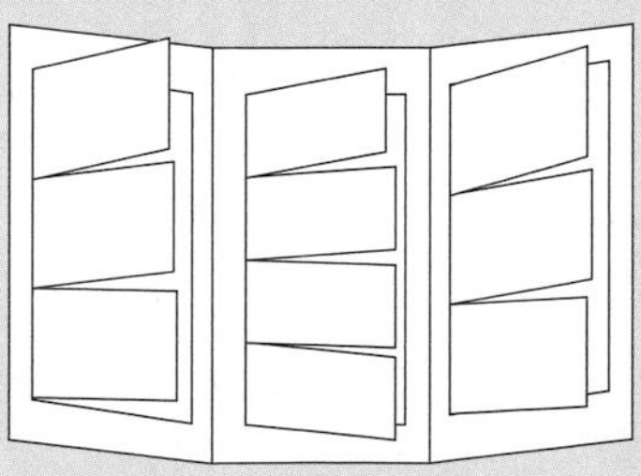

Variations

A Make a trifold by folding the paper into thirds vertically or horizontally.

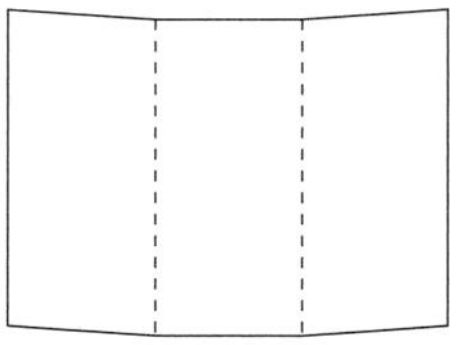

B Make a trifold book. Unfold it and draw a Venn diagram on the inside.

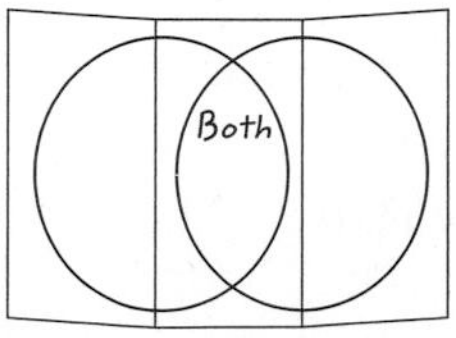

Two or Three-Pockets Foldable® By Dinah Zike

Step 1 Fold up the long side of a horizontal sheet of paper about 5 cm.

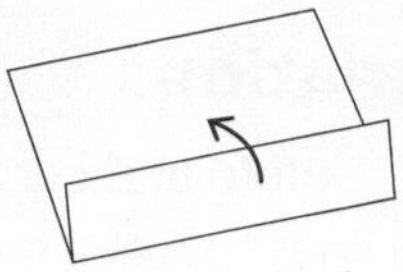

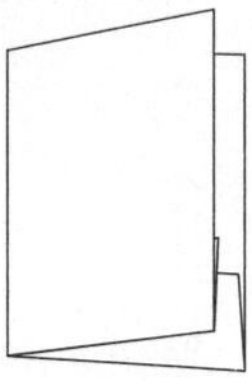

Step 2 Fold the paper in half.

Step 3 Open the paper and glue or staple the outer edges to make two compartments.

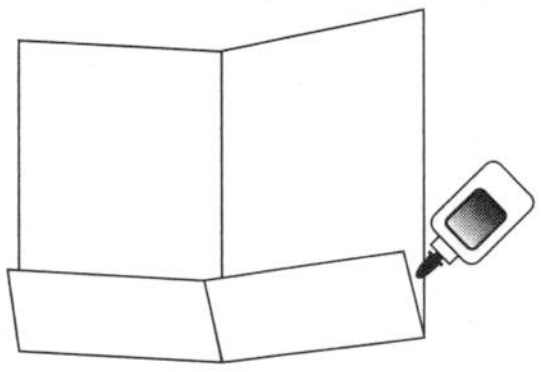

Variations

A Make a multi-page booklet by gluing several pocket books together.

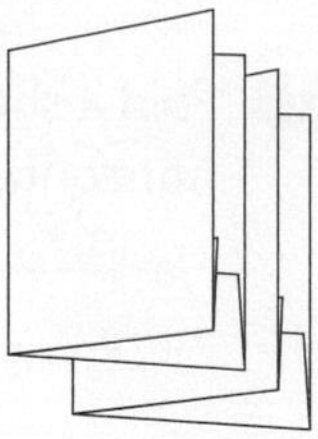

B Make a three-pocket book by using a trifold (see previous instructions).

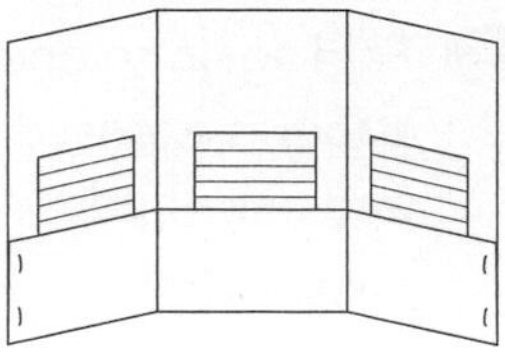

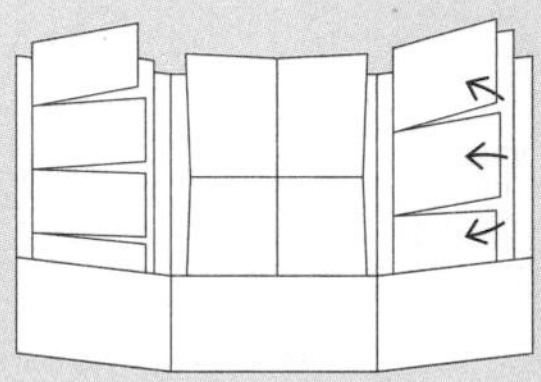

PROJECT FORMAT
Use 11″ × 17″ or 12″ × 18″ paper and fold it horizontally to make a large multi-pocket project.

Matchbook Foldable® By Dinah Zike

Step 1 Fold a sheet of paper almost in half and make the back edge about 1–2 cm longer than the front edge.

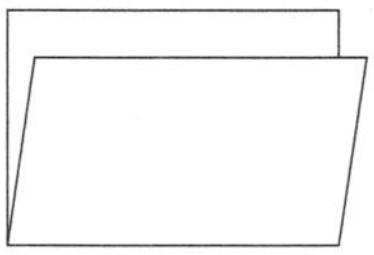

Step 2 Find the midpoint of the shorter flap.

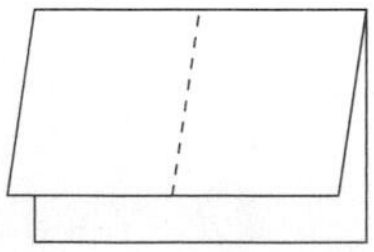

Step 3 Open the paper and cut the short side along the fold lines making two tabs.

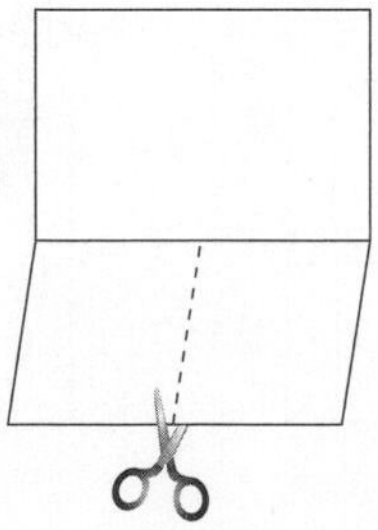

Step 4 Close the book and fold the tab over the short side.

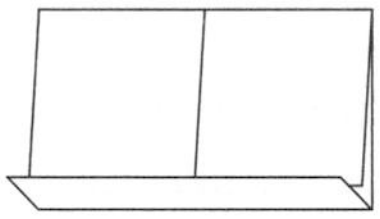

Variations

A Make a single-tab matchbook by skipping Steps 2 and 3.

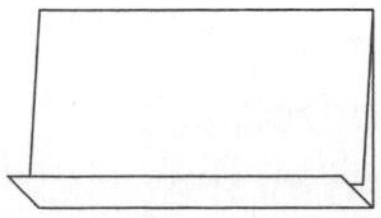

B Make two smaller matchbooks by cutting the single-tab matchbook in half.

Shutterfold Foldable® By Dinah Zike

Step 1 Begin as if you were folding a vertical sheet of paper in half, but instead of creasing the paper, pinch it to show the midpoint.

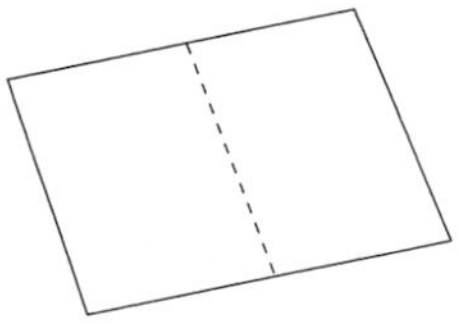

Step 2 Fold the top and bottom to the middle and crease the folds.

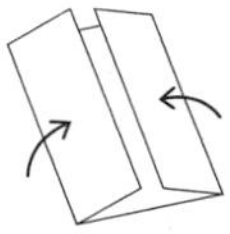

PROJECT FORMAT
Use 11″ × 17″ or 12″ × 18″ paper and fold it to make a large shutterfold project.

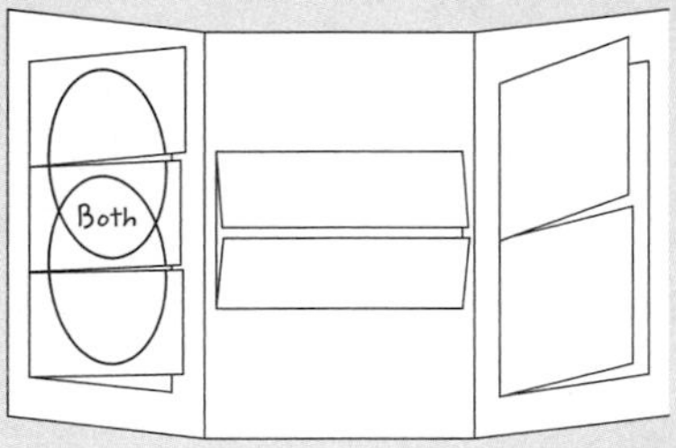

Variations

A Use the shutterfold on the horizontal axis.

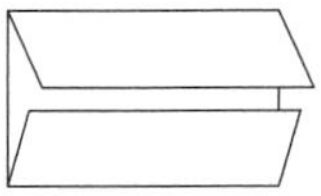

B Create a center tab by leaving .5–2 cm between the flaps in Step 2.

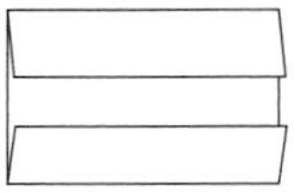

Four-Door Foldable® By Dinah Zike

Step 1 Make a shutterfold (see above).

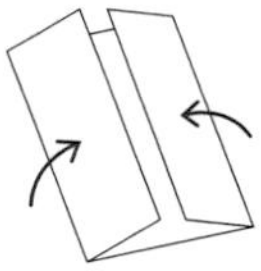

Step 2 Fold the sheet of paper in half.

Step 3 Open the last fold and cut along the inside fold lines to make four tabs.

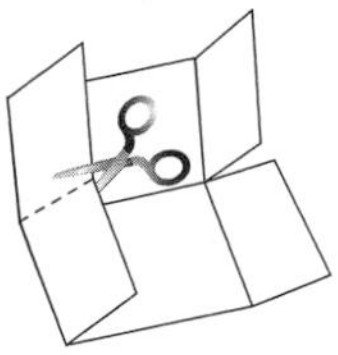

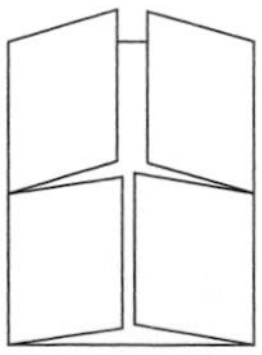

Variations

A Use the four-door book on the opposite axis.

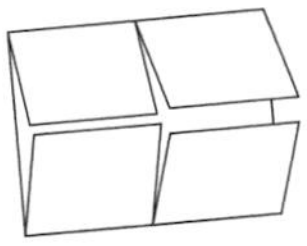

B Create a center tab by leaving .5–2 cm between the flaps in Step 1.

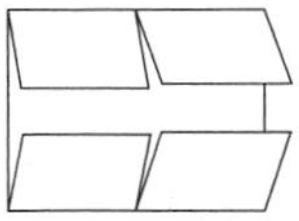

Bound Book Foldable® By Dinah Zike

Step 1 Fold three sheets of paper in half. Place the papers in a stack, leaving about .5 cm between each top fold. Mark all three sheets about 3 cm from the outer edges.

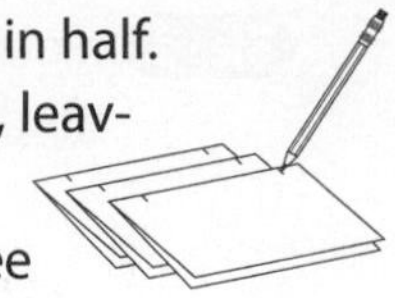

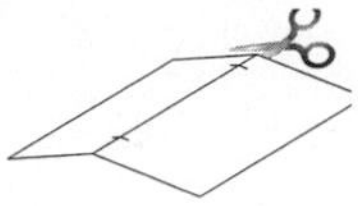

Step 2 Using two of the sheets, cut from the outer edges to the marked spots on each side. On the other sheet, cut between the marked spots.

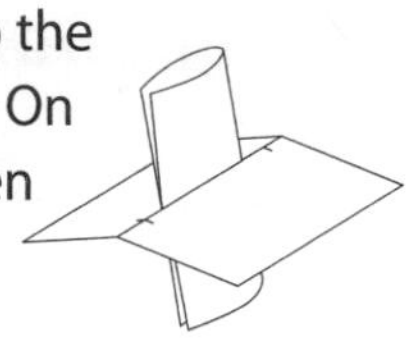

Step 3 Take the two sheets from Step 1 and slide them through the cut in the third sheet to make a 12-page book.

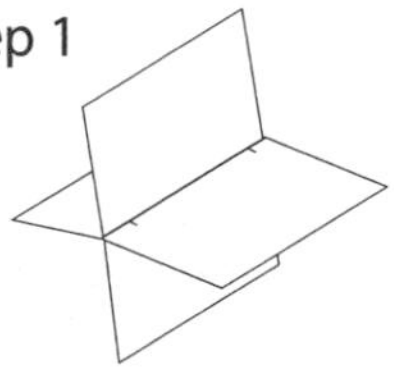

Step 4 Fold the bound pages in half to form a book.

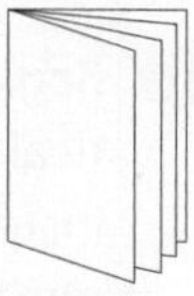

Variation

A Use two sheets of paper to make an eight-page book, or increase the number of pages by using more than three sheets.

PROJECT FORMAT

Use two or more sheets of 11″ × 17″ or 12″ × 18″ paper and fold it to make a large bound book project.

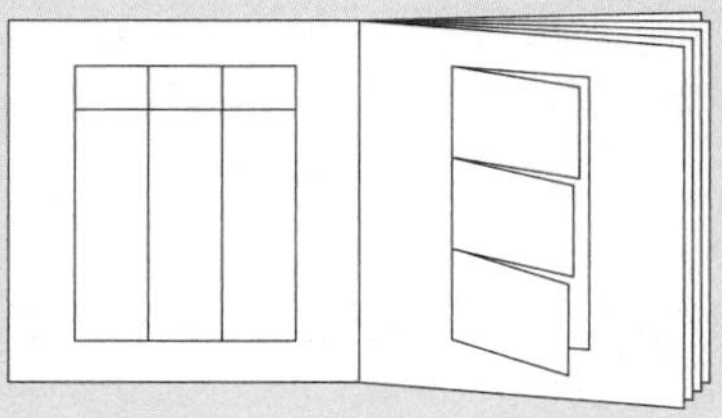

Accordian Foldable® By Dinah Zike

Step 1 Fold the selected paper in half vertically, like a *hamburger*.

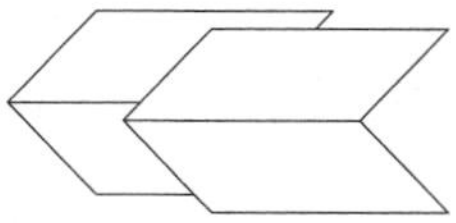

Step 2 Cut each sheet of folded paper in half along the fold lines.

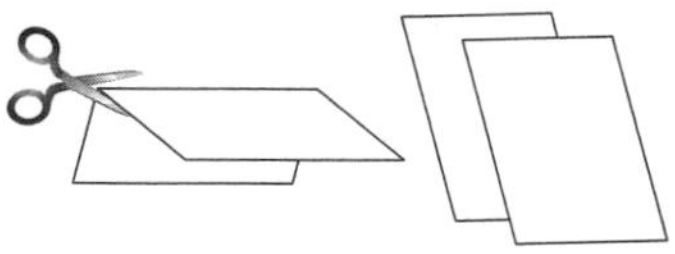

Step 3 Fold each half-sheet almost in half, leaving a 2 cm tab at the top.

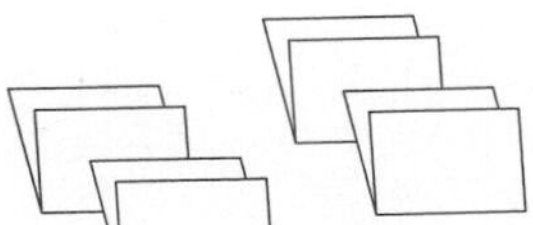

Step 4 Fold the top tab over the short side, then fold it in the opposite direction.

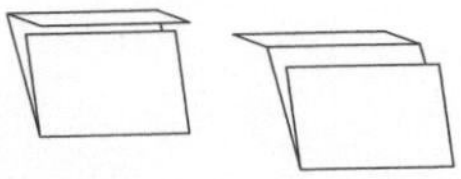

Variations

A Glue the straight edge of one paper inside the tab of another sheet. Leave a tab at the end of the book to add more pages.

B Tape the straight edge of one paper to the tab of another sheet, or just tape the straight edges of nonfolded paper end to end to make an accordian.

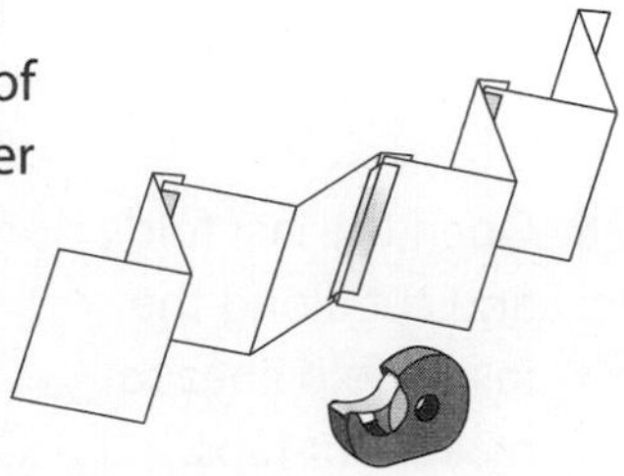

C Use whole sheets of paper to make a large accordian.

Layered Foldable® By Dinah Zike

Step 1 Stack two sheets of paper about 1–2 cm apart. Keep the right and left edges even.

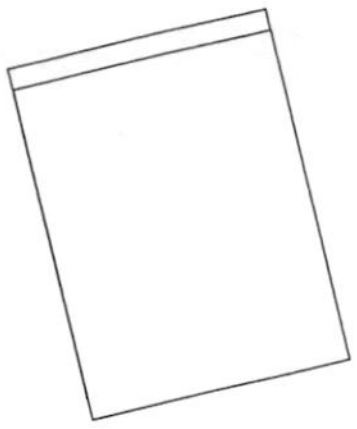

Step 2 Fold up the bottom edges to to form four tabs. Crease the fold to hold the tabs in place.

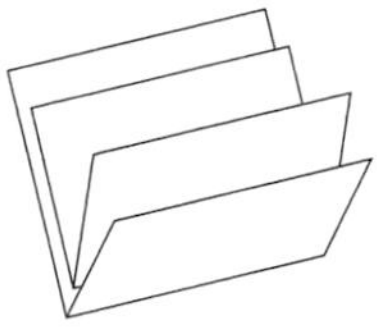

Step 3 Staple along the folded edge, or open and glue the papers together at the fold line.

Variations

A Rotate the book so the fold is at the top or to the side.

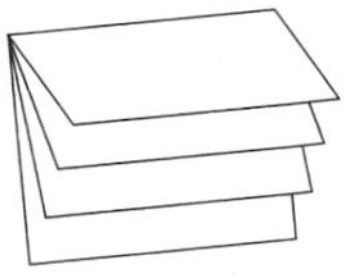

B Extend the book by using more than two sheets of paper.

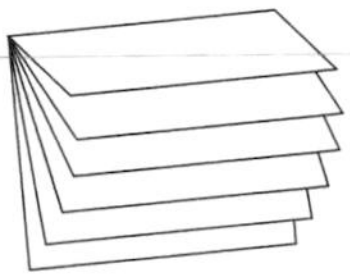

Envelope Foldable® By Dinah Zike

Step 1 Fold a sheet of paper into a *taco*. Cut off the tab at the top.

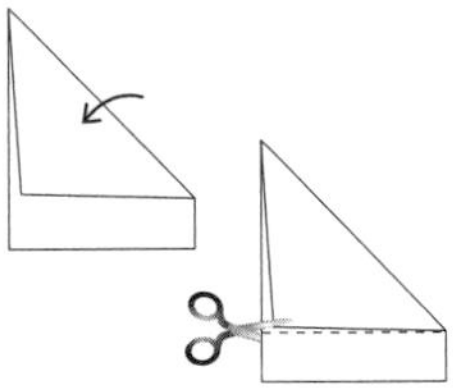

Step 2 Open the *taco* and fold it the opposite way making another *taco* and X-fold pattern on the sheet of paper.

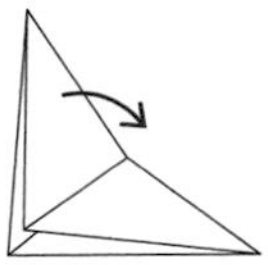

Step 3 Cut a map, illustration or diagram to fit the inside of the envelope.

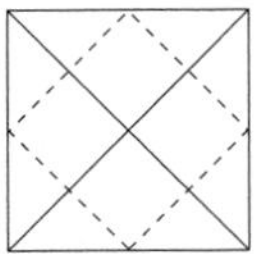

Step 4 Use the outside tabs for labels and inside tabs for writing information.

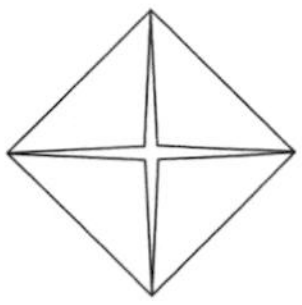

Variations

A Use 11″ × 17″ or 12″ × 18″ paper to make a large envelope.

B Cut off the points of the four tabs to make a window in the middle of the book.

Sentence Strip Foldable® By Dinah Zike

Step 1 Fold two sheets of paper in half vertically, like a *hamburger*.

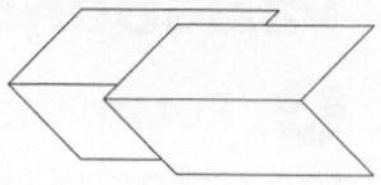

Step 2 Unfold and cut along fold lines making four half sheets.

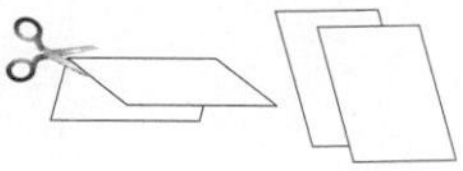

Step 3 Fold each half sheet in half horizontally, like a *hotdog*.

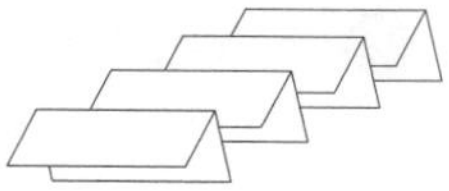

Step 4 Stack folded horizontal sheets evenly and staple together on the left side.

Step 5 Open the top flap of the first sentence strip and make a cut about 2 cm from the stapled edge to the fold line. This forms a flap that can be raisied and lowered. Repeat this step for each sentence strip.

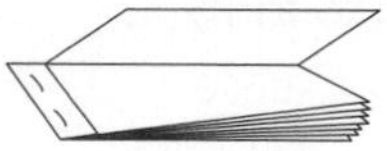

Variations

A Expand this book by using more than two sheets of paper.

B Use whole sheets of paper to make large books.

Pyramid Foldable® By Dinah Zike

Step 1 Fold a sheet of paper into a *taco*. Crease the fold line, but do not cut it off.

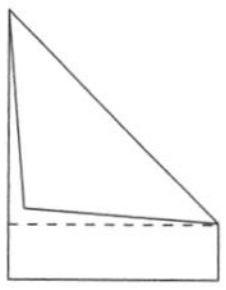

Step 2 Open the folded sheet and refold it like a *taco* in the opposite direction to create an X-fold pattern.

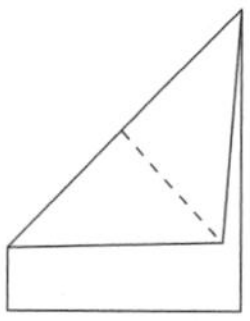

Step 3 Cut one fold line as shown, stopping at the center of the X-fold to make a flap.

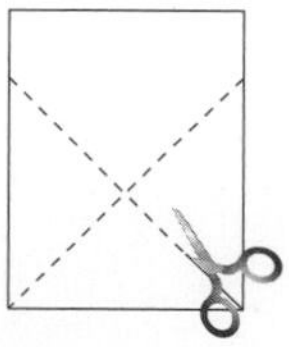

Step 4 Outline the fold lines of the X-fold. Label the three front sections and use the inside spaces for notes. Use the tab for the title.

Step 5 Glue the tab into a project book or notebook. Use the space under the pyramid for other information.

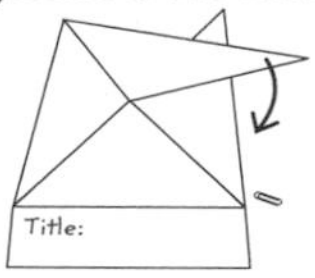

Step 6 To display the pyramid, fold the flap under and secure with a paper clip, if needed.

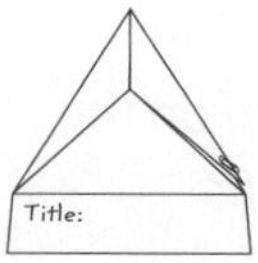

Single-Pocket or One-Pocket Foldable® By Dinah Zike

Step 1 Using a large piece of paper on a vertical axis, fold the bottom edge of the paper upwards, about 5 cm.

Step 2 Glue or staple the outer edges to make a large pocket.

PROJECT FORMAT
Use 11″ × 17″ or 12″ × 18″ paper and fold it vertically or horizontally to make a large pocket project.

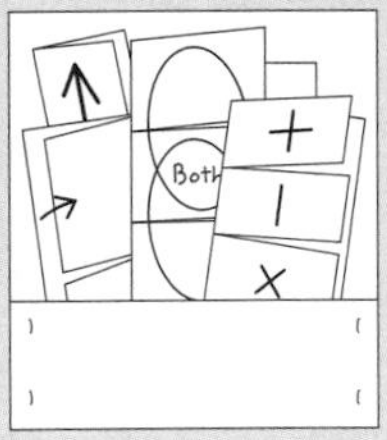

Variations

A Make the one-pocket project using the paper on the horizontal axis.

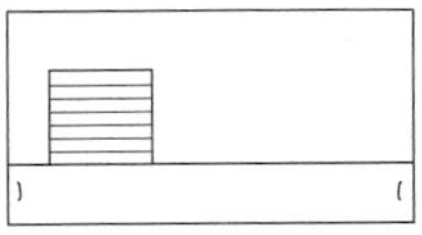

B To store materials securely inside, fold the top of the paper almost to the center, leaving about 2–4 cm between the paper edges. Slip the Foldables through the opening and under the top and bottom pockets.

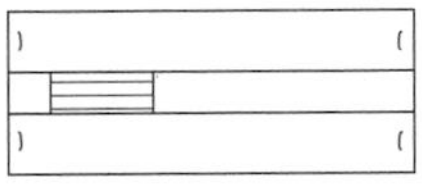

Multi-Tab Foldable® By Dinah Zike

Step 1 Fold a sheet of notebook paper in half like a *hotdog*.

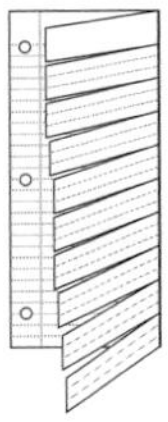

Step 2 Open the paper and on one side cut every third line. This makes ten tabs on wide ruled notebook paper and twelve tabs on college ruled.

Step 3 Label the tabs on the front side and use the inside space for definitions, or other information.

Variation

A Make a tab for a title by folding the paper so the holes remain uncovered. This allows the notebook Foldable to be stored in a three-hole binder.

PERIODIC TABLE OF THE ELEMENTS

Element	Hydrogen
Atomic number	1
Symbol	H
Atomic mass	1.01
State of matter	

Gas
Liquid
Solid
Synthetic

A column in the periodic table is called a **group.**

A row in the periodic table is called a **period.**

	1	2	3	4	5	6	7	8	9
1	Hydrogen 1 **H** 1.01								
2	Lithium 3 **Li** 6.94	Beryllium 4 **Be** 9.01							
3	Sodium 11 **Na** 22.99	Magnesium 12 **Mg** 24.31							
4	Potassium 19 **K** 39.10	Calcium 20 **Ca** 40.08	Scandium 21 **Sc** 44.96	Titanium 22 **Ti** 47.87	Vanadium 23 **V** 50.94	Chromium 24 **Cr** 52.00	Manganese 25 **Mn** 54.94	Iron 26 **Fe** 55.85	Cobalt 27 **Co** 58.93
5	Rubidium 37 **Rb** 85.47	Strontium 38 **Sr** 87.62	Yttrium 39 **Y** 88.91	Zirconium 40 **Zr** 91.22	Niobium 41 **Nb** 92.91	Molybdenum 42 **Mo** 95.96	Technetium 43 **Tc** (98)	Ruthenium 44 **Ru** 101.07	Rhodium 45 **Rh** 102.91
6	Cesium 55 **Cs** 132.91	Barium 56 **Ba** 137.33	Lanthanum 57 **La** 138.91	Hafnium 72 **Hf** 178.49	Tantalum 73 **Ta** 180.95	Tungsten 74 **W** 183.84	Rhenium 75 **Re** 186.21	Osmium 76 **Os** 190.23	Iridium 77 **Ir** 192.22
7	Francium 87 **Fr** (223)	Radium 88 **Ra** (226)	Actinium 89 **Ac** (227)	Rutherfordium 104 **Rf** (267)	Dubnium 105 **Db** (268)	Seaborgium 106 **Sg** (271)	Bohrium 107 **Bh** (272)	Hassium 108 **Hs** (270)	Meitnerium 109 **Mt** (276)

The number in parentheses is the mass number of the longest lived isotope for that element.

Lanthanide series	Cerium 58 **Ce** 140.12	Praseodymium 59 **Pr** 140.91	Neodymium 60 **Nd** 144.24	Promethium 61 **Pm** (145)	Samarium 62 **Sm** 150.36	Europium 63 **Eu** 151.96
Actinide series	Thorium 90 **Th** 232.04	Protactinium 91 **Pa** 231.04	Uranium 92 **U** 238.03	Neptunium 93 **Np** (237)	Plutonium 94 **Pu** (244)	Americium 95 **Am** (243)

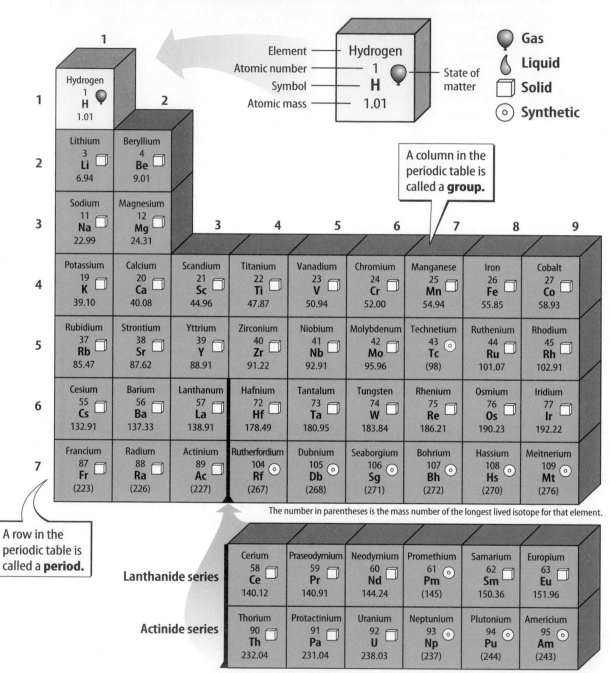

- Metal
- Metalloid
- Nonmetal
- Recently discovered

10	11	12	13	14	15	16	17	18
								Helium 2 **He** 4.00
			Boron 5 **B** 10.81	Carbon 6 **C** 12.01	Nitrogen 7 **N** 14.01	Oxygen 8 **O** 16.00	Fluorine 9 **F** 19.00	Neon 10 **Ne** 20.18
			Aluminum 13 **Al** 26.98	Silicon 14 **Si** 28.09	Phosphorus 15 **P** 30.97	Sulfur 16 **S** 32.07	Chlorine 17 **Cl** 35.45	Argon 18 **Ar** 39.95
Nickel 28 **Ni** 58.69	Copper 29 **Cu** 63.55	Zinc 30 **Zn** 65.38	Gallium 31 **Ga** 69.72	Germanium 32 **Ge** 72.64	Arsenic 33 **As** 74.92	Selenium 34 **Se** 78.96	Bromine 35 **Br** 79.90	Krypton 36 **Kr** 83.80
Palladium 46 **Pd** 106.42	Silver 47 **Ag** 107.87	Cadmium 48 **Cd** 112.41	Indium 49 **In** 114.82	Tin 50 **Sn** 118.71	Antimony 51 **Sb** 121.76	Tellurium 52 **Te** 127.60	Iodine 53 **I** 126.90	Xenon 54 **Xe** 131.29
Platinum 78 **Pt** 195.08	Gold 79 **Au** 196.97	Mercury 80 **Hg** 200.59	Thallium 81 **Tl** 204.38	Lead 82 **Pb** 207.20	Bismuth 83 **Bi** 208.98	Polonium 84 **Po** (209)	Astatine 85 **At** (210)	Radon 86 **Rn** (222)
Darmstadtium 110 **Ds** (281)	Roentgenium 111 **Rg** (280)	Copernicium 112 **Cn** (285)	Ununtrium * 113 **Uut** (284)	Ununquadium * 114 **Uuq** (289)	Ununpentium * 115 **Uup** (288)	Ununhexium * 116 **Uuh** (293)		Ununoctium * 118 **Uuo** (294)

* The names and symbols for elements 113-116 and 118 are temporary. Final names will be selected when the elements' discoveries are verified.

Gadolinium 64 **Gd** 157.25	Terbium 65 **Tb** 158.93	Dysprosium 66 **Dy** 162.50	Holmium 67 **Ho** 164.93	Erbium 68 **Er** 167.26	Thulium 69 **Tm** 168.93	Ytterbium 70 **Yb** 173.05	Lutetium 71 **Lu** 174.97
Curium 96 **Cm** (247)	Berkelium 97 **Bk** (247)	Californium 98 **Cf** (251)	Einsteinium 99 **Es** (252)	Fermium 100 **Fm** (257)	Mendelevium 101 **Md** (258)	Nobelium 102 **No** (259)	Lawrencium 103 **Lr** (262)

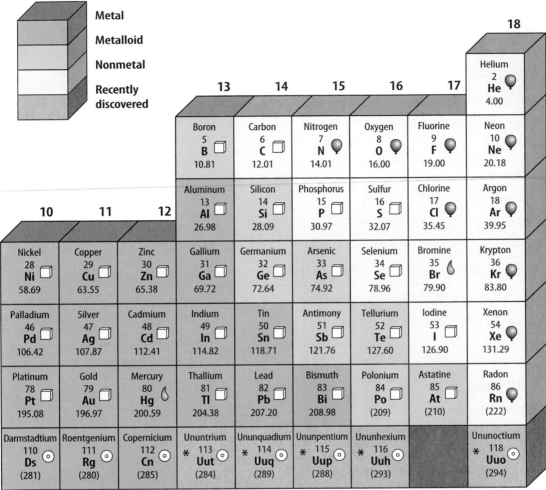

Topographic Map Symbols

Topographic Map Symbols	
Primary highway, hard surface	Index contour
Secondary highway, hard surface	Supplementary contour
Light-duty road, hard or improved surface	Intermediate contour
Unimproved road	Depression contours
Railroad: single track	
Railroad: multiple track	Boundaries: national
Railroads in juxtaposition	State
	County, parish, municipal
Buildings	Civil township, precinct, town, barrio
cem Schools, church, and cemetery	Incorporated city, village, town, hamlet
Buildings (barn, warehouse, etc.)	Reservation, national or state
Wells other than water (labeled as to type)	Small park, cemetery, airport, etc.
Tanks: oil, water, etc. (labeled only if water)	Land grant
Located or landmark object; windmill	Township or range line, U.S. land survey
Open pit, mine, or quarry; prospect	
	Township or range line, approximate location
Marsh (swamp)	
Wooded marsh	Perennial streams
Woods or brushwood	Elevated aqueduct
Vineyard	Water well and spring
Land subject to controlled inundation	Small rapids
Submerged marsh	Large rapids
Mangrove	Intermittent lake
Orchard	Intermittent stream
Scrub	Aqueduct tunnel
Urban area	Glacier
	Small falls
x7369 Spot elevation	Large falls
670 Water elevation	Dry lake bed

Rocks

Rocks		
Rock Type	**Rock Name**	**Characteristics**
Igneous (intrusive)	Granite	Large mineral grains of quartz, feldspar, hornblende, and mica. Usually light in color.
	Diorite	Large mineral grains of feldspar, hornblende, and mica. Less quartz than granite. Intermediate in color.
	Gabbro	Large mineral grains of feldspar, augite, and olivine. No quartz. Dark in color.
Igneous (extrusive)	Rhyolite	Small mineral grains of quartz, feldspar, hornblende, and mica, or no visible grains. Light in color.
	Andesite	Small mineral grains of feldspar, hornblende, and mica or no visible grains. Intermediate in color.
	Basalt	Small mineral grains of feldspar, augite, and possibly olivine or no visible grains. No quartz. Dark in color.
	Obsidian	Glassy texture. No visible grains. Volcanic glass. Fracture looks like broken glass.
	Pumice	Frothy texture. Floats in water. Usually light in color.
Sedimentary (detrital)	Conglomerate	Coarse grained. Gravel or pebble-size grains.
	Sandstone	Sand-sized grains 1/16 to 2 mm.
	Siltstone	Grains are smaller than sand but larger than clay.
	Shale	Smallest grains. Often dark in color. Usually platy.
Sedimentary (chemical or organic)	Limestone	Major mineral is calcite. Usually forms in oceans and lakes. Often contains fossils.
	Coal	Forms in swampy areas. Compacted layers of organic material, mainly plant remains.
Sedimentary (chemical)	Rock Salt	Commonly forms by the evaporation of seawater.
Metamorphic (foliated)	Gneiss	Banding due to alternate layers of different minerals, of different colors. Parent rock often is granite.
	Schist	Parallel arrangement of sheetlike minerals, mainly micas. Forms from different parent rocks.
	Phyllite	Shiny or silky appearance. May look wrinkled. Common parent rocks are shale and slate.
	Slate	Harder, denser, and shinier than shale. Common parent rock is shale.
Metamorphic (nonfoliated)	Marble	Calcite or dolomite. Common parent rock is limestone.
	Soapstone	Mainly of talc. Soft with greasy feel.
	Quartzite	Hard with interlocking quartz crystals. Common parent rock is sandstone.

Minerals

Minerals					
Mineral (formula)	**Color**	**Streak**	**Hardness Pattern**	**Breakage Properties**	**Uses and Other**
Graphite (C)	black to gray	black to gray	1–1.5	basal cleavage (scales)	pencil lead, lubricants for locks, rods to control some small nuclear reactions, battery poles
Galena (PbS)	gray	gray to black	2.5	cubic cleavage perfect	source of lead, used for pipes, shields for X rays, fishing equipment sinkers
Hematite (Fe_2O_3)	black or reddish-brown	reddish-brown	5.5–6.5	irregular fracture	source of iron; converted to pig iron, made into steel
Magnetite (Fe_3O_4)	black	black	6	conchoidal fracture	source of iron, attracts a magnet
Pyrite (FeS_2)	light, brassy, yellow	greenish-black	6–6.5	uneven fracture	fool's gold
Talc ($Mg_3 Si_4O_{10} (OH)_2$)	white, greenish	white	1	cleavage in one direction	used for talcum powder, sculptures, paper, and tabletops
Gypsum ($CaSO_4 \cdot 2H_2O$)	colorless, gray, white, brown	white	2	basal cleavage	used in plaster of paris and dry wall for building construction
Sphalerite (ZnS)	brown, reddish-brown, greenish	light to dark brown	3.5–4	cleavage in six directions	main ore of zinc; used in paints, dyes, and medicine
Muscovite ($KAl_3Si_3 O_{10}(OH)_2$)	white, light gray, yellow, rose, green	colorless	2–2.5	basal cleavage	occurs in large, flexible plates; used as an insulator in electrical equipment, lubricant
Biotite ($K(Mg,Fe)_3 (AlSi_3O_{10}) (OH)_2$)	black to dark brown	colorless	2.5–3	basal cleavage	occurs in large, flexible plates
Halite ($NaCl$)	colorless, red, white, blue	colorless	2.5	cubic cleavage	salt; soluble in water; a preservative

Minerals

Mineral (formula)	Color	Streak	Hardness	Breakage Pattern	Uses and Other Properties
Calcite ($CaCO_3$)	colorless, white, pale blue	colorless, white	3	cleavage in three directions	fizzes when HCl is added; used in cements and other building materials
Dolomite ($CaMg(CO_3)_2$)	colorless, white, pink, green, gray, black	white	3.5–4	cleavage in three directions	concrete and cement; used as an ornamental building stone
Fluorite (CaF_2)	colorless, white, blue, green, red, yellow, purple	colorless	4	cleavage in four directions	used in the manufacture of optical equipment; glows under ultraviolet light
Hornblende ($(CaNa)_{2\text{-}3}(Mg,Al,Fe)_5\text{-}(Al,Si)_2Si_6O_{22}(OH)_2$)	green to black	gray to white	5–6	cleavage in two directions	will transmit light on thin edges; 6-sided cross section
Feldspar ($(KAlSi_3O_8)$ $(NaAlSi_3O_8)$, $(CaAl_2Si_2O_8)$)	colorless, white to gray, green	colorless	6	two cleavage planes meet at 90° angle	used in the manufacture of ceramics
Augite ($((Ca,Na)(Mg,Fe,Al)(Al,Si)_2O_6)$)	black	colorless	6	cleavage in two directions	square or 8-sided cross section
Olivine ($((Mg,Fe)_2SiO_4)$)	olive, green	none	6.5–7	conchoidal fracture	gemstones, refractory sand
Quartz (SiO_2)	colorless, various colors	none	7	conchoidal fracture	used in glass manufacture, electronic equipment, radios, computers, watches, gemstones

Weather Map Symbols

Sample Station Model

Type of high clouds

Type of middle clouds

Temperature (F)

Type of precipitation

Wind speed and direction

Location of weather station

Barometric pressure in millibars with initial 9 or 10 omitted (1,024.7)

247

128

Change in barometric pressure in last 3 h

Total percentage of sky covered by clouds

Type of low clouds

Dew point temperature (°F)

31

**

30

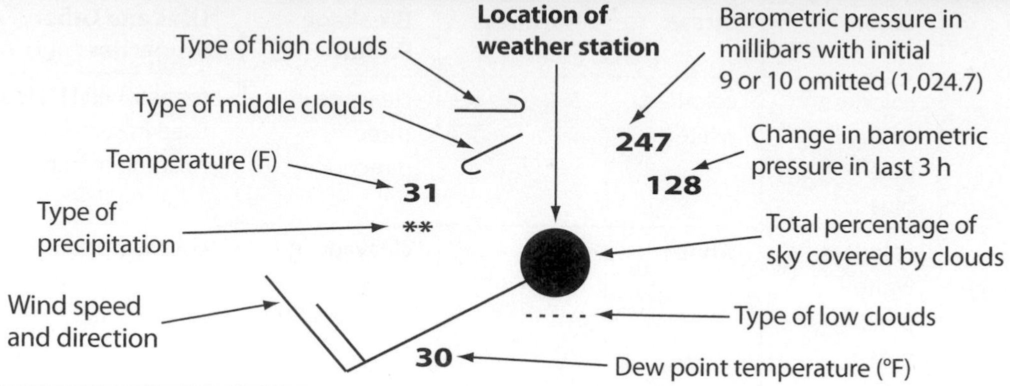

Sample Plotted Report at Each Station

Precipitation		Wind Speed and Direction		Sky Coverage		Some Types of High Clouds	
≡	Fog	○	0 calm	○	No cover		Scattered cirrus
★	Snow	/	1–2 knots	◐	1/10 or less		Dense cirrus in patches
●	Rain	∨	3–7 knots	◕	2/10 to 3/10		Veil of cirrus covering entire sky
⊺	Thunderstorm	∨	8–12 knots	◑	4/10		Cirrus not covering entire sky
'	Drizzle	∨	13–17 knots	◐	–		
▽	Showers	∨	18–22 knots	◕	6/10		
		∨	23–27 knots	◕	7/10		
		∨	48–52 knots	◑	Overcast with openings		
		1 knot = 1.852 km/h		●	Completely overcast		

Some Types of Middle Clouds		Some Types of Low Clouds		Fronts and Pressure Systems	
	Thin altostratus layer	⌒	Cumulus of fair weather	Ⓗ or High Ⓛ or Low	Center of high- or low-pressure system
	Thick altostratus layer	∪	Stratocumulus	▲▲▲▲	Cold front
	Thin altostratus in patches	- - - - -	Fractocumulus of bad weather	●●●●	Warm front
	Thin altostratus in bands	—	Stratus of fair weather	▲●▲▲	Occluded front
				●▲●▲	Stationary front

Use and Care of a Microscope

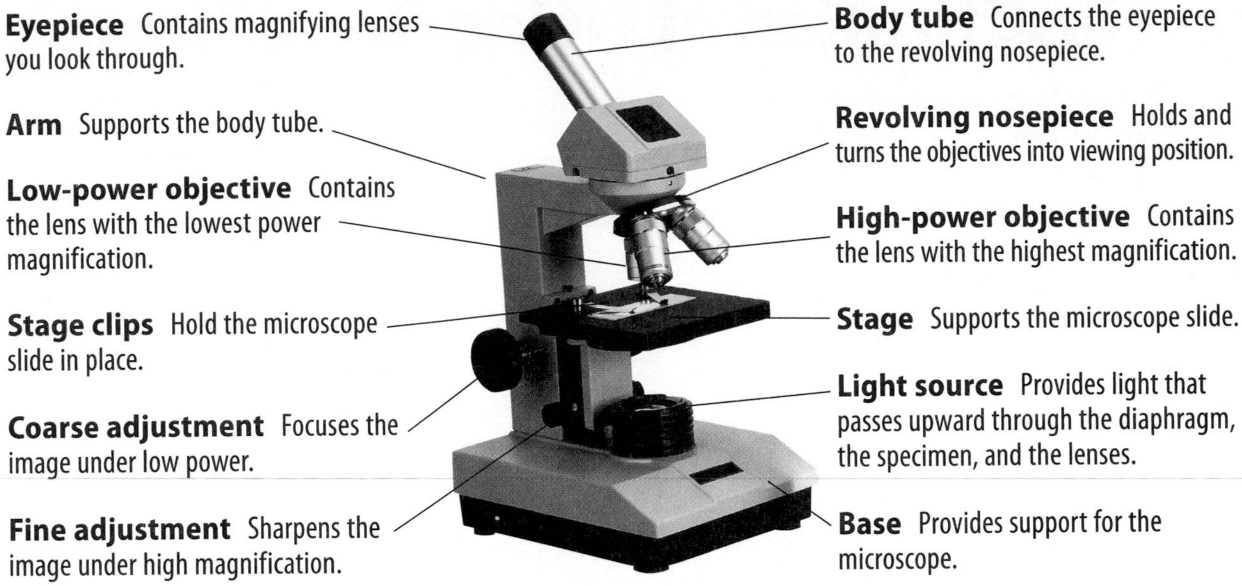
Eyepiece Contains magnifying lenses you look through.
Arm Supports the body tube.
Low-power objective Contains the lens with the lowest power magnification.
Stage clips Hold the microscope slide in place.
Coarse adjustment Focuses the image under low power.
Fine adjustment Sharpens the image under high magnification.
Body tube Connects the eyepiece to the revolving nosepiece.
Revolving nosepiece Holds and turns the objectives into viewing position.
High-power objective Contains the lens with the highest magnification.
Stage Supports the microscope slide.
Light source Provides light that passes upward through the diaphragm, the specimen, and the lenses.
Base Provides support for the microscope.

Caring for a Microscope

1. Always carry the microscope holding the arm with one hand and supporting the base with the other hand.
2. Don't touch the lenses with your fingers.
3. The coarse adjustment knob is used only when looking through the lowest-power objective lens. The fine adjustment knob is used when the high-power objective is in place.
4. Cover the microscope when you store it.

Using a Microscope

1. Place the microscope on a flat surface that is clear of objects. The arm should be toward you.
2. Look through the eyepiece. Adjust the diaphragm so light comes through the opening in the stage.
3. Place a slide on the stage so the specimen is in the field of view. Hold it firmly in place by using the stage clips.
4. Always focus with the coarse adjustment and the low-power objective lens first. After the object is in focus on low power, turn the nosepiece until the high-power objective is in place. Use ONLY the fine adjustment to focus with the high-power objective lens.

Making a Wet-Mount Slide

1. Carefully place the item you want to look at in the center of a clean, glass slide. Make sure the sample is thin enough for light to pass through.
2. Use a dropper to place one or two drops of water on the sample.
3. Hold a clean coverslip by the edges and place it at one edge of the water. Slowly lower the coverslip onto the water until it lies flat.
4. If you have too much water or a lot of air bubbles, touch the edge of a paper towel to the edge of the coverslip to draw off extra water and draw out unwanted air.

Diversity of Life: Classification of Living Organisms

A six-kingdom system of classification of organisms is used today. Two kingdoms—Kingdom Archaebacteria and Kingdom Eubacteria—contain organisms that do not have a nucleus and that lack membrane-bound structures in the cytoplasm of their cells. The members of the other four kingdoms have a cell or cells that contain a nucleus and structures in the cytoplasm, some of which are surrounded by membranes. These kingdoms are Kingdom Protista, Kingdom Fungi, Kingdom Plantae, and Kingdom Animalia.

Kingdom Archaebacteria

one-celled; some absorb food from their surroundings; some are photosynthetic; some are chemosynthetic; many are found in extremely harsh environments including salt ponds, hot springs, swamps, and deep-sea hydrothermal vents

Kingdom Eubacteria

one-celled; most absorb food from their surroundings; some are photosynthetic; some are chemosynthetic; many are parasites; many are round, spiral, or rod-shaped; some form colonies

Kingdom Protista

Phylum Euglenophyta one-celled; photosynthetic or take in food; most have one flagellum; euglenoids

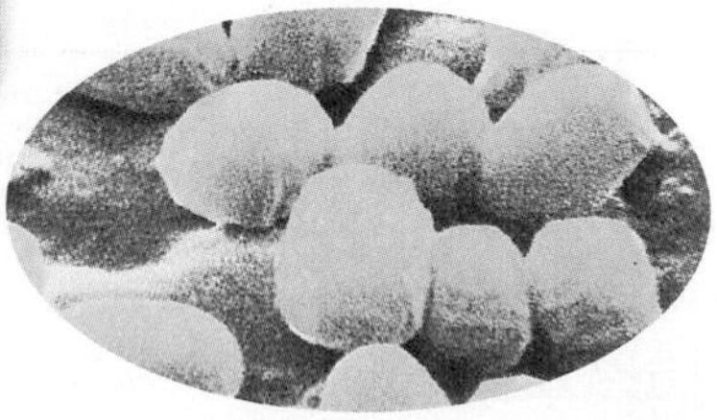

Kingdom Eubacteria
Bacillus anthracis

Phylum Chlorophyta
Desmids

Phylum Bacillariophyta one-celled; photosynthetic; have unique double shells made of silica; diatoms

Phylum Dinoflagellata one-celled; photosynthetic; contain red pigments; have two flagella; dinoflagellates

Phylum Chlorophyta one-celled, many-celled, or colonies; photosynthetic; contain chlorophyll; live on land, in freshwater, or salt water; green algae

Phylum Rhodophyta most are many-celled; photosynthetic; contain red pigments; most live in deep, saltwater environments; red algae

Phylum Phaeophyta most are many-celled; photosynthetic; contain brown pigments; most live in saltwater environments; brown algae

Phylum Rhizopoda one-celled; take in food; are free-living or parasitic; move by means of pseudopods; amoebas

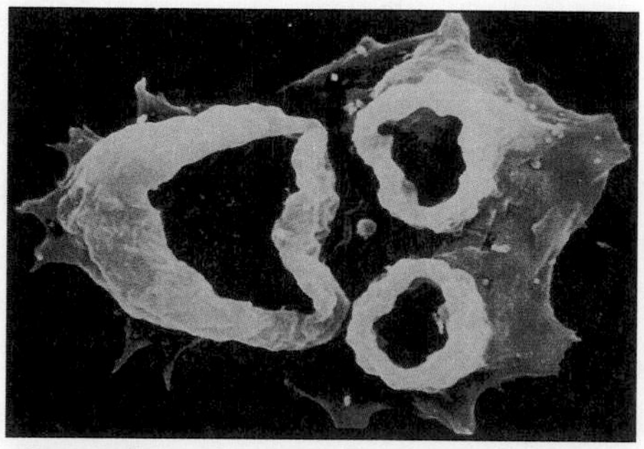

Amoeba

Phylum Zoomastigina one-celled; take in food; free-living or parasitic; have one or more flagella; zoomastigotes

Phylum Ciliophora one-celled; take in food; have large numbers of cilia; ciliates

Phylum Sporozoa one-celled; take in food; have no means of movement; are parasites in animals; sporozoans

Phylum Myxomycota
Slime mold

Phylum Oomycota
Phytophthora infestans

Phyla Myxomycota and Acrasiomycota one- or many-celled; absorb food; change form during life cycle; cellular and plasmodial slime molds

Phylum Oomycota many-celled; are either parasites or decomposers; live in freshwater or salt water; water molds, rusts and downy mildews

Kingdom Fungi

Phylum Zygomycota many-celled; absorb food; spores are produced in sporangia; zygote fungi; bread mold

Phylum Ascomycota one- and many-celled; absorb food; spores produced in asci; sac fungi; yeast

Phylum Basidiomycota many-celled; absorb food; spores produced in basidia; club fungi; mushrooms

Phylum Deuteromycota members with unknown reproductive structures; imperfect fungi; *Penicillium*

Phylum Mycophycota organisms formed by symbiotic relationship between an ascomycote or a basidiomycote and green alga or cyanobacterium; lichens

Lichens

Kingdom Plantae

Divisions Bryophyta (mosses), **Anthocerophyta** (hornworts), **Hepaticophyta** (liverworts), **Psilophyta** (whisk ferns) many-celled nonvascular plants; reproduce by spores produced in capsules; green; grow in moist, land environments

Division Lycophyta many-celled vascular plants; spores are produced in conelike structures; live on land; are photosynthetic; club mosses

Division Arthrophyta vascular plants; ribbed and jointed stems; scalelike leaves; spores produced in conelike structures; horsetails

Division Pterophyta vascular plants; leaves called fronds; spores produced in clusters of sporangia called sori; live on land or in water; ferns

Division Ginkgophyta deciduous trees; only one living species; have fan-shaped leaves with branching veins and fleshy cones with seeds; ginkgoes

Division Cycadophyta palmlike plants; have large, featherlike leaves; produces seeds in cones; cycads

Division Coniferophyta deciduous or evergreen; trees or shrubs; have needlelike or scalelike leaves; seeds produced in cones; conifers

Division Anthophyta
Tomato plant

Division Gnetophyta shrubs or woody vines; seeds are produced in cones; division contains only three genera; gnetum

Division Anthophyta dominant group of plants; flowering plants; have fruits with seeds

Kingdom Animalia

Phylum Porifera aquatic organisms that lack true tissues and organs; are asymmetrical and sessile; sponges

Phylum Cnidaria radially symmetrical organisms; have a digestive cavity with one opening; most have tentacles armed with stinging cells; live in aquatic environments singly or in colonies; includes jellyfish, corals, hydra, and sea anemones

Phylum Platyhelminthes bilaterally symmetrical worms; have flattened bodies; digestive system has one opening; parasitic and free-living species; flatworms

Division Bryophyta
Liverwort

Phylum Platyhelminthes
Flatworm

Phylum Chordata

Phylum Nematoda round, bilaterally symmetrical body; have digestive system with two openings; free-living forms and parasitic forms; roundworms

Phylum Mollusca soft-bodied animals, many with a hard shell and soft foot or footlike appendage; a mantle covers the soft body; aquatic and terrestrial species; includes clams, snails, squid, and octopuses

Phylum Annelida bilaterally symmetrical worms; have round, segmented bodies; terrestrial and aquatic species; includes earthworms, leeches, and marine polychaetes

Phylum Arthropoda largest animal group; have hard exoskeletons, segmented bodies, and pairs of jointed appendages; land and aquatic species; includes insects, crustaceans, and spiders

Phylum Echinodermata marine organisms; have spiny or leathery skin and a water-vascular system with tube feet; are radially symmetrical; includes sea stars, sand dollars, and sea urchins

Phylum Chordata organisms with internal skeletons and specialized body systems; most have paired appendages; all at some time have a notochord, nerve cord, gill slits, and a post-anal tail; include fish, amphibians, reptiles, birds, and mammals

Glossary/Glosario

Multilingual eGlossary

A science multilingual glossary is available on the science website. The glossary includes the following languages.

Arabic	Hmong	Tagalog
Bengali	Korean	Urdu
Chinese	Portuguese	Vietnamese
English	Russian	
Haitian Creole	Spanish	

Cómo usar el glosario en español:

1. Busca el término en inglés que desees encontrar.
2. El término en español, junto con la definición, se encuentran en la columna de la derecha.

Pronunciation Key

Use the following key to help you sound out words in the glossary.

a	back (BAK)	**ew**	food (FEWD)
ay	day (DAY)	**yoo**	pure (PYOOR)
ah	father (FAH thur)	**yew**	few (FYEW)
ow	flower (FLOW ur)	**uh**	comma (CAH muh)
ar	car (CAR)	**u (+ con)**	rub (RUB)
e	less (LES)	**sh**	shelf (SHELF)
ee	leaf (LEEF)	**ch**	nature (NAY chur)
ih	trip (TRIHP)	**g**	gift (GIHFT)
i (i + com + e)	idea (i DEE uh)	**j**	gem (JEM)
oh	go (GOH)	**ing**	sing (SING)
aw	soft (SAWFT)	**zh**	vision (VIH zhun)
or	orbit (OR buht)	**k**	cake (KAYK)
oy	coin (COYN)	**s**	seed, cent (SEED, SENT)
oo	foot (FOOT)	**z**	zone, raise (ZOHN, RAYZ)

English — **A** — **Español**

abrasion/amplitude — **abrasión/amplitud**

abrasion: the grinding away of rock or other surfaces as particles carried by wind, water, or ice scrape against them. (p. 334)

abrasión: desgaste de una roca o de otras superficies a medida que las partículas transportadas por el viento, el agua o el hielo las raspan. (pág. 334)

acceleration: a measure of the change in velocity during a period of time. (p. 50)

aceleración: medida del cambio de velocidad durante un período de tiempo. (pág. 50)

accuracy: a description of how close a measurement is to an accepted or true value. (p. NOS 12)

exactitud: descripción de qué tan cerca está una medida a un valor aceptable. (pág. NOS 12)

active transport: the movement of substances through a cell membrane using the cell's energy. (p. 408)

transporte activo: movimiento de sustancias a través de la membrana celular usando la energía de la célula. (pág. 408)

amplitude: the maximum distance a wave varies from its rest position. (p. 124)

amplitud: distancia máxima que varía una onda desde su posición de reposo. (pág. 124)

asthenosphere (as THE nuh sfir): the partially melted portion of the mantle below the lithosphere. (p. 174)

astenosfera: porción parcialmente fundida del manto debajo de la litosfera. (pág. 174)

B

balanced forces: forces acting on an object that combine and form a net force of zero. (p. 61)

biochemical rock: sedimentary rock that was formed by organisms or contains the remains of organisms. (p. 299)

biota: all of the organisms that live in a region. (p. 367)

fuerzas en equilibrio: fuerzas que actúan sobre un objeto, se combinan y forman una fuerza neta de cero. (pág. 61)

roca bioquímica: roca sedimentaria formada por organismos o que contiene restos de organismos. (pág. 299)

biota: todos los organismos que viven en una región. (pág. 367)

C

carbohydrate (kar boh HI drayt): a macromolecule made up of one or more sugar molecules, which are composed of carbon, hydrogen, and oxygen; usually the body's major source of energy. (p. 391)

cell cycle: a cycle of growth, development, and division that most cells in an organism go through. (p. 429)

cell differentiation (dihf uh ren shee AY shun): the process by which cells become different types of cells. (p. 443)

cell membrane: a flexible covering that protects the inside of a cell from the environment outside the cell. (p. 369)

cell theory: the theory that states that all living things are made of one or more cells, the cell is the smallest unit of life, and all new cells come from preexisting cells. (p. 388)

cell wall: a stiff structure outside the cell membrane that protects a cell from attack by viruses and other harmful organisms. (p. 396)

cellular respiration: a series of chemical reactions that convert the energy in food molecules into a usable form of energy called ATP. (p. 413)

cementation: a process in which minerals dissolved in water crystallize between sediment grains. (p. 296)

carbohidrato: macromolécula constituida de una o más moléculas de azúcar, las cuales están compuestas de carbono, hidrógeno y oxígeno; usualmente es la mayor fuente de energía del cuerpo. (pág. 391)

ciclo celular: ciclo de crecimiento, desarrollo y división por el que pasan la mayoría de células de un organismo. (pág. 429)

diferenciación celular: proceso por el cual las células se convierten en diferentes tipos de células. (pág. 443)

membrana celular: cubierta flexible que protege el interior de una célula del ambiente externo de la célula. (pág. 369)

teoría celular: teoría que establece que todos los seres vivos están constituidos de una o más células (la célula es la unidad más pequeña de vida) y que las células nuevas provienen de células preexistentes. (pág. 388)

pared celular: estructura rígida en el exterior de la membrana celular que protege la célula del ataque de virus y otros organismos dañinos. (pág. 396)

respiración celular: serie de reacciones químicas que convierten la energía de las moléculas de alimento en una forma de energía utilizable llamada ATP. (pág. 413)

cementación: proceso por el cual los minerales disueltos en agua se cristalizan entre granos de sedimento. (pág. 296)

Cenozoic era: the youngest era of the Phanerozoic eon. (p. 243)

centromere: a structure that holds sister chromatids together. (p. 432)

chemical energy: energy that is stored in and released from the bonds between atoms. (p. 10)

chemical rock: sedimentary rock that forms when minerals crystallize directly from water. (p. 298)

chemical weathering: the process that changes the composition of rocks and minerals due to exposure to the environment. (p. 358)

chloroplast (KLOR uh plast): a membrane-bound organelle that uses light energy and makes food—a sugar called glucose—from water and carbon dioxide in a process known as photosynthesis. (p. 401)

clast: a broken piece or fragment that makes up a clastic rock. (p. 297)

clastic (KLAH stik) rock: sedimentary rock that is made up of broken pieces of minerals and rock fragments. (p. 297)

climate: the long-term average weather conditions that occur in a particular region. (p. 366)

closed system: a system that does not exchange matter or energy with the environment. (p. 21)

coal swamp: an oxygen-poor environment where, over a period of time, decaying plant material changes into coal. (p. 246)

compaction: a process in which the weight from the layers of sediment forces out fluids and decreases the space between sediment grains. (p. 296)

compression: region of a longitudinal wave where the particles of the medium are closest together. (p. 143)

conduction (kuhn DUK shun): the transfer of thermal energy due to collisions between particles. (p. 31)

constants: the factors in an experiment that remain the same. (p. NOS 18)

era Cenozoica: era más joven del eón Fanerozoico. (pág. 243)

centrómero: estructura que mantiene unidas las cromátidas hermanas. (pág. 432)

energía química: energía almacenada en y liberada por los enlaces entre los átomos. (pág. 10)

roca química: roca sedimentaria que se forma cuando los minerales se cristalizan directamente del agua. (pág. 298)

meteorización química: proceso que cambia la composición de las rocas y los minerales debido a la exposición al medioambiente. (pág. 358)

cloroplasto: organelo limitado por una membrana que usa la energía lumínica para producir alimento –un azúcar llamado glucosa– del agua y del dióxido de carbono en un proceso llamado fotosíntesis. (pág. 401)

clasto: pedazo partido o fragmentado que forma una roca clástica. (pág. 297)

roca clástica: roca sedimentaria formada por pedazos partidos de minerales y fragmentos de rocas. (pág. 297)

clima: promedio a largo plazo de las condiciones del tiempo atmosférico de una región en particular. (pág. 366)

sistema cerrado: sistema que no intercambia materia o energía con el ambiente. (pág. 21)

pantano de carbón: medioambiente pobre en oxígeno donde, al paso de un período de tiempo, el material en descomposición de plantas, se transforma en carbón. (pág. 246)

compactación: proceso por el cual el peso de las capas de sedimento extrae los fluidos y reduce el espacio entre los granos de sedimento. (pág. 296)

compresión: región de una onda longitudinal donde las partículas del medio están más cerca. (pág. 143)

conducción: transferencia de energía térmica debido a colisiones entre partículas. (pág. 31)

constantes: factores en un experimento que permanecen iguales. (pág. NOS 18)

contact force: a push or a pull on one object by another object that is touching it. (p. 58)

contact metamorphism: formation of a metamorphic rock caused by magma coming into contact with existing rock. (p. 306)

continental drift: Wegener's hypothesis which suggested that the continents are in constant motion on Earth's surface. (p. 199)

convection: the circulation of particles within a material caused by differences in thermal energy and density (p. 220); the transfer of thermal energy by the movement of particles from one part of a material to another. (p. 31)

convergent plate boundary: the boundary between two plates that move toward each other. (p. 217)

core: the dense metallic center of Earth. (p. 176)

critical thinking: comparing what you already know with information you are given in order to decide whether you agree with it. (p. NOS 8)

crust: the brittle, rocky outer layer of Earth. (p. 173)

cytokinesis (si toh kuh NEE sus): a process during which the cytoplasm and its contents divide. (p. 433)

cytoplasm: the liquid part of a cell inside the cell membrane; contains salts and other molecules. (p. 397)

cytoskeleton: a network of threadlike proteins joined together that gives a cell its shape and helps it move. (p. 397)

fuerza de contacto: empuje o arrastre ejercido sobre un objeto por otro que lo está tocando. (pág. 58)

metamorfismo de contacto: formación de roca metamórfica causada por el contacto del magma con la roca existente. (pág. 306)

deriva continental: hipótesis de Wegener que sugirió que los continentes están en constante movimiento en la superficie de la Tierra. (pág. 199)

convección: circulación de partículas en el interior de un material causada por diferencias en la energía térmica y la densidad (pág. 220); transferencia de energía térmica por el movimiento de partículas de una parte de la materia a otra. (pág. 31)

límite convergente de placas: límite entre dos placas que se acercan una hacia la otra. (pág. 217)

núcleo: centro de la Tierra denso y metálico. (pág. 176)

pensamiento crítico: comparación que se hace cuando se sabe algo acerca de información nueva, y se decide si se está o no de acuerdo con ella. (pág. NOS 8)

corteza: capa frágil y rocosa superficial de la Tierra. (pág. 173)

citocinesis: proceso durante el cual el citoplasma y sus contenidos se dividen. (pág. 433)

citoplasma: fluido en el interior de una célula que contiene sales y otras moléculas. (pág. 397)

citoesqueleto: red de proteínas en forma de filamentos unidos que le da forma a la célula y le ayuda a moverse. (pág. 397)

D

daughter cells: the two new cells that result from mitosis and cytokinesis. (p. 433)

decibel: the unit used to measure sound intensity or loudness. (p. 145)

decomposition: the breaking down of dead organisms and organic waste. (p. 365)

delta: a large deposit of sediment that forms where a stream enters a large body of water. (p. 332)

células hija: las dos células nuevas que resultan de la mitosis y la citocinesis. (pág. 433)

decibel: unidad usada para medir la intensidad o el volumen del sonido. (pág. 145)

descomposición: degradación de organismos muertos y desecho orgánico. (pág. 365)

delta: depósito grande de sedimento que se forma donde una corriente entra a un cuerpo grande de agua. (pág. 332)

density: the mass per unit volume of a substance. (p. 167)

densidad: cantidad de masa por unidad de volumen de una sustancia. (pág. 167)

dependent variable: the factor a scientist observes or measures during an experiment. (p. NOS 18)

variable dependiente: factor que el científico observa o mide durante un experimento. (pág. NOS 18)

deposition: the laying down or settling of eroded material. (p. 323)

deposición: establecimiento o asentamiento de material erosionado. (pág. 323)

description: a spoken or written summary of an observation. (p. NOS 10)

descripción: resumen oral o escrito de una observación de. (pág. NOS 10)

diffusion: the movement of substances from an area of higher concentration to an area of lower concentration. (p. 406)

difusión: movimiento de sustancias de un área de mayor concentración a un área de menor concentración. (pág. 406)

dinosaur: dominant Mesozoic land vertebrates that walked with their legs positioned directly below their hips. (p. 254)

dinosaurio: vertebrados dominantes de la tierra del Mesozoico que caminaban con las extremidades ubicadas justo debajo de las caderas. (pág. 254)

displacement: the difference between the initial, or starting, position and the final position of an object that has moved. (p. 48)

desplazamiento: diferencia entre la posición inicial, o salida, y la final de un objeto que se ha movido. (pág. 48)

distance: the total length of your path. (p. 48)

distancia: longitud total de un trayecto. (pág. 48)

divergent plate boundary: the boundary between two plates that move away from each other. (p. 217)

límite divergente de placas: límite entre dos placas que se alejan una de la otra. (pág. 217)

dune: a pile of windblown sand. (p. 334)

duna: montón de arena que el viento transporta. (pág. 334)

E

efficiency: the ratio of output work to input work. (p. 95)

eficiencia: relación entre energía invertida y energía útil. (pág. 95)

electric energy: energy carried by an electric current. (p. 11)

energía eléctrica: energía transportada por una corriente eléctrica. (pág. 11)

electromagnetic wave: a transverse wave that can travel through empty space and through matter. (p. 120)

onda electromagnética: onda transversal que puede viajar a través del espacio vacío y de la materia. (pág. 120)

endocytosis (en duh si TOH sus): the process during which a cell takes in a substance by surrounding it with the cell membrane. (p. 408)

endocitosis: proceso durante el cual una célula absorbe una sustancia rodeándola con la membrana celular. (pág. 408)

energy: the ability to cause change. (p. 9)

energía: capacidad de ocasionar cambio. (pág. 9)

energy transfer: the process of moving energy from one object to another without changing form. (p. 19)

transferencia de energía: proceso por el cual se mueve energía de un objeto a otro sin cambiar de forma. (pág. 19)

energy transformation: the conversion of one form of energy to another. (p. 13)

transformación de energía: conversión de una forma de energía a otra. (pág. 13)

eon: the longest unit of geologic time (p. 235)

eón: unidad más larga del tiempo geológico. (pág. 235)

epoch: a division of geologic time smaller than a period. (p. 235)
era: a large division of geologic time, but smaller than an eon. (p. 235)
erosion: the moving of weathered material, or sediment, from one location to another. (p. 321)
exocytosis (ek soh si TOH sus): the process during which a cell's vesicles release their contents outside the cell. (p. 408)
explanation: an interpretation of observations. (p. NOS 10)
extrusive rock: igneous rock that forms when volcanic material erupts, cools, and crystallizes on Earth's surface. (p. 290)

época: división del tiempo geológico más pequeña que un período. (pág. 235)
era: división grande del tiempo geológico, pero más pequeña que un eón. (pág. 235)
erosión: transporte de material meteorizado, o de sedimento, de un lugar a otro. (pág. 321)
exocitosis: proceso durante el cual las vesículas de una célula liberan sus contenidos fuera de la célula. (pág. 408)
explicación: interpretación que se hace de las observaciones. (pág. NOS 10)
roca extrusiva: roca ígnea que se forma cuando el material volcánico sale, se enfría y se cristaliza en la superficie de la Tierra. (pág. 290)

F

facilitated diffusion: the process by which molecules pass through a cell membrane using special proteins called transport proteins. (p. 407)
fermentation: a reaction that eukaryotic and prokaryotic cells can use to obtain energy from food when oxygen levels are low. (p. 414)
foliated rock: rock that contains parallel layers of flat and elongated minerals. (p. 305)
force: a push or a pull on an object. (p. 57)
force pair: the forces two objects apply to each other. (p. 69)
frequency: the number of wavelengths that pass by a point each second. (p. 123)
friction: a contact force that resists the sliding motion of two surfaces that are touching. (p. 59)
fulcrum: the point about which a lever pivots. (p. 100)

difusión facilitada: proceso por el cual las moléculas pasan a través de la membrana celular usando proteínas especiales, llamadas proteínas de transporte. (pág. 407)
fermentación: reacción que las células eucarióticas y procarióticas usan para obtener energía del alimento cuando los niveles de oxígeno son bajos. (pág. 414)
roca foliada: roca que contiene capas paralelas de minerales planos y alargados. (pág. 305)
fuerza: empuje o arrastre ejercido sobre un objeto. (pág. 57)
par de fuerzas: fuerzas que dos objetos se aplican entre sí. (pág. 69)
frecuencia: número de longitudes de onda que pasan por un punto cada segundo. (pág. 123)
fricción: fuerza de contacto que resiste el movimiento de dos superficies que están en contacto. (pág. 59)
fulcro: punto alrededor del cual gira una palanca. (pág. 100)

G

geographic isolation: the separation of a population of organisms from the rest of its species due to some physical barrier such as a mountain range or an ocean. (p. 238)

aislamiento geográfico: separación de una población de organismos del resto de su especie debido a alguna barrera física, tal como una cordillera o un océano. (pág. 238)

geosphere: the solid part of Earth. (p. 164)

glacial grooves: grooves in solid rock formations made by rocks that are carried by glaciers. (p. 261)

glacier: a large mass of ice, formed by snow accumulation on land, that moves slowly across Earth's surface. (p. 341)

glycolysis: a process by which glucose, a sugar, is broken down into smaller molecules. (p. 413)

grain: an individual particle in a rock. (p. 281)

gravity: an attractive force that exists between all objects that have mass. (pp. 59, 165)

geosfera: parte sólida de la Tierra. (pág. 164)

surcos glaciales: surcos en las formaciones de roca sólida producidos por las rocas transportadas por los glaciares. (pág. 261)

glaciar: masa enorme de hielo, formada por la acumulación de nieve en la tierra, que se mueve lentamente por la superficie de la Tierra. (pág. 341)

glucólisis: proceso por el cual la glucosa, un azúcar, se divide en moléculas más pequeñas. (pág. 413)

grano: partícula individual de una roca. (pág. 281)

gravedad: fuerza de atracción que existe entre todos los objetos que tienen masa. (pág. 59, 165)

H

heat: the movement of thermal energy from a region of higher temperature to a region of lower temperature. (p. 30)

Holocene epoch: the current epoch of geologic time which began 10,000 years ago. (p. 259)

horizons: layers of soil formed from the movement of the products of weathering. (p. 358)

hypothesis: a possible explanation for an observation that can be tested by scientific investigations. (p. NOS 4)

calor: movimiento de energía térmica desde una región de alta temperatura a una región de baja temperatura. (pág. 30)

Holoceno: época actual del tiempo geológico que comenzó hace 10.000 años. (pág. 259)

horizontes: capas de suelo formadas por el movimiento de productos meteorizados. (pág. 358)

hipótesis: explicación posible de una observación que se puede probar por medio de investigaciones científicas. (pág. NOS 4)

I

ice age: a period of time when a large portion of Earth's surface is covered by glaciers. (p. 261)

inclined plane: a simple machine that consists of a ramp, or a flat, sloped surface. (p. 103)

independent variable: the factor that is changed by the investigator to observe how it affects a dependent variable. (p. NOS 18)

inertia (ihn UR shuh): the tendency of an object to resist a change in motion. (p. 65)

inference: a logical explanation of an observation that is drawn from prior knowledge or experience. (p. NOS 4)

era del hielo: período de tiempo cuando los glaciares cubren una gran porción de la superficie de la Tierra. (pág. 261)

plano inclinado: máquina simple que consiste en una rampa, o superficie plana inclinada. (pág. 103)

variable independiente: factor que el investigador cambia para observar cómo afecta la variable dependiente. (pág. NOS 18)

inercia: tendencia de un objeto a resistir un cambio en el movimiento. (pág. 65)

inferencia: explicación lógica de una observación que se extrae de un conocimiento previo o experiencia. (pág. NOS 4)

infrared wave: an electromagnetic wave that has a wavelength shorter than a microwave but longer than visible light. (p. 132)

onda infrarroja: onda electromagnética que tiene una longitud de onda más corta que la de una microonda, pero más larga que la de la luz visible. (pág. 132)

inland sea: a body of water formed when ocean water floods continents. (p. 244)

mar interior: cuerpo de agua formado cuando el agua del océano inunda los continentes. (pág. 244)

intensity: the amount of energy that passes through a square meter of space in one second. (p. 136)

intensidad: cantidad de energía que atraviesa un metro cuadrado de espacio en un segundo. (pág. 136)

International System of Units (SI): the internationally accepted system of measurement. (p. NOS 10)

Sistema Internacional de Unidades (SI): sistema de medidas aceptado internacionalmente. (pág. NOS 10)

interphase: the period during the cell cycle of a cell's growth and development. (p. 430)

interfase: período durante el ciclo celular del crecimiento y desarrollo de una célula. (pág. 430)

intrusive rock: igneous rock that forms as magma cools underground. (p. 291)

roca intrusiva: roca ígnea que se forma cuando el magma se enfría bajo el suelo. (pág. 291)

K

kinetic energy: energy due to motion. (p. 11)

energía cinética: energía debida al movimiento. (pág. 11)

L

land bridge: a landform that connects two continents that were previously separated. (p. 238)

puente terrestre: accidente geográfico que conecta dos continentes que anteriormente estaban separados. (pág. 238)

landform: a topographic feature formed by processes that shape Earth's surface. (p. 182)

accidente geográfico: característica topográfica formada por procesos que moldean la superficie de la Tierra. (pág. 182)

landslide: rapid, downhill movement of soil, loose rocks, and boulders. (p. 339)

deslizamiento de tierra: movimiento rápido del suelo, rocas sueltas y canto rodado, pendiente abajo. (pág. 339)

lava: magma that erupts onto Earth's surface. (p. 283)

lava: magma que llega a la superficie de la Tierra. (pág. 283)

law of conservation of energy: law that states that energy can be transformed from one form to another, but it cannot be created or destroyed. (p. 18)

ley de la conservación de la energía: ley que plantea que la energía puede transformarse de una forma a otra, pero no puede crearse ni destruirse. (pág. 18)

lever: a simple machine that consists of a bar that pivots, or rotates, around a fixed point. (p. 100)

palanca: máquina simple que consiste en una barra que gira, o rota, alrededor de un punto fijo. (pág. 100)

lipid: a large macromolecule that does not dissolve in water. (p. 391)

lípido: macromolécula extensa que no se disuelve en agua. (pág. 391)

lithosphere (LIH thuh sfihr): the rigid outermost layer of Earth that includes the uppermost mantle and crust. (pp. 174, 216)

loess (LUHS): a crumbly, windblown deposit of silt and clay. (p. 334)

longitudinal (lahn juh TEWD nul) wave: a wave in which the disturbance is parallel to the direction the wave travels. (p. 121)

longshore current: a current that flows parallel to the shoreline. (p. 331)

litosfera: capa rígida más externa de la Tierra que incluye el manto superior y la corteza. (pág. 174, 216)

loess: depósito quebradizo de limo y arcilla transportados por el viento. (pág. 334)

onda longitudinal: onda en la que la perturbación es paralela a la dirección en que viaja la onda. (pág. 121)

corriente costera: corriente que fluye paralela a la costa. (pág. 331)

M

macromolecule: substance that forms from joining many small molecules together. (p. 389)

magma: molten rock stored beneath Earth's surface. (p. 283)

magnetic reversal: an event that causes a magnetic field to reverse direction. (p. 210)

magnetosphere: the outer part of Earth's magnetic field that interacts with charged particles. (p. 177)

mantle: the thick middle layer in the solid part of Earth. (p. 174)

mass extinction: the extinction of many species on Earth within a short period of time. (p. 237)

mass wasting: the downhill movement of a large mass of rocks or soil due to gravity. (p. 338)

meander: a broad, C-shaped curve in a stream. (p. 330)

mechanical advantage: the ratio of a machine's output force produced to the input force applied. (p. 94)

mechanical energy: sum of the potential energy and the kinetic energy in a system. (p. 12)

mechanical wave: a wave that can travel only through matter. (p. 120)

mechanical weathering: physical processes that naturally break rocks into smaller pieces. (p. 356)

mega-mammal: large mammal of the Cenozoic era. (p. 262)

Mesozoic era: the middle era of the Phanerozoic eon. (p. 243)

macromolécula: sustancia que se forma al unir muchas moléculas pequeñas. (pág. 389)

magma: roca derretida almacenada debajo de la superficie de la Tierra. (pág. 283)

inversión magnética: evento que causa que un campo magnético invierta su dirección. (pág. 210)

magnetosfera: parte externa del campo magnético de la Tierra que interactúa con partículas cargadas. (pág. 177)

manto: capa delgada central de la parte sólida de la Tierra. (pág. 174)

extinción en masa: extinción de muchas especies en la Tierra dentro de un período de tiempo corto. (pág. 237)

transporte en masa: movimiento cuesta debajo de gran cantidad de roca o suelo debido a la fuerza de gravedad. (pág. 338)

meandro: curva pronunciada en forma de C en un arroyo. (pág. 330)

ventaja mecánica: relación entre la fuerza útil que produce una máquina con la fuerza aplicada. (pág. 94)

energía mecánica: suma de la energía potencial y de la energía cinética en un sistema. (pág. 12)

onda mecánica: onda que puede viajar sólo a través de la materia. (pág. 120)

meteorización mecánica: proceso físico natural mediante el cual se rompe una roca en pedazos más pequeños. (pág. 356)

mega mamífero: mamífero enorme de la era Cenozoica. (pág. 262)

era Mesozoica: era media del eón Fanerozoico. (pág. 243)

metamorphism: process that affects the structure or composition of a rock in a solid state as a result of changes in temperature, pressure, or the addition of chemical fluids. (p. 303)

metamorfismo: proceso que afecta la estructura o composición de una roca en estado sólido como resultado de cambios en la temperatura, la presión, o por la adición de fluidos químicos. (pág. 303)

mid-ocean ridge: long, narrow mountain range on the ocean floor; formed by magma at divergent plate boundaries. (p. 207)

dorsal oceánica: cordillera larga y angosta en el lecho del océano, formada por magma en los límites de las placas divergentes. (pág. 207)

mitosis (mi TOH sus): a process during which the nucleus and its contents divide. (p. 433)

mitosis: proceso durante el cual el núcleo y sus contenidos se divide. (pág. 433)

moraine: a mound or ridge of unsorted sediment deposited by a glacier. (p. 342)

morrena: monte o colina de sedimento sin clasificar depositado por un glacial. (pág. 342)

motion: the process of changing position. (p. 47)

movimiento: proceso de cambiar de posición. (pág. 47)

mountain: landform with high relief and high elevation. (p. 185)

montaña: accidente geográfico de alto relieve y elevación alta. (pág. 185)

N

Newton's first law of motion: law that states that if the net force acting on an object is zero, the motion of the object does not change. (p. 65)

primera ley del movimiento de Newton: ley que establece que si la fuerza neta ejercida sobre un objeto es cero, el movimiento de dicho objeto no cambia. (pág. 65)

Newton's second law of motion: law that states that the acceleration of an object is equal to the new force exerted on the object divided by the object's mass. (p. 68)

segunda ley del movimiento de Newton: ley que establece que la aceleración de un objeto es igual a la fuerza neta que actúa sobre él divida por su masa. (pág. 68)

Newton's third law of motion: law that states that for every action there is an equal and opposite reaction. (p. 69)

tercera ley del movimiento de Newton: ley que establece que para cada acción hay una reacción igual en dirección opuesta. (pág. 69)

noncontact force: a force that one object applies to another object without touching it. (p. 58)

fuerza de no contacto: fuerza que un objeto puede aplicar sobre otro sin tocarlo. (pág. 58)

non-foliated rock: metamorphic rock with mineral grains that have a random, interlocking texture. (p. 305)

roca no foliada: roca metamórfica con granos de mineral que tienen una textura entrelazada al azar. (pág. 305)

nonrenewable energy resource: an energy resource that is available in limited amounts or that is used faster than it can be replaced in nature. (p. 24)

recurso energético no renovable: recurso energético disponible en cantidades limitadas o que se usa más rápido de lo que se repone en la naturaleza. (pág. 24)

normal polarity: when magnetized objects, such as compass needles, orient themselves to point north. (p. 210)

polaridad normal: ocurre cuando los objetos magnetizados, tales como las agujas de la brújula, se orientan a sí mismas para apuntar al norte. (pág. 210)

nuclear energy: energy stored in and released from the nucleus of an atom. (p. 10)

energía nuclear: energía almacenada en y liberada por el núcleo de un átomo. (pág. 10)

nucleic acid: a macromolecule that forms when long chains of molecules called nucleotides join together. (p. 390)

ácido nucléico: macromolécula que se forma cuando cadenas largas de moléculas llamadas nucleótidos se unen. (pág. 390)

nucleus: part of a eukaryotic cell that directs cell activity and contains genetic information stored in DNA. (p. 399)

núcleo: parte de la célula eucariótica que gobierna la actividad celular y contiene la información genética almacenada en el ADN. (pág. 399)

O

observation: the act of using one or more of your senses to gather information and take note of what occurs. (p. NOS 4)

observación: acción de usar uno o más sentidos para reunir información y tomar notar de lo que ocurre. (pág. NOS 4)

opaque: a material through which light does not pass. (p. 134)

opaco: material por el que no pasa la luz. (pág. 134)

open system: a system that exchanges matter or energy with the environment. (p. 21)

sistema abierto: sistema que intercambia materia o energía con el ambiente. (pág. 21)

organ: a group of different tissues working together to perform a particular job. (p. 446)

órgano: grupo de diferentes tejidos que trabajan juntos para realizar una función específica. (pág. 446)

organelle: membrane-surrounded component of a eukaryotic cell with a specialized function. (p. 398)

organelo: componente de una célula eucariótica rodeado de una membrana con una función especializada. (pág. 398)

organic matter: remains of something that was once alive. (p. 364)

materia orgánica: restos de algo que una vez estuvo vivo. (pág. 364)

organ system: a group of organs that work together and perform a specific task. (p. 447)

sistema de órganos: grupo de órganos que trabajan juntos y realizar una función específica. (pág. 447)

osmosis: the diffusion of water molecules only through a membrane. (p. 406)

ósmosis: difusión de las moléculas de agua únicamente a través de una membrana. (pág. 406)

outwash: layered sediment deposited by streams of water that flow from a melting glacier. (p. 342)

sandur: capas de sedimentos depositados por las corrientes de agua que fluyen de un glaciar en deshielo. (pág. 342)

oxidation: the process that combines the element oxygen with other elements or molecules. (p. 359)

oxidación: proceso por el cual se combina el elemento oxígeno con otros elementos o moléculas. (pág. 359)

P

Paleozoic era: the oldest era of the Phanerozoic eon. (p. 243)

era Paleozoica: era más antigua del eón Fanerozoico. (pág. 243)

Pangaea (pan JEE uh): name given to a supercontinent that began to break apart approximately 200 million years ago. (p. 199)

Pangea: nombre dado a un supercontinente que empezó a separarse hace aproximadamente 200 millones de años. (pág. 199)

parent material: the starting material of soil consisting of rock or sediment that is subject to weathering. (p. 366)

passive transport: the movement of substances through a cell membrane without using the cell's energy. (p. 405)

period: a unit of geologic time smaller than an era. (p. 235)

photosynthesis: a series of chemical reactions that convert light energy, water, and CO_2 into the food-energy molecule glucose and give off oxygen. (p. 415)

pitch: the perception of how high or low a sound is; related to the frequency of a sound wave. (p. 143)

plain: landform with low relief and low elevation. (p. 184)

plastic deformation: the permanent change in shape of rocks caused by bending or folding. (p. 304)

plateau: an area with low relief and high elevation. (p. 185)

plate tectonics: theory that Earth's surface is broken into large, rigid pieces that move with respect to each other. (p. 215)

Pleistocene epoch: the first epoch of the Quaternary period. (p. 261)

plesiosaur: Mesozoic marine reptile with a small head, long neck, and flippers. (p. 255)

pores: small holes and spaces in soil. (p. 364)

potential (puh TEN chul) energy: stored energy due to the interactions between objects or particles. (p. 9)

power: the rate at which work is done. (p. 87)

precision: a description of how similar or close measurements are to each other. (p. NOS 12)

prediction: a statement of what will happen next in a sequence of events. (p. NOS 5)

protein: a long chain of amino acid molecules; contains carbon, hydrogen, oxygen, nitrogen, and sometimes sulfur. (p. 391)

material parental: material original del suelo compuesto de roca o sedimento sujeto a meteorización. (pág. 366)

transporte pasivo: movimiento de sustancias a través de una membrana celular sin usar la energía de la célula. (pág. 405)

período: unidad del tiempo geológico más pequeña que una era. (pág. 235)

fotosíntesis: serie de reacciones químicas que convierten la energía lumínica, el agua y el CO_2 en glucosa, una molécula de energía alimentaria, y libera oxígeno. (pág. 415)

tono: percepción de qué tan alto o bajo es el sonido; relacionado con la frecuencia de la onda sonora. (pág. 143)

plano: accidente geográfico de bajo relieve y baja elevación. (pág. 184)

deformación plástica: cambio permanente en la forma de las rocas causado por el doblamiento o el plegado. (pág. 304)

meseta: área de bajo relieve y alta elevación. (pág. 185)

tectónica de placas: teoría que afirma que la superficie de la Tierra está divida en piezas enormes y rígidas que se mueven una con respecto a la otra. (pág. 215)

época del Pleistoceno: primera época del período Cuaternario. (pág. 261)

plesiosaurio: reptil marino del Mesozoico de cabeza pequeña, cuello largo y aletas. (pág. 255)

poros: huecos y espacios pequeños en el suelo. (pág. 364)

energía potencial: energía almacenada debido a las interacciones entre objetos o partículas. (pág. 9)

potencia: velocidad a la que se hace trabajo. (pág. 87)

precisión: sescripción de qué tan similar o cercana están las mediciones una de otra. (pág. NOS 12)

predicción: afirmación de lo que ocurrirá a continuación en una secuencia de eventos. (pág. NOS 5)

proteína: larga cadena de aminoácidos; contiene carbono, hidrógeno, oxígeno, nitrógeno y, algunas veces, sulfuro. (pág. 391)

pterosaur: Mesozoic flying reptile with large, batlike wings. (p. 255)

pterosaurio: reptil volador del Mesozoico de alas grandes parecidas a las del murciélago. (pág. 255)

pulley: a simple machine that consists of a grooved wheel with a rope or cable wrapped around it. (p. 105)

polea: máquina simple que consiste en una rueda acanalada rodeada por una cuerda o cable. (pág. 105)

R

radiant energy: energy carried by an electromagnetic wave. (p. 14)

energía radiante: energía que transporta una onda electromagnética. (pág. 14)

radiation: the transfer of thermal energy by electromagnetic waves. (p. 31)

radiación: transferencia de energía térmica por ondas electromagnéticas. (pág. 31)

radio wave: a low-frequency, low-energy electromagnetic wave that has a wavelength longer than about 30 cm. (p. 131)

onda de radio: onda electromagnética de baja frecuencia y baja energía que tiene una longitud de onda mayor de más o menos 30 cm. (pág. 131)

rarefaction (rayr uh FAK shun): region of a longitudinal wave where the particles of the medium are farthest apart. (p. 143)

rarefacción: region de una onda longitudinal donde las partículas del medio están más alejadas. (pág. 143)

reference point: the starting point you use to describe the motion or the position of an object. (p. 47)

punto de referencia: punto que se escoge para describir el movimiento o posición de un objeto. (pág. 47)

refraction: the change in direction of a wave as it changes speed in moving from one medium to another. (p. 126)

refracción: cambio en la dirección de una onda a medida que cambia de rapidez al moverse de un medio a otro. (pág. 126)

regional metamorphism: formation of metamorphic rock bodies that are hundreds of square kilometers in size. (p. 306)

metamorfismo regional: formación de cuerpos de rocas metamórficas que son del tamaño de cientos de kilómetros cuadrados. (pág. 306)

renewable energy resource: an energy resource that is replaced as fast as, or faster than, it is used. (p. 22)

recurso energético renovable: recurso energético que se repone tan rápido, o más rápido, de lo que se consume. (pág. 22)

reversed polarity: when magnetized objects reverse direction and orient themselves to point south. (p. 210)

polaridad inversa: ocurre cuando los objetos magnetizados invierten la dirección y se orientan a sí mismos para apuntar al sur. (pág. 210)

ridge push: the process that results when magma rises at a mid-ocean ridge and pushes oceanic plates in two different directions away from the ridge. (p. 221)

empuje de dorsal: proceso que resulta cuando el magma se levanta en la dorsal oceánica y empuja las placas oceánicas en dos direcciones diferentes, lejos de la dorsal. (pág. 221)

rock: a naturally occurring solid composed of minerals, rock fragments, and sometimes other materials such as organic matter. (p. 281)

roca: sólido de origen natural compuesto de minerales, acumulación de fragmentos y algunas veces de otros materiales como materia orgánica. (pág. 281)

rock cycle: the series of processes that change one type of rock into another type of rock. (p. 284)

ciclo geológico: series de procesos que cambian un tipo de roca en otro tipo de roca. (pág. 284)

S

science: the investigation and exploration of natural events and of the new information that results from those investigations. (p. NOS 2)

ciencia: la investigación y exploración de los eventos naturales y de la información nueva que es el resultado de estas investigaciones. (pág. NOS 2)

scientific law: a rule that describes a pattern in nature. (p. NOS 7)

ley científica: regla que describe un patrón dado en la naturaleza. (pág. NOS 7)

scientific theory: an explanation of observations or events that is based on knowledge gained from many observations and investigations. (p. NOS 7)

teoría científica: explicación de observaciones o eventos con base en conocimiento obtenido de muchas observaciones e investigaciones. (pág. NOS 7)

screw: a simple machine that consists of an inclined plane wrapped around a cylinder. (p. 104)

tornillo: máquina simple que consiste en un plano inclinado incrustado alrededor de un cilindro. (pág. 104)

seafloor spreading: the process by which new oceanic crust forms along a mid-ocean ridge and older oceanic crust moves away from the ridge. (p. 208)

expansión del lecho marino: proceso mediante el cual se forma corteza oceánica nueva en la dorsal oceánica, y la corteza oceánica vieja se aleja de la dorsal. (pág. 208)

sediment: rock material that forms when rocks are broken down into smaller pieces or dissolved in water as rocks erode. (p. 283)

sedimento: material rocoso formado cuando las rocas se rompen en piezas pequeñas o se disuelven en agua al erosionarse. (pág. 283)

significant digits: the number of digits in a measurement that are known with a certain degree of reliability. (p. NOS 13)

cifras significativas: número de dígitos que se conoce con cierto grado de fiabilidad en una medida. (pág. NOS 13)

simple machine: a machine that does work using one movement. (p. 99)

máquina simple: máquina que hace trabajo con un movimiento. (pág. 99)

sister chromatids: two identical chromosomes that make up a duplicated chromosome. (p. 432)

cromátidas hermanas: dos cromosomas idénticos que constituyen un cromosoma duplicado. (pág. 432)

slab pull: the process that results when a dense oceanic plate sinks beneath a more buoyant plate along a subduction zone, pulling the rest of the plate that trails behind it. (p. 221)

convergencia de placas: proceso que resulta cuando una placa oceánica densa se hunde debajo de una placa flotante en una zona de subducción, arrastrando el resto de la placa detrás suyo. (pág. 221)

soil: a mixture of weathered rock, rock fragments, decayed organic matter, water, and air. (p. 364)

suelo: mezcla de roca meteorizada, fragmentos de rocas, materia orgánica descompuesta, agua y aire. (pág. 364)

sound energy: energy carried by sound waves. (p. 13)

energía sonora: energía que transportan las ondas sonoras. (pág. 13)

speed: the distance an object moves divided by the time it takes to move that distance. (p. 48)

rapidez: distancia que un objeto recorre dividida por el tiempo que éste tarda en recorrer dicha distancia. (pág. 48)

sphere: a ball shape with all points on the surface at an equal distance from the center. (p. 163)

stem cell: an unspecialized cell that is able to develop into many different cell types. (p. 444)

subduction: the process that occurs when one tectonic plate moves under another tectonic plate. (p. 217)

supercontinent: an ancient landmass which separated into present-day continents. (p. 247)

esfera: figura de bola cuyos puntos en la superficie están ubicados a una distancia igual del centro. (pág. 163)

célula madre: célula no especializada que tiene la capacidad de desarrollarse en diferentes tipos de células. (pág. 444)

subducción: proceso que ocurre cuando una placa tectónica se mueve debajo de otra placa tectónica. (pág. 217)

supercontinente: antigua masa de tierra que se dividió en los continentes actuales. (pág. 247)

T

talus: a pile of angular rocks and sediment from a rockfall. (p. 339)

technology: the practical use of scientific knowledge, especially for industrial or commercial use. (p. NOS 6)

temperature: the measure of the average kinetic energy of the particles in a material. (p. 29)

texture: a rock's grain size and the way the grains fit together. (p. 282)

thermal conductor: a material through which thermal energy flows quickly. (p. 34)

thermal energy: the sum of the kinetic energy and the potential energy of the particles that make up an object. (p. 12)

thermal insulator: a material through which thermal energy flows slowly. (p. 34)

till: a mixture of various sizes of sediment that has been deposited by a glacier. (p. 342)

tissue: a group of similar types of cells that work together to carry out specific tasks. (p. 445)

topography: the shape and steepness of the landscape. (p. 367)

transform plate boundary: the boundary between two plates that slide past each other. (p. 217)

translucent: a material that allows most of the light that strikes it to pass through, but through which objects appear blurry. (p. 134)

talus: montón de rocas angulares y sedimentos de un derrumbe de montaña. (pág. 339)

tecnología: uso práctico del conocimiento científico, especialmente para uso industrial o comercial. (pág. NOS 6)

temperatura: medida de la energía cinética promedio de las partículas de un material. (pág. 29)

textura: tamaño del grano de una roca y la forma como los granos encajan. (pág. 282)

conductor térmico: material en el cual la energía térmica se mueve con rapidez. (pág. 34)

energía térmica: suma de la energía cinética y potencial de las partículas que componen un objeto. (pág. 12)

aislante térmico: material a través del cual la energía térmica fluye con lentitud. (pág. 34)

till: mezcla de varios tamaños de sedimento depositado por un glaciar. (pág. 342)

tejido: grupo de tipos similares de células que trabajan juntas para llevar a cabo diferentes funciones. (pág. 445)

topografía: forma e inclinación del paisaje. (pág. 367)

límite de placas transcurrente: límite entre dos placas que se deslizan una con respecto a la otra. (pág. 217)

translúcido: material que permite el paso de la mayor cantidad de luz que lo toca, pero a través del cual los objetos se ven borrosos. (pág. 134)

transparent: a material that allows almost all of the light striking it to pass through, and through which objects can be seen clearly. (p. 134)

transverse wave: a wave in which the disturbance is perpendicular to the direction the wave travels. (p. 121)

transparente: material que permite el paso de la mayor cantidad de luz que lo toca, y a través del cual los objetos pueden verse con nitidez. (pág. 134)

onda transversal: onda en la que la perturbación es perpendicular a la dirección en que viaja la onda. (pág. 121)

U

ultraviolet wave: an electromagnetic wave that has a slightly shorter wavelength and higher frequency than visible light. (p. 132)

unbalanced forces: forces acting on an object that combine and form a net force that is not zero. (p. 61)

onda ultravioleta: onda electromagnética que tiene una longitud de onda ligeramente menor y mayor frecuencia que la luz visible. (pág. 132)

fuerzas no balanceadas: fuerzas que actúan sobre un objeto, se combinan y forman una fuerza neta diferente de cero. (pág. 61)

V

vaporization: the change of state from a liquid to a gas. (p. 33)

variable: any factor that can have more than one value. (p. NOS 18)

velocity: the speed and the direction of a moving object. (p. 49)

volcanic glass: rock that forms when lava cools too quickly to form crystals. (p. 290)

vaporización: cambio de estado líquido a gaseoso. (pág. 33)

variable: cualquier factor que tenga más de un valor. (pág. NOS 18)

velocidad: rapidez y dirección de un objeto en movimiento. (pág. 49)

vidrio volcánico: roca que se forma como resultado del enfriamiento muy rápido de la lava, formando cristales. (pág. 290)

W

wave: a disturbance that transfers energy from one place to another without transferring matter. (p. 13)

weathering: the mechanical and chemical processes that change Earth's surface over time. (p. 355)

wedge: a simple machine that consists of an inclined plane with one or two sloping sides; it is used to split or separate an object. (p. 104)

wheel and axle: a simple machine that consists of an axle attached to the center of a larger wheel, so that the shaft and wheel rotate together. (p. 102)

work: the amount of energy used as a force moves an object over a distance. (pp. 19, 83)

onda: perturbación que transfiere energía de un lugar a otro sin transferir materia. (pág. 13)

meteorización: procesos mecánicos y químicos que con el paso del tiempo cambian la superficie de la Tierra. (pág. 355)

cuña: máquina simple que consiste en un plano inclinado con uno o dos lados inclinados; se usa para partir o separar un objeto. (pág. 104)

rueda y eje: máquina simple que consiste en un eje insertado en el centro de una rueda grande, de manera que el eje y la rueda rotan juntos. (pág. 102)

trabajo: cantidad de energía usada como fuerza que mueve un objeto a cierta distancia. (pág. 19, 83)

Index

Italic numbers = illustration/photo **Bold numbers = vocabulary term**
lab = indicates entry is used in a lab on this page

A

B

C

H

I

J

K

N

X

Y

Credits

Art Acknowledgments: MCA+, Argosy, Cindy Shaw, Mapping Specialists Ltd.

Photo Credits

Cover Morales Morales/Photolibrary; **ix** (b)Fancy Photography/Veer; **vii** Ransom Studios; **NOS 02–03** Images & Stories/Alamy; **NOS 04** (l)Kelly Jett/Alamy, (r)Natural Visions/Alamy; **NOS 05** (t)MARK MOFFETT/MINDEN PICTURES/National Geographic Stock, (c)Frans Lanting/CORBIS (b)Hank Morgan - Rainbow/Science Faction/CORBIS; **NOS 06** Lynn Keddie/Photolibrary; **NOS 07** Jose Luis Pelaez, Inc./CORBIS; **NOS 08** (t)David S. Holloway/Getty Images, (c)Klaus Guldbrandsen/Photo Researchers, (b)Giovanni Chaves-Portilla/Fundación Ecodiversidad Colombia; **NOS 09** Dennis Kunkel Microscopy, Inc./PHOTOTAKE/Alamy; **NOS 11** Plush Studios/Getty Images; **NOS 12** (tl)Henry Groskinsky/Time & Life Pictures/Getty Images, (tr)Noel Hendrickson/Getty Image, (b)Georgette Douwma/Getty Images; **NOS 13** (t)Charlie Munsey/CORBIS, (b)Bill Hatcher/National Geographic/Getty Images; **NOS 14** Richard Peters/Alamy; **NOS 15** PETE OXFORD/MINDEN PICTURES/National Geographic Stock; **NOS 18** (tl)Charles D. Winters/Photo Researchers, (tr)Matt Meadows, (c)Louis Rosenstock/The McGraw-Hill Companies, (bl)David Chasey/Getty Images, (br)Biosphoto/NouN/Peter Arnold, Inc.; **NOS 19** (t)Lauren Burke/Getty Images, (b)Richard T. Nowitz/CORBIS; **NOS 20** (tl)Stockbyte/Getty Images, (tr)Don Farrall/Getty Images, (bl)Medicimage/Visulas Unlimited, Inc., (br)Hutchings Photography/Digital Light Source; **NOS 21** (l to r, t to b)Hutchings Photography/Digital Light Source, (1,3)The Mcgraw-Hill Companies; **NOS 22** NREL/US Department of Energy/Photo Researchers; **NOS 23** (l)akg-images, (r)Stefan Puchner/UPPA/Photoshot; **NOS 24** (l)Tom & Therisa Stack/Tom Stack & Associates, (r)Jan Hinsch/Photo Researchers; **NOS 25** (t)Peter Ginter/Getty Images, (c)Andrew Kaufman, (b)Ashley Cooper/Alamy; **NOS 26** Colin Braley/AP Images; **NOS 28** Mark E. Gibson/CORBIS; **NOS 29** Courtesy Seambiotic Ltd; **NOS 30** (l to r, t to b)Hutchings Photography/Digital Light Source, (1)The Mcgraw-Hill Companies; **NOS 31** Images & Stories/Alamy; **4** (cw from top, 2,3)CORBIS, (4)fStop/PunchStock, (5)Digital Archive Japan/Alamy, (6)Photodisc/Getty Images; **5** (bl,bc,)Lyn Hughes/CORBIS, (br)U.S. Air Force photo by Lisa M. Macias; **6–7** Frank Lukasseck/CORBIS; **8** Juniors Bildarchiv/photolibrary.com; **9** (t)Hutchings Photography/Digital Light Source, (b)Dimitri Vervitsiotis/Getty Images; **10** (t)David Young-Wolff/Getty Images, (b)Digital Vision/PunchStock; **11** (tl, tc)i love images/Alamy, (tr)Asia Images Group Pte Ltd/Alamy; (b)Hutchings Photography/Digital Light Source; **12** David Stoecklein/CORBIS; **13** (l)Royalty-Free/CORBIS, (r)Hutchings Photography/Digital Light Source; **15** (tl)Dimitri Vervitsiotis/Getty Images, (r)Tommaso di Girolamo/age fotostock, (bl)David Stoecklein/CORBIS; **16** (t)Hutchings Photography/Digital Light Source, (c)The Mcgraw-Hill Companies, (b)Hutchings Photography/Digital Light Source; **17** David Tipling/Minden Pictures; **18** Hutchings Photography/Digital Light Source; **19** MOODBOARD/age fotostock; **20** Hutchings Photography/Digital Light Source; **21** (l)Transtock, (inset)Frederic Charpentier/Alamy; **22** (t)JOSE MANUEL RIBEIRO/Reuters/Landov, (b)Thinkstock/Masterfile; **23** (t)Harald Sund/Getty Images, (c)Roger Ressmeyer/CORBIS, (b)AP Photo/Heribert Proepper; **25** (tl)MOODBOARD/age footstock, (cl)Transtock, (r)The McGraw-Hill Companies, (bl)Thinkstock/Masterfile; **26** (tl)Adrian Sherratt/Alamy, (bl)MIXA/Alamy, (br)Brand X Pictures/PunchStock, (bkgd)Richard Clark/photolibrary.com; **27** Adam Jones/Visuals Unlimited, Inc.; **28** Foodfolio/age fotostock; **29** (l)Sue Flood/Getty Images, (r)David Taylor/Photo Researchers, Inc.; **30** foodfolio/Alamy; **32** The McGraw-Hill Companies; **33** (l)Charles D. Winters/Photo Researchers, Inc., (r)Thomas Sbampato/Alaskastock/photolibrary.com; **34** (l)Scientifica/Visuals Unlimited, Inc., (r)Hutchings Photography/Digital Light Source; **35** (tl)Adam Jones/Visuals Unlimited, Inc., (r)Thomas Sbampato/photolibrary.com, (bl)Scientifica/Visuals Unlimited, Inc.; **36** (tl,r,bl)Hutchings Photography/Digital Light Source, (cl)Macmillan/McGraw-Hill; **37** Hutchings Photography/Digital Light Source; **38** (t)Juniors Bildarchiv/photolibrary.com, (c)JOSE MANUEL RIBEIRO/Reuters/Landov, (b)Thomas Sbampato/photolibrary.com; **40** (l)Gavin Hellier/Getty Images, (r)Jupiterimages/Getty Images; **41** (l)David Madison/Getty Images, (r)Frank Lukasseck/CORBIS; **44–45** AFP/Getty Images; **46** Hill Street Studios/Getty Images; **47** (t)Hutchings Photography/Digital Light Source, (t)Nancy Ney/Getty Images; **50** Hutchings Photography/Digital Light Source; **52** PAUL NICKLEN/National Geographic Stock; **54** Nancy Ney/Getty Images; **56** Visuals Unlimited/CORBIS; **57** (t)Hutchings Photography/Digital Light Source, (c)Anthony-Masterson/Getty Images, (b)Per Breiehagen/Getty Images; **58** (tl)Visual Cuisines/Getty Images, (tc)Photodisc/Alamy, (tr)Floresco Productions/CORBIS, (bl)Mark Spowart/Alamy, (bc)sciencephotos/Alamy, (br)Steve Casimiro/Getty Images; **59** (t)Hutchings Photography/Digital Light Source, (b)David Madison/Getty Images; **62** sciencephotos/Alamy; **63** (r)Hutchings Photography/Digital Light Source; **64** imac/Alamy; **65** Hutchings Photography/Digital Light Source; **66** (tl,tr)Bernd Mellmann/Alamy, (b)Hutchings Photography/Digital Light Source; **67** (tl,tr)camera lucida lifestyle/Alamy, (b)Richard Green/Alamy; **68** skip caplan/Alamy; **69** (t)Uwe Krejci/Getty Images, (b)The McGraw-Hill Companies, Inc./Jill Braaten, photographer; **70** (t)DEX IMAGE/Getty Images, (c)Masterfile, (b)Nikki O'Keefe Images/Getty Images; **71** (t)Per Breiehagen/Getty Images, (c)skip caplan/Alamy, (b)The McGraw-Hill Companies, Inc./Jill Braaten, photographer; **72** (5,6)The Mcgraw-Hill Companies, (others)Hutchings Photography/Digital Light Source; **73** Hutchings Photography/Digital Light Source; **74** (t)sciencephotos/Alamy, (b)skip caplan/Alamy; **77** (l)NASA, (r)AFP/Getty Images; **80–81** Neil Duncan/photolibrary.com; **81** Malcolm Fife/Getty Images; **82** (t)Hutchings Photography/Digital Light Source, (bl,br)JUPITERIMAGES/Brand X/Alamy; **85–86** Hutchings Photography/Digital Light Source; **88** (tl,r)JUPITERIMAGES/Brand X/Alamy, (cl,bl)Hutchings Photography/Digital Light Source; **89** (t)P.H. Emerson/George Eastman House/Getty Images, (c)Hulton Archive/Getty Images, (b)Bridgeman Art Library/SuperStock, (inset)Eduardo M. Rivero/age fotostock; **90** Philip and Karen Smith/Getty Images; **91** (t)Hutchings Photography/Digital Light Source, (c)Clive Streeter/Getty Images; (b)CORBIS; **92** (t)Hutchings Photography/Digital Light Source, (bl,br)The McGraw-Hill Companies; **93** (t)Steve Gorton/Dorling Kindersley/Getty Images, (c)Sean Justice/Getty Images, (b)Dorling Kindersley; **95** Glowimages/Getty Images; **96** (tl)Clive Streeter/Getty Images, (cl,cr)The McGraw-Hill Companies, (bl)Glowimages/Getty Images, (br)Sean Justice/Getty Images; **97** (t to b)Hutchings Photography/Digital Light Source, (4)Macmillan/McGraw-Hill; **98** SoloStock Travel/Alamy; **99** (t,bl)The McGraw-Hill Companies, (cl)Bob Elsdale, (c)Rod McLean/Alamy, (cr)David Papazian Photography Inc./Jupiterimages, (bc)F. Schussler/PhotoLink/Getty Images, (br)Susan E. Degginger/Alamy; **100** (t)Jupiterimages, (c)Digital Vision/Alamy, (b)Andy Aitchison/CORBIS; **102** (tl)Matt Carr/Getty Images, (tc)Maurilio Cheli/epa/CORBIS, (tr)liquidlibrary/PictureQuest, (b)JUPITERIMAGES/Brand X/Alamy; **104** (t)Mark Douet/Getty Images, (b)Reimar/Alamy; **105** Hutchings Photography/Digital Light Source; **106** (t)imagebroker/Alamy, (b)Brand Z/Alamy; **107** (tl)F. Schussler/PhotoLink/Getty Images, (cl)Digital Vision/Alamy, (r)CORBIS, (bl)Mark Douet/Getty Images; **108** (t to b)Hutchings Photography/Digital Light Source, (2,3)The McGraw-Hill Companies; **109** Hutchings Photography/Digital Light Source; **110** (t)Hutchings Photography/Digital Light Source, (c)Steve Gorton/Dorling Kindersley/Getty Images, (b)Jupiterimages; **113** (l)Hutchings Photography/Digital Light Source, (r)Neil Duncan/photolibrary.com; **116–117** imac/Alamy; **118** redbrickstock.com/Alamy; **119** (t)Hutchings Photography/Digital Light Source, (b)Comstock/PunchStock; **120** Don Farrall/Getty Images; **123** Hutchings Photography/Digital Light Source; **126** Richard Megna, Fundamental Photographs, NYC; **127** (t)Comstock/PunchStock, (b)Richard Megna, Fundamental Photographs, NYC; **128** (t to b)Hutchings

Credits

Photography/Digital Light Source, (2,3,4)The Mcgraw-Hill Companies, Momentum Creative Group/Alamy Images; **129** Heike Odermatt/Foto Natura/Minden Pictures; **130** Hutchings Photography/Digital Light Source; **132** imagebroker/Alamy; **133** Photo montage by Nick Veasey/Getty Images; **134** Helena Karlsson/Getty Images; **136** (t,b)Todd Carlson; **137** Alan Bolesta/age fotostock; **139** (t)imagebroker/Alamy, (c)Helena Karlsson/Getty Images, (b)Alan Bolesta/age fotostock; **140** (t)Data courtesy Marc Imhoff of NASA GSFC and Christopher Elvidge of NOAA NGDC. Image by Craig Mayhew and Robert Simmon, NASA, (bl)Domino/Getty Images, (br)SW Productions/Getty Images; **141** Sean Justice; **142, 144** Hutchings Photography/Digital Light Source; **147** (t)Sean Justice, (b)Hutchings Photography/Digital Light Source; **148** (t to b)The McGraw-Hill Companies; **149** John Bentley/Alamy; **150** (t)Don Farrall/Getty Images, (b)Heike Odermatt/Foto Natura/Minden Pictures; **153** imac/Alamy; **158** Jason Reed/Photodisc/Getty Images; **159** Edwin Stranner/Photolibrary; **160–161** Robert Postma/age fotostock; **163** Bloomimage/CORBIS; **163** Hutchings Photography/Digital Light Source; **164** (tl)Brand X Pictures/PunchStock, (tr)Gary Vestal/Getty Images, (c)NASA, (bl)CORBIS/SuperStock, (br)age fotostock/SuperStock; **166** Hutchings Photography/Digital Light Source; **168** Gary Vestal/Getty Images; **169** (tr)The Natural History Museum/Alamy, AMNH; **170** Stephen Alvarez/Getty Images; **171, 173** Hutchings Photography/Digital Light Source; **174–175** (inset)NASA, (bkgd)StockTrek/Getty Images; **177** (b)NASA Marshall Space Flight Center (NASA-MSFC); **179** (t to b)Hutchings Photography/Digital Light Source, (4)Macmillan/McGraw-Hill; **180** David Gralian/Alamy; **181, 183** Hutchings Photography/Digital Light Source; **184** (t)Medioimages/Photodisc/Getty Images, (b)Jonathan Andrew/CORBIS; **185** (l)Yann Arthus-Bertrand/CORBIS, (tr)Jane Sweeney/Getty Images, (cr)CORBIS; **187** (t)CORBIS, (b)Yann Arthus-Bertrand/CORBIS; **188** (t to b) Hutchings Photography/Digital Light Source, (3,4,5)Macmillan/McGraw-Hill; **189** Hutchings Photography/Digital Light Source; **190** (t)Bloomimage/CORBIS, (c)Stephen Alvarez/Getty Images, (b)David Gralian/Alamy; **193** Robert Postma/age fotostock; **196–197** Arctic-Images/Getty Images; **198** Oddur Sigurdsson/Visuals Unlimited, Inc.; **199** Hutchings Photography/Digital Light Source; **201** Walter Geiersperger/CORBIS; **202** Tim Fitzharris/Minden Pictures; **203** Hutchings Photography/Digital Light Source; **205** (l)Peter Johnson/CORBIS, (r)Clare Flemming; **206** Science Source/Photo Researchers; **207** Hutchings Photography/Digital Light Source; **208, 212** Image courtesy of Submarine Ring of Fire 2002 Exploration, NOAA-OE.; **213** (t to b)Hutchings Photography/Digital Light Source, (3)Macmillan/McGraw-Hill, (r)Dr. Peter Sloss, formerly of NGDC/NOAA/NGDC; **214** NASA; **215** Hutchings Photography/Digital Light Source; **218** (t to b)Dr. Ken MacDonald/Photo Researchers, Inc., (2)Lloyd Cluff/CORBIS, (3)Jim Richardson/CORBIS, (4)Tony Waltham/Getty Images; **220, 223** Richard Megna/Fundamental Photographs; **224** (t to b,tr,cr,br) Hutchings Photography/Digital Light Source, (2,3,4)The McGraw-Hill Companies; **232–233** Kevin Schafer/CORBIS; **234** (t)Joseph Szkodzinski/Getty Images, Francois Gohier/Photo Researchers, Inc.; **235** Hutchings Photography/Digital Light Source; **236** (tl)Andy Crawford/Getty Images, (tr,bl)DK Limited/CORBIS; **237** Jonathan Blair/CORBIS; **238** (t)Hutchings Photography/Digital Light Source, (bl)Robert Clay/Alamy, (bc)Panoramic Images/Getty Images, (br)Tom Bean/CORBIS; **239** 2007 Photograph of Ediacara Biota diorama at Smithsonian Institute/Joshua Sherurcij; **240** (t)Andy Crawford/Getty Images, (b)Panoramic Images/Getty Images; **241** (tl)Andrew Ward/Life File/Getty Images, (tc)DK Limited/CORBIS, (tr)Tom Bean/CORBIS, (bl)John Cancalosi/Alamy; **242** Mark Steinmetz; **243** Hutchings Photography/Digital Light Source; **245** (b)DEA PICTURE LIBRARY/Getty Images; **246** The Field Museum, GEO85637c; **247** Hutchings Photography/Digital Light Source; **248** The Field Museum, GEO85637c; **249** Photodisc/Getty Images; **250** DEA PICTURE LIBRARY/Getty Images; **251, 254** Hutchings Photography/Digital Light Source; **255** (t)Naturfoto Honal/CORBIS, (b)Nigel Reed QEDimages/Alamy; **257** (tl)Jin Meng, (tr)(br)American Museum of Natural History, (bl)AMNH/Denis Finnin; **258** Nik Wheeler/CORBIS; **259** Hutchings Photography/Digital Light Source; **261** Mark Steinmetz; **262** Sinclair Stammers/Photo Researchers, Inc.; **264** (t)Ariadne Van Zandbergen/Lonely Planet Images, Inc., (b)Getty Images; **265** Ariadne Van Zandbergen/Lonely Planet Images, Inc.; **266** (t to b)Hutchings Photography/Digital Light Source, (2,4)Macmillan/McGraw-Hill; **270** Tom Bean/CORBIS; **271** Kevin Schafer/CORBIS; **278–279** Steve Allen/Getty Images; **280** Robert Harding Picture Library Ltd/Alamy; **281** (t)Hutchings Photography/Digital Light Source, (b)Momatiuk - Eastcott/CORBIS; **282** (tl)Colin Keates/Dorling Kindersley, Courtesy of the Natural History Museum, London, (cl)Andreas Einsiedel/Dorling Kindersley, (b)Nancy Simmerman/Getty Images; **283** Eastcott/CORBIS; **284** (tl)Brent Turner/BLT Productions, (bl,br)Macmillan/McGraw-Hill; **285** Hutchings Photography/Digital Light Source; **286** (tl)Momatiuk - Eastcott/CORBIS, (cl)George Bernard/Photo Researchers; **287** (t)Jeff Vanuga/CORBIS, (cl)Sarah Fowler, (cr)The McGraw-Hill Companies Inc./Ken Cavanagh Photographer, (br)Scientifica/Getty Images; **288** Philippe Bourseiller/Getty Images; **289** (t)Hutchings Photography/Digital Light Source, (b)Kevin Fleming/CORBIS; **290** (tl)Harry Taylor/Getty Images, (cl)Tony Lilley/Alamy, (b)Hutchings Photography/Digital Light Source; **291** (tl)The McGraw-Hill Companies Inc./Ken Cavanagh Photographer, (tr)Mark Schneider/Getty Images; **292** (tl)Colin Keates/Getty Images, (tr)RF Company/Alamy, Albert Copley/Visuals Unlimited/Alamy, (cr)Joyce Photographics/Photo Researchers, Inc., (bl)Mike Dunning/Dorling Kindersley, (br)Mark Schneider/Getty Images; **293** (tl)Joyce Photographics/Photo Researchers, Inc., (cl)Harry Taylor/Getty Images, (r)Mike Dunning/Dorling Kindersley, (bl)Kevin Fleming/CORBIS; **294** (t to b)Macmillan/McGraw-Hill, (5)Hutchings Photography/Digital Light Source; **295** Panoramic Images/Getty Images; **296** (tr,cr,br)Macmillan/McGraw-Hill, (bl)Momatiuk - Eastcott/CORBIS; **297** (l)Andreas Einsiedel/Dorling Kindersley, (r)Visuals Unlimited/CORBIS; **298** National Geographic/Getty Images; **299** (l to r)PhotoStock-Israel/Alamy, (2)Frank Blackburn/Alamy, (3)DEA/C.BEVILACQUA/Getty Images, (4)Andreas Einsiedel/Dorling Kindersley, (5)Nearby/Alamy, (6)Mark Schneider/Getty Images; **300** (t)Visuals Unlimited/CORBIS, (c)National Geographic/Getty Images, (b)Andreas Einsiedel/Dorling Kindersley; **301** (t to b)Macmillan/McGraw-Hill, (7)Hutchings Photography/Digital Light Source; **302** Visuals Unlimited/CORBIS; **303–304** Hutchings Photography/Digital Light Source; **305** Visuals Unlimited/CORBIS; **306** (t to b)Macmillan/McGraw-Hill, (2)Steve Gorton/Getty Images, (3)RF Company/Alamy, (4)Mark A. Schneider/Photo Researchers, Inc., (5)Dr. Parvinder Sethi/The McGraw-Hill Companies, (6)Andrew J. Martinez/Photo Researchers, Inc., (7)The McGraw-Hill Companies Inc./Ken Cavanagh Photographer; **307** (t)Visuals Unlimited/CORBIS, (c)Andrew J. Martinez/Photo Researchers, Inc., (b)Macmillan/McGraw-Hill; **308** (6)Hutchings Photography/Digital Light Source, (others)Macmillan/McGraw-Hill; **309** (t,c,b)Macmillan/McGraw-Hill, (bl)The McGraw-Hill Companies Inc./Ken Cavanagh Photographer; **310** (tl)Momatiuk - Eastcott/CORBIS, (cl)National Geographic/Getty Images, (cr)Mike Dunning/Dorling Kindersley, (br)Macmillan/McGraw-Hill; **312** (l)Macmillan/McGraw-Hill, (r)PhotoStock-Israel/Alamy; **313** Steve Allen/Getty Images; **316–317** Beate Muenter/PhotoLibrary; **317** (t)Creatas/PunchStock, (b)Glen Allison/Getty Images; **318** Hutchings Photography/Digital Light Source; **320** (b)Image Source; **321** (tl)Medioimages/Photodisc/Getty Images, (tr)Photodisc/SuperStock, (b)Hutchings Photography/Digital Light Source; **322** (tl)Pixoi Ltd/Alamy, (cl)Stephen Reynolds, (bl,bc,br)Photo by Stan Celestian; **323** DEA/F. BARBAGALLO/Getty Images; **324** (c)CORBIS, (b)Adam Jones/Getty Images; **325** (t)Dr. Marli Miller/Getty Images, (b)Patrick Durand/CORBIS SYGMA; **326** (t)Image Source (c)Stephen Reynolds, (b)Photodisc/SuperStock; **327** Jeff Foott/Getty Images; **328** Theo Allofs/Getty Images; **329** (l to r, t to b)Harald Sund/Photographer's Choice/Getty Images, (2)Steve Hamblin/CORBIS, (3)Image Source/Getty Images, (4)Michael Melford/Getty Images, (5)Robert Glusic/Photodisc/Getty Images,

Credits

(6)CORBIS, (7)Dirk Anschutz 2007/Getty Images; **330** (t)Michael Melford/Getty Images, (bl)Digital Archive Japan/Alamy, (bc)Connie Coleman/Photographer's Choice/Getty Images, (br)Image Source/Getty Images; **331** (t)Karl Johaentges/Getty Images, (b)Steve Hamblin/CORBIS; **332** CORBIS; **333** (t)Tony Hopewell/Getty Images, (b)Getty Images; **334** (t)Robert Glusic/Photodisc/Getty Images, (b)Harald Sund/Photographer's Choice/Getty Images; **335** (tl)Digital Archive Japan/Alamy, (cl)CORBIS, (bl)Harald Sund/Photographer's Choice/Getty Images, (br)Image Source/Getty Images; **336** (t to b,6)Macmillan/McGraw-Hill; **337** Getty Images; **338** Hutchings Photography/Digital Light Source; **339** (l)Dr. Marli Miller/Getty Images, (c)Getty Images, (r)Dr. Marli Miller/Getty Images; **340** (t)Getty Images, (b)Hutchings Photography/Digital Light Source; **341** DEA/G.SIOEN/Getty Images; **343** (t)Getty Images, (b)Dr. Marli Miller/Getty Images; **344** (t to b,2) Macmillan/McGraw-Hill, (2)Macmillan/McGraw-Hill; **345** J.T. McGill/U.S. Geological Survey; **346** (t)Joseph Szkodzinski/Getty Images, (c)Michael Melford/Getty Images, (b)Dr. Marli Miller/Getty Images; **348** Dr. Marli Miller/Getty Images; **349** Beate Muenter/PhotoLibrary; **352–353** Robert Harding Picture Library Ltd/Alamy; **354** Masterfile Royalty-Free; **355** Hutchings Photography/Digital Light Source; **356** (l,r)Hutchings Photography/Digital Light Source; **357** (t to b)Richard Hamilton Smith/CORBIS, (2)altrendo nature/Getty Images, (3)Peter Arnold, Inc./Alamy, (4)Guy Edwardes/Getty Images; **358** (l)Worldwide Picture Library/Alamy, (r)Dr. Marli Miller/Getty Images; **359** (l)MARTIN LAND/SCIENCE PHOTO LIBRARY, (r)Hutchings Photography/Digital Light Source; **360** Paul Stutzman/National Institute of Standards and Technology; **361** (tl)altrendo nature/Getty Images, (cl)Hutchings Photography/Digital Light Source, (r)Worldwide Picture Library/Alamy, (bl)Dr. Marli Miller/Getty Images; **362** (t to b)Hutchings Photography/Digital Light Source, (3)Macmillan/McGraw-Hill; **363** Lester Lefkowitz/CORBIS; **364–365** Hutchings Photography/Digital Light Source; **368, 371** Matthew Ward/Getty Images; **372** (t to b)Macmillan/McGraw-Hill, (r)USDA/NRCS and SWSD-UnF, (4,5,7)Hutchings Photography/Digital Light Source; **373** (l)USDA, (r)Tom Reinsch/USDA-NRCS; **374** Richard Hamilton Smith/CORBIS; **377** Robert Harding Picture Library Ltd/Alamy; **382** (t)Living Art Enterprises/Photo Researchers, Inc., (cl)BSIP/Photo Researchers, Inc., (cr)Michael Matisse/Getty Images, (cr)PHANIE/Photo Researchers, Inc.; **384** (c)Dr. Donald Fawcett/Visuals Unlimited/Getty Images; **384–385** Dr. Dennis Kunkel/Visuals Unlimited/Getty Images; **386** Tui De Roy/Minden Pictures; **387** (t)Hutchings Photography/Digital Light Source, (c)Bon Appetit/Alamy, (b)Omikron/Photo Researchers; **388** (tl)Tim Fitzharris/Minden Pictures/Getty Images, (tc)Biophoto Associates/Photo Researchers, (tr)James M. Bell/Photo Researchers, (bl, bc, br)Dr. Richard Kessel & Dr. Gene Shih/Visuals Unlimited/Getty Images; **389** FoodCollection/SuperStock; **390** Dr. Gopal Murti/Photo Researchers; **391** Ed Reschke/Peter Arnold, Inc.; **392** (t)James M. Bell/Photo Researchers, (b)Dr. Gopal Murti/Photo Researchers; **393** (l)VICTOR SHAHIN, PROF. DR. H.OBERLEITHNER, UNIVERSITY HOSPITAL OF MUENSTER/Photo Researchers, (r)NASA-JPL; **394** Eye of Science/Photo Researchers; **395** Hutchings Photography/Digital Light Source; **397** SPL/Photo Researchers; **398** Hutchings Photography/Digital Light Source; **399** Dr. Donald Fawcett/Visuals Unlimited/Getty Images; **400** (l)Dr. Donald Fawcett/Visuals Unlimited/Getty Images, (r)Dennis Kunkel/Phototake; **401** (l)Dr. R. Howard Berg/Visuals Unlimited/Getty Images, (r)Dennis Kunkel/Phototake; **402** Dr. R. Howard Berg/Visuals Unlimited/Getty Images; **403** (c)Macmillan/McGraw-Hill, (others)Hutchings Photography/Digital Light Source; **404** LIU JIN/AFP/Getty Images; **405** Macmillan/McGraw-Hill; **407** Hutchings Photography/Digital Light Source; **411** (c)Macmillan/McGraw-Hill, (others)Hutchings Photography/Digital Light Source; **412** Colin Milkins/Photolibrary; **413** Hutchings Photography/Digital Light Source; **415** (t)Biology Media/Photo Researchers, (b)Andrew Syred/Photo Researchers; **416** Michael & Patricia Fogden/Minden Pictures; **417** Biology Media/Photo Researchers; **418** (tc,bc)Macmillan/McGraw-Hill, (others)Hutchings Photography/Digital Light Source; **420** Dr. Richard Kessel & Dr. Gene Shih/Visuals Unlimited/Getty Images; **423** Dr. Dennis Kunkel/Visuals Unlimited/Getty Images; **426–427** Robert Pickett/CORBIS; **428** Michael Abbey/Photo Researchers; **429** (t)Hutchings Photography/Digital Light Source, (b)Bill Brooks/Alamy; **431** (bl)Ed Reschke/Peter Arnold, Inc., (br)Biophoto Associates/Photo Researchers, (others)Dr. Richard Kessel & Dr. Gene Shih/Visuals Unlimited; **433** Don W. Fawcett/Photo Researchers; **434–435** Ed Reschke/Peter Arnold, Inc.; **436** (l)P.M. Motta & D. Palermo/Photo Researchers, (r)Manfred Kage/Peter Arnold, Inc.; **437** Hutchings Photography/Digital Light Source; **438** (t)Biophoto Associates/Photo Researchers, (b)P.M. Motta & D. Palermo/Photo Researchers; **439** (l)Alex Wilson/Marshall University/AP Images, (r)Bananastock/Alamy; **440** (inset)Biosphoto/Lopez Georges/Peter Arnold, Inc., (bkgd)Biosphoto/Bringard Denis/Peter Arnold, Inc.; **441** (t)Hutchings Photography/Digital Light Source, (c)Steve Gschmeissner/Photo Researchers, (b)Cyril Ruoso/ JH Editorial/Minden Pictures; **442** (t)Wim van Egmond/Visuals Unlimited/Getty Images, (c)Jeff Vanuga/CORBIS, (b)Alfred Pasieka/Photo Researchers; **445** (l)Biophoto Associates/Photo Researchers, (r)Andrew Syred/Photo Researchers; **446** (inset)Ed Reschke/Peter Arnold, Inc., (bkgd)Michael Drane/Alamy; **447** Hutchings Photography/Digital Light Source; **449** Wim van Egmond/Visuals Unlimited/Getty Images; **450–451** Hutchings Photography/Digital Light Source; **455** Robert Pickett/CORBIS; **SR-0–SR-1** (bkgd)Gallo Images - Neil Overy/Getty Images; **SR-2** Hutchings Photography/Digital Light Source; **SR-6** Michell D. Bridwell/PhotoEdit; **SR-7** (t)The McGraw-Hill Companies, (b)Dominic Oldershaw; **SR-8** StudiOhio; **SR-9** Timothy Fuller; **SR-10** Aaron Haupt; **SR-12** KS Studios; **SR-13, SR-47** Matt Meadows; **SR-48** (c)NIBSC/Photo Researchers, Inc., (r)Science VU/Drs. D.T. John & T.B. Cole/Visuals Unlimited, Inc., Stephen Durr; **SR-49** (t)Mark Steinmetz, (r)Andrew Syred/Science Photo Library/Photo Researchers, (br)Rich Brommer; **SR-50** (l)Lynn Keddie/Photolibrary, (tr)G.R. Roberts, David Fleetham/Visuals Unlimited/Getty Images; **SR-51** Gallo Images/CORBIS.